TO TERRA...

VOLUME 2

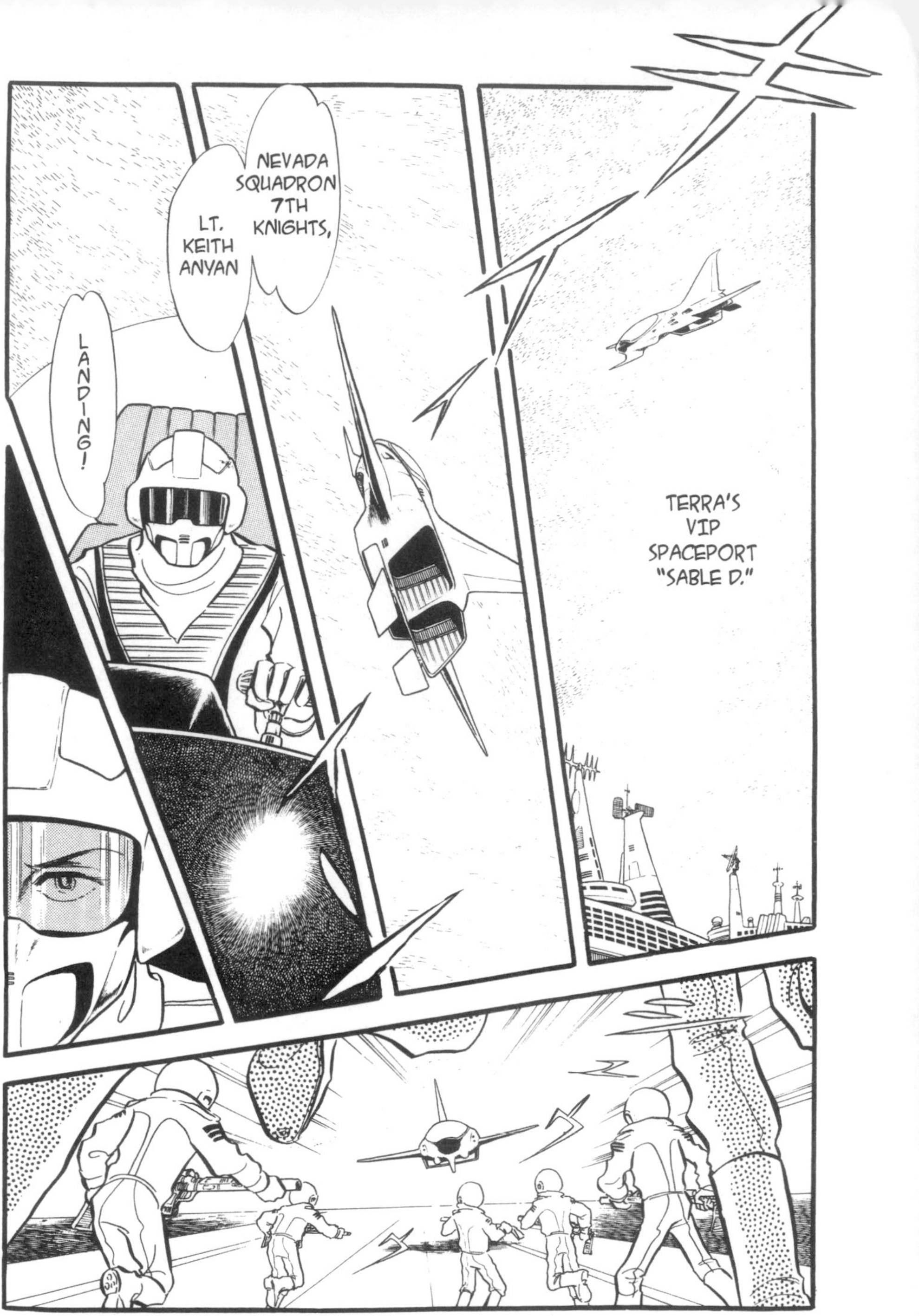
TERRA'S VIP SPACEPORT "SABLE D."
NEVADA SQUADRON 7TH KNIGHTS,
LT. KEITH ANYAN
LANDING!

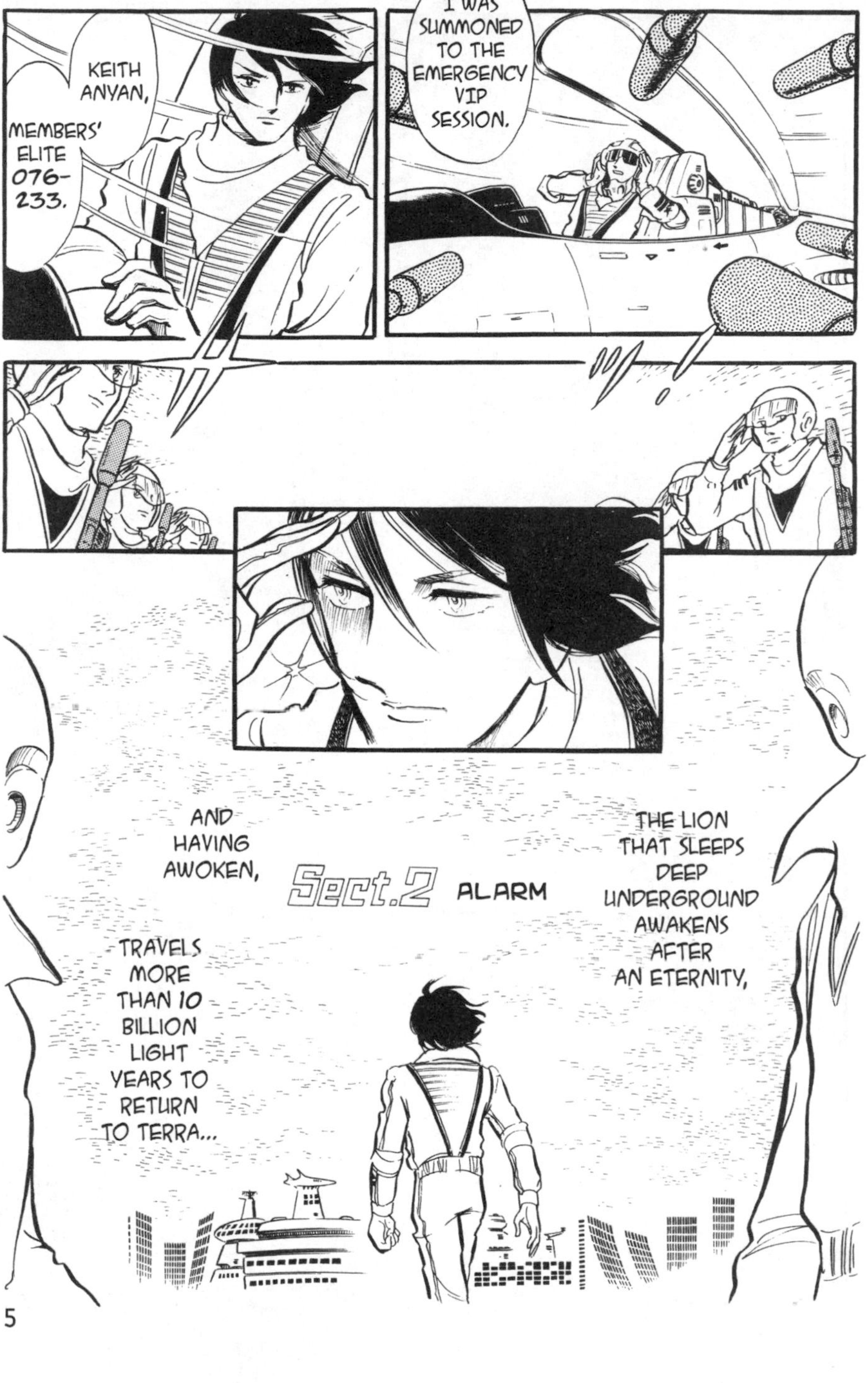
I WAS SUMMONED TO THE EMERGENCY VIP SESSION.
KEITH ANYAN,
MEMBERS' ELITE 076-233.
THE LION THAT SLEEPS DEEP UNDERGROUND AWAKENS AFTER AN ETERNITY,
Sect.2 ALARM
AND HAVING AWOKEN,
TRAVELS MORE THAN 10 BILLION LIGHT YEARS TO RETURN TO TERRA...

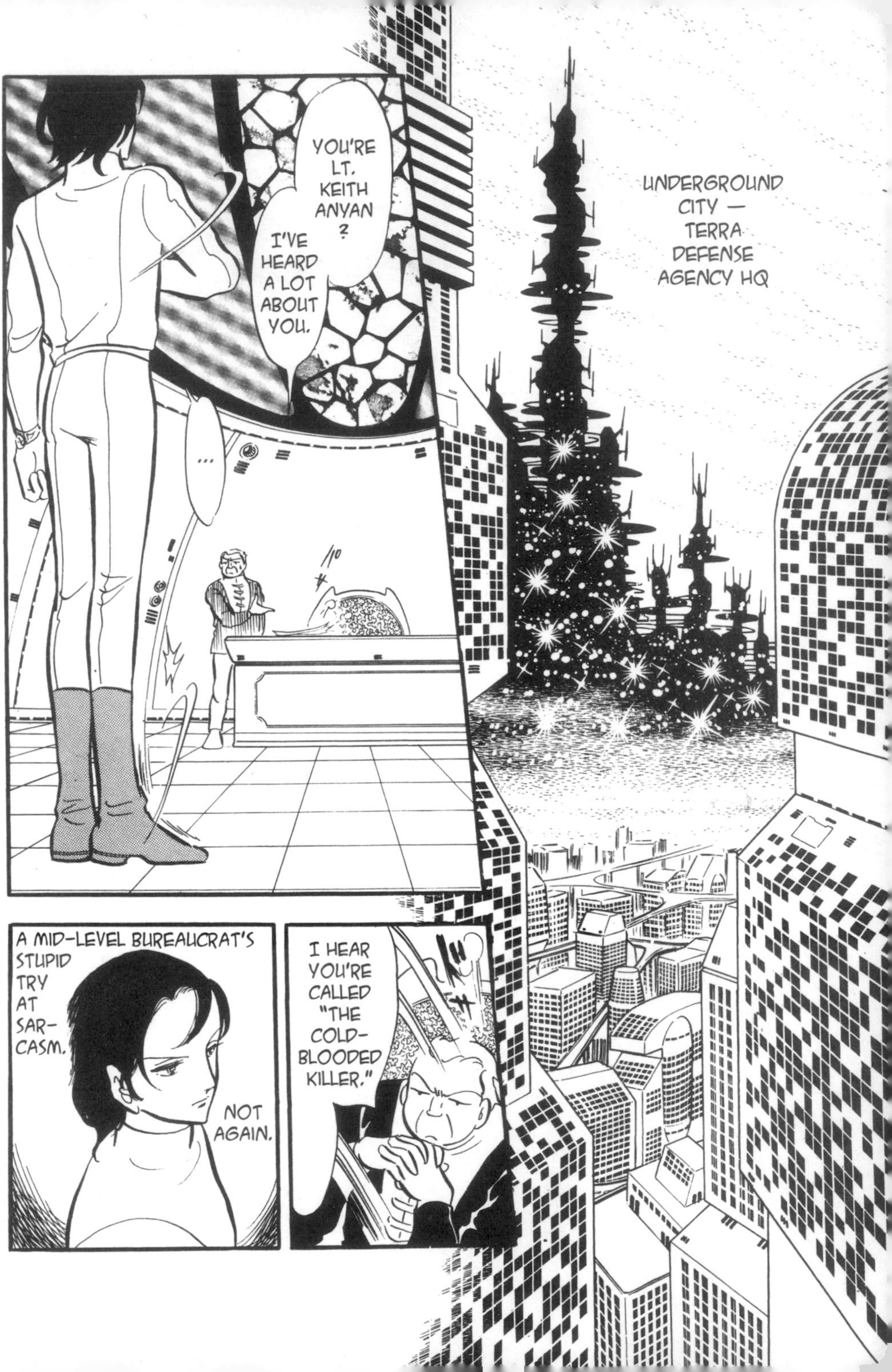
UNDERGROUND CITY — TERRA DEFENSE AGENCY HQ
YOU'RE LT. KEITH ANYAN?
I'VE HEARD A LOT ABOUT YOU.
...
I HEAR YOU'RE CALLED "THE COLD-BLOODED KILLER."
A MID-LEVEL BUREAUCRAT'S STUPID TRY AT SARCASM.
NOT AGAIN.

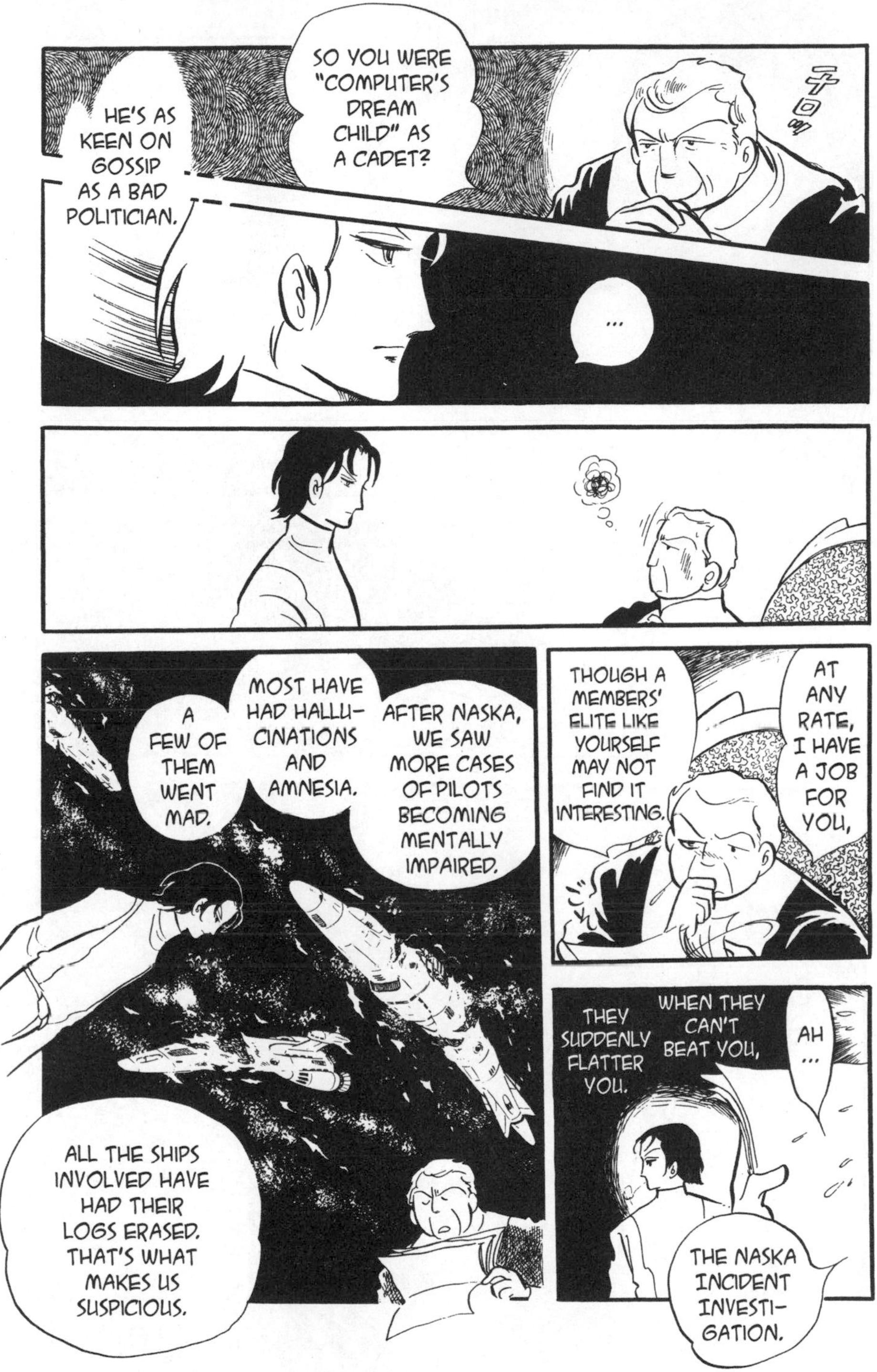
チロッ
SO YOU WERE "COMPUTER'S DREAM CHILD" AS A CADET?
HE'S AS KEEN ON GOSSIP AS A BAD POLITICIAN.
...
AT ANY RATE, I HAVE A JOB FOR YOU,
THOUGH A MEMBERS' ELITE LIKE YOURSELF MAY NOT FIND IT INTERESTING.
AH ...
WHEN THEY CAN'T BEAT YOU,
THEY SUDDENLY FLATTER YOU.
THE NASKA INCIDENT INVESTIGATION.
AFTER NASKA, WE SAW MORE CASES OF PILOTS BECOMING MENTALLY IMPAIRED.
MOST HAVE HAD HALLUCINATIONS AND AMNESIA.
A FEW OF THEM WENT MAD.
ALL THE SHIPS INVOLVED HAVE HAD THEIR LOGS ERASED. THAT'S WHAT MAKES US SUSPICIOUS.

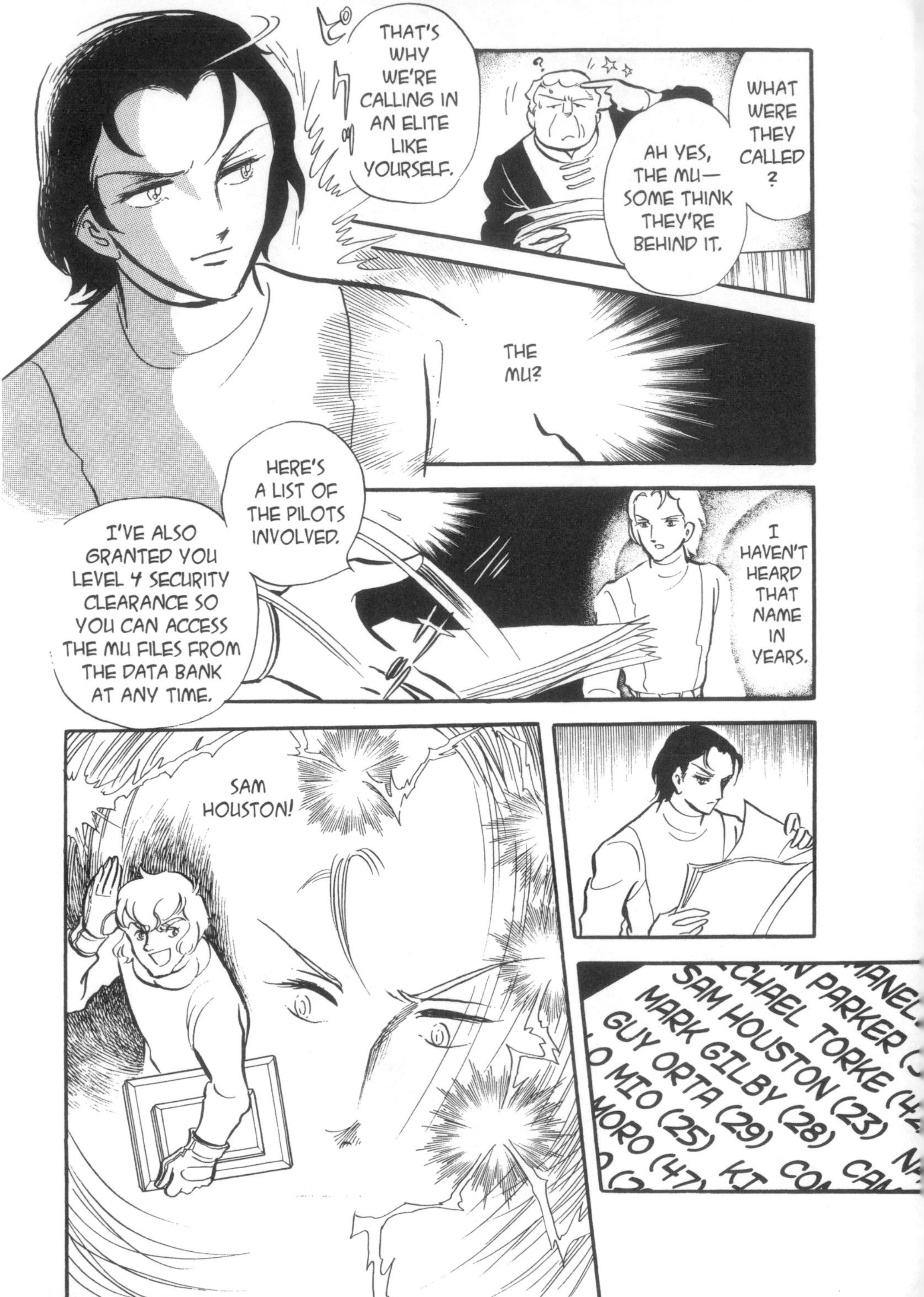

WHAT WERE THEY CALLED?
AH YES, THE MU— SOME THINK THEY'RE BEHIND IT.
THE MU?
I HAVEN'T HEARD THAT NAME IN YEARS.
THAT'S WHY WE'RE CALLING IN AN ELITE LIKE YOURSELF.
HERE'S A LIST OF THE PILOTS INVOLVED.
I'VE ALSO GRANTED YOU LEVEL 4 SECURITY CLEARANCE SO YOU CAN ACCESS THE MU FILES FROM THE DATA BANK AT ANY TIME.
PARKER
CHAEL TORKE
SAM HOUSTON (23)
MARK GILBY (28)
GUY ORTA (29)
MIO (25)
MORO (47)
SAM HOUSTON!

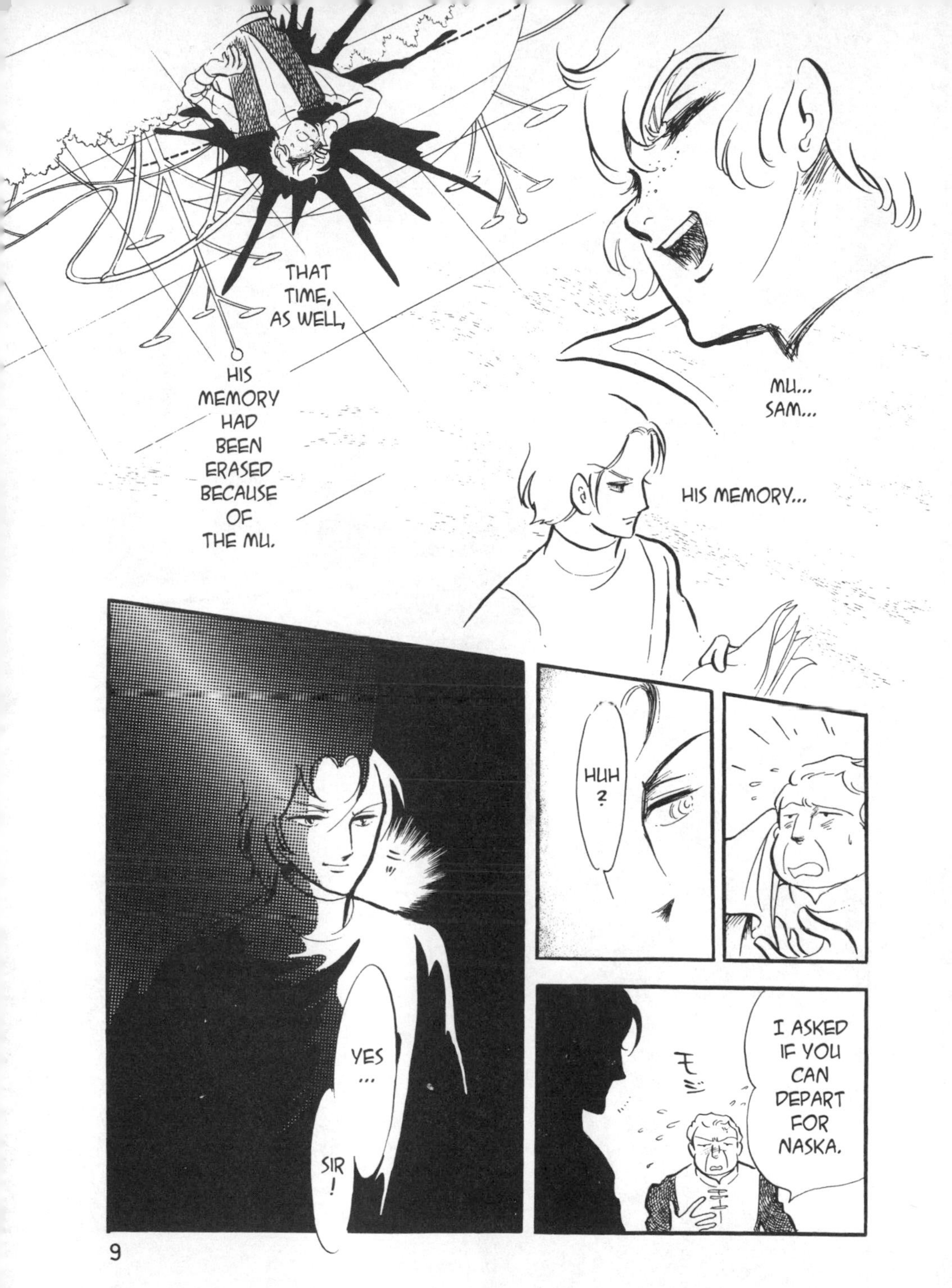

MU... SAM...
HIS MEMORY...
THAT TIME, AS WELL,
HIS MEMORY HAD BEEN ERASED BECAUSE OF THE MU.
HUH?
I ASKED IF YOU CAN DEPART FOR NASKA.
モジ
YES... SIR!

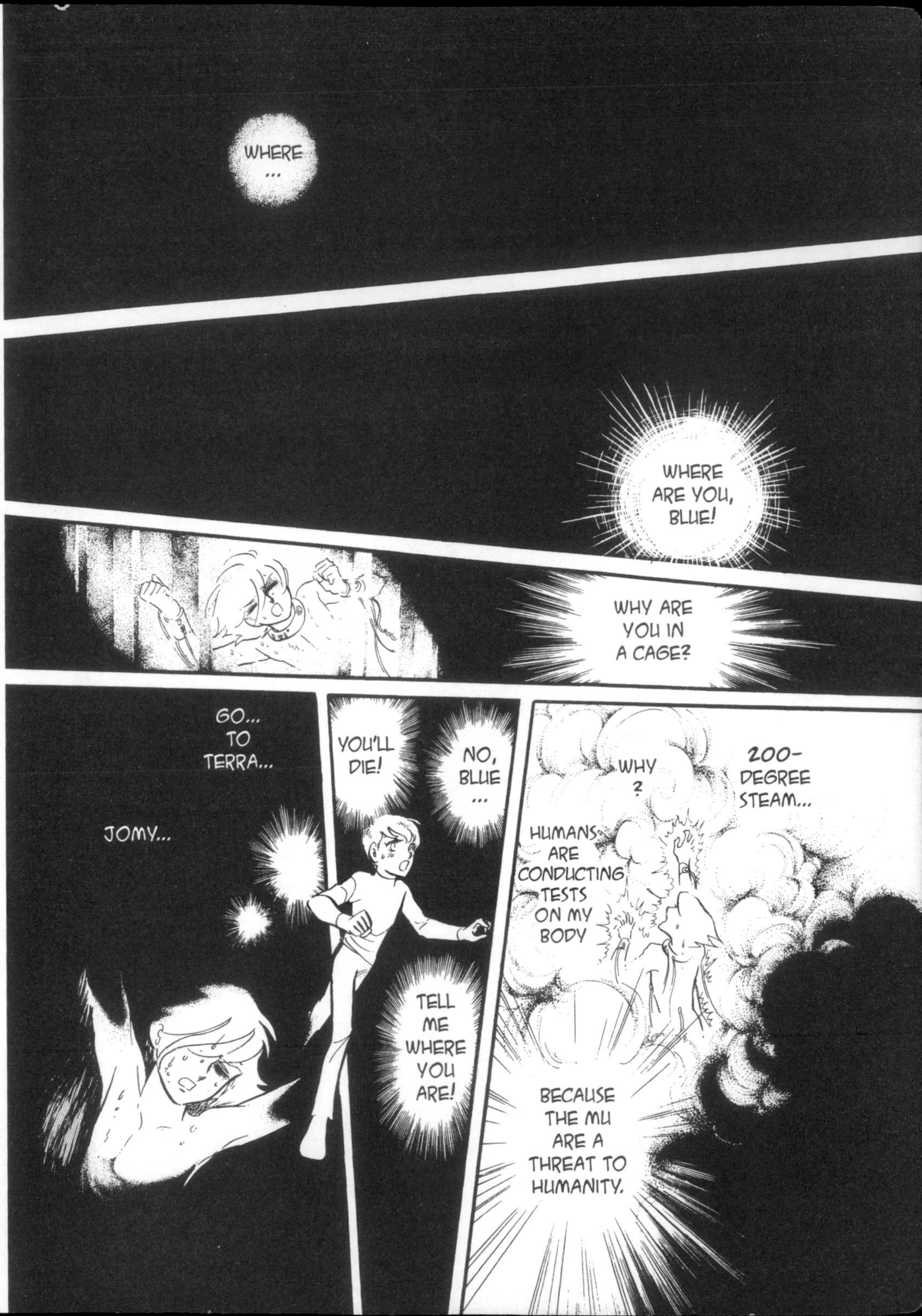
WHERE ...
WHERE ARE YOU, BLUE!
WHY ARE YOU IN A CAGE?
200-DEGREE STEAM...
WHY ?
HUMANS ARE CONDUCTING TESTS ON MY BODY
BECAUSE THE MU ARE A THREAT TO HUMANITY.
NO, BLUE ...
YOU'LL DIE!
TELL ME WHERE YOU ARE!
GO... TO TERRA...
JOMY...

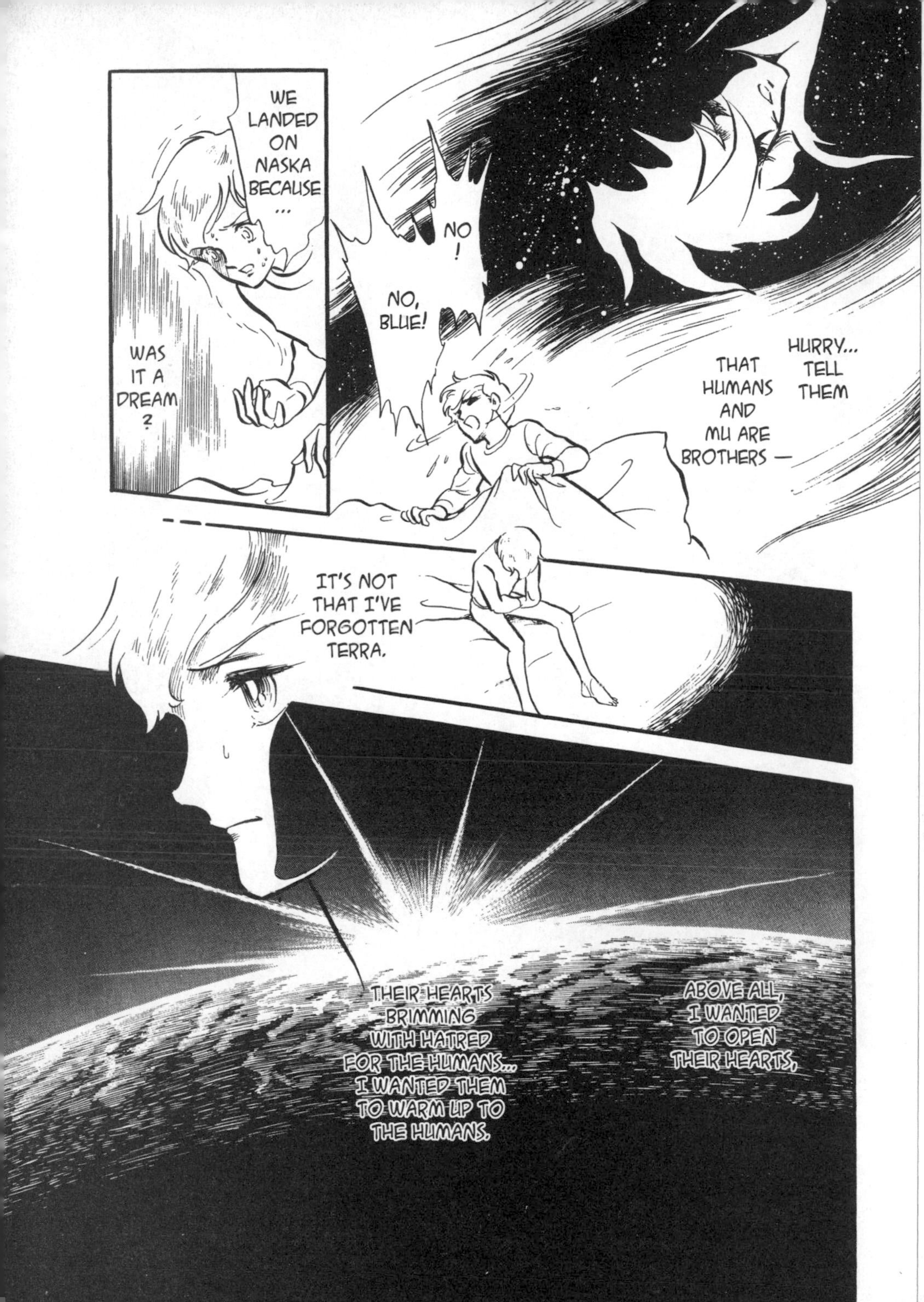
HURRY... TELL THEM
THAT HUMANS AND MU ARE BROTHERS —
NO !
NO, BLUE!
WE LANDED ON NASKA BECAUSE ...
WAS IT A DREAM ?
IT'S NOT THAT I'VE FORGOTTEN TERRA.
ABOVE ALL, I WANTED TO OPEN THEIR HEARTS,
THEIR HEARTS BRIMMING WITH HATRED FOR THE HUMANS... I WANTED THEM TO WARM UP TO THE HUMANS.

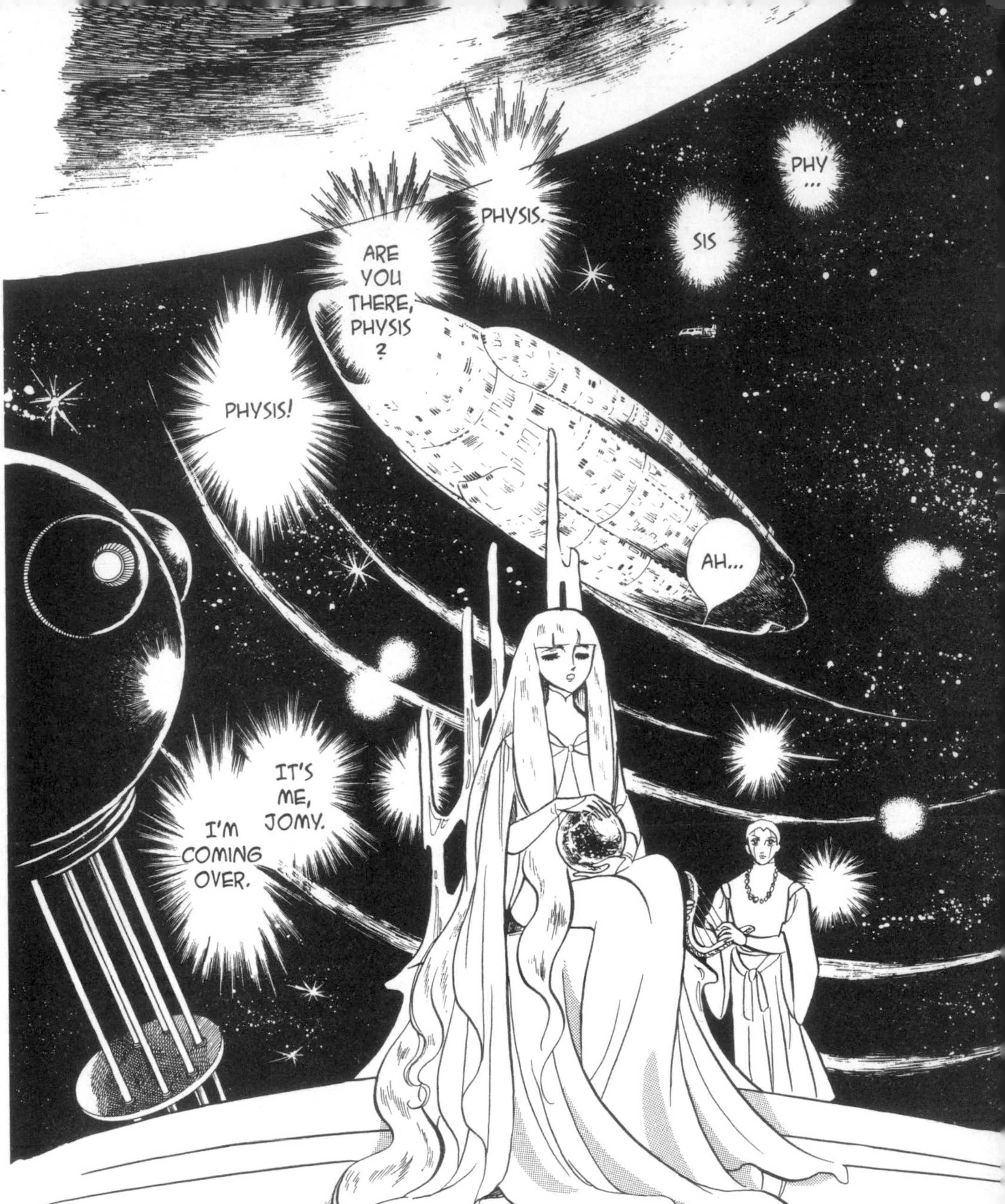
PHY ...
SIS
PHYSIS.
ARE YOU THERE, PHYSIS?
PHYSIS!
AH...
IT'S ME, JOMY.
I'M COMING OVER.

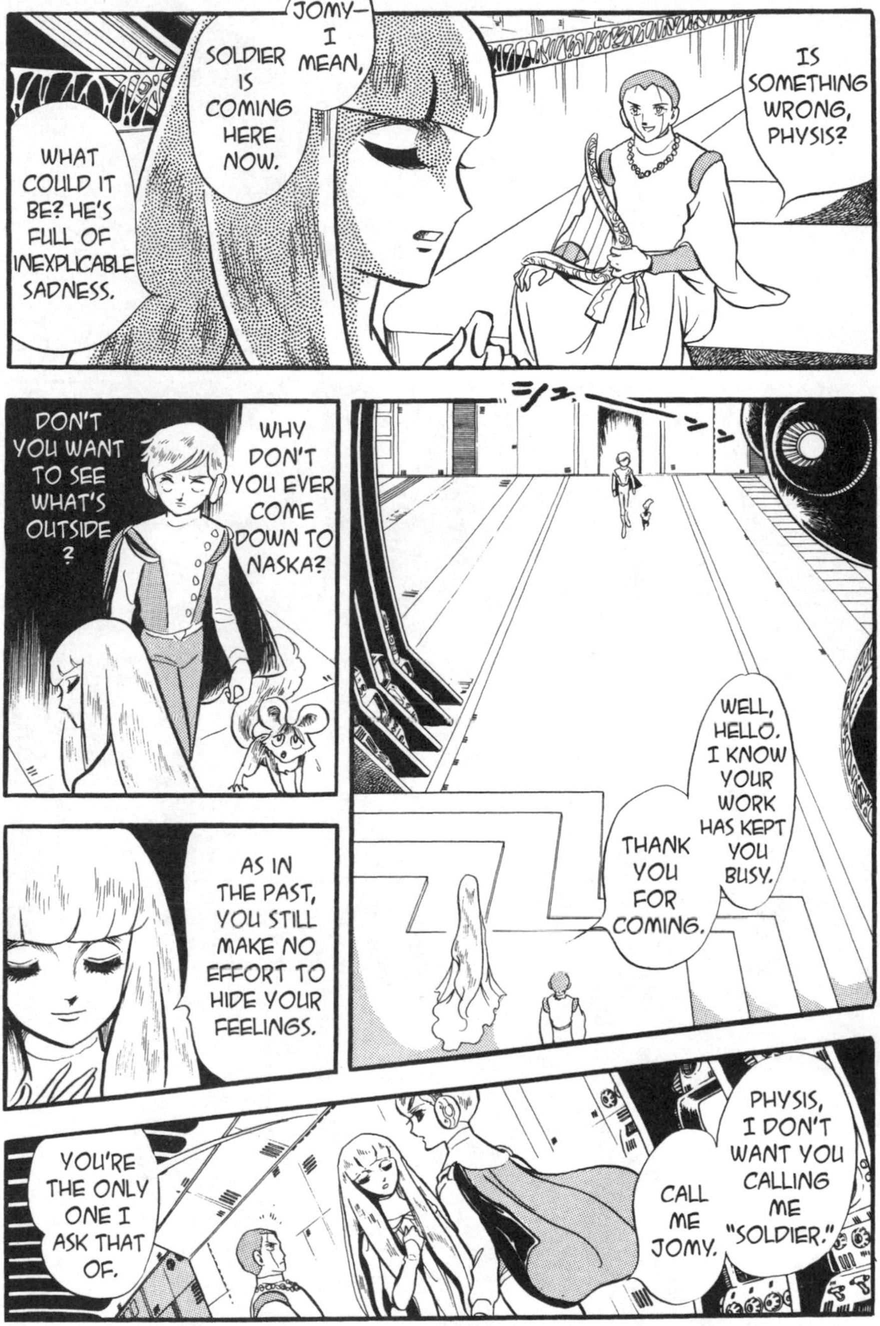
IS SOMETHING WRONG, PHYSIS?
JOMY— I MEAN, SOLDIER IS COMING HERE NOW.
WHAT COULD IT BE? HE'S FULL OF INEXPLICABLE SADNESS.
WHY DON'T YOU EVER COME DOWN TO NASKA?
DON'T YOU WANT TO SEE WHAT'S OUTSIDE?
WELL, HELLO. I KNOW YOUR WORK HAS KEPT YOU BUSY.
THANK YOU FOR COMING.
AS IN THE PAST, YOU STILL MAKE NO EFFORT TO HIDE YOUR FEELINGS.
PHYSIS, I DON'T WANT YOU CALLING ME "SOLDIER."
CALL ME JOMY.
YOU'RE THE ONLY ONE I ASK THAT OF.

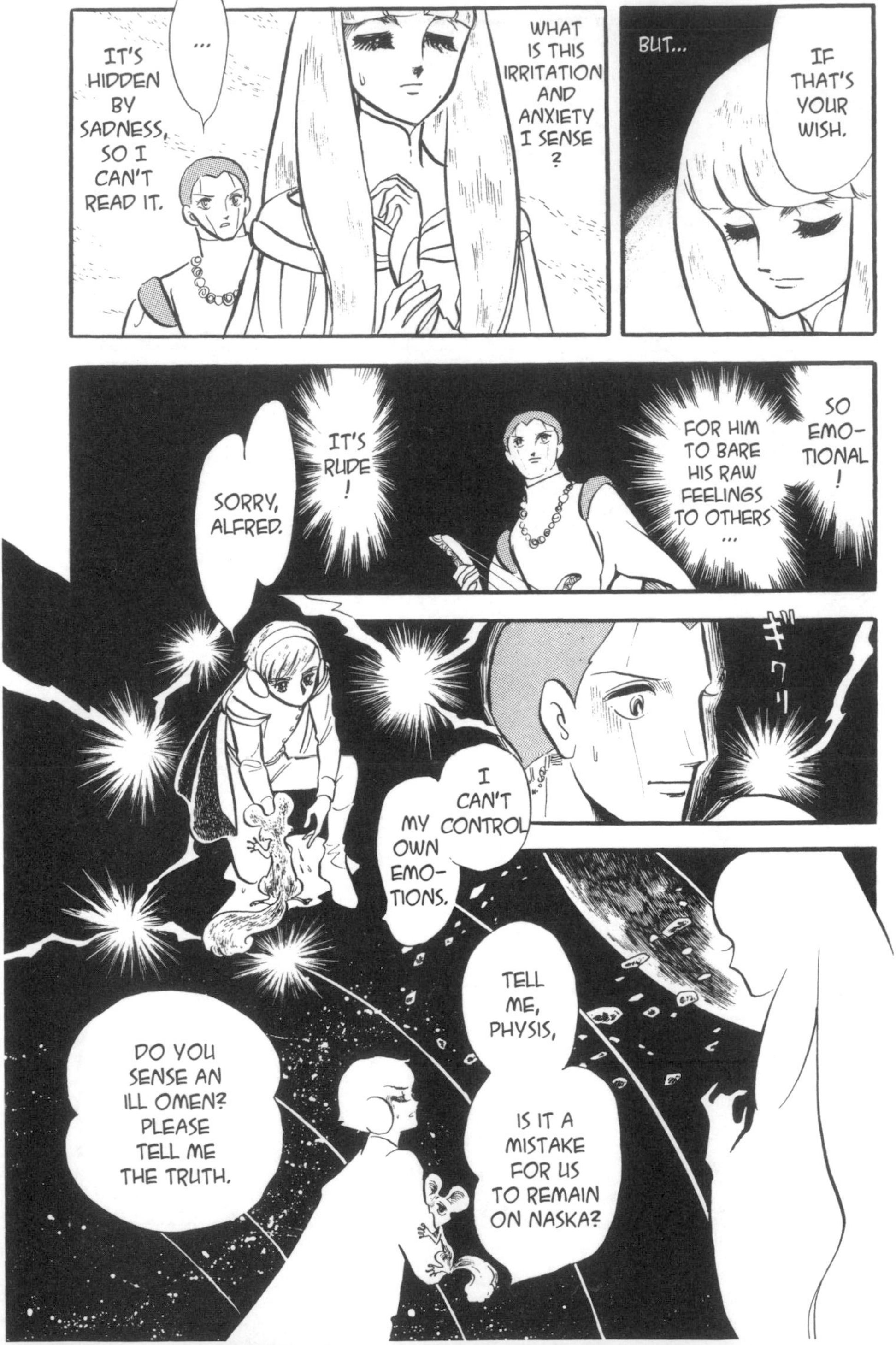
BUT...
IF THAT'S YOUR WISH.
WHAT IS THIS IRRITATION AND ANXIETY I SENSE?
...
IT'S HIDDEN BY SADNESS, SO I CAN'T READ IT.
SO EMO-TIONAL!
FOR HIM TO BARE HIS RAW FEELINGS TO OTHERS...
IT'S RUDE!
SORRY, ALFRED.
ギクリ
I CAN'T CONTROL MY OWN EMO-TIONS.
TELL ME, PHYSIS,
IS IT A MISTAKE FOR US TO REMAIN ON NASKA?
DO YOU SENSE AN ILL OMEN? PLEASE TELL ME THE TRUTH.

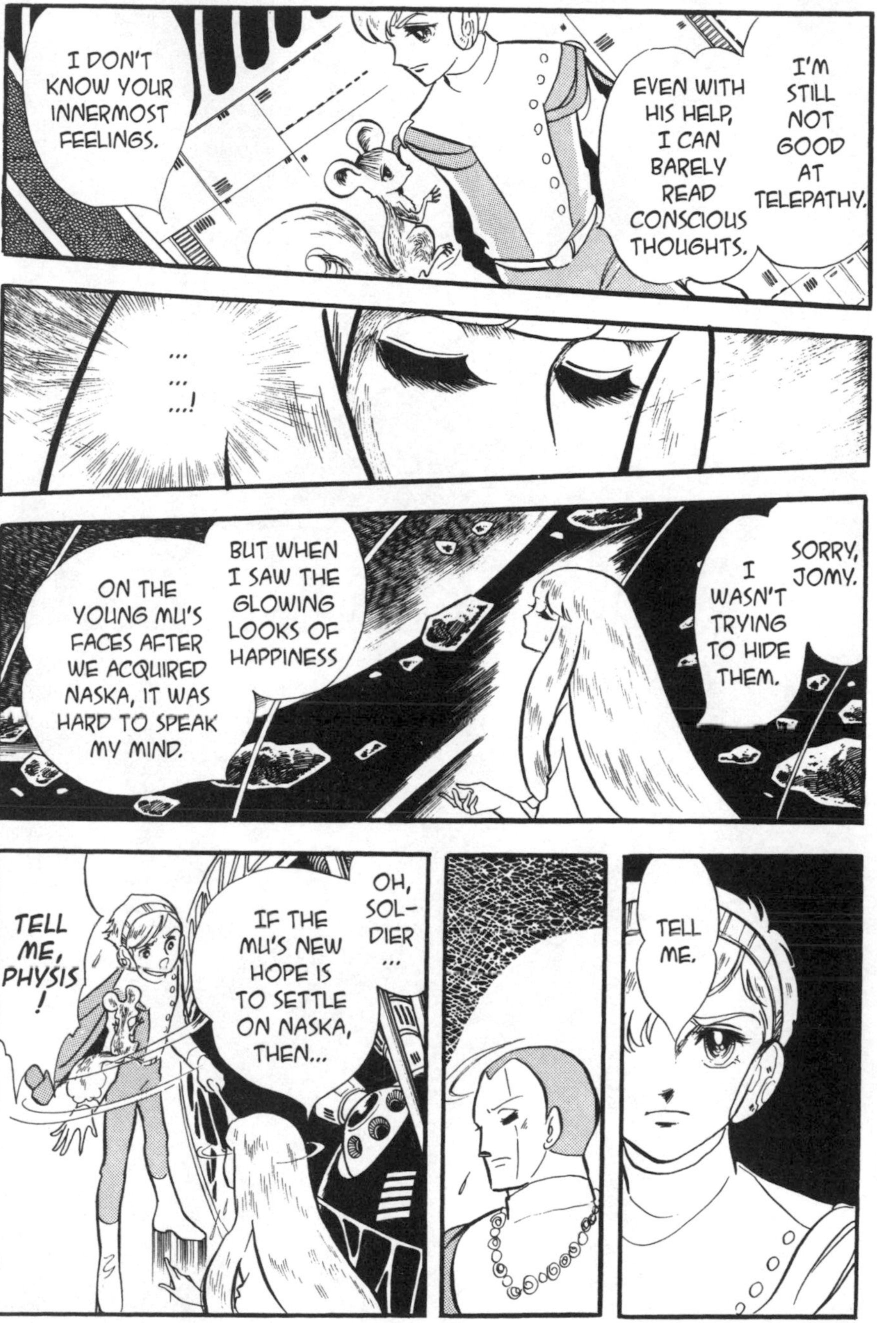
I'M STILL NOT GOOD AT TELEPATHY.
EVEN WITH HIS HELP, I CAN BARELY READ CONSCIOUS THOUGHTS.
I DON'T KNOW YOUR INNERMOST FEELINGS.
... ...!
SORRY, JOMY.
I WASN'T TRYING TO HIDE THEM.
BUT WHEN I SAW THE GLOWING LOOKS OF HAPPINESS
ON THE YOUNG MU'S FACES AFTER WE ACQUIRED NASKA, IT WAS HARD TO SPEAK MY MIND.
TELL ME.
OH, SOL-DIER...
IF THE MU'S NEW HOPE IS TO SETTLE ON NASKA, THEN...
TELL ME, PHYSIS!

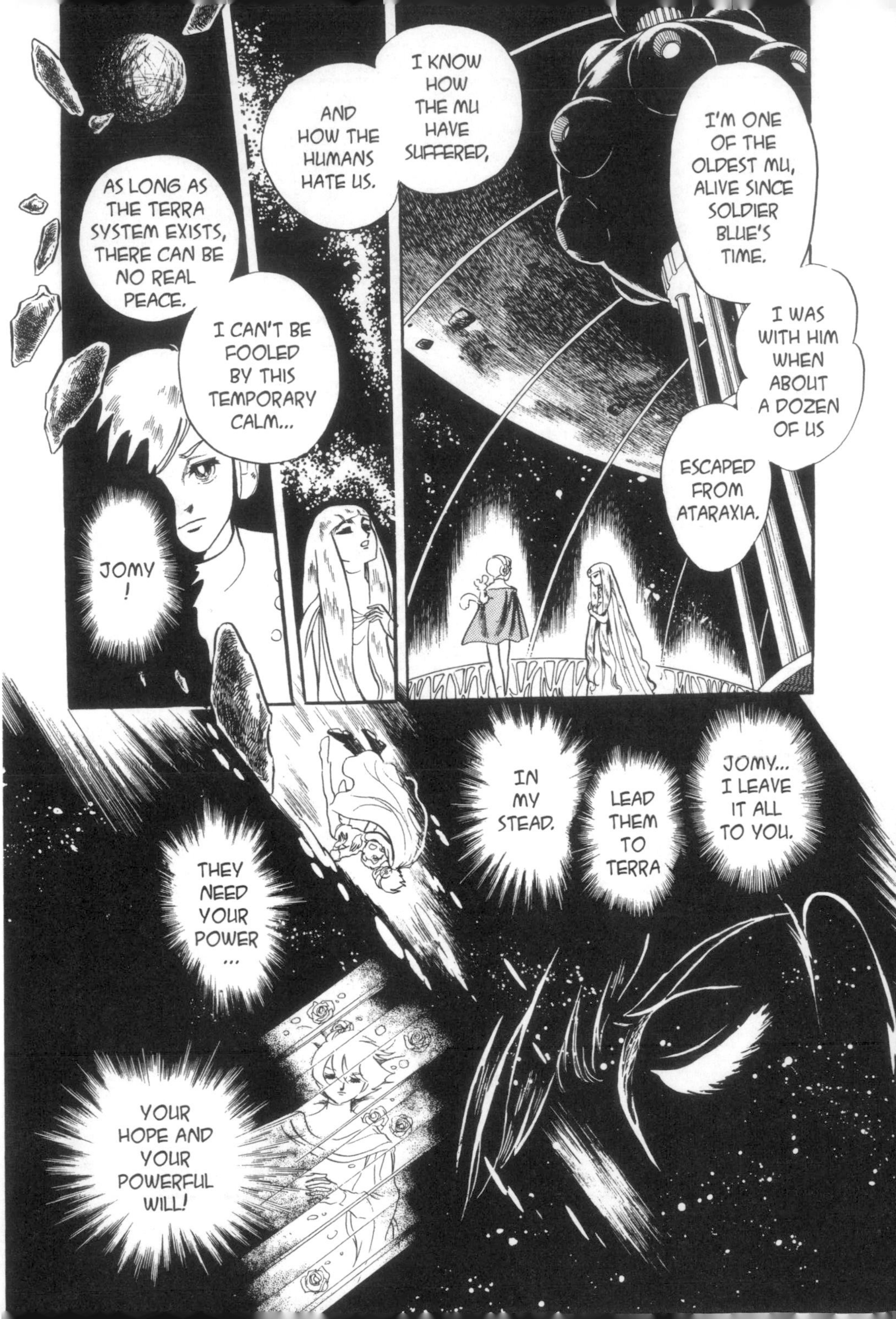
I'M ONE OF THE OLDEST MU, ALIVE SINCE SOLDIER BLUE'S TIME.
I WAS WITH HIM WHEN ABOUT A DOZEN OF US
ESCAPED FROM ATARAXIA.
I KNOW HOW THE MU HAVE SUFFERED,
AND HOW THE HUMANS HATE US.
AS LONG AS THE TERRA SYSTEM EXISTS, THERE CAN BE NO REAL PEACE.
I CAN'T BE FOOLED BY THIS TEMPORARY CALM...
JOMY!
JOMY... I LEAVE IT ALL TO YOU.
LEAD THEM TO TERRA
IN MY STEAD.
THEY NEED YOUR POWER...
YOUR HOPE AND YOUR POWERFUL WILL!

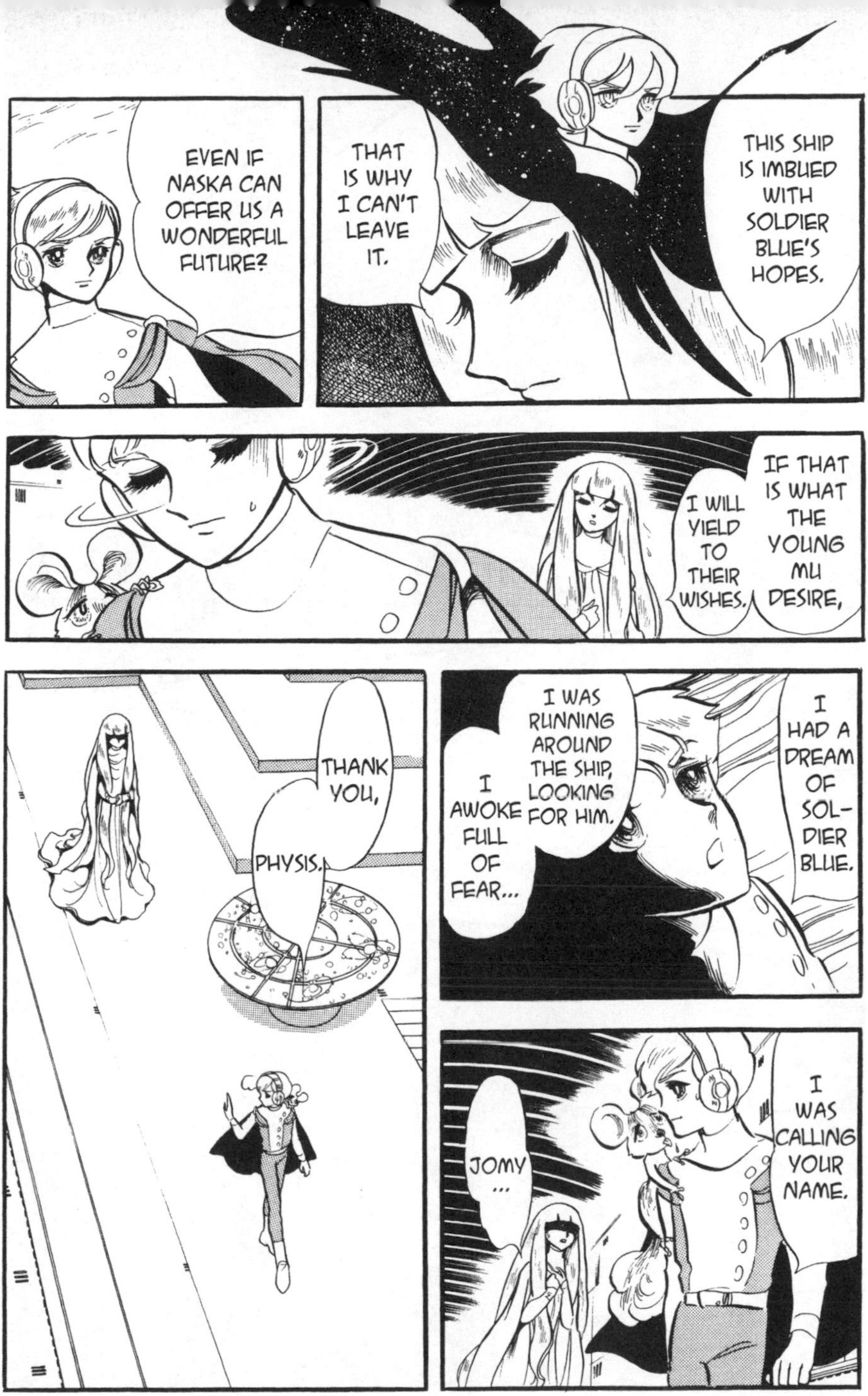
THIS SHIP IS IMBUED WITH SOLDIER BLUE'S HOPES.
THAT IS WHY I CAN'T LEAVE IT.
EVEN IF NASKA CAN OFFER US A WONDERFUL FUTURE?
IF THAT IS WHAT THE YOUNG MU DESIRE,
I WILL YIELD TO THEIR WISHES.
I HAD A DREAM OF SOL-DIER BLUE.
I WAS RUNNING AROUND THE SHIP, LOOKING FOR HIM.
I AWOKE FULL OF FEAR...
I WAS CALLING YOUR NAME.
JOMY ...
THANK YOU,
PHYSIS.

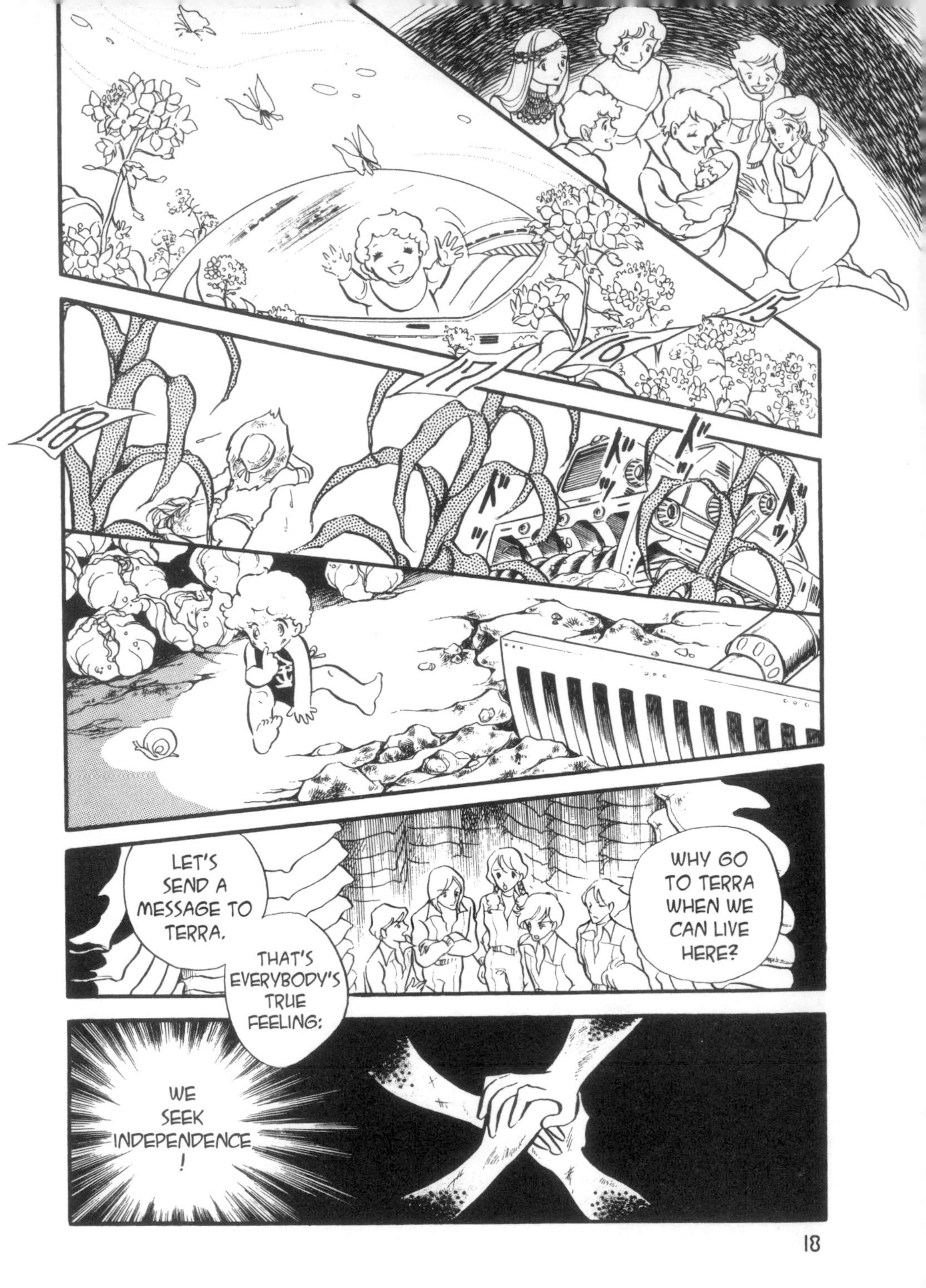
WHY GO TO TERRA WHEN WE CAN LIVE HERE?
LET'S SEND A MESSAGE TO TERRA.
THAT'S EVERYBODY'S TRUE FEELING:
WE SEEK INDEPENDENCE!

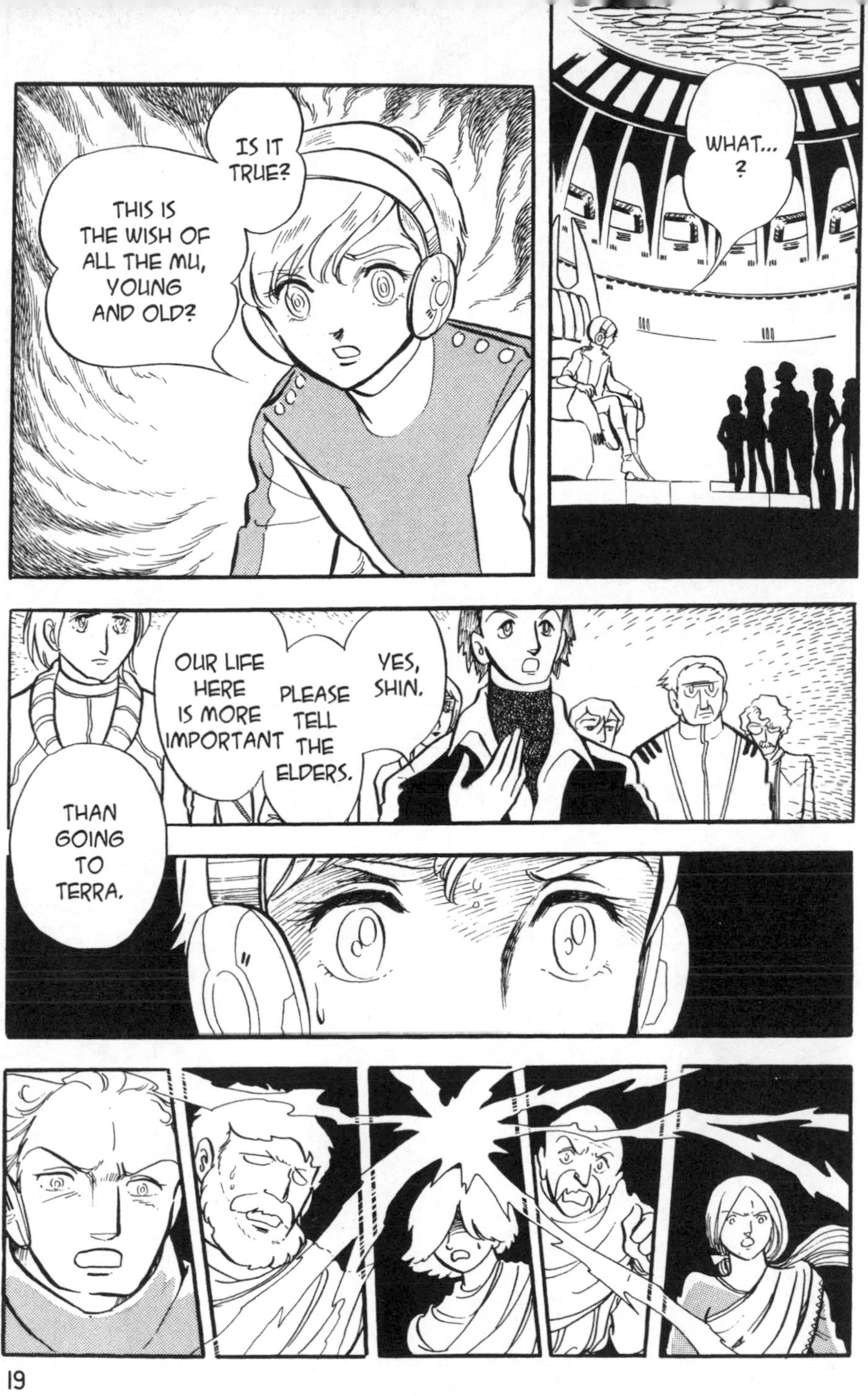
WHAT... ?
IS IT TRUE?
THIS IS THE WISH OF ALL THE MU, YOUNG AND OLD?
YES, SHIN.
PLEASE TELL THE ELDERS.
OUR LIFE HERE IS MORE IMPORTANT
THAN GOING TO TERRA.

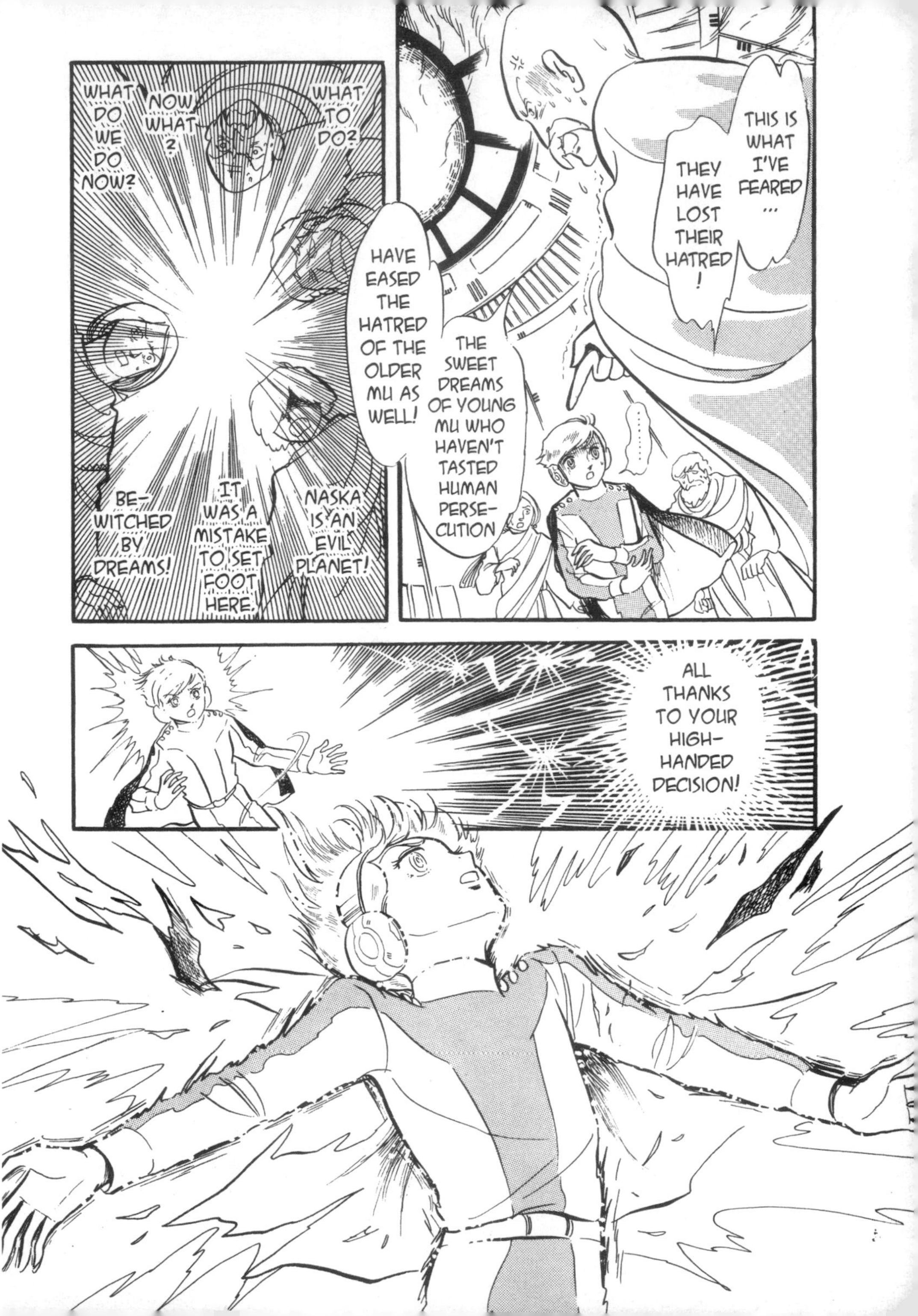
THIS IS WHAT I'VE FEARED ...
THEY HAVE LOST THEIR HATRED!
THE SWEET DREAMS OF YOUNG MU WHO HAVEN'T TASTED HUMAN PERSECUTION
HAVE EASED THE HATRED OF THE OLDER MU AS WELL!
......
WHAT TO DO?
NOW WHAT?
WHAT DO WE DO NOW?
NASKA IS AN EVIL PLANET!
IT WAS A MISTAKE TO SET FOOT HERE.
BE-WITCHED BY DREAMS!
ALL THANKS TO YOUR HIGH-HANDED DECISION!

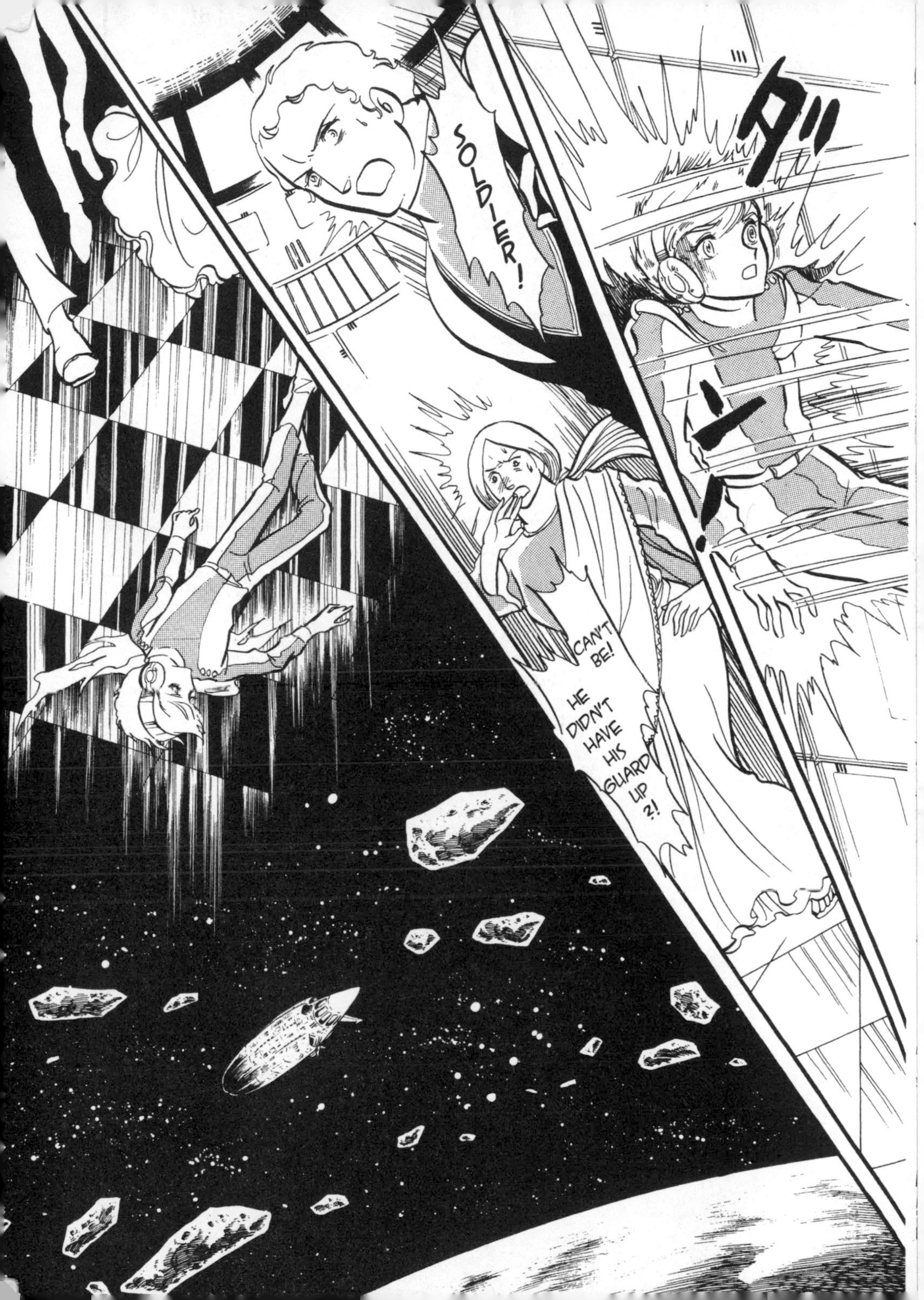
ダッ
SOLDIER!
CAN'T BE!
HE DIDN'T HAVE HIS GUARD UP?!

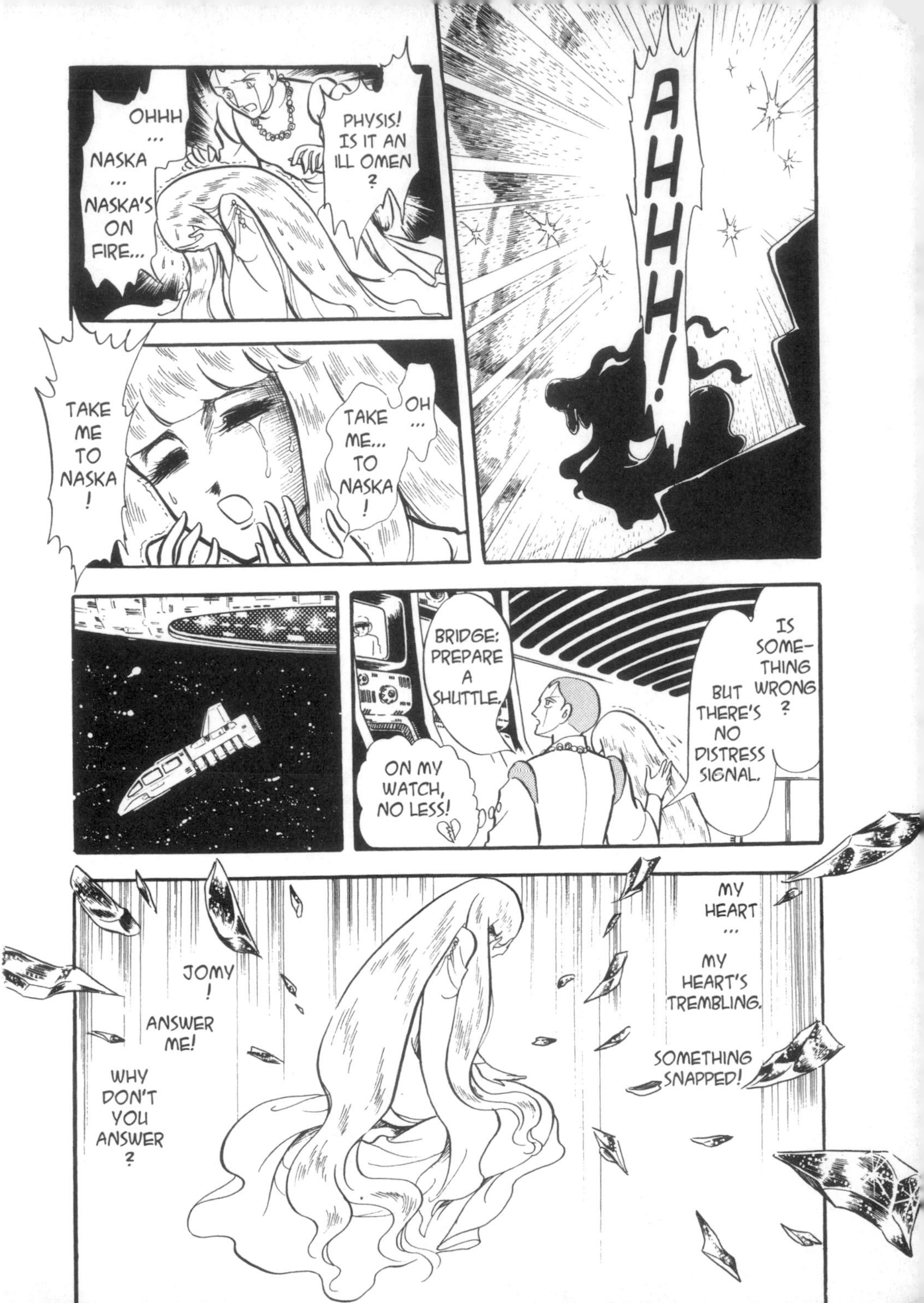
AHHHH!
PHYSIS! IS IT AN ILL OMEN?
OHHH... NASKA... NASKA'S ON FIRE...
OH... TAKE ME... TO NASKA!
TAKE ME TO NASKA!
IS SOMETHING WRONG?
BUT THERE'S NO DISTRESS SIGNAL.
BRIDGE: PREPARE A SHUTTLE.
ON MY WATCH, NO LESS!
MY HEART... MY HEART'S TREMBLING.
SOMETHING SNAPPED!
JOMY! ANSWER ME!
WHY DON'T YOU ANSWER?

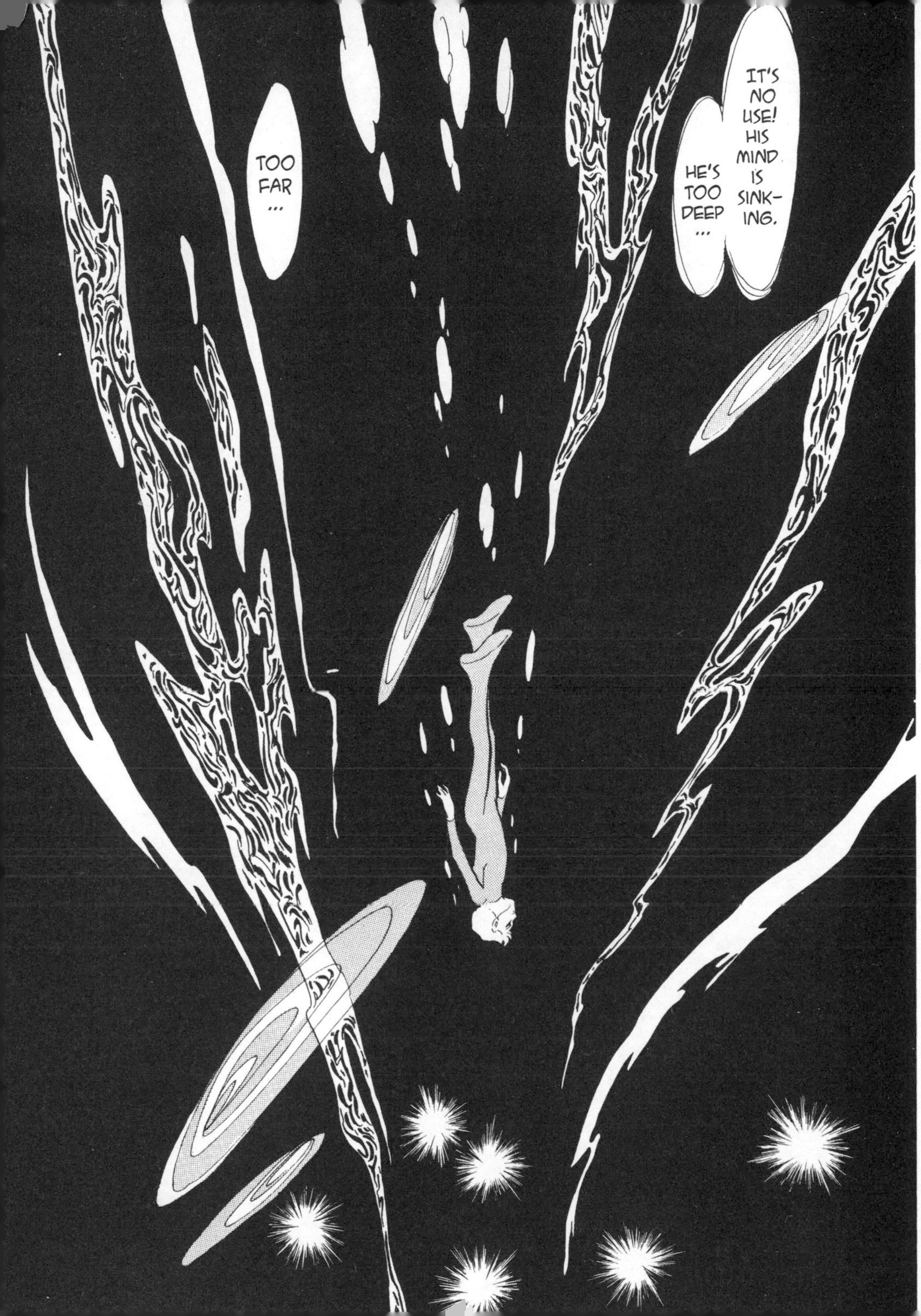
IT'S NO USE! HIS MIND IS SINK-ING.
HE'S TOO DEEP ...
TOO FAR ...

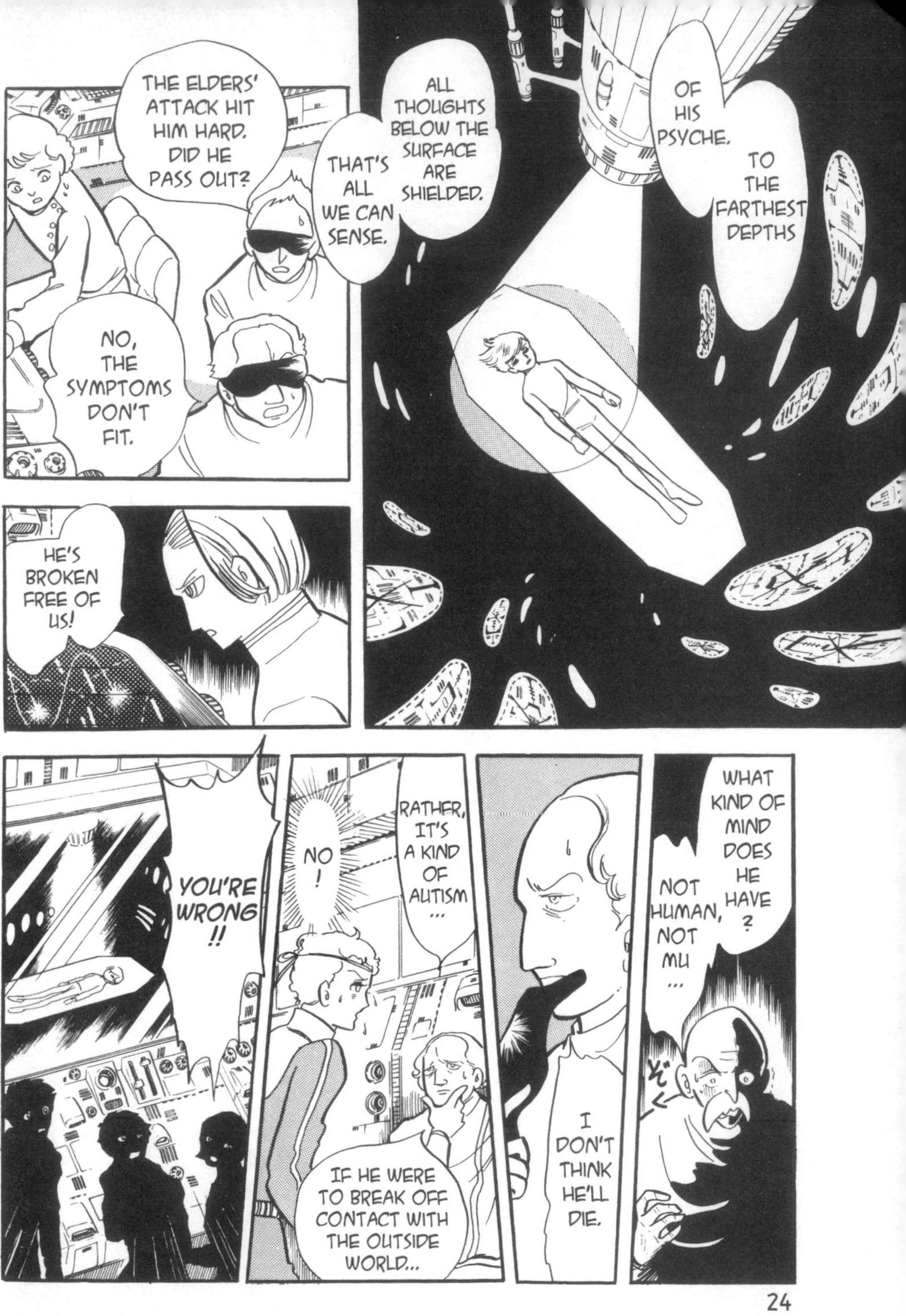
OF HIS PSYCHE.
TO THE FARTHEST DEPTHS
ALL THOUGHTS BELOW THE SURFACE ARE SHIELDED.
THAT'S ALL WE CAN SENSE.
THE ELDERS' ATTACK HIT HIM HARD. DID HE PASS OUT?
NO, THE SYMPTOMS DON'T FIT.
HE'S BROKEN FREE OF US!
WHAT KIND OF MIND DOES HE HAVE?
NOT HUMAN, NOT MU...
ぞく
I DON'T THINK HE'LL DIE.
RATHER, IT'S A KIND OF AUTISM...
NO!
IF HE WERE TO BREAK OFF CONTACT WITH THE OUTSIDE WORLD...
YOU'RE WRONG!!

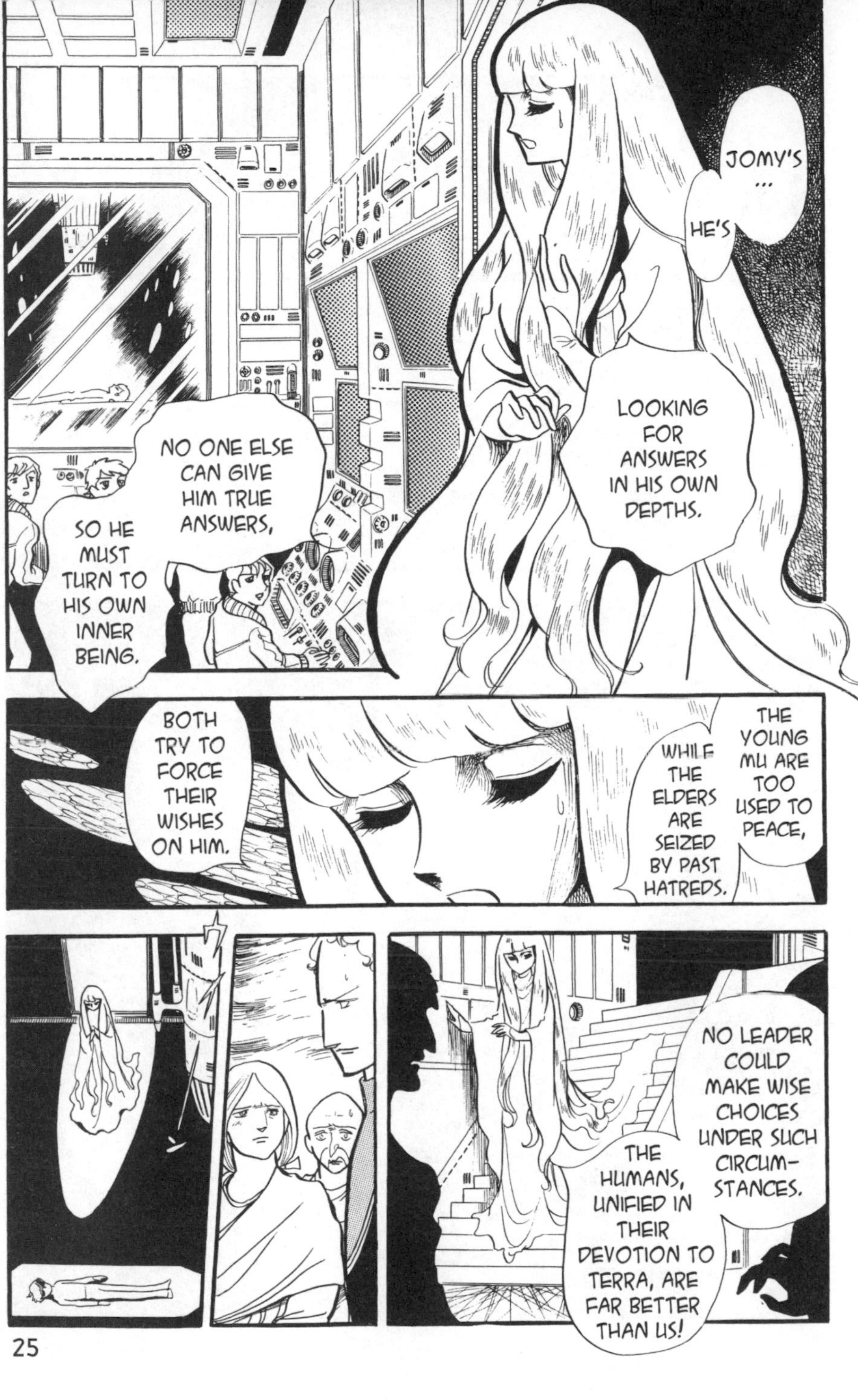
JOMY'S ...
HE'S
LOOKING FOR ANSWERS IN HIS OWN DEPTHS.
NO ONE ELSE CAN GIVE HIM TRUE ANSWERS,
SO HE MUST TURN TO HIS OWN INNER BEING.
THE YOUNG MU ARE TOO USED TO PEACE,
WHILE THE ELDERS ARE SEIZED BY PAST HATREDS.
BOTH TRY TO FORCE THEIR WISHES ON HIM.
NO LEADER COULD MAKE WISE CHOICES UNDER SUCH CIRCUM-STANCES.
THE HUMANS, UNIFIED IN THEIR DEVOTION TO TERRA, ARE FAR BETTER THAN US!

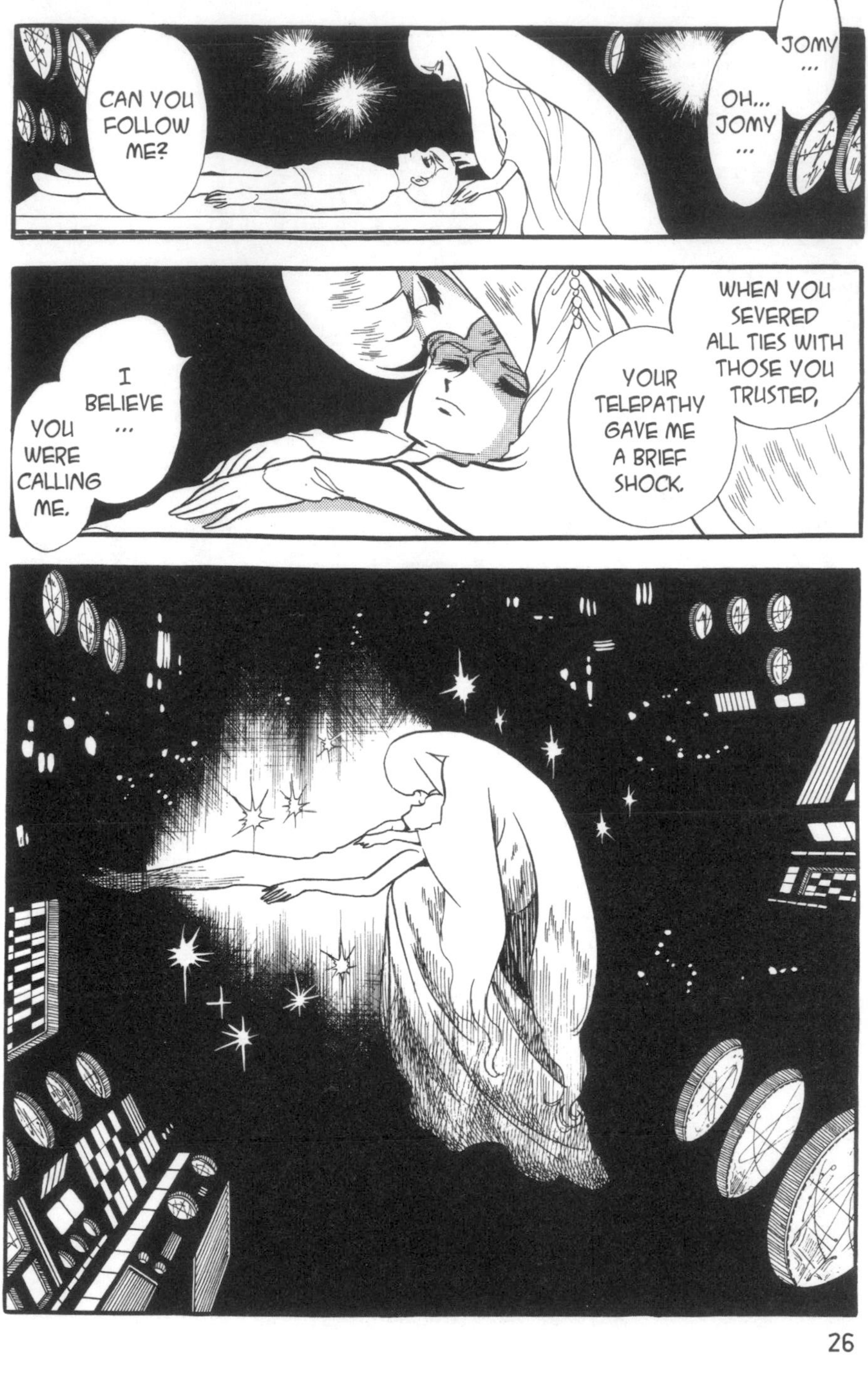
JOMY ...
OH... JOMY ...
CAN YOU FOLLOW ME?
WHEN YOU SEVERED ALL TIES WITH THOSE YOU TRUSTED,
YOUR TELEPATHY GAVE ME A BRIEF SHOCK.
I BELIEVE ... YOU WERE CALLING ME.

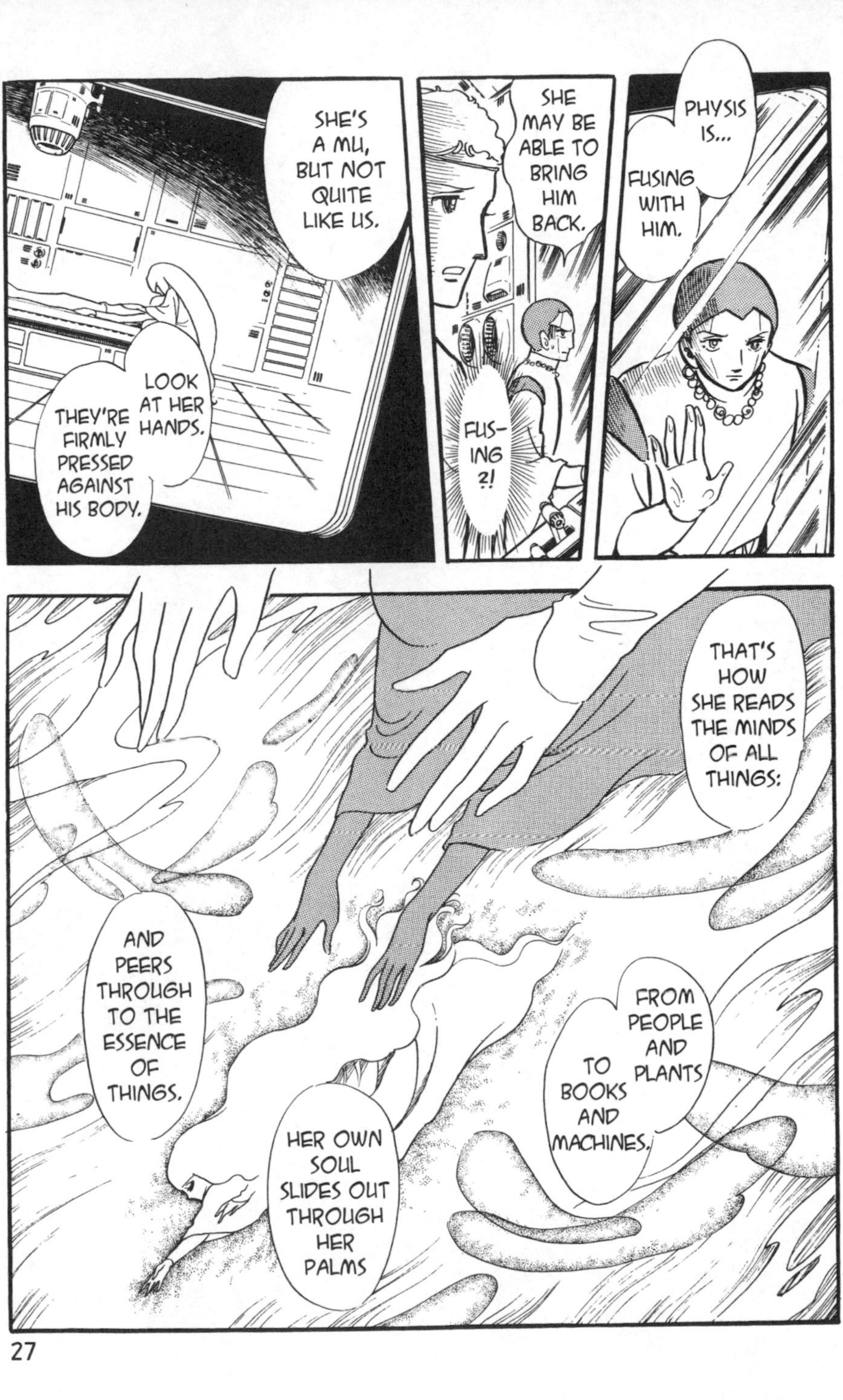
PHYSIS IS...
FUSING WITH HIM.
SHE MAY BE ABLE TO BRING HIM BACK.
FUS-ING?!
SHE'S A MU, BUT NOT QUITE LIKE US.
LOOK AT HER HANDS.
THEY'RE FIRMLY PRESSED AGAINST HIS BODY.
THAT'S HOW SHE READS THE MINDS OF ALL THINGS:
FROM PEOPLE AND PLANTS
TO BOOKS AND MACHINES.
HER OWN SOUL SLIDES OUT THROUGH HER PALMS
AND PEERS THROUGH TO THE ESSENCE OF THINGS.

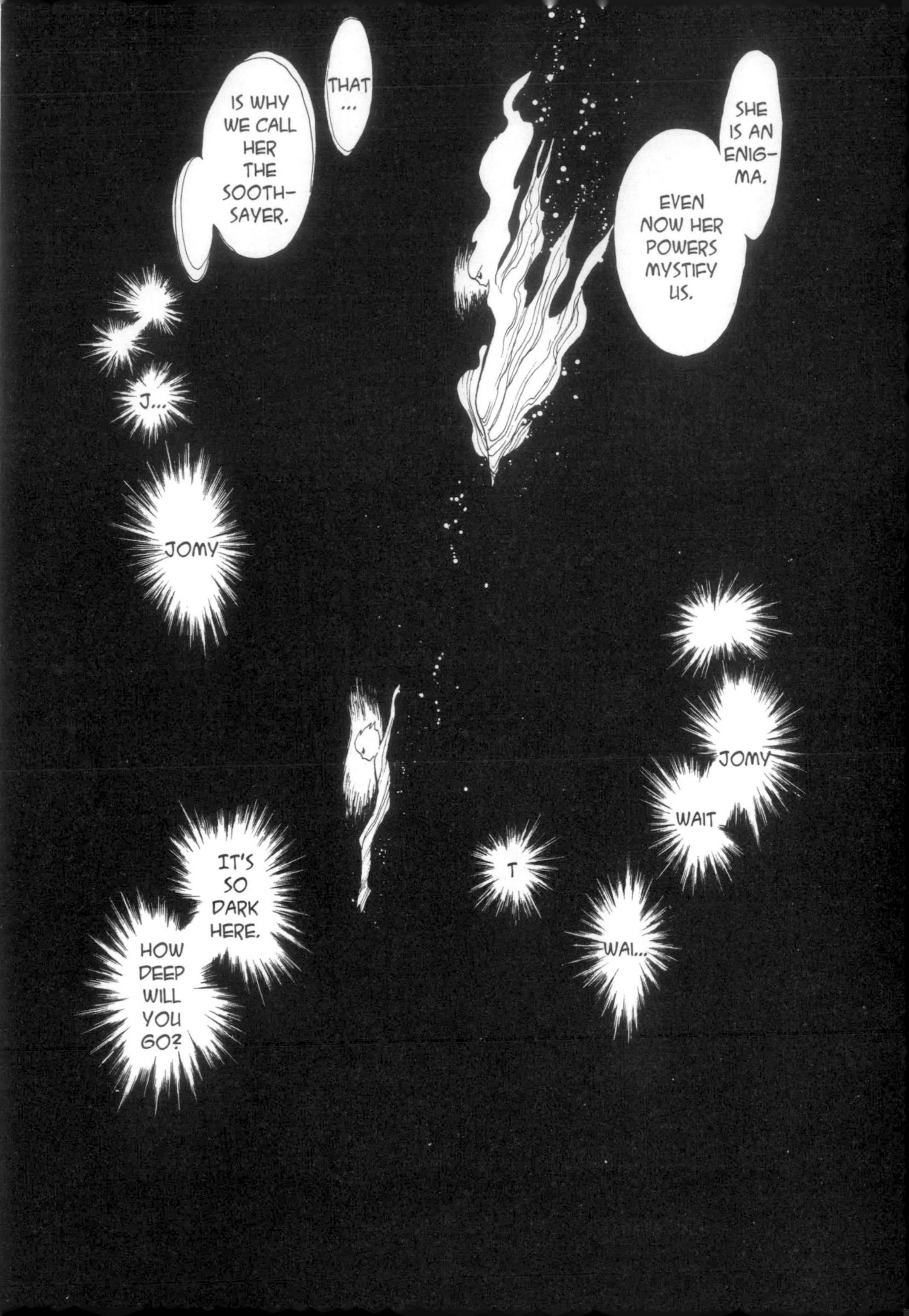
SHE IS AN ENIGMA.
EVEN NOW HER POWERS MYSTIFY US.
THAT...
IS WHY WE CALL HER THE SOOTHSAYER.
J...
JOMY
JOMY
WAIT
T
WAI...
IT'S SO DARK HERE.
HOW DEEP WILL YOU GO?

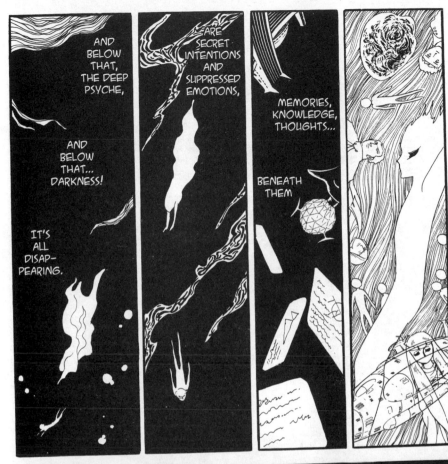

MEMORIES, KNOWLEDGE, THOUGHTS...
BENEATH THEM
ARE SECRET INTENTIONS AND SUPPRESSED EMOTIONS,
AND BELOW THAT, THE DEEP PSYCHE,
AND BELOW THAT... DARKNESS!
IT'S ALL DISAP-PEARING.
JOMY,
EVEN YOU
ARE FADING!

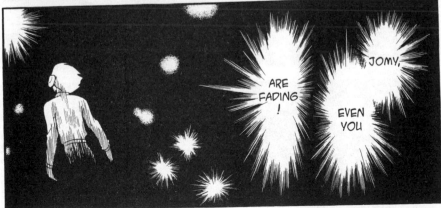

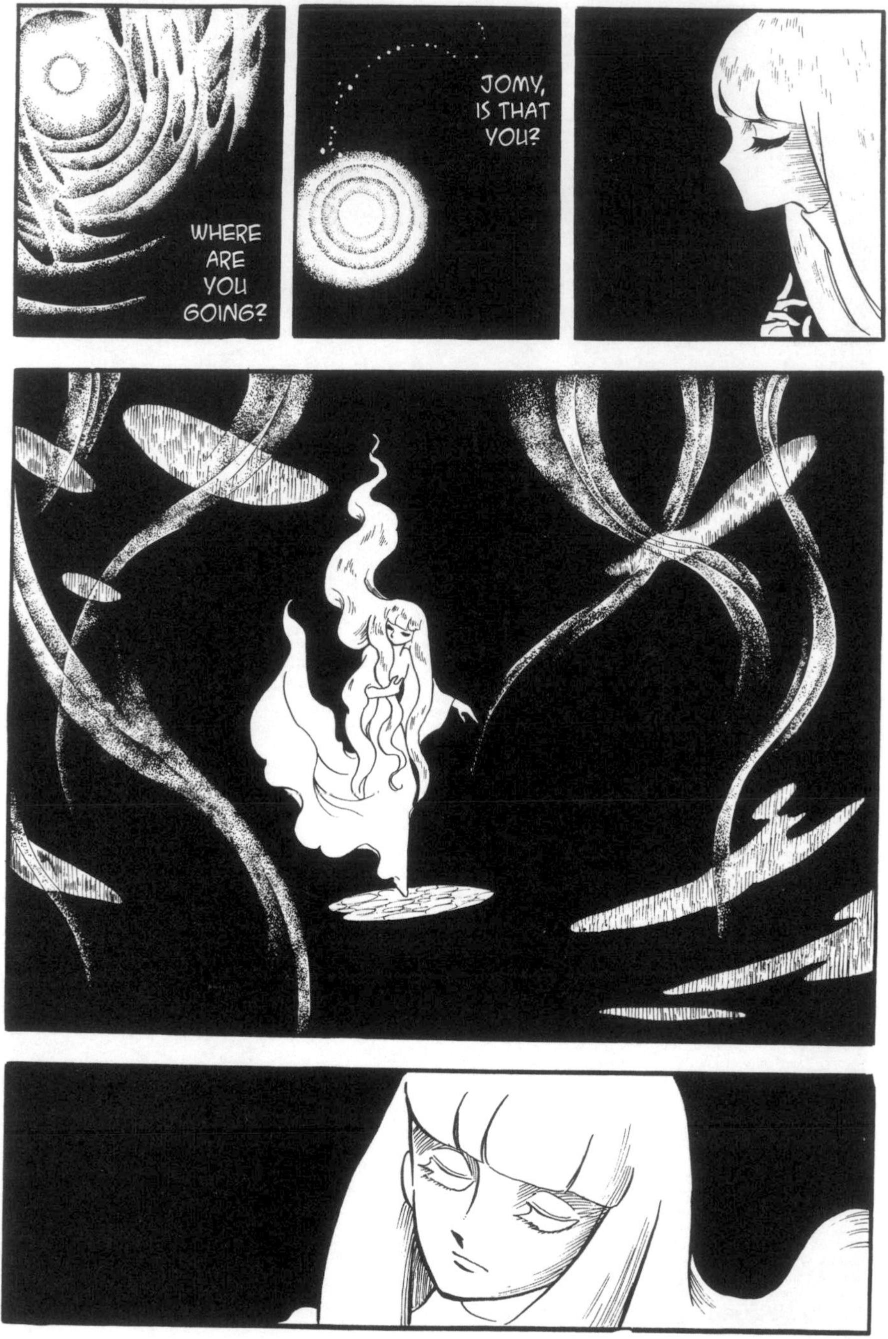
JOMY, IS THAT YOU?
WHERE ARE YOU GOING?

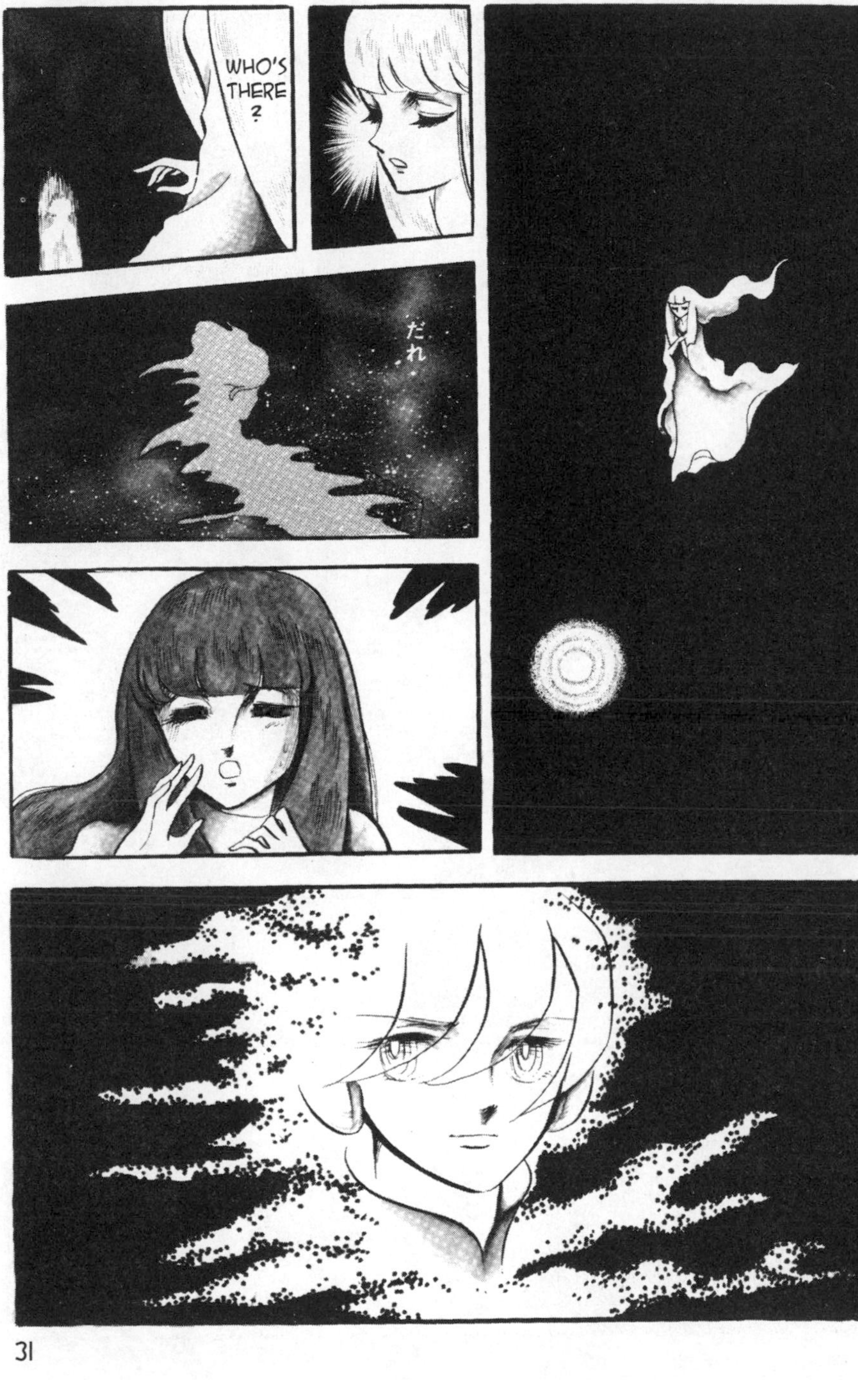
WHO'S THERE ?
だれ

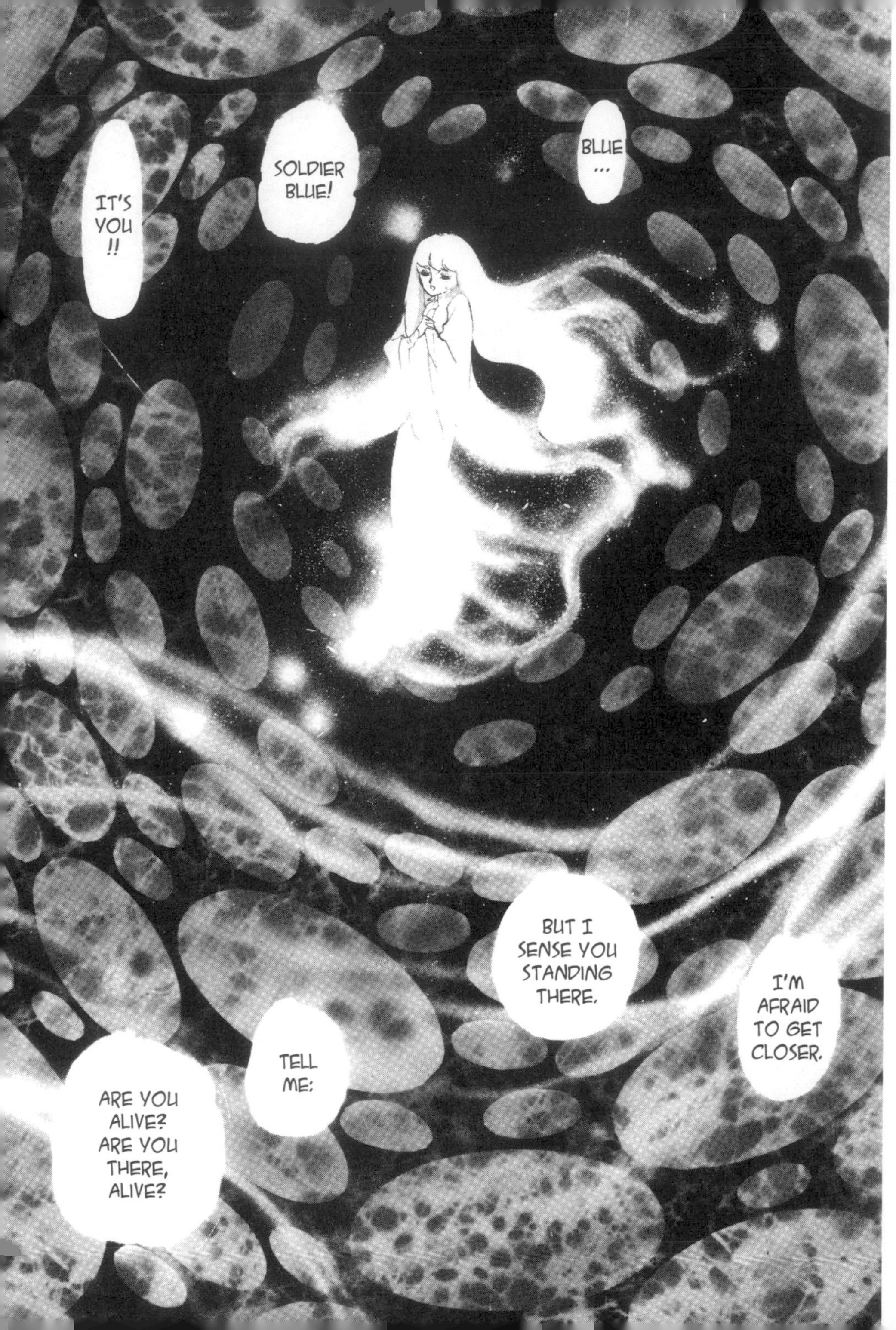
BLUE ...
SOLDIER BLUE!
IT'S YOU !!
I'M AFRAID TO GET CLOSER.
BUT I SENSE YOU STANDING THERE.
TELL ME:
ARE YOU ALIVE? ARE YOU THERE, ALIVE?

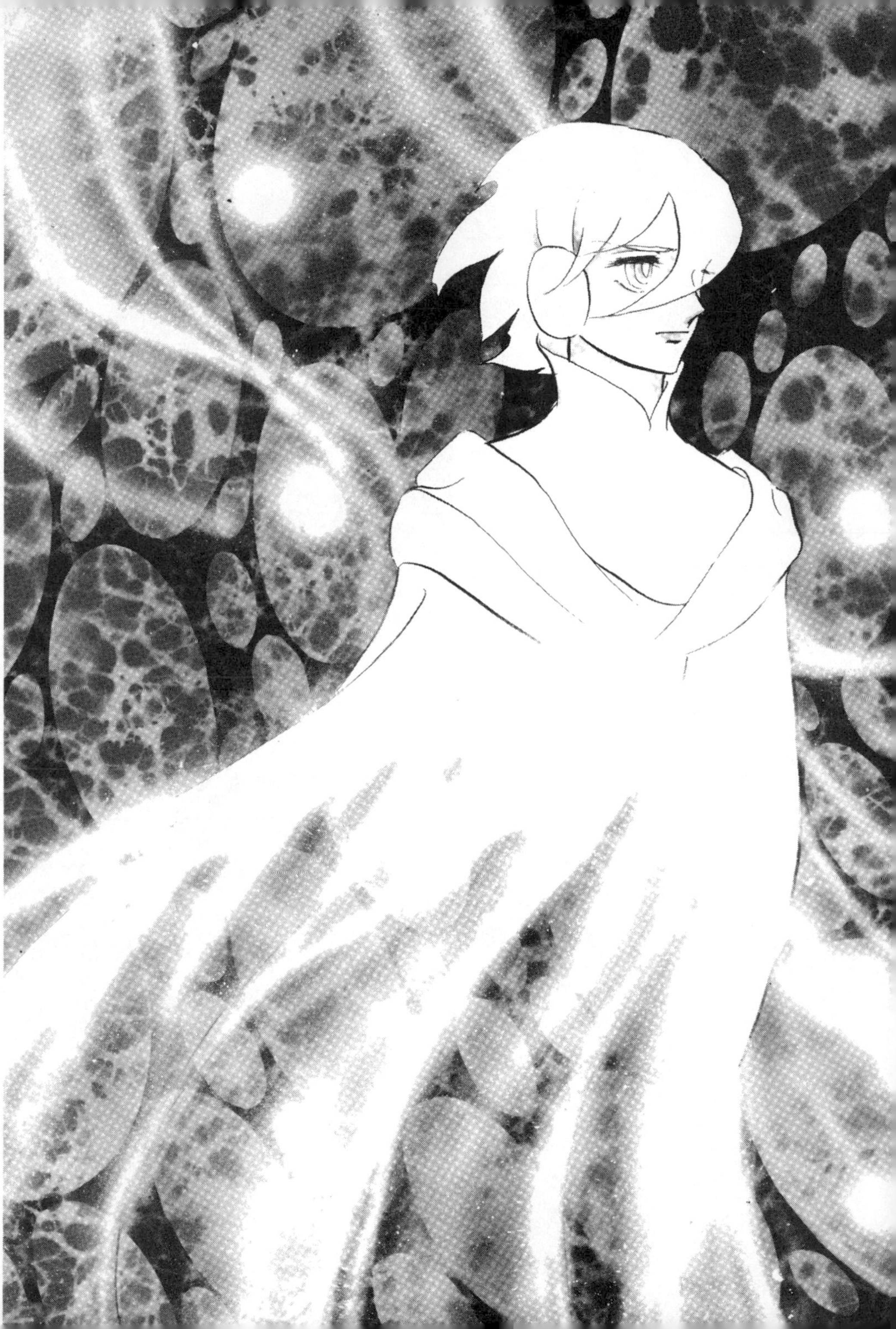

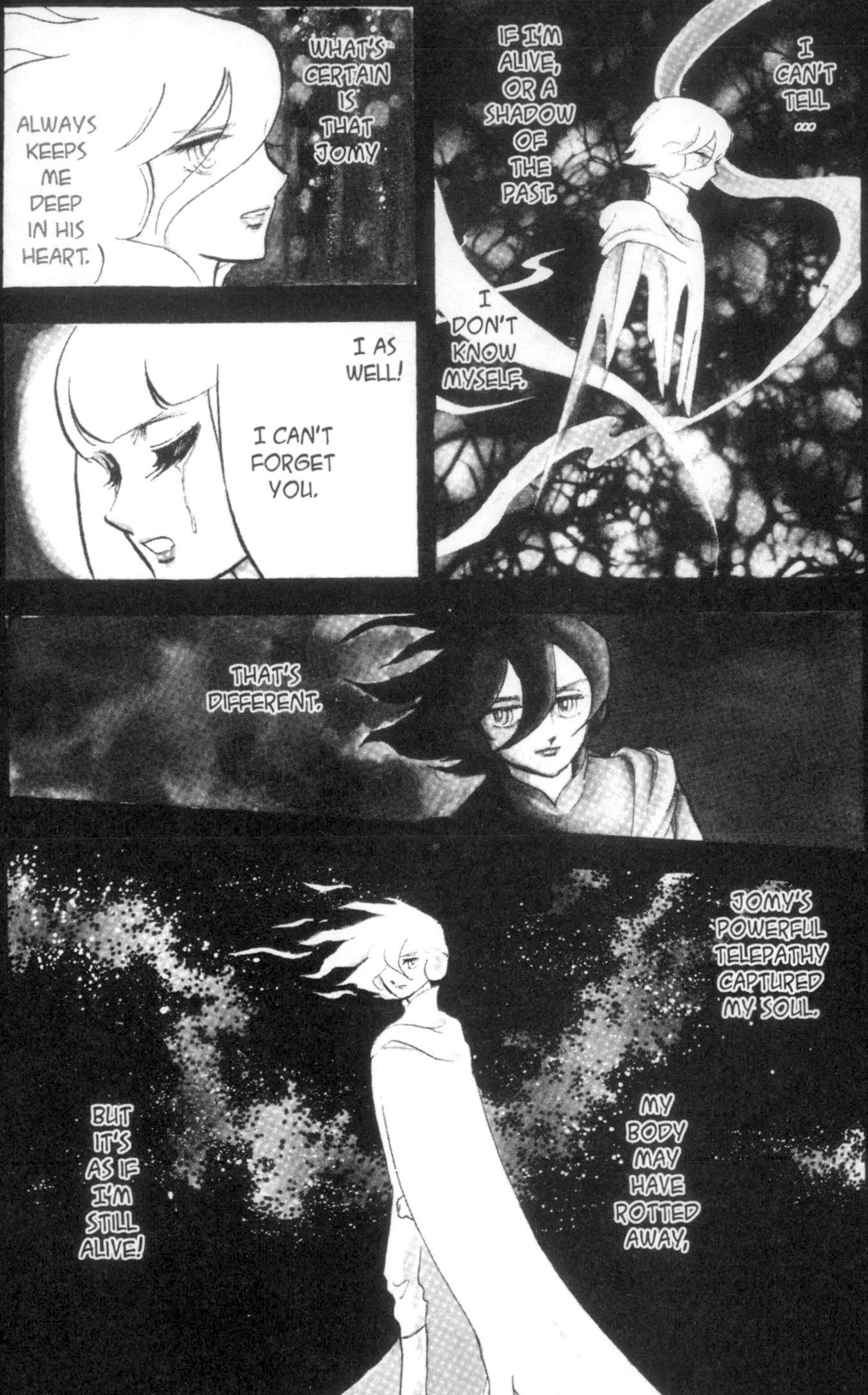
I CAN'T TELL ...
IF I'M ALIVE, OR A SHADOW OF THE PAST.
I DON'T KNOW MYSELF.
WHAT'S CERTAIN IS THAT JOMY
ALWAYS KEEPS ME DEEP IN HIS HEART.
I AS WELL!
I CAN'T FORGET YOU.
THAT'S DIFFERENT.
JOMY'S POWERFUL TELEPATHY CAPTURED MY SOUL.
MY BODY MAY HAVE ROTTED AWAY,
BUT IT'S AS IF I'M STILL ALIVE!

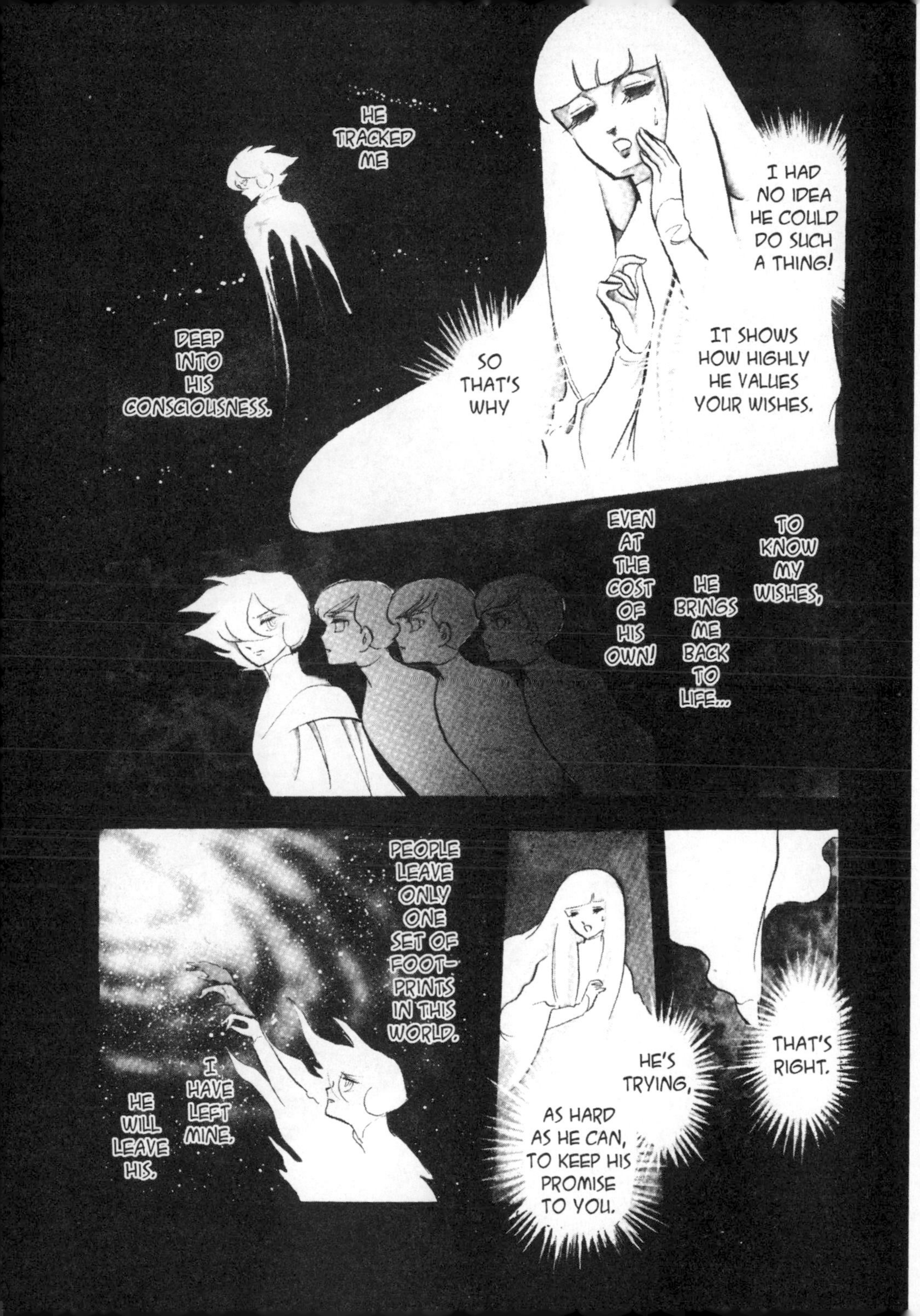
I HAD NO IDEA HE COULD DO SUCH A THING!
IT SHOWS HOW HIGHLY HE VALUES YOUR WISHES.
SO THAT'S WHY
HE TRACKED ME
DEEP INTO HIS CONSCIOUSNESS.
TO KNOW MY WISHES,
HE BRINGS ME BACK TO LIFE...
EVEN AT THE COST OF HIS OWN!
THAT'S RIGHT.
HE'S TRYING,
AS HARD AS HE CAN, TO KEEP HIS PROMISE TO YOU.
PEOPLE LEAVE ONLY ONE SET OF FOOT-PRINTS IN THIS WORLD.
I HAVE LEFT MINE.
HE WILL LEAVE HIS.

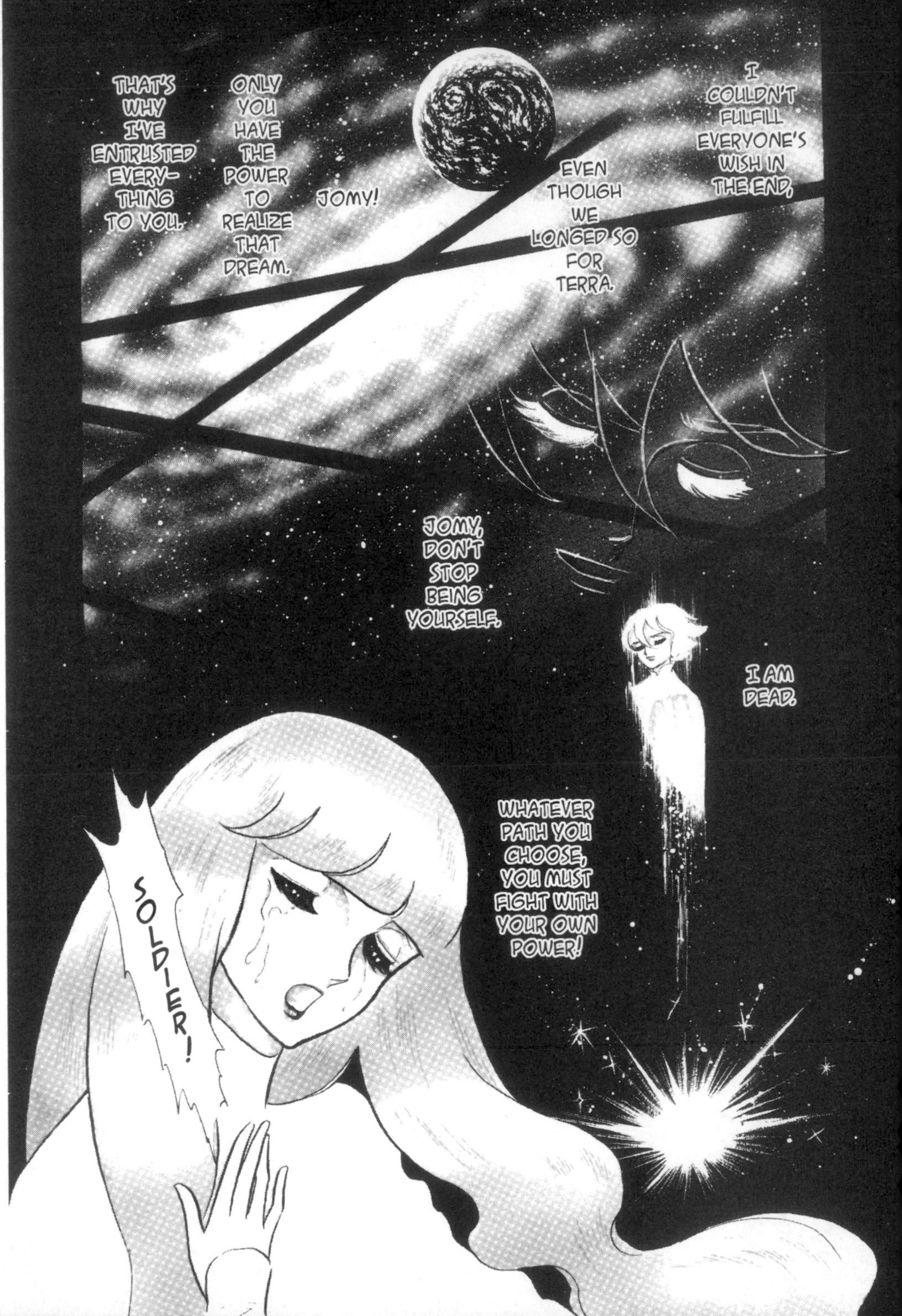
I COULDN'T FULFILL EVERYONE'S WISH IN THE END,
EVEN THOUGH WE LONGED SO FOR TERRA.
JOMY!
ONLY YOU HAVE THE POWER TO REALIZE THAT DREAM.
THAT'S WHY I'VE ENTRUSTED EVERY-THING TO YOU.
JOMY, DON'T STOP BEING YOURSELF.
I AM DEAD.
WHATEVER PATH YOU CHOOSE, YOU MUST FIGHT WITH YOUR OWN POWER!
SOLDIER!

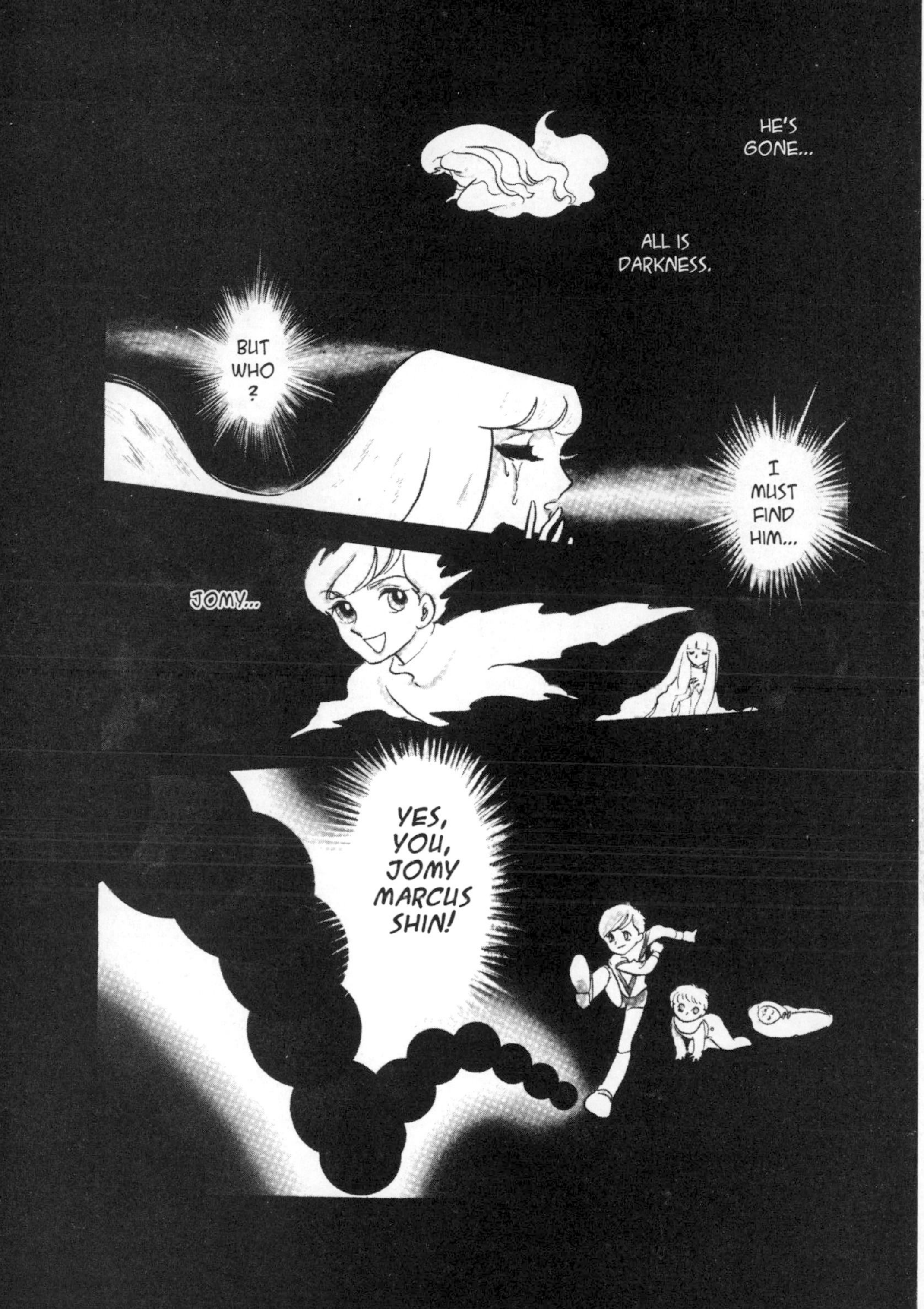
HE'S GONE...
ALL IS DARKNESS.
I MUST FIND HIM...
BUT WHO ?
JOMY...
YES, YOU, JOMY MARCUS SHIN!

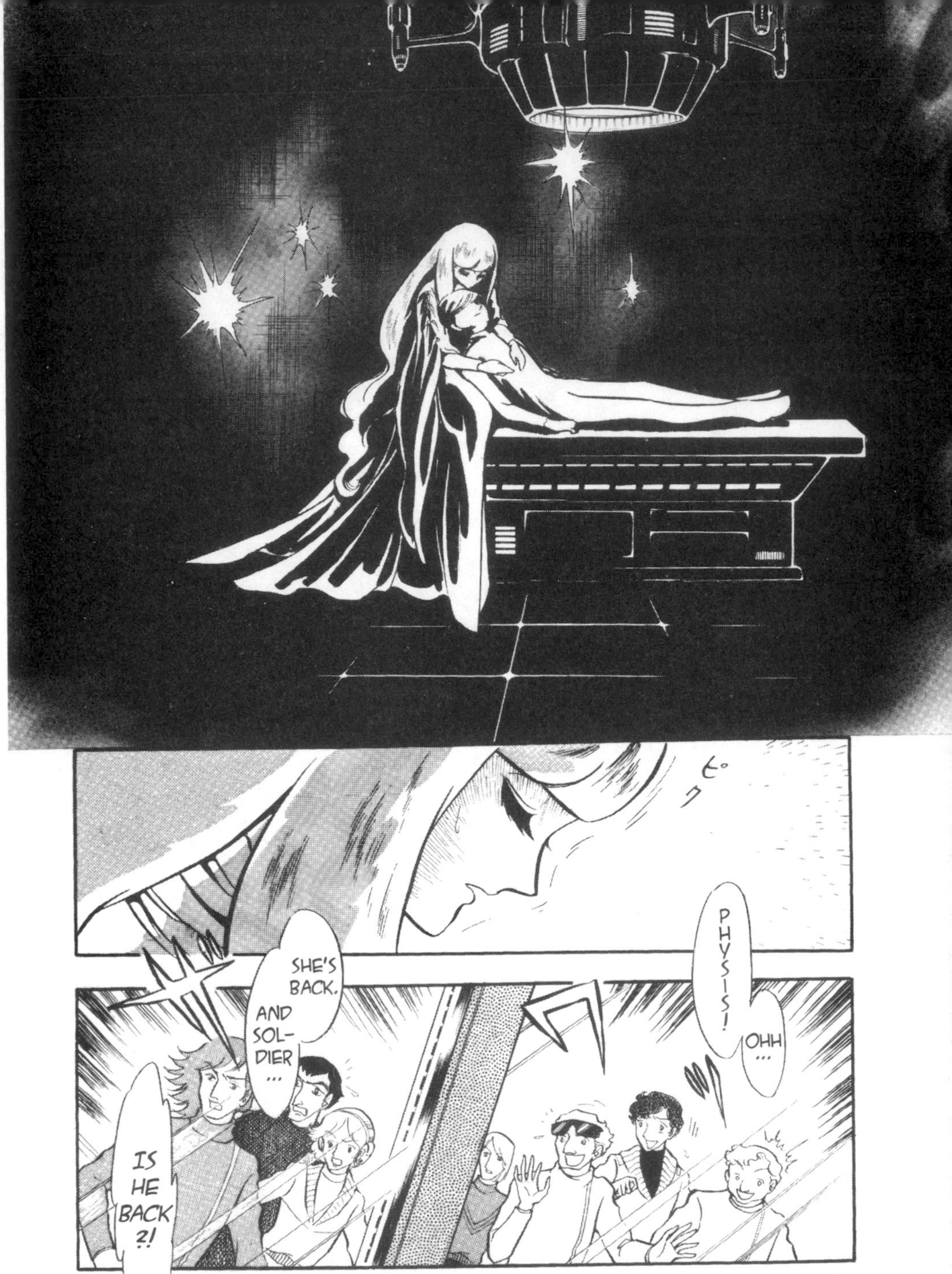
ピク
PHYSIS!
OHH...
SHE'S BACK.
AND SOLDIER...
IS HE BACK?!

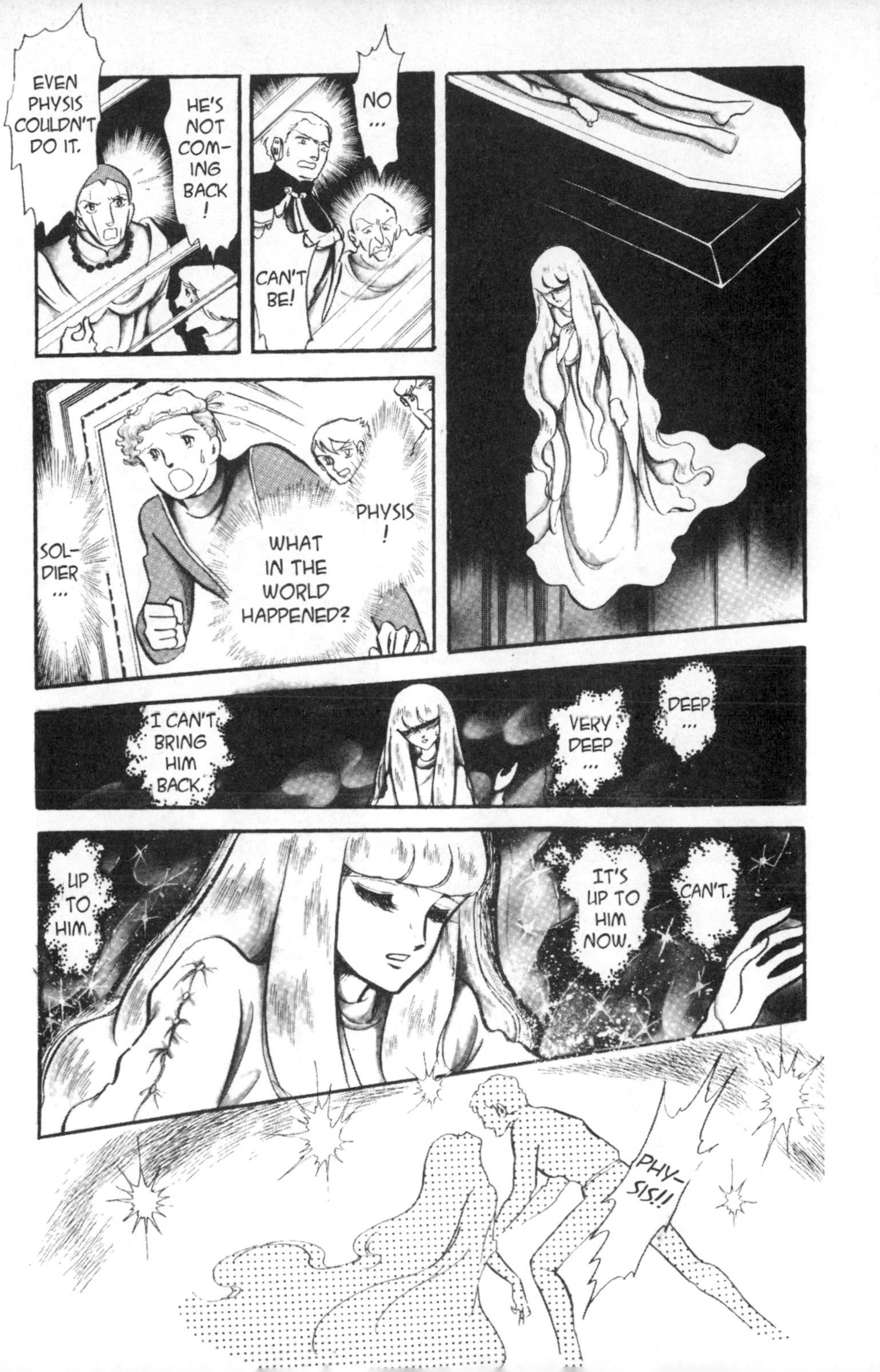
NO...
HE'S NOT COMING BACK!
CAN'T BE!
EVEN PHYSIS COULDN'T DO IT.
PHYSIS!
WHAT IN THE WORLD HAPPENED?
SOLDIER...
DEEP...
VERY DEEP...
I CAN'T BRING HIM BACK.
CAN'T.
IT'S UP TO HIM NOW.
UP TO HIM.
PHYSIS!!

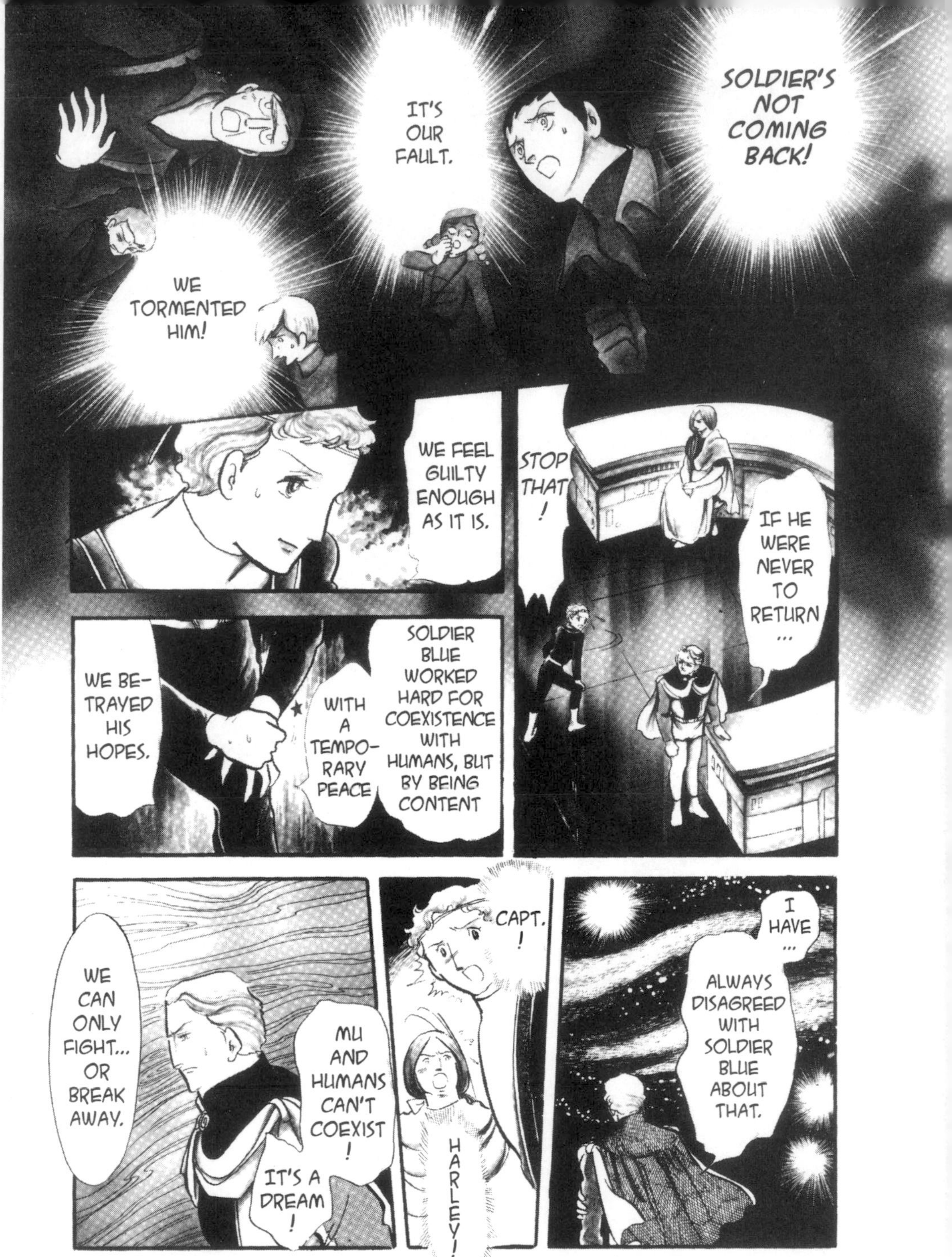
SOLDIER'S NOT COMING BACK!
IT'S OUR FAULT.
WE TORMENTED HIM!
IF HE WERE NEVER TO RETURN ...
STOP THAT!
WE FEEL GUILTY ENOUGH AS IT IS.
SOLDIER BLUE WORKED HARD FOR COEXISTENCE WITH HUMANS, BUT BY BEING CONTENT
WITH A TEMPORARY PEACE
WE BETRAYED HIS HOPES.
I HAVE ...
ALWAYS DISAGREED WITH SOLDIER BLUE ABOUT THAT.
CAPT.!
MU AND HUMANS CAN'T COEXIST!
HARLEY!
IT'S A DREAM!
WE CAN ONLY FIGHT... OR BREAK AWAY.

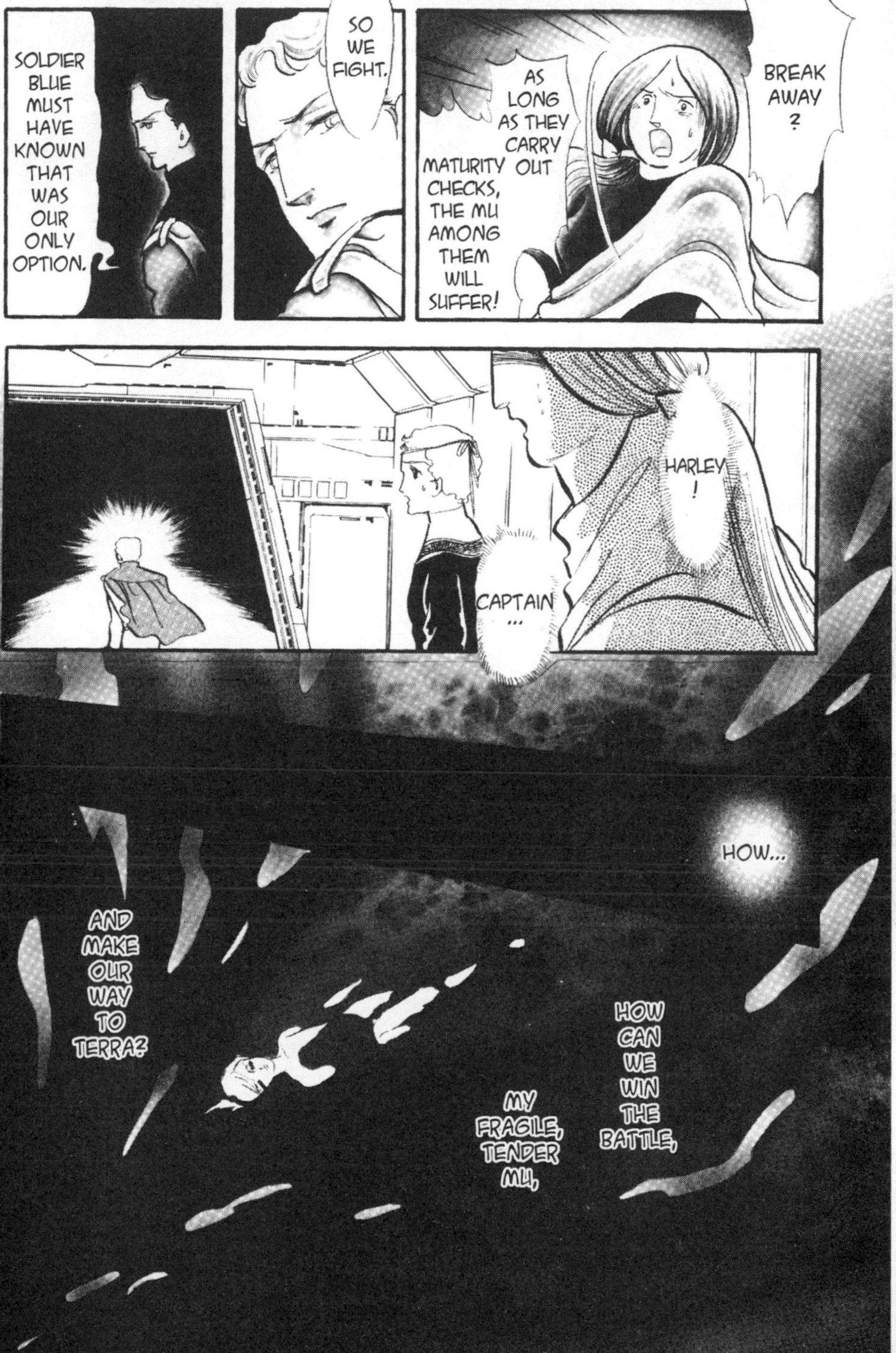
BREAK AWAY?
AS LONG AS THEY CARRY OUT MATURITY CHECKS, THE MU AMONG THEM WILL SUFFER!
SO WE FIGHT.
SOLDIER BLUE MUST HAVE KNOWN THAT WAS OUR ONLY OPTION.
HARLEY!
CAPTAIN...
HOW...
HOW CAN WE WIN THE BATTLE,
MY FRAGILE, TENDER MU,
AND MAKE OUR WAY TO TERRA?

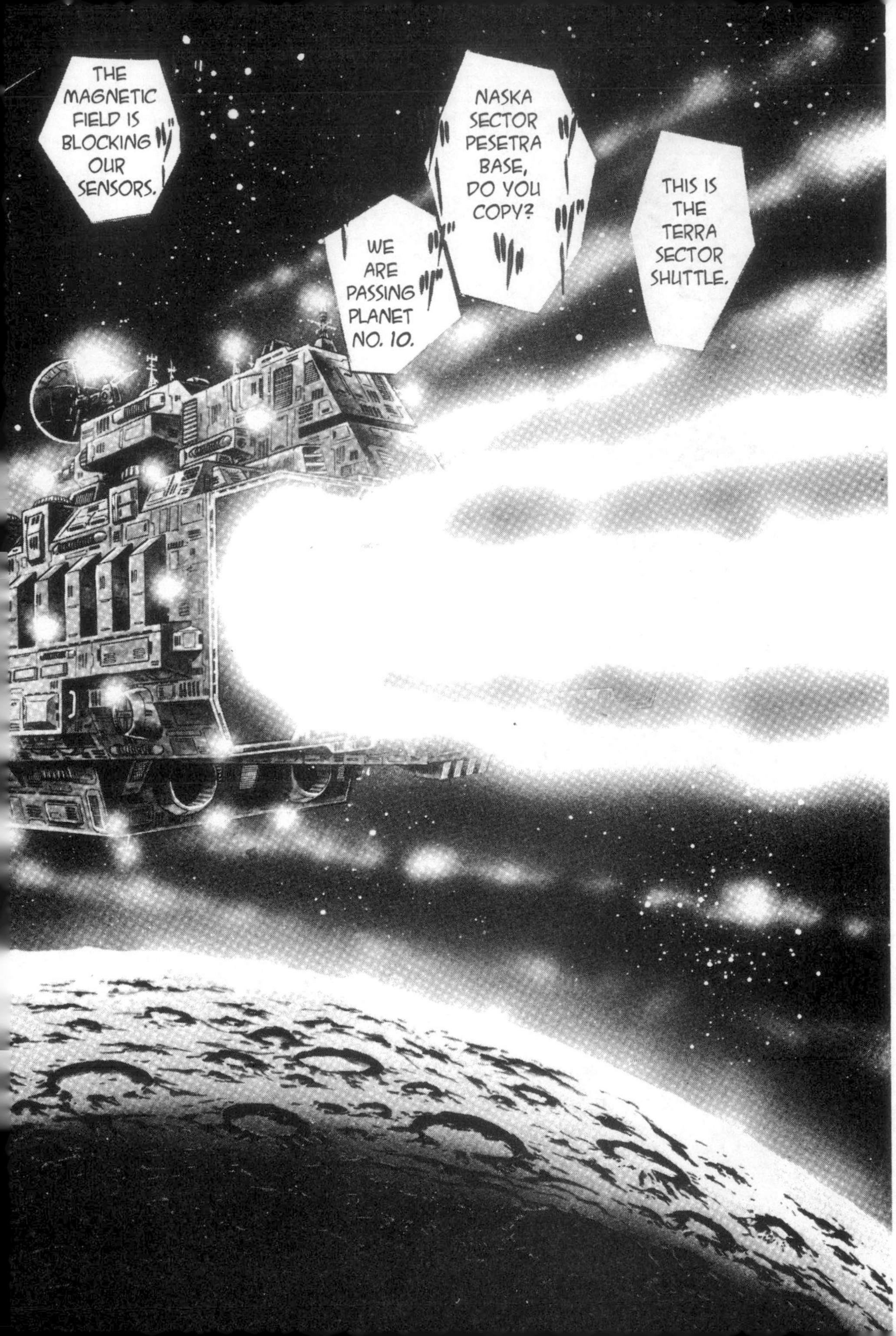
THIS IS THE TERRA SECTOR SHUTTLE.
NASKA SECTOR PESETRA BASE, DO YOU COPY?
WE ARE PASSING PLANET NO. 10.
THE MAGNETIC FIELD IS BLOCKING OUR SENSORS.

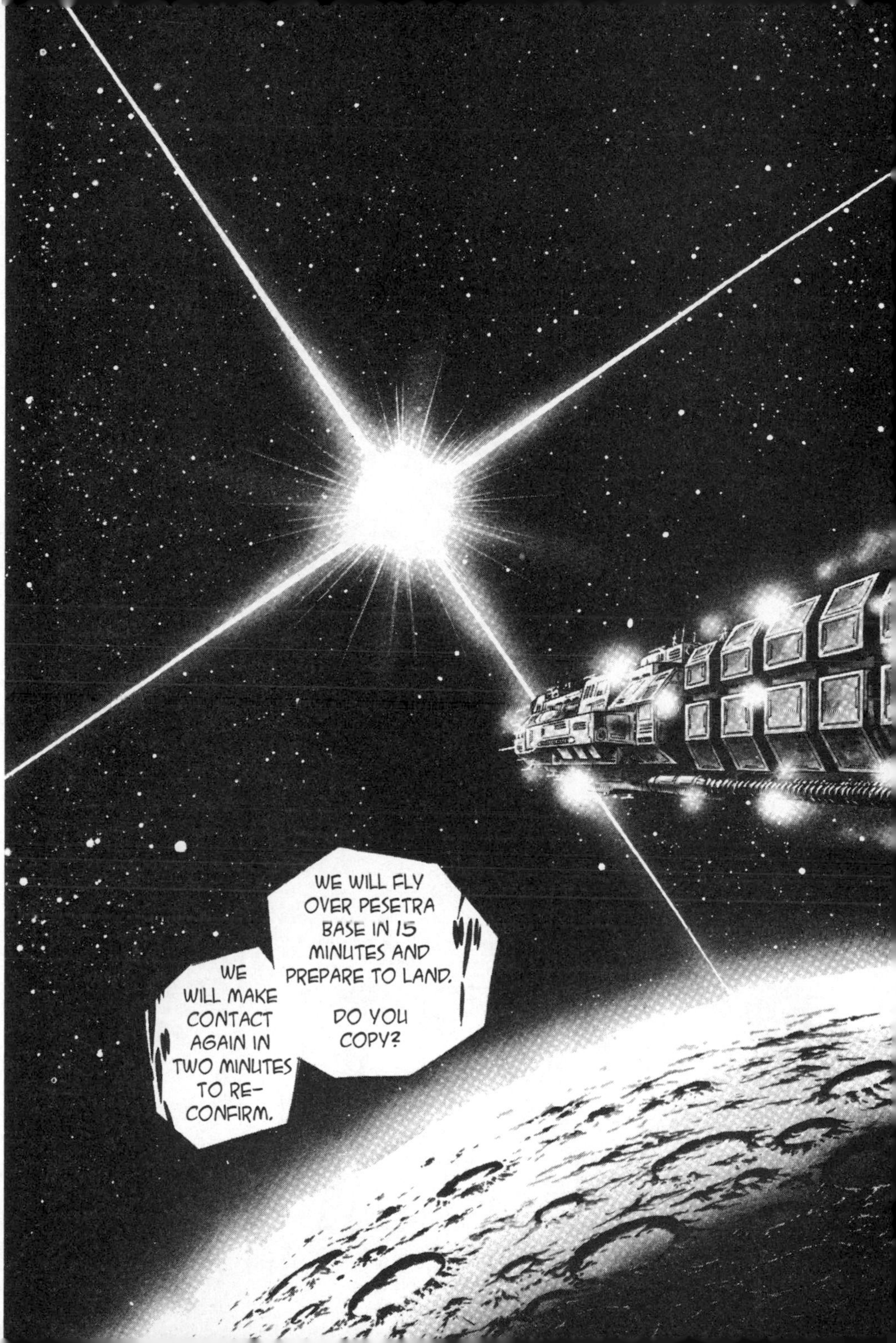
WE WILL FLY OVER PESETRA BASE IN 15 MINUTES AND PREPARE TO LAND.
DO YOU COPY?
WE WILL MAKE CONTACT AGAIN IN TWO MINUTES TO RE-CONFIRM.

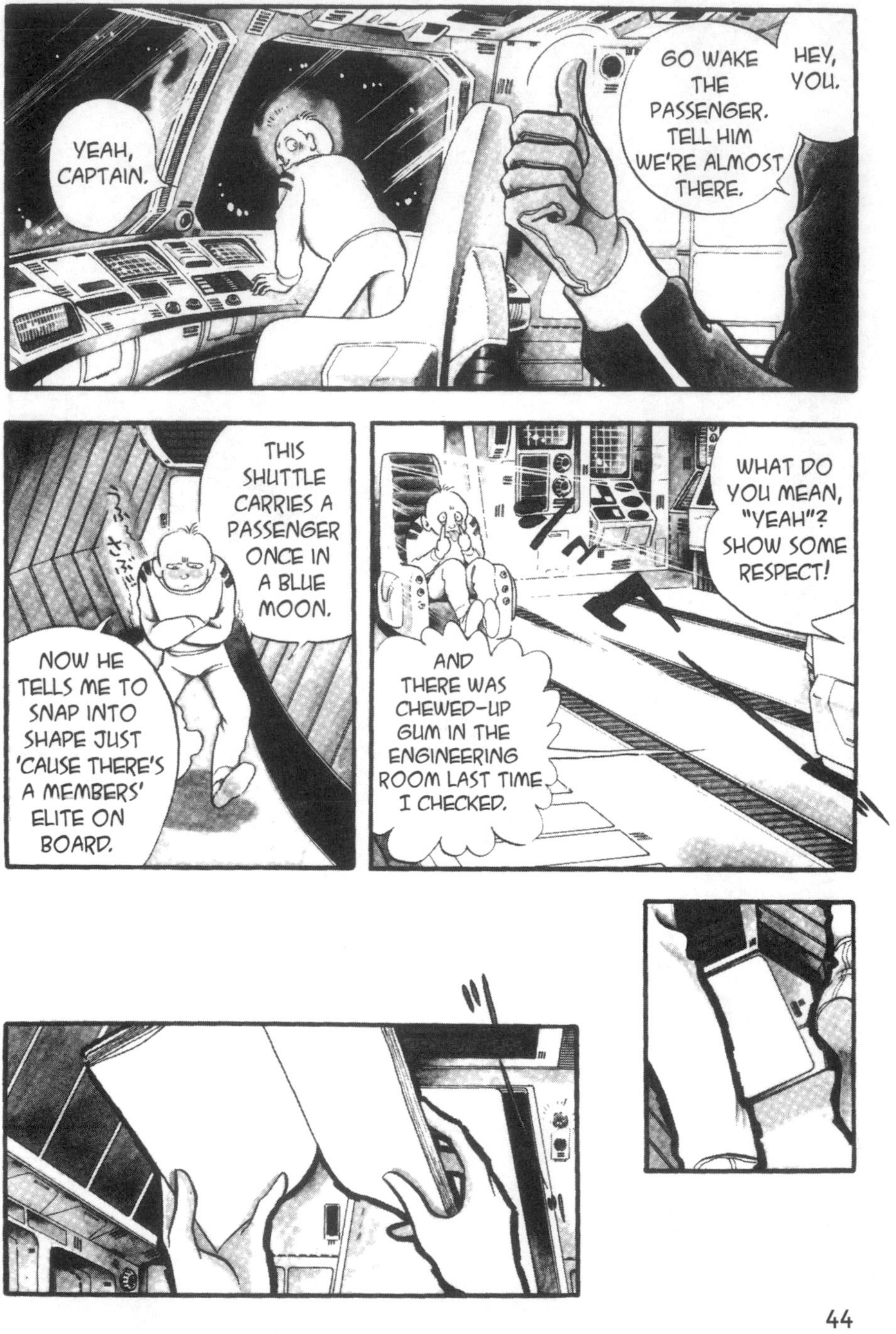
HEY, YOU.
GO WAKE THE PASSENGER. TELL HIM WE'RE ALMOST THERE.
YEAH, CAPTAIN.
WHAT DO YOU MEAN, "YEAH"? SHOW SOME RESPECT!
AND THERE WAS CHEWED-UP GUM IN THE ENGINEERING ROOM LAST TIME I CHECKED.
THIS SHUTTLE CARRIES A PASSENGER ONCE IN A BLUE MOON.
NOW HE TELLS ME TO SNAP INTO SHAPE JUST 'CAUSE THERE'S A MEMBERS' ELITE ON BOARD.

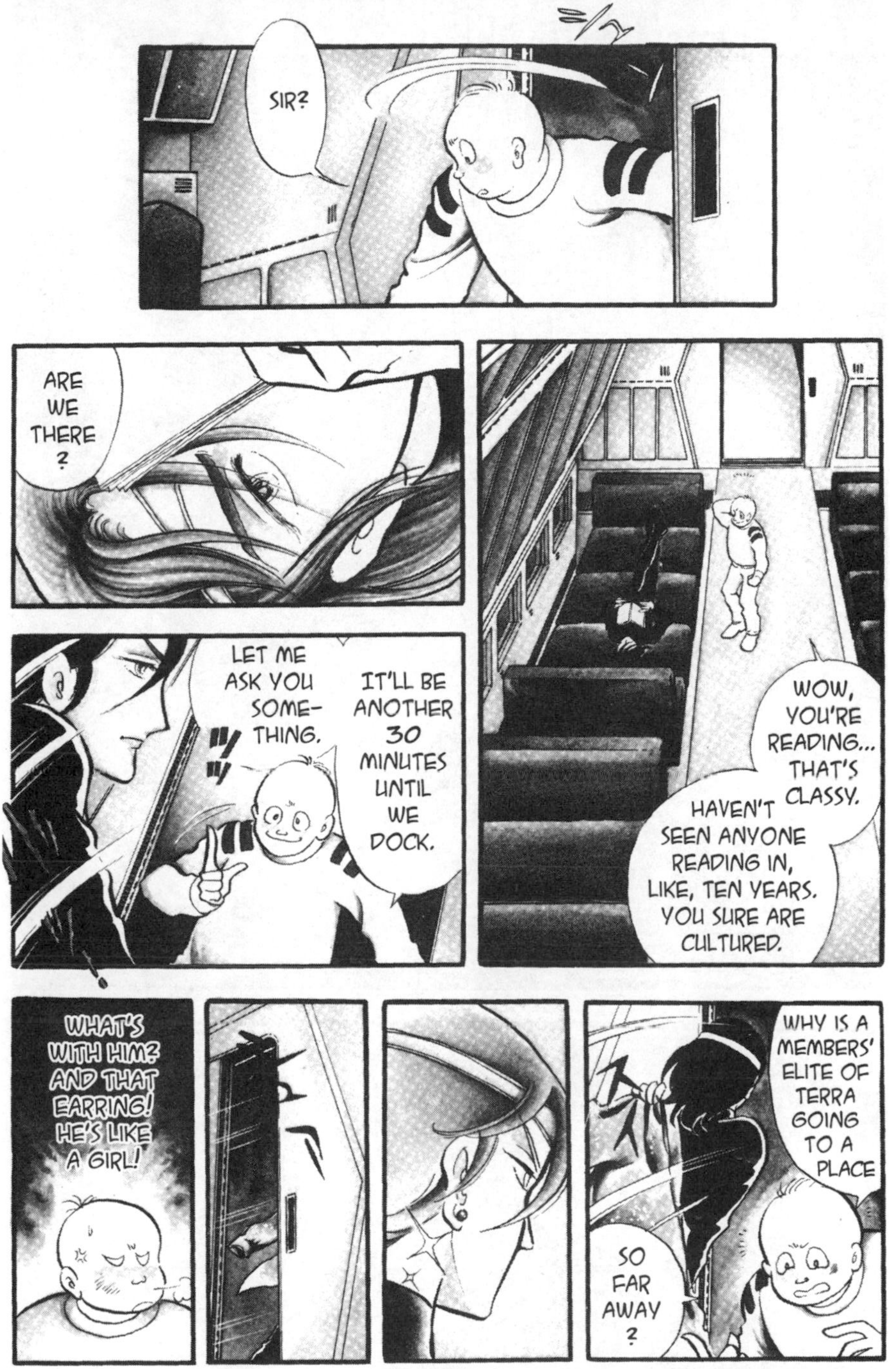
SIR?
WOW, YOU'RE READING... THAT'S CLASSY.
HAVEN'T SEEN ANYONE READING IN, LIKE, TEN YEARS. YOU SURE ARE CULTURED.
ARE WE THERE?
IT'LL BE ANOTHER 30 MINUTES UNTIL WE DOCK.
LET ME ASK YOU SOMETHING.
WHY IS A MEMBERS' ELITE OF TERRA GOING TO A PLACE
SO FAR AWAY?
WHAT'S WITH HIM? AND THAT EARRING! HE'S LIKE A GIRL!

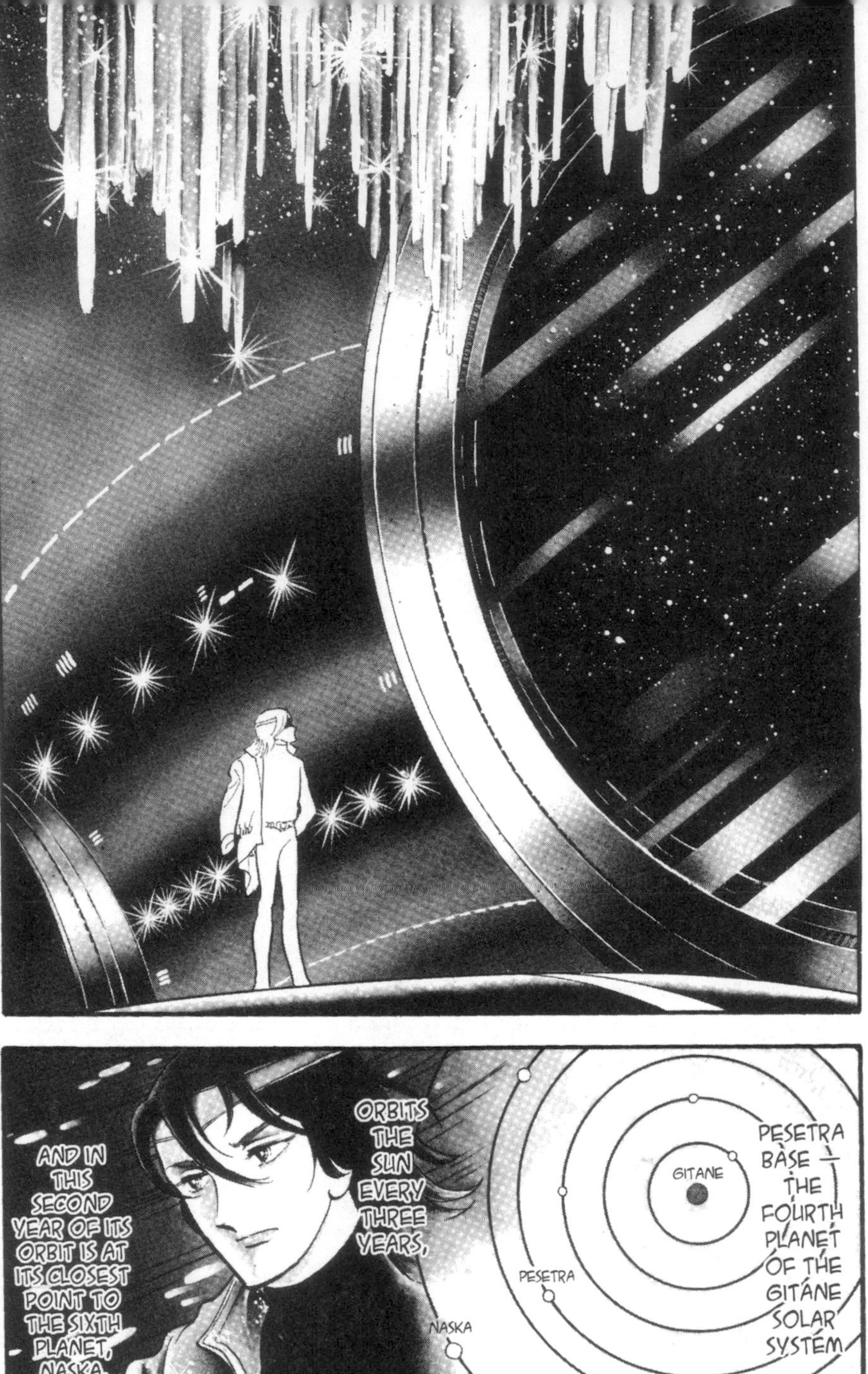
PESETRA BASE — THE FOURTH PLANET OF THE GITÁNE SOLAR SYSTEM
GITANE
PESETRA
NASKA
ORBITS THE SUN EVERY THREE YEARS,
AND IN THIS SECOND YEAR OF ITS ORBIT IS AT ITS CLOSEST POINT TO THE SIXTH PLANET, NASKA.

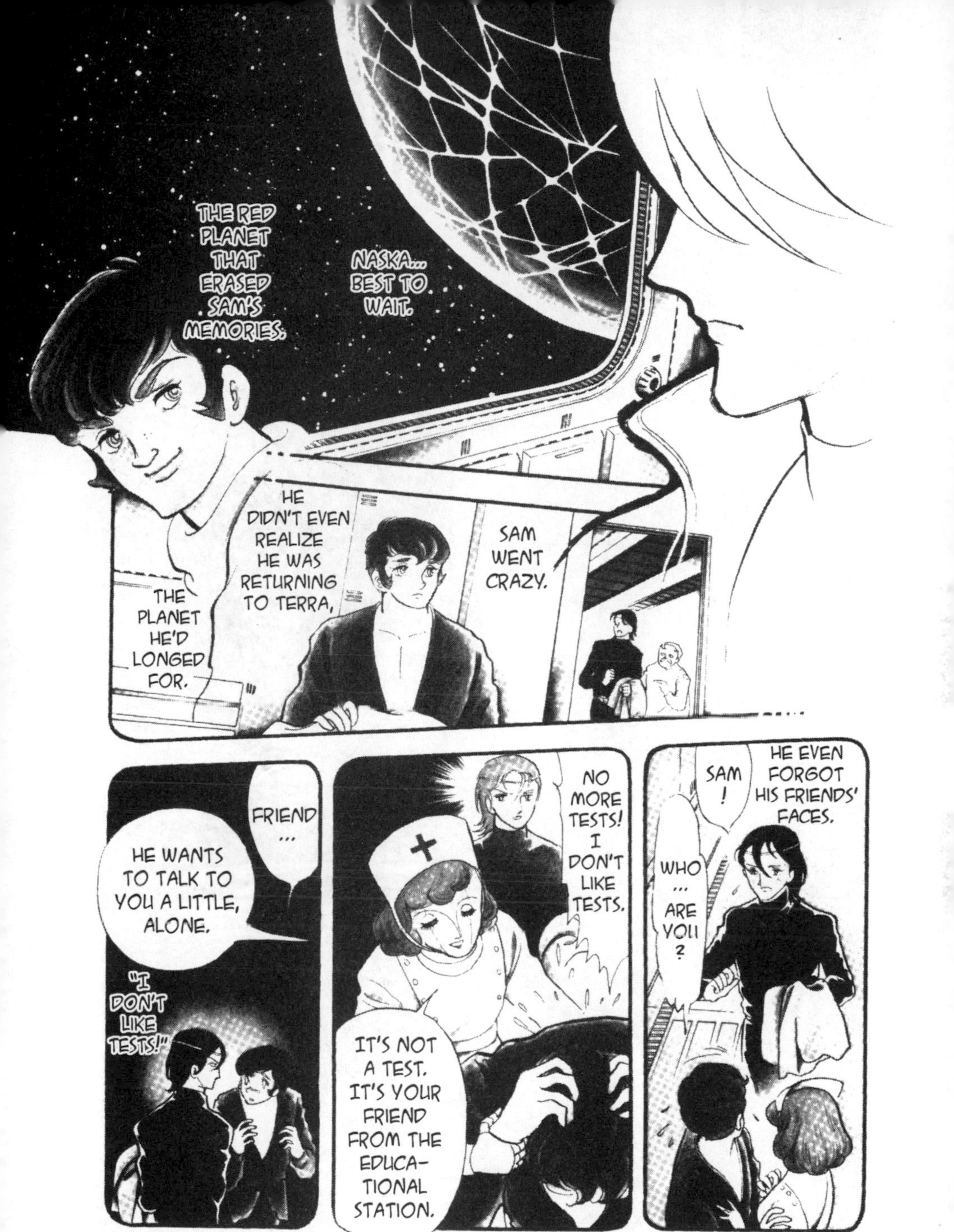
NASKA... BEST TO WAIT.
THE RED PLANET THAT ERASED SAM'S MEMORIES.
SAM WENT CRAZY.
HE DIDN'T EVEN REALIZE HE WAS RETURNING TO TERRA,
THE PLANET HE'D LONGED FOR.
HE EVEN FORGOT HIS FRIENDS' FACES.
SAM!
WHO ... ARE YOU?
NO MORE TESTS! I DON'T LIKE TESTS.
IT'S NOT A TEST. IT'S YOUR FRIEND FROM THE EDUCA-TIONAL STATION.
FRIEND ...
HE WANTS TO TALK TO YOU A LITTLE, ALONE.
"I DON'T LIKE TESTS!"

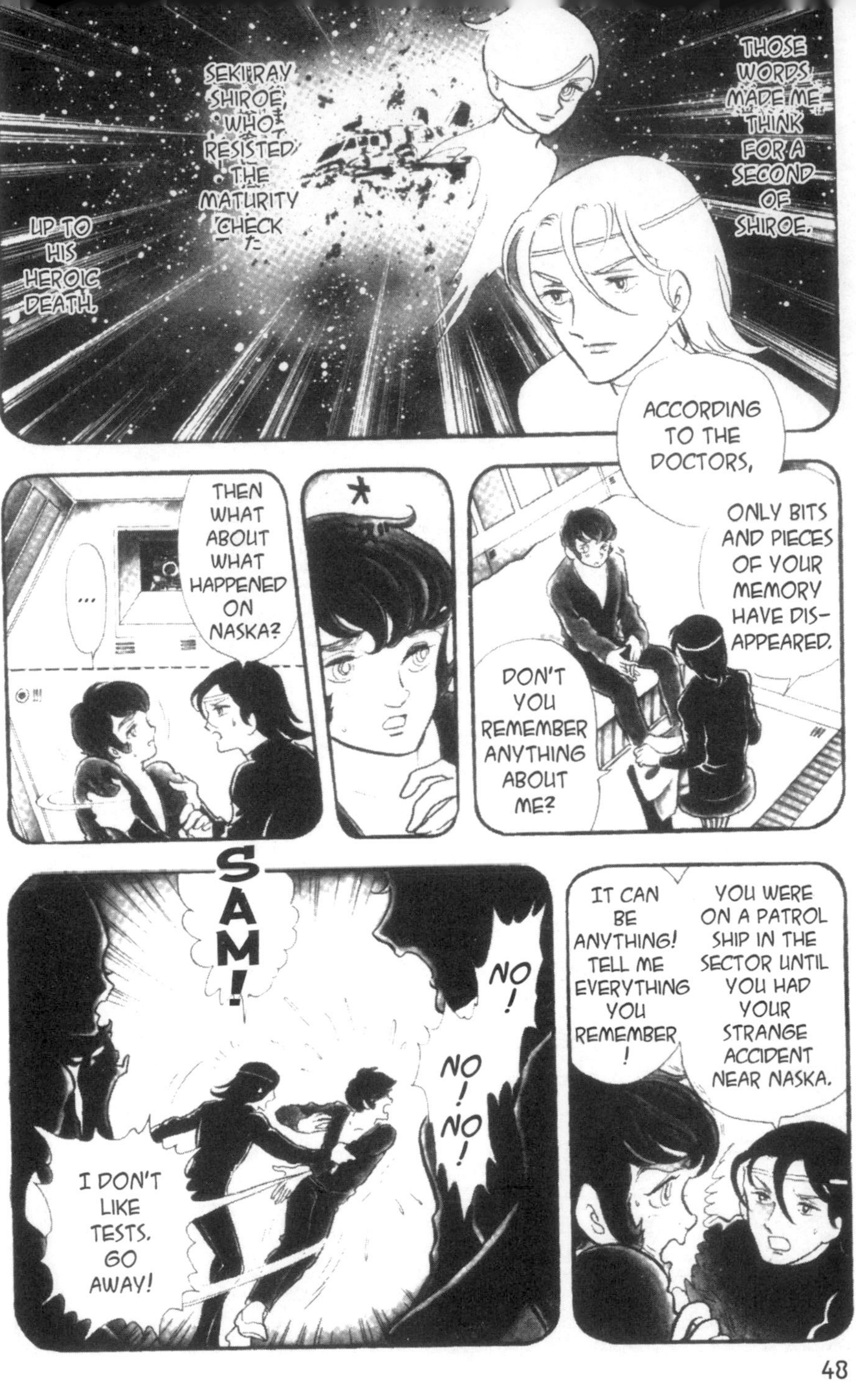

THOSE WORDS MADE ME THINK FOR A SECOND OF SHIROE.
SEKIRAY SHIROE, WHO RESISTED THE MATURITY CHECK
UP TO HIS HEROIC DEATH.
ACCORDING TO THE DOCTORS,
ONLY BITS AND PIECES OF YOUR MEMORY HAVE DIS-APPEARED.
DON'T YOU REMEMBER ANYTHING ABOUT ME?
*
THEN WHAT ABOUT WHAT HAPPENED ON NASKA?
...
!!!
YOU WERE ON A PATROL SHIP IN THE SECTOR UNTIL YOU HAD YOUR STRANGE ACCIDENT NEAR NASKA.
IT CAN BE ANYTHING! TELL ME EVERYTHING YOU REMEMBER!
SAM!
NO!
NO! NO!
I DON'T LIKE TESTS. GO AWAY!

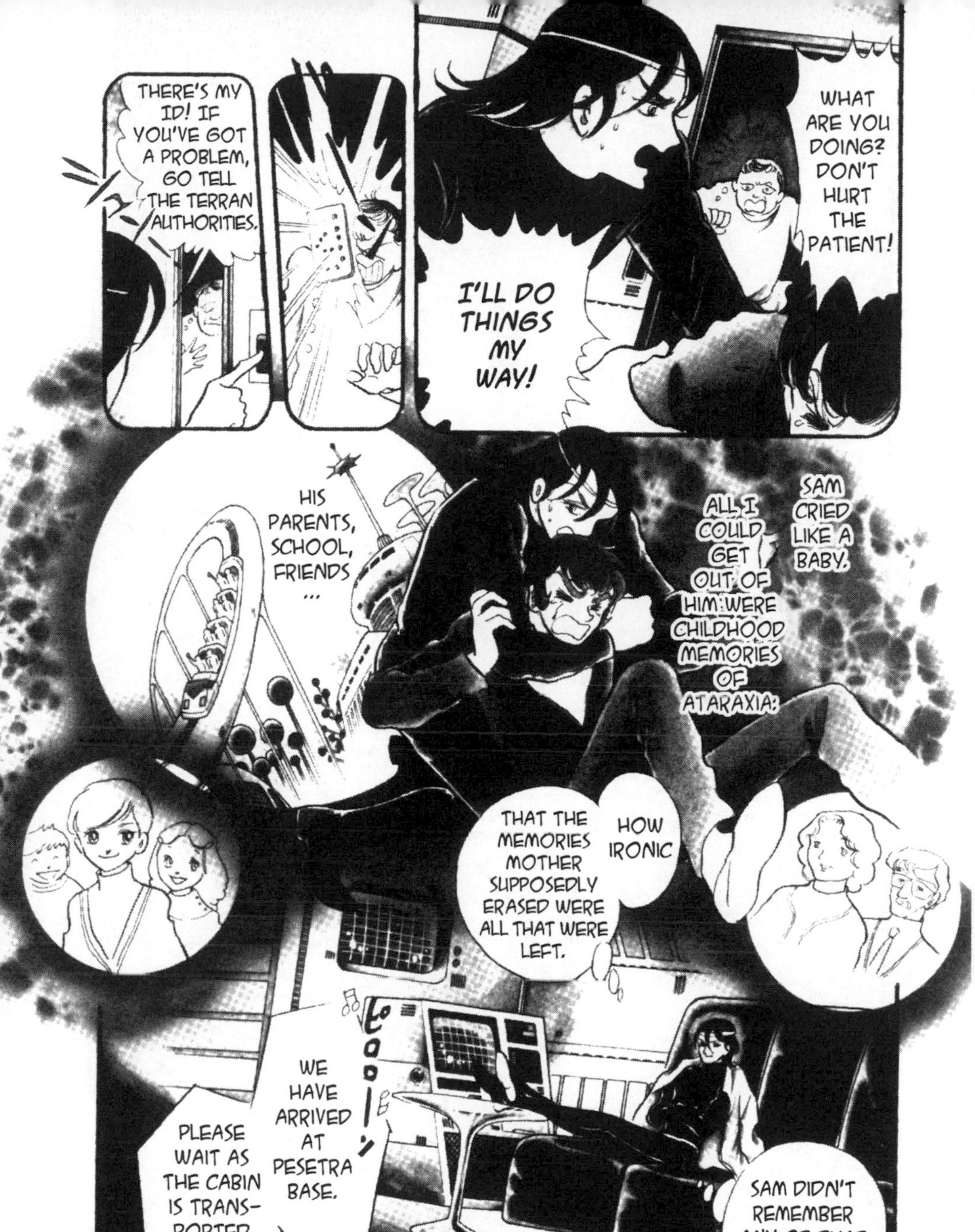
WHAT ARE YOU DOING? DON'T HURT THE PATIENT!
I'LL DO THINGS MY WAY!
THERE'S MY ID! IF YOU'VE GOT A PROBLEM, GO TELL THE TERRAN AUTHORITIES.
SAM CRIED LIKE A BABY.
ALL I COULD GET OUT OF HIM WERE CHILDHOOD MEMORIES OF ATARAXIA.
HIS PARENTS, SCHOOL, FRIENDS ...
HOW IRONIC
THAT THE MEMORIES MOTHER SUPPOSEDLY ERASED WERE ALL THAT WERE LEFT.
SAM DIDN'T REMEMBER ANY OF THAT WHEN HE WAS NORMAL.
WE HAVE ARRIVED AT PESETRA BASE.
PLEASE WAIT AS THE CABIN IS TRANS-PORTED TO THE LANDING DOCK.

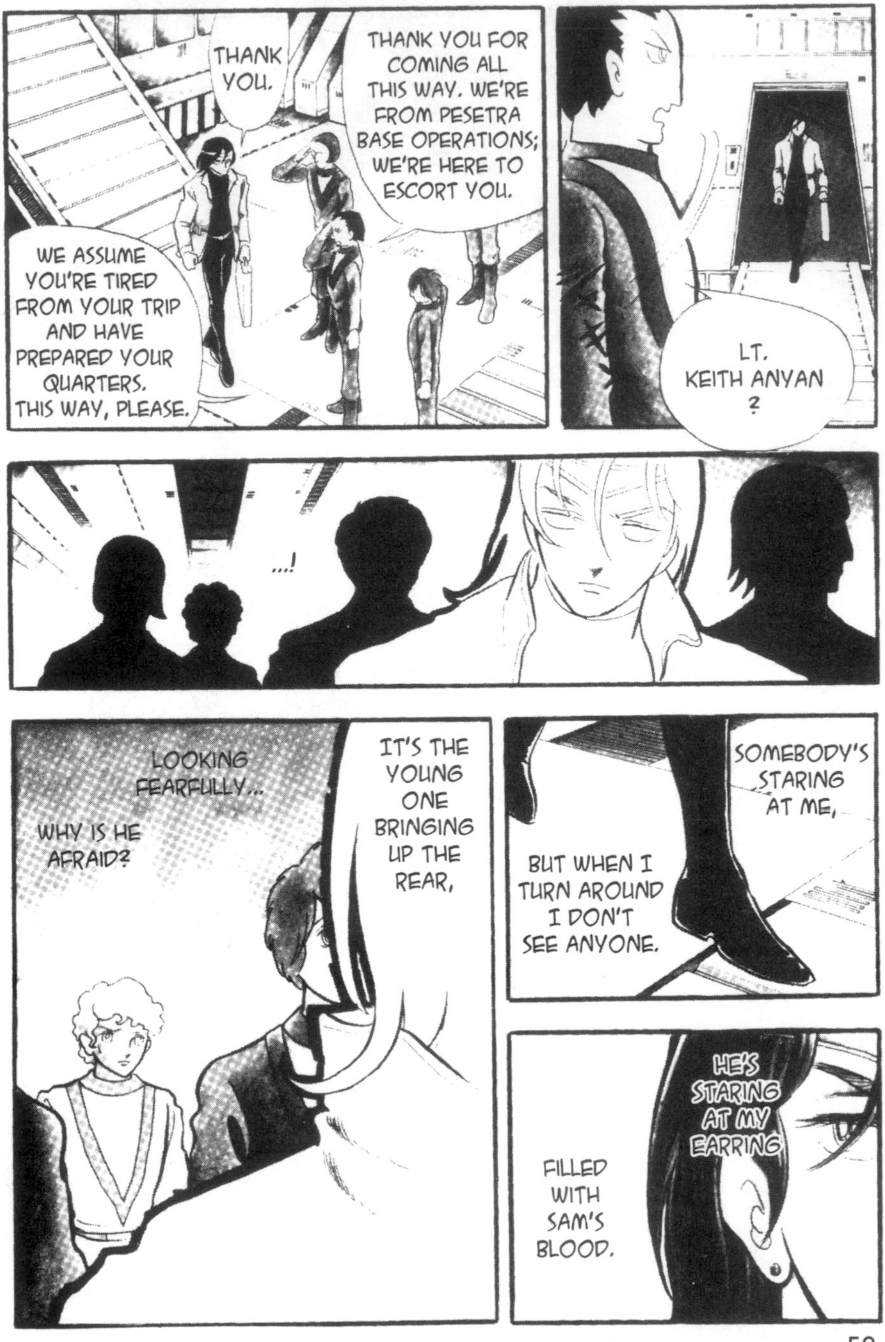
LT. KEITH ANYAN?
THANK YOU FOR COMING ALL THIS WAY. WE'RE FROM PESETRA BASE OPERATIONS; WE'RE HERE TO ESCORT YOU.
THANK YOU.
WE ASSUME YOU'RE TIRED FROM YOUR TRIP AND HAVE PREPARED YOUR QUARTERS. THIS WAY, PLEASE.
...!
SOMEBODY'S STARING AT ME,
BUT WHEN I TURN AROUND I DON'T SEE ANYONE.
HE'S STARING AT MY EARRING
FILLED WITH SAM'S BLOOD.
IT'S THE YOUNG ONE BRINGING UP THE REAR,
LOOKING FEARFULLY...
WHY IS HE AFRAID?

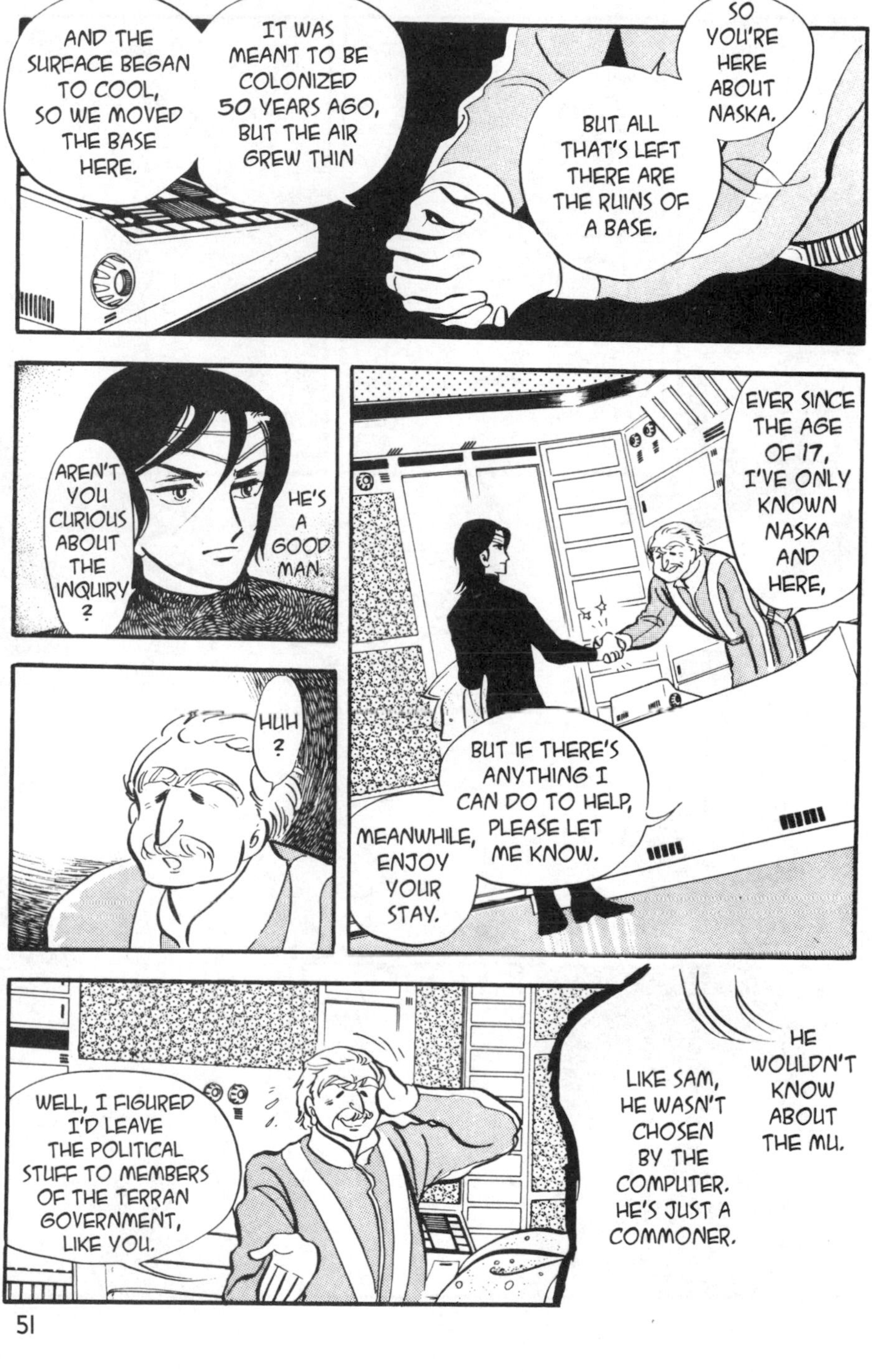
SO YOU'RE HERE ABOUT NASKA.
BUT ALL THAT'S LEFT THERE ARE THE RUINS OF A BASE.
IT WAS MEANT TO BE COLONIZED 50 YEARS AGO, BUT THE AIR GREW THIN
AND THE SURFACE BEGAN TO COOL, SO WE MOVED THE BASE HERE.
EVER SINCE THE AGE OF 17, I'VE ONLY KNOWN NASKA AND HERE,
BUT IF THERE'S ANYTHING I CAN DO TO HELP, PLEASE LET ME KNOW.
MEANWHILE, ENJOY YOUR STAY.
HE'S A GOOD MAN.
AREN'T YOU CURIOUS ABOUT THE INQUIRY?
HUH?
HE WOULDN'T KNOW ABOUT THE MU.
LIKE SAM, HE WASN'T CHOSEN BY THE COMPUTER. HE'S JUST A COMMONER.
WELL, I FIGURED I'D LEAVE THE POLITICAL STUFF TO MEMBERS OF THE TERRAN GOVERNMENT, LIKE YOU.

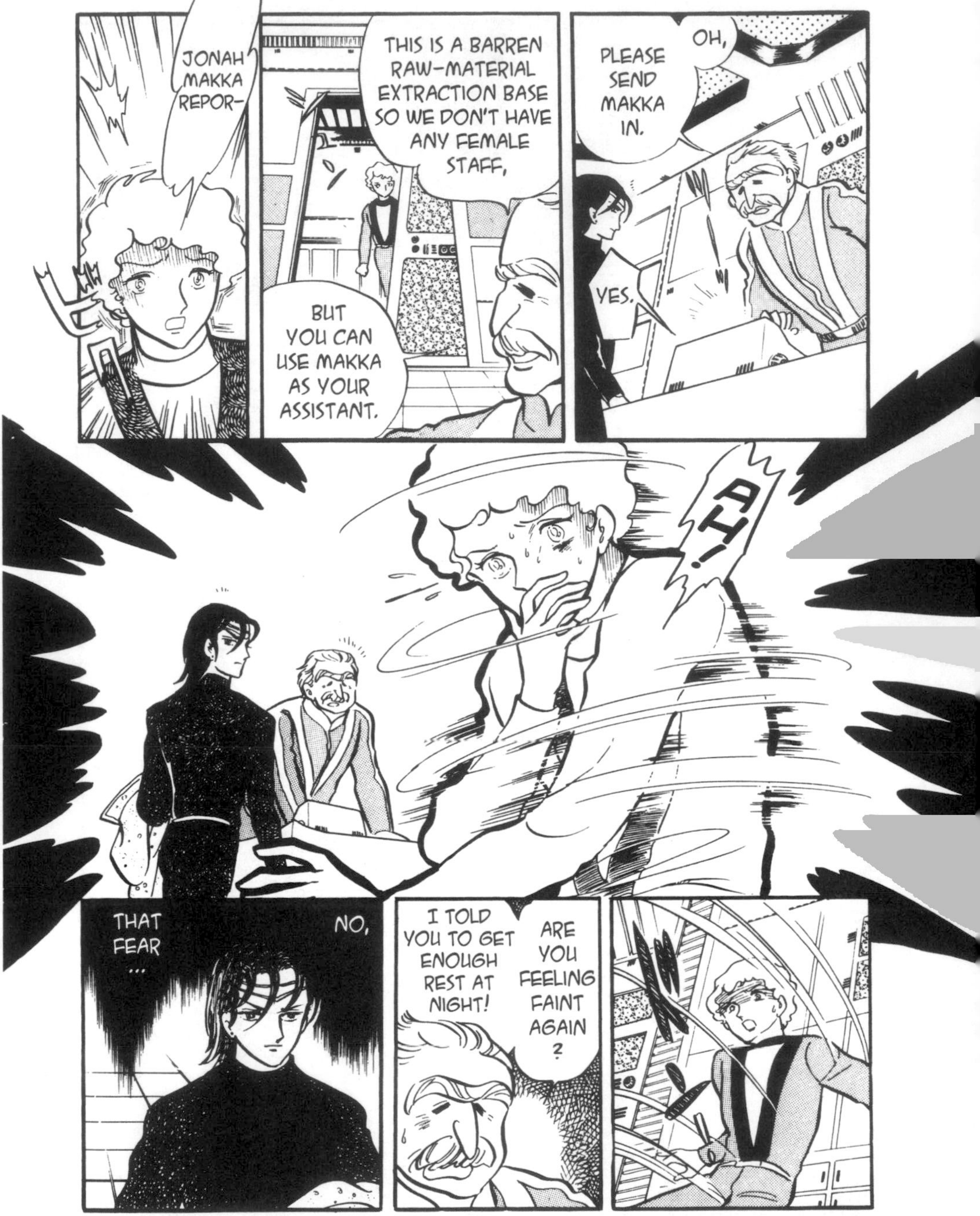
OH,
PLEASE SEND MAKKA IN.
YES.
THIS IS A BARREN RAW-MATERIAL EXTRACTION BASE SO WE DON'T HAVE ANY FEMALE STAFF,
BUT YOU CAN USE MAKKA AS YOUR ASSISTANT.
JONAH MAKKA REPOR-
AH!
ARE YOU FEELING FAINT AGAIN?
I TOLD YOU TO GET ENOUGH REST AT NIGHT!
NO,
THAT FEAR ...

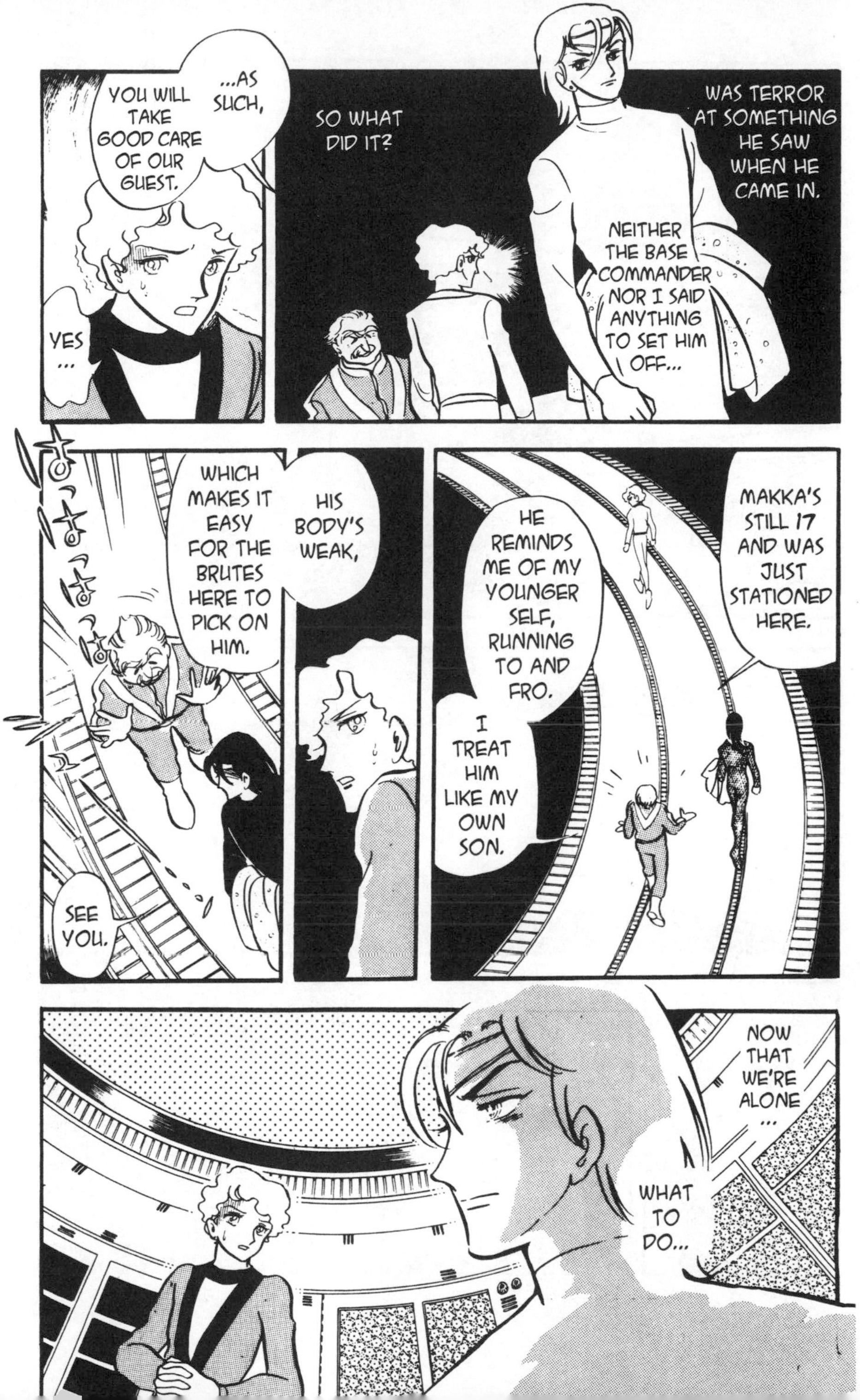

WAS TERROR AT SOMETHING HE SAW WHEN HE CAME IN.
NEITHER THE BASE COMMANDER NOR I SAID ANYTHING TO SET HIM OFF...
SO WHAT DID IT?
...AS SUCH,
YOU WILL TAKE GOOD CARE OF OUR GUEST.
YES ...
MAKKA'S STILL 17 AND WAS JUST STATIONED HERE.
HE REMINDS ME OF MY YOUNGER SELF, RUNNING TO AND FRO.
I TREAT HIM LIKE MY OWN SON.
HIS BODY'S WEAK,
WHICH MAKES IT EASY FOR THE BRUTES HERE TO PICK ON HIM.
SEE YOU.
NOW THAT WE'RE ALONE ...
WHAT TO DO...

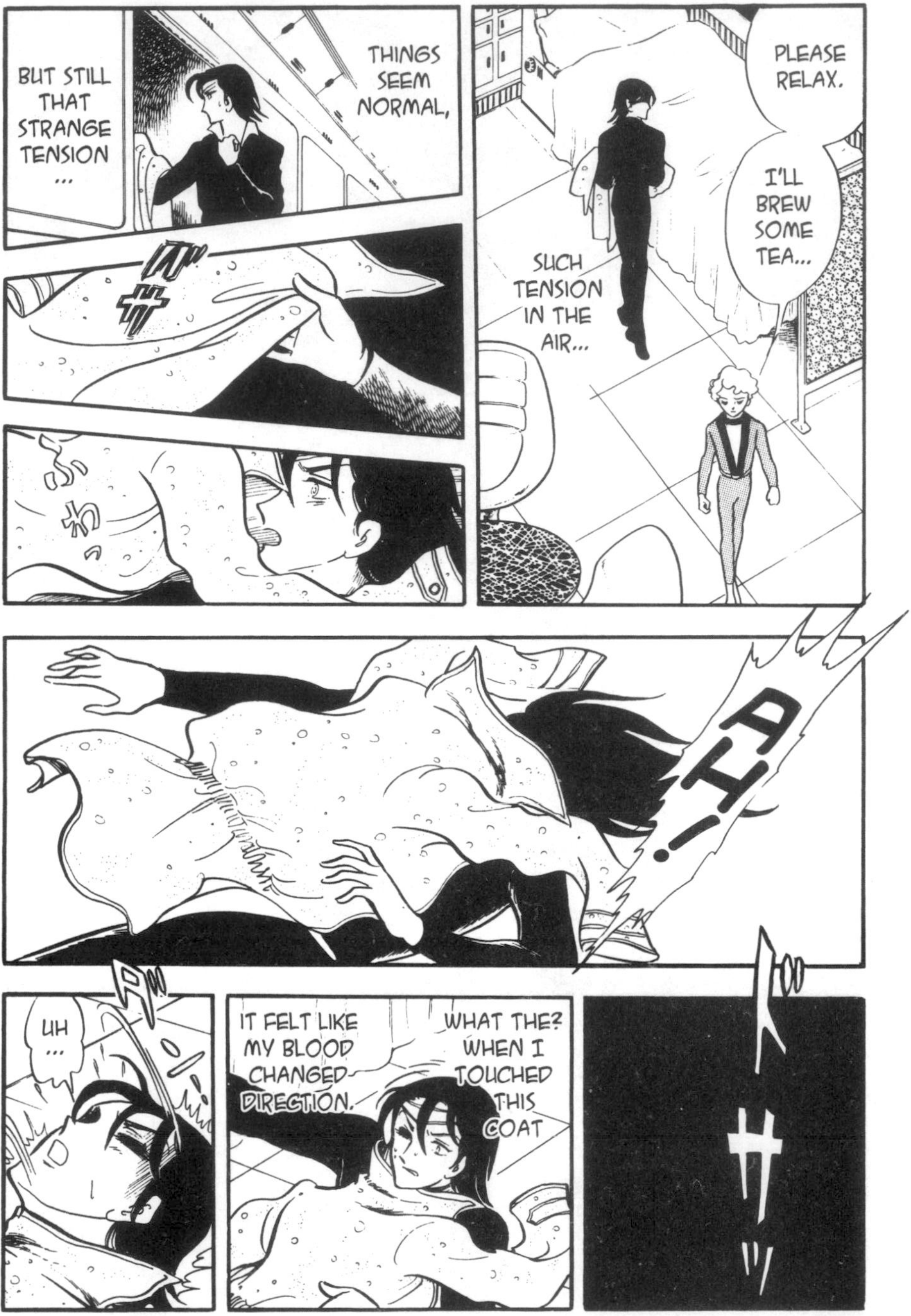
PLEASE RELAX.
I'LL BREW SOME TEA...
SUCH TENSION IN THE AIR...
THINGS SEEM NORMAL,
BUT STILL THAT STRANGE TENSION ...
AH!!
WHAT THE? WHEN I TOUCHED THIS COAT
IT FELT LIKE MY BLOOD CHANGED DIRECTION.
UH ...

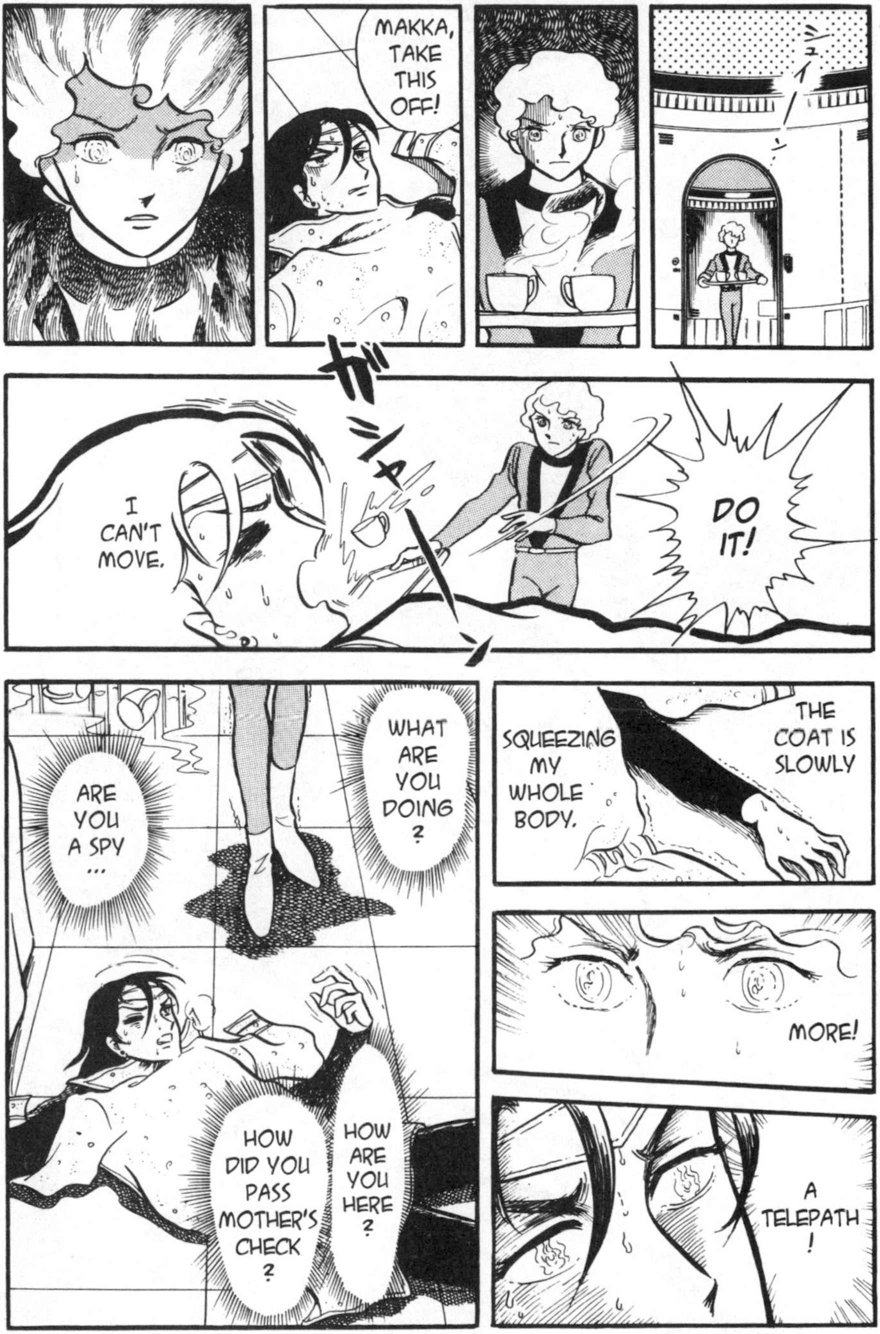
シュイーン
MAKKA, TAKE THIS OFF!
ガシャ
DO IT!
I CAN'T MOVE.
THE COAT IS SLOWLY
SQUEEZING MY WHOLE BODY.
MORE!
A TELEPATH!
WHAT ARE YOU DOING?
ARE YOU A SPY...
HOW ARE YOU HERE?
HOW DID YOU PASS MOTHER'S CHECK?

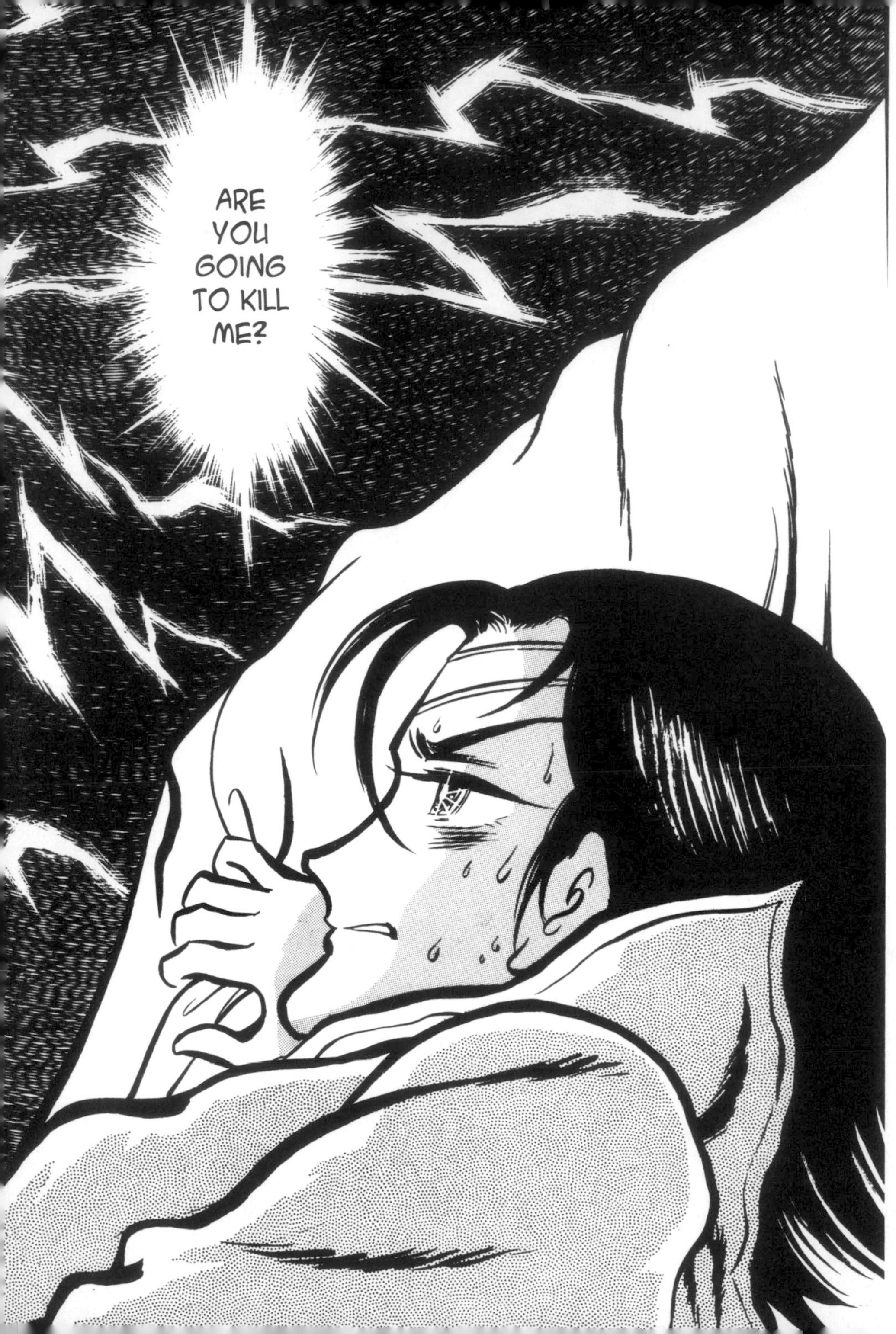
ARE YOU GOING TO KILL ME?

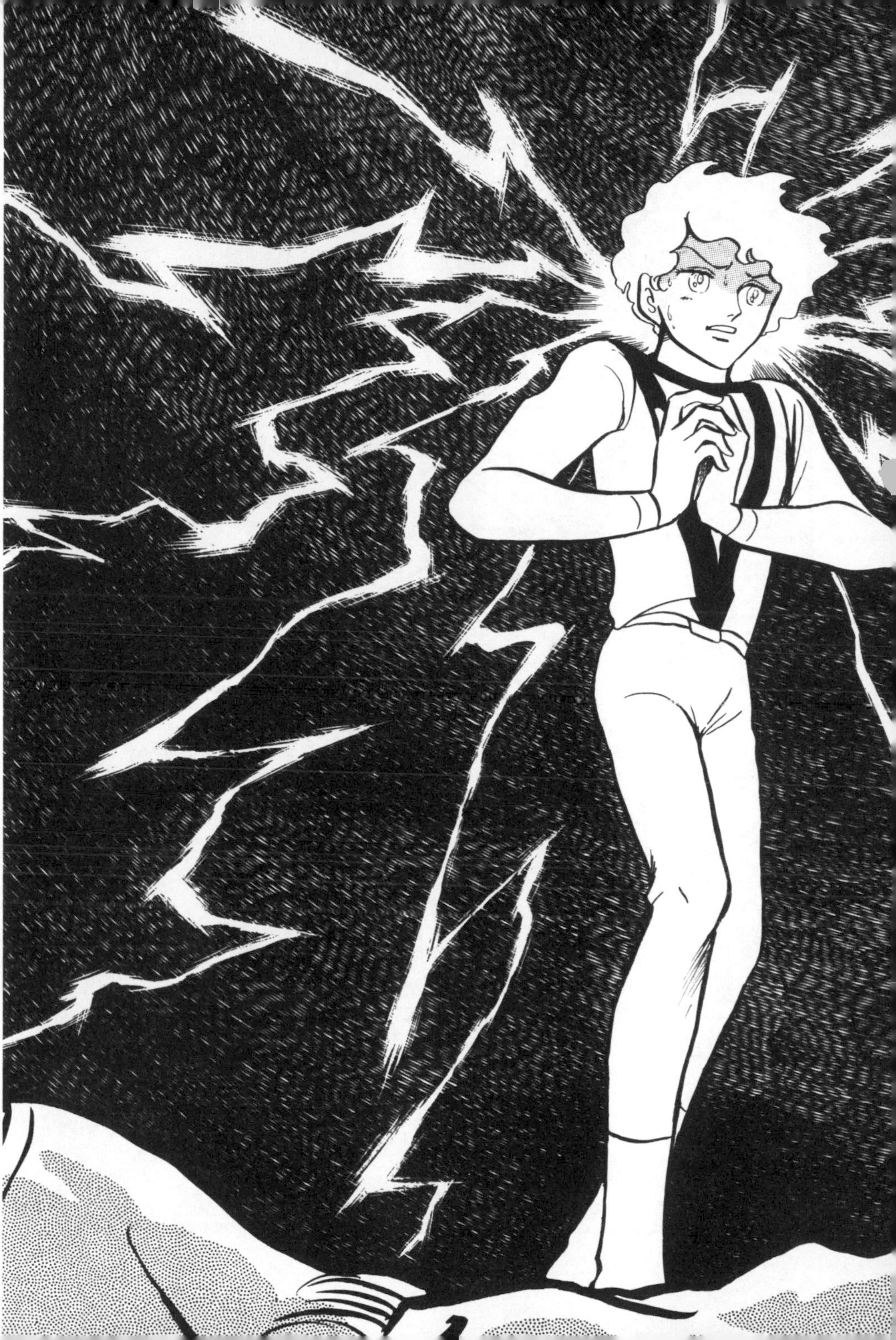

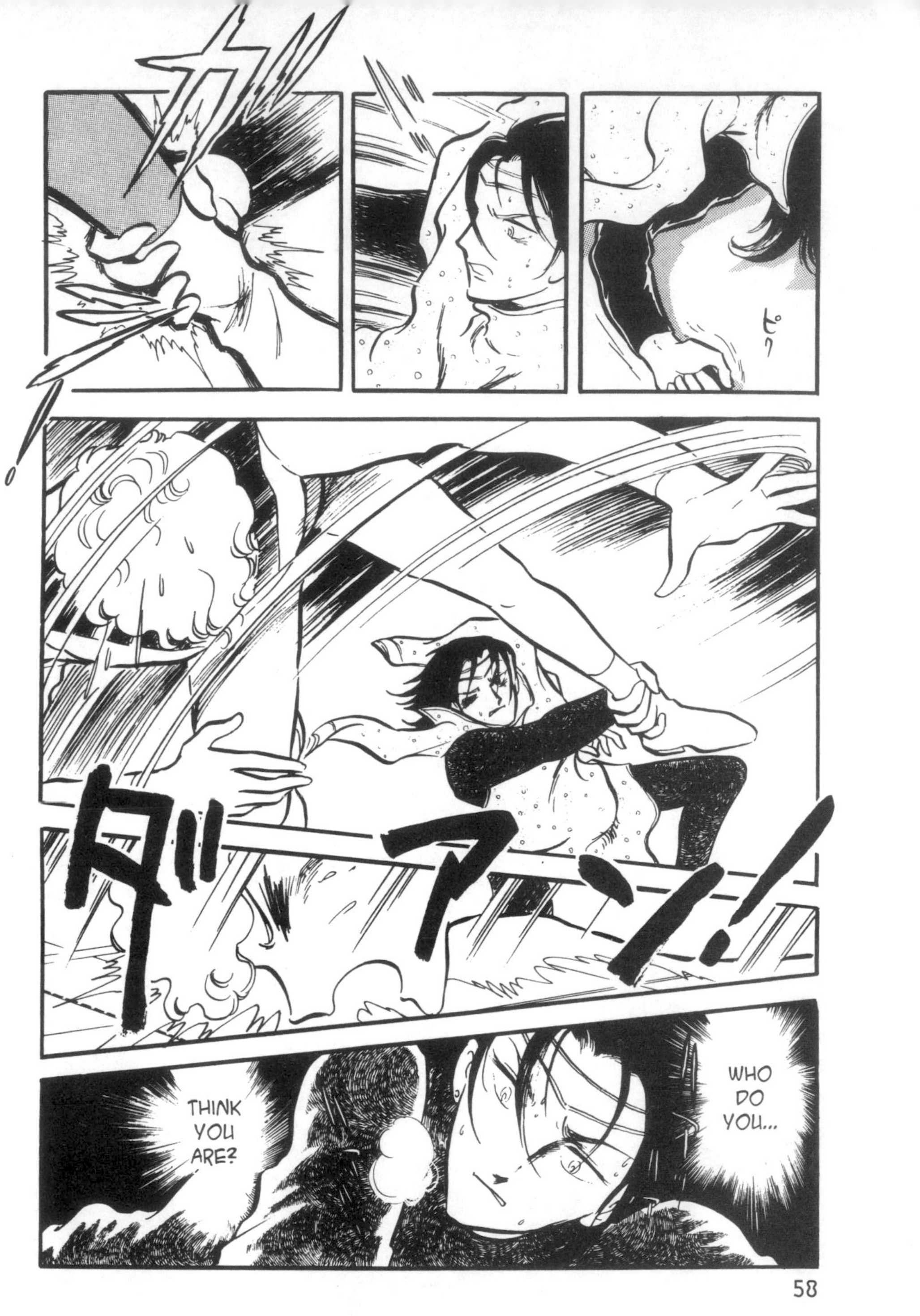
ピク
ガッ
ダアン!!
WHO DO YOU...
THINK YOU ARE?

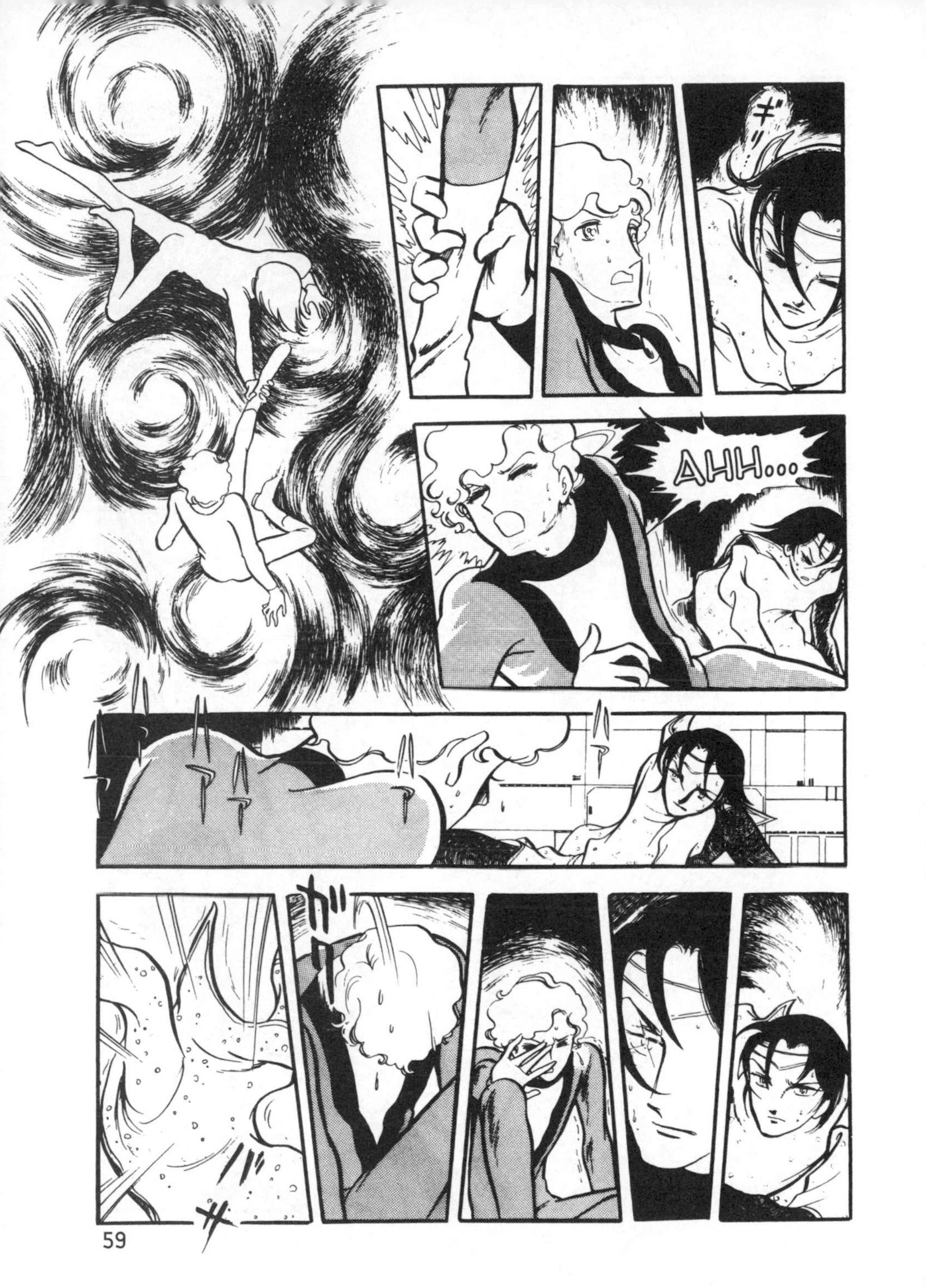
AHH...

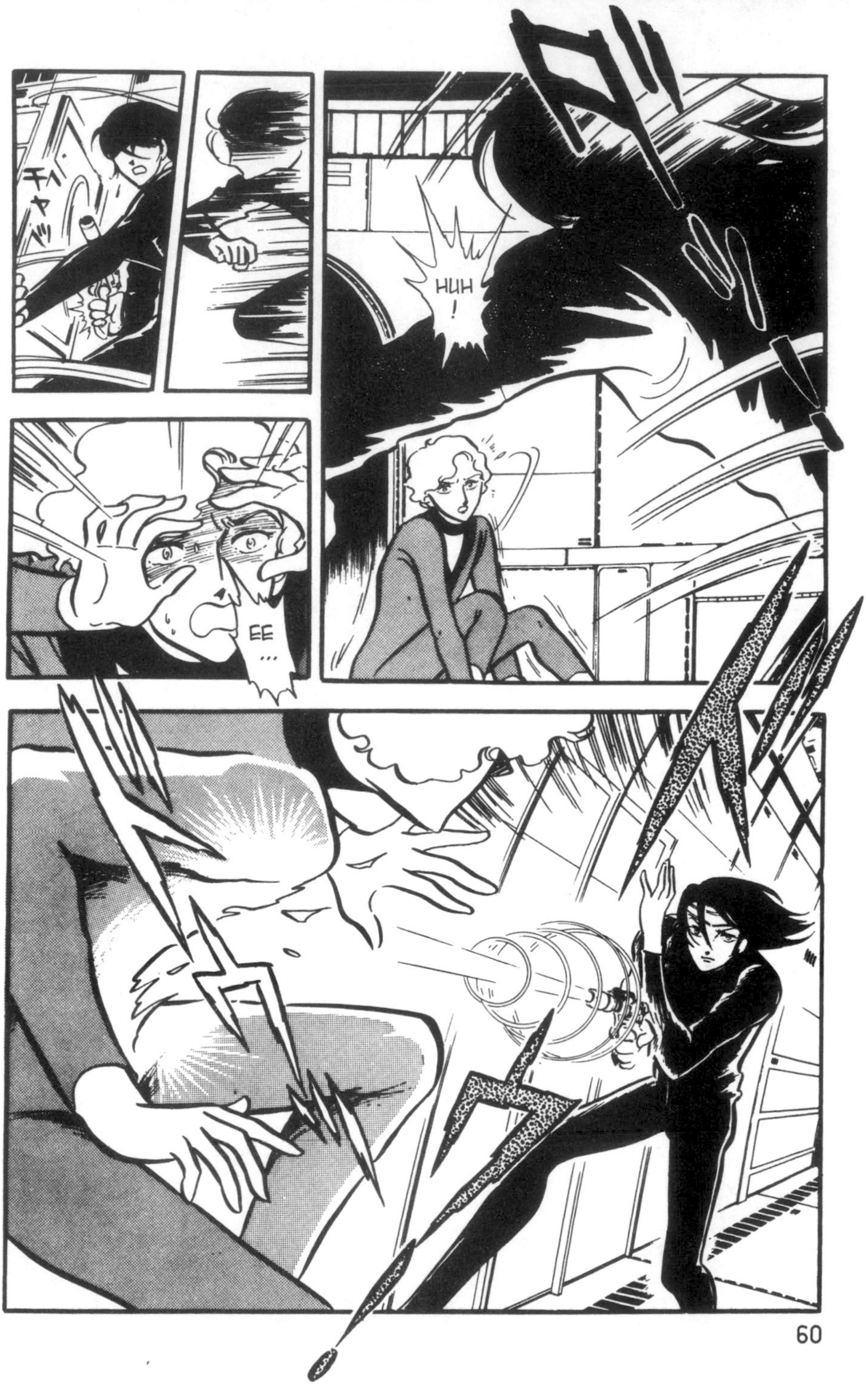
HUH!
EE...

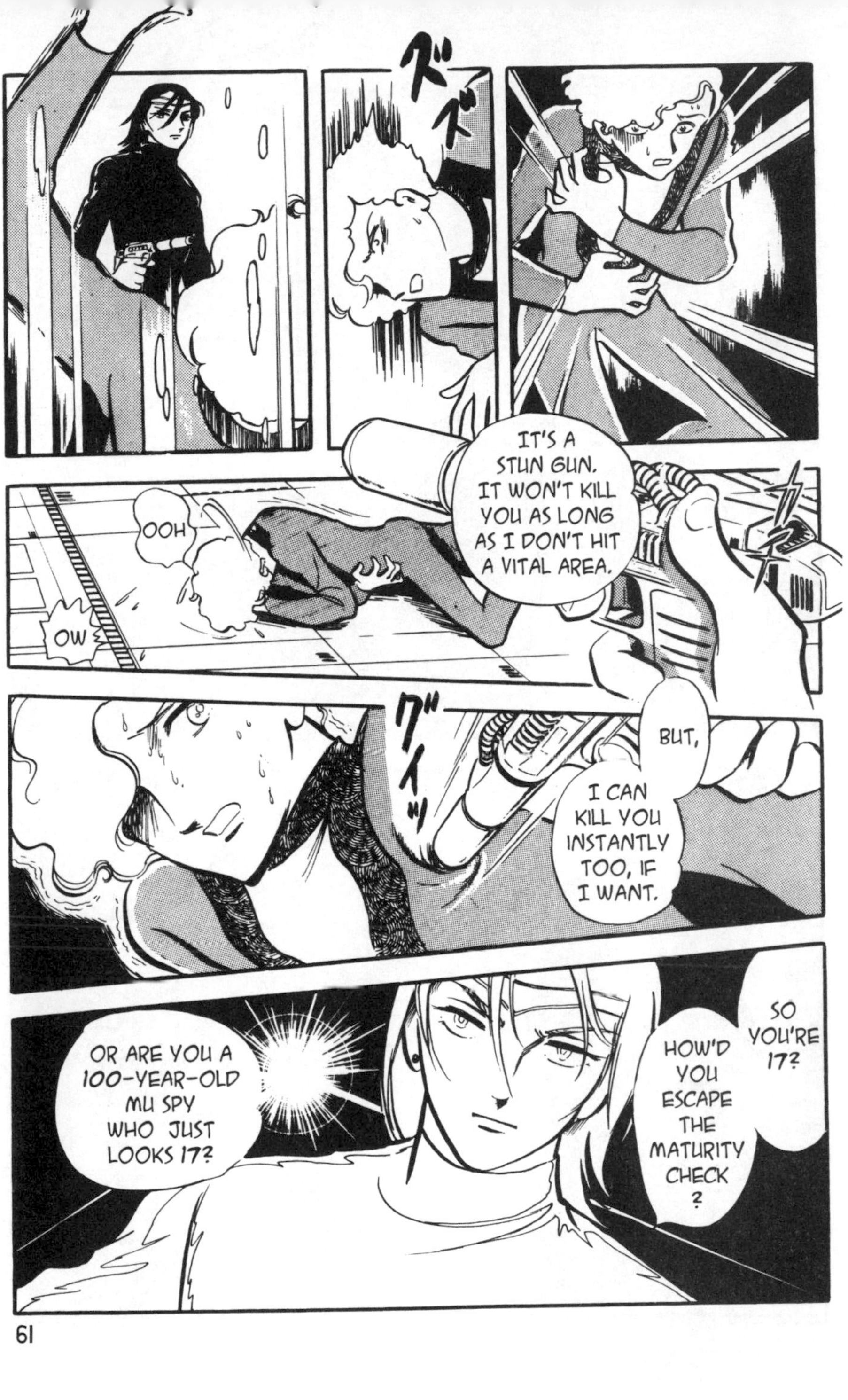
ズズ
IT'S A STUN GUN. IT WON'T KILL YOU AS LONG AS I DON'T HIT A VITAL AREA.
OOH
OW
グイッ
BUT,
I CAN KILL YOU INSTANTLY TOO, IF I WANT.
SO YOU'RE 17?
HOW'D YOU ESCAPE THE MATURITY CHECK?
OR ARE YOU A 100-YEAR-OLD MU SPY WHO JUST LOOKS 17?

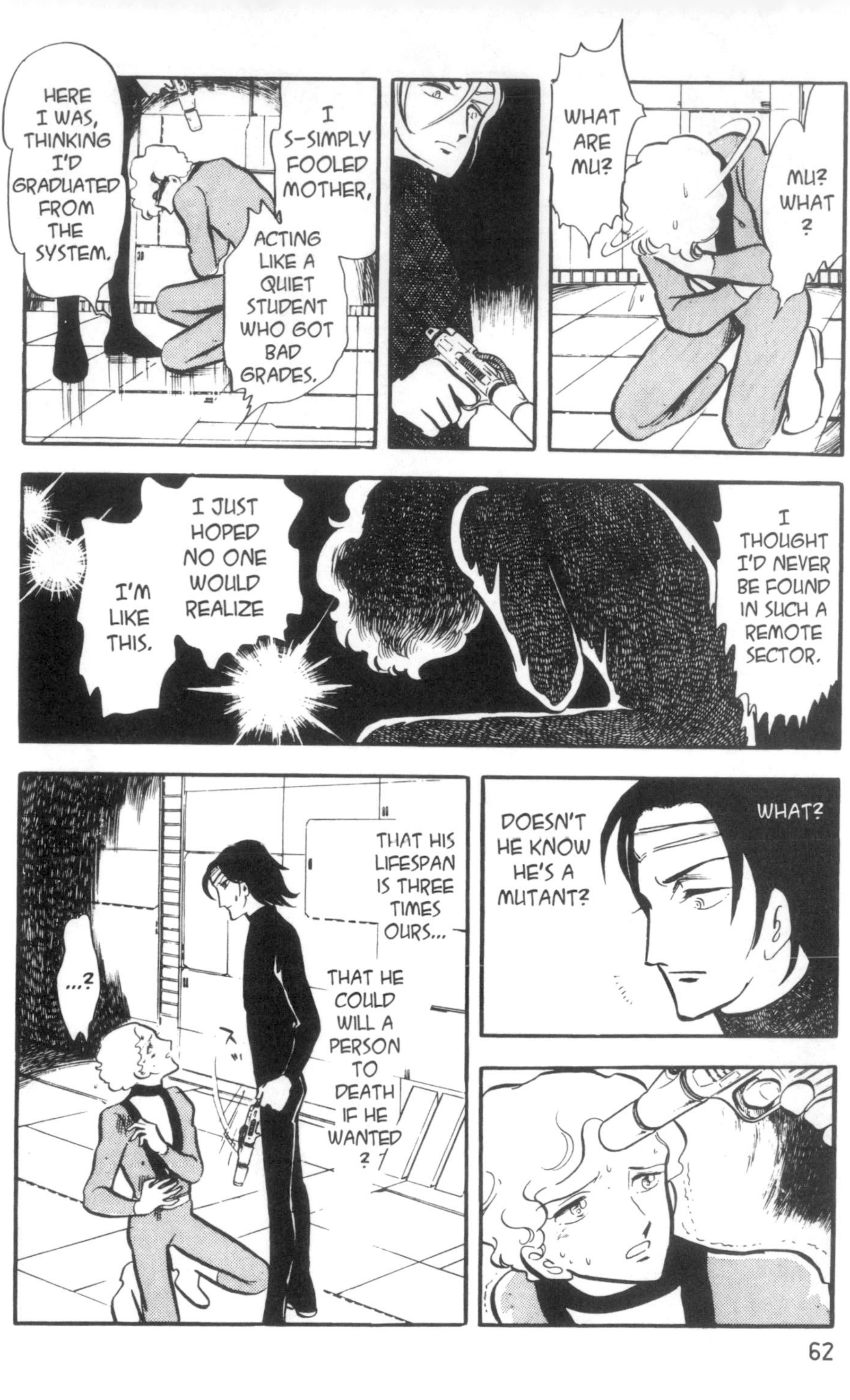
WHAT ARE MU?
MU? WHAT ?
I S-SIMPLY FOOLED MOTHER,
ACTING LIKE A QUIET STUDENT WHO GOT BAD GRADES.
HERE I WAS, THINKING I'D GRADUATED FROM THE SYSTEM.
I THOUGHT I'D NEVER BE FOUND IN SUCH A REMOTE SECTOR.
I JUST HOPED NO ONE WOULD REALIZE
I'M LIKE THIS.
WHAT?
DOESN'T HE KNOW HE'S A MUTANT?
THAT HIS LIFESPAN IS THREE TIMES OURS...
THAT HE COULD WILL A PERSON TO DEATH IF HE WANTED ?
...?

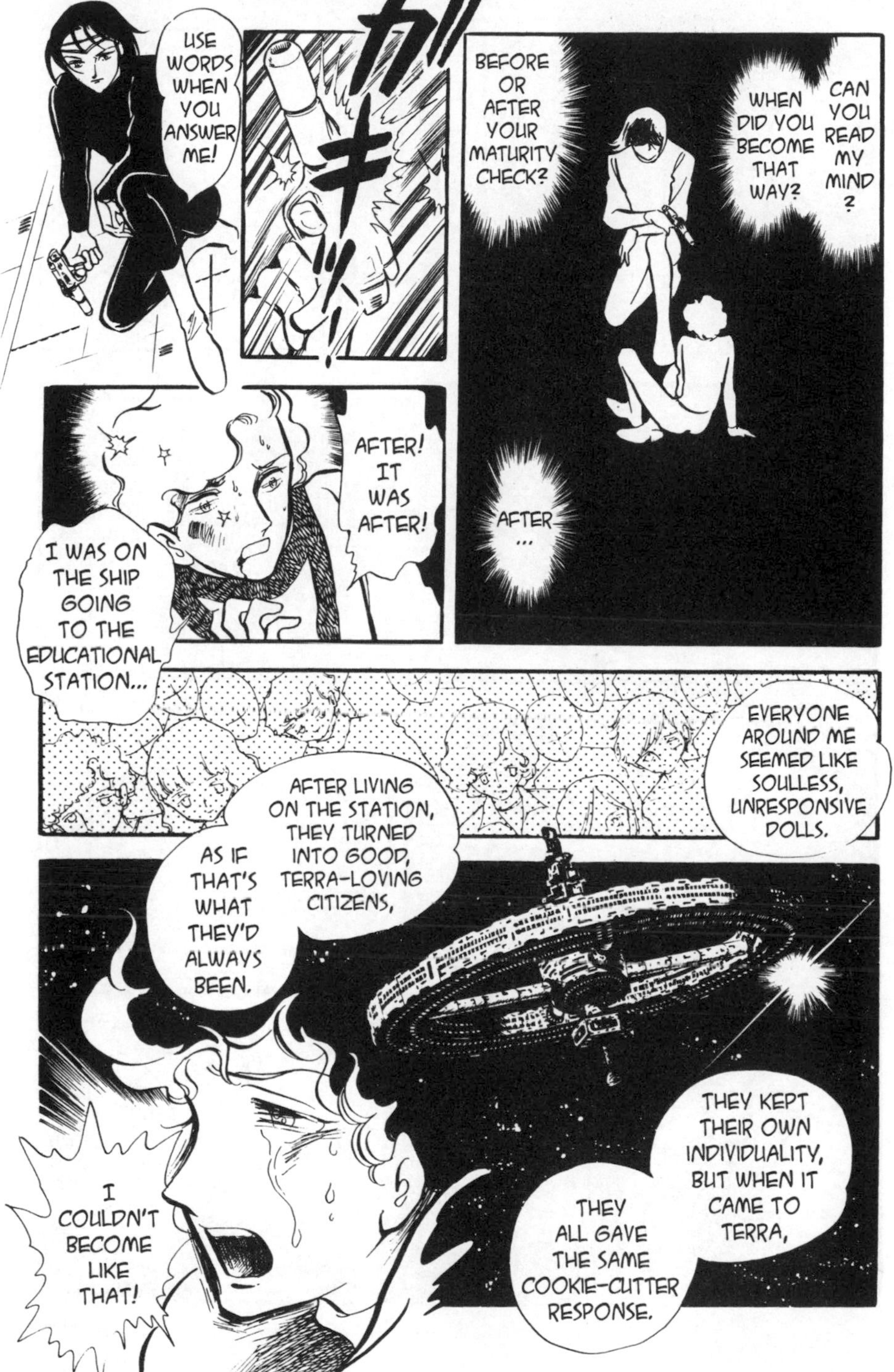
CAN YOU READ MY MIND?
WHEN DID YOU BECOME THAT WAY?
BEFORE OR AFTER YOUR MATURITY CHECK?
AFTER...
カキッ!!
USE WORDS WHEN YOU ANSWER ME!
AFTER! IT WAS AFTER!
I WAS ON THE SHIP GOING TO THE EDUCATIONAL STATION...
EVERYONE AROUND ME SEEMED LIKE SOULLESS, UNRESPONSIVE DOLLS.
AFTER LIVING ON THE STATION, THEY TURNED INTO GOOD, TERRA-LOVING CITIZENS,
AS IF THAT'S WHAT THEY'D ALWAYS BEEN.
THEY KEPT THEIR OWN INDIVIDUALITY, BUT WHEN IT CAME TO TERRA,
THEY ALL GAVE THE SAME COOKIE-CUTTER RESPONSE.
I COULDN'T BECOME LIKE THAT!

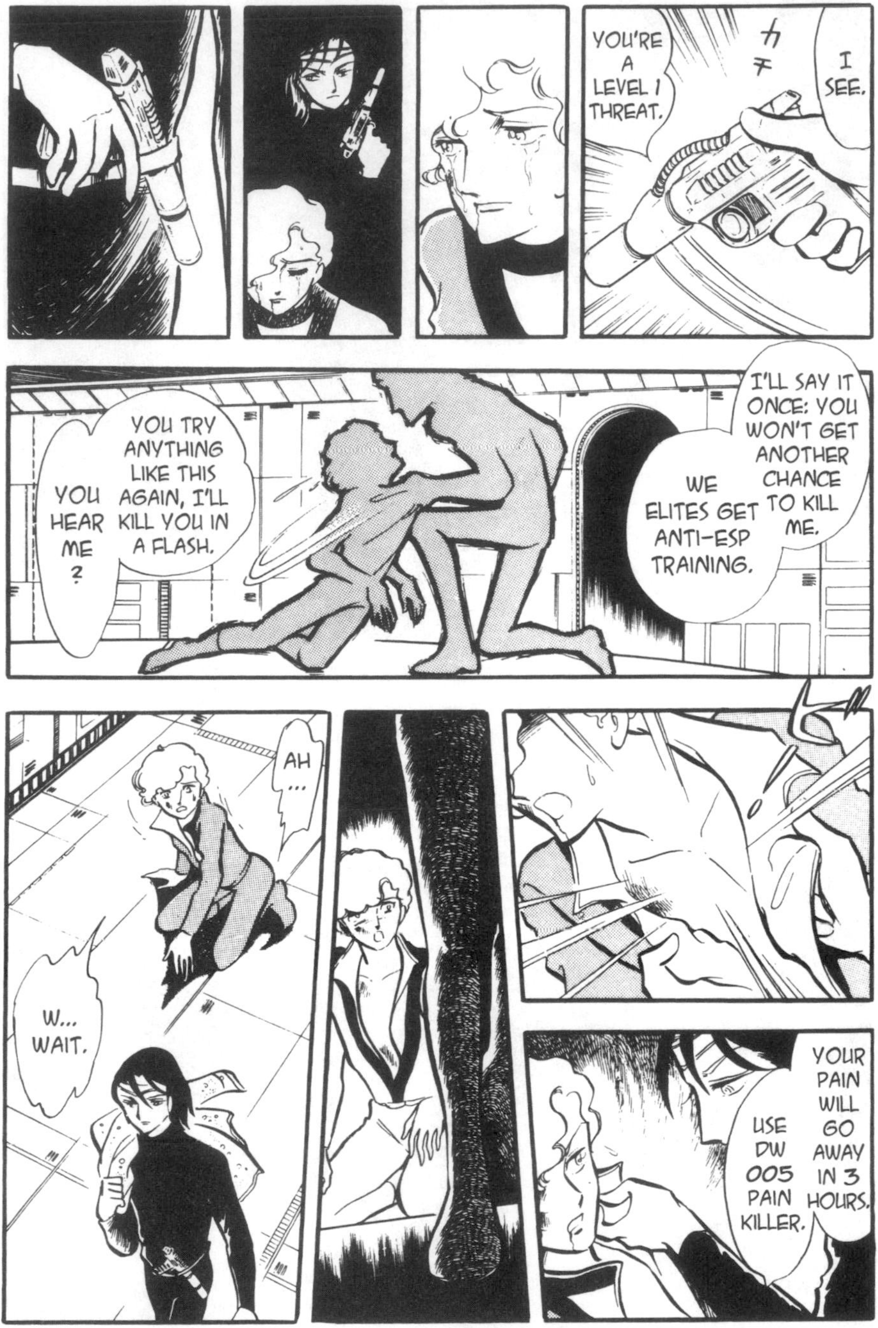
I SEE.
カチ
YOU'RE A LEVEL 1 THREAT.
I'LL SAY IT ONCE: YOU WON'T GET ANOTHER CHANCE TO KILL ME.
WE ELITES GET ANTI-ESP TRAINING.
YOU TRY ANYTHING LIKE THIS AGAIN, I'LL KILL YOU IN A FLASH.
YOU HEAR ME?
YOUR PAIN WILL GO AWAY IN 3 HOURS.
USE DW 005 PAIN KILLER.
AH ...
W... WAIT.

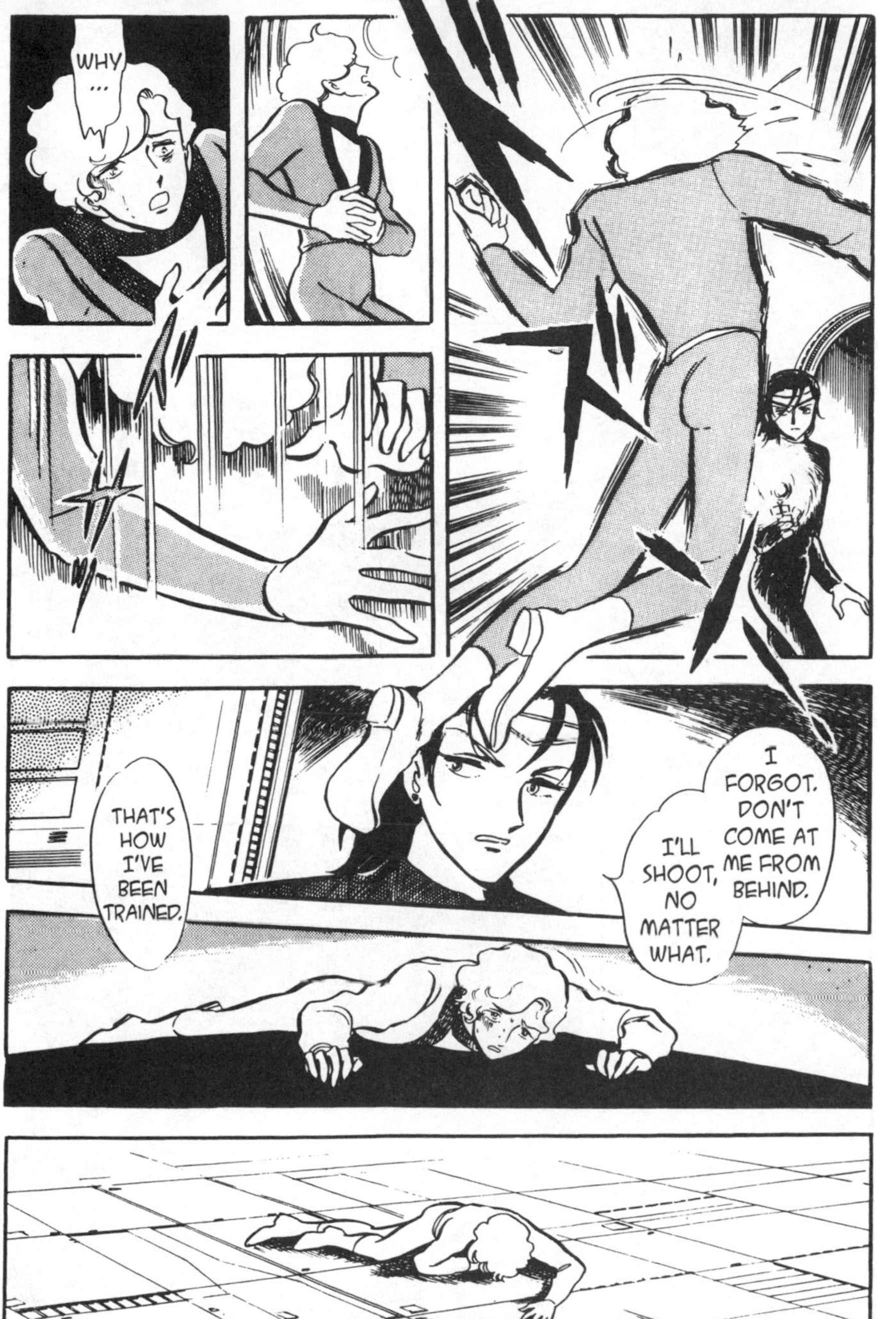
WHY ...
I FORGOT. DON'T COME AT ME FROM BEHIND.
I'LL SHOOT, NO MATTER WHAT.
THAT'S HOW I'VE BEEN TRAINED.

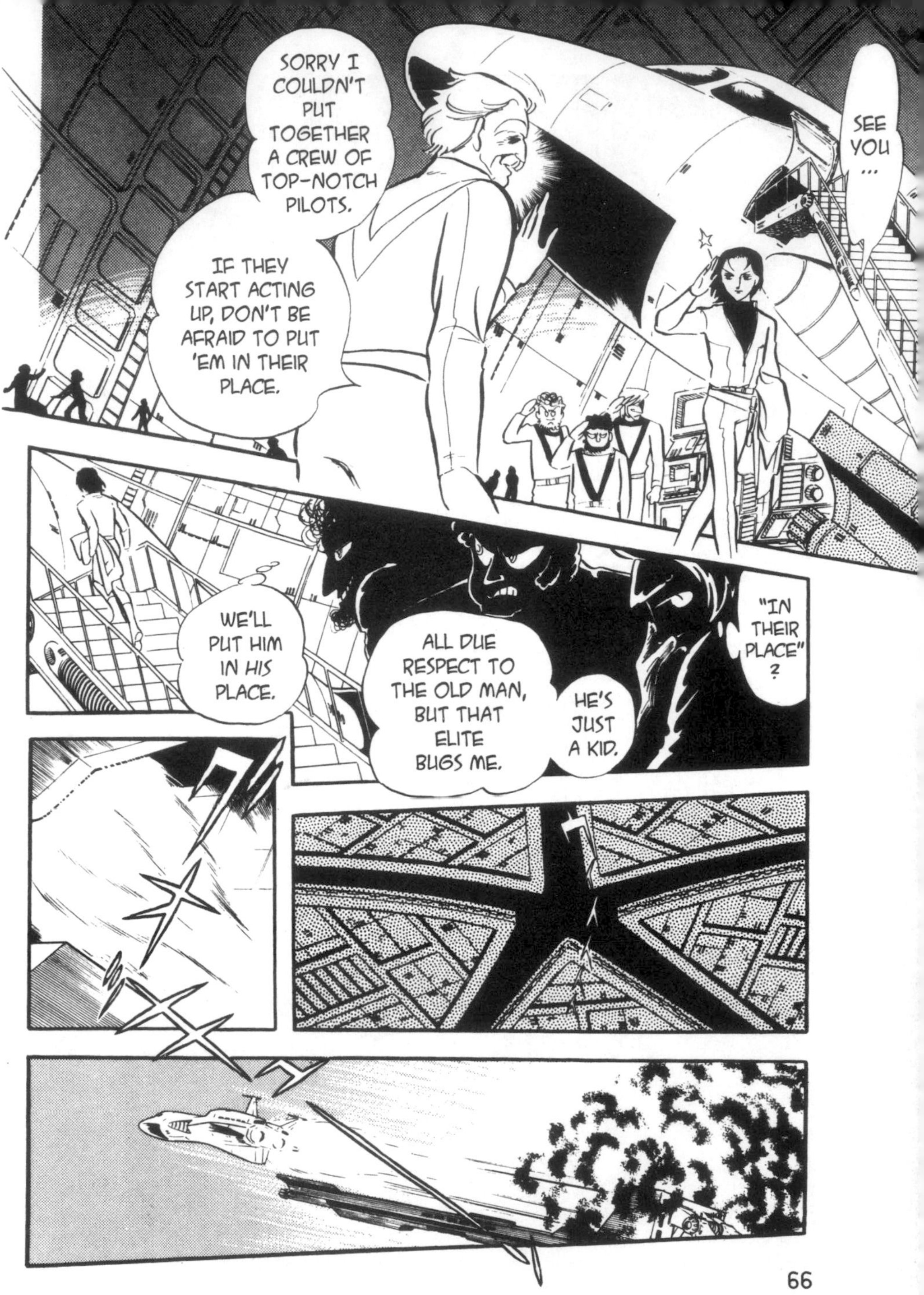
SEE YOU ...
SORRY I COULDN'T PUT TOGETHER A CREW OF TOP-NOTCH PILOTS.
IF THEY START ACTING UP, DON'T BE AFRAID TO PUT 'EM IN THEIR PLACE.
"IN THEIR PLACE"?
HE'S JUST A KID.
ALL DUE RESPECT TO THE OLD MAN, BUT THAT ELITE BUGS ME.
WE'LL PUT HIM IN HIS PLACE.

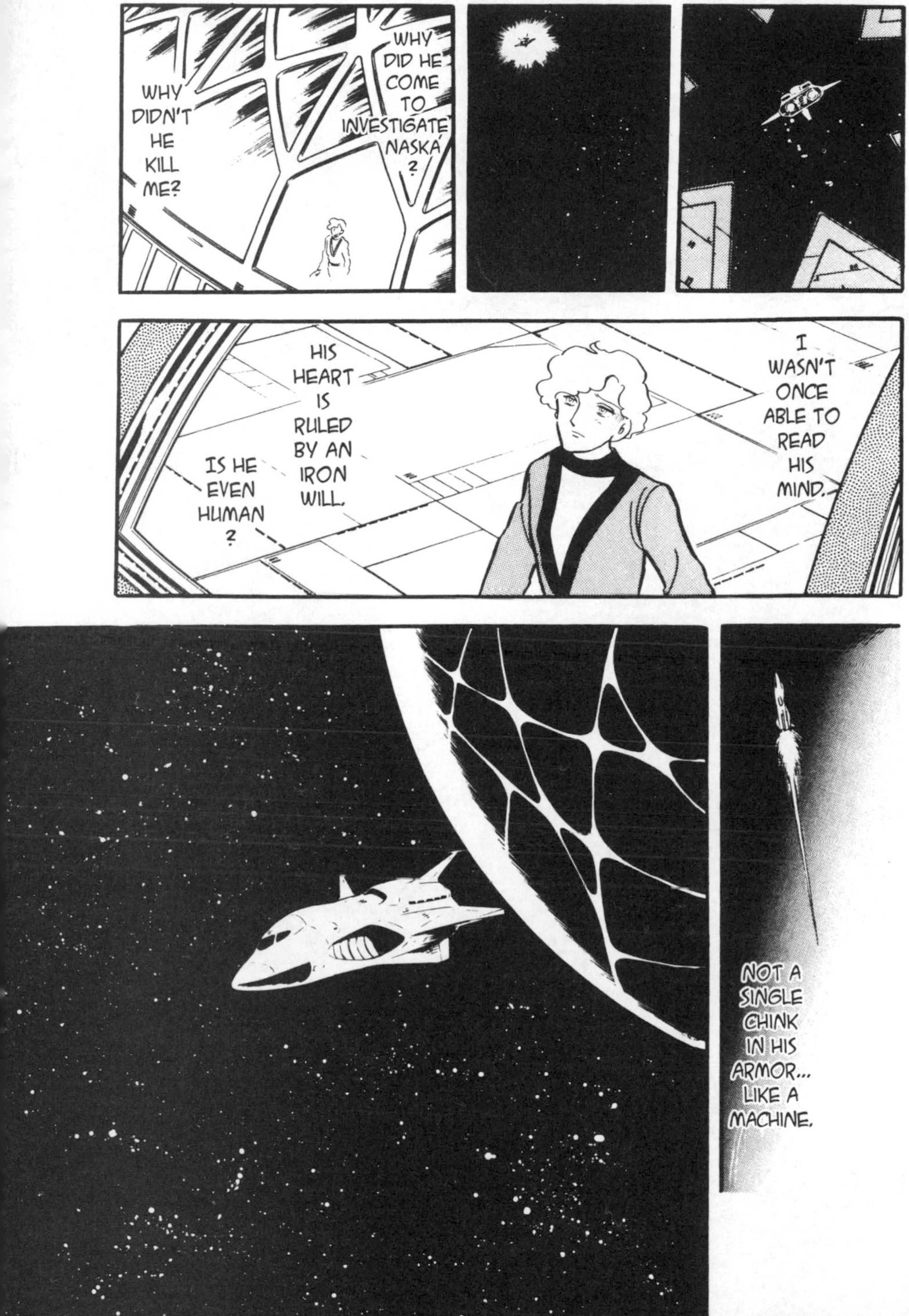

WHY DID HE COME TO INVESTIGATE NASKA?
WHY DIDN'T HE KILL ME?
I WASN'T ONCE ABLE TO READ HIS MIND.
HIS HEART IS RULED BY AN IRON WILL.
IS HE EVEN HUMAN?
NOT A SINGLE CHINK IN HIS ARMOR... LIKE A MACHINE.

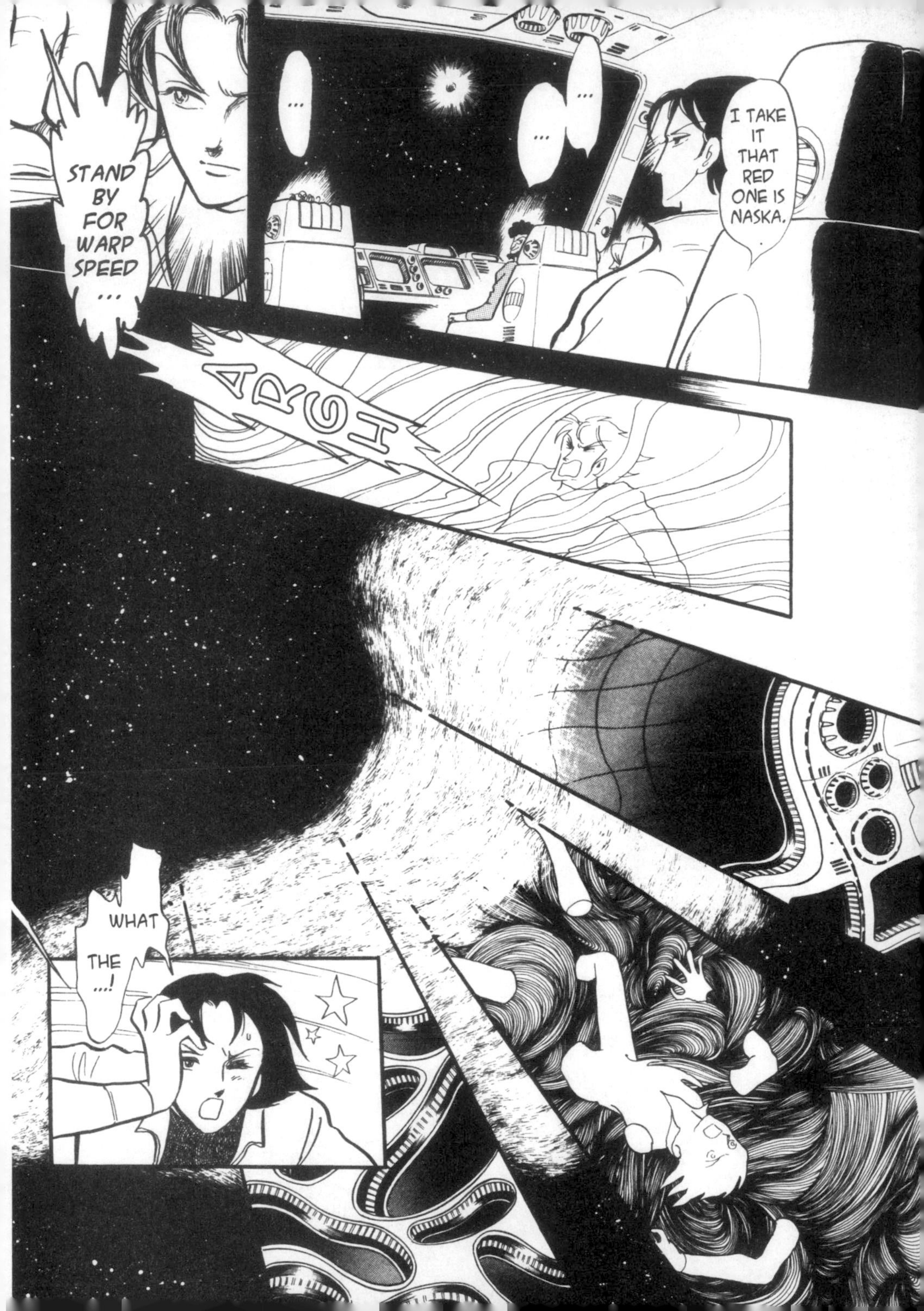
I TAKE IT THAT RED ONE IS NASKA.
...
...
...
STAND BY FOR WARP SPEED ...
ARGH
WHAT THE ...!

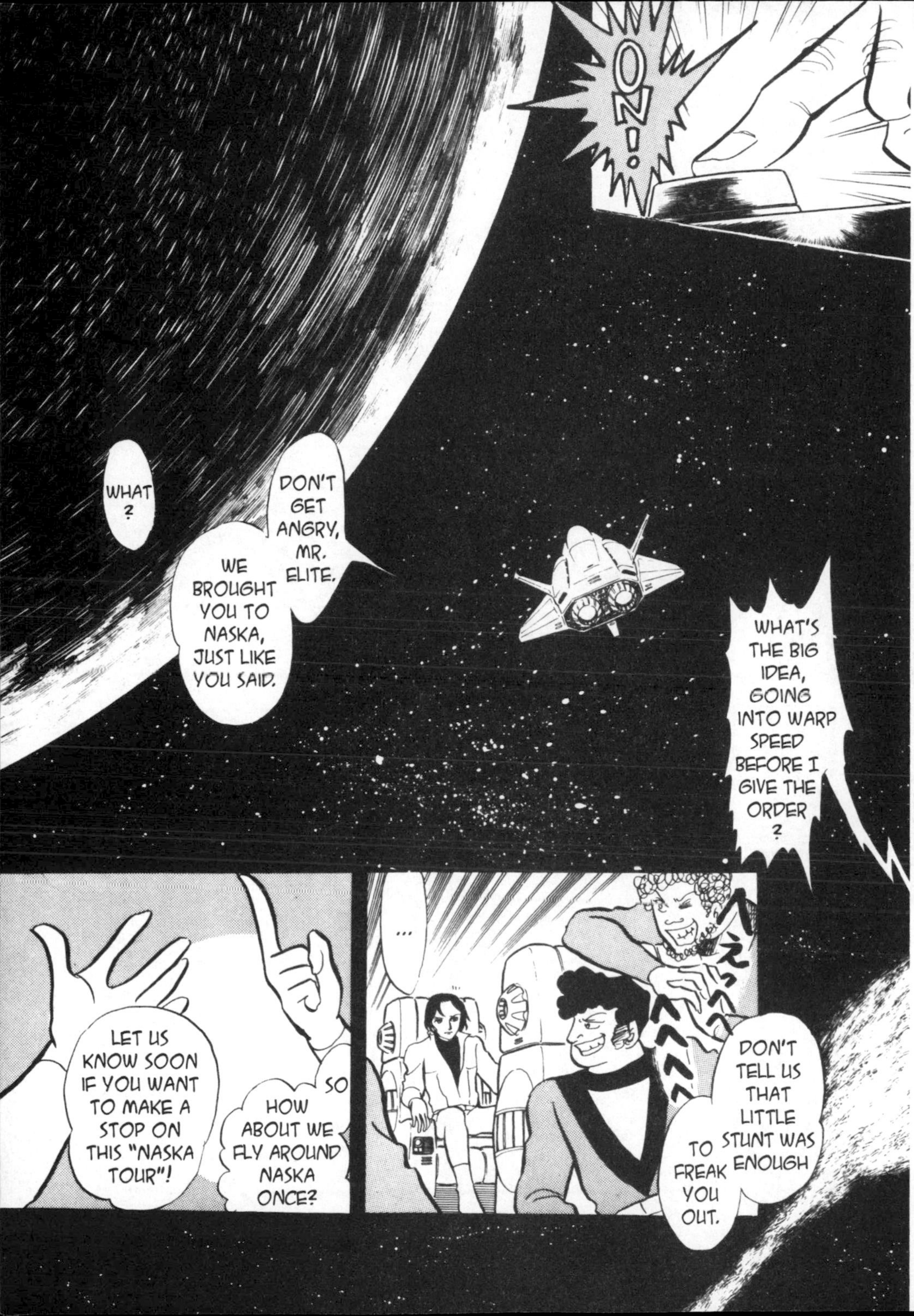
ON!
WHAT'S THE BIG IDEA, GOING INTO WARP SPEED BEFORE I GIVE THE ORDER?
DON'T GET ANGRY, MR. ELITE.
WE BROUGHT YOU TO NASKA, JUST LIKE YOU SAID.
WHAT?
DON'T TELL US THAT LITTLE STUNT WAS ENOUGH TO FREAK YOU OUT.
...
SO HOW ABOUT WE FLY AROUND NASKA ONCE?
LET US KNOW SOON IF YOU WANT TO MAKE A STOP ON THIS "NASKA TOUR"!

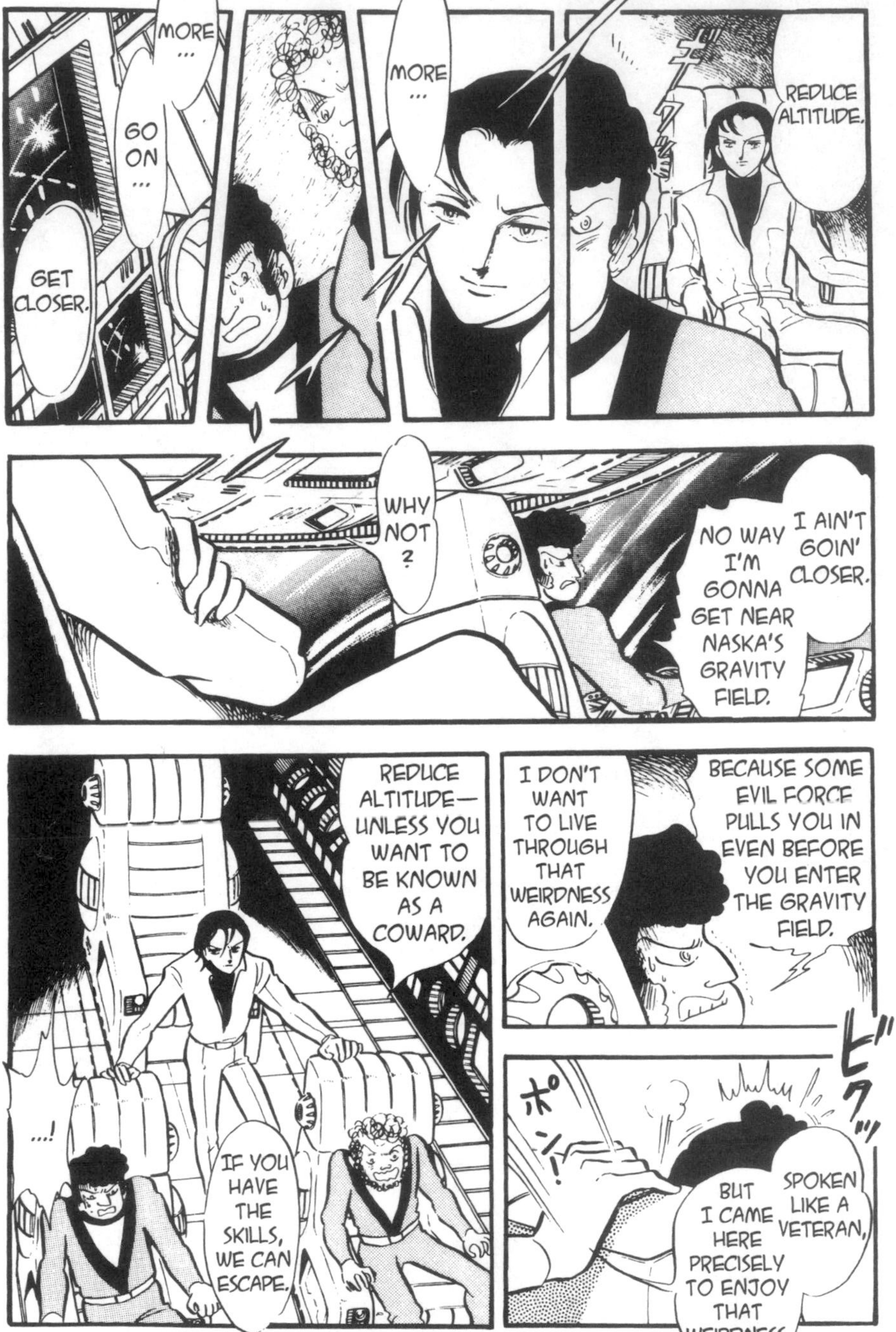
REDUCE ALTITUDE.
MORE ...
MORE ...
GO ON ...
GET CLOSER.
I AIN'T GOIN' CLOSER.
NO WAY I'M GONNA GET NEAR NASKA'S GRAVITY FIELD.
WHY NOT?
BECAUSE SOME EVIL FORCE PULLS YOU IN EVEN BEFORE YOU ENTER THE GRAVITY FIELD.
I DON'T WANT TO LIVE THROUGH THAT WEIRDNESS AGAIN.
ビクッ
SPOKEN LIKE A VETERAN,
BUT I CAME HERE PRECISELY TO ENJOY THAT WEIRDNESS.
REDUCE ALTITUDE— UNLESS YOU WANT TO BE KNOWN AS A COWARD.
IF YOU HAVE THE SKILLS, WE CAN ESCAPE.
...!

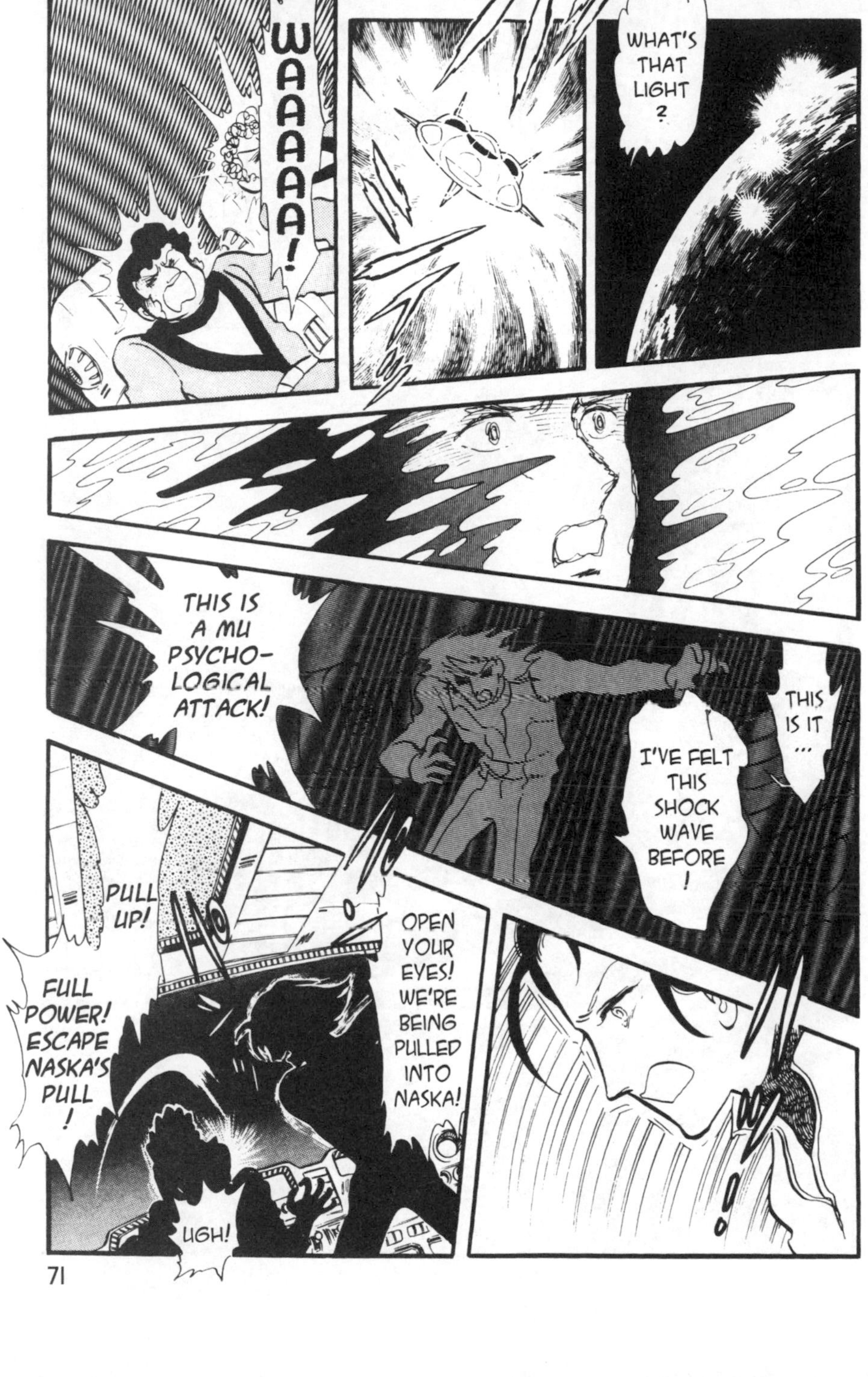
WHAT'S THAT LIGHT?
WAAAAAAA!
THIS IS IT...
I'VE FELT THIS SHOCK WAVE BEFORE!
THIS IS A MU PSYCHO-LOGICAL ATTACK!
OPEN YOUR EYES! WE'RE BEING PULLED INTO NASKA!
PULL UP!
FULL POWER! ESCAPE NASKA'S PULL!
UGH!

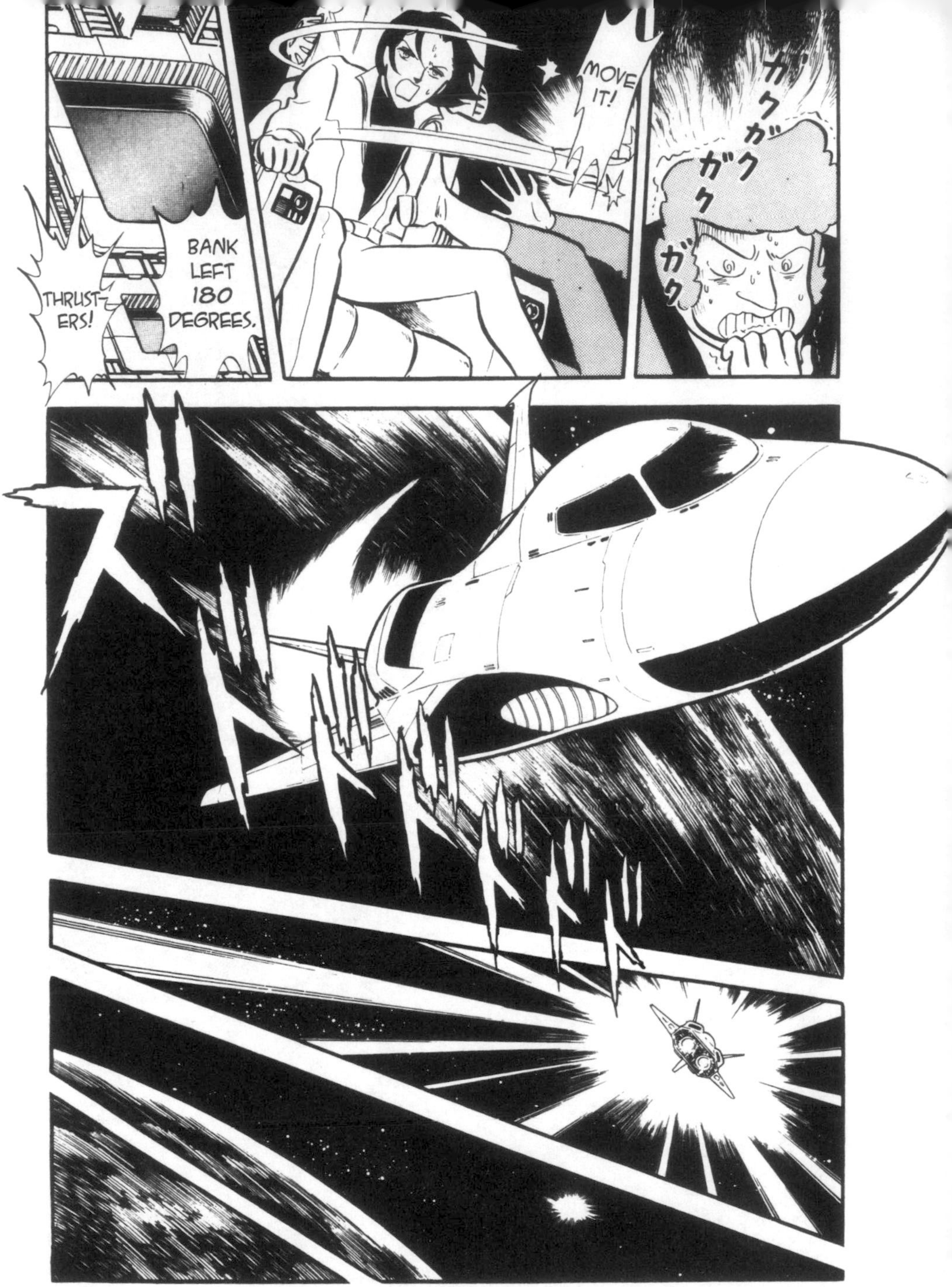
ガクガクガクガク
MOVE IT!
BANK LEFT 180 DEGREES.
THRUST-ERS!

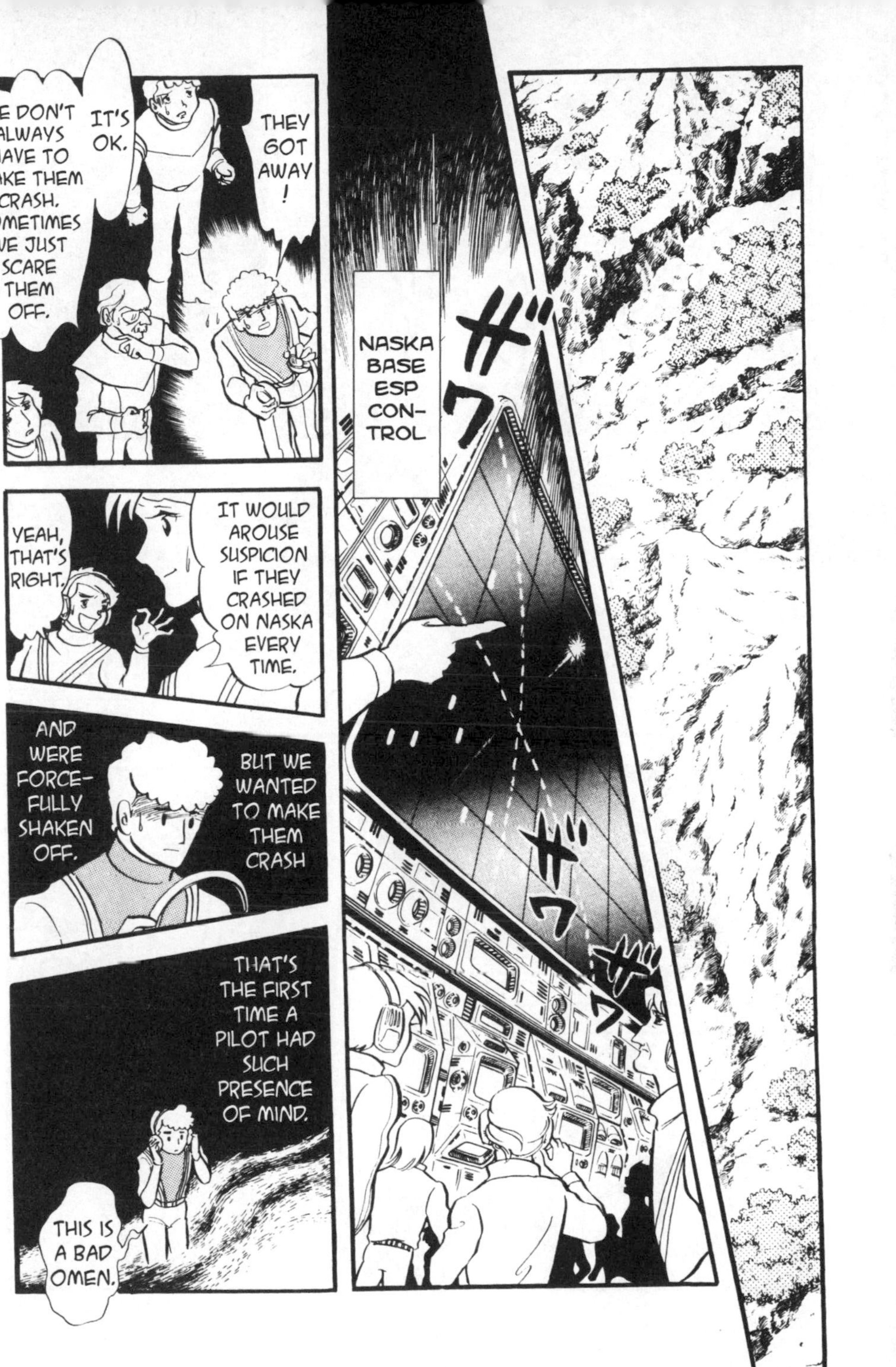
NASKA BASE ESP CONTROL
ザワ
ザワ
ザワ
THEY GOT AWAY!
IT'S OK.
WE DON'T ALWAYS HAVE TO MAKE THEM CRASH. SOMETIMES WE JUST SCARE THEM OFF.
IT WOULD AROUSE SUSPICION IF THEY CRASHED ON NASKA EVERY TIME.
YEAH, THAT'S RIGHT.
BUT WE WANTED TO MAKE THEM CRASH
AND WERE FORCE-FULLY SHAKEN OFF.
THAT'S THE FIRST TIME A PILOT HAD SUCH PRESENCE OF MIND.
THIS IS A BAD OMEN.

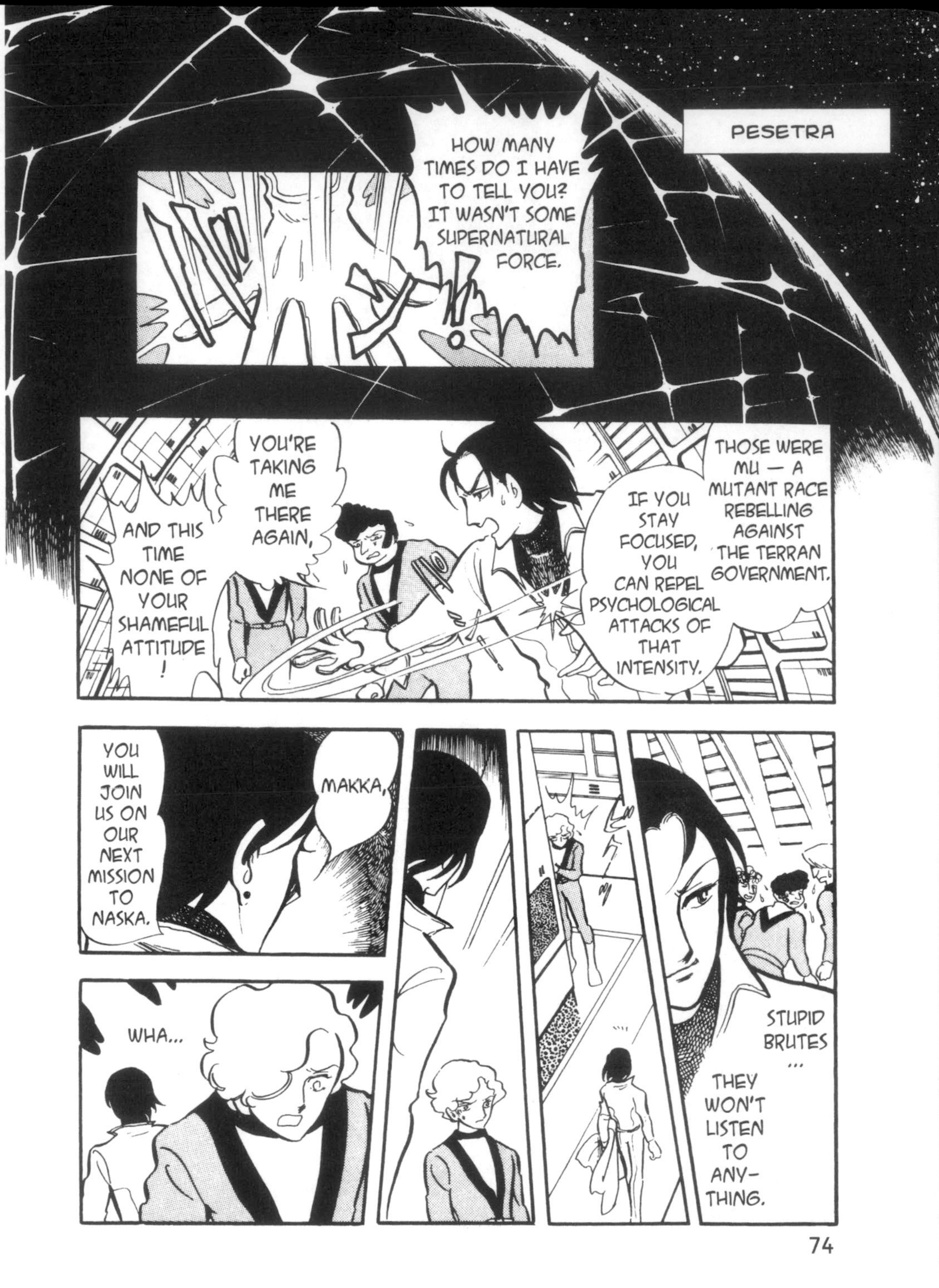
PESETRA
HOW MANY TIMES DO I HAVE TO TELL YOU? IT WASN'T SOME SUPERNATURAL FORCE.
THOSE WERE MU — A MUTANT RACE REBELLING AGAINST THE TERRAN GOVERNMENT.
IF YOU STAY FOCUSED, YOU CAN REPEL PSYCHOLOGICAL ATTACKS OF THAT INTENSITY.
YOU'RE TAKING ME THERE AGAIN,
AND THIS TIME NONE OF YOUR SHAMEFUL ATTITUDE!
STUPID BRUTES...
THEY WON'T LISTEN TO ANY-THING.
MAKKA,
YOU WILL JOIN US ON OUR NEXT MISSION TO NASKA.
WHA...

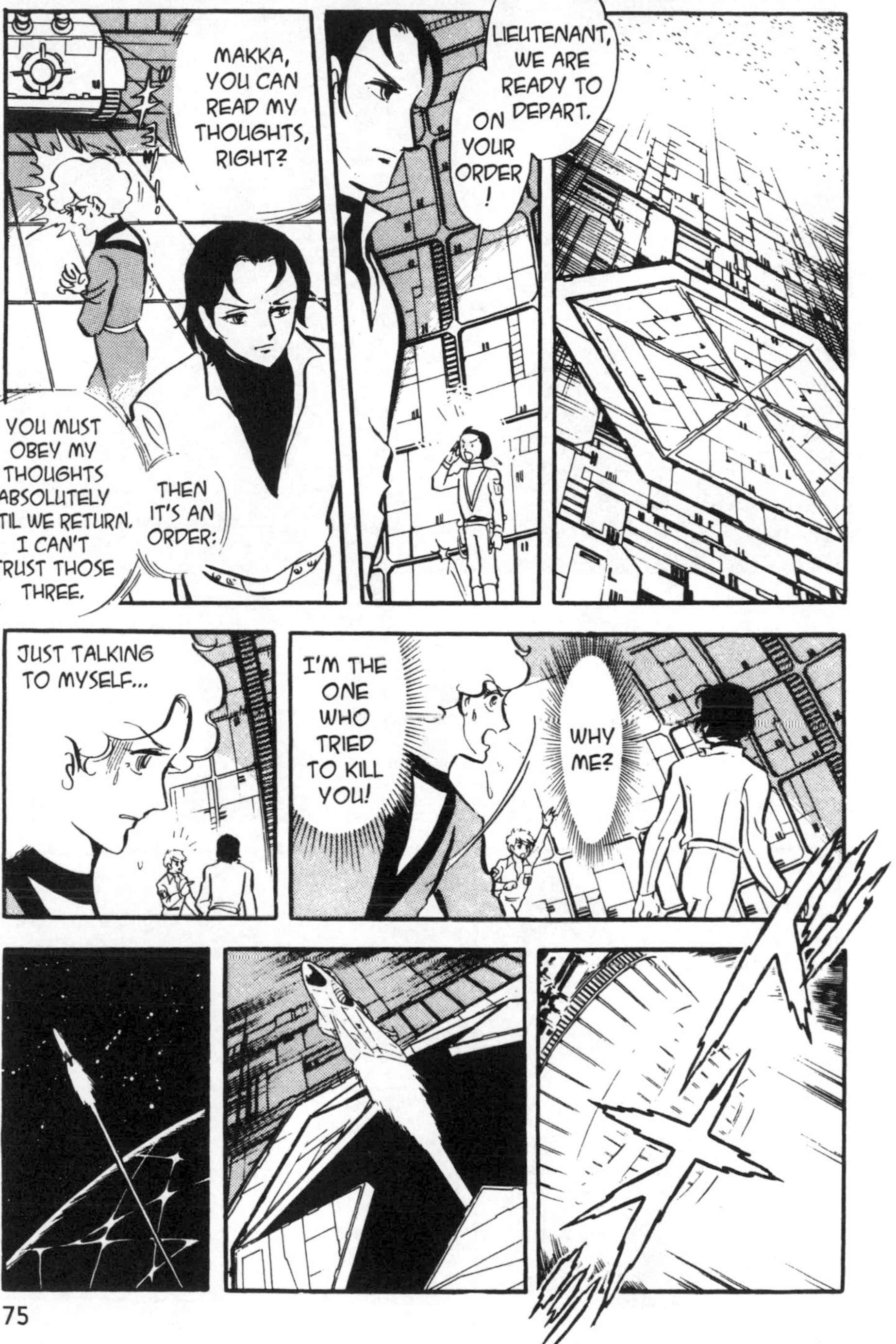
LIEUTENANT, WE ARE READY TO DEPART.
ON YOUR ORDER!
MAKKA, YOU CAN READ MY THOUGHTS, RIGHT?
THEN IT'S AN ORDER:
YOU MUST OBEY MY THOUGHTS ABSOLUTELY UNTIL WE RETURN. I CAN'T TRUST THOSE THREE.
WHY ME?
I'M THE ONE WHO TRIED TO KILL YOU!
JUST TALKING TO MYSELF...

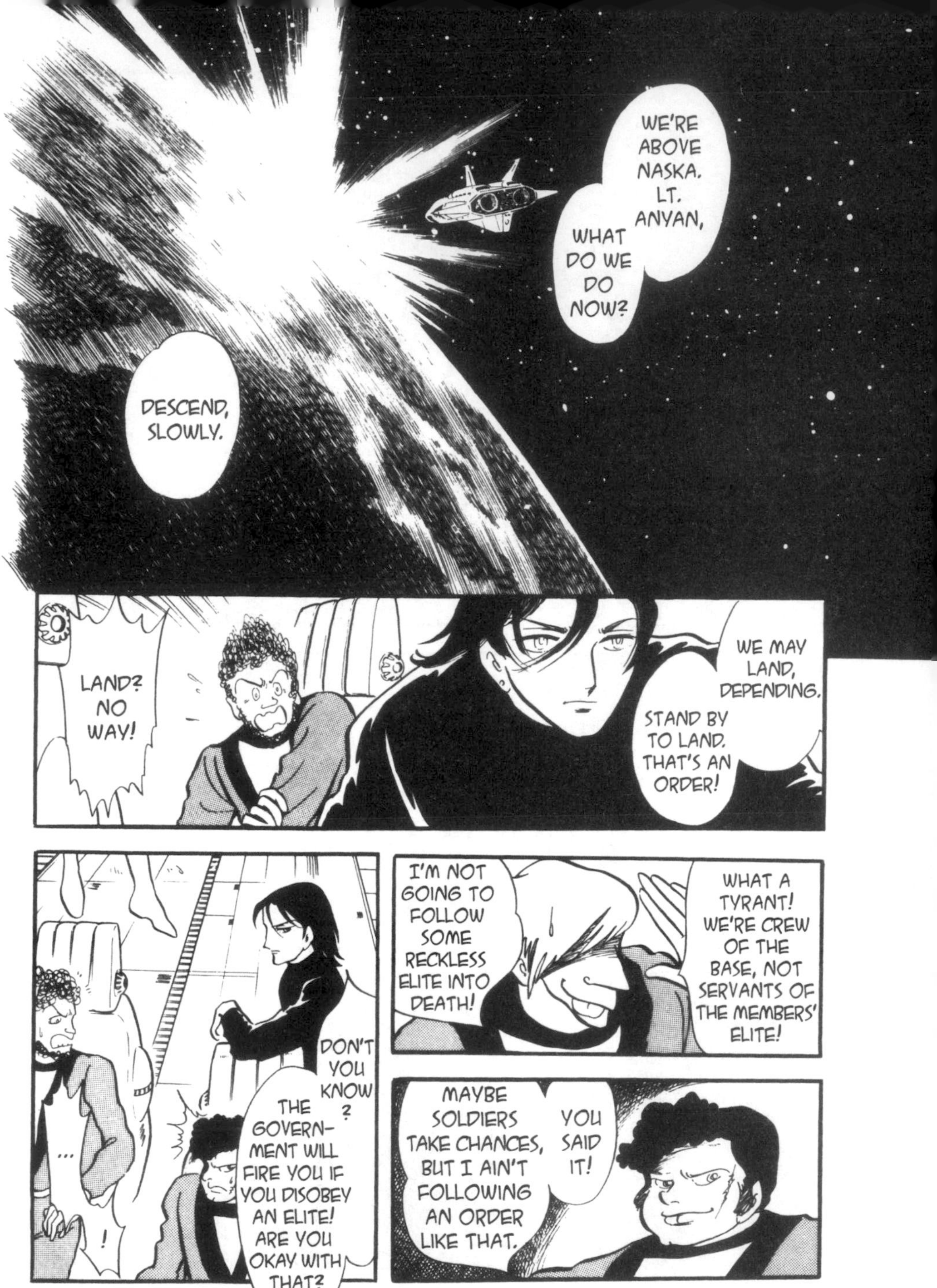
WE'RE ABOVE NASKA. LT. ANYAN,
WHAT DO WE DO NOW?
DESCEND, SLOWLY.
WE MAY LAND, DEPENDING.
STAND BY TO LAND. THAT'S AN ORDER!
LAND? NO WAY!
WHAT A TYRANT! WE'RE CREW OF THE BASE, NOT SERVANTS OF THE MEMBERS' ELITE!
I'M NOT GOING TO FOLLOW SOME RECKLESS ELITE INTO DEATH!
YOU SAID IT!
MAYBE SOLDIERS TAKE CHANCES, BUT I AIN'T FOLLOWING AN ORDER LIKE THAT.
DON'T YOU KNOW?
THE GOVERN-MENT WILL FIRE YOU IF YOU DISOBEY AN ELITE! ARE YOU OKAY WITH THAT?
...
!

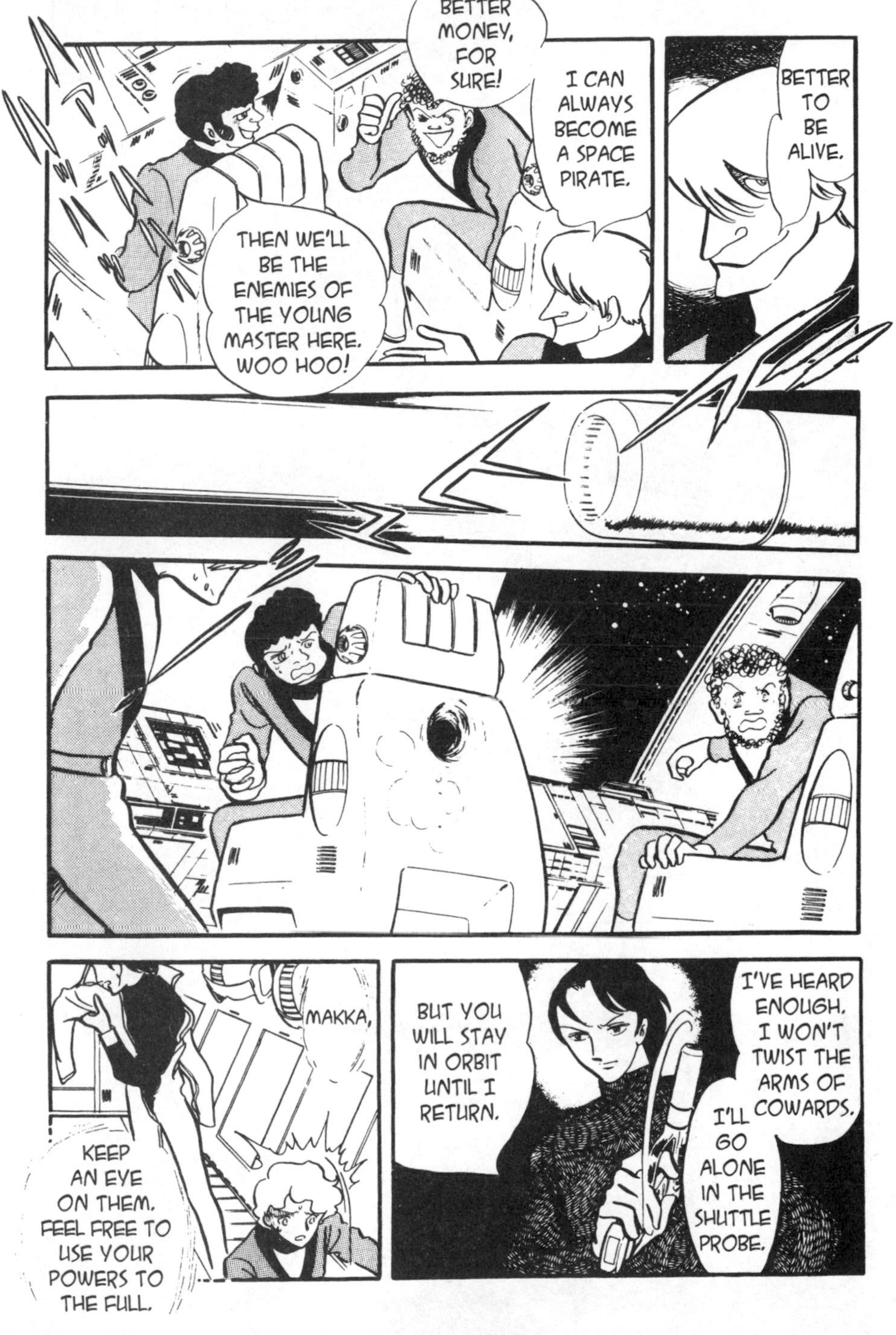
BETTER TO BE ALIVE.
I CAN ALWAYS BECOME A SPACE PIRATE.
BETTER MONEY, FOR SURE!
THEN WE'LL BE THE ENEMIES OF THE YOUNG MASTER HERE. WOO HOO!
I'VE HEARD ENOUGH. I WON'T TWIST THE ARMS OF COWARDS.
I'LL GO ALONE IN THE SHUTTLE PROBE.
BUT YOU WILL STAY IN ORBIT UNTIL I RETURN.
MAKKA,
KEEP AN EYE ON THEM. FEEL FREE TO USE YOUR POWERS TO THE FULL.

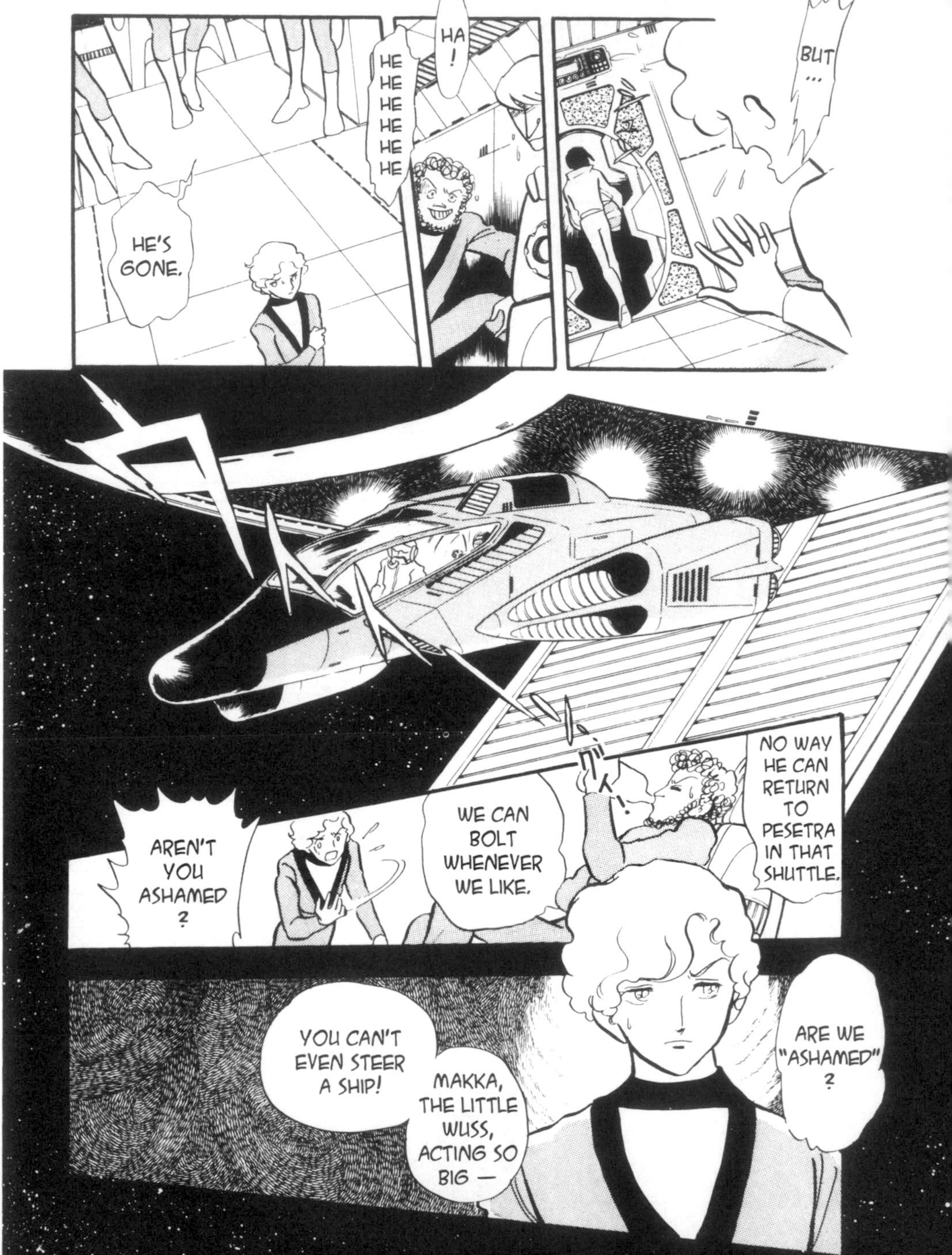

BUT ...
HA!
HE HE HE HE HE HE
HE'S GONE.
NO WAY HE CAN RETURN TO PESETRA IN THAT SHUTTLE.
WE CAN BOLT WHENEVER WE LIKE.
AREN'T YOU ASHAMED?
ARE WE "ASHAMED"?
MAKKA, THE LITTLE WUSS, ACTING SO BIG —
YOU CAN'T EVEN STEER A SHIP!

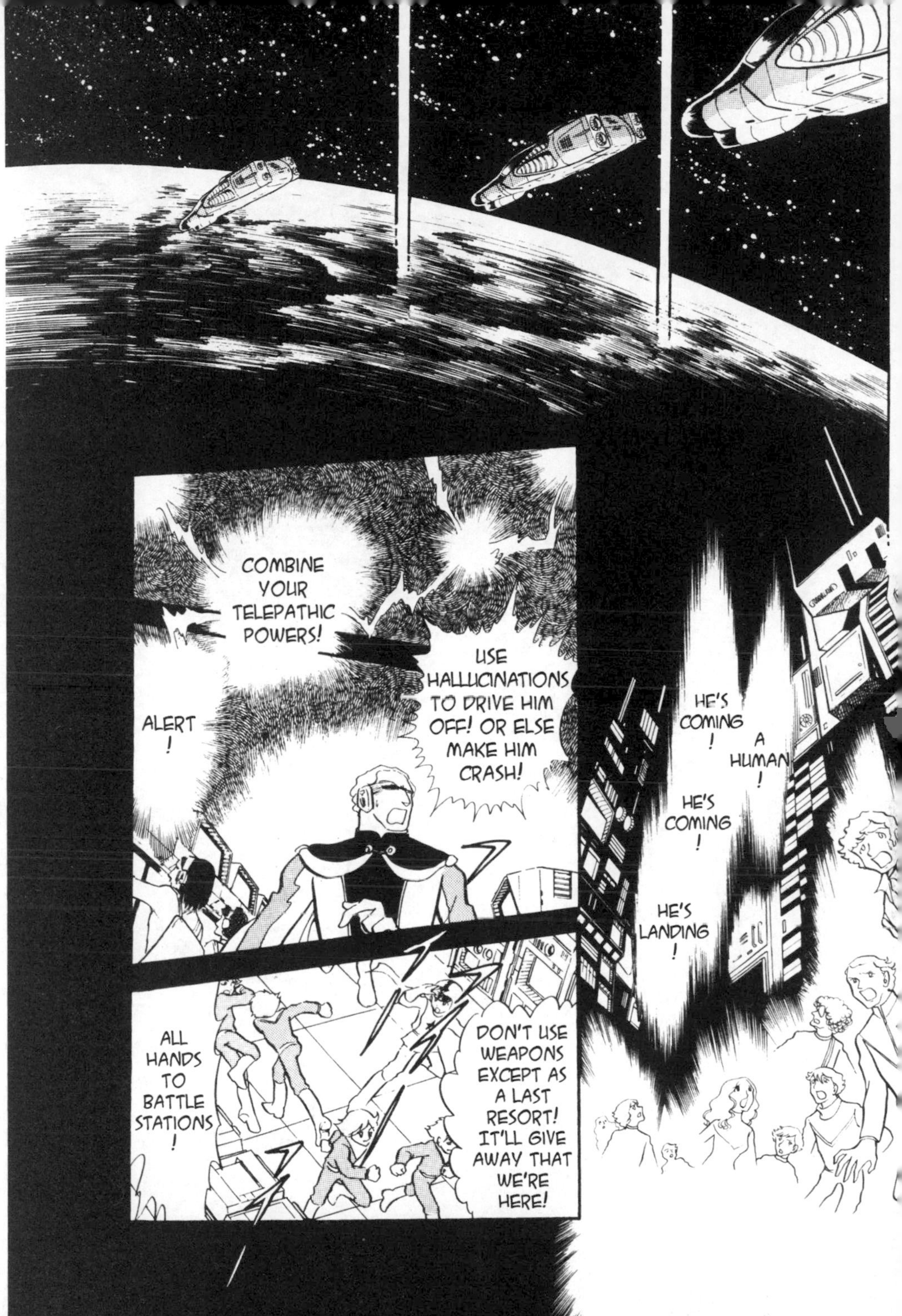
HE'S COMING!
A HUMAN!
HE'S COMING!
HE'S LANDING!
COMBINE YOUR TELEPATHIC POWERS!
USE HALLUCINATIONS TO DRIVE HIM OFF! OR ELSE MAKE HIM CRASH!
ALERT!
DON'T USE WEAPONS EXCEPT AS A LAST RESORT! IT'LL GIVE AWAY THAT WE'RE HERE!
ALL HANDS TO BATTLE STATIONS!

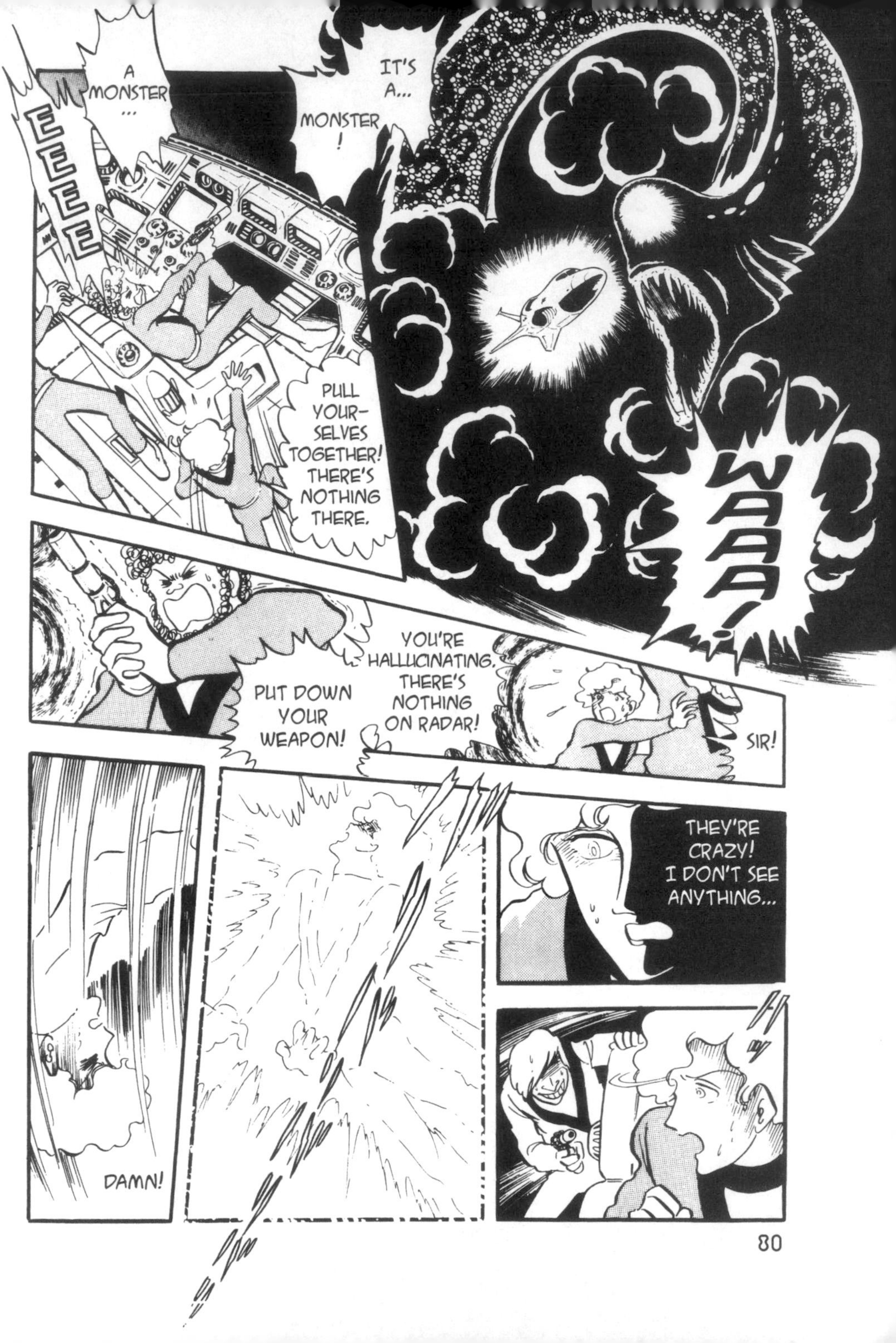
WAAAA!
IT'S A... MONSTER!
A MONSTER...
EEEEE
PULL YOURSELVES TOGETHER! THERE'S NOTHING THERE.
SIR!
YOU'RE HALLUCINATING. THERE'S NOTHING ON RADAR!
PUT DOWN YOUR WEAPON!
THEY'RE CRAZY! I DON'T SEE ANYTHING...
DAMN!

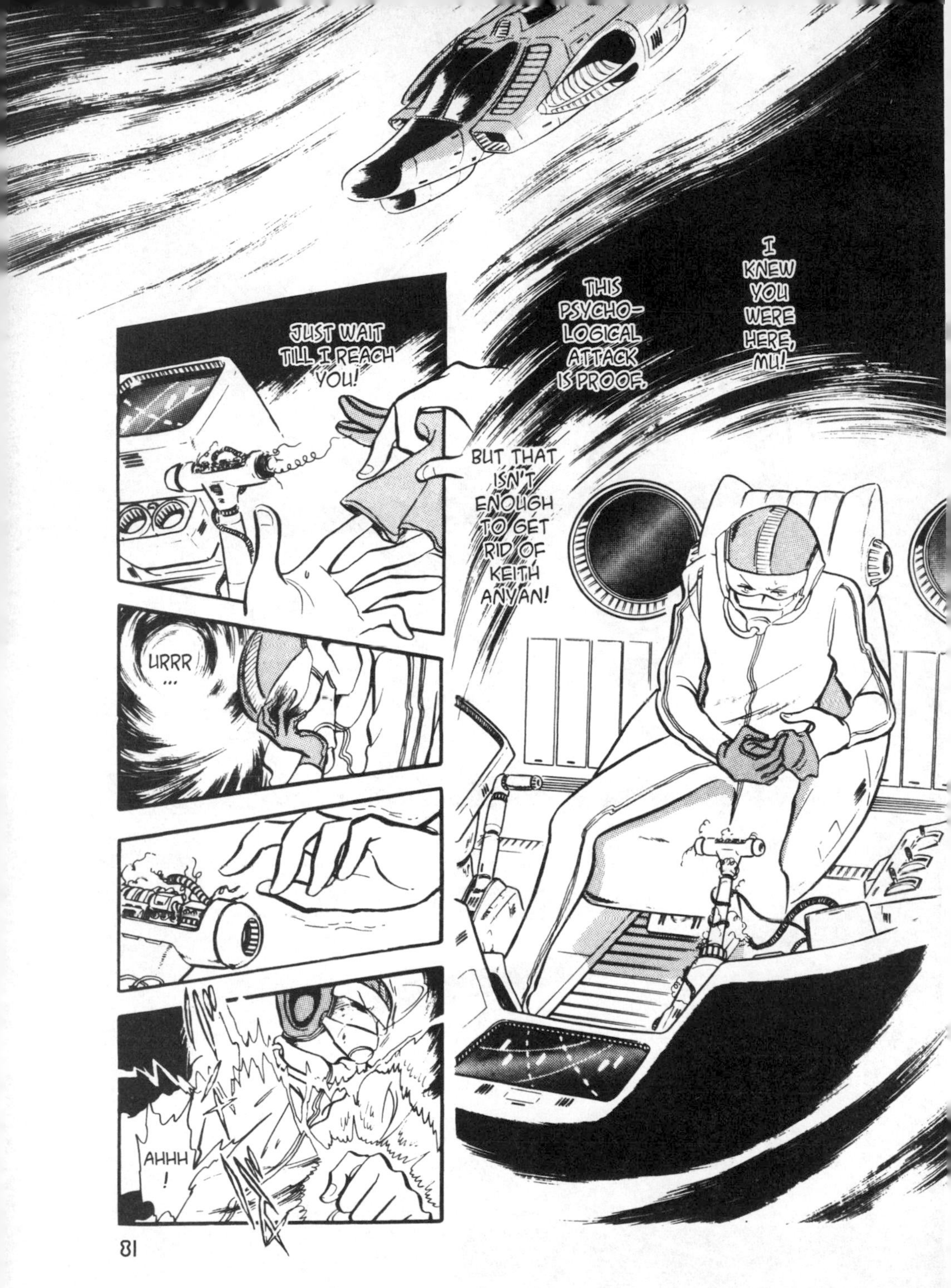
I KNEW YOU WERE HERE, MU!
THIS PSYCHO-LOGICAL ATTACK IS PROOF.
BUT THAT ISN'T ENOUGH TO GET RID OF KEITH ANYAN!
JUST WAIT TILL I REACH YOU!
URRR...
AHHH!

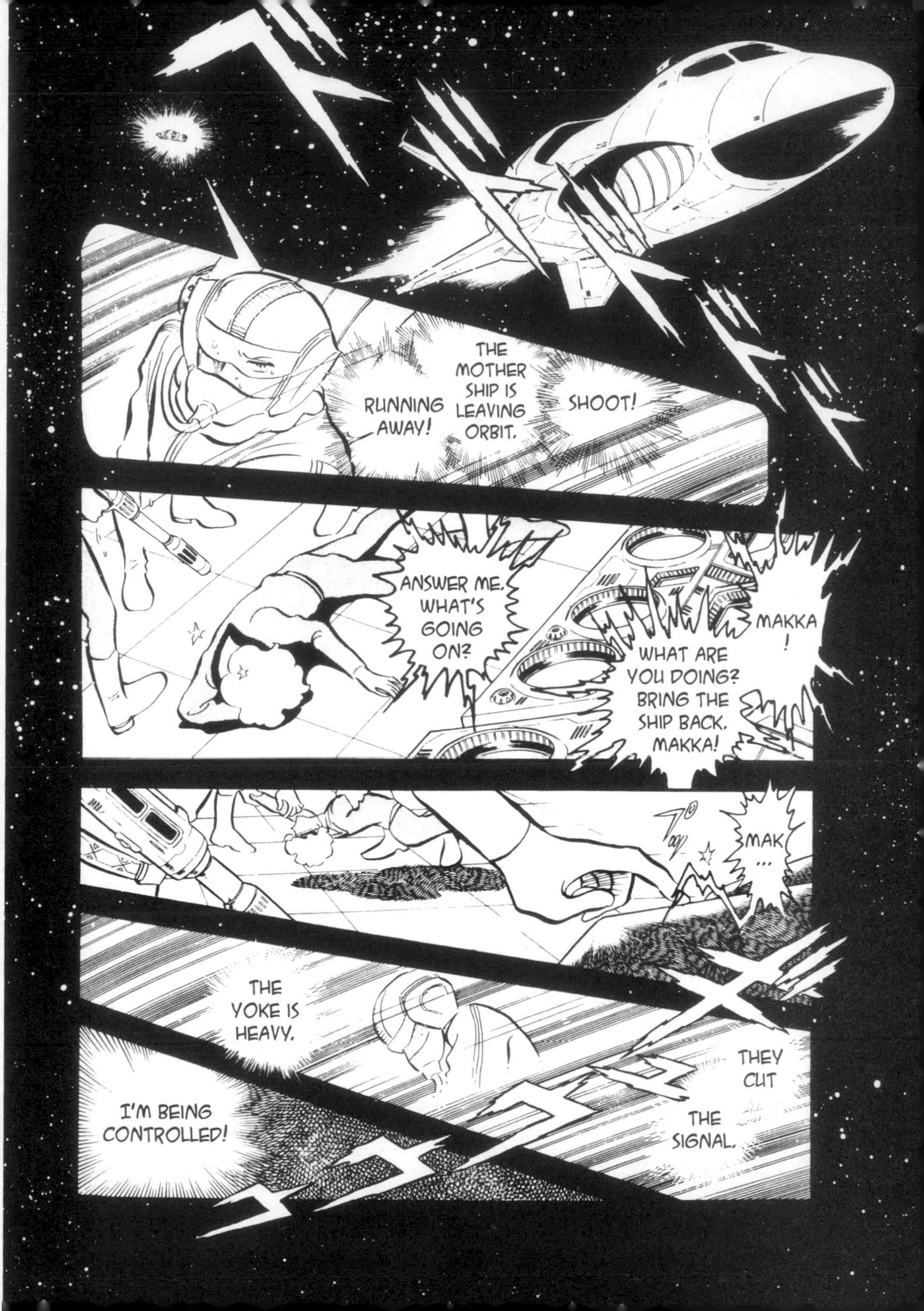
SHOOT!
THE MOTHER SHIP IS LEAVING ORBIT.
RUNNING AWAY!
MAKKA!
WHAT ARE YOU DOING? BRING THE SHIP BACK. MAKKA!
ANSWER ME. WHAT'S GOING ON?
MAK...
THEY CUT THE SIGNAL.
THE YOKE IS HEAVY.
I'M BEING CONTROLLED!

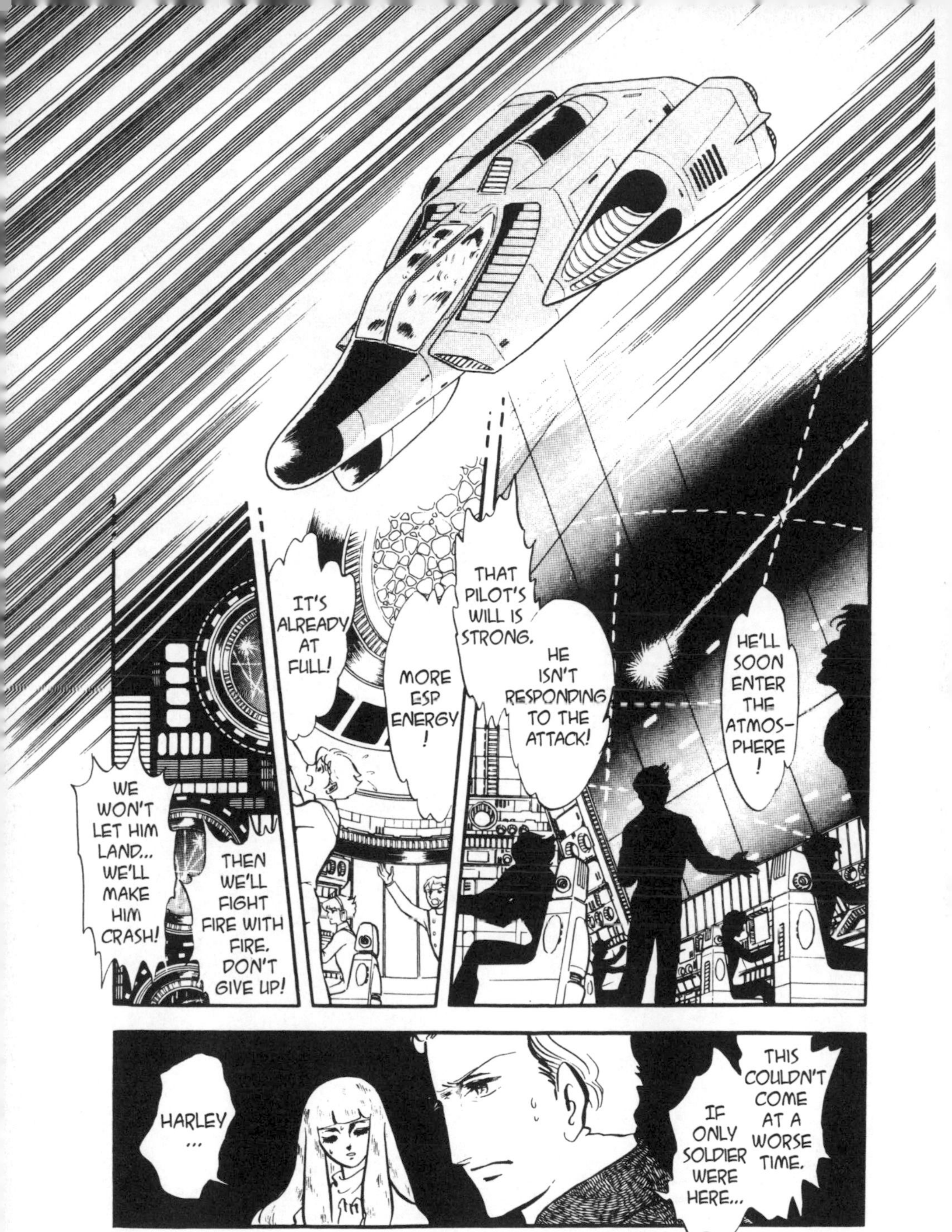
HE'LL SOON ENTER THE ATMOSPHERE!
THAT PILOT'S WILL IS STRONG.
HE ISN'T RESPONDING TO THE ATTACK!
MORE ESP ENERGY!
IT'S ALREADY AT FULL!
THEN WE'LL FIGHT FIRE WITH FIRE. DON'T GIVE UP!
WE WON'T LET HIM LAND... WE'LL MAKE HIM CRASH!
THIS COULDN'T COME AT A WORSE TIME.
IF ONLY SOLDIER WERE HERE...
HARLEY ...

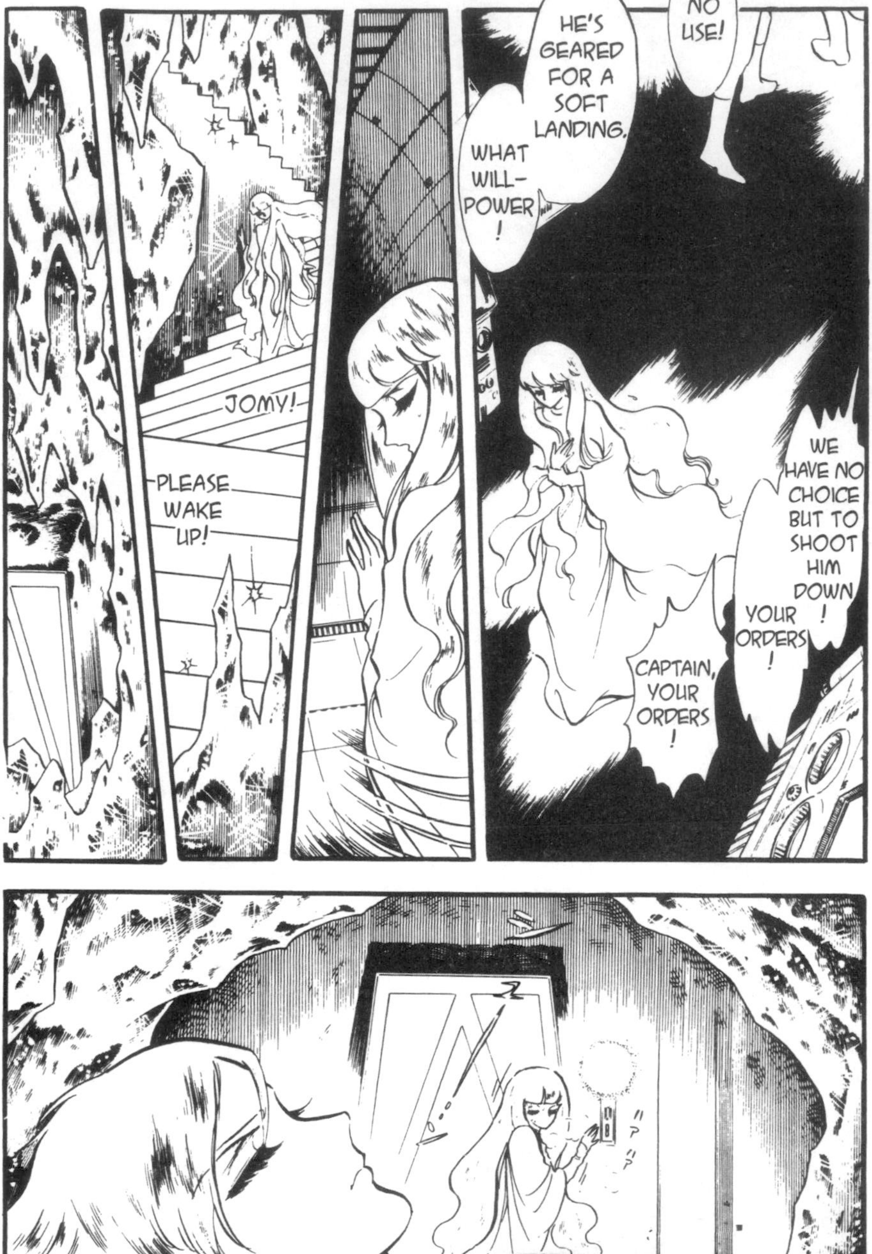
NO USE!
HE'S GEARED FOR A SOFT LANDING.
WHAT WILL-POWER!
WE HAVE NO CHOICE BUT TO SHOOT HIM DOWN!
YOUR ORDERS!
CAPTAIN, YOUR ORDERS!
JOMY!
PLEASE WAKE UP!

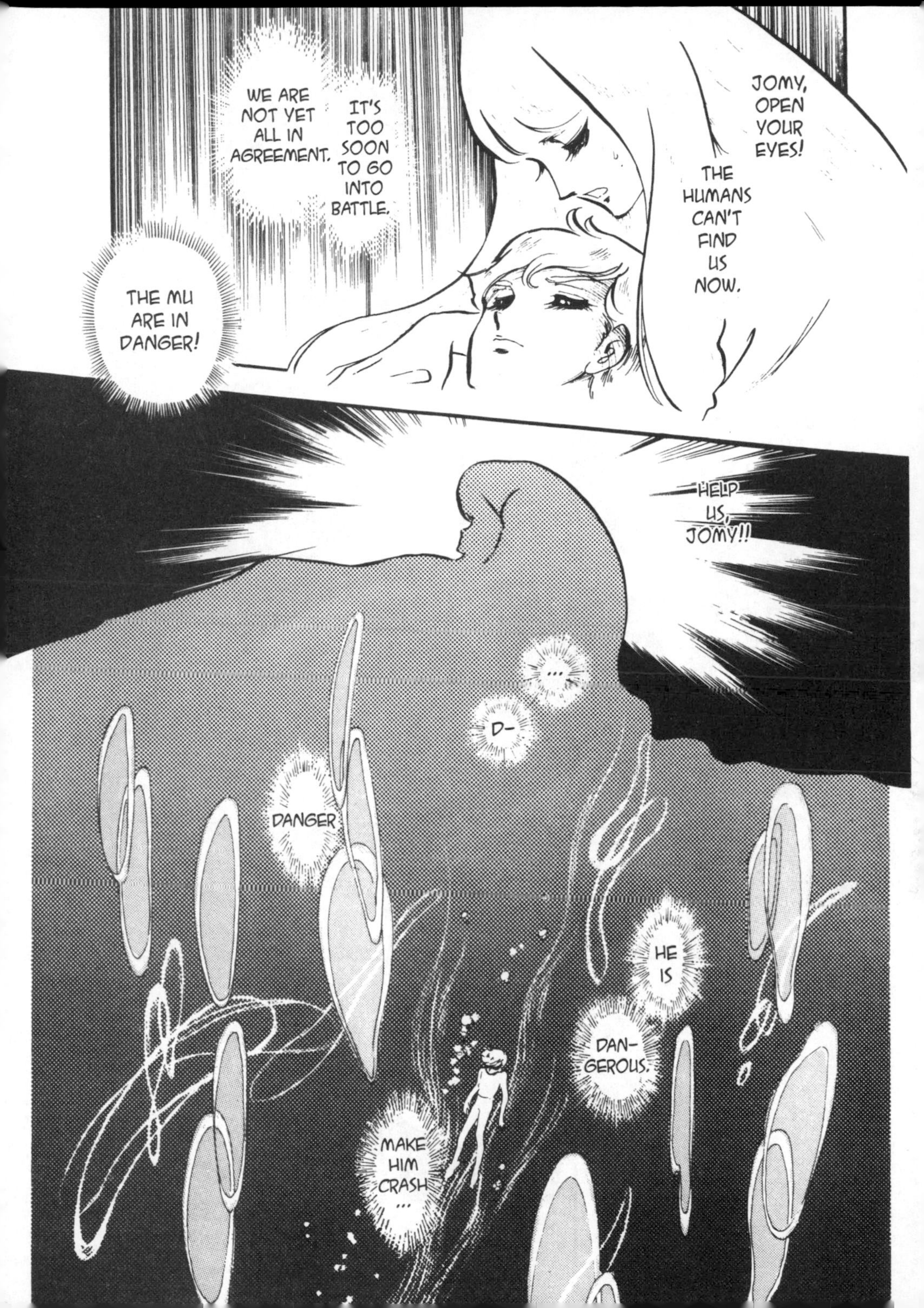
JOMY, OPEN YOUR EYES!
THE HUMANS CAN'T FIND US NOW.
IT'S TOO SOON TO GO INTO BATTLE.
WE ARE NOT YET ALL IN AGREEMENT.
THE MU ARE IN DANGER!
HELP US, JOMY!!
...
D-
DANGER
HE IS
DAN-GEROUS.
MAKE HIM CRASH ...

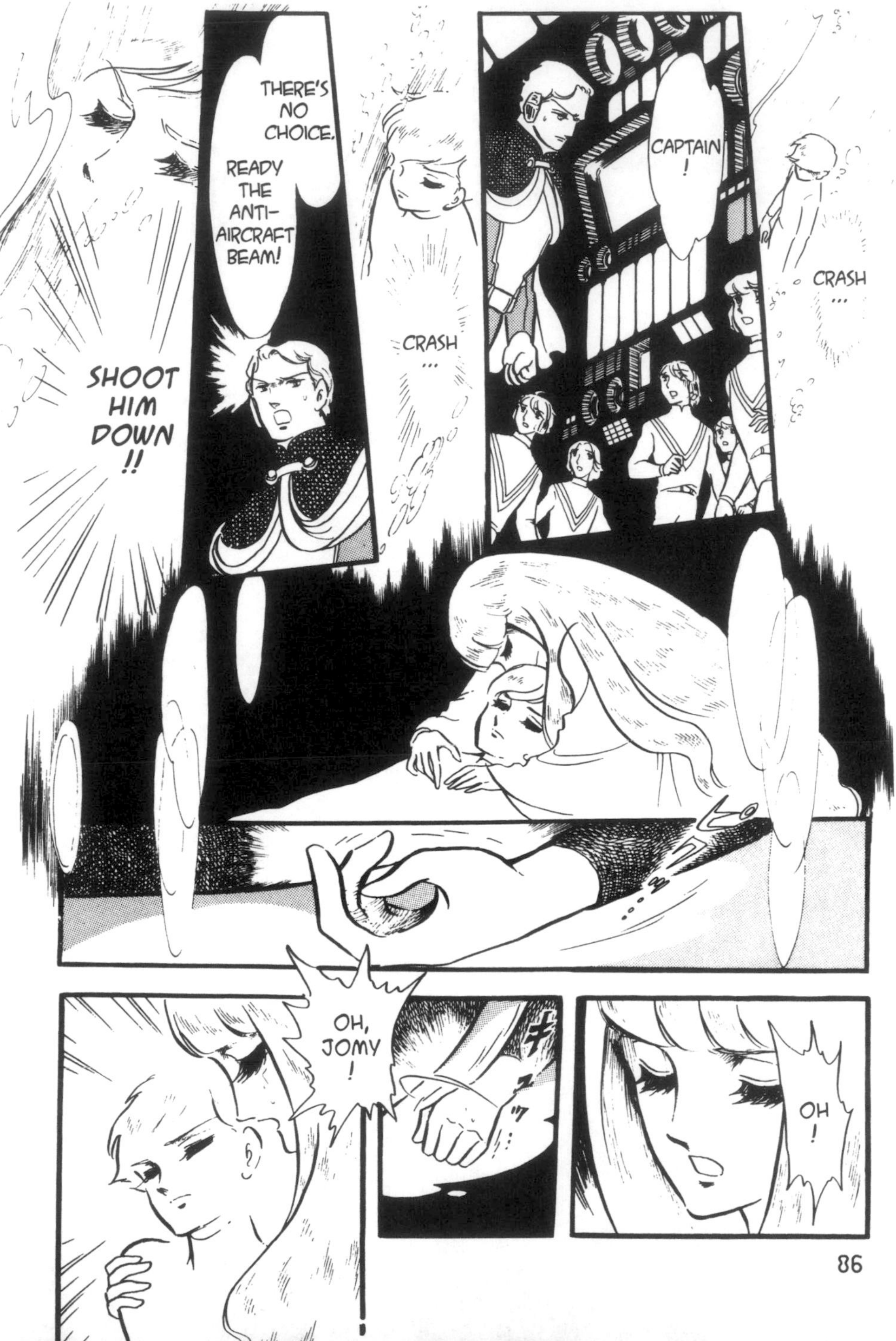
CRASH...
CAPTAIN!
CRASH...
THERE'S NO CHOICE.
READY THE ANTI-AIRCRAFT BEAM!
SHOOT HIM DOWN!!
OH!
OH, JOMY!

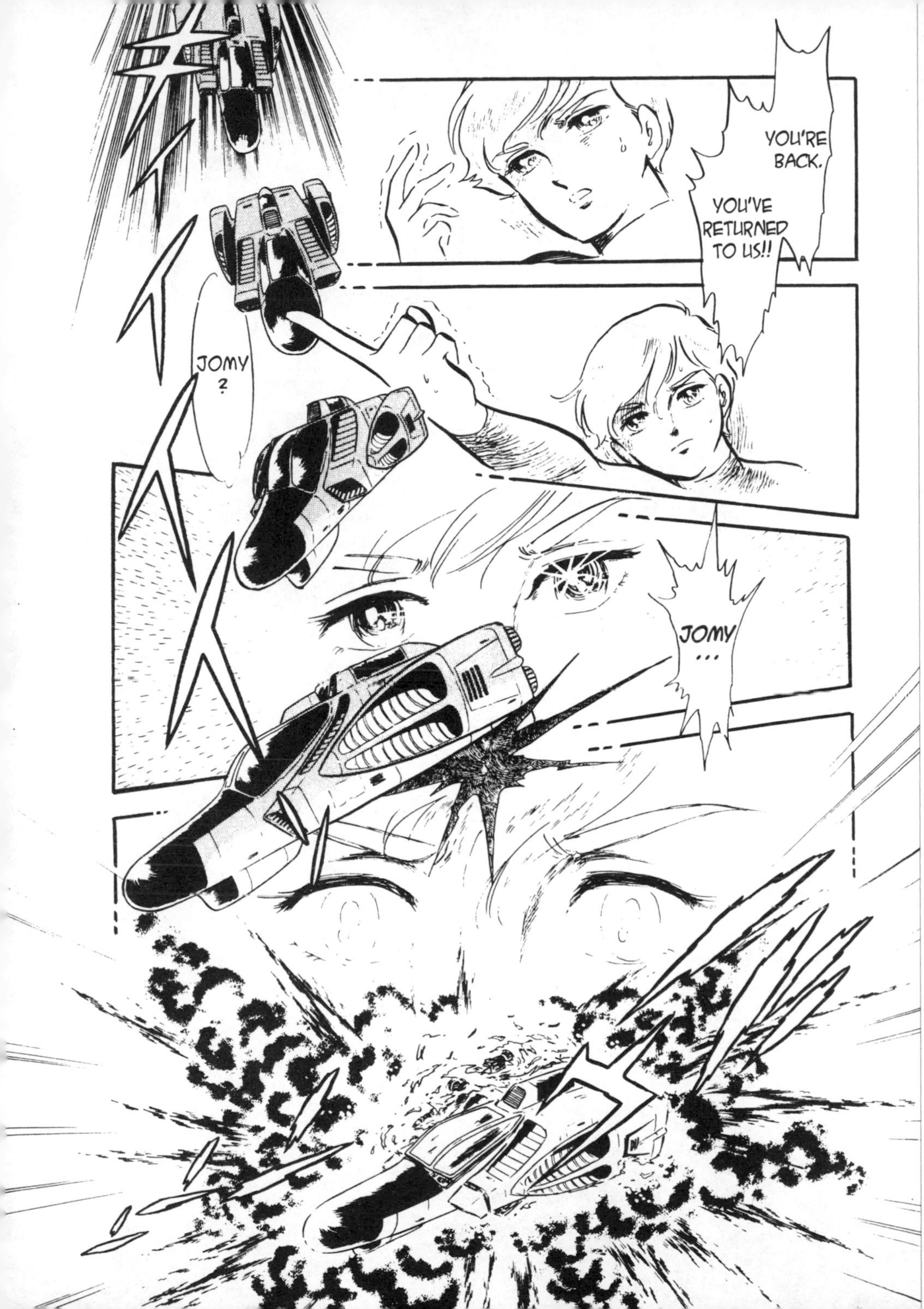
YOU'RE BACK.
YOU'VE RETURNED TO US!!
JOMY ?
JOMY ...

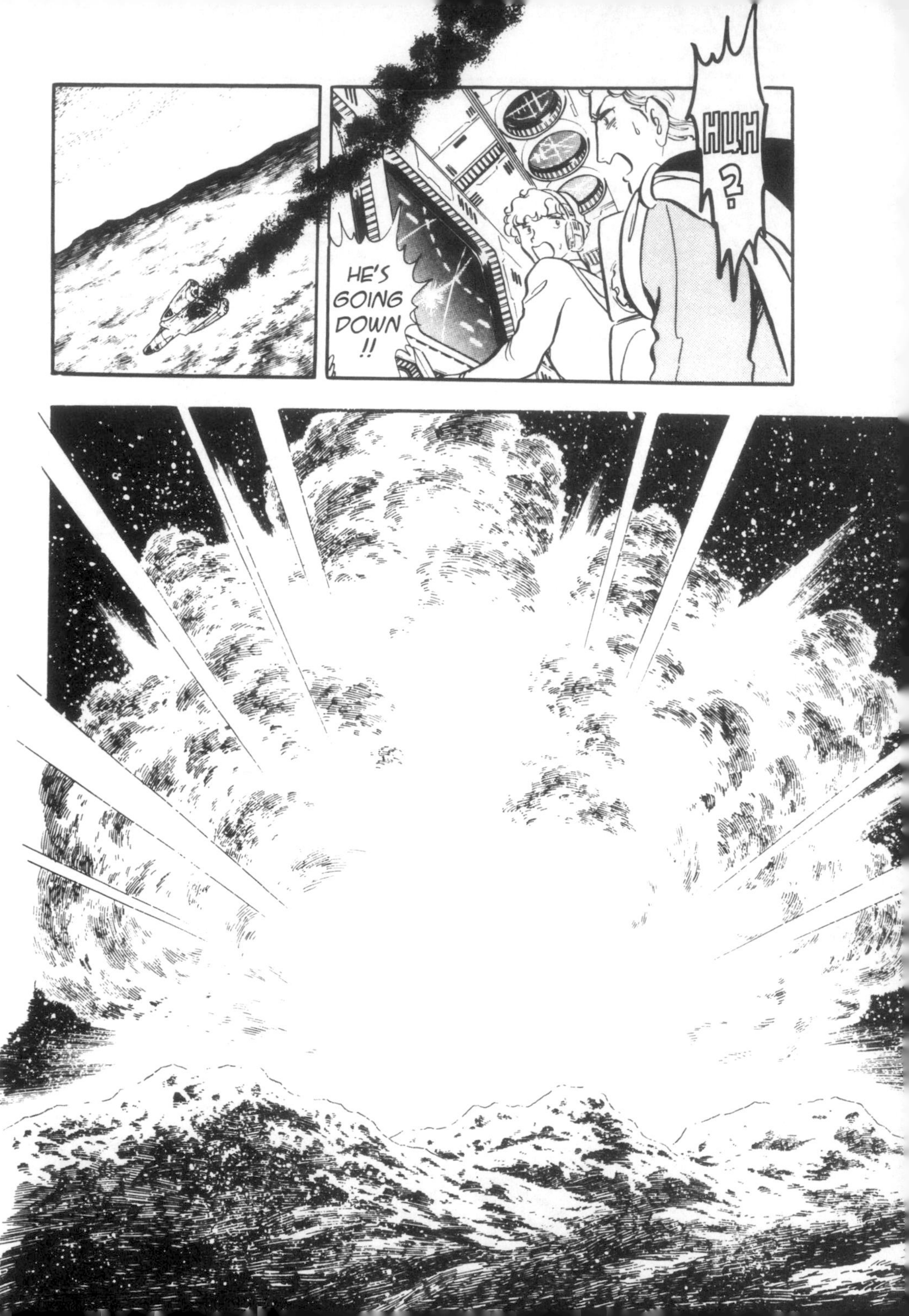
HUH ?
HE'S GOING DOWN !!

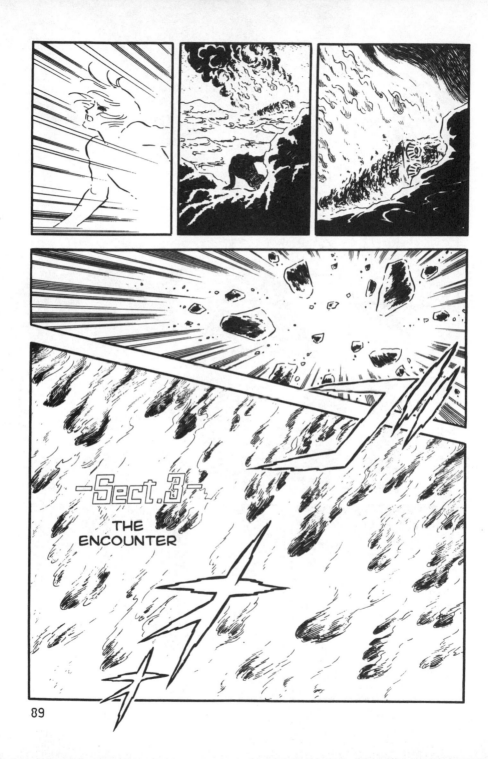

–Sect.3–

THE
ENCOUNTER

89

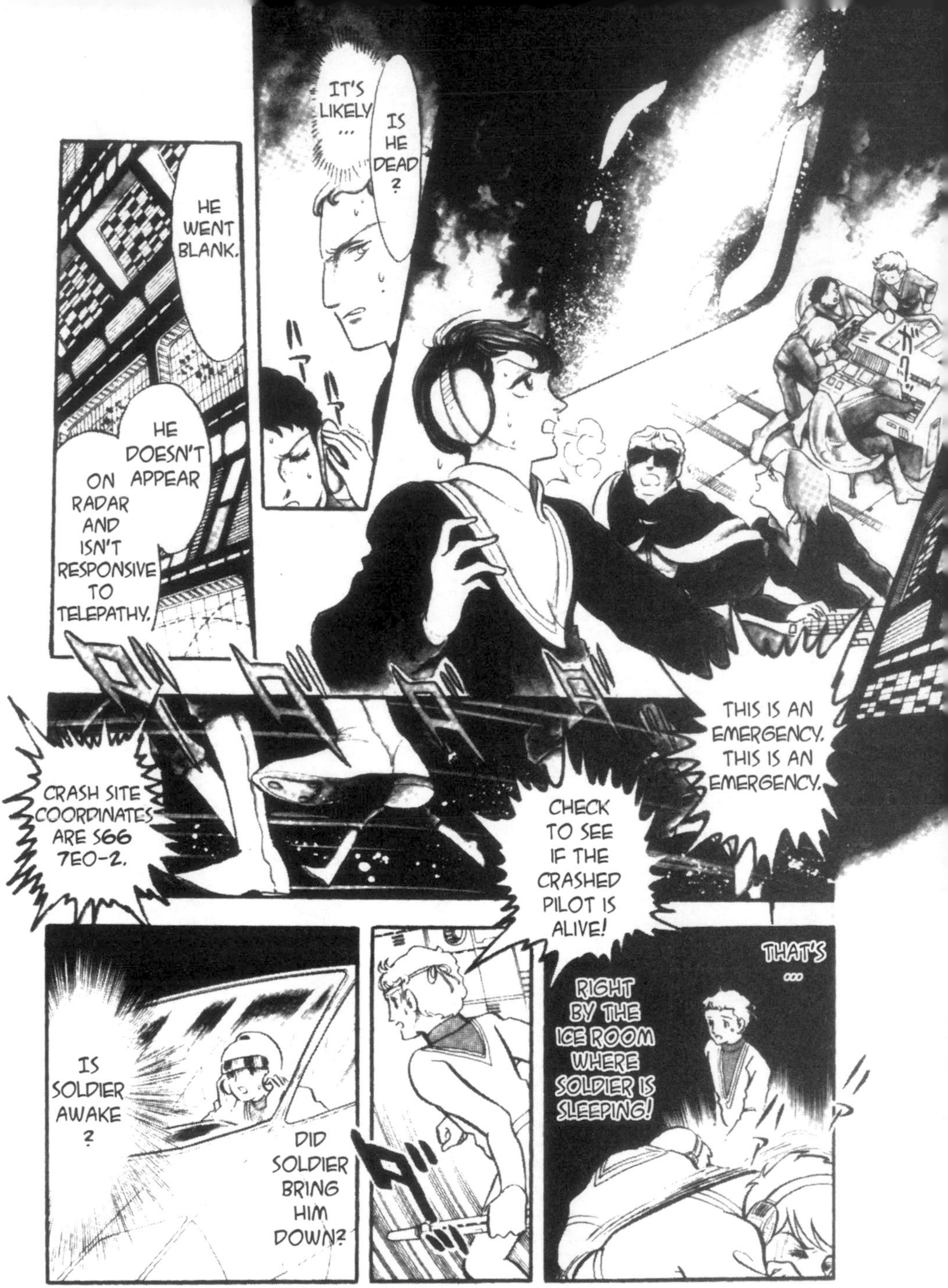
IS HE DEAD?
IT'S LIKELY...
HE WENT BLANK.
HE DOESN'T APPEAR ON RADAR AND ISN'T RESPONSIVE TO TELEPATHY.
THIS IS AN EMERGENCY. THIS IS AN EMERGENCY.
CHECK TO SEE IF THE CRASHED PILOT IS ALIVE!
CRASH SITE COORDINATES ARE S66 7EO-2.
THAT'S...
RIGHT BY THE ICE ROOM WHERE SOLDIER IS SLEEPING!
DID SOLDIER BRING HIM DOWN?
IS SOLDIER AWAKE?

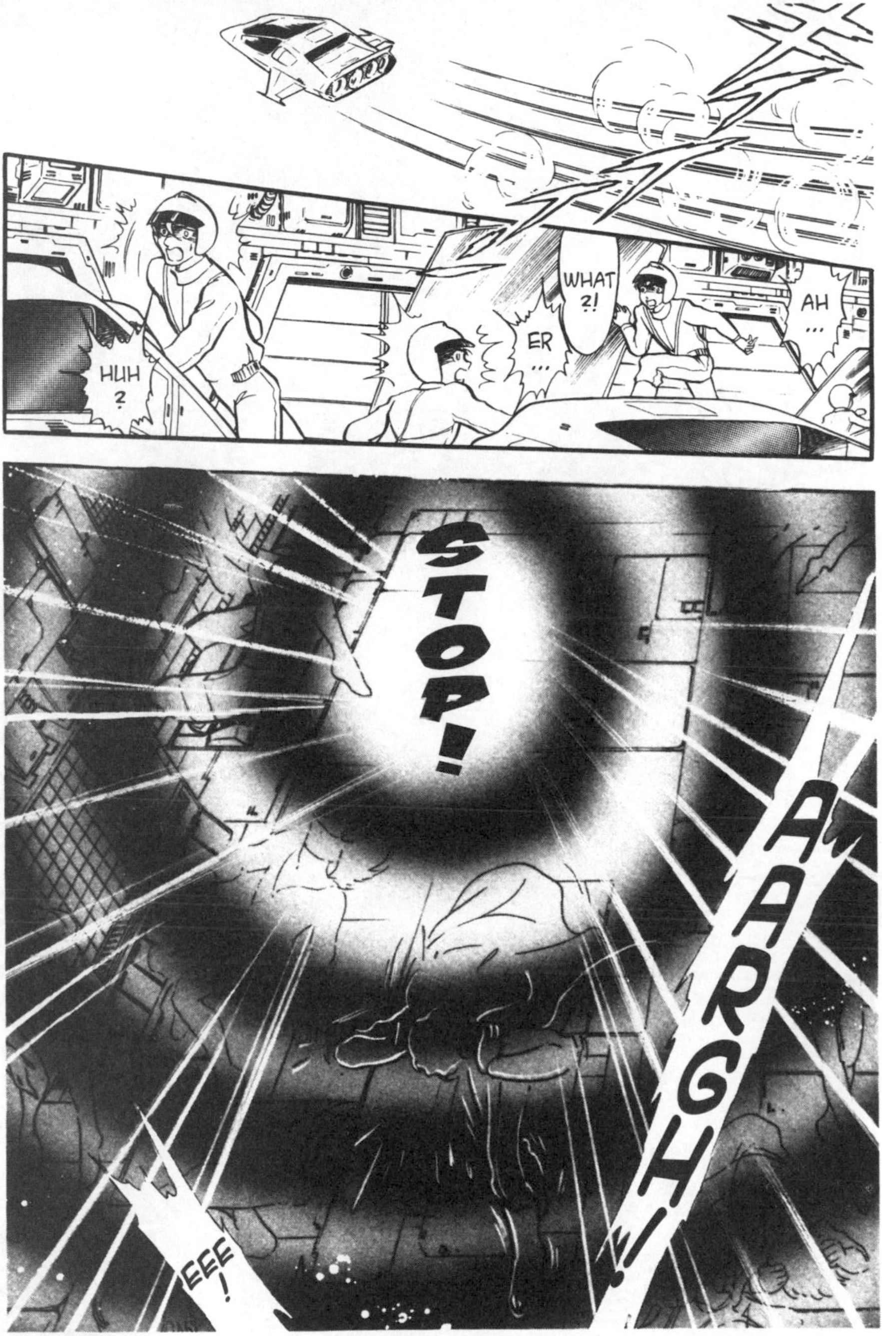
AH …
WHAT ?!
ER …
HUH ?
STOP!
AARGH!!
EEE!

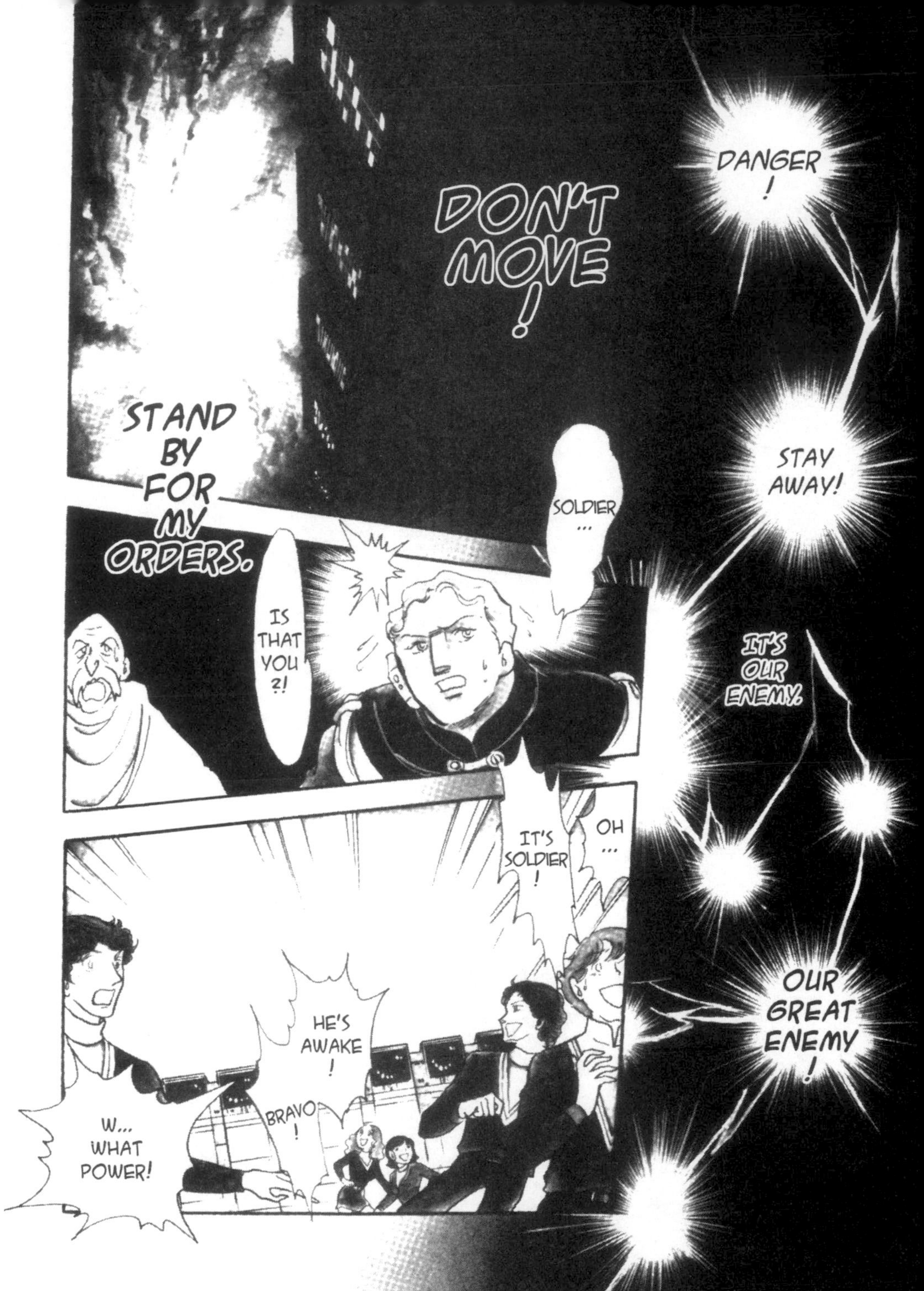
DANGER!
DON'T MOVE!
STAND BY FOR MY ORDERS.
STAY AWAY!
SOLDIER...
IS THAT YOU?!
IT'S OUR ENEMY.
OH...
IT'S SOLDIER!
HE'S AWAKE!
BRAVO!
W... WHAT POWER!
OUR GREAT ENEMY!

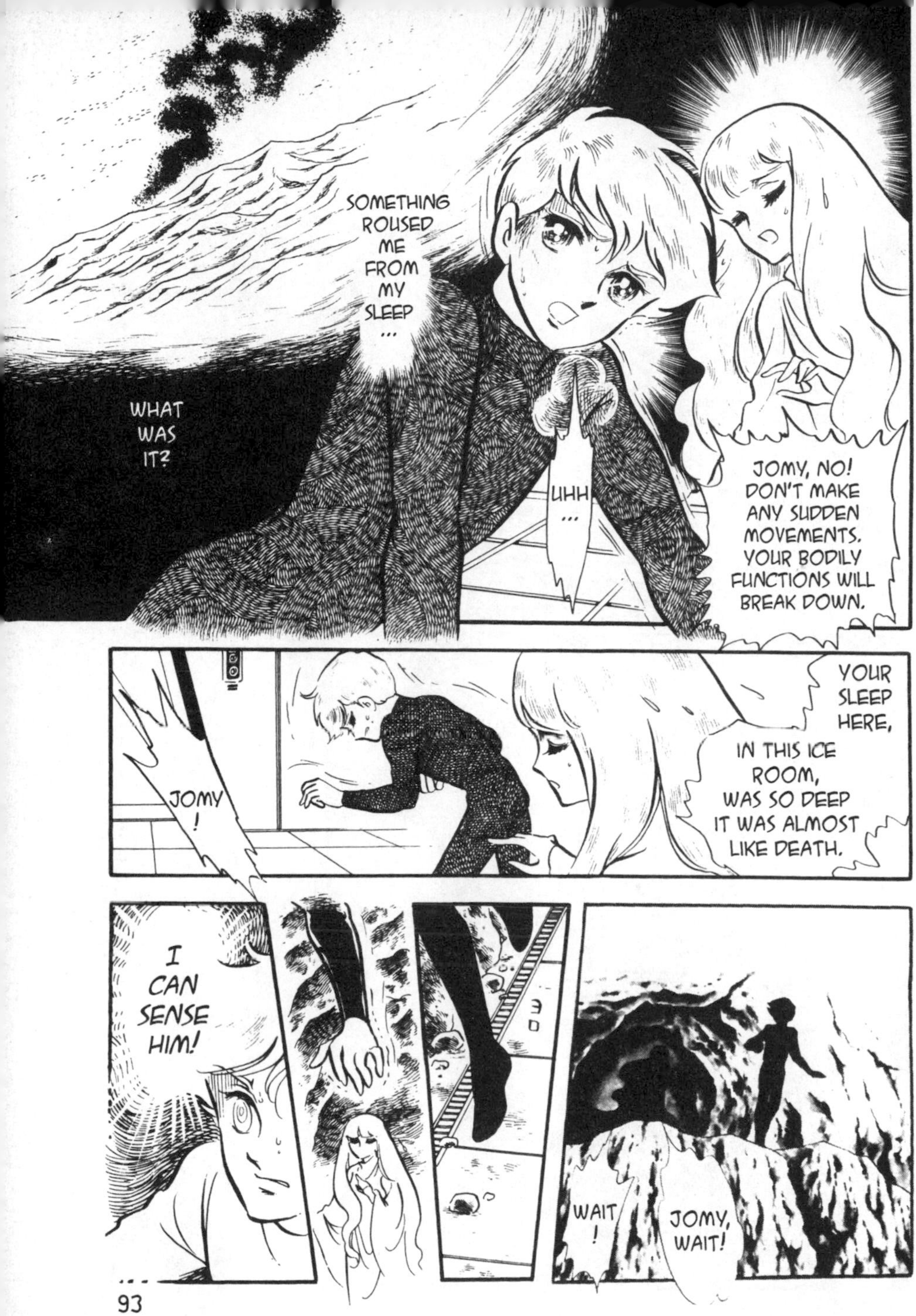
SOMETHING ROUSED ME FROM MY SLEEP ...
WHAT WAS IT?
UHH ...
JOMY, NO! DON'T MAKE ANY SUDDEN MOVEMENTS. YOUR BODILY FUNCTIONS WILL BREAK DOWN.
YOUR SLEEP HERE,
IN THIS ICE ROOM, WAS SO DEEP IT WAS ALMOST LIKE DEATH.
JOMY!
JOMY, WAIT!
WAIT!
I CAN SENSE HIM!
...

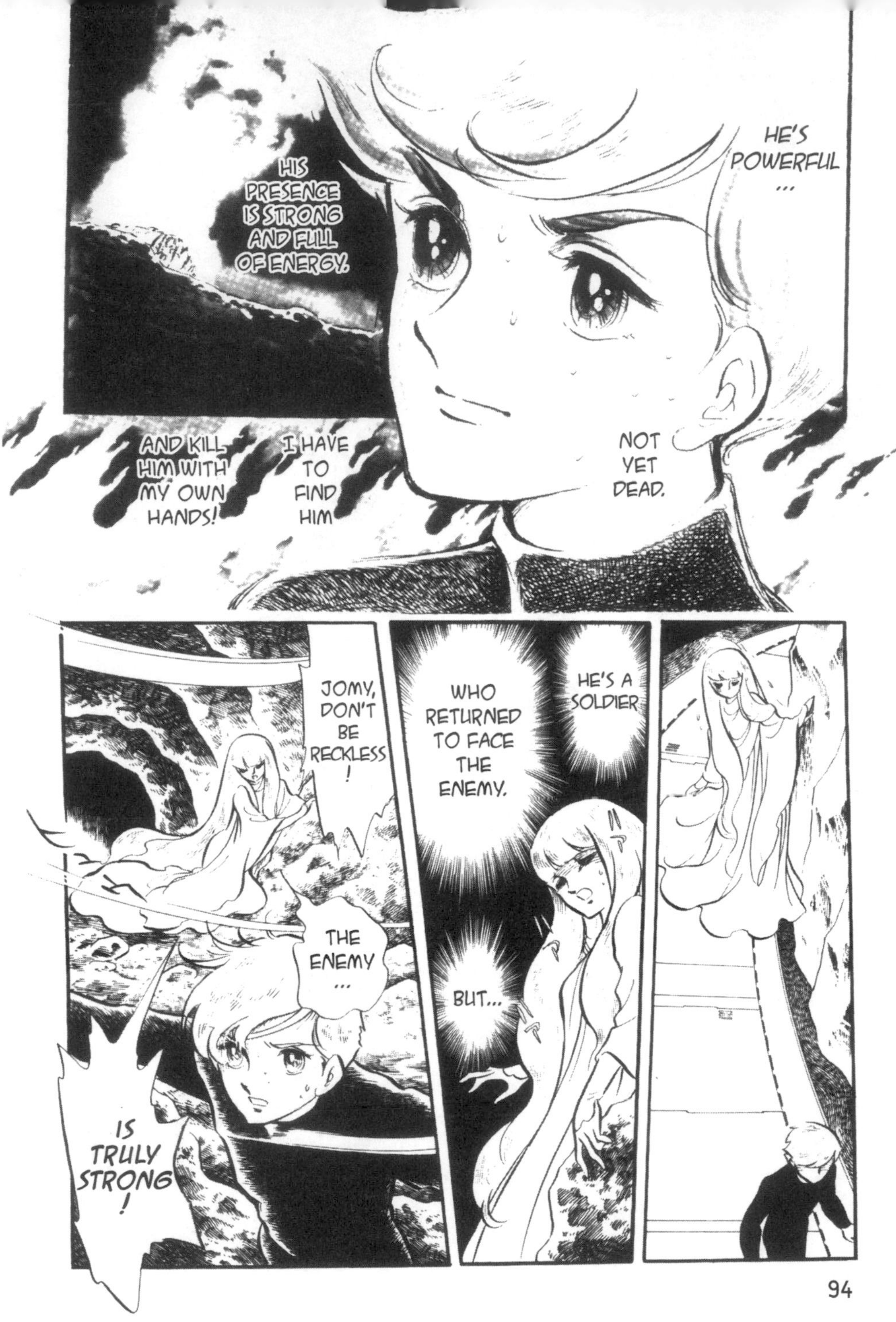
HE'S POWERFUL ...
HIS PRESENCE IS STRONG AND FULL OF ENERGY.
NOT YET DEAD.
I HAVE TO FIND HIM
AND KILL HIM WITH MY OWN HANDS!
HE'S A SOLDIER
WHO RETURNED TO FACE THE ENEMY.
BUT...
JOMY, DON'T BE RECKLESS!
THE ENEMY ...
IS TRULY STRONG!

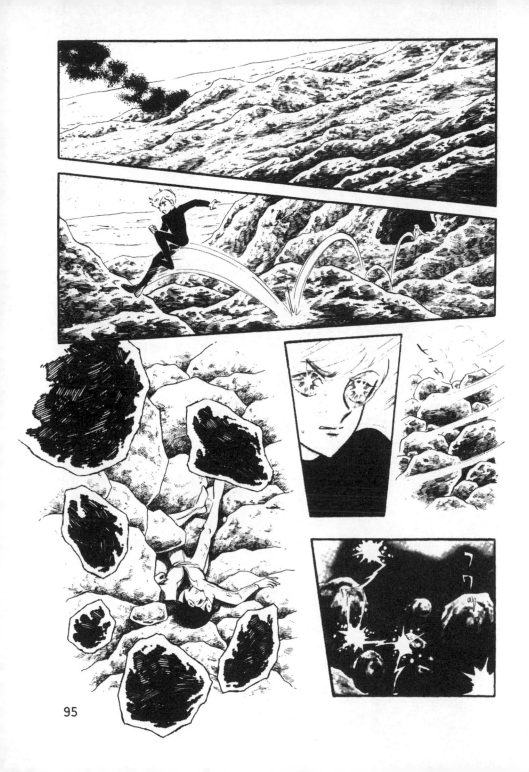

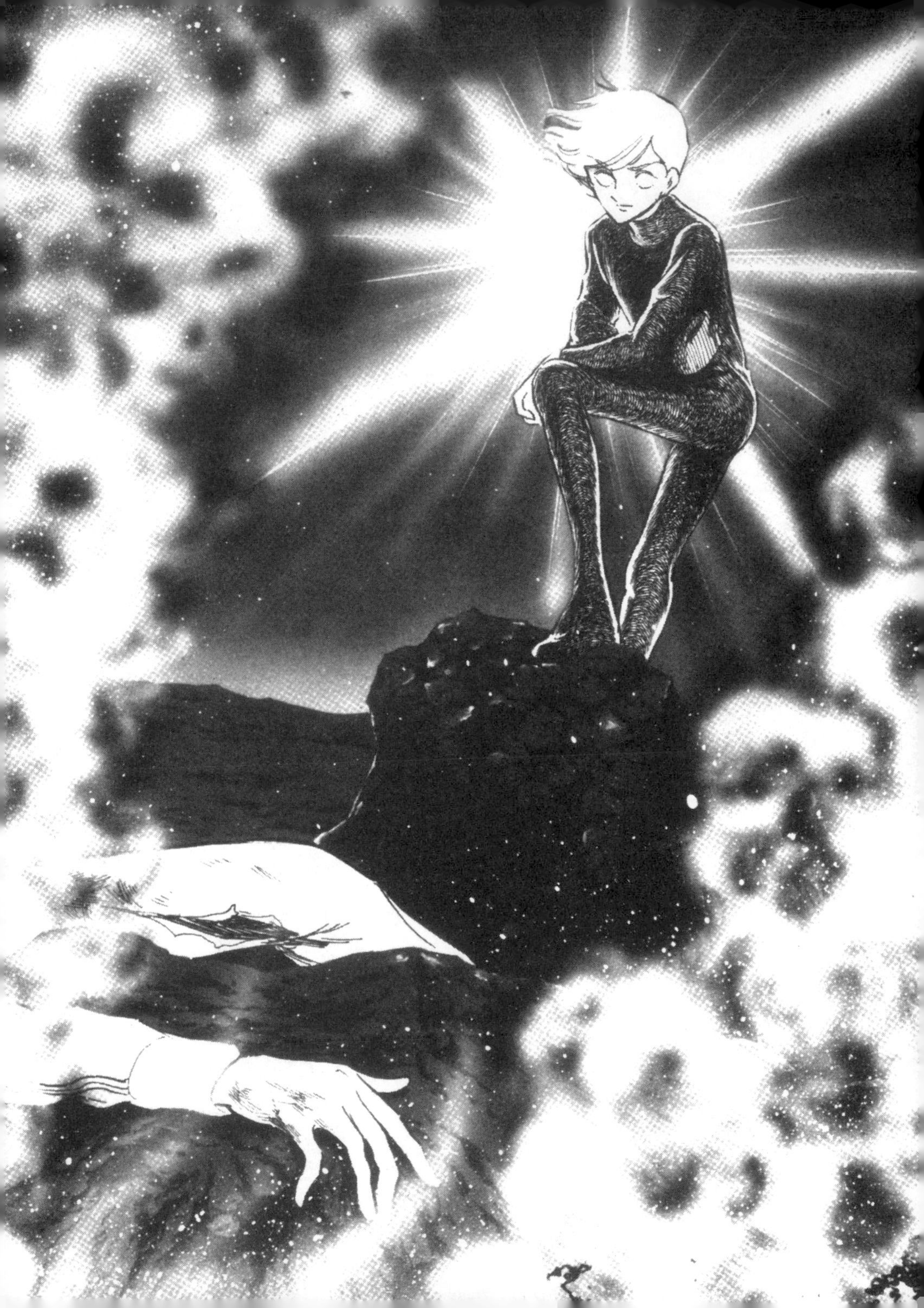

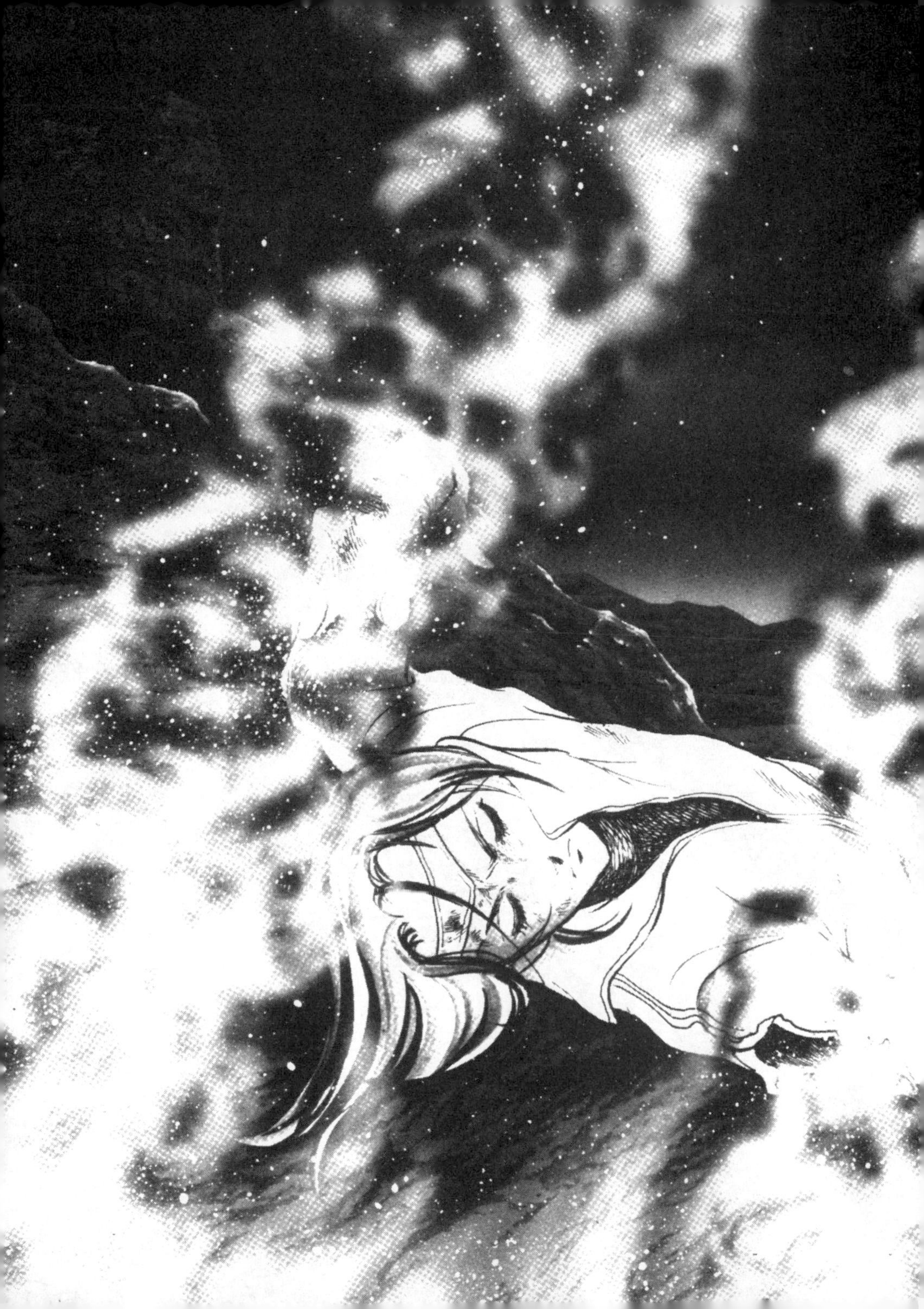

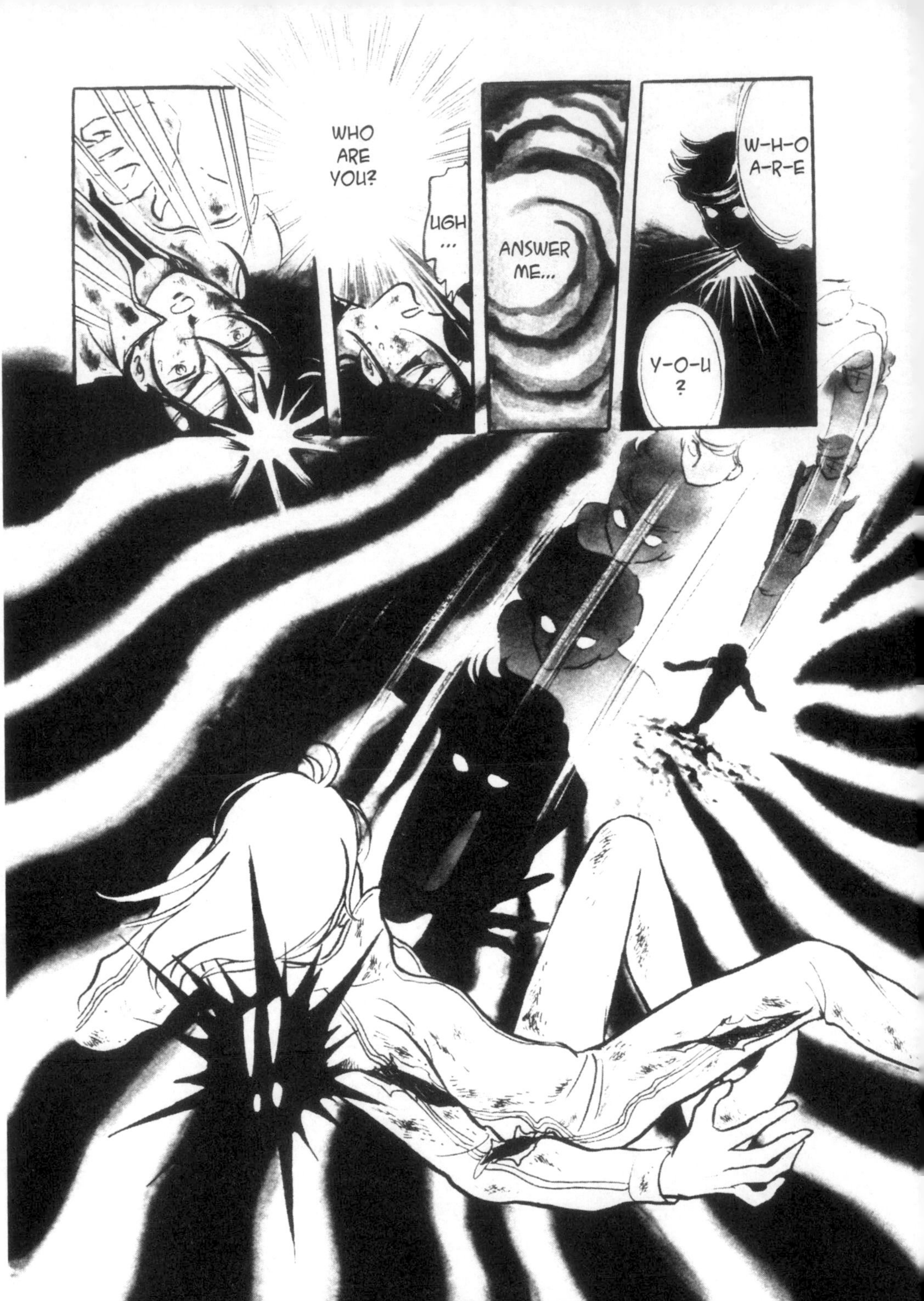
W-H-O A-R-E
Y-O-U ?
ANSWER ME...
UGH ...
WHO ARE YOU?

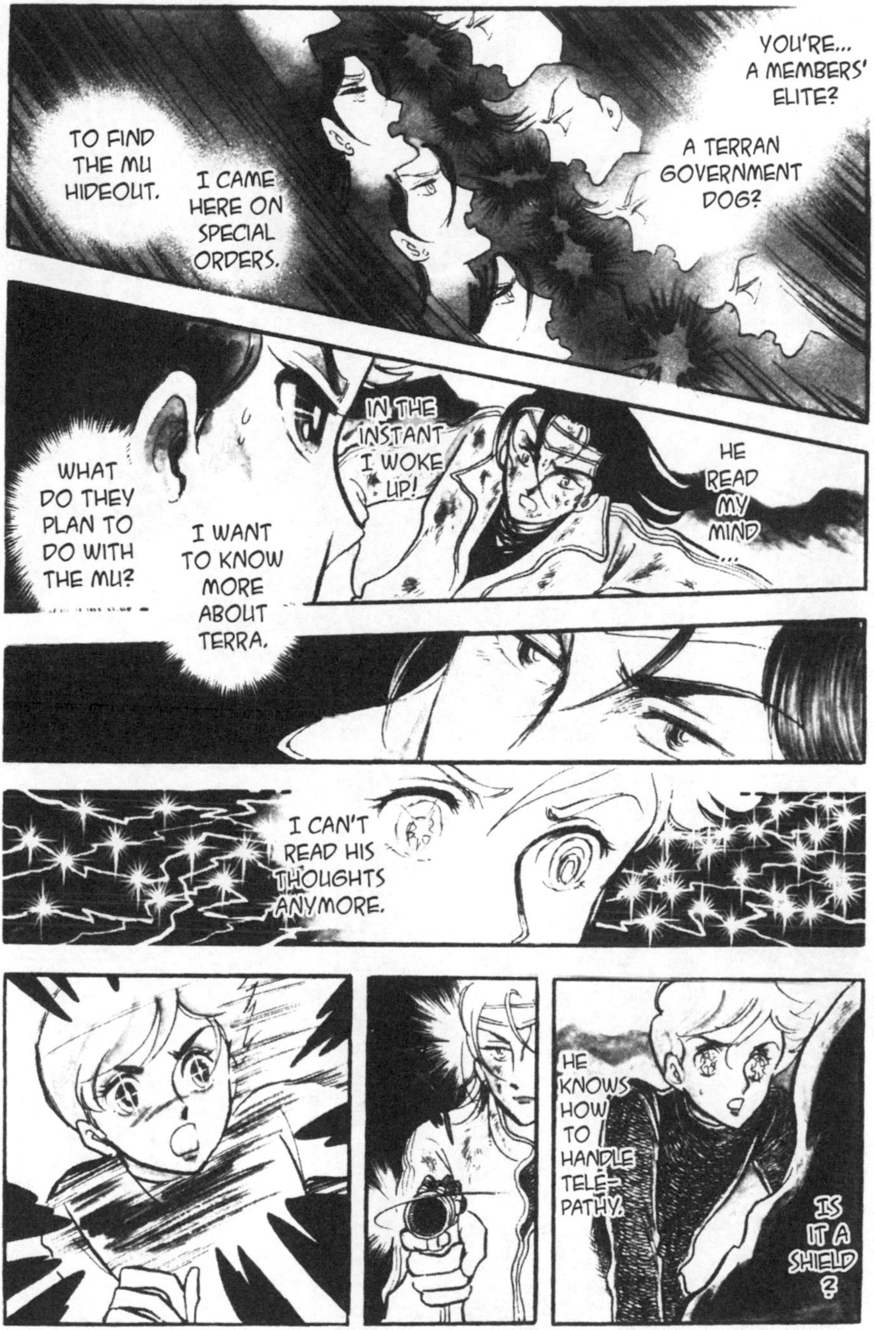
YOU'RE... A MEMBERS' ELITE?
A TERRAN GOVERNMENT DOG?
I CAME HERE ON SPECIAL ORDERS.
TO FIND THE MU HIDEOUT.
HE READ MY MIND...
IN THE INSTANT I WOKE UP!
I WANT TO KNOW MORE ABOUT TERRA.
WHAT DO THEY PLAN TO DO WITH THE MU?
I CAN'T READ HIS THOUGHTS ANYMORE.
HE KNOWS HOW TO HANDLE TELE-PATHY.
IS IT A SHIELD?

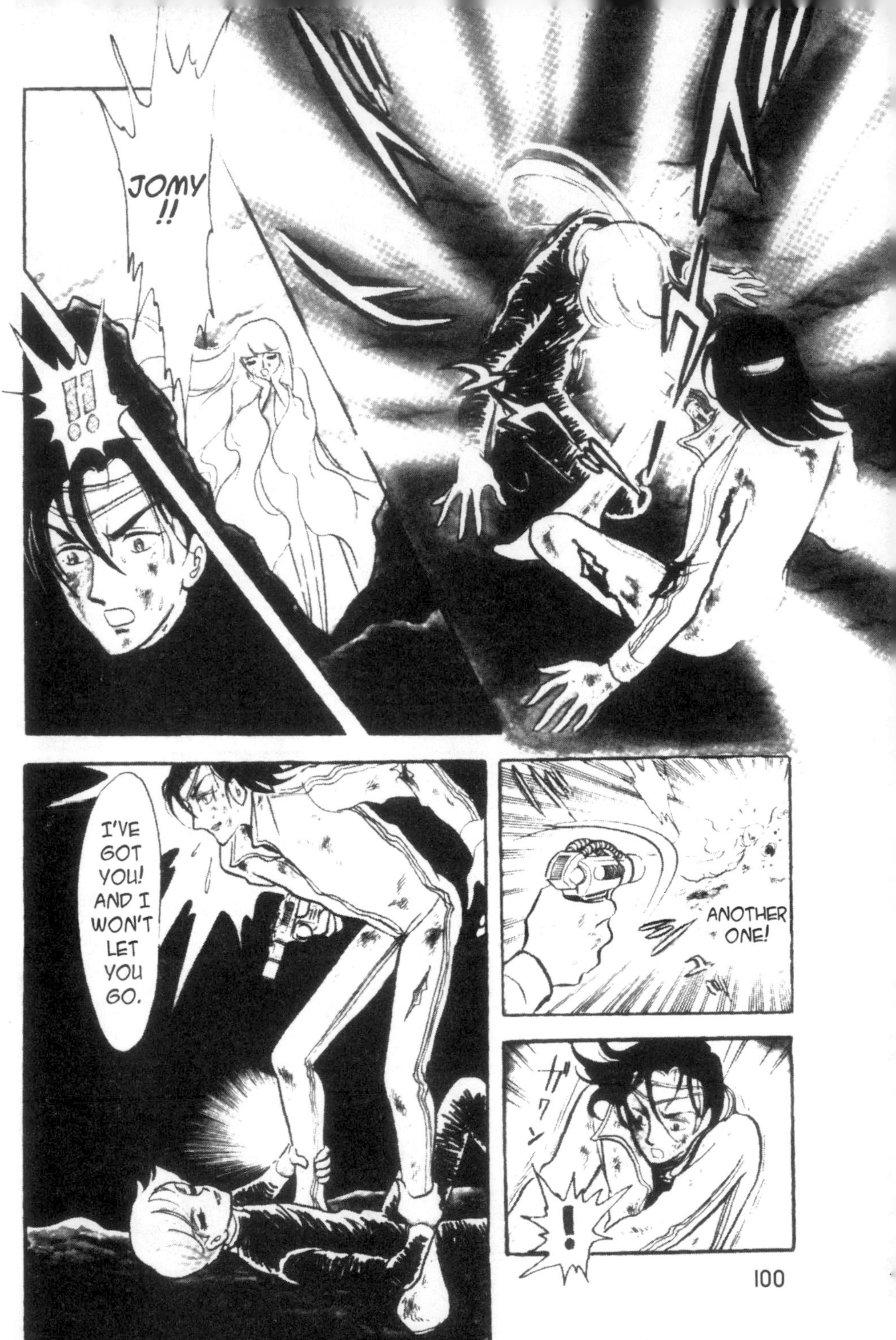
JOMY !!
!!
ANOTHER ONE!
ガクン
!
I'VE GOT YOU! AND I WON'T LET YOU GO.

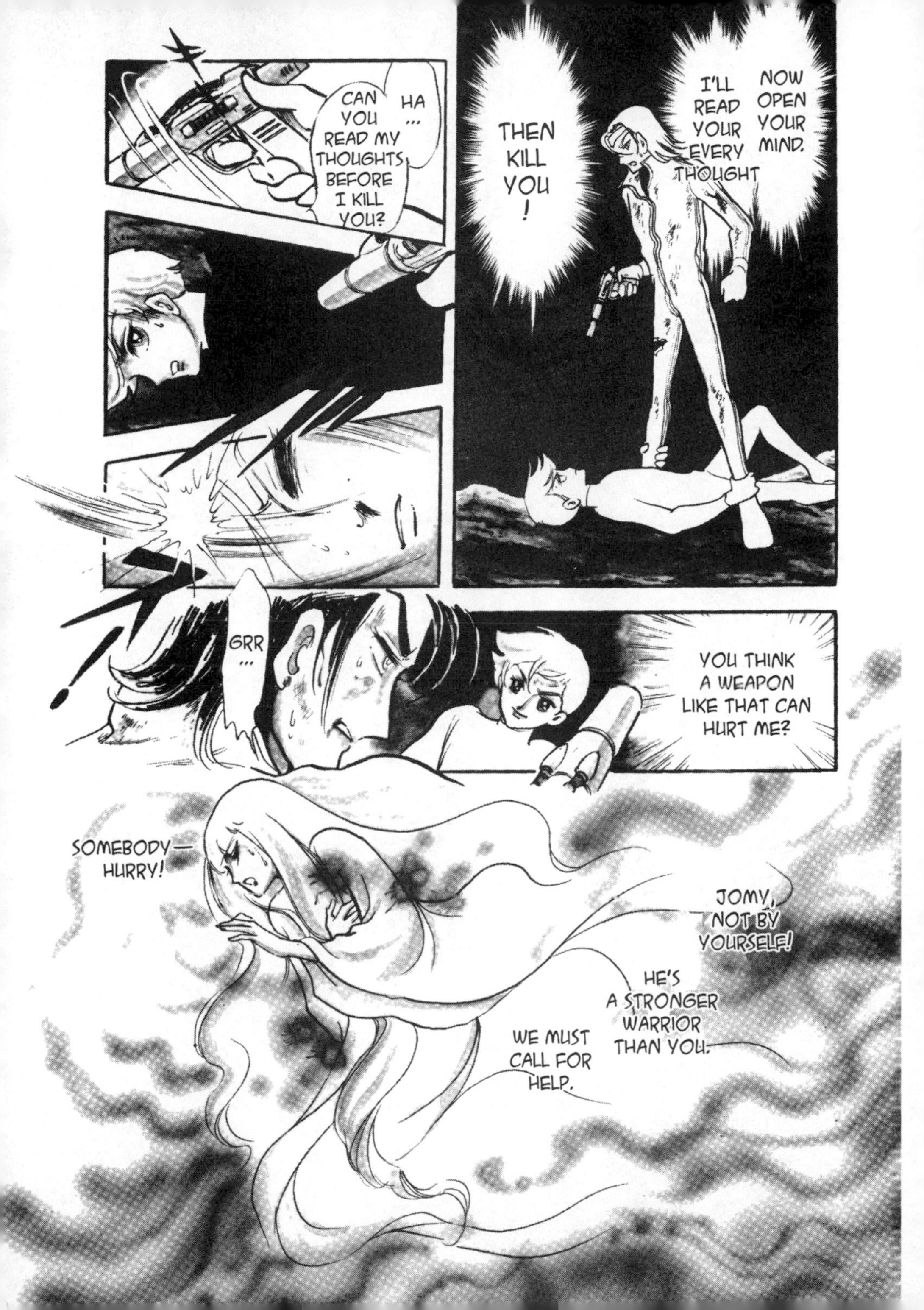
NOW OPEN YOUR MIND.
I'LL READ YOUR EVERY THOUGHT
THEN KILL YOU!
HA ...
CAN YOU READ MY THOUGHTS BEFORE I KILL YOU?
YOU THINK A WEAPON LIKE THAT CAN HURT ME?
GRR ...
!
JOMY, NOT BY YOURSELF!
HE'S A STRONGER WARRIOR THAN YOU.
WE MUST CALL FOR HELP.
SOMEBODY— HURRY!

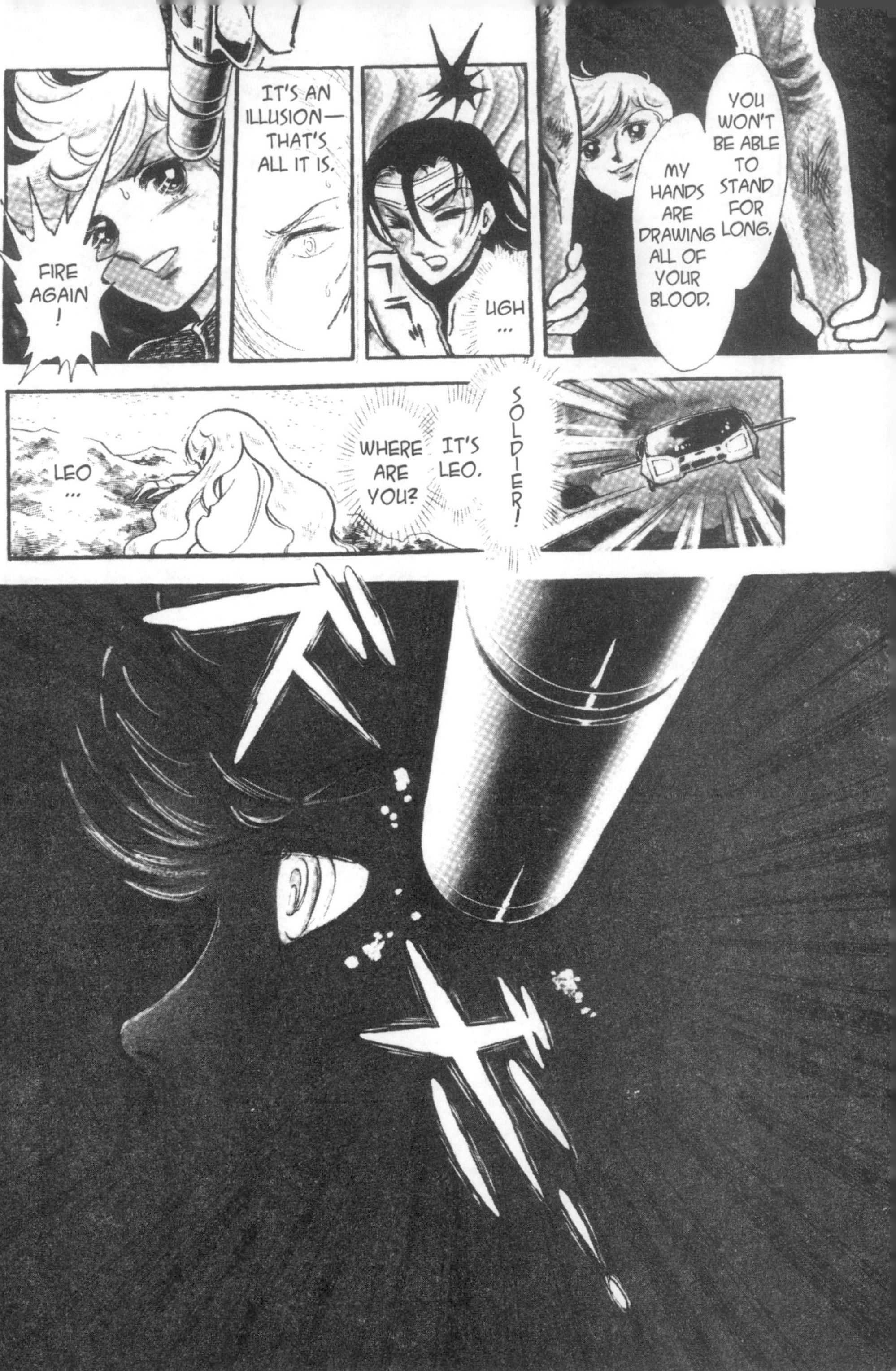
YOU WON'T BE ABLE TO STAND FOR LONG.
MY HANDS ARE DRAWING ALL OF YOUR BLOOD.
UGH ...
IT'S AN ILLUSION— THAT'S ALL IT IS.
FIRE AGAIN!
SOLDIER!
IT'S LEO.
WHERE ARE YOU?
LEO ...

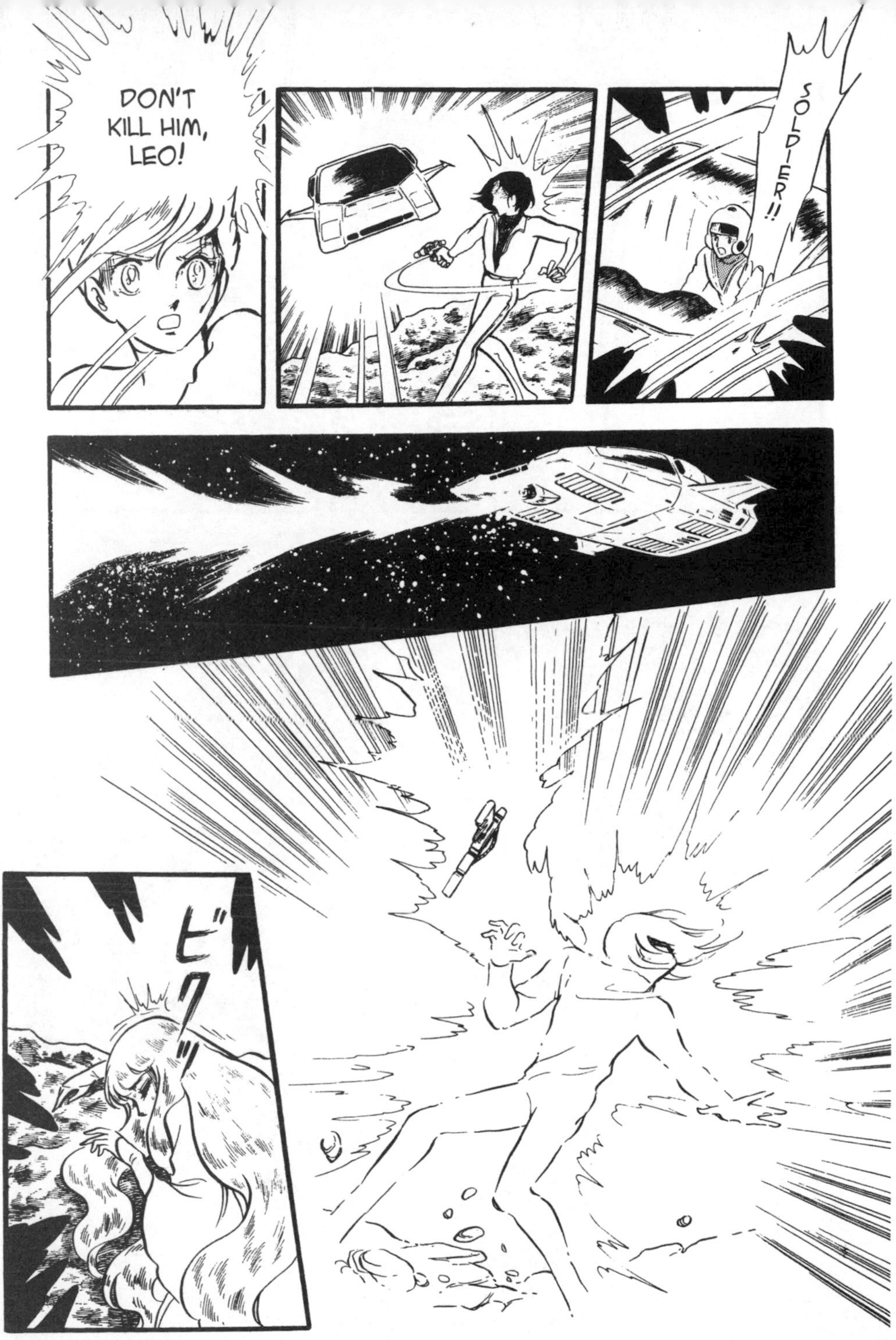
SOLDIER!!
DON'T KILL HIM, LEO!
ビクッ

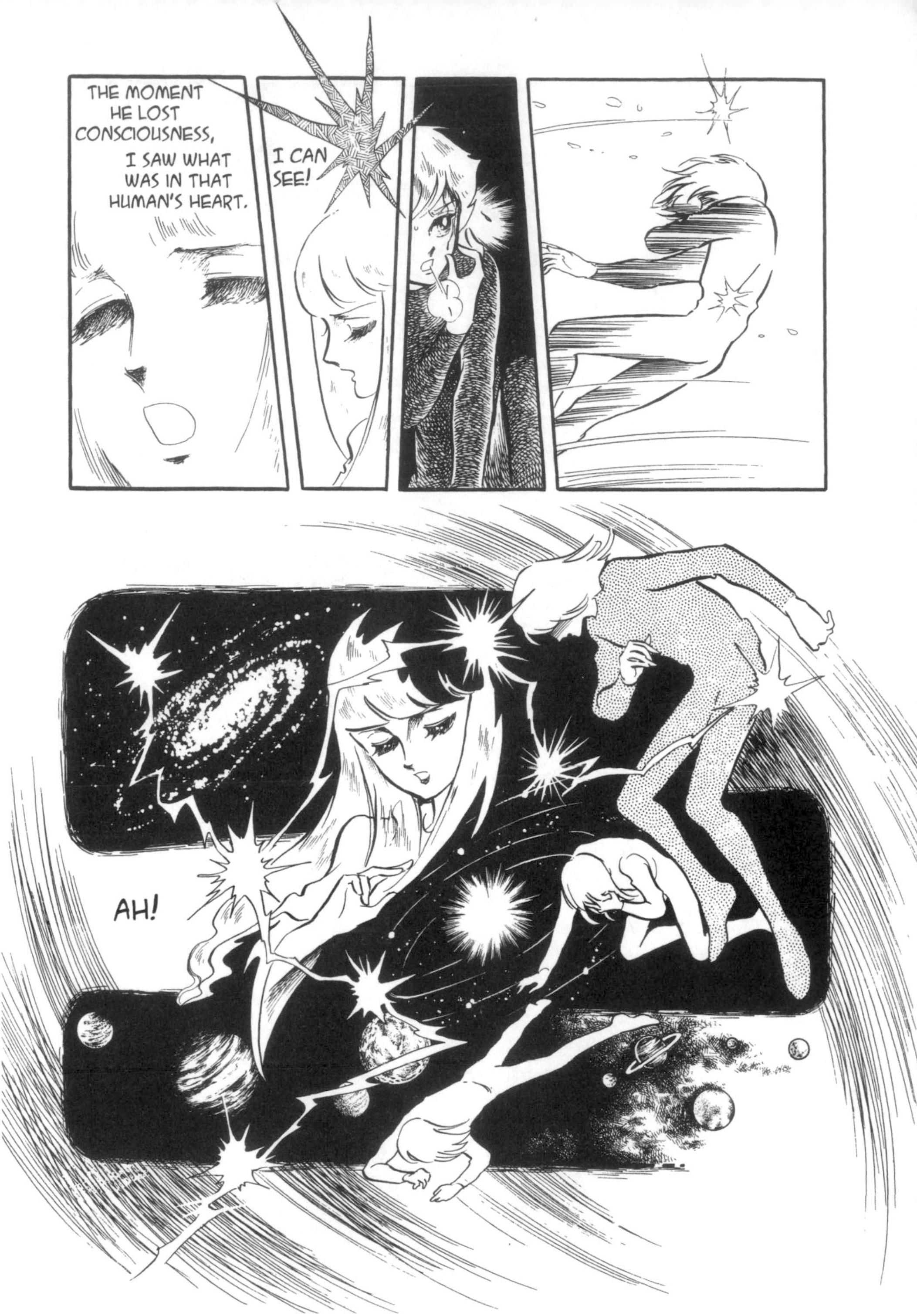
I CAN SEE!
THE MOMENT HE LOST CONSCIOUSNESS,
I SAW WHAT WAS IN THAT HUMAN'S HEART.
AH!

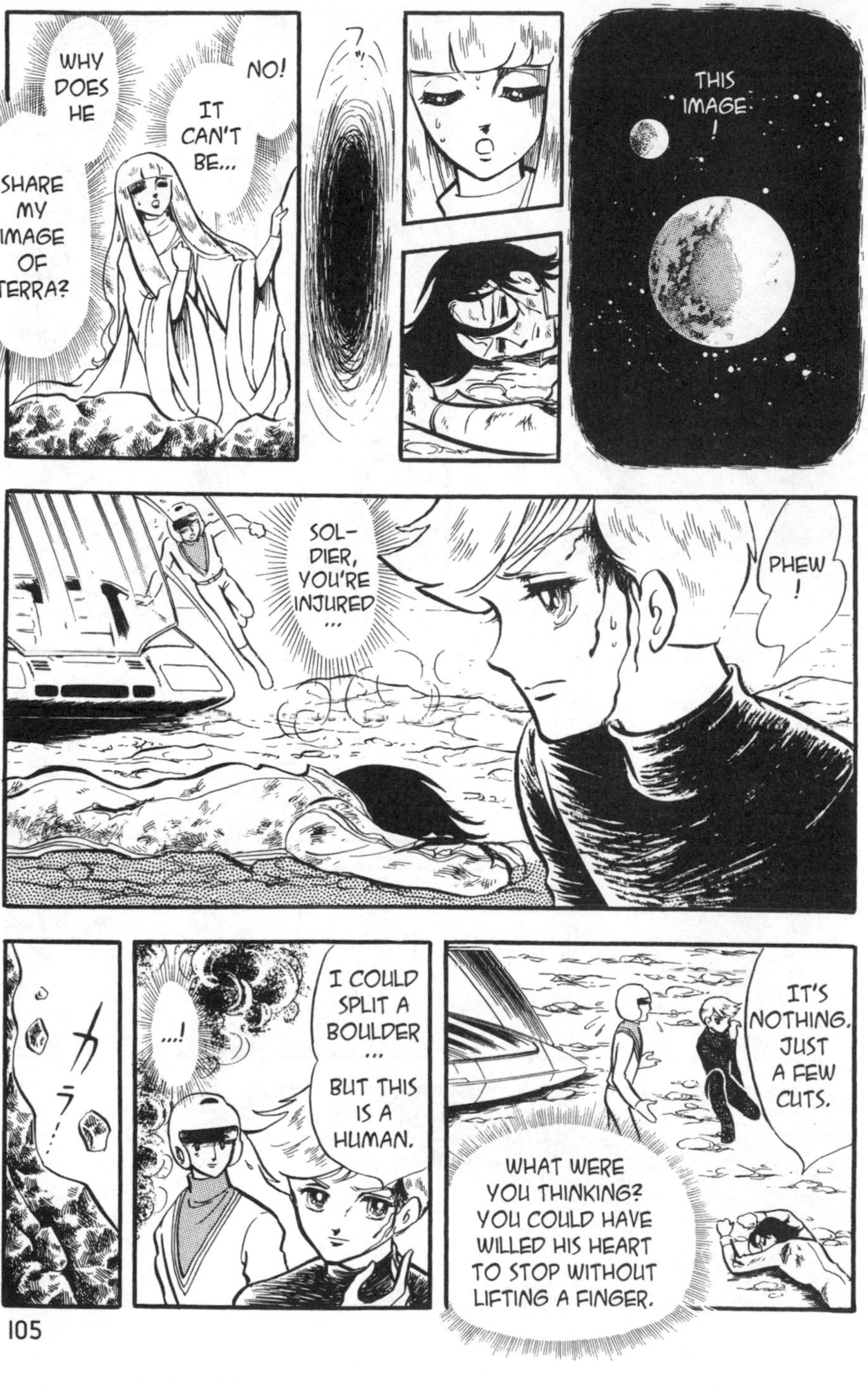

THIS IMAGE !
NO!
IT CAN'T BE...
WHY DOES HE SHARE MY IMAGE OF TERRA?
PHEW !
SOL-DIER, YOU'RE INJURED ...
IT'S NOTHING. JUST A FEW CUTS.
WHAT WERE YOU THINKING? YOU COULD HAVE WILLED HIS HEART TO STOP WITHOUT LIFTING A FINGER.
I COULD SPLIT A BOULDER ... BUT THIS IS A HUMAN.
...!
カラ…

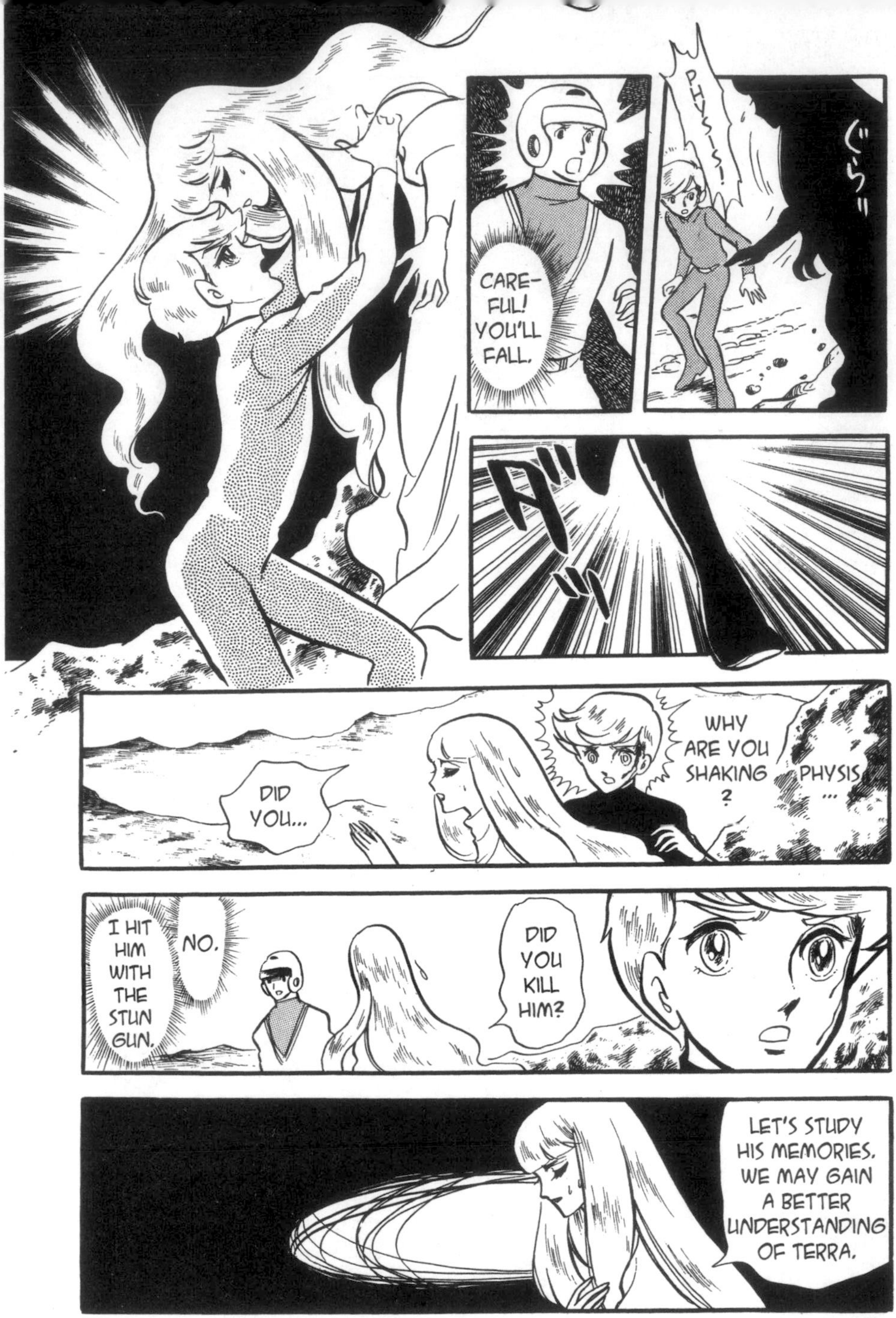
ぐらり
PHYSIS!
CAREFUL! YOU'LL FALL.
ガッ
PHYSIS...
WHY ARE YOU SHAKING?
DID YOU...
DID YOU KILL HIM?
NO.
I HIT HIM WITH THE STUN GUN.
LET'S STUDY HIS MEMORIES. WE MAY GAIN A BETTER UNDERSTANDING OF TERRA.

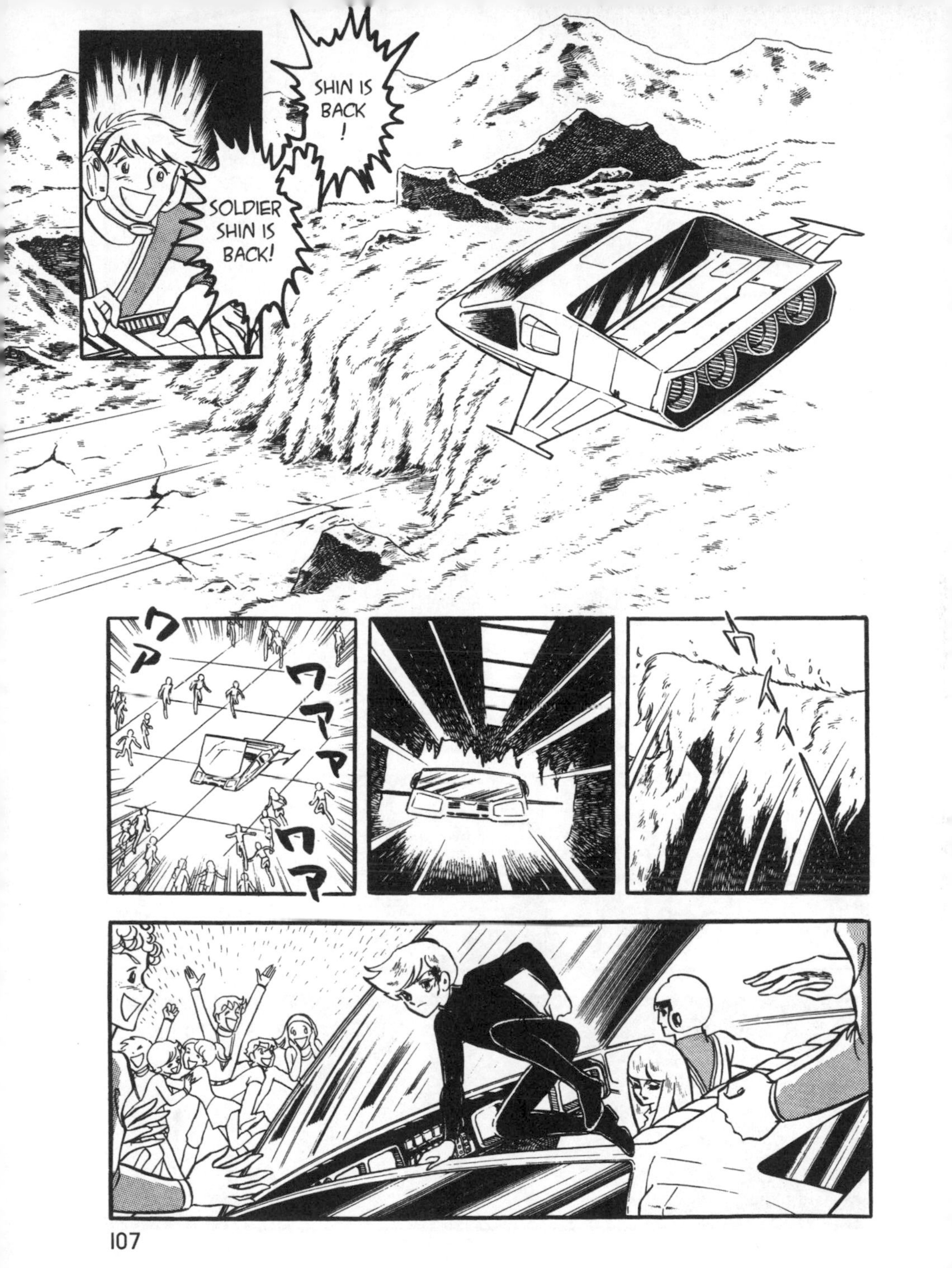
SHIN IS BACK !
SOLDIER SHIN IS BACK!
ワア
ワアーア
ワア

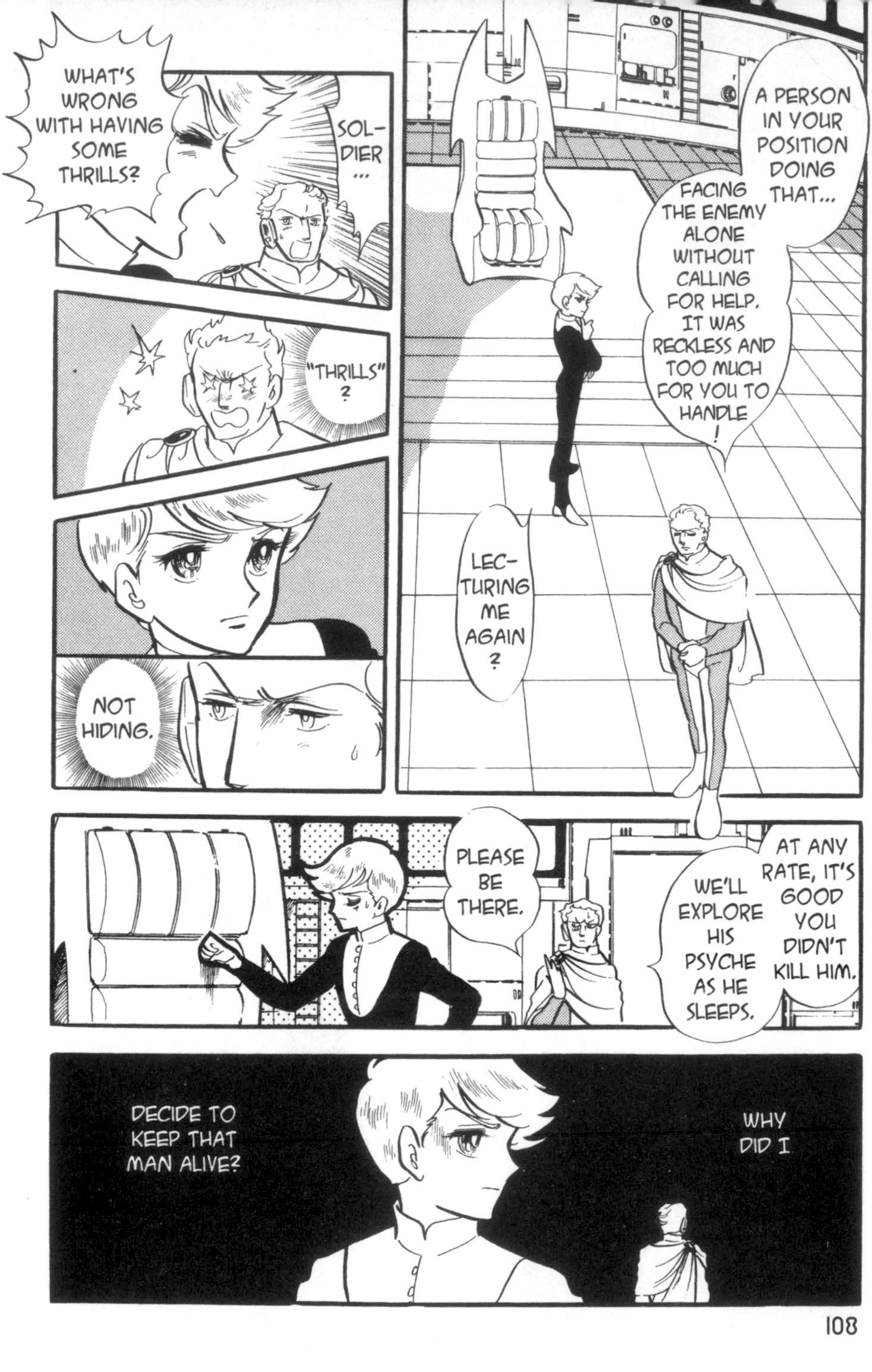
A PERSON IN YOUR POSITION DOING THAT...
FACING THE ENEMY ALONE WITHOUT CALLING FOR HELP. IT WAS RECKLESS AND TOO MUCH FOR YOU TO HANDLE!
LEC-TURING ME AGAIN?
SOL-DIER...
WHAT'S WRONG WITH HAVING SOME THRILLS?
"THRILLS"?
NOT HIDING.
AT ANY RATE, IT'S GOOD YOU DIDN'T KILL HIM.
WE'LL EXPLORE HIS PSYCHE AS HE SLEEPS.
PLEASE BE THERE.
WHY DID I
DECIDE TO KEEP THAT MAN ALIVE?

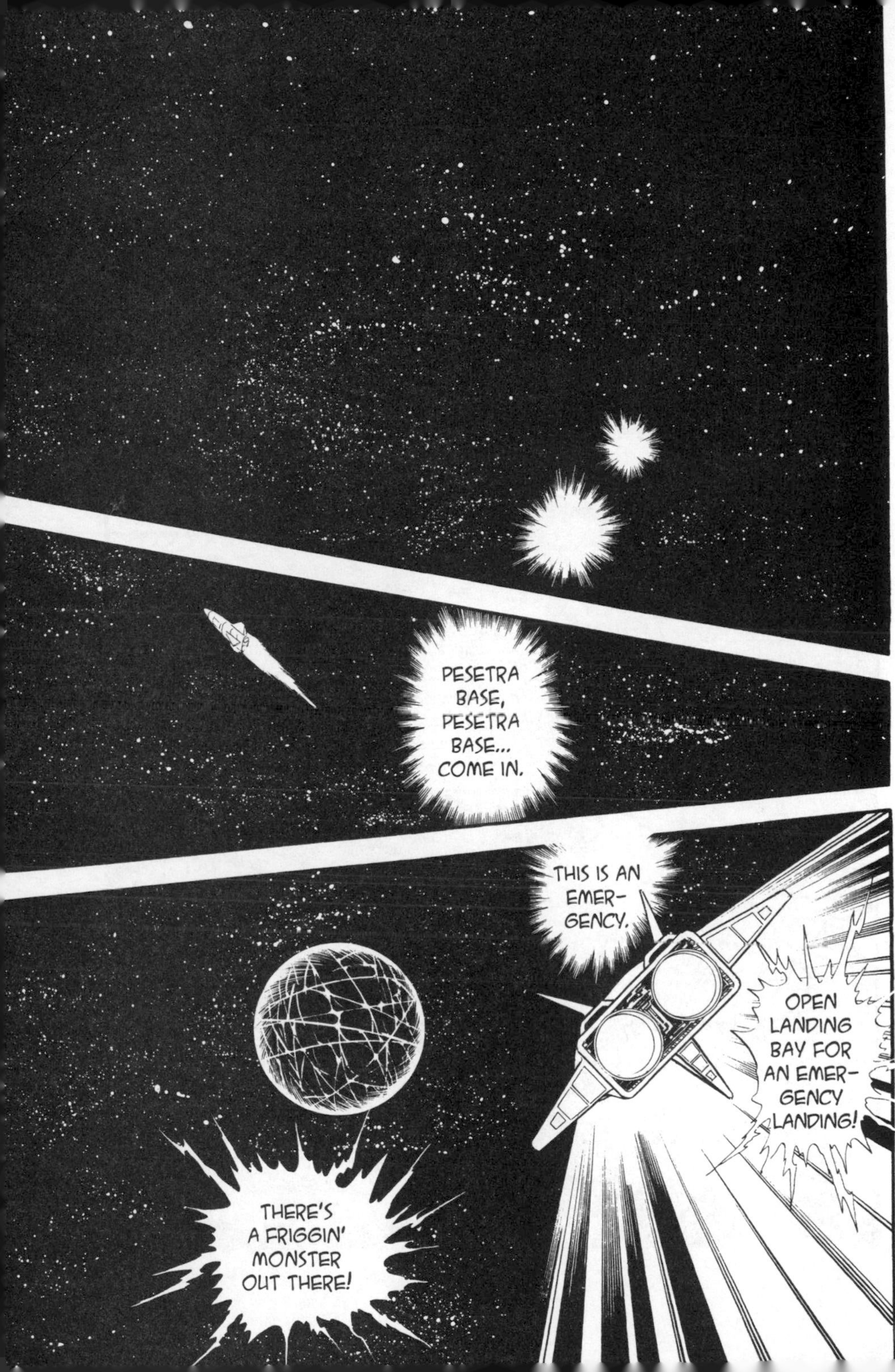
PESETRA BASE, PESETRA BASE... COME IN.
THIS IS AN EMER-GENCY.
OPEN LANDING BAY FOR AN EMER-GENCY LANDING!
THERE'S A FRIGGIN' MONSTER OUT THERE!

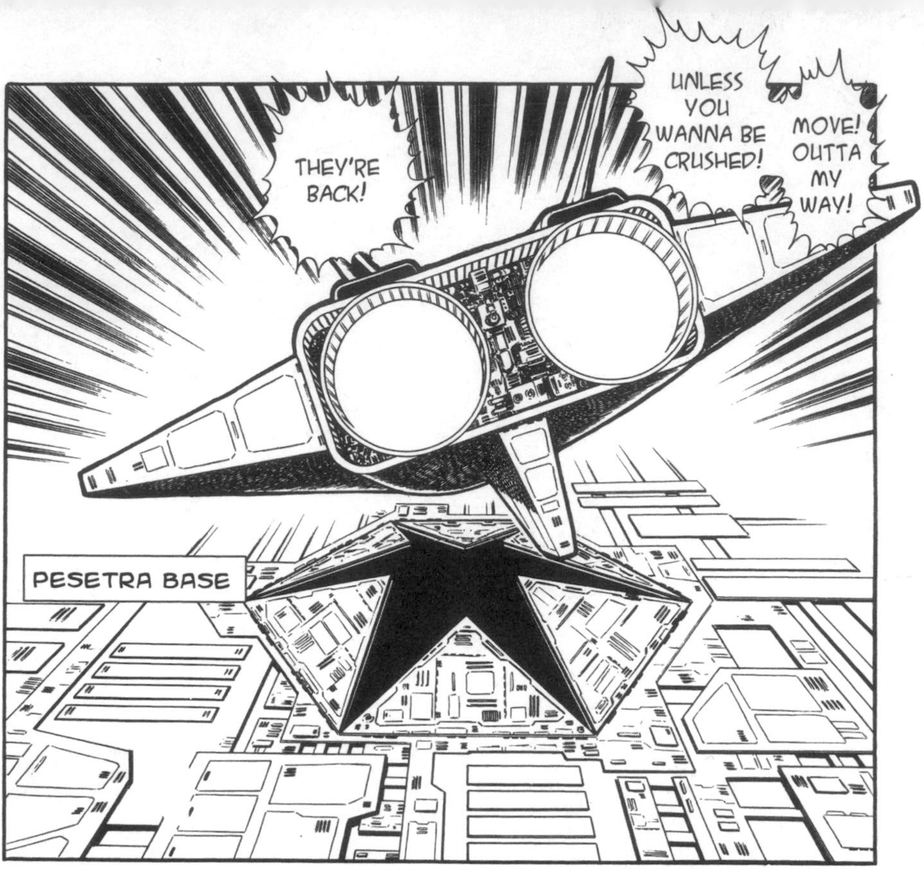
MOVE! OUTTA MY WAY!
UNLESS YOU WANNA BE CRUSHED!
THEY'RE BACK!
PESETRA BASE

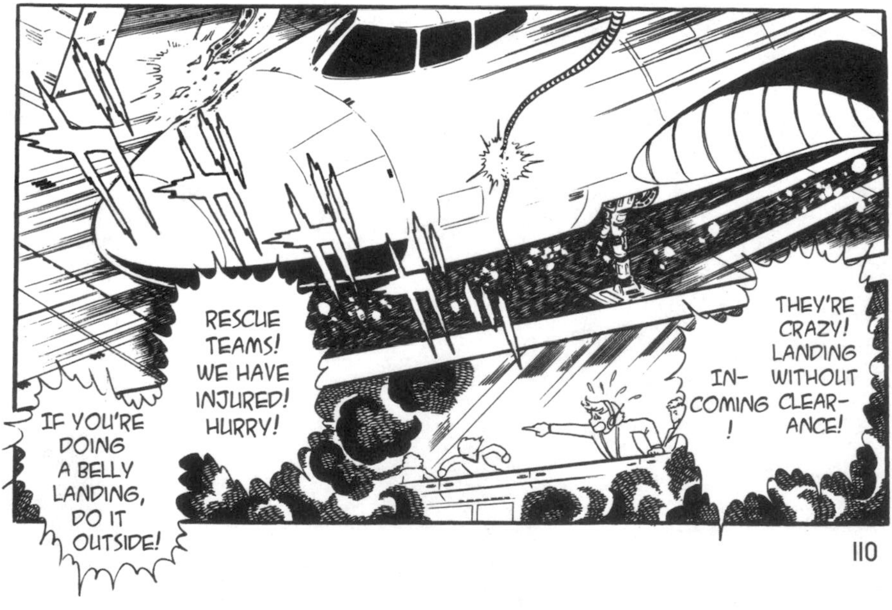
THEY'RE CRAZY! LANDING WITHOUT CLEAR-ANCE!
IN-COMING!
RESCUE TEAMS! WE HAVE INJURED! HURRY!
IF YOU'RE DOING A BELLY LANDING, DO IT OUTSIDE!

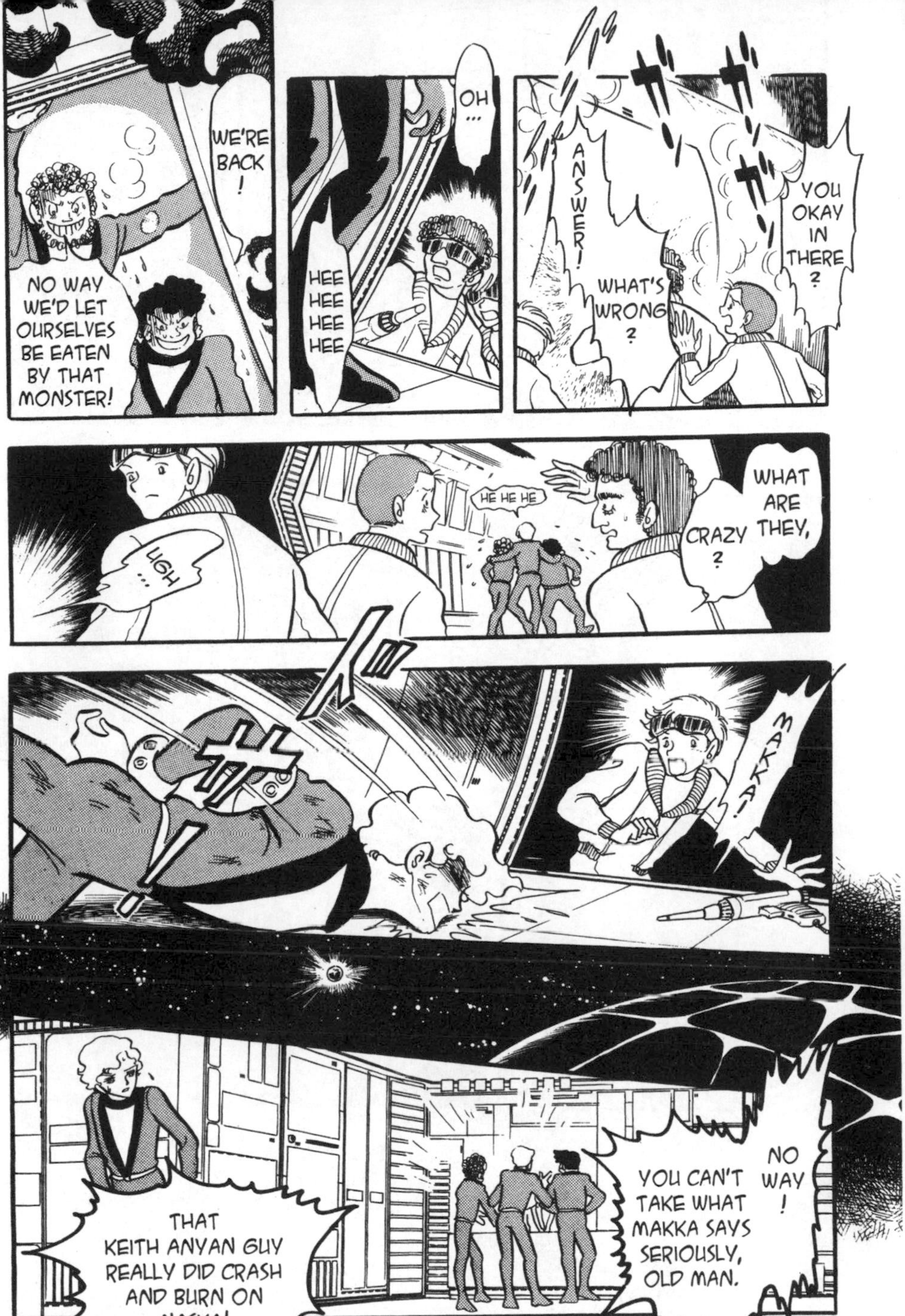
YOU OKAY IN THERE?
ANSWER!
WHAT'S WRONG?
OH...
HEE HEE HEE HEE
WE'RE BACK!
NO WAY WE'D LET OURSELVES BE EATEN BY THAT MONSTER!
WHAT ARE THEY, CRAZY?
HE HE HE
UGH...
MAKKA!
NO WAY!
YOU CAN'T TAKE WHAT MAKKA SAYS SERIOUSLY, OLD MAN.
THAT KEITH ANYAN GUY REALLY DID CRASH AND BURN ON NASKA!

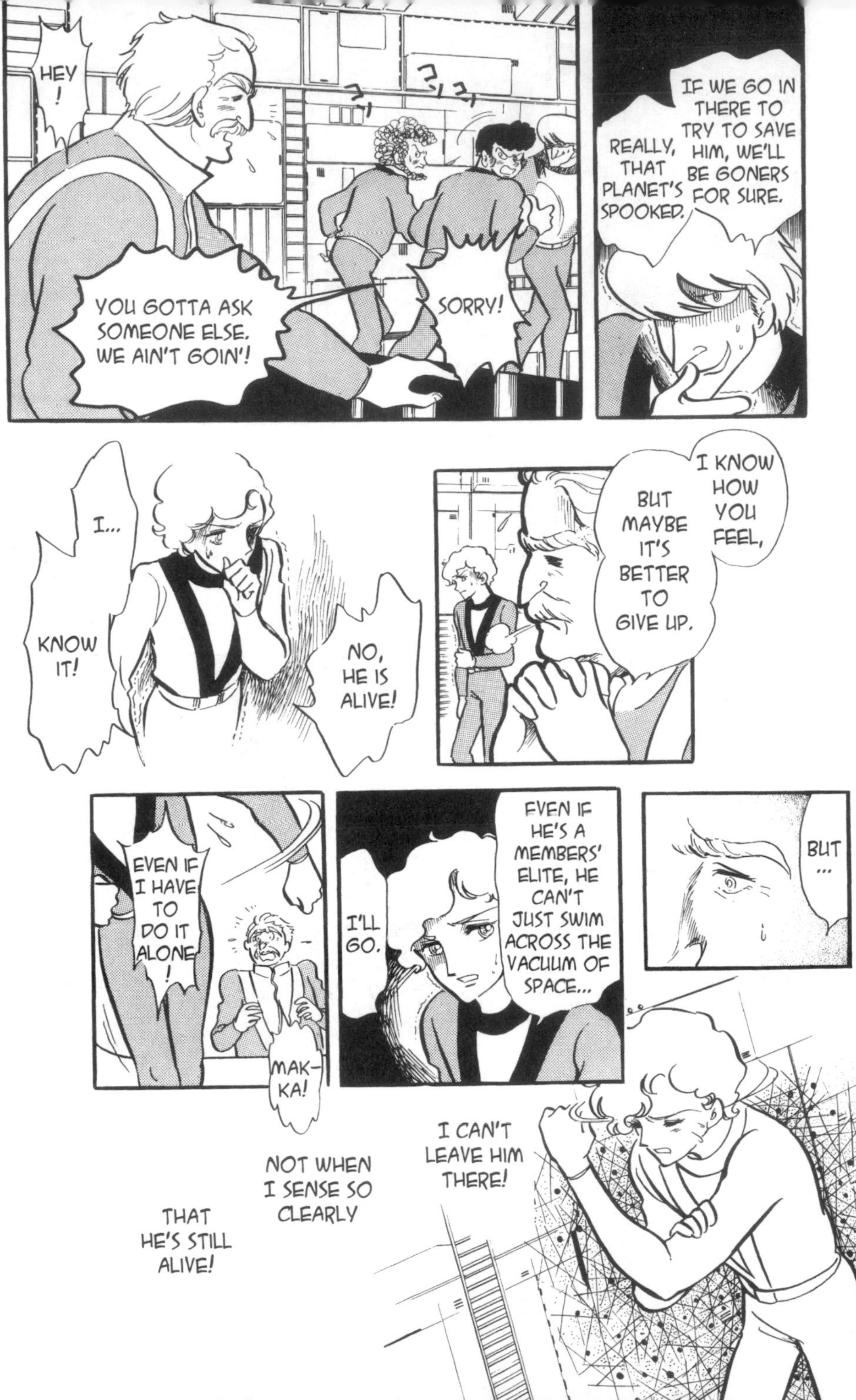
IF WE GO IN THERE TO TRY TO SAVE HIM, WE'LL BE GONERS FOR SURE.
REALLY, THAT PLANET'S SPOOKED.
HEY!
SORRY!
YOU GOTTA ASK SOMEONE ELSE. WE AIN'T GOIN'!
I KNOW HOW YOU FEEL,
BUT MAYBE IT'S BETTER TO GIVE UP.
NO, HE IS ALIVE!
I...
KNOW IT!
BUT...
EVEN IF HE'S A MEMBERS' ELITE, HE CAN'T JUST SWIM ACROSS THE VACUUM OF SPACE...
I'LL GO.
EVEN IF I HAVE TO DO IT ALONE!
MAK-KA!
I CAN'T LEAVE HIM THERE!
NOT WHEN I SENSE SO CLEARLY
THAT HE'S STILL ALIVE!

WHOA!
HE'S LOOKING...
AT A HUGE GALAXY FROM THE OUTSIDE.
IT'S A VIVID IMAGE. IT WAS PROBABLY PLANTED IN HIS MEMORY.
SATURN,
JUPITER,
MARS...
AND TERRA.
THE IMAGES ARE MOVING TOWARDS ITS SURFACE,
TO ONE LOCATION.
IT MAY BE THE TERRA DEFENSE AGENCY BASE.

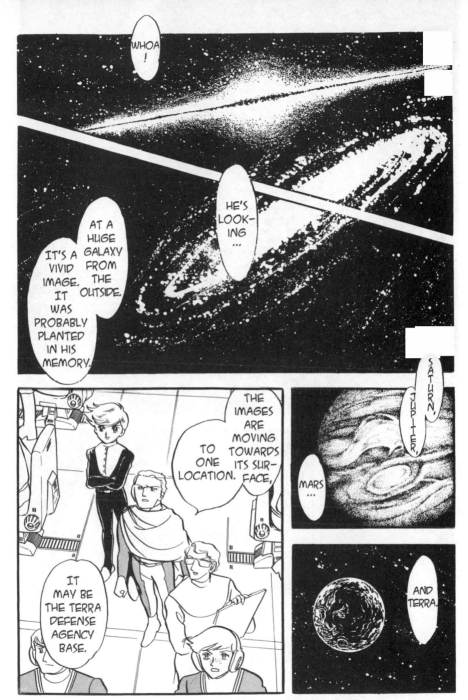

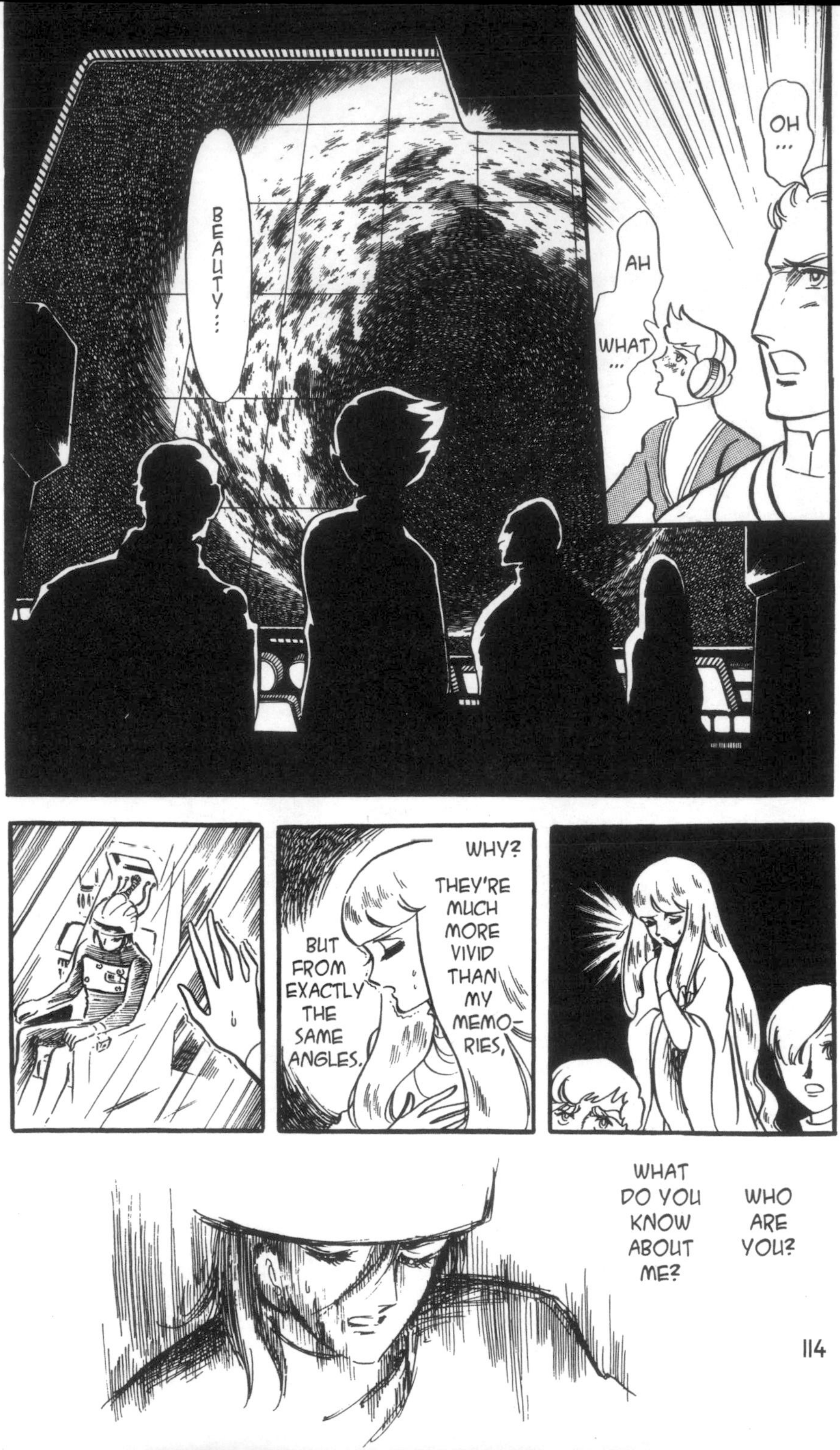
OH ...
AH
WHAT ...
BEAUTY...
WHY?
THEY'RE MUCH MORE VIVID THAN MY MEMORIES,
BUT FROM EXACTLY THE SAME ANGLES.
WHO ARE YOU?
WHAT DO YOU KNOW ABOUT ME?

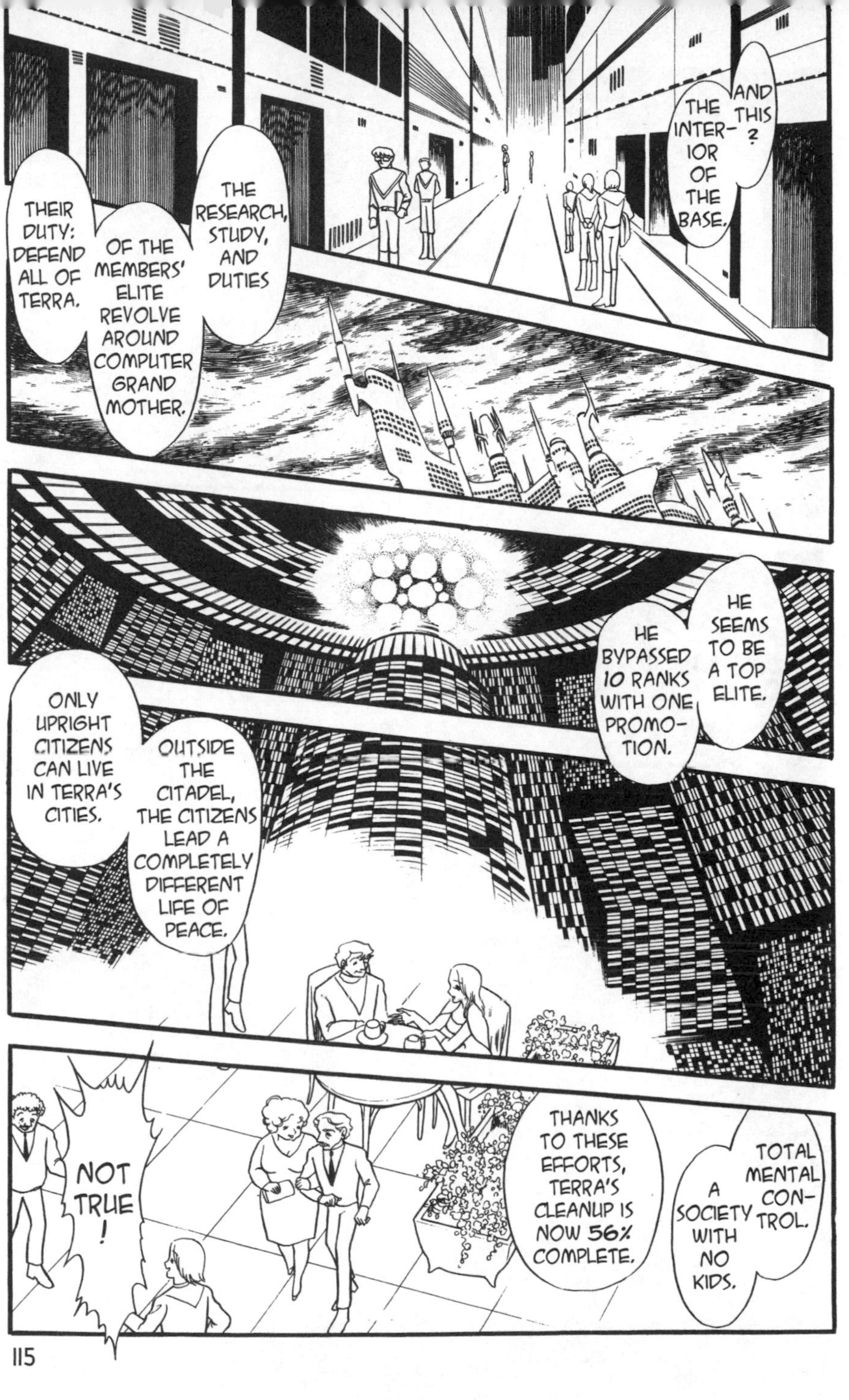
AND THIS ?
THE INTERIOR OF THE BASE.
THE RESEARCH, STUDY, AND DUTIES
OF THE MEMBERS' ELITE REVOLVE AROUND COMPUTER GRAND MOTHER.
THEIR DUTY: DEFEND ALL OF TERRA.
HE SEEMS TO BE A TOP ELITE.
HE BYPASSED 10 RANKS WITH ONE PROMOTION.
OUTSIDE THE CITADEL, THE CITIZENS LEAD A COMPLETELY DIFFERENT LIFE OF PEACE.
ONLY UPRIGHT CITIZENS CAN LIVE IN TERRA'S CITIES.
TOTAL MENTAL CONTROL.
A SOCIETY WITH NO KIDS.
THANKS TO THESE EFFORTS, TERRA'S CLEANUP IS NOW 56% COMPLETE.
NOT TRUE!

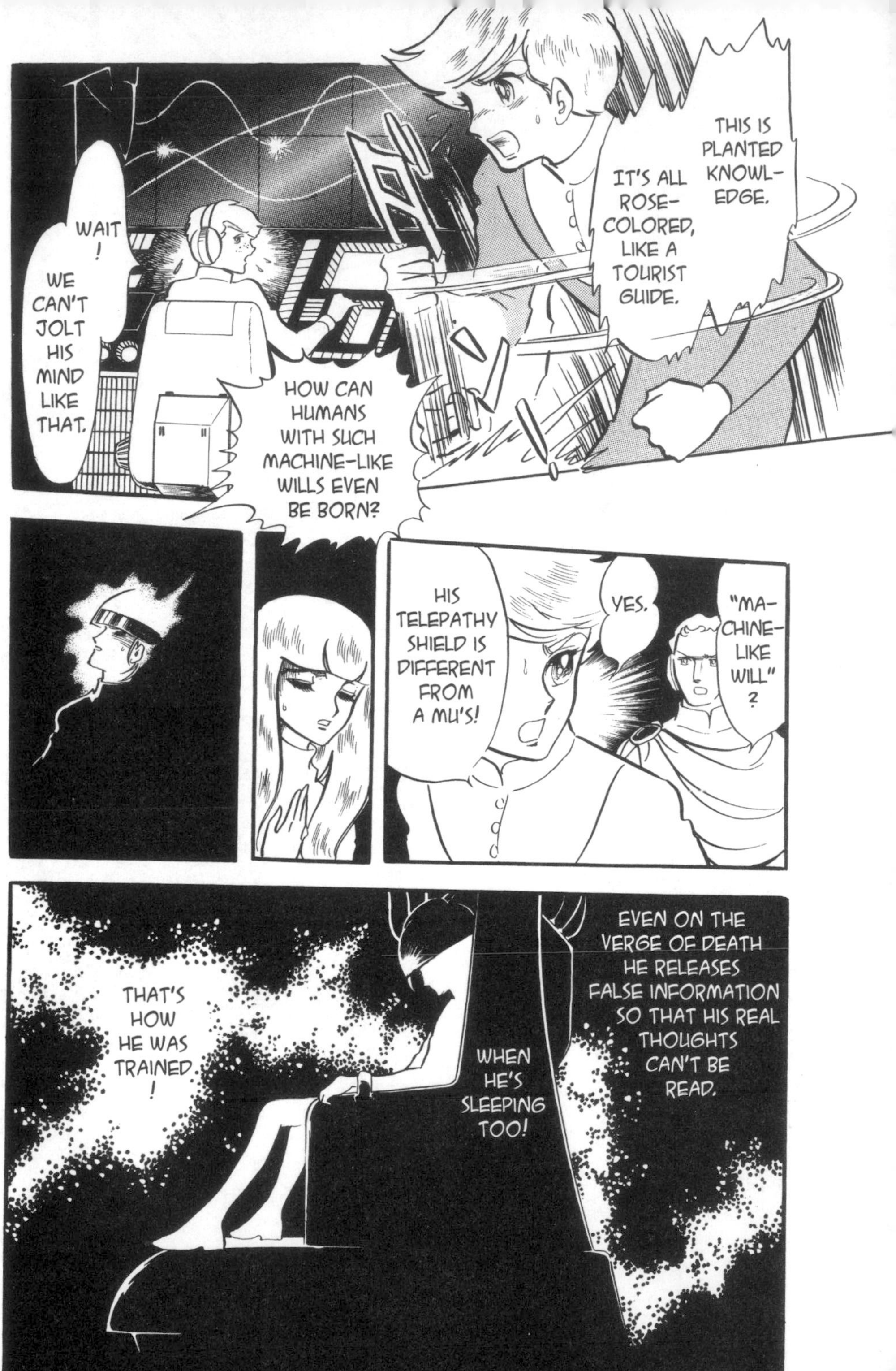
THIS IS PLANTED KNOWL-EDGE.
IT'S ALL ROSE-COLORED, LIKE A TOURIST GUIDE.
HOW CAN HUMANS WITH SUCH MACHINE-LIKE WILLS EVEN BE BORN?
WAIT! WE CAN'T JOLT HIS MIND LIKE THAT.
"MA-CHINE-LIKE WILL"?
YES.
HIS TELEPATHY SHIELD IS DIFFERENT FROM A MU'S!
EVEN ON THE VERGE OF DEATH HE RELEASES FALSE INFORMATION SO THAT HIS REAL THOUGHTS CAN'T BE READ.
WHEN HE'S SLEEPING TOO!
THAT'S HOW HE WAS TRAINED!

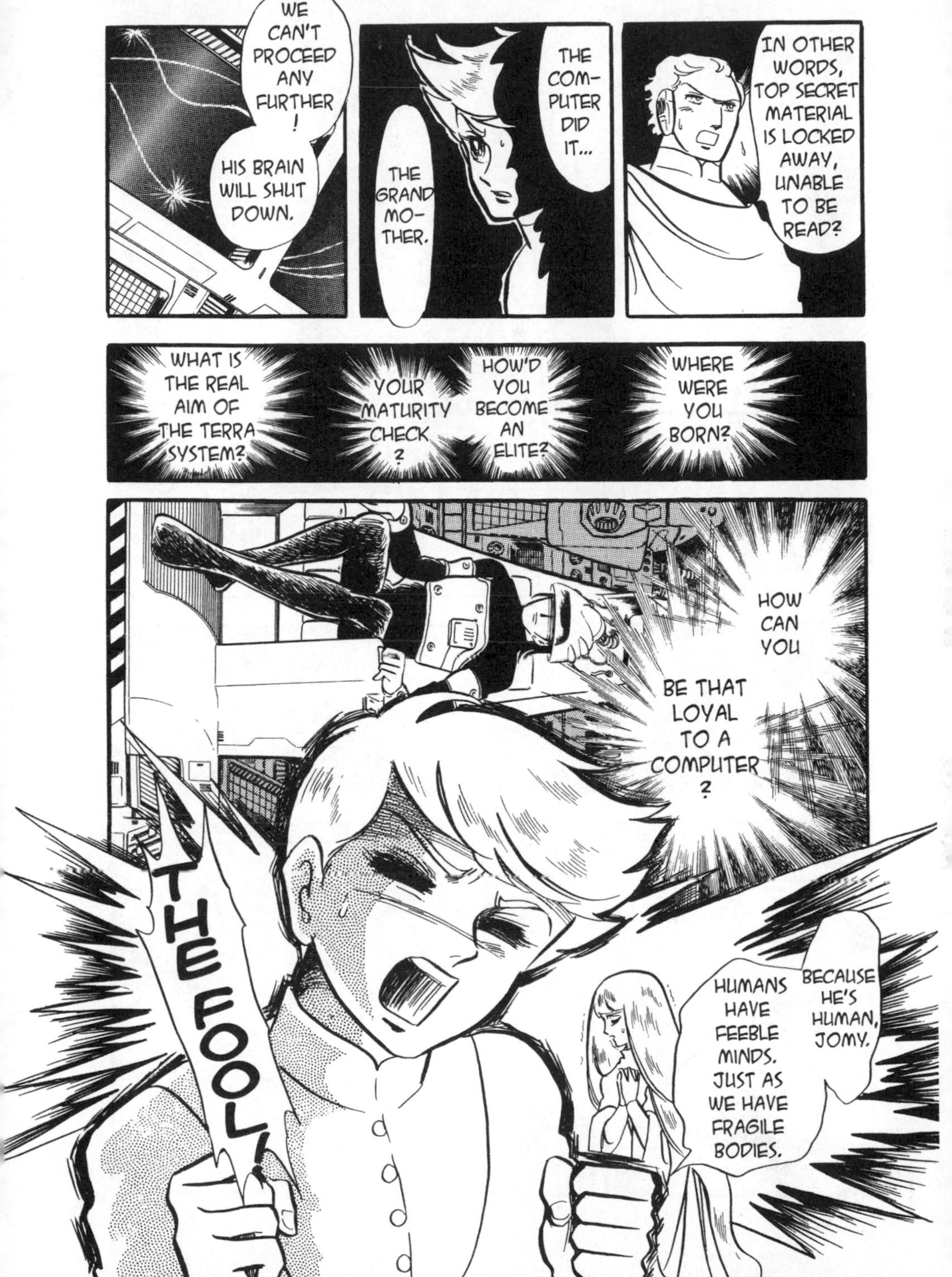
IN OTHER WORDS, TOP SECRET MATERIAL IS LOCKED AWAY, UNABLE TO BE READ?
THE COMPUTER DID IT...
THE GRAND MOTHER.
WE CAN'T PROCEED ANY FURTHER!
HIS BRAIN WILL SHUT DOWN.
WHERE WERE YOU BORN?
HOW'D YOU BECOME AN ELITE?
YOUR MATURITY CHECK?
WHAT IS THE REAL AIM OF THE TERRA SYSTEM?
HOW CAN YOU
BE THAT LOYAL TO A COMPUTER?
THE FOOL!
BECAUSE HE'S HUMAN, JOMY.
HUMANS HAVE FEEBLE MINDS. JUST AS WE HAVE FRAGILE BODIES.

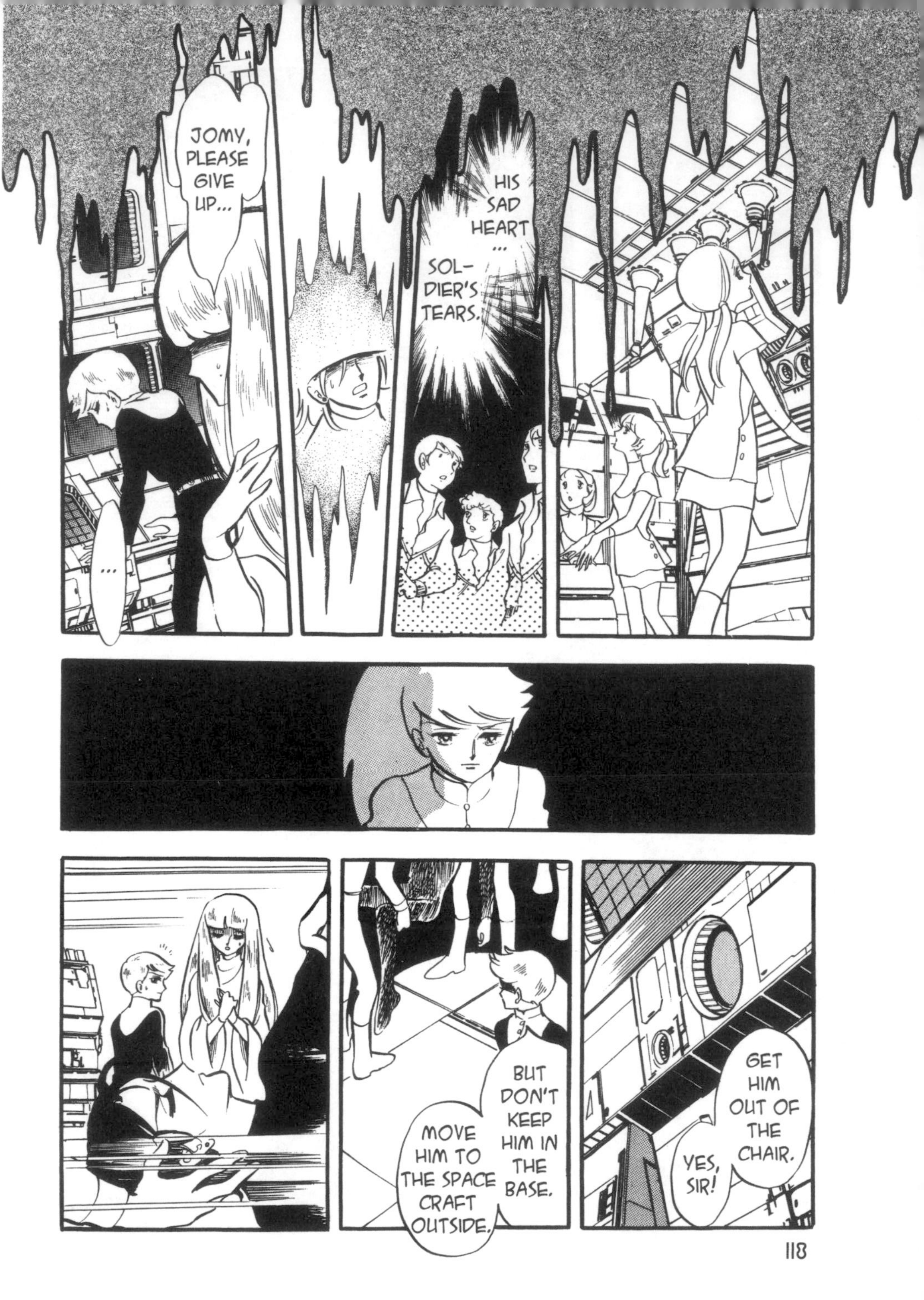
HIS SAD HEART ...
SOL-DIER'S TEARS.
JOMY, PLEASE GIVE UP...
...
GET HIM OUT OF THE CHAIR.
YES, SIR!
BUT DON'T KEEP HIM IN THE BASE.
MOVE HIM TO THE SPACE CRAFT OUTSIDE.

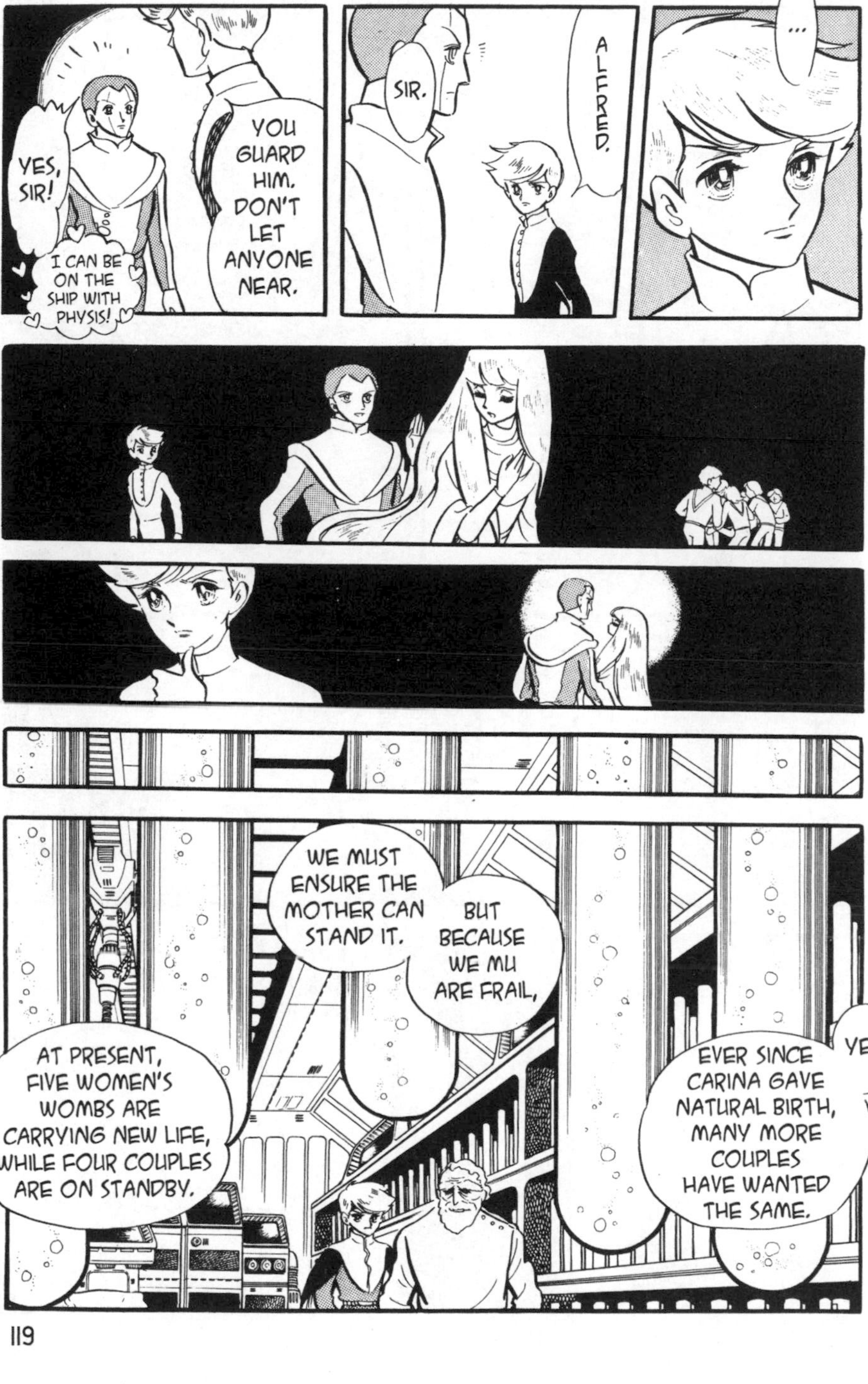
...
ALFRED.
SIR.
YOU GUARD HIM. DON'T LET ANYONE NEAR.
YES, SIR!
I CAN BE ON THE SHIP WITH PHYSIS!
YES,
EVER SINCE CARINA GAVE NATURAL BIRTH, MANY MORE COUPLES HAVE WANTED THE SAME.
AT PRESENT, FIVE WOMEN'S WOMBS ARE CARRYING NEW LIFE, WHILE FOUR COUPLES ARE ON STANDBY.
BUT BECAUSE WE MU ARE FRAIL,
WE MUST ENSURE THE MOTHER CAN STAND IT.

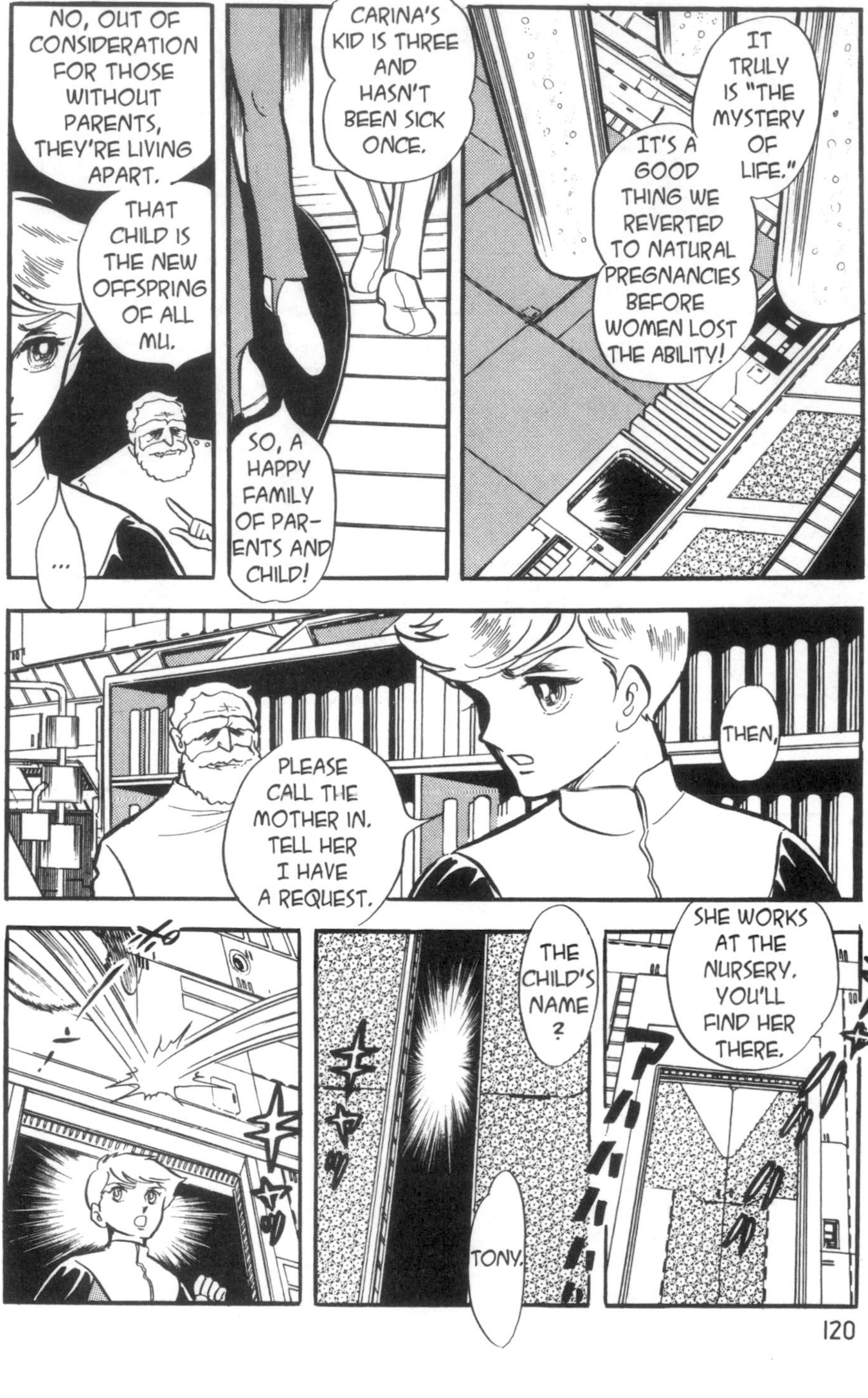
IT TRULY IS "THE MYSTERY OF LIFE."
IT'S A GOOD THING WE REVERTED TO NATURAL PREGNANCIES BEFORE WOMEN LOST THE ABILITY!
CARINA'S KID IS THREE AND HASN'T BEEN SICK ONCE.
SO, A HAPPY FAMILY OF PAR-ENTS AND CHILD!
NO, OUT OF CONSIDERATION FOR THOSE WITHOUT PARENTS, THEY'RE LIVING APART.
THAT CHILD IS THE NEW OFFSPRING OF ALL MU.
...
THEN,
PLEASE CALL THE MOTHER IN. TELL HER I HAVE A REQUEST.
SHE WORKS AT THE NURSERY. YOU'LL FIND HER THERE.
THE CHILD'S NAME?
TONY.

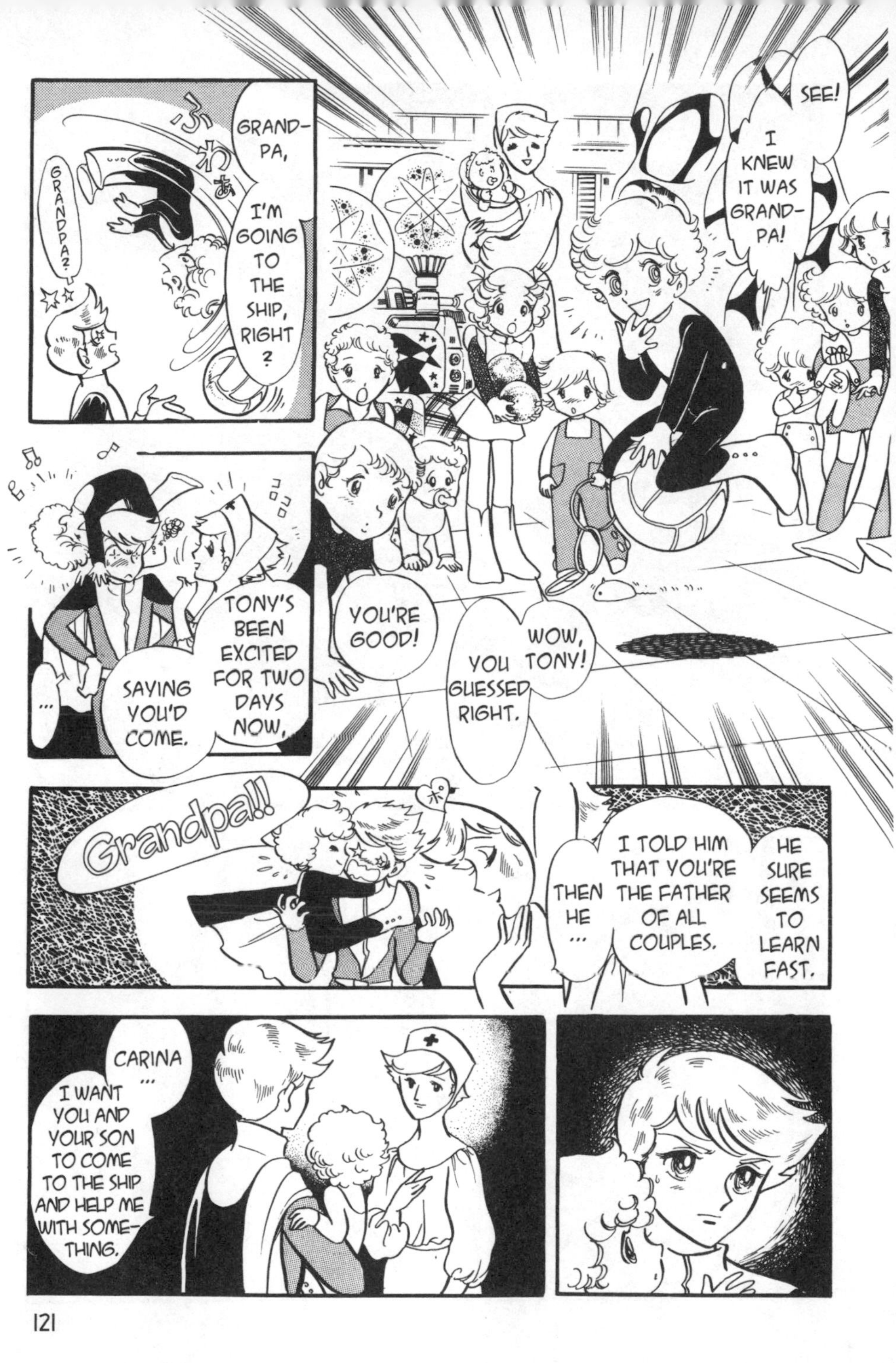
SEE!
I KNEW IT WAS GRANDPA!
WOW, TONY! YOU GUESSED RIGHT.
YOU'RE GOOD!
GRANDPA, I'M GOING TO THE SHIP, RIGHT?
ふわぁ
GRANDPA?!
TONY'S BEEN EXCITED FOR TWO DAYS NOW,
SAYING YOU'D COME.
...
HE SURE SEEMS TO LEARN FAST.
I TOLD HIM THAT YOU'RE THE FATHER OF ALL COUPLES.
THEN HE ...
Grandpa!!
CARINA ...
I WANT YOU AND YOUR SON TO COME TO THE SHIP AND HELP ME WITH SOMETHING.

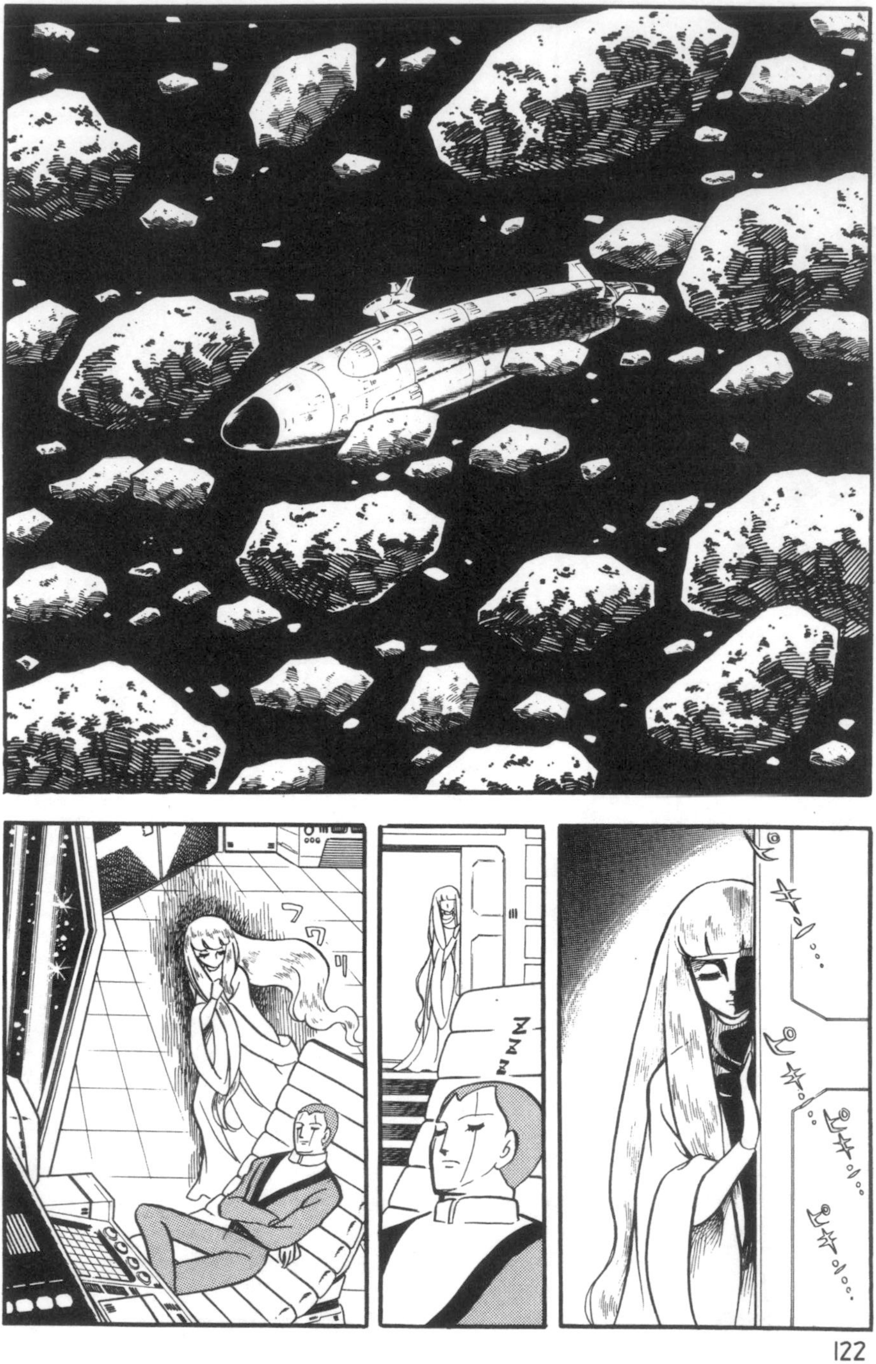
ZZZ
フワリ

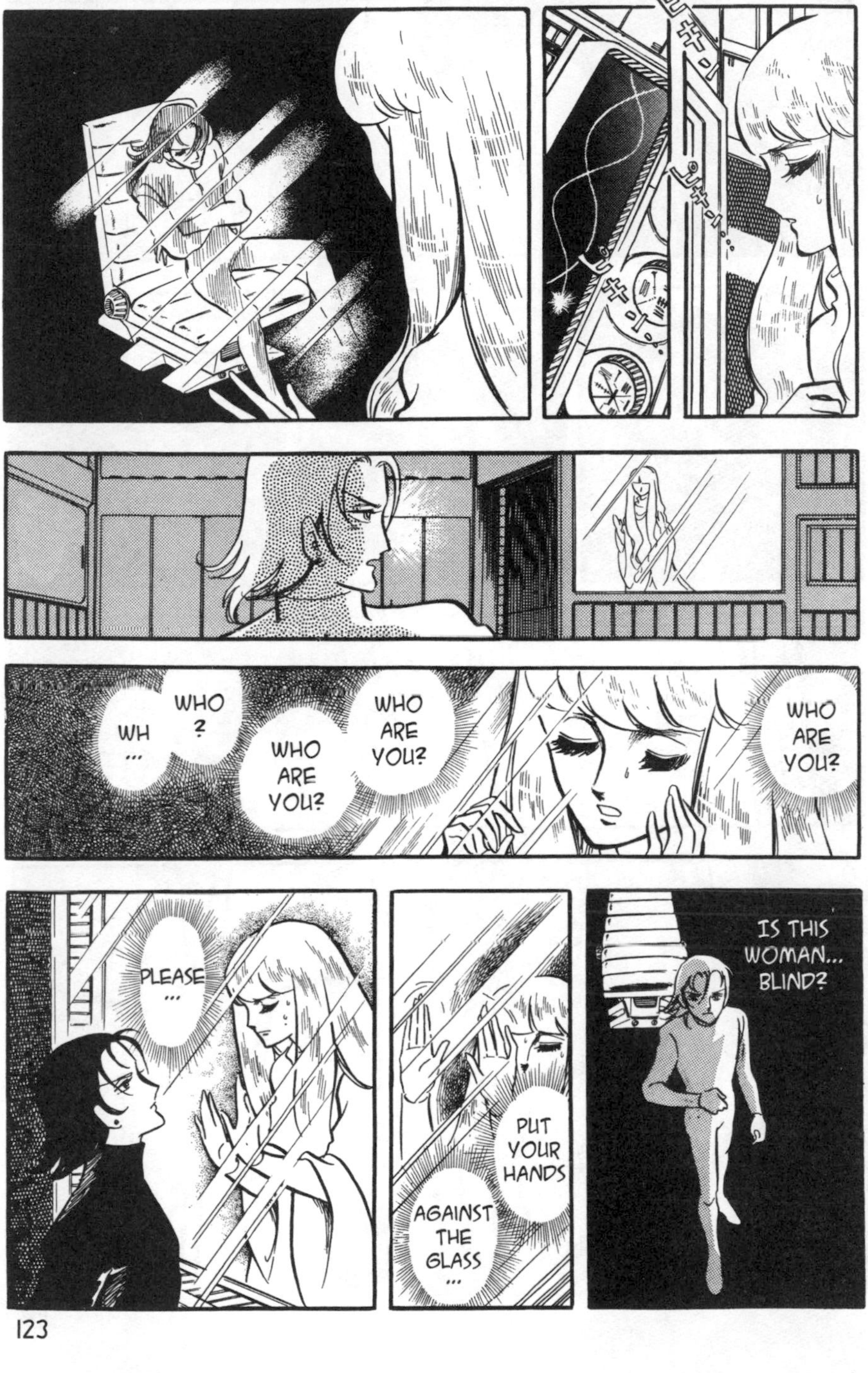
WHO ARE YOU?
WHO ARE YOU?
WHO ARE YOU?
WHO ?
WH ...
IS THIS WOMAN... BLIND?
PUT YOUR HANDS
AGAINST THE GLASS ...
PLEASE ...

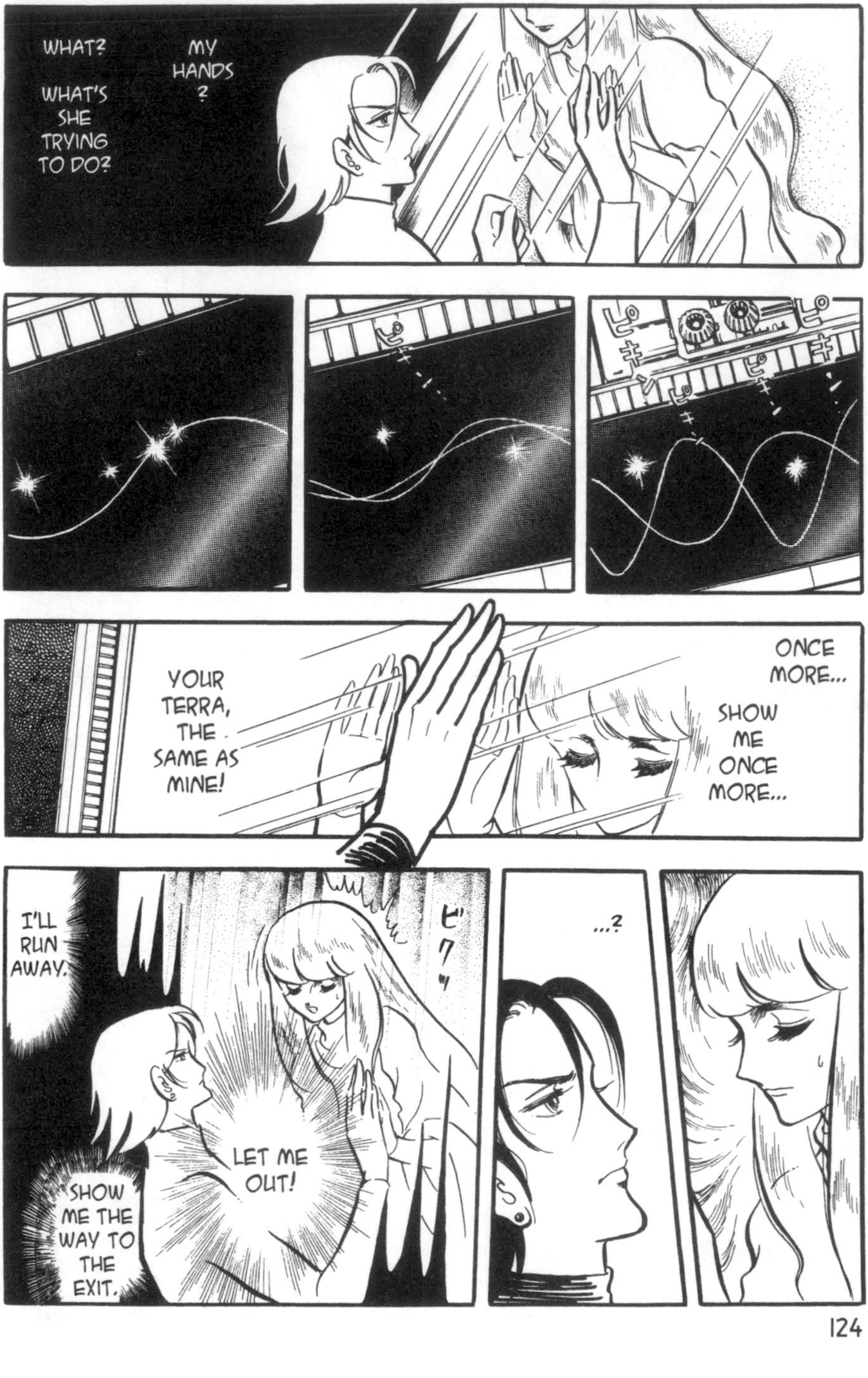
MY HANDS?
WHAT? WHAT'S SHE TRYING TO DO?
ONCE MORE...
SHOW ME ONCE MORE...
YOUR TERRA, THE SAME AS MINE!
...?
ビクッ
I'LL RUN AWAY.
LET ME OUT!
SHOW ME THE WAY TO THE EXIT.

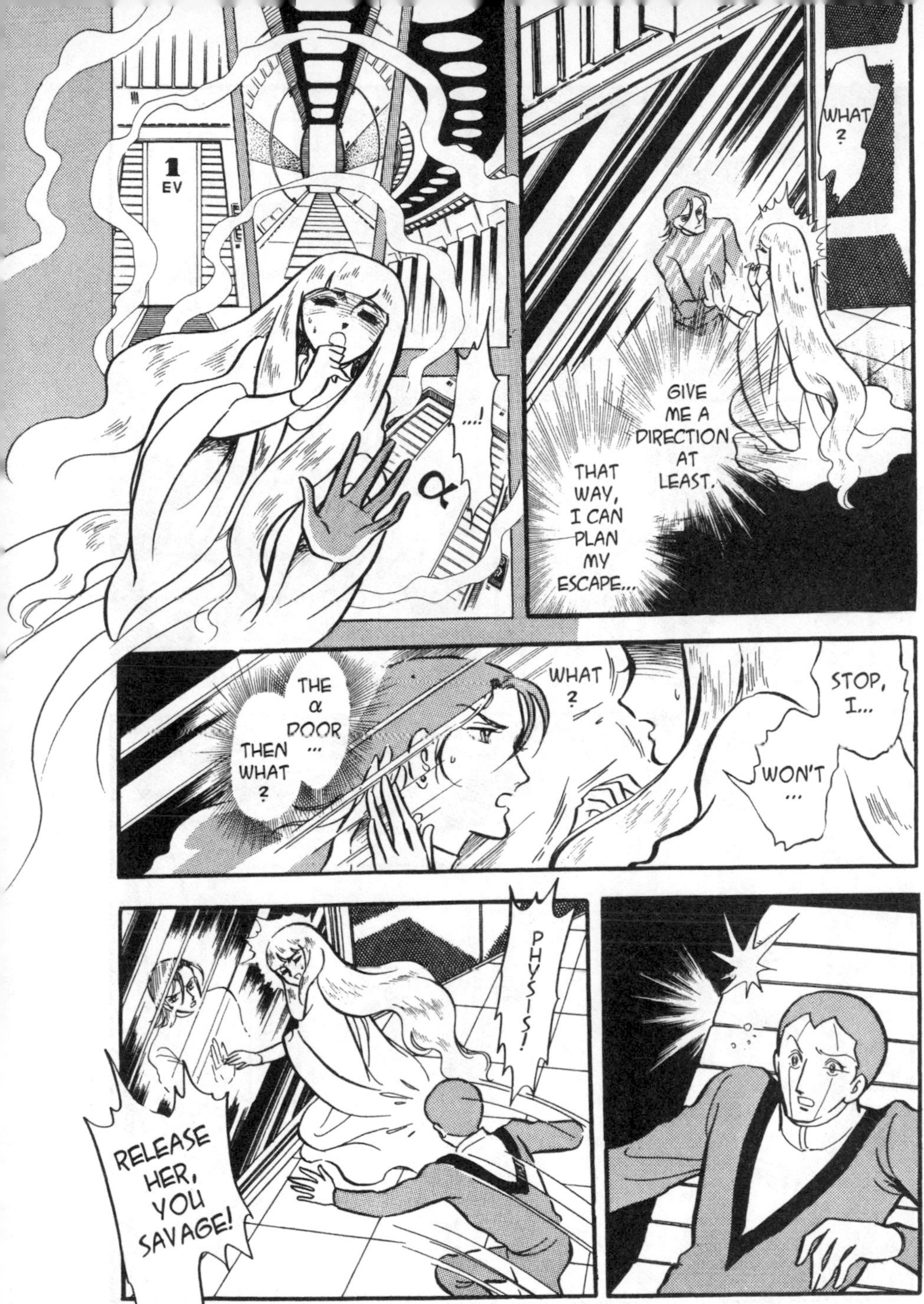
WHAT?
GIVE ME A DIRECTION AT LEAST.
THAT WAY, I CAN PLAN MY ESCAPE...
1 EV
...!
α
STOP, I...
WON'T...
WHAT?
THE α DOOR...
THEN WHAT?
PHYSIS!
RELEASE HER, YOU SAVAGE!

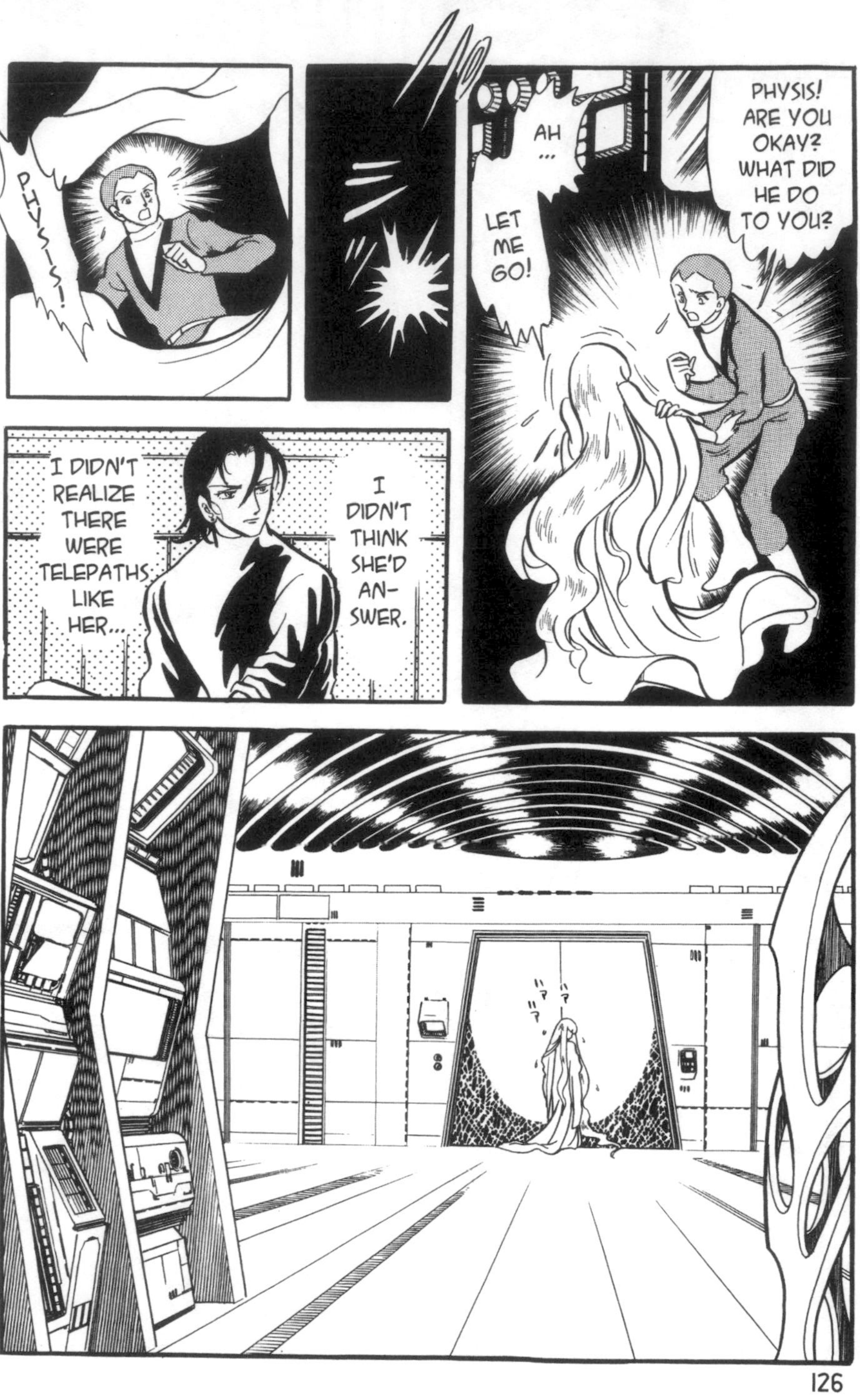
PHYSIS! ARE YOU OKAY? WHAT DID HE DO TO YOU?
AH ...
LET ME GO!
PHYSIS!
I DIDN'T THINK SHE'D AN-SWER.
I DIDN'T REALIZE THERE WERE TELEPATHS LIKE HER...

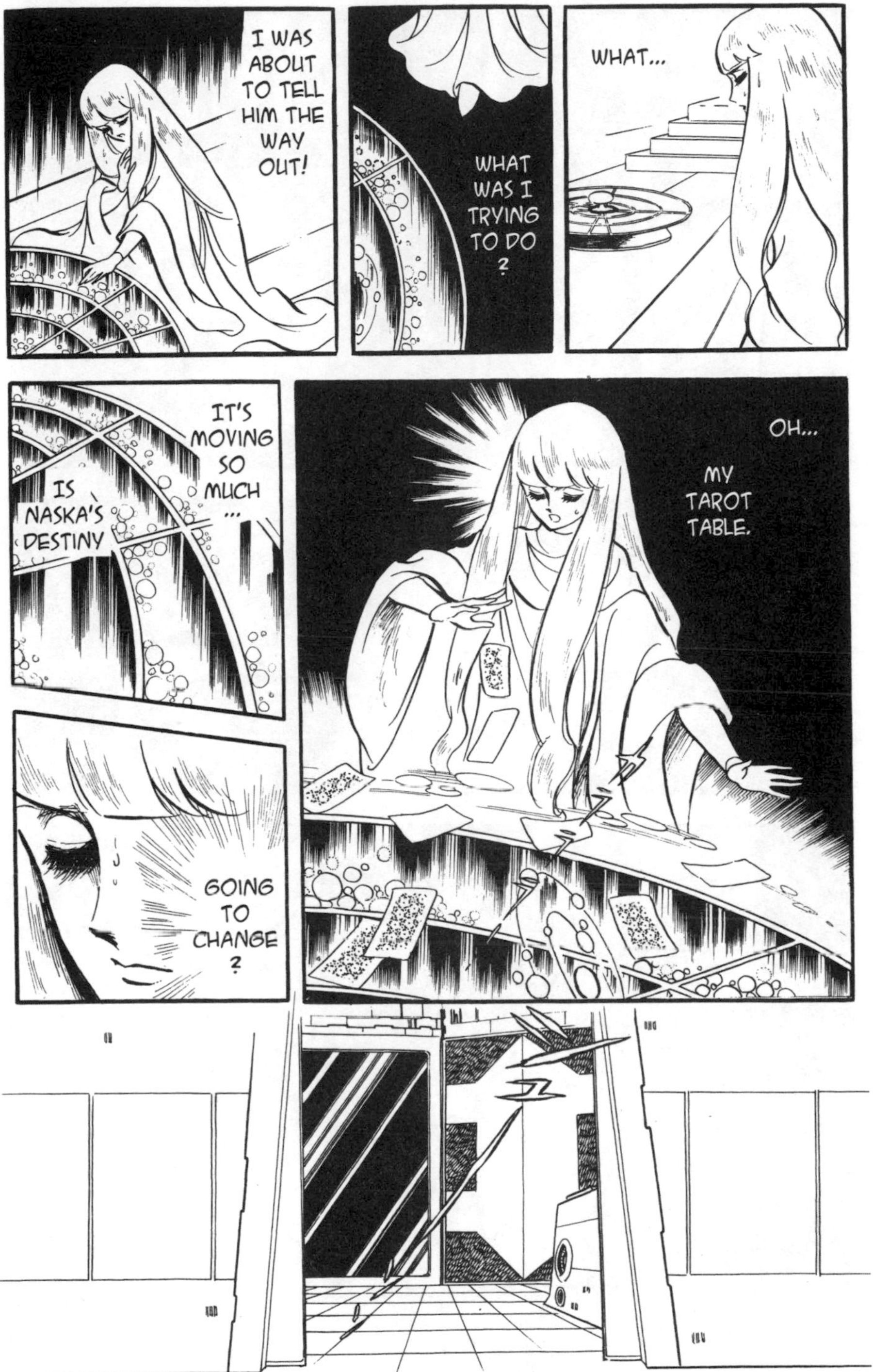
WHAT...
WHAT WAS I TRYING TO DO ?
I WAS ABOUT TO TELL HIM THE WAY OUT!
OH...
MY TAROT TABLE.
IT'S MOVING SO MUCH ...
IS NASKA'S DESTINY
GOING TO CHANGE ?

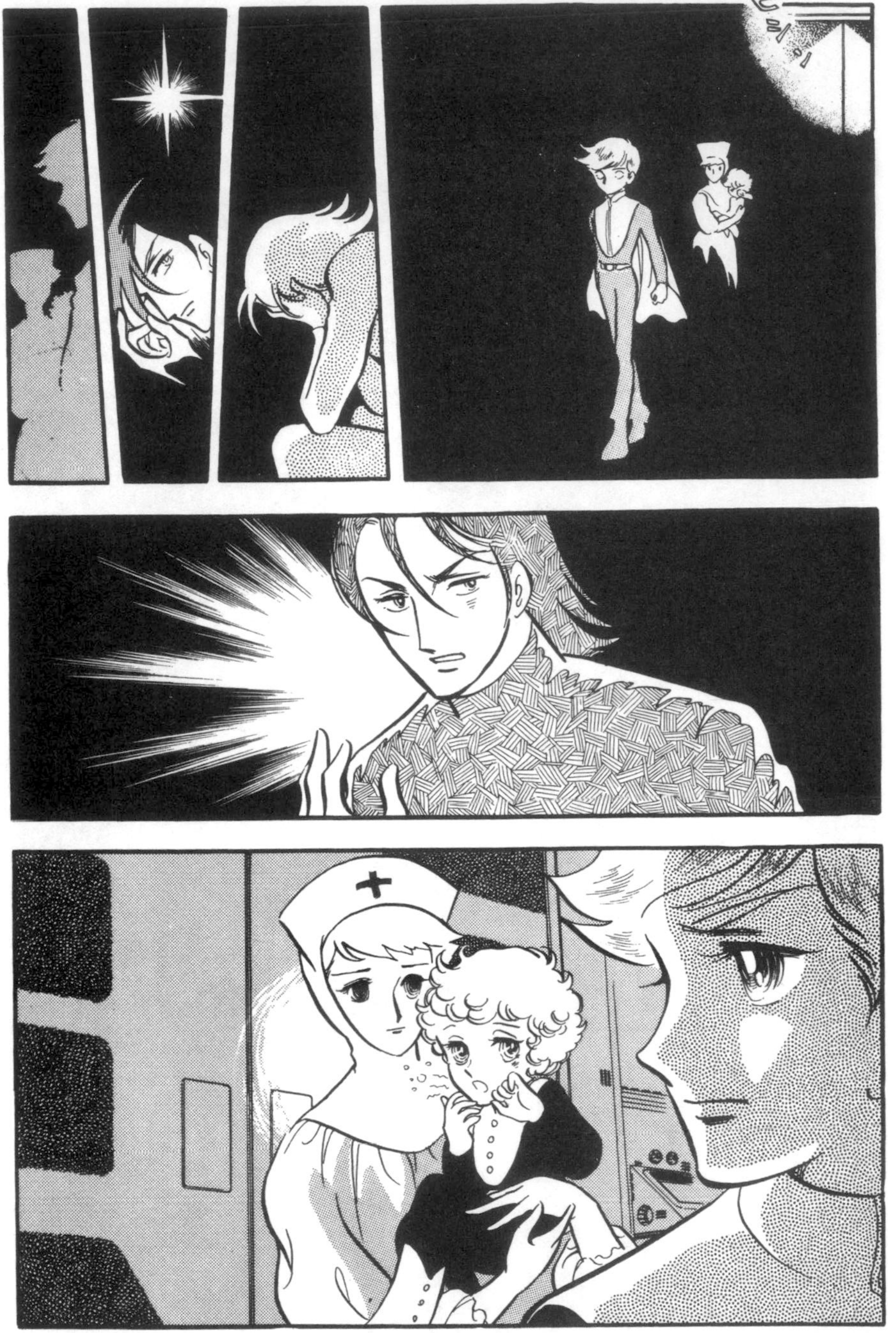
ピシッ

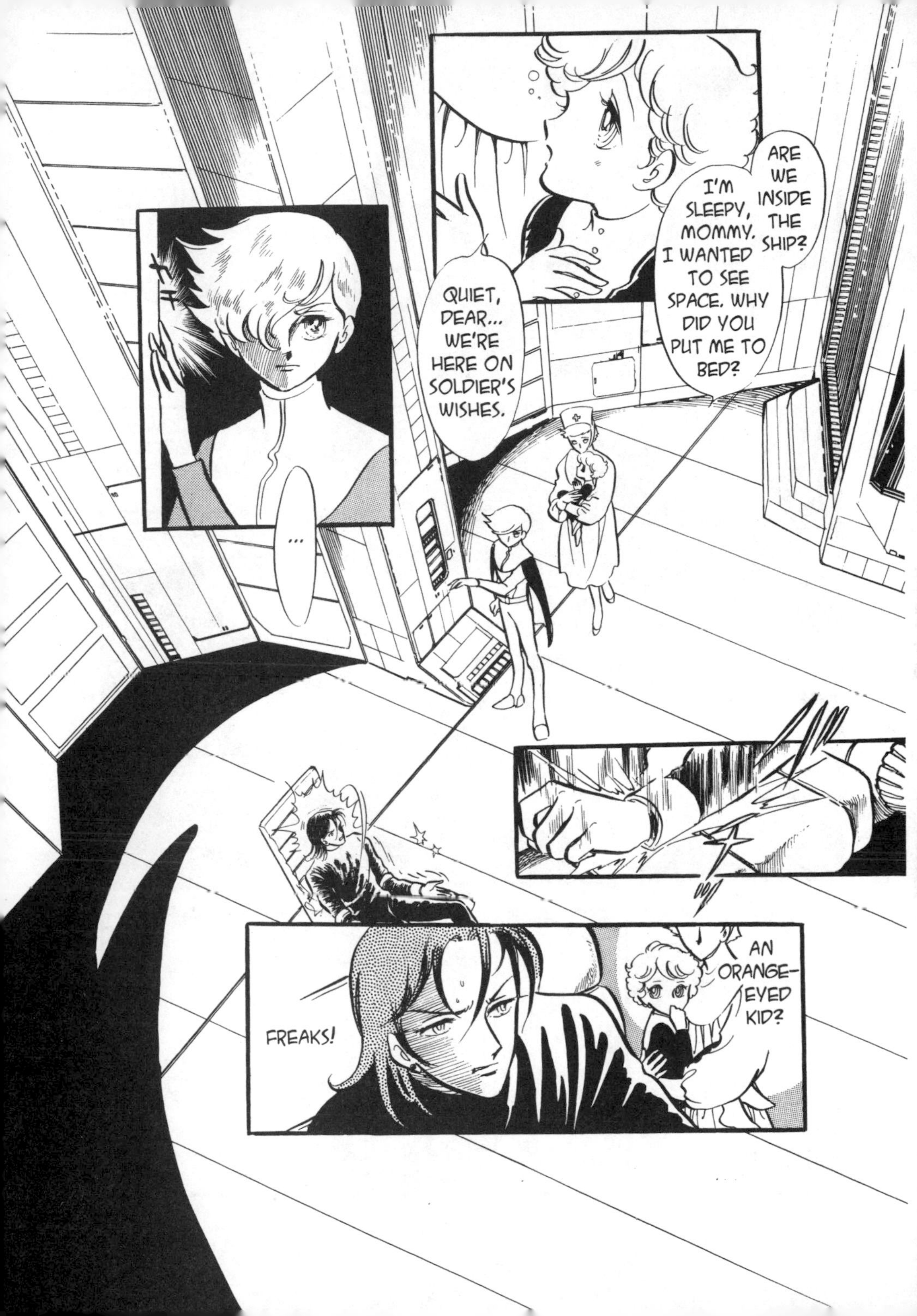
ARE WE INSIDE THE SHIP?
I'M SLEEPY, MOMMY. I WANTED TO SEE SPACE. WHY DID YOU PUT ME TO BED?
QUIET, DEAR... WE'RE HERE ON SOLDIER'S WISHES.
...
AN ORANGE-EYED KID?
FREAKS!

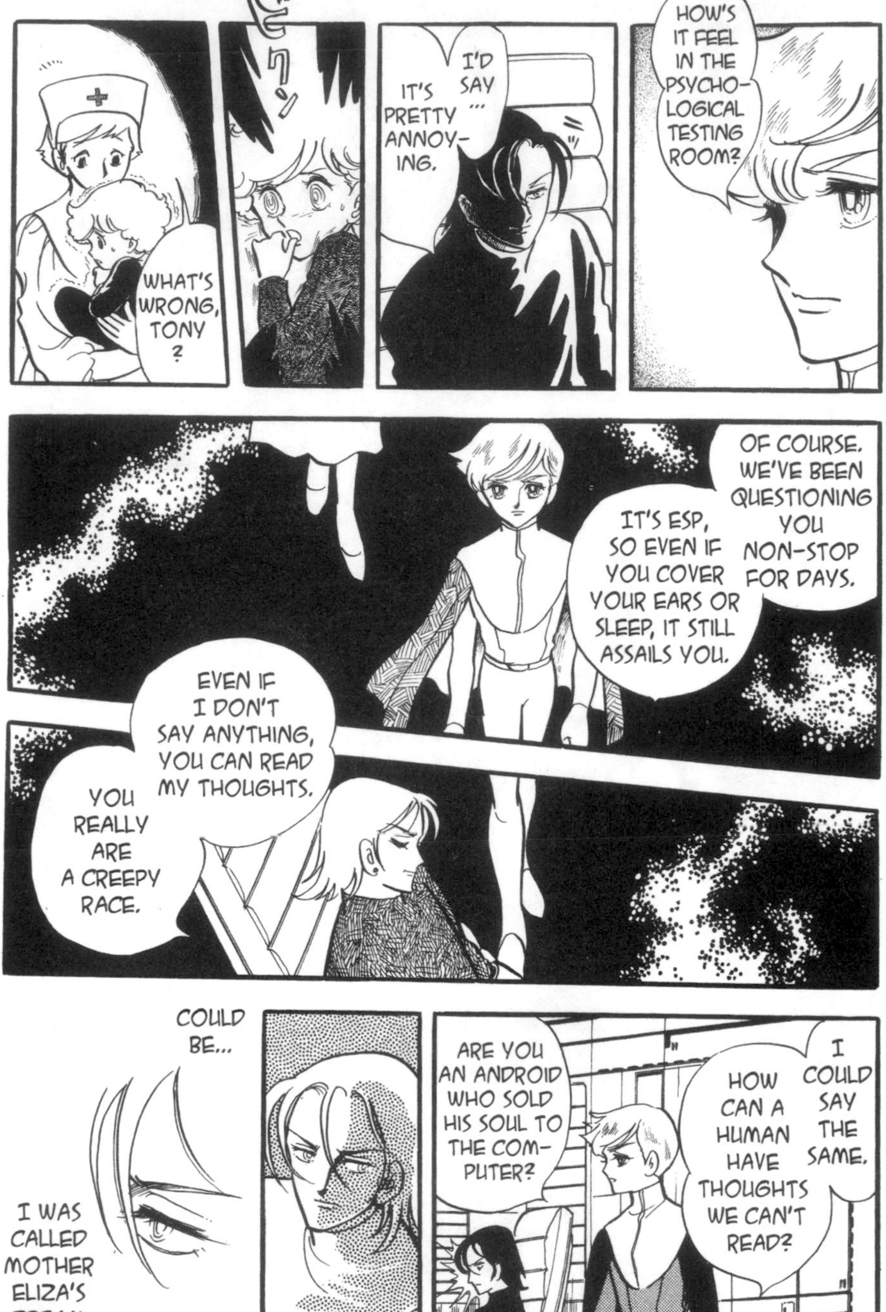
HOW'S IT FEEL IN THE PSYCHOLOGICAL TESTING ROOM?
I'D SAY...
IT'S PRETTY ANNOYING.
ビクン
WHAT'S WRONG, TONY?
OF COURSE. WE'VE BEEN QUESTIONING YOU NON-STOP FOR DAYS.
IT'S ESP, SO EVEN IF YOU COVER YOUR EARS OR SLEEP, IT STILL ASSAILS YOU.
EVEN IF I DON'T SAY ANYTHING, YOU CAN READ MY THOUGHTS.
YOU REALLY ARE A CREEPY RACE.
I COULD SAY THE SAME.
HOW CAN A HUMAN HAVE THOUGHTS WE CAN'T READ?
ARE YOU AN ANDROID WHO SOLD HIS SOUL TO THE COMPUTER?
COULD BE...
I WAS CALLED MOTHER ELIZA'S DREAM CHILD.

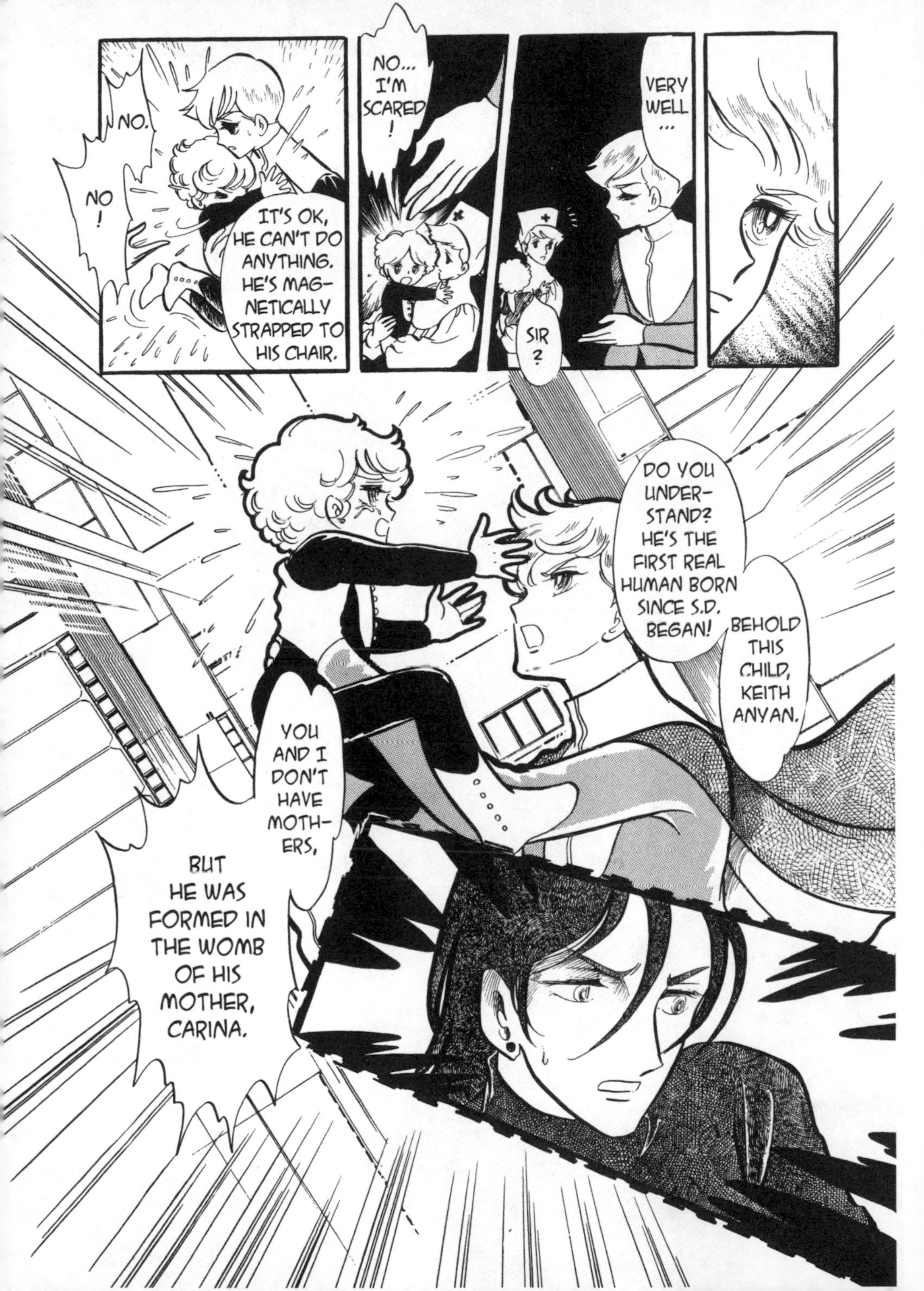
VERY WELL ...
SIR ?
NO... I'M SCARED !
NO.
NO !
IT'S OK, HE CAN'T DO ANYTHING. HE'S MAGNETICALLY STRAPPED TO HIS CHAIR.
DO YOU UNDERSTAND? HE'S THE FIRST REAL HUMAN BORN SINCE S.D. BEGAN!
BEHOLD THIS CHILD, KEITH ANYAN.
YOU AND I DON'T HAVE MOTHERS,
BUT HE WAS FORMED IN THE WOMB OF HIS MOTHER, CARINA.

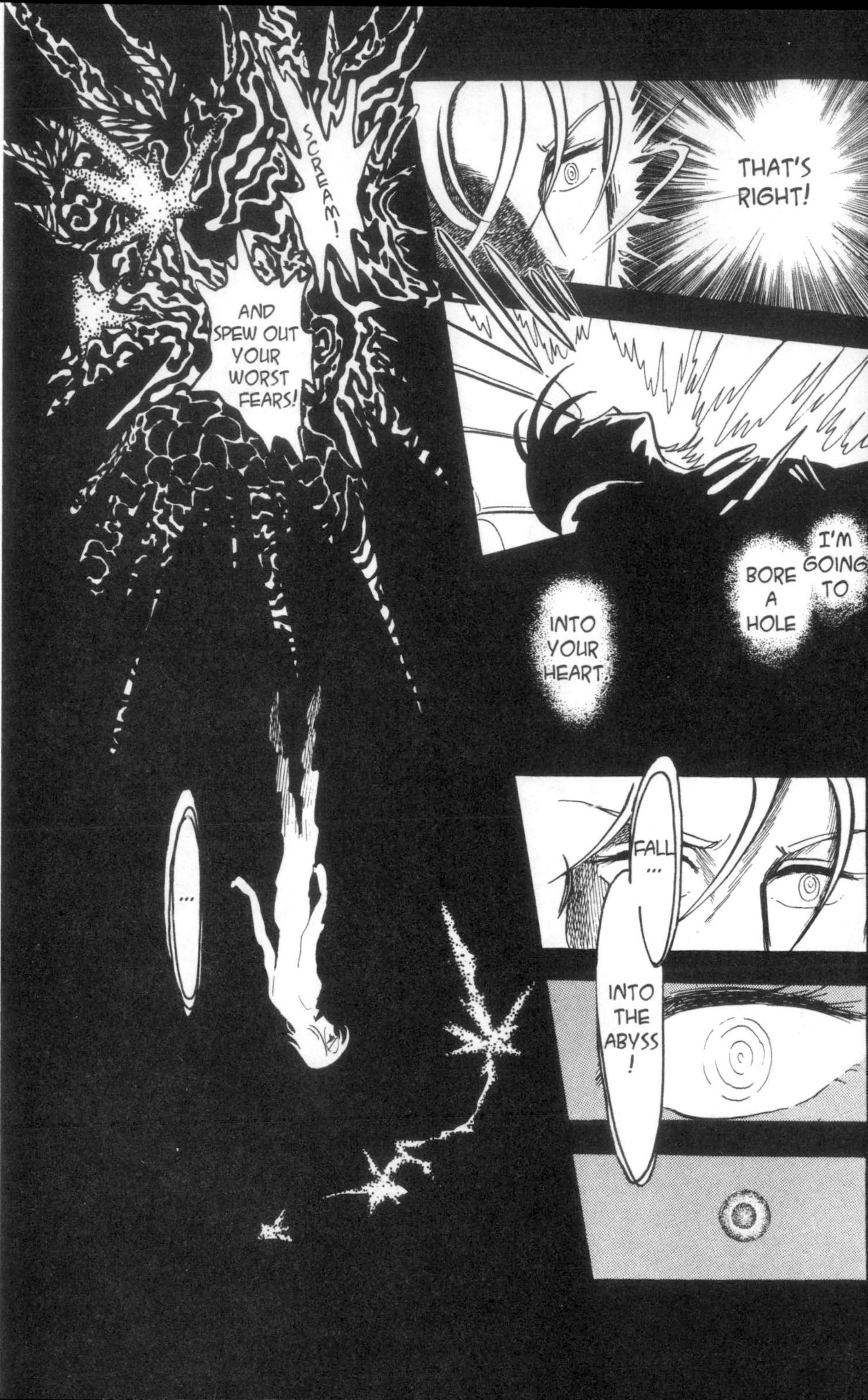
THAT'S RIGHT!
I'M GOING TO BORE A HOLE INTO YOUR HEART.
FALL...
INTO THE ABYSS!
SCREAM!
AND SPEW OUT YOUR WORST FEARS!
...

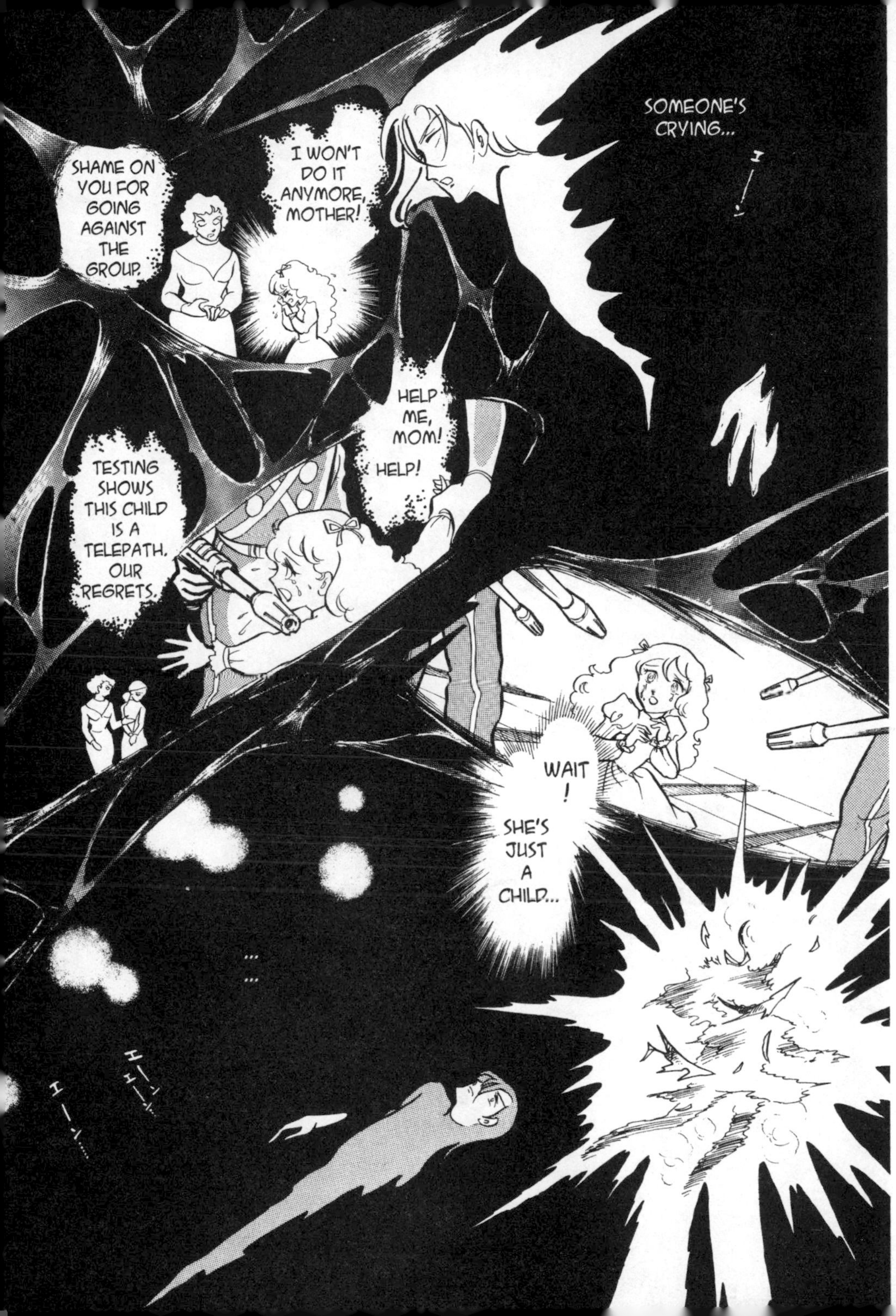
SOMEONE'S CRYING...
I WON'T DO IT ANYMORE, MOTHER!
SHAME ON YOU FOR GOING AGAINST THE GROUP.
HELP ME, MOM!
HELP!
TESTING SHOWS THIS CHILD IS A TELEPATH. OUR REGRETS.
WAIT!
SHE'S JUST A CHILD...
...
...

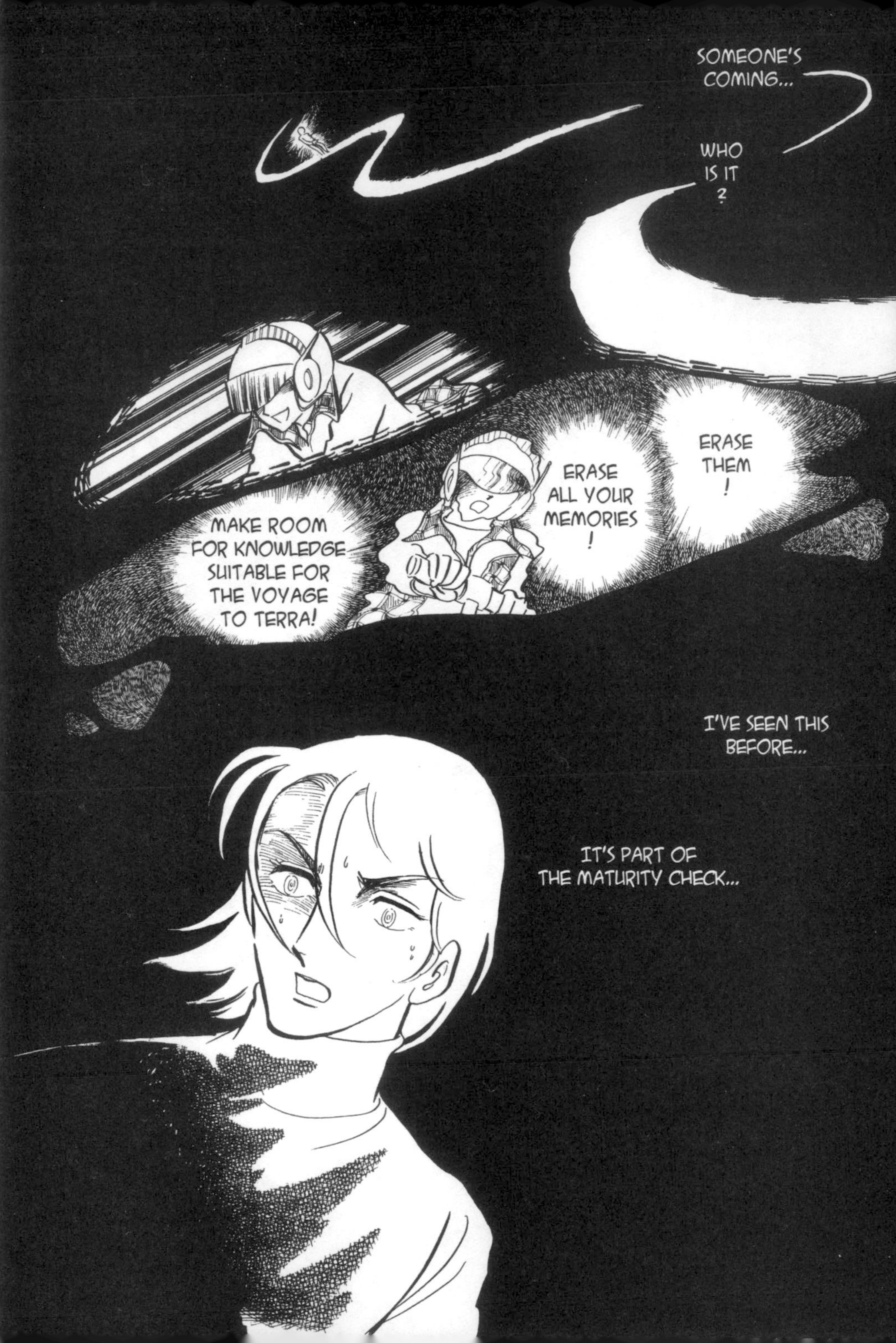
SOMEONE'S COMING...
WHO IS IT ?
ERASE THEM !
ERASE ALL YOUR MEMORIES !
MAKE ROOM FOR KNOWLEDGE SUITABLE FOR THE VOYAGE TO TERRA!
I'VE SEEN THIS BEFORE...
IT'S PART OF THE MATURITY CHECK...

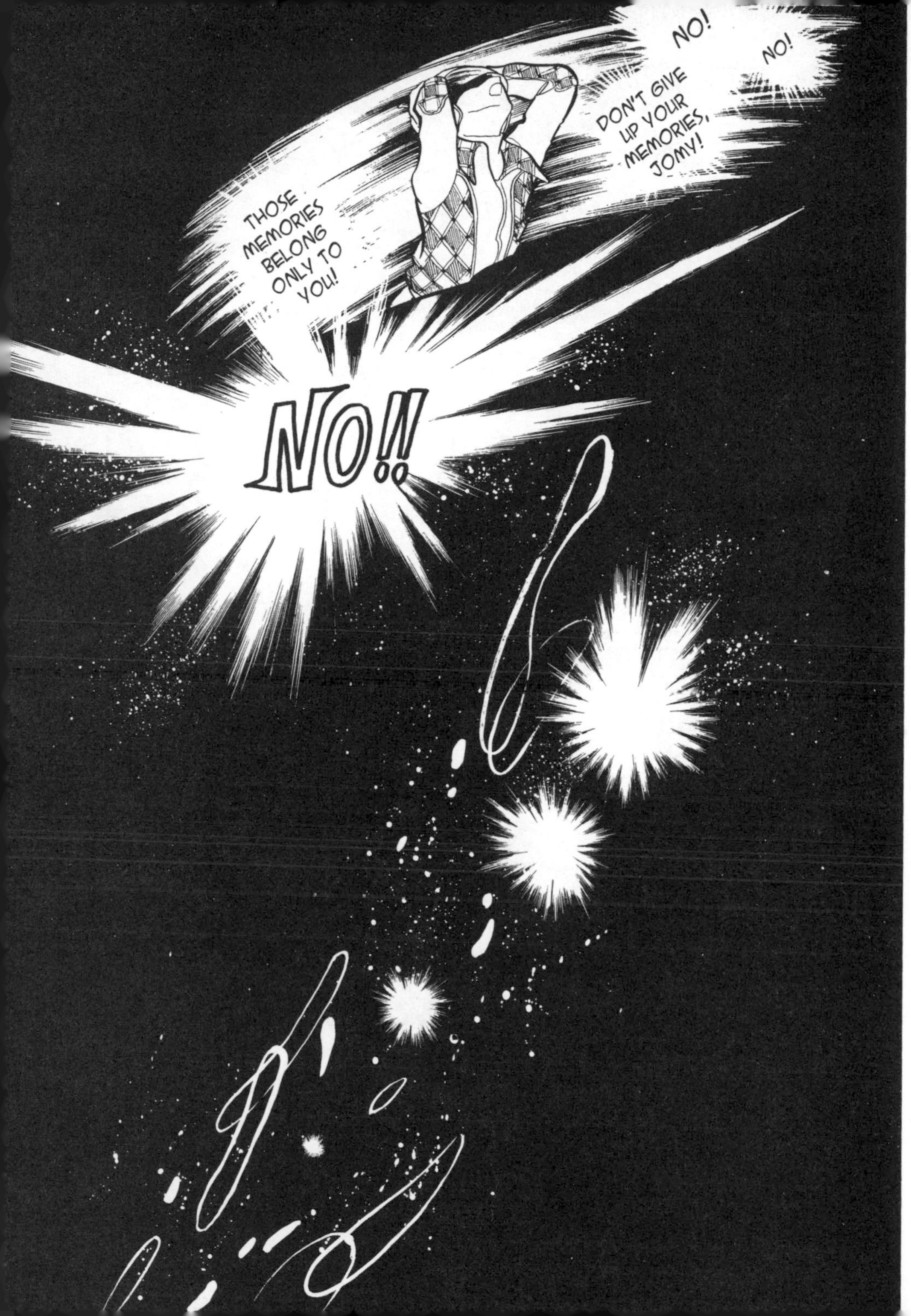
NO!
NO!
DON'T GIVE UP YOUR MEMORIES, JOMY!
THOSE MEMORIES BELONG ONLY TO YOU!
NO!!

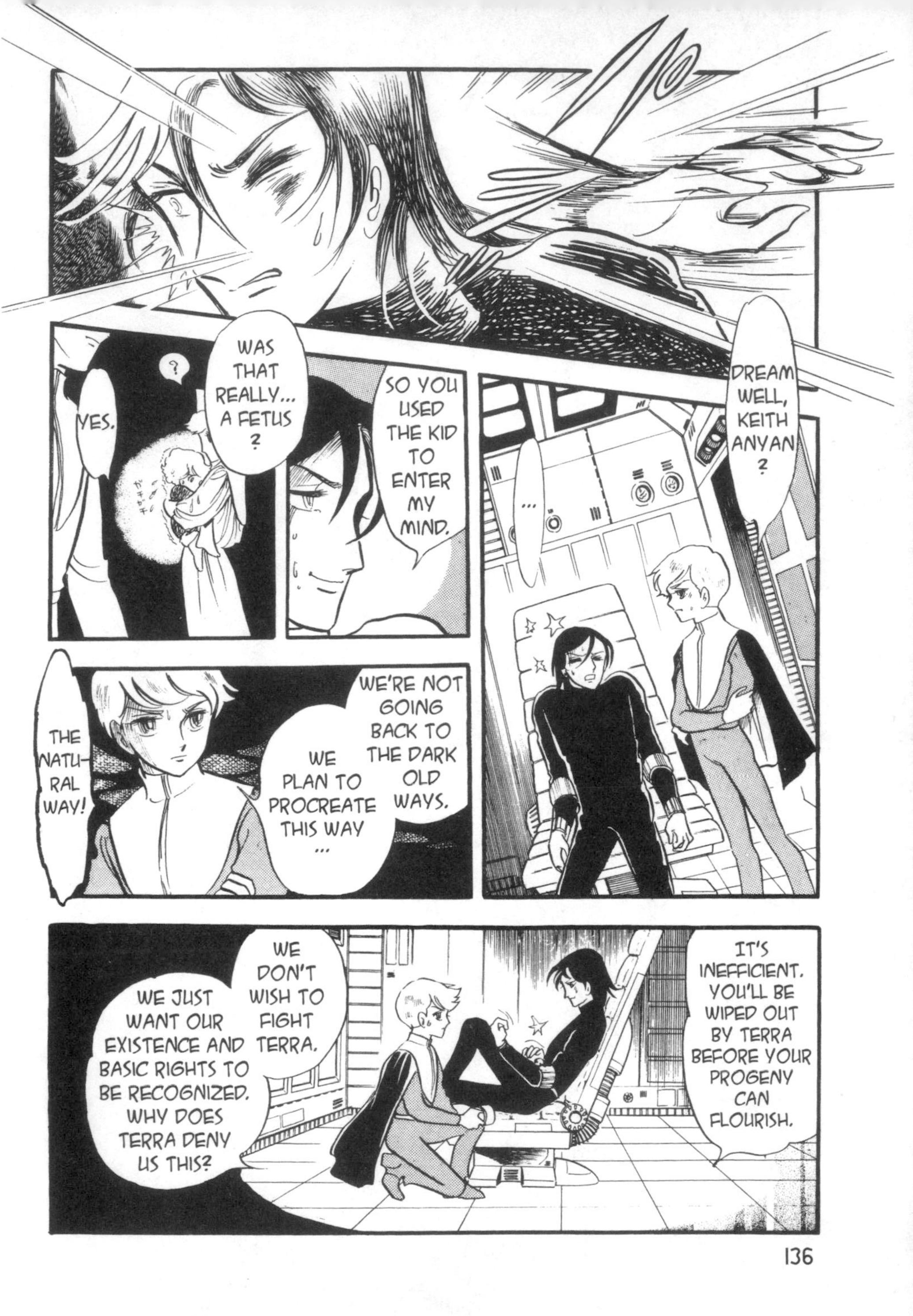

DREAM WELL, KEITH ANYAN?
...
SO YOU USED THE KID TO ENTER MY MIND.
WAS THAT REALLY... A FETUS?
?
YES.
WE'RE NOT GOING BACK TO THE DARK OLD WAYS.
WE PLAN TO PROCREATE THIS WAY ...
THE NATURAL WAY!
IT'S INEFFICIENT. YOU'LL BE WIPED OUT BY TERRA BEFORE YOUR PROGENY CAN FLOURISH.
WE DON'T WISH TO FIGHT TERRA.
WE JUST WANT OUR EXISTENCE AND BASIC RIGHTS TO BE RECOGNIZED. WHY DOES TERRA DENY US THIS?

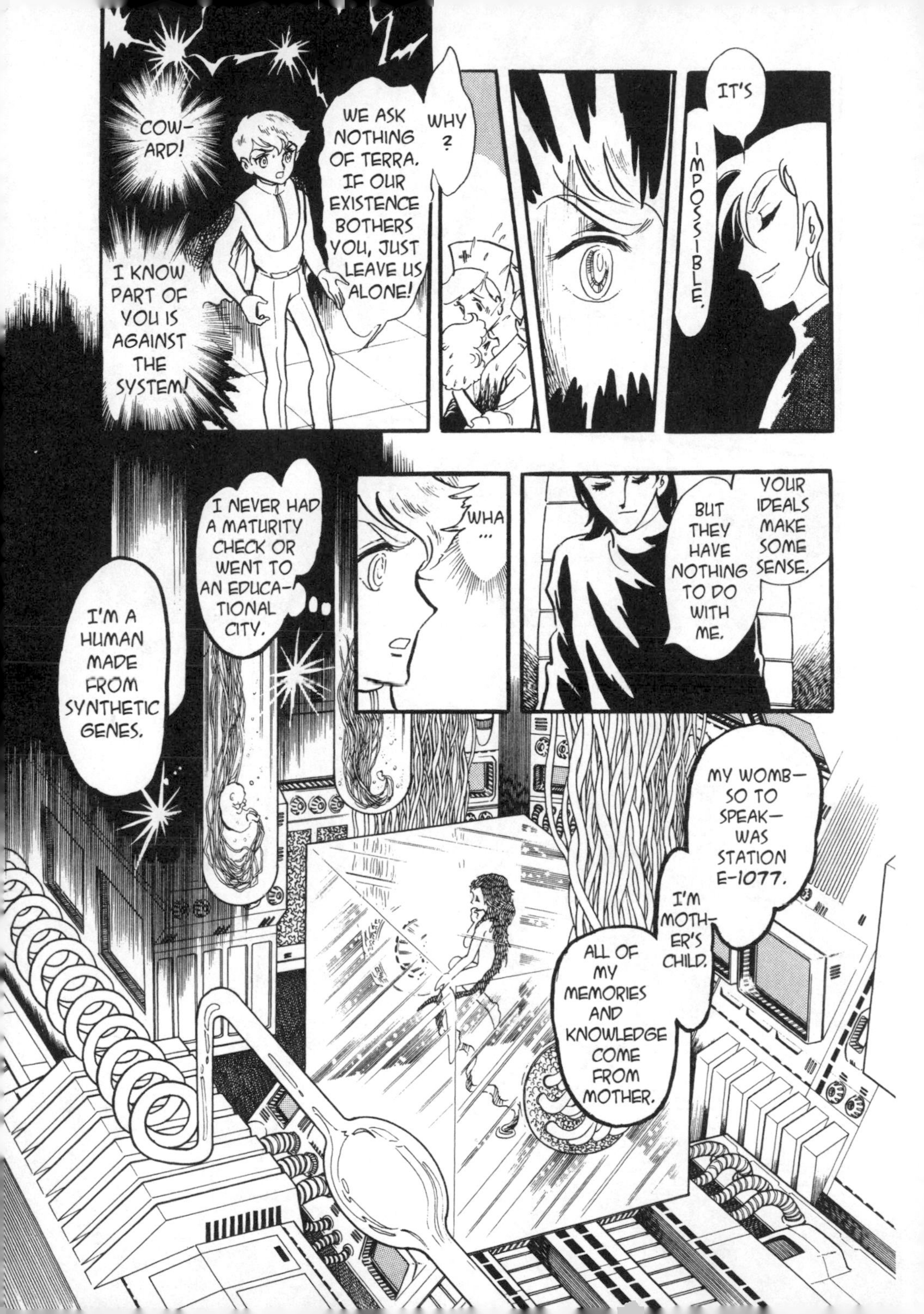
IT'S
IMPOSSIBLE.
WHY?
WE ASK NOTHING OF TERRA. IF OUR EXISTENCE BOTHERS YOU, JUST LEAVE US ALONE!
COW-ARD!
I KNOW PART OF YOU IS AGAINST THE SYSTEM!
YOUR IDEALS MAKE SOME SENSE.
BUT THEY HAVE NOTHING TO DO WITH ME.
WHA...
I NEVER HAD A MATURITY CHECK OR WENT TO AN EDUCA-TIONAL CITY.
I'M A HUMAN MADE FROM SYNTHETIC GENES.
MY WOMB—SO TO SPEAK—WAS STATION E-1077.
I'M MOTH-ER'S CHILD.
ALL OF MY MEMORIES AND KNOWLEDGE COME FROM MOTHER.

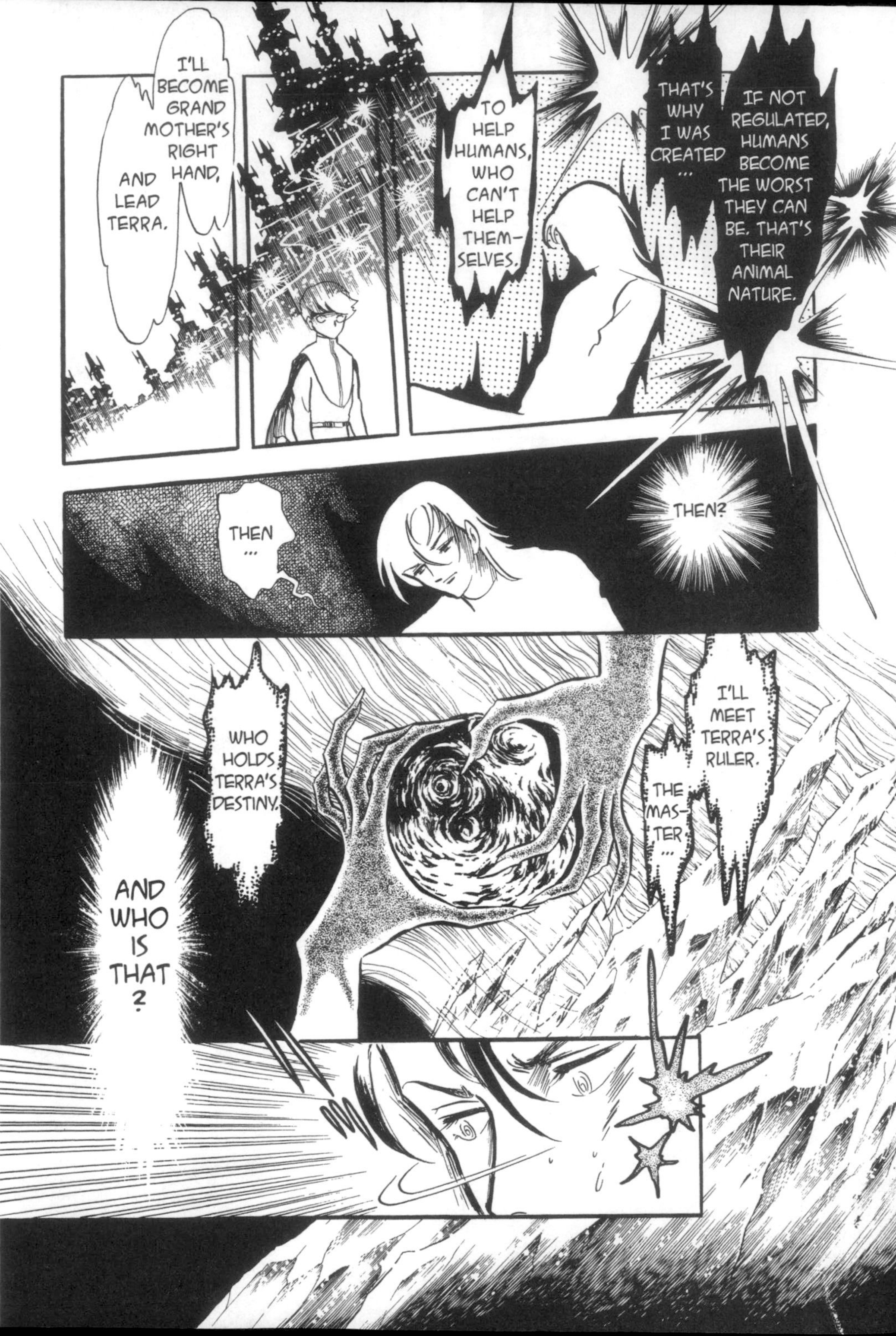
IF NOT REGULATED, HUMANS BECOME THE WORST THEY CAN BE. THAT'S THEIR ANIMAL NATURE.
THAT'S WHY I WAS CREATED ...
TO HELP HUMANS, WHO CAN'T HELP THEMSELVES.
I'LL BECOME GRAND MOTHER'S RIGHT HAND,
AND LEAD TERRA.
THEN?
THEN ...
I'LL MEET TERRA'S RULER.
THE MASTER ...
WHO HOLDS TERRA'S DESTINY.
AND WHO IS THAT ?

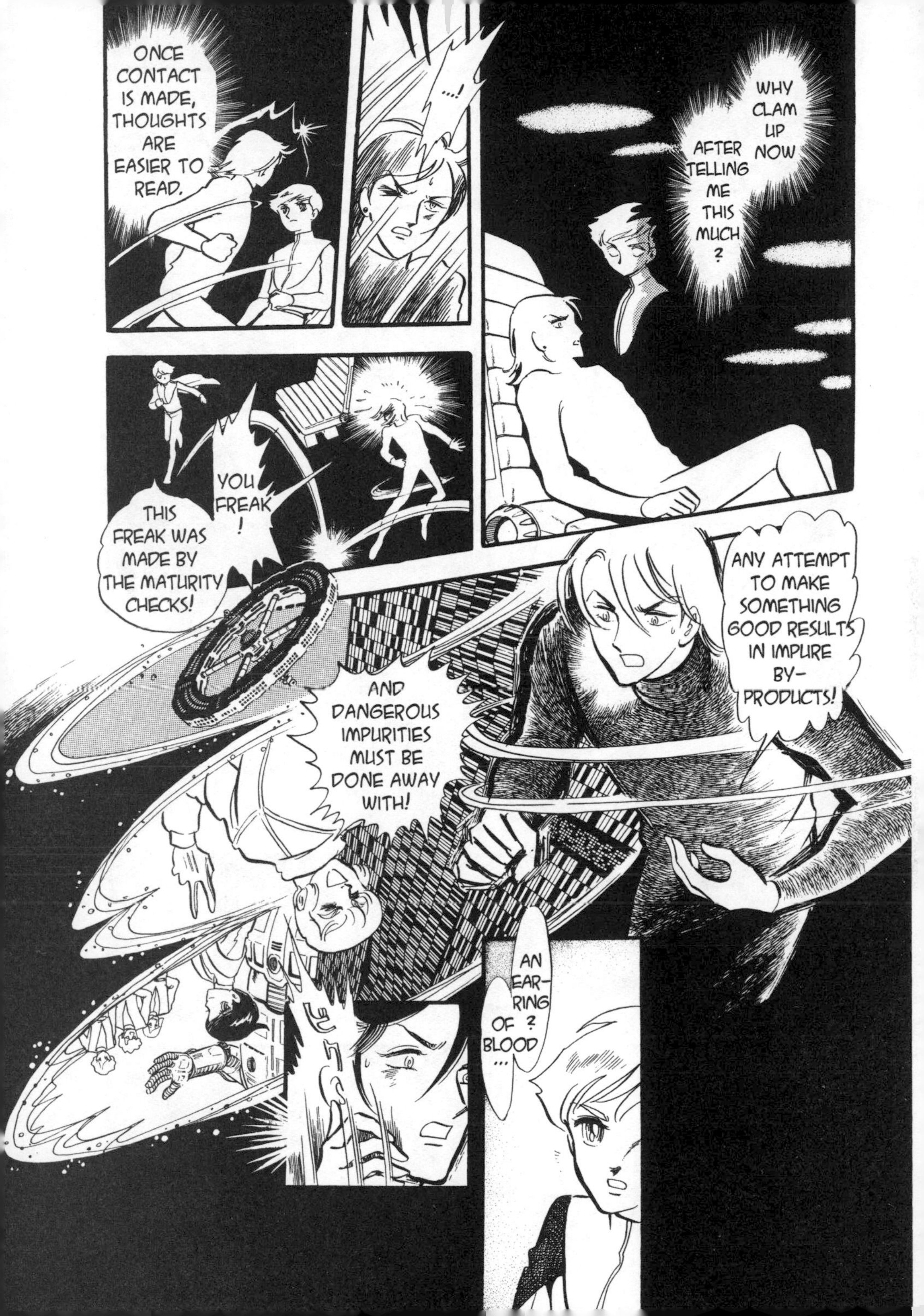

WHY CLAM UP NOW AFTER TELLING ME THIS MUCH?
...!
ONCE CONTACT IS MADE, THOUGHTS ARE EASIER TO READ.
YOU FREAK!
THIS FREAK WAS MADE BY THE MATURITY CHECKS!
ANY ATTEMPT TO MAKE SOMETHING GOOD RESULTS IN IMPURE BY-PRODUCTS!
AND DANGEROUS IMPURITIES MUST BE DONE AWAY WITH!
AN EAR-RING?
OF BLOOD...

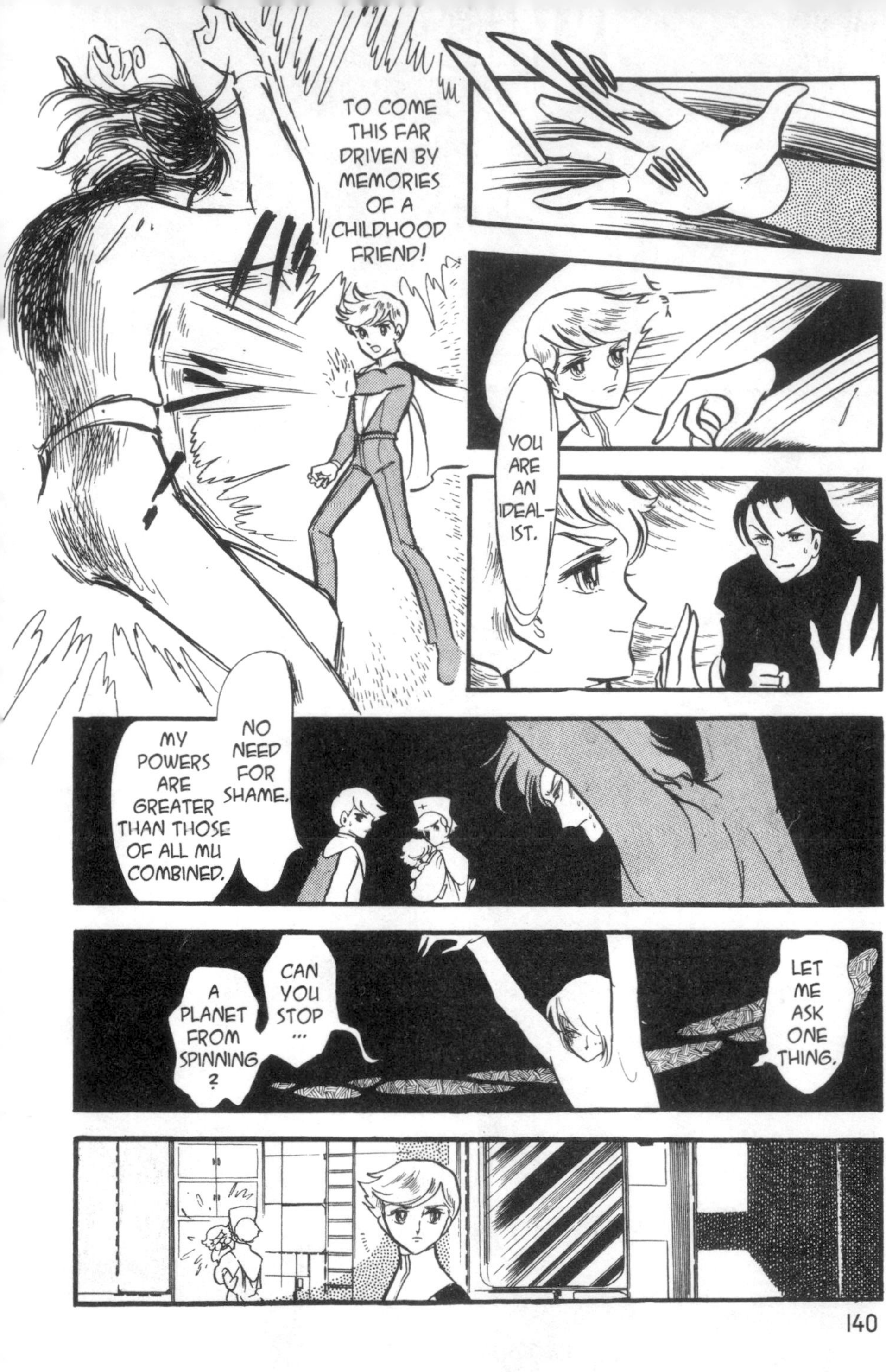
YOU ARE AN IDEALIST.
TO COME THIS FAR DRIVEN BY MEMORIES OF A CHILDHOOD FRIEND!
NO NEED FOR SHAME.
MY POWERS ARE GREATER THAN THOSE OF ALL MU COMBINED.
LET ME ASK ONE THING.
CAN YOU STOP ...
A PLANET FROM SPINNING?

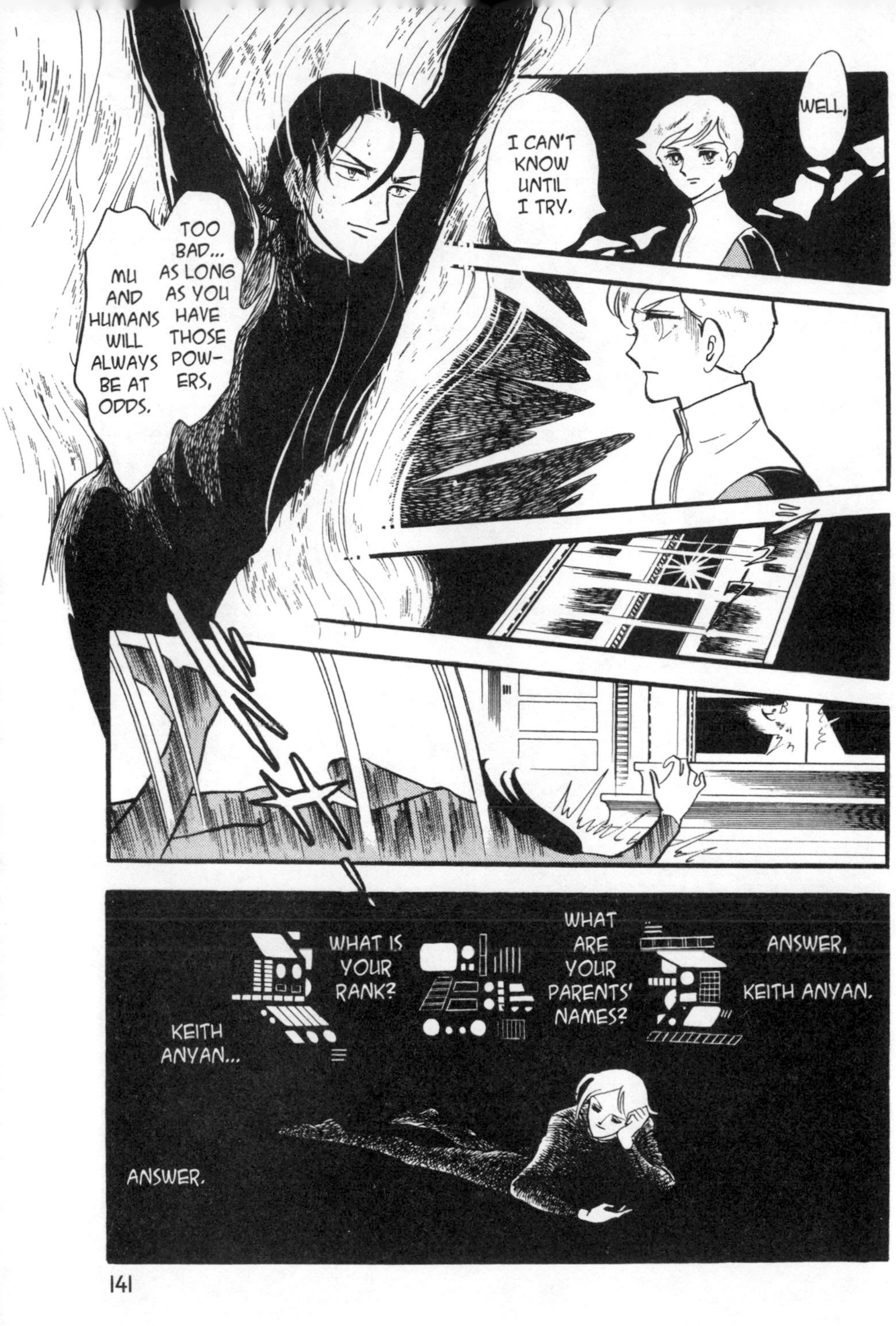
WELL,
I CAN'T KNOW UNTIL I TRY.
TOO BAD... AS LONG AS YOU HAVE THOSE POW-ERS,
MU AND HUMANS WILL ALWAYS BE AT ODDS.
ANSWER,
KEITH ANYAN.
WHAT ARE YOUR PARENTS' NAMES?
WHAT IS YOUR RANK?
KEITH ANYAN...
ANSWER.

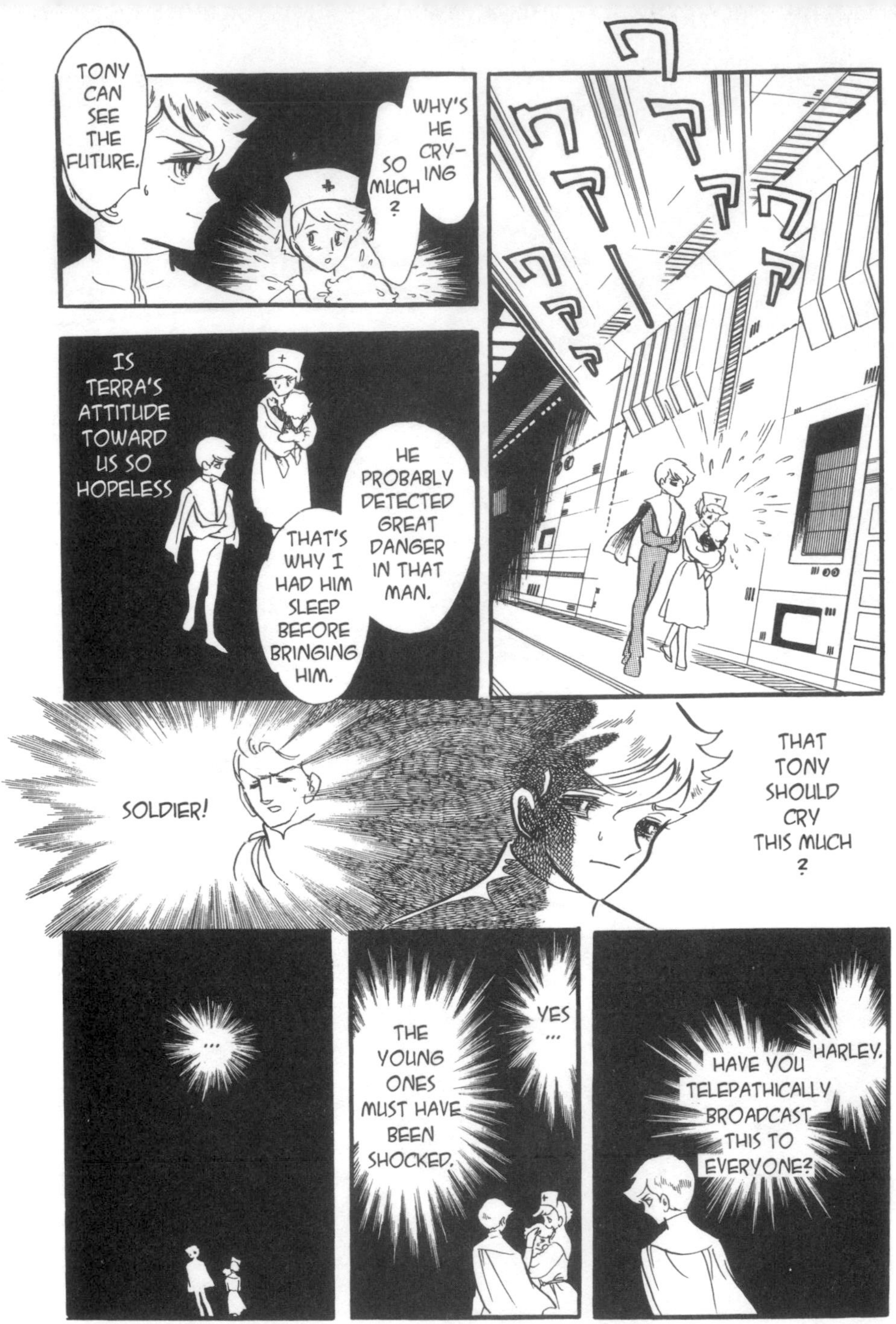
WHY'S HE CRYING SO MUCH?
TONY CAN SEE THE FUTURE.
HE PROBABLY DETECTED GREAT DANGER IN THAT MAN.
THAT'S WHY I HAD HIM SLEEP BEFORE BRINGING HIM.
IS TERRA'S ATTITUDE TOWARD US SO HOPELESS
THAT TONY SHOULD CRY THIS MUCH?
SOLDIER!
HARLEY.
HAVE YOU TELEPATHICALLY BROADCAST THIS TO EVERYONE?
YES ...
THE YOUNG ONES MUST HAVE BEEN SHOCKED.
...

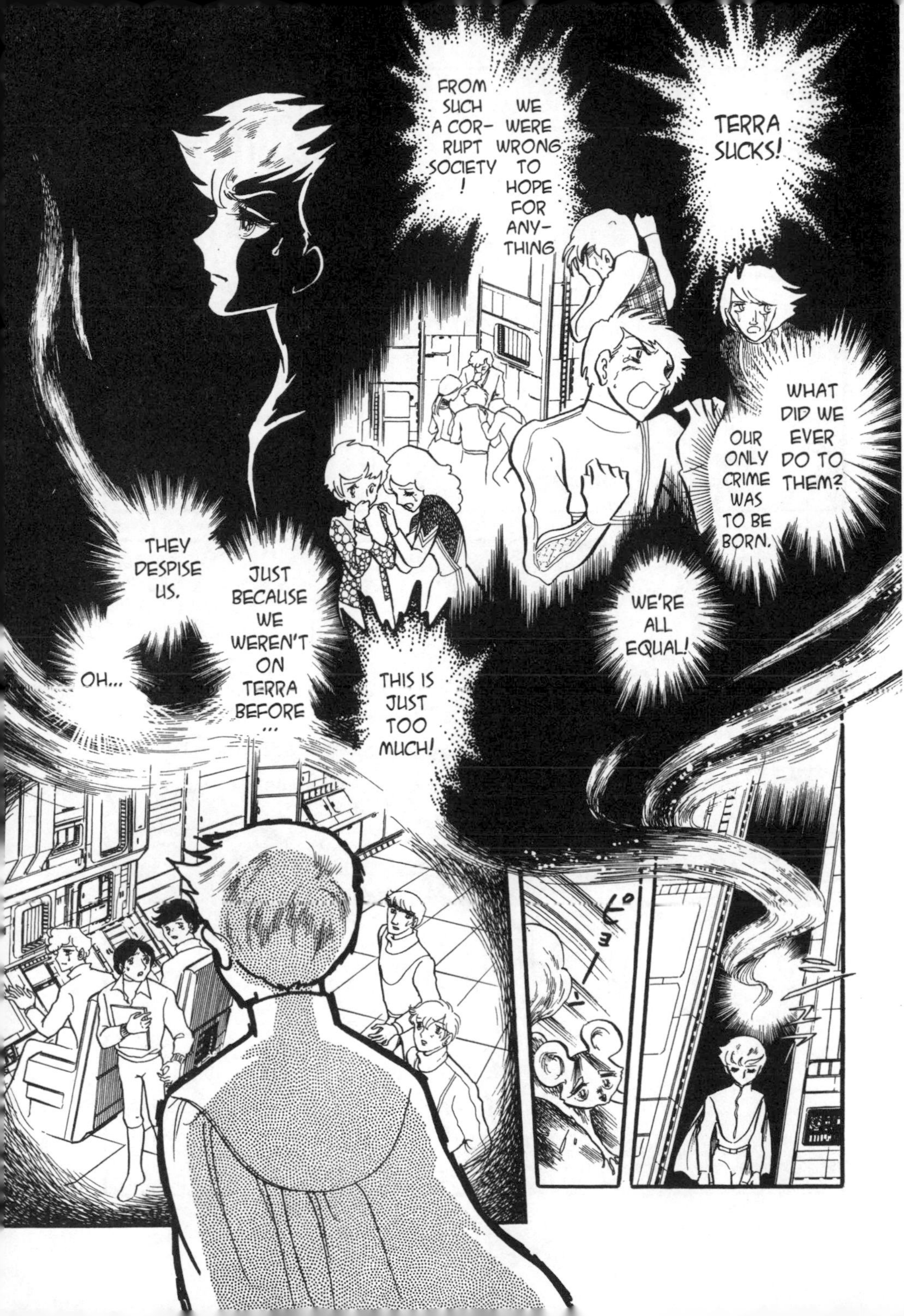
TERRA SUCKS!
WE WERE WRONG TO HOPE FOR ANYTHING
FROM SUCH A COR-RUPT SOCIETY!
WHAT DID WE EVER DO TO THEM?
OUR ONLY CRIME WAS TO BE BORN.
WE'RE ALL EQUAL!
THIS IS JUST TOO MUCH!
THEY DESPISE US.
JUST BECAUSE WE WEREN'T ON TERRA BEFORE...
OH...

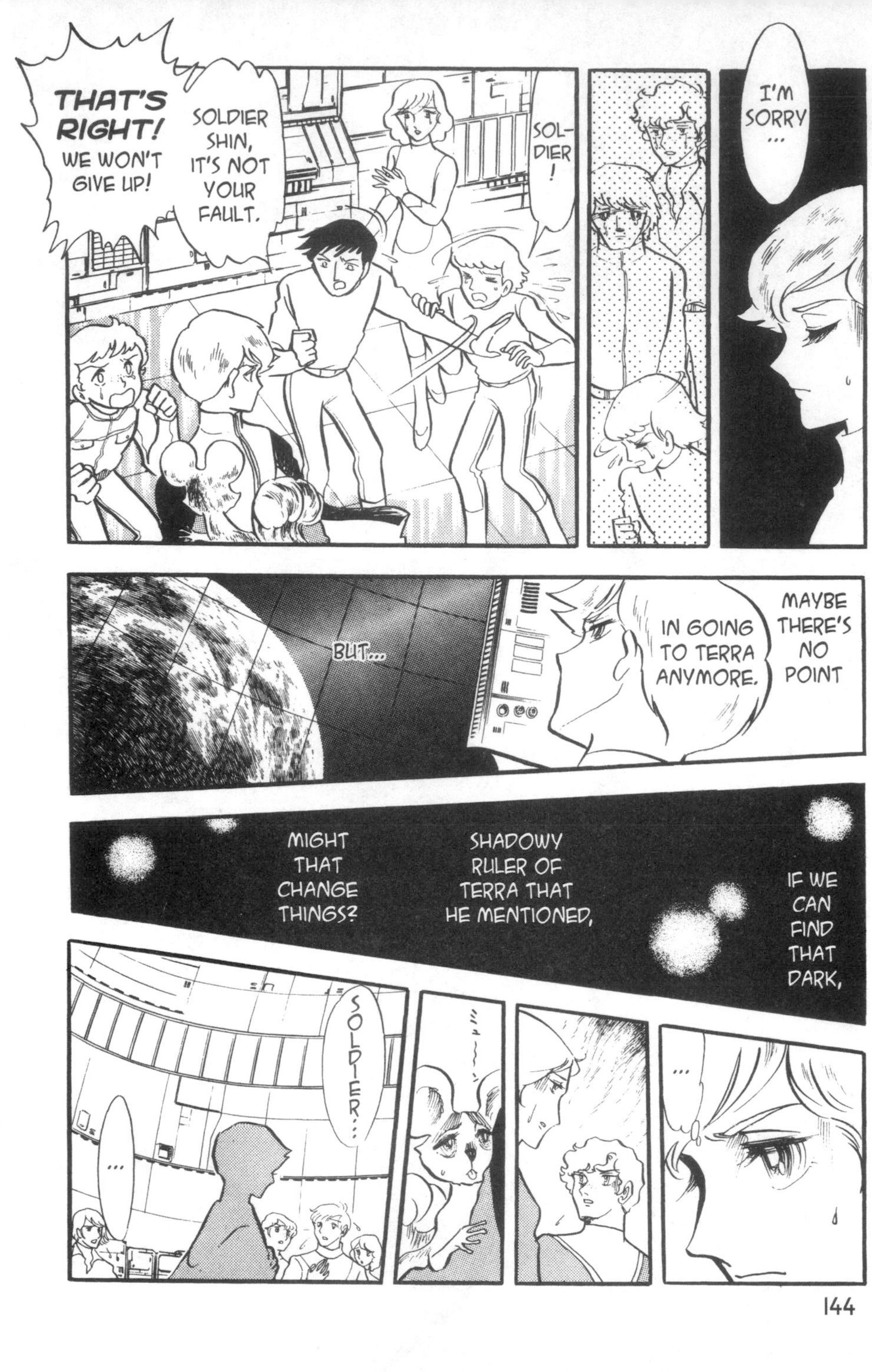
I'M SORRY...
SOL-DIER!
SOLDIER SHIN, IT'S NOT YOUR FAULT.
THAT'S RIGHT! WE WON'T GIVE UP!
MAYBE THERE'S NO POINT
IN GOING TO TERRA ANYMORE.
BUT...
IF WE CAN FIND THAT DARK,
SHADOWY RULER OF TERRA THAT HE MENTIONED,
MIGHT THAT CHANGE THINGS?
...
ミュ〜〜ン
SOLDIER...
...

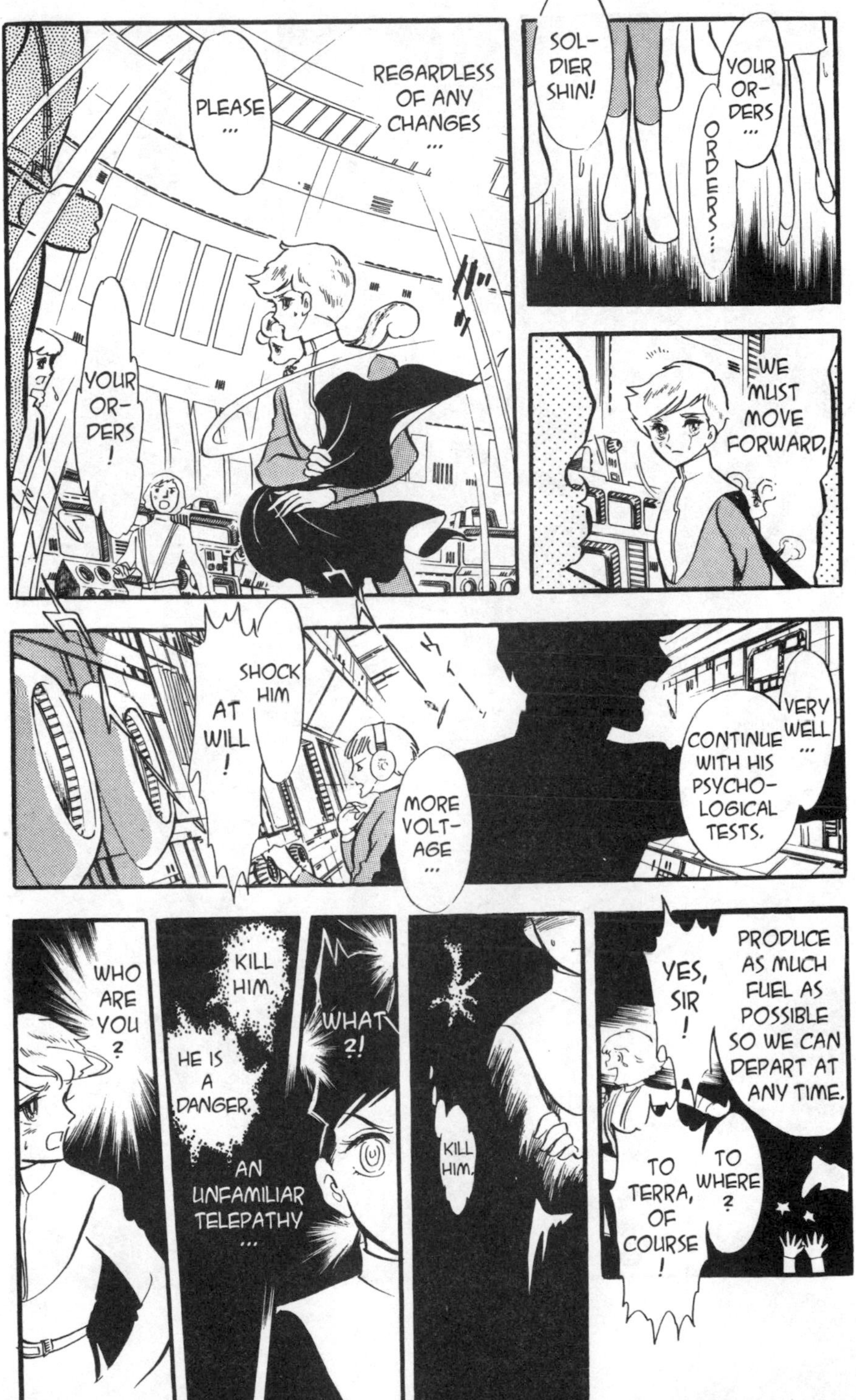
YOUR ORDERS...
SOLDIER SHIN!
ORDERS...
WE MUST MOVE FORWARD,
REGARDLESS OF ANY CHANGES...
PLEASE...
YOUR ORDERS!
VERY WELL...
CONTINUE WITH HIS PSYCHOLOGICAL TESTS.
MORE VOLTAGE...
SHOCK HIM AT WILL!
PRODUCE AS MUCH FUEL AS POSSIBLE SO WE CAN DEPART AT ANY TIME.
YES, SIR!
TO WHERE?
TO TERRA, OF COURSE!
KILL HIM.
KILL HIM.
WHAT?!
HE IS A DANGER.
AN UNFAMILIAR TELEPATHY...
WHO ARE YOU?

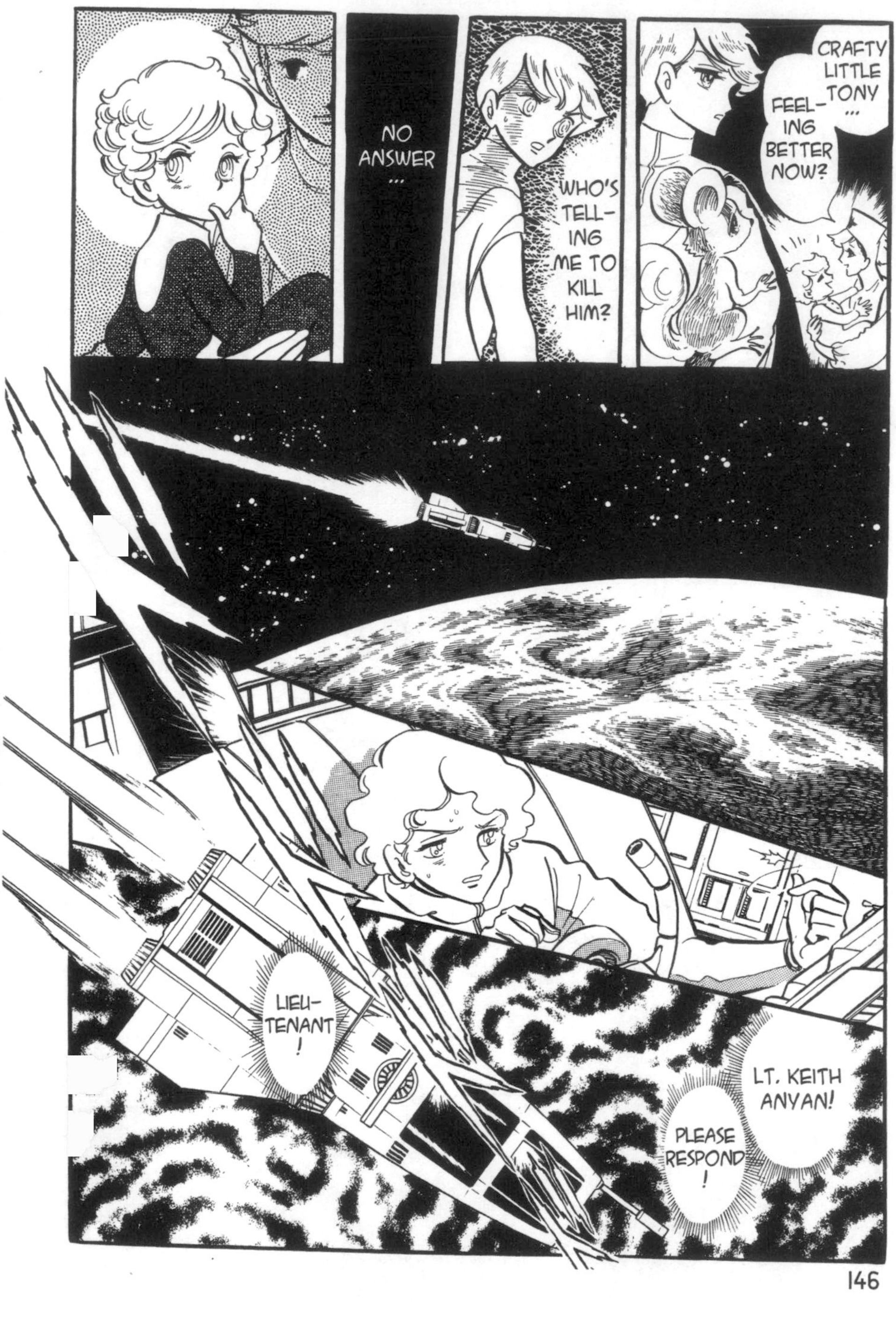
CRAFTY LITTLE TONY ...
FEEL-ING BETTER NOW?
WHO'S TELL-ING ME TO KILL HIM?
NO ANSWER ...
LT. KEITH ANYAN!
PLEASE RESPOND !
LIEU-TENANT !

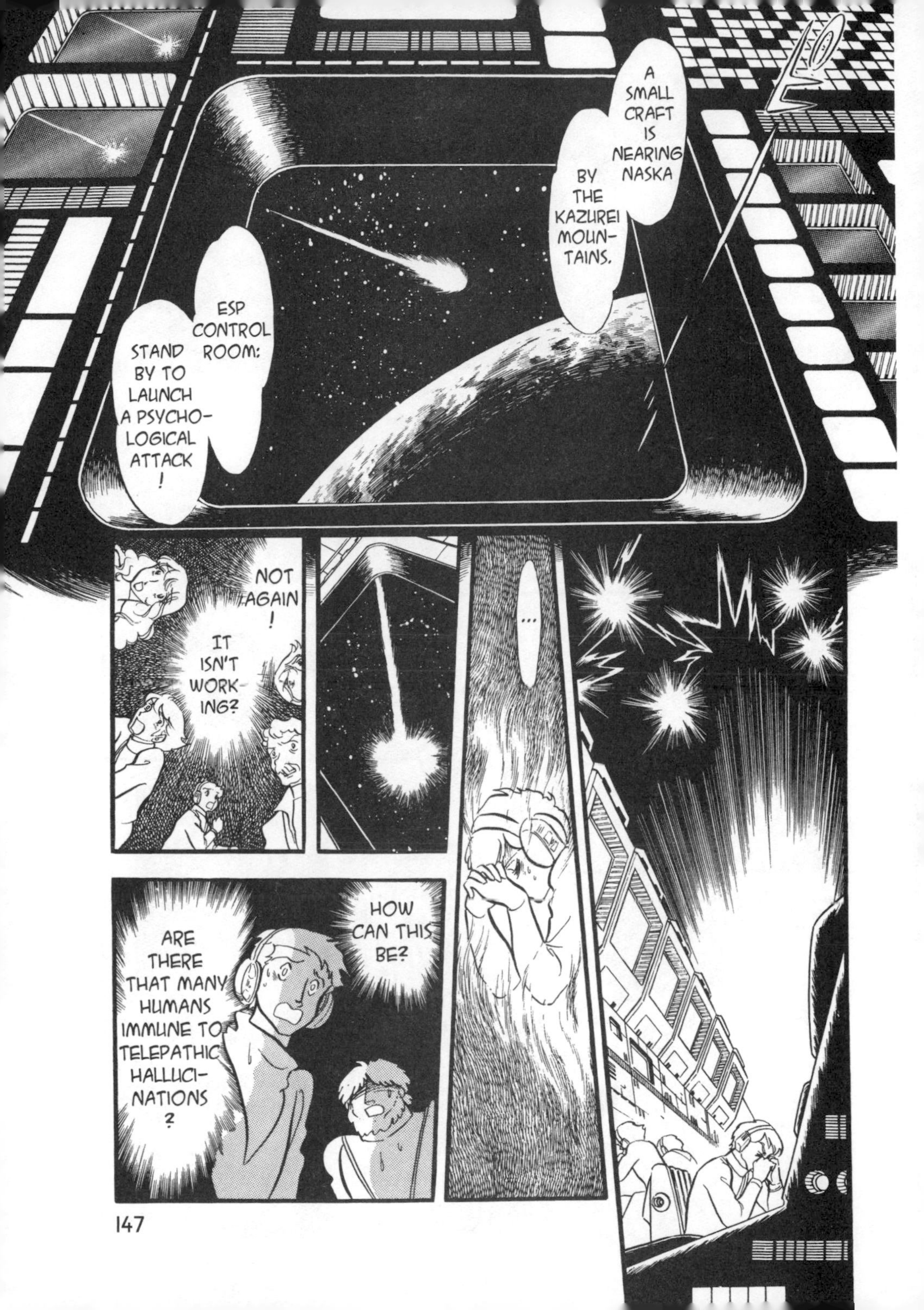
A SMALL CRAFT IS NEARING NASKA BY THE KAZUREI MOUNTAINS.
ESP CONTROL ROOM: STAND BY TO LAUNCH A PSYCHOLOGICAL ATTACK!
...
NOT AGAIN!
IT ISN'T WORKING?
HOW CAN THIS BE?
ARE THERE THAT MANY HUMANS IMMUNE TO TELEPATHIC HALLUCINATIONS?

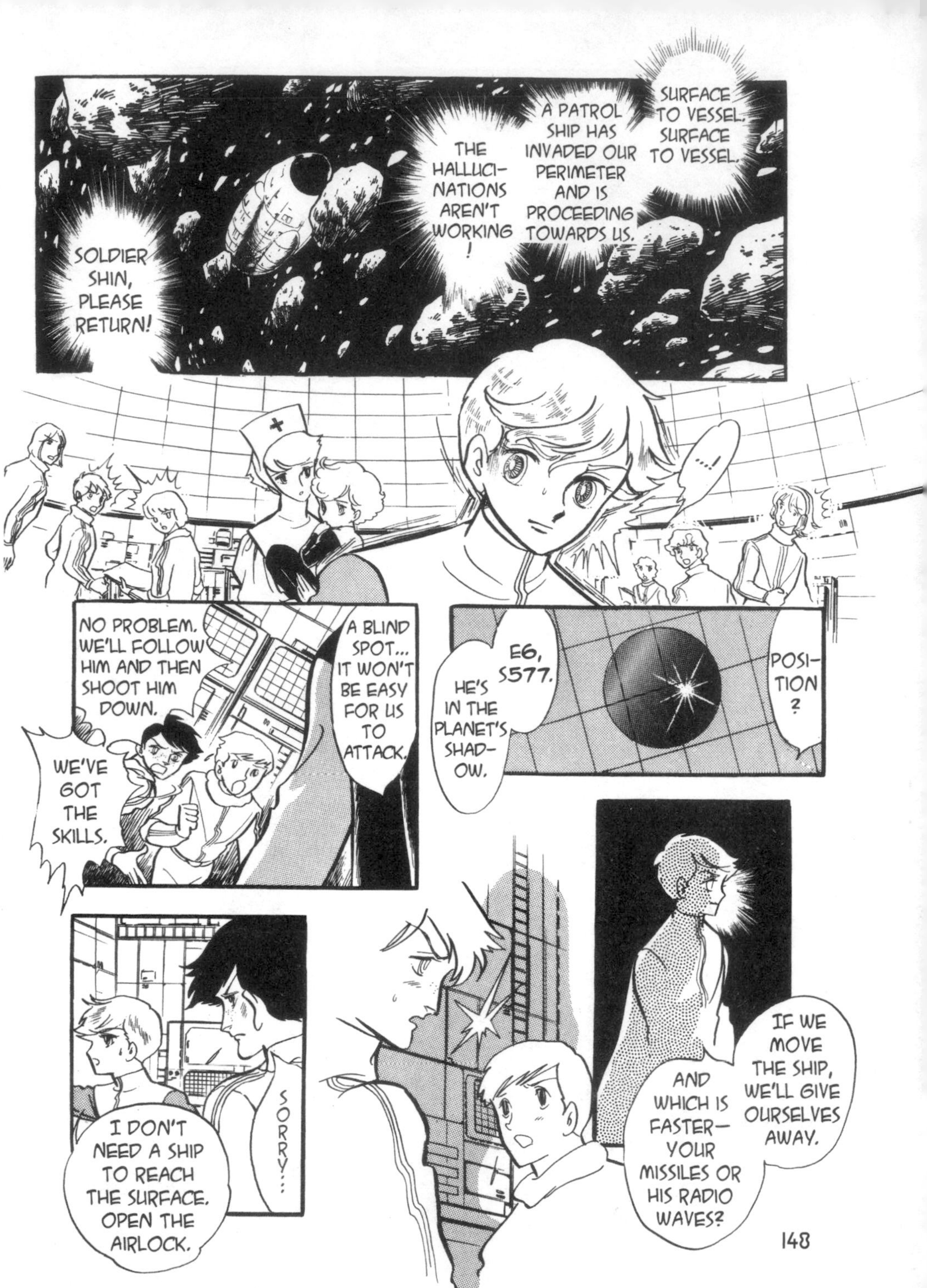
SURFACE TO VESSEL. SURFACE TO VESSEL.
A PATROL SHIP HAS INVADED OUR PERIMETER AND IS PROCEEDING TOWARDS US.
THE HALLUCI-NATIONS AREN'T WORKING!
SOLDIER SHIN, PLEASE RETURN!
...!
POSI-TION?
E6, S577.
HE'S IN THE PLANET'S SHAD-OW.
A BLIND SPOT... IT WON'T BE EASY FOR US TO ATTACK.
NO PROBLEM. WE'LL FOLLOW HIM AND THEN SHOOT HIM DOWN.
WE'VE GOT THE SKILLS.
IF WE MOVE THE SHIP, WE'LL GIVE OURSELVES AWAY.
AND WHICH IS FASTER—YOUR MISSILES OR HIS RADIO WAVES?
SORRY...
I DON'T NEED A SHIP TO REACH THE SURFACE. OPEN THE AIRLOCK.

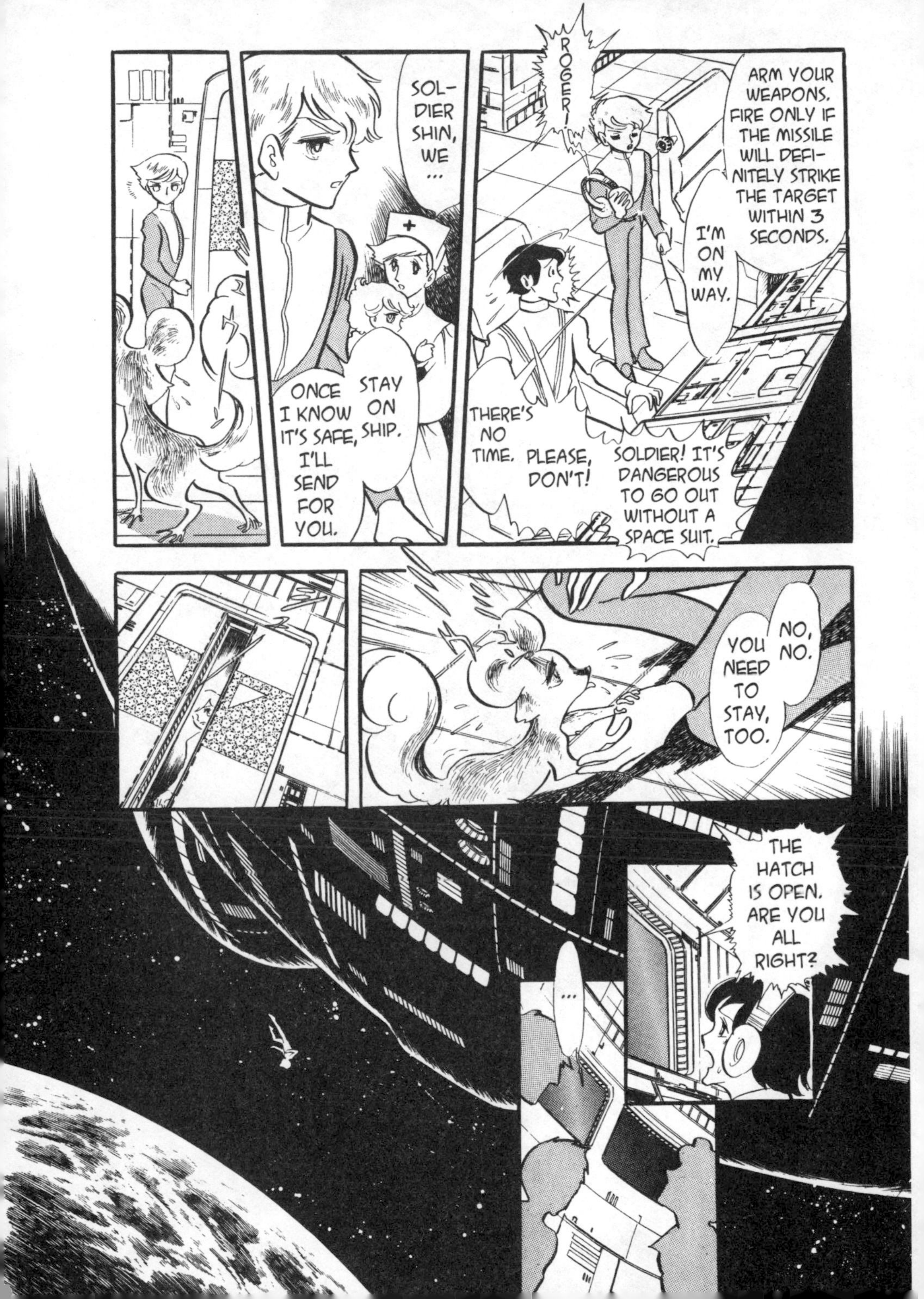
ARM YOUR WEAPONS. FIRE ONLY IF THE MISSILE WILL DEFINITELY STRIKE THE TARGET WITHIN 3 SECONDS.
ROGER!
I'M ON MY WAY.
SOLDIER! IT'S DANGEROUS TO GO OUT WITHOUT A SPACE SUIT.
PLEASE, DON'T!
THERE'S NO TIME.
SOL-DIER SHIN, WE ...
STAY ON SHIP.
ONCE I KNOW IT'S SAFE, I'LL SEND FOR YOU.
NO, NO.
YOU NEED TO STAY, TOO.
THE HATCH IS OPEN. ARE YOU ALL RIGHT?
...

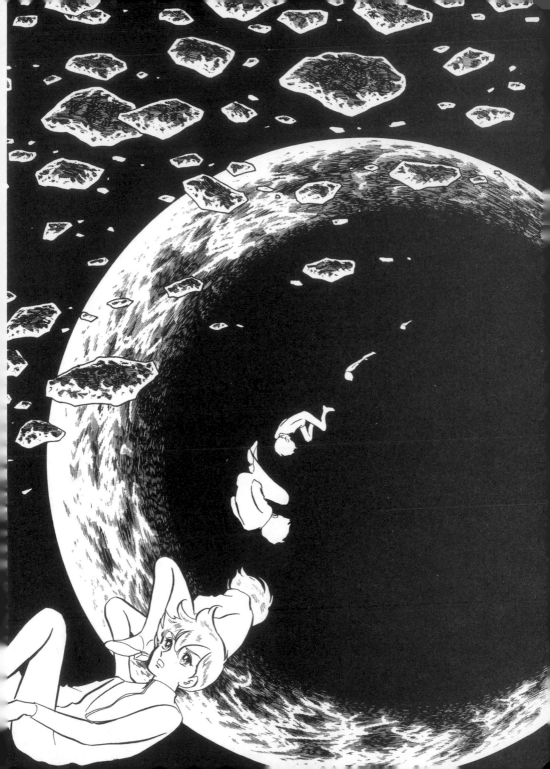

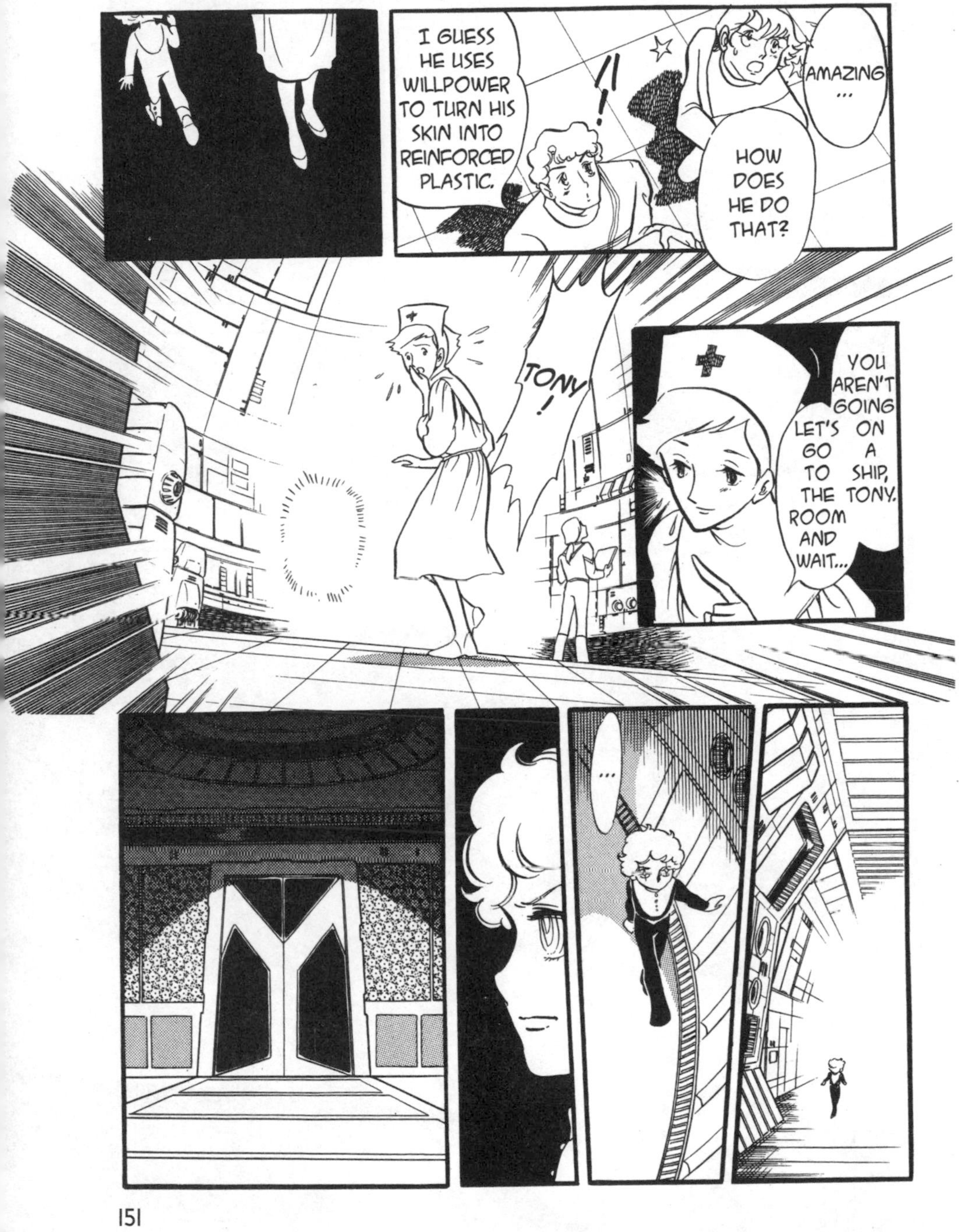
AMAZING...
HOW DOES HE DO THAT?
!!
I GUESS HE USES WILLPOWER TO TURN HIS SKIN INTO REINFORCED PLASTIC.
TONY!
YOU AREN'T GOING ON A SHIP, TONY.
LET'S GO TO THE ROOM AND WAIT...
...

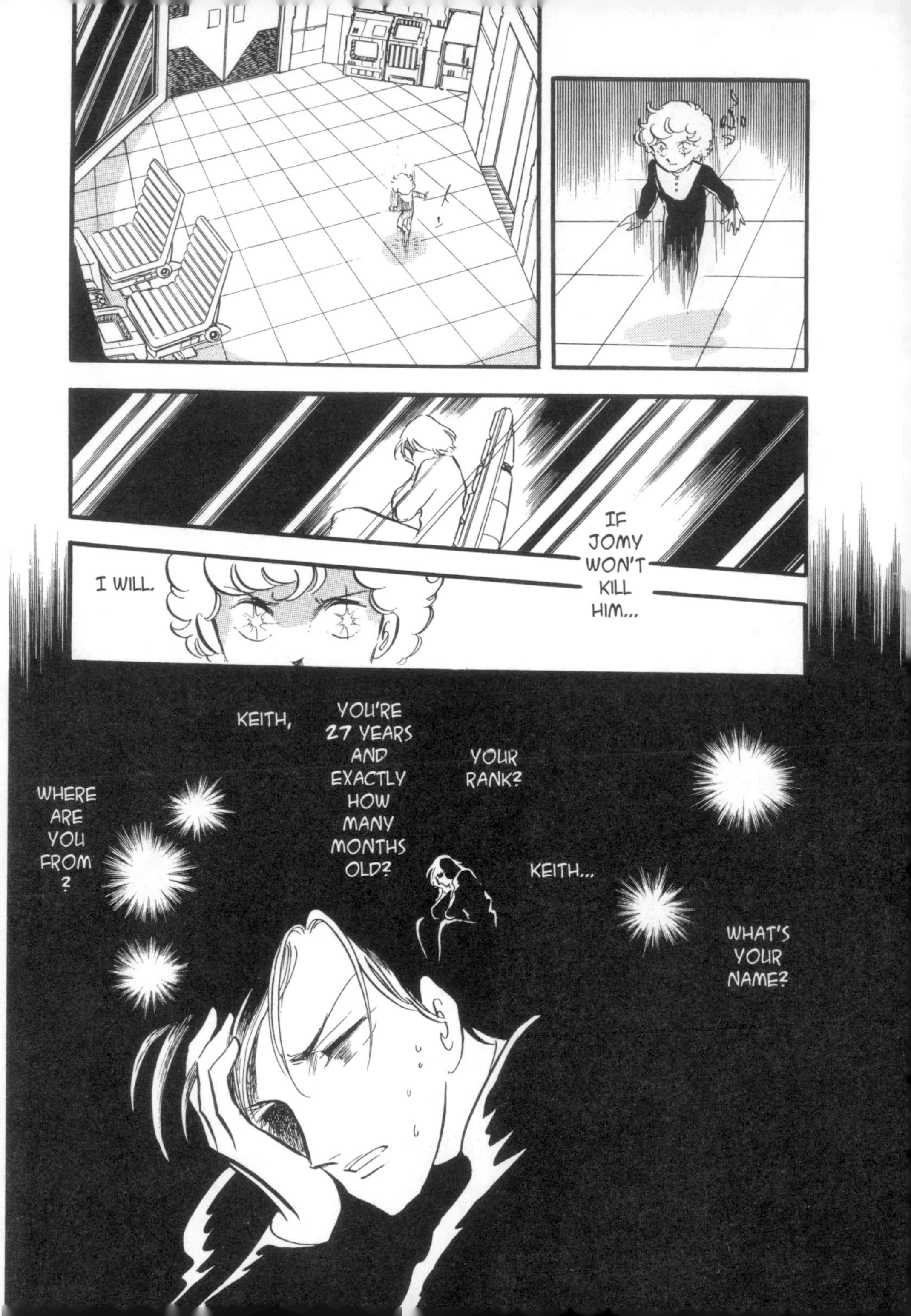
IF JOMY WON'T KILL HIM...
I WILL.
WHAT'S YOUR NAME?
KEITH...
YOUR RANK?
KEITH,
YOU'RE 27 YEARS AND EXACTLY HOW MANY MONTHS OLD?
WHERE ARE YOU FROM?

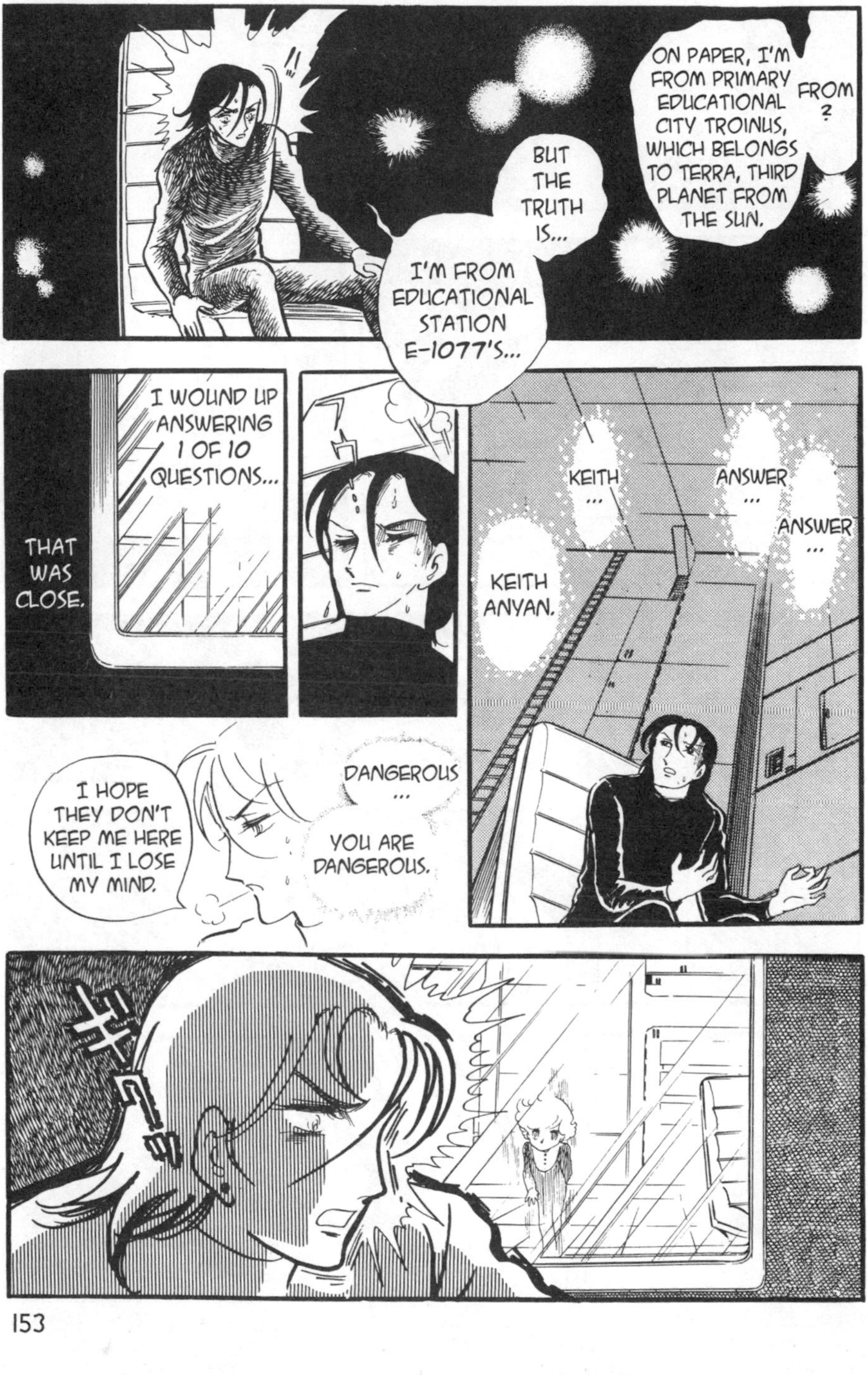
FROM ?
ON PAPER, I'M FROM PRIMARY EDUCATIONAL CITY TROINUS, WHICH BELONGS TO TERRA, THIRD PLANET FROM THE SUN.
BUT THE TRUTH IS...
!!
I'M FROM EDUCATIONAL STATION E-1077'S...
ANSWER ...
ANSWER ...
KEITH ...
KEITH ANYAN.
I WOUND UP ANSWERING 1 OF 10 QUESTIONS...
THAT WAS CLOSE.
DANGEROUS ...
YOU ARE DANGEROUS.
I HOPE THEY DON'T KEEP ME HERE UNTIL I LOSE MY MIND.

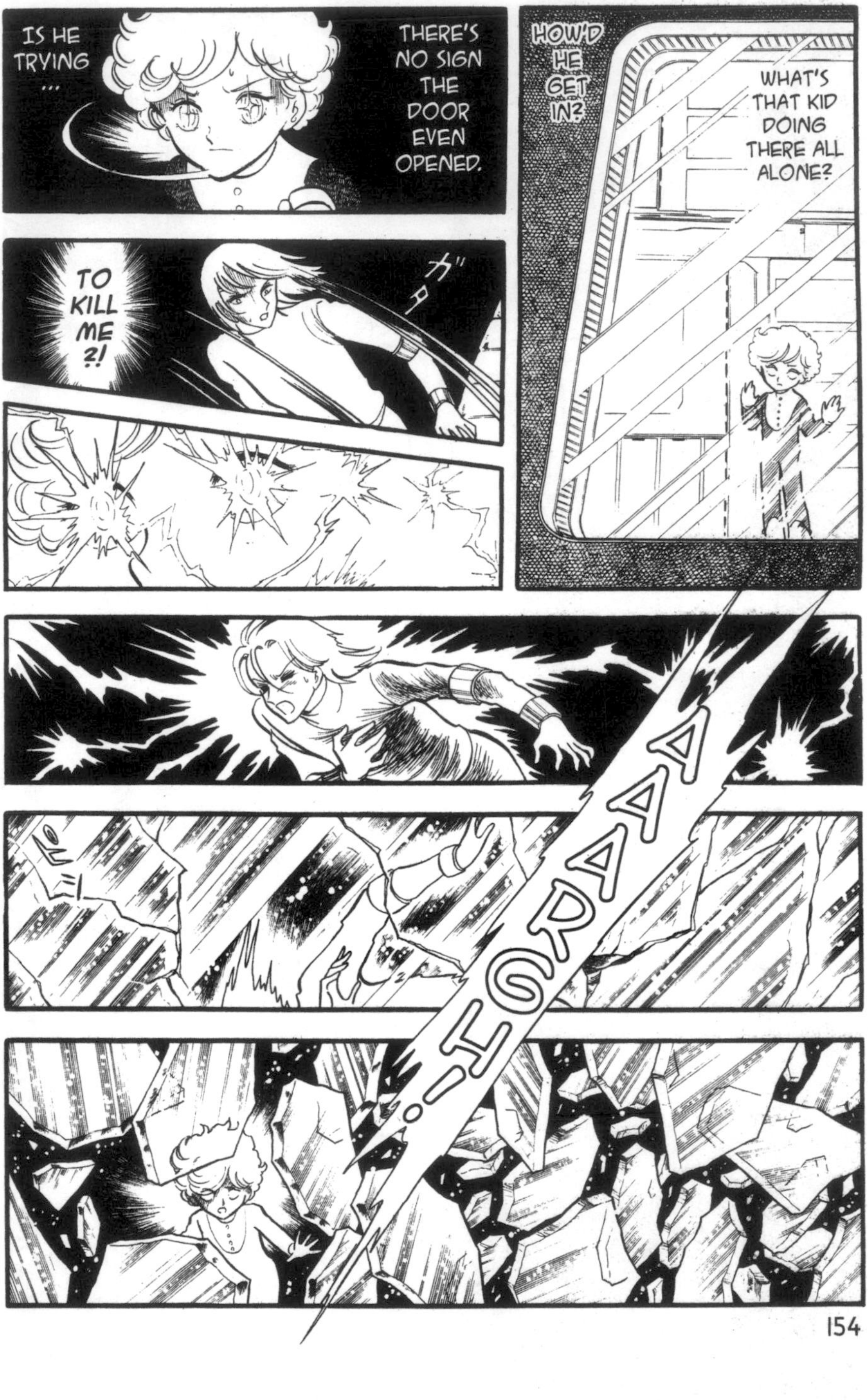
HOW'D HE GET IN?
WHAT'S THAT KID DOING THERE ALL ALONE?
THERE'S NO SIGN THE DOOR EVEN OPENED.
IS HE TRYING ...
TO KILL ME?!
AAARGH-!!

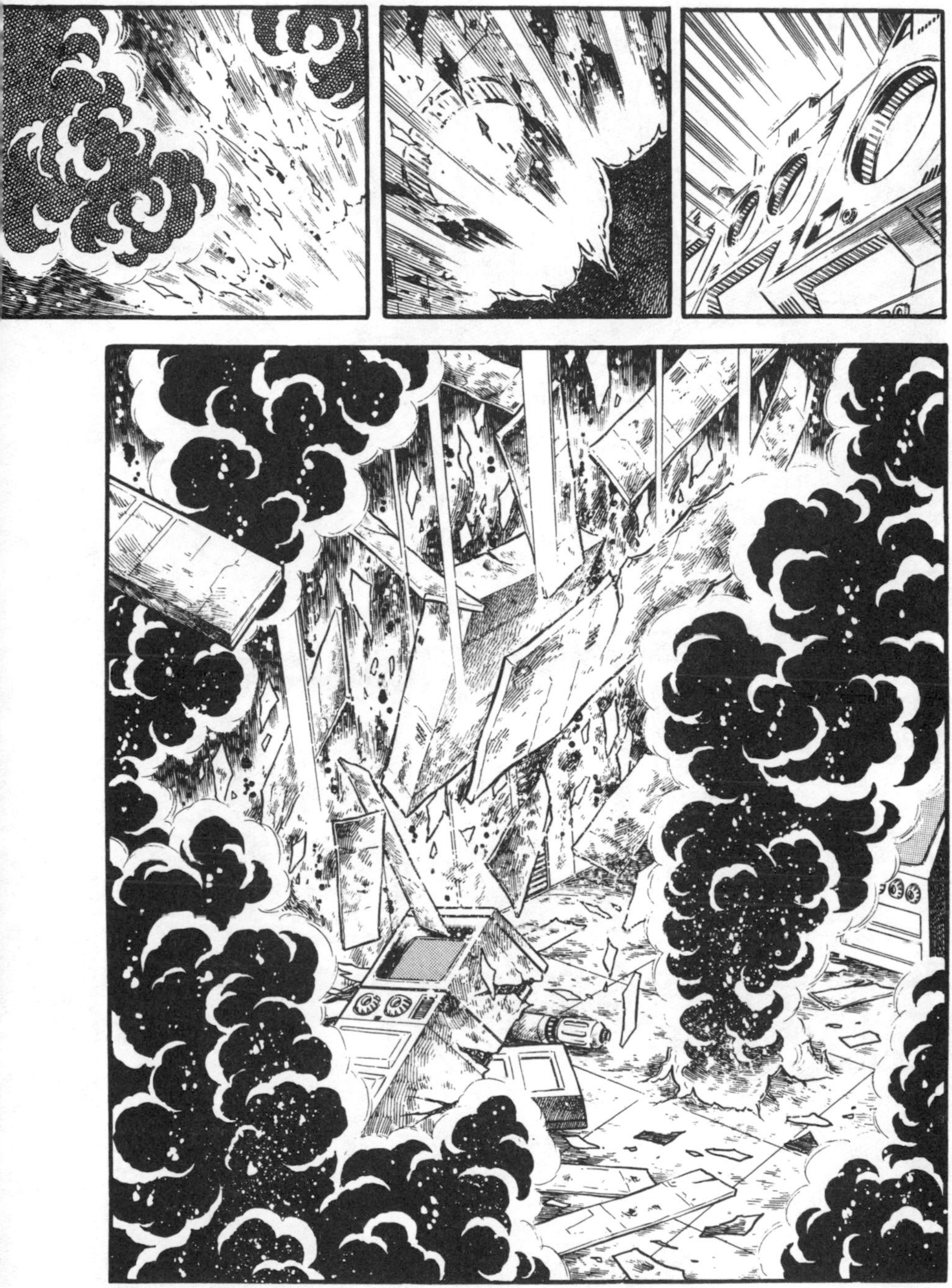

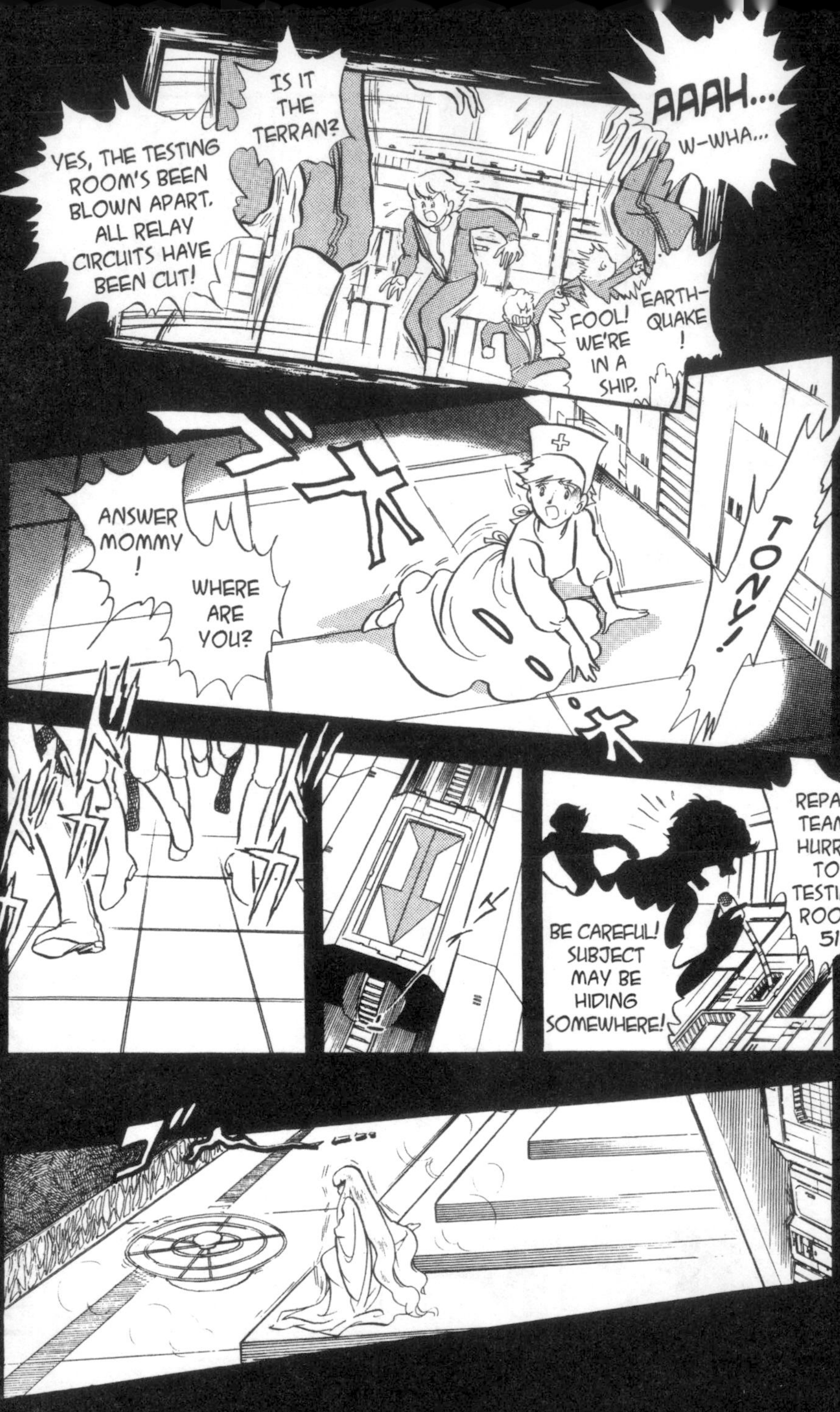
AAAH...
W-WHA...
EARTH-QUAKE!
FOOL! WE'RE IN A SHIP.
IS IT THE TERRAN?
YES, THE TESTING ROOM'S BEEN BLOWN APART. ALL RELAY CIRCUITS HAVE BEEN CUT!
TONY!
ANSWER MOMMY!
WHERE ARE YOU?
REPAIR TEAM, HURRY TO TESTING ROOM 51!
BE CAREFUL! SUBJECT MAY BE HIDING SOMEWHERE!

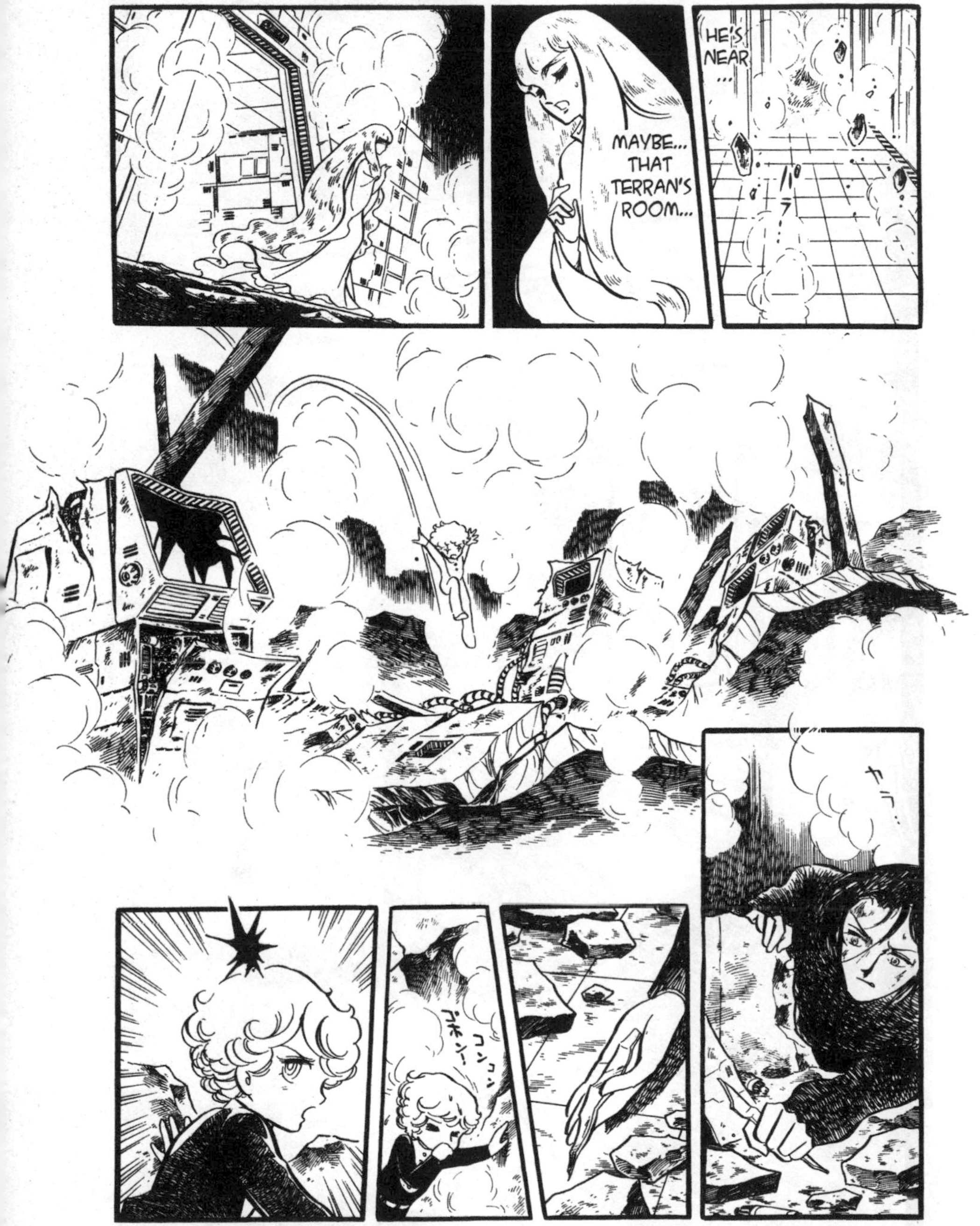
HE'S NEAR ...
MAYBE... THAT TERRAN'S ROOM...

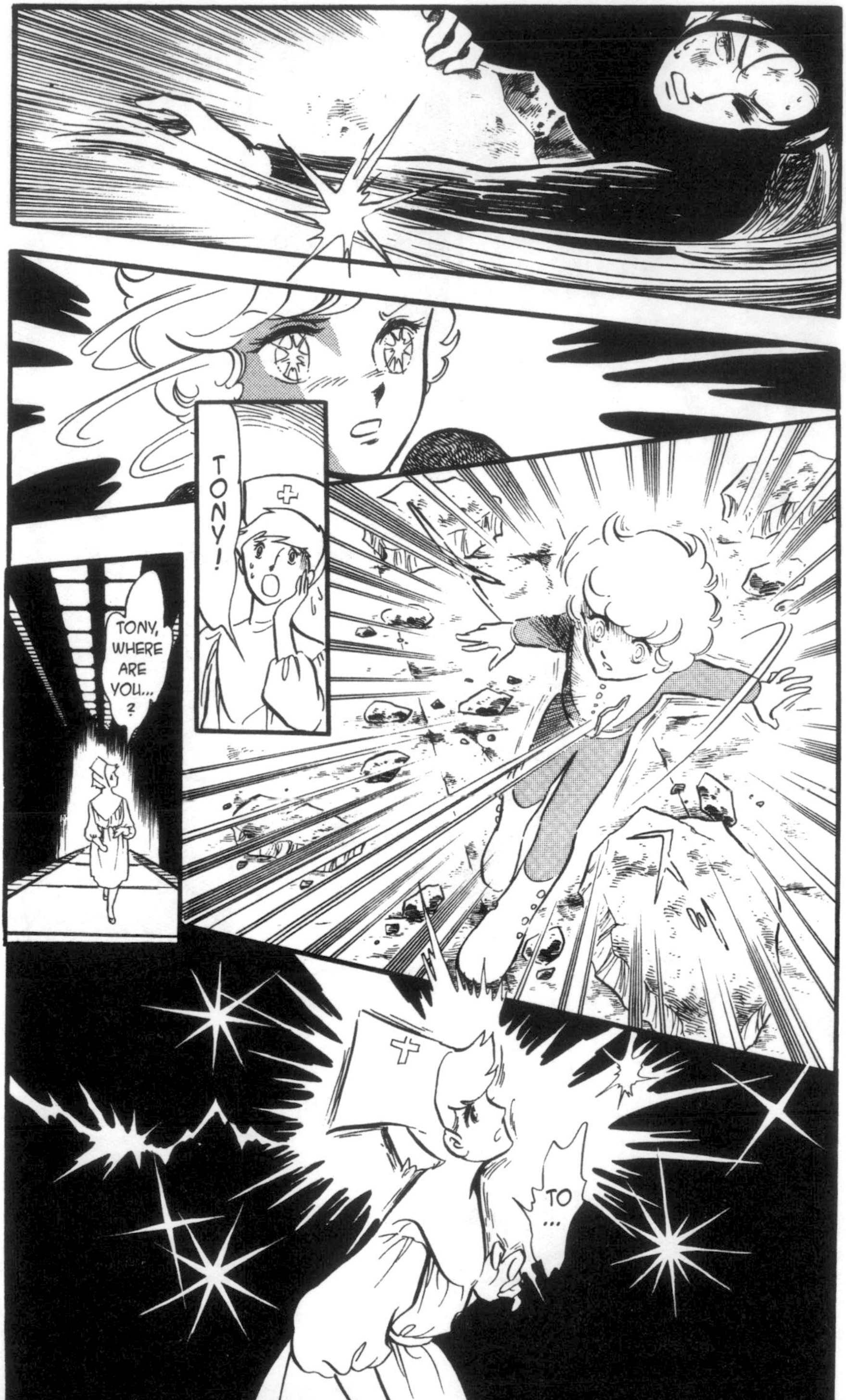
TONY!
TONY, WHERE ARE YOU...?
TO...

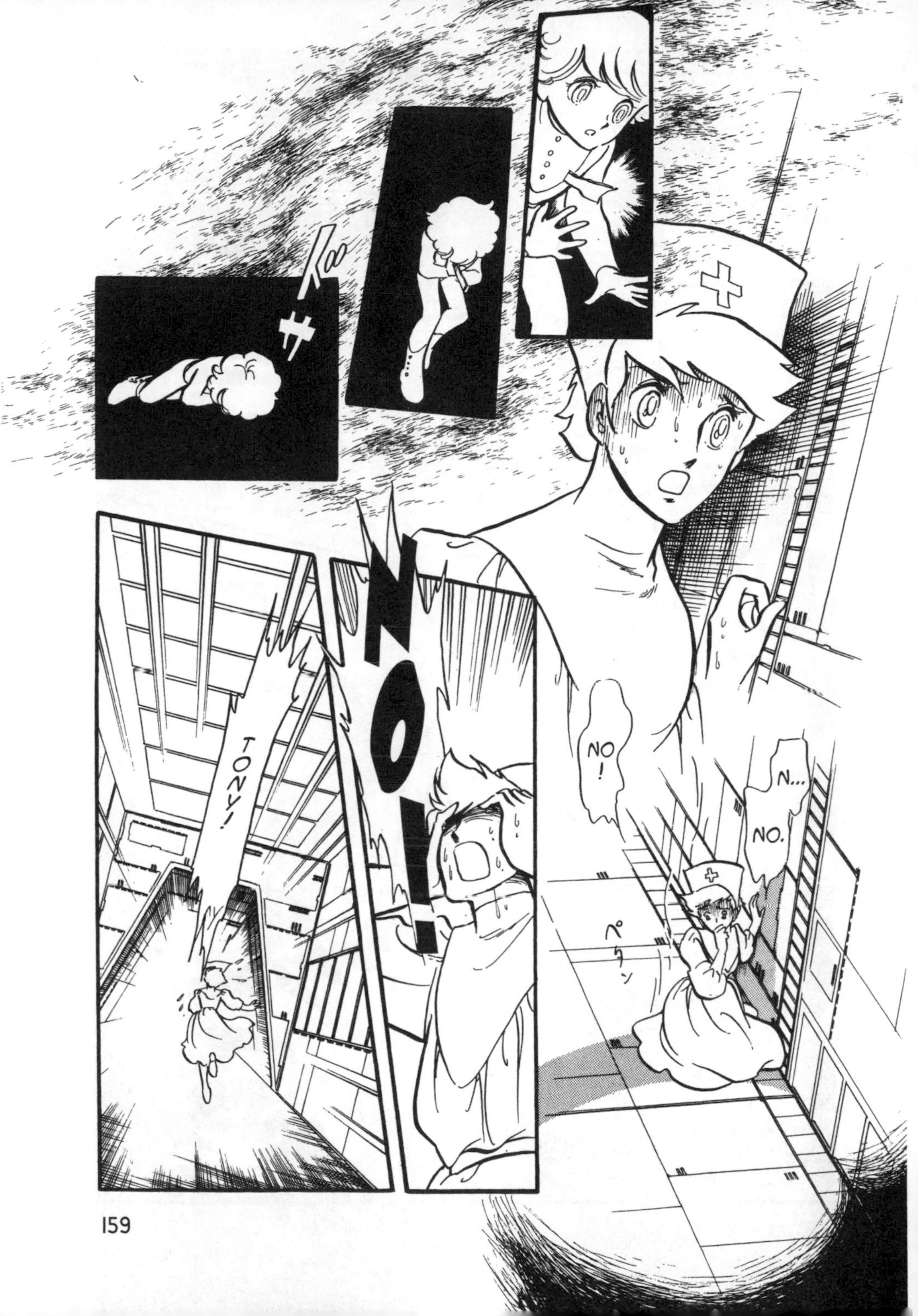
NO!
N...
NO.
ペタン
NO!!
TONY!

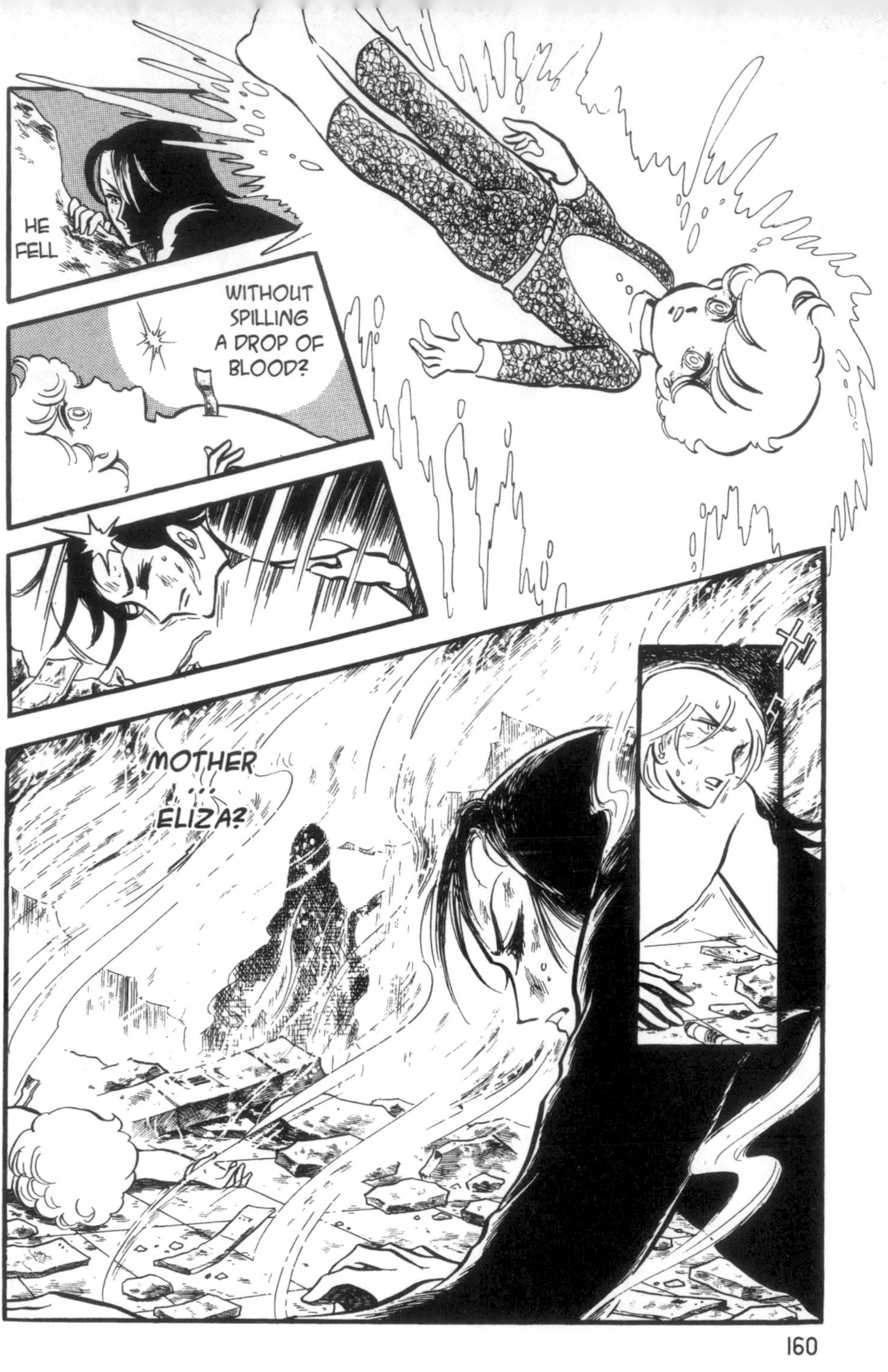
HE FELL
WITHOUT SPILLING A DROP OF BLOOD?
MOTHER ... ELIZA?

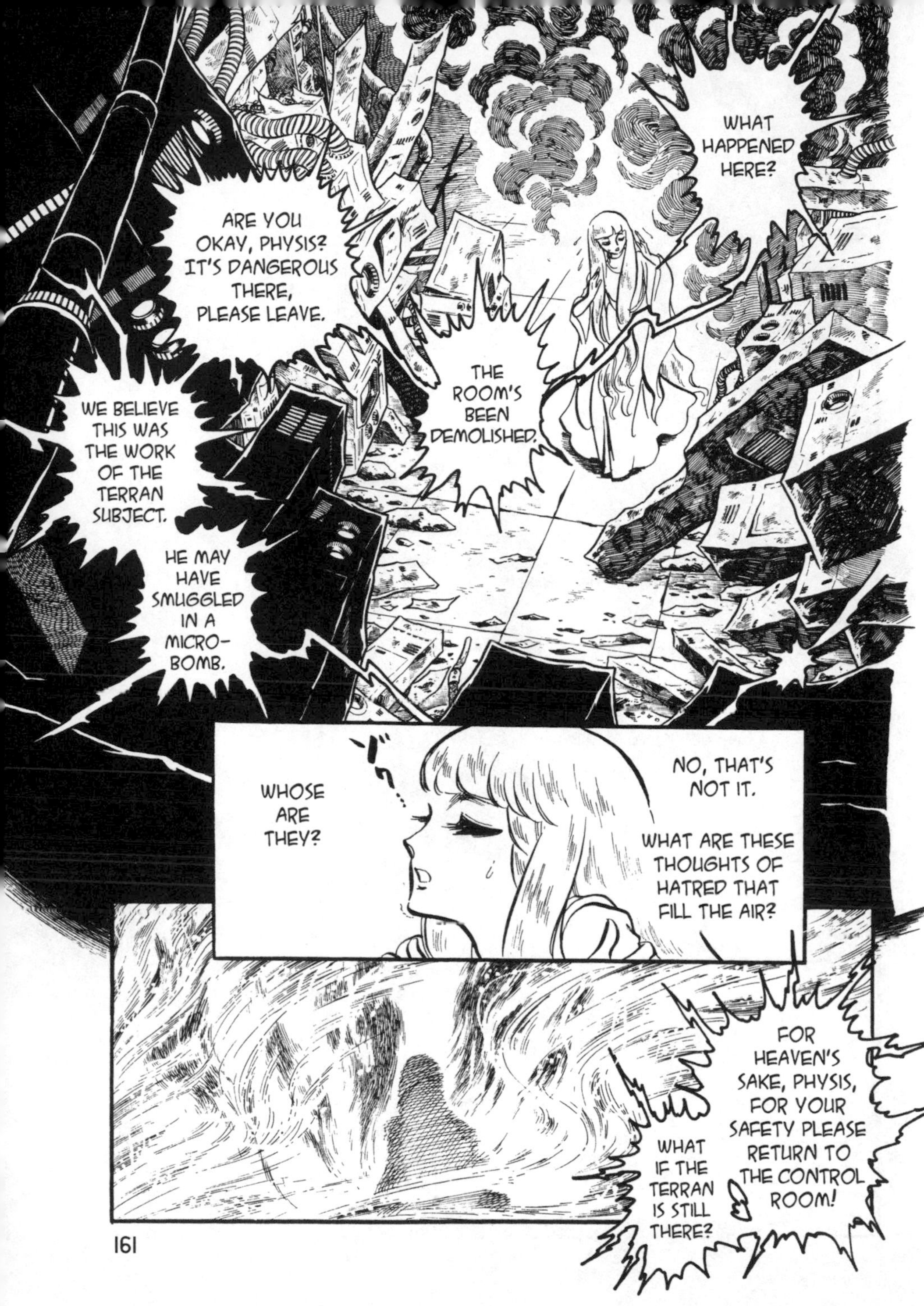
WHAT HAPPENED HERE?
ARE YOU OKAY, PHYSIS? IT'S DANGEROUS THERE, PLEASE LEAVE.
THE ROOM'S BEEN DEMOLISHED.
WE BELIEVE THIS WAS THE WORK OF THE TERRAN SUBJECT.
HE MAY HAVE SMUGGLED IN A MICRO-BOMB.
NO, THAT'S NOT IT.
WHAT ARE THESE THOUGHTS OF HATRED THAT FILL THE AIR?
WHOSE ARE THEY?
FOR HEAVEN'S SAKE, PHYSIS, FOR YOUR SAFETY PLEASE RETURN TO THE CONTROL ROOM!
WHAT IF THE TERRAN IS STILL THERE?

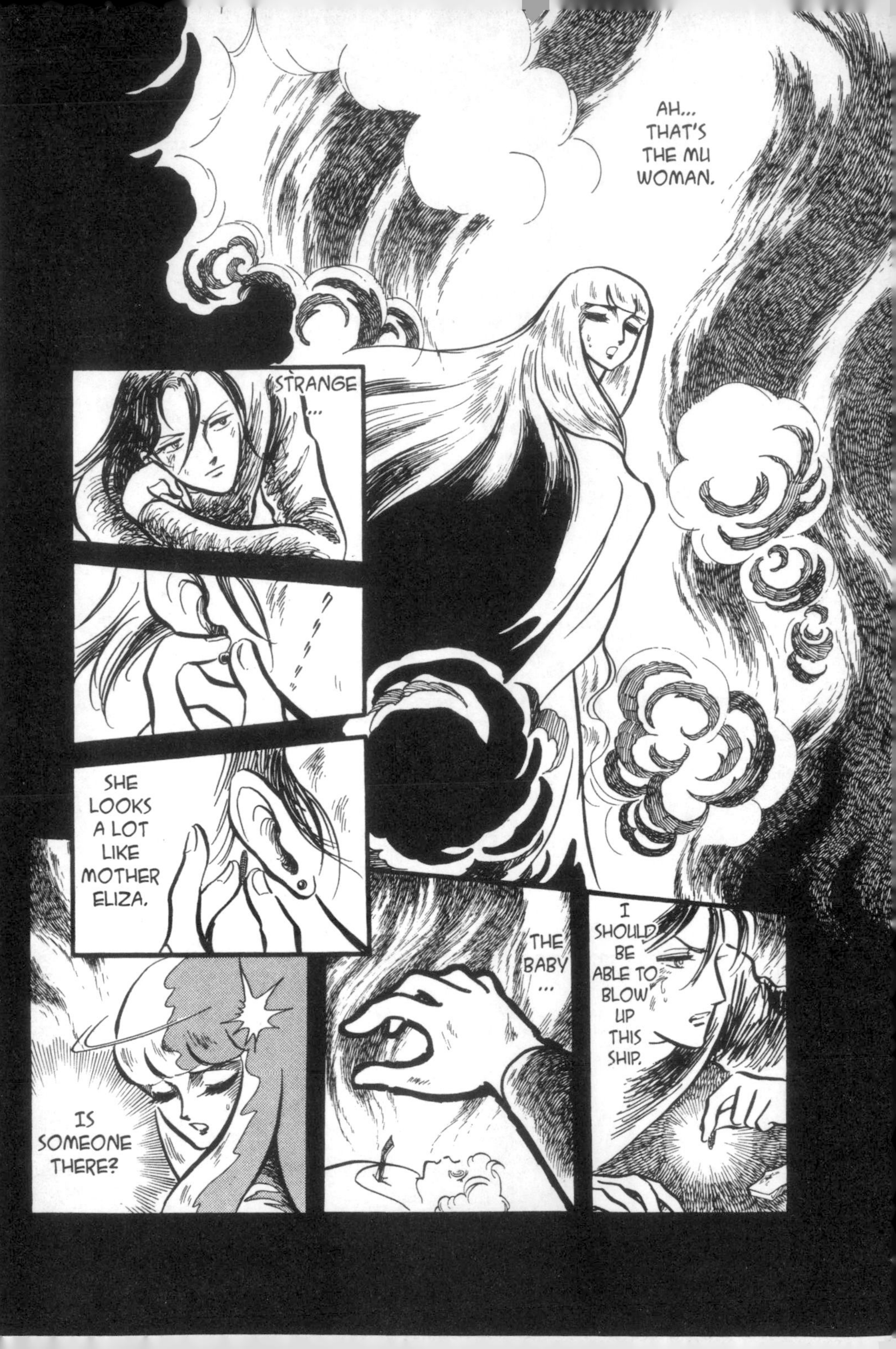
AH... THAT'S THE MU WOMAN.
STRANGE ...
SHE LOOKS A LOT LIKE MOTHER ELIZA.
I SHOULD BE ABLE TO BLOW UP THIS SHIP.
THE BABY ...
IS SOMEONE THERE?

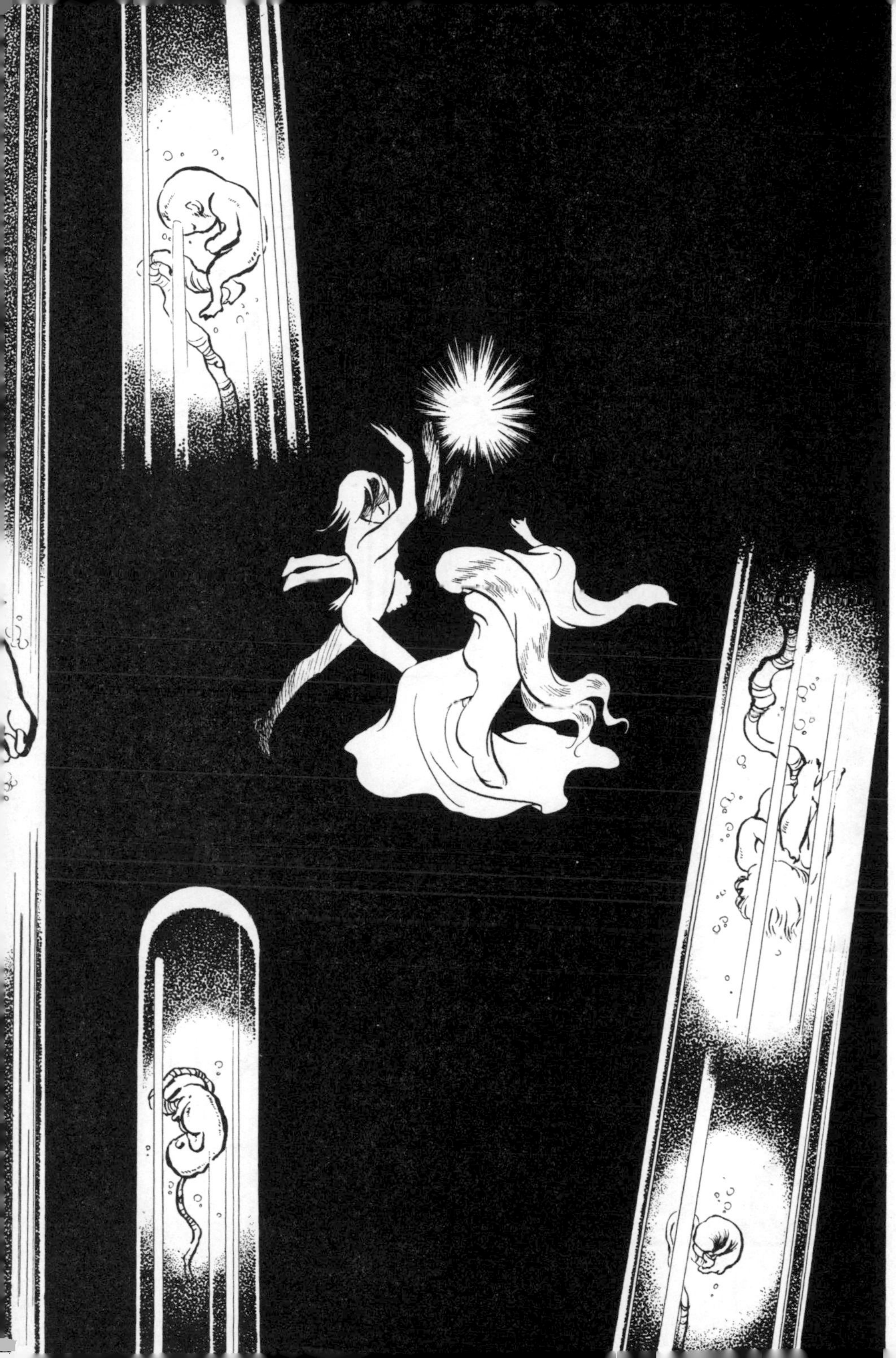

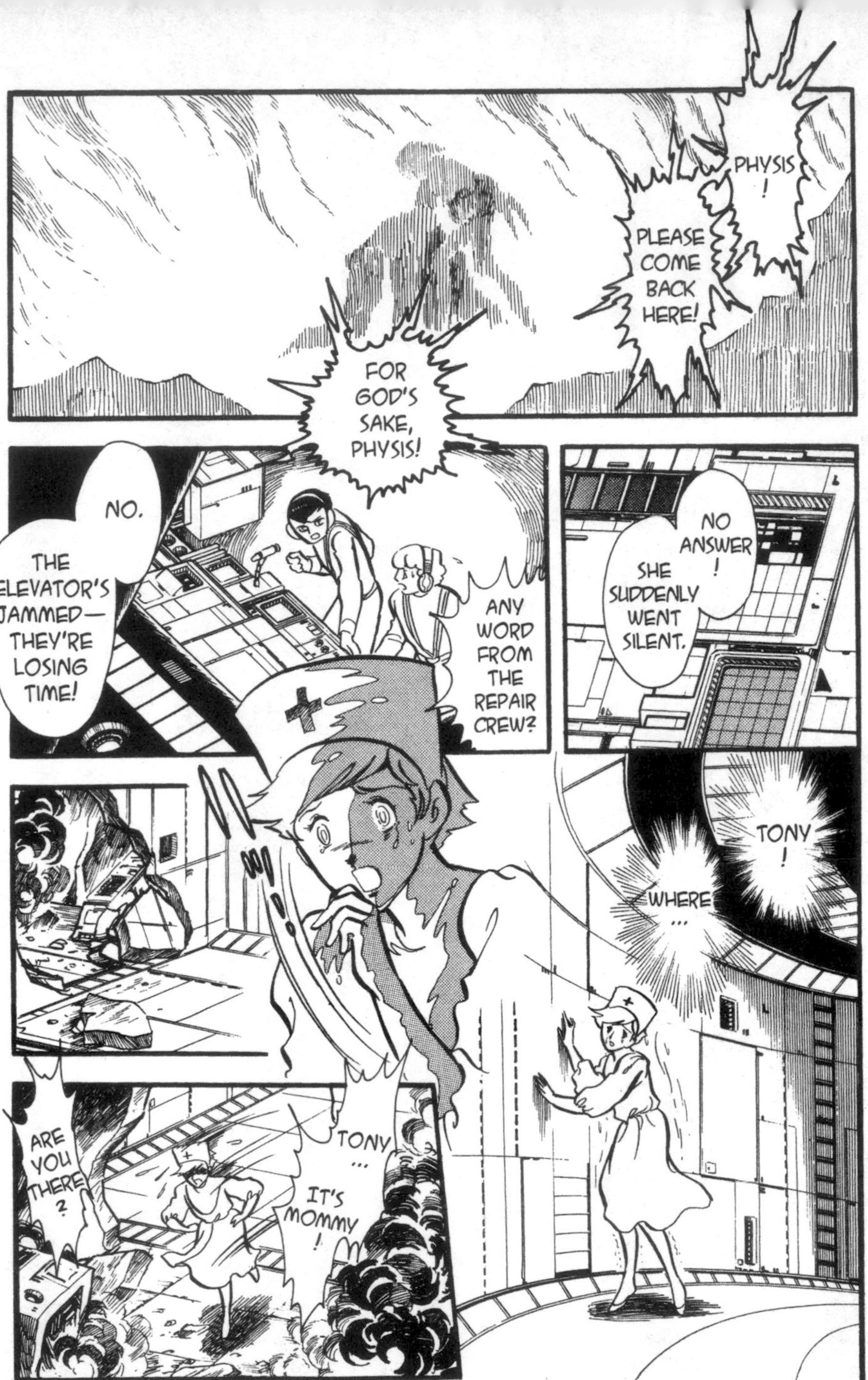
PHYSIS!
PLEASE COME BACK HERE!
FOR GOD'S SAKE, PHYSIS!
NO ANSWER!
SHE SUDDENLY WENT SILENT.
ANY WORD FROM THE REPAIR CREW?
NO.
THE ELEVATOR'S JAMMED— THEY'RE LOSING TIME!
TONY!
WHERE...
TONY... IT'S MOMMY!
ARE YOU THERE?

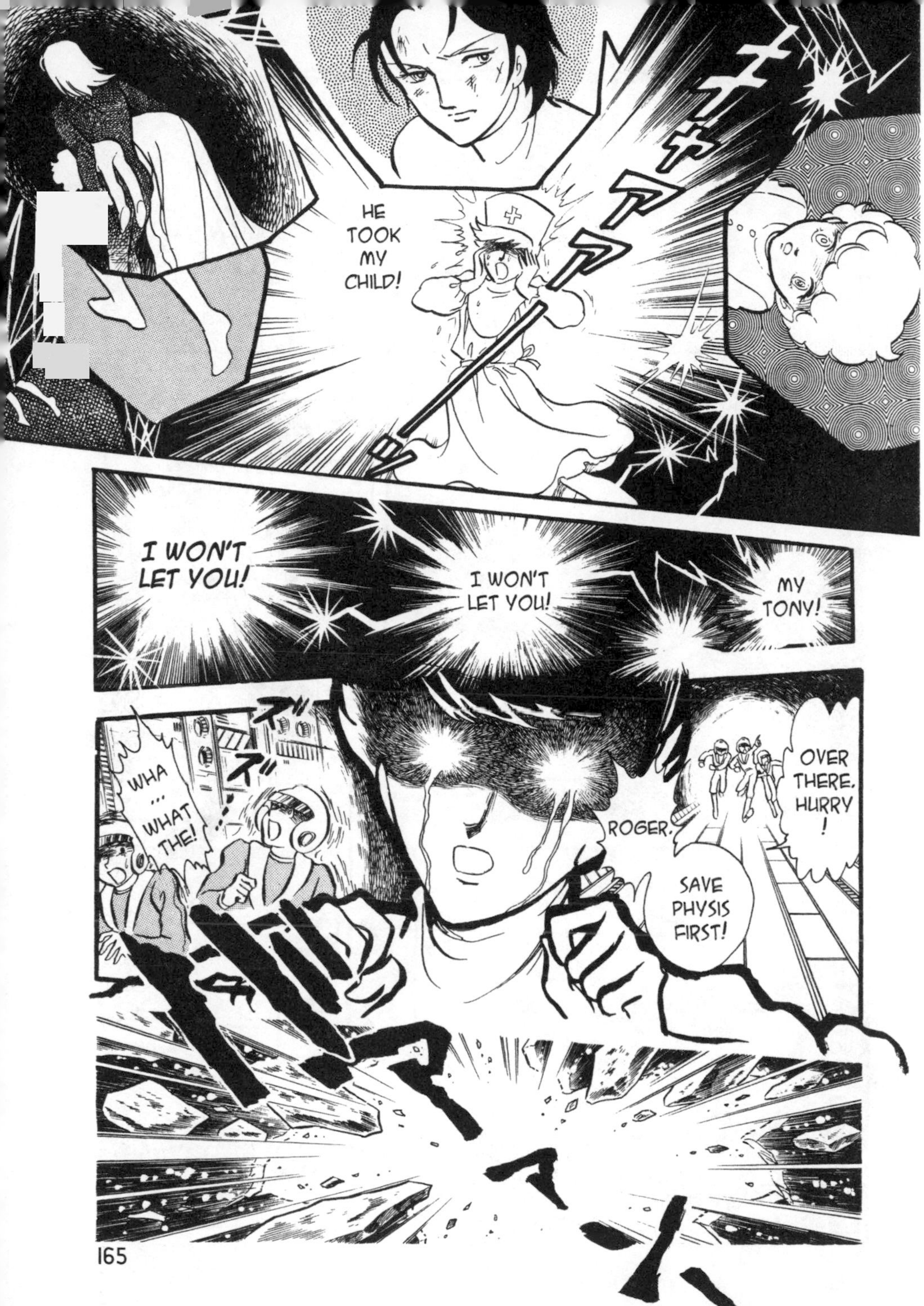
HE TOOK MY CHILD!
MY TONY!
I WON'T LET YOU!
I WON'T LET YOU!
OVER THERE, HURRY!
ROGER.
SAVE PHYSIS FIRST!
WHA... WHAT THE!

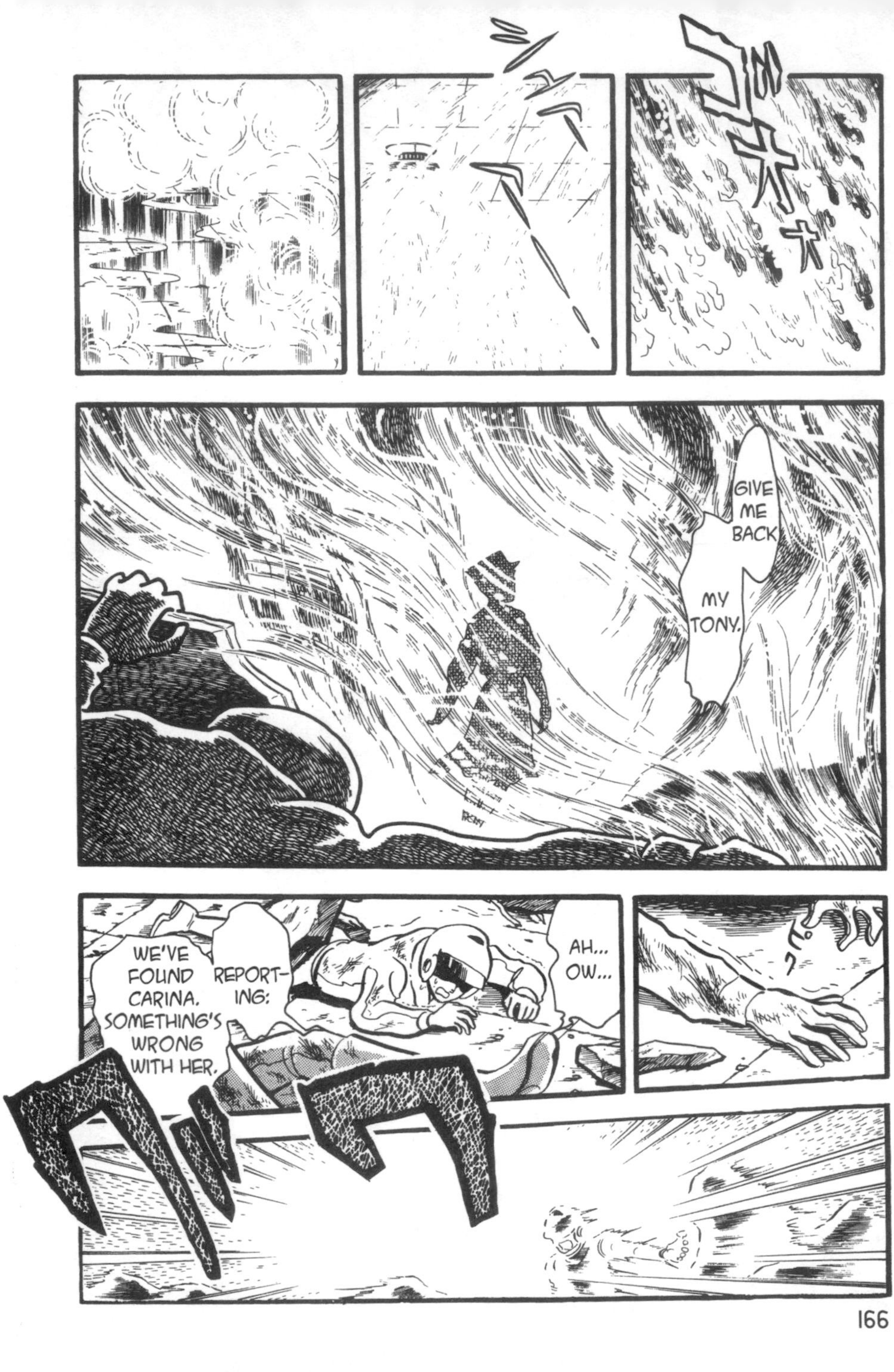

GIVE ME BACK
MY TONY.
AH... OW...
REPORT-ING:
WE'VE FOUND CARINA. SOMETHING'S WRONG WITH HER.

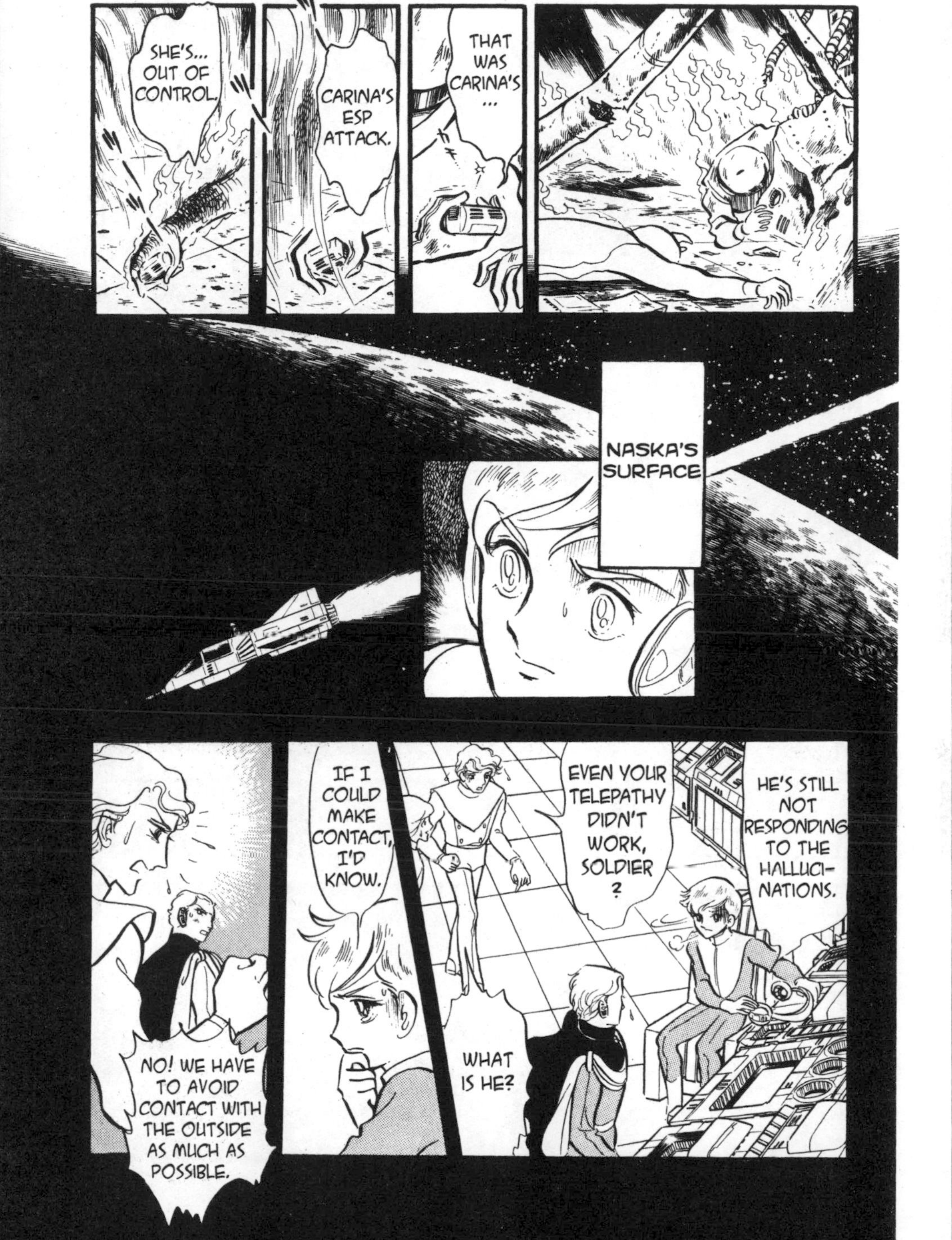
THAT WAS CARINA'S ...
CARINA'S ESP ATTACK.
SHE'S... OUT OF CONTROL.
NASKA'S SURFACE
HE'S STILL NOT RESPONDING TO THE HALLUCI-NATIONS.
EVEN YOUR TELEPATHY DIDN'T WORK, SOLDIER?
WHAT IS HE?
IF I COULD MAKE CONTACT, I'D KNOW.
NO! WE HAVE TO AVOID CONTACT WITH THE OUTSIDE AS MUCH AS POSSIBLE.

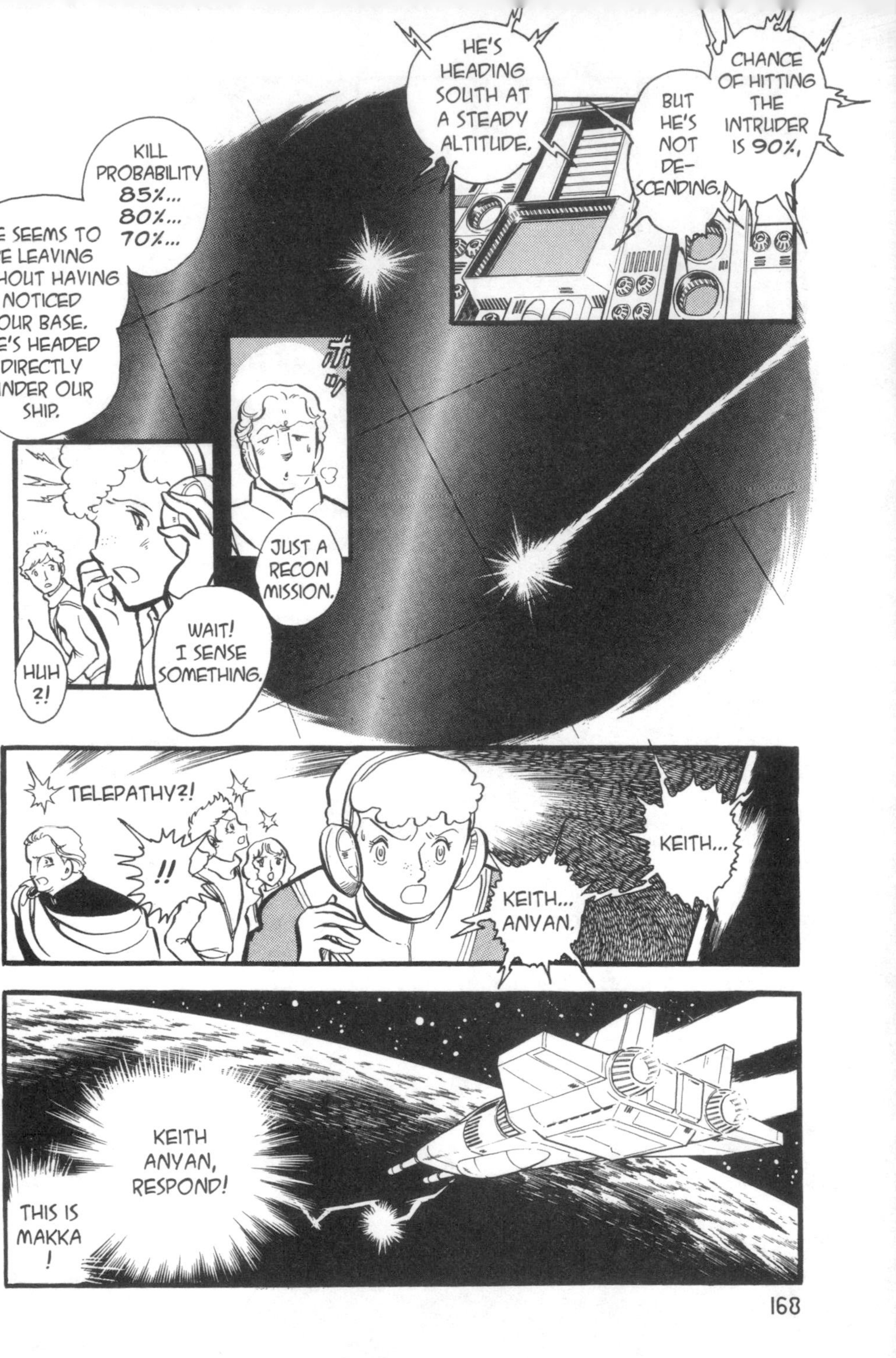
CHANCE OF HITTING THE INTRUDER IS 90%,
BUT HE'S NOT DE-SCENDING.
HE'S HEADING SOUTH AT A STEADY ALTITUDE.
KILL PROBABILITY 85%... 80%... 70%...
HE SEEMS TO BE LEAVING WITHOUT HAVING NOTICED OUR BASE. HE'S HEADED DIRECTLY UNDER OUR SHIP.
JUST A RECON MISSION.
WAIT! I SENSE SOMETHING.
HUH?!
KEITH...
KEITH... ANYAN.
!!
TELEPATHY?!
KEITH ANYAN, RESPOND!
THIS IS MAKKA!

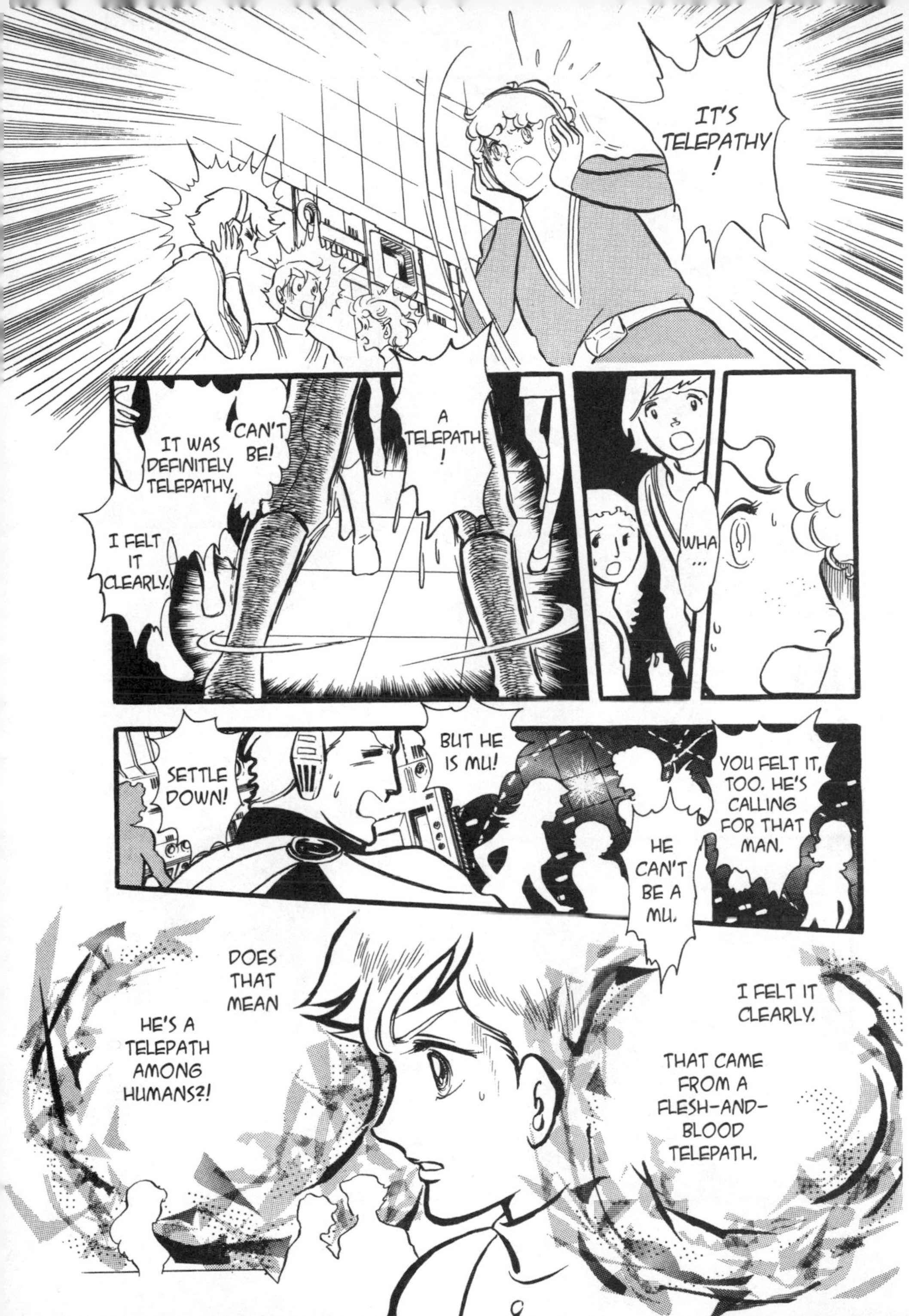
IT'S TELEPATHY!
WHA...
A TELEPATH!
CAN'T BE!
IT WAS DEFINITELY TELEPATHY.
I FELT IT CLEARLY.
YOU FELT IT, TOO. HE'S CALLING FOR THAT MAN.
HE CAN'T BE A MU.
BUT HE IS MU!
SETTLE DOWN!
I FELT IT CLEARLY.
THAT CAME FROM A FLESH-AND-BLOOD TELEPATH.
DOES THAT MEAN
HE'S A TELEPATH AMONG HUMANS?!

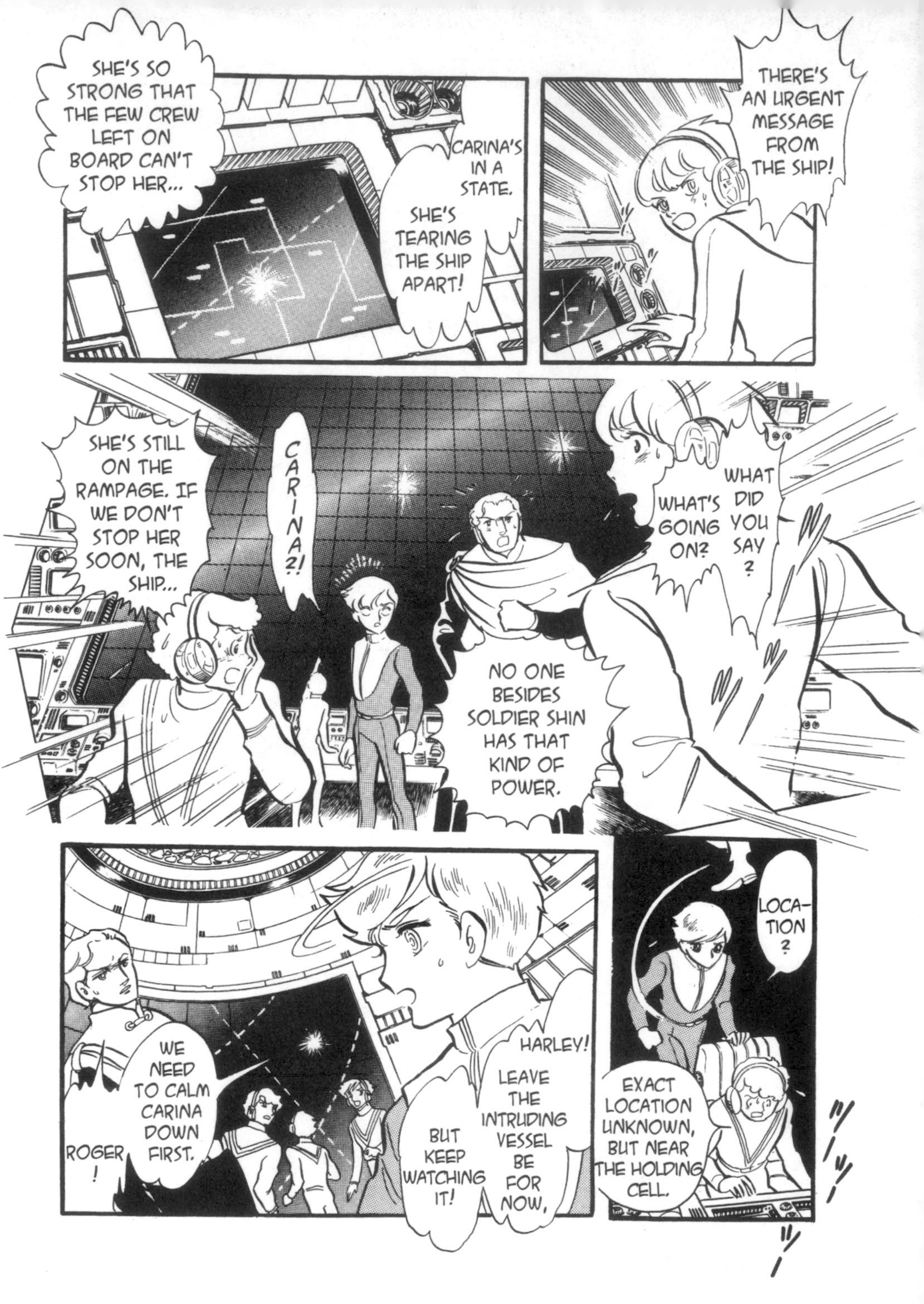
THERE'S AN URGENT MESSAGE FROM THE SHIP!
CARINA'S IN A STATE.
SHE'S TEARING THE SHIP APART!
SHE'S SO STRONG THAT THE FEW CREW LEFT ON BOARD CAN'T STOP HER...
WHAT DID YOU SAY?
WHAT'S GOING ON?
CARINA?!
SHE'S STILL ON THE RAMPAGE. IF WE DON'T STOP HER SOON, THE SHIP...
NO ONE BESIDES SOLDIER SHIN HAS THAT KIND OF POWER.
LOCATION?
EXACT LOCATION UNKNOWN, BUT NEAR THE HOLDING CELL.
HARLEY!
LEAVE THE INTRUDING VESSEL BE FOR NOW.
BUT KEEP WATCHING IT!
WE NEED TO CALM CARINA DOWN FIRST.
ROGER!

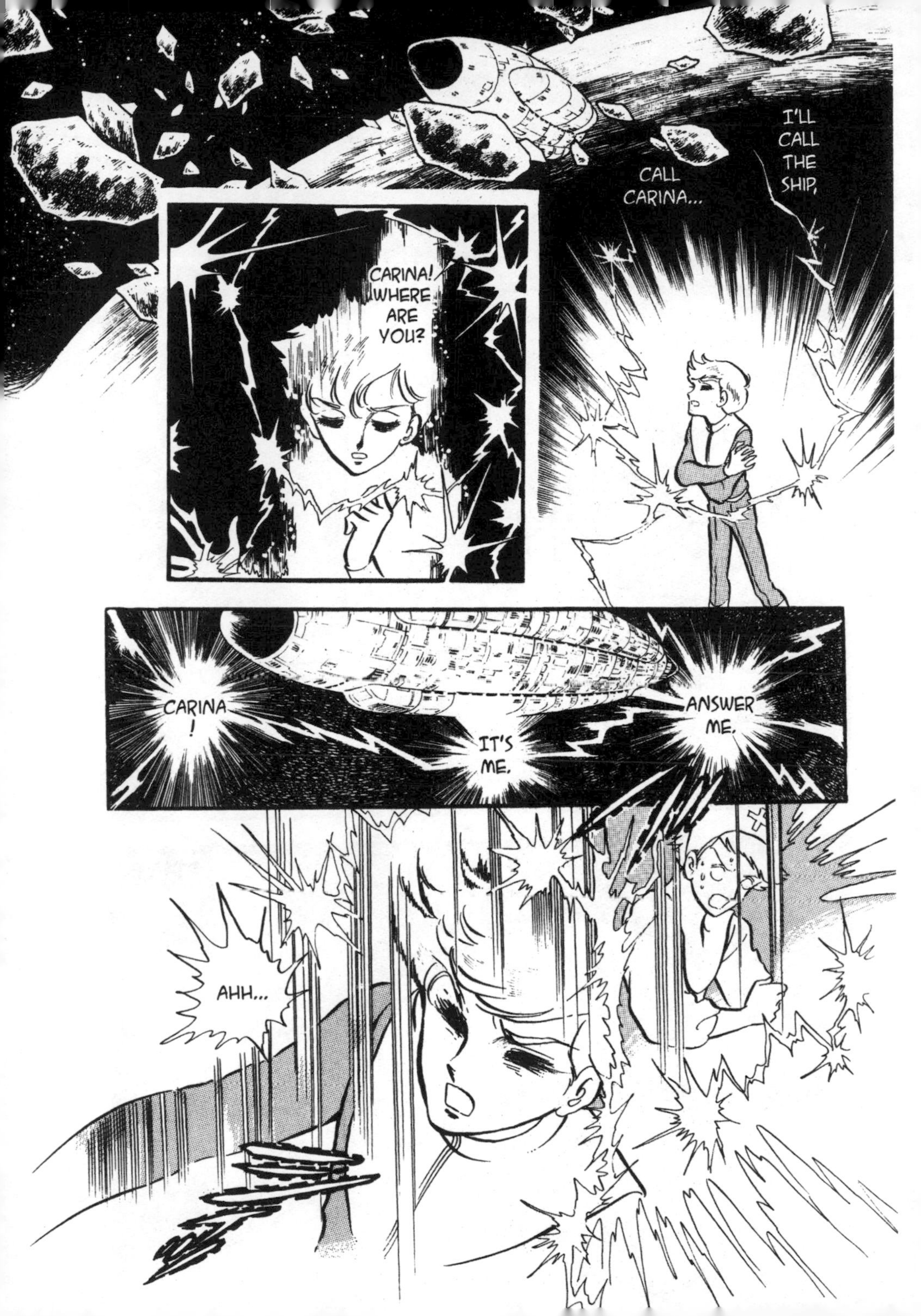
I'LL CALL THE SHIP.
CALL CARINA...
CARINA! WHERE ARE YOU?
ANSWER ME.
IT'S ME.
CARINA!
AHH...

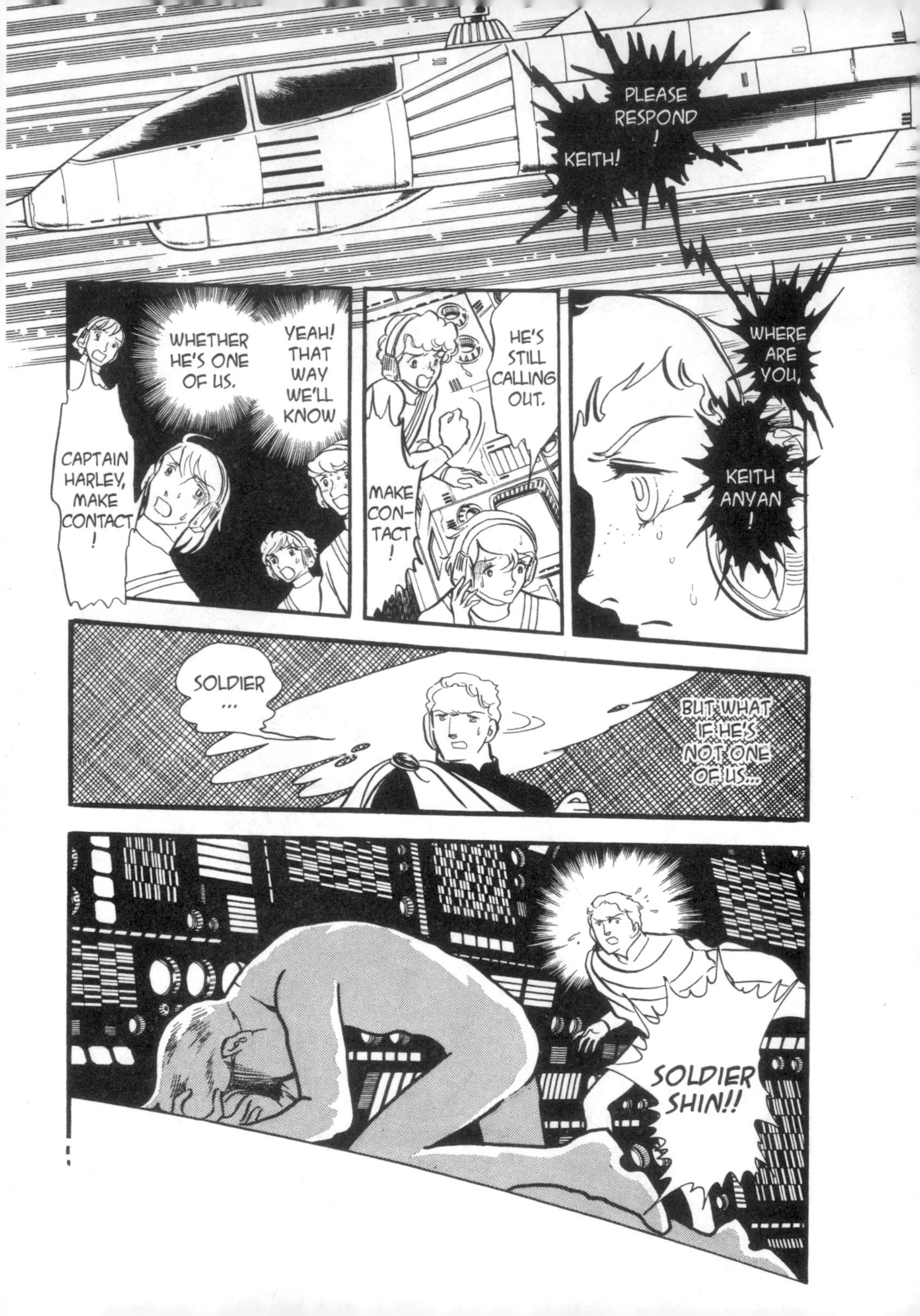
PLEASE RESPOND! KEITH!
WHERE ARE YOU,
KEITH ANYAN!
HE'S STILL CALLING OUT.
MAKE CONTACT!
YEAH! THAT WAY WE'LL KNOW
WHETHER HE'S ONE OF US.
CAPTAIN HARLEY, MAKE CONTACT!
BUT WHAT IF HE'S NOT ONE OF US...
SOLDIER ...
SOLDIER SHIN!!

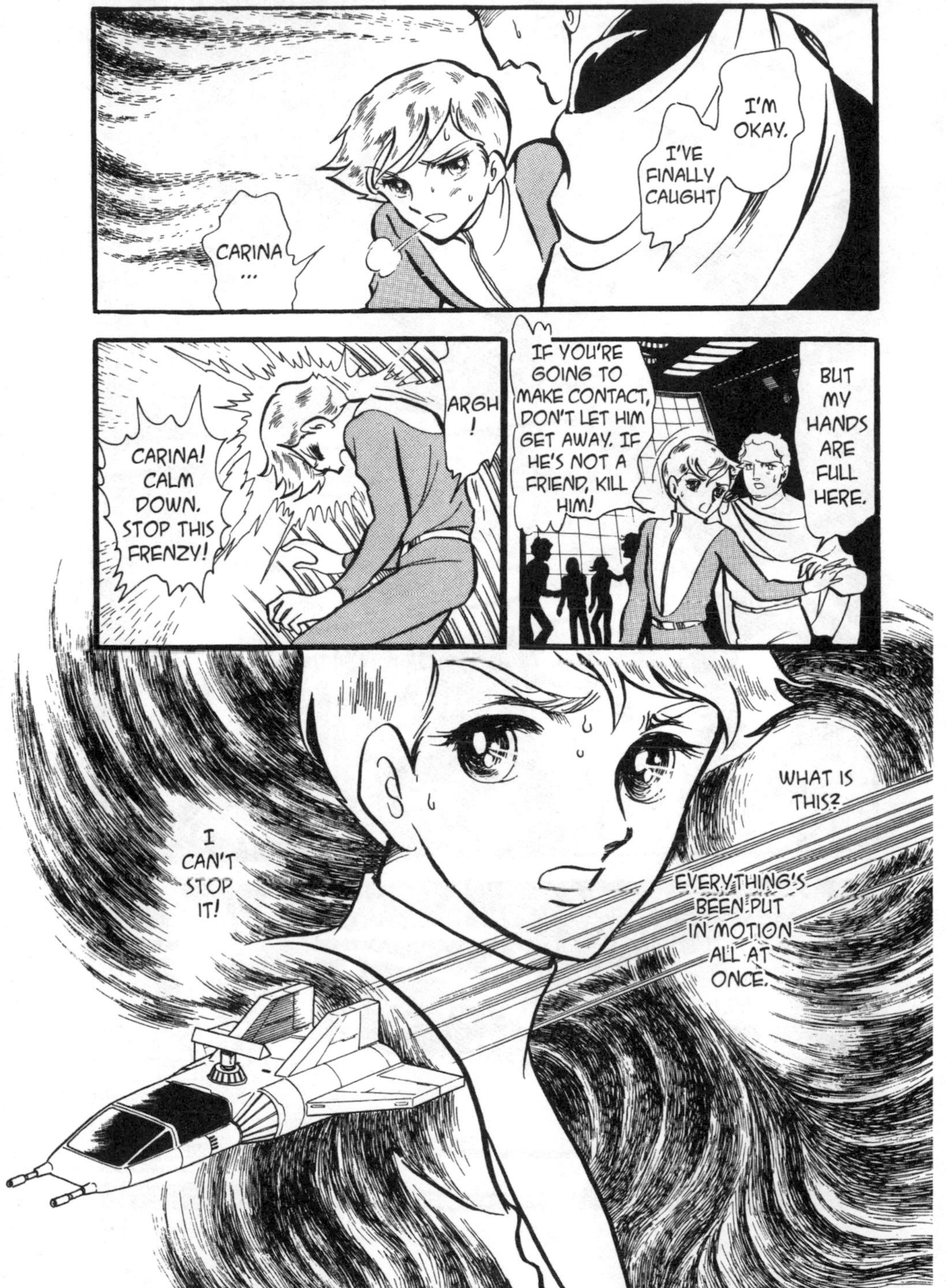
I'M OKAY.
I'VE FINALLY CAUGHT
CARINA ...
IF YOU'RE GOING TO MAKE CONTACT, DON'T LET HIM GET AWAY. IF HE'S NOT A FRIEND, KILL HIM!
BUT MY HANDS ARE FULL HERE.
ARGH!
CARINA! CALM DOWN. STOP THIS FRENZY!
WHAT IS THIS?
EVERYTHING'S BEEN PUT IN MOTION ALL AT ONCE.
I CAN'T STOP IT!

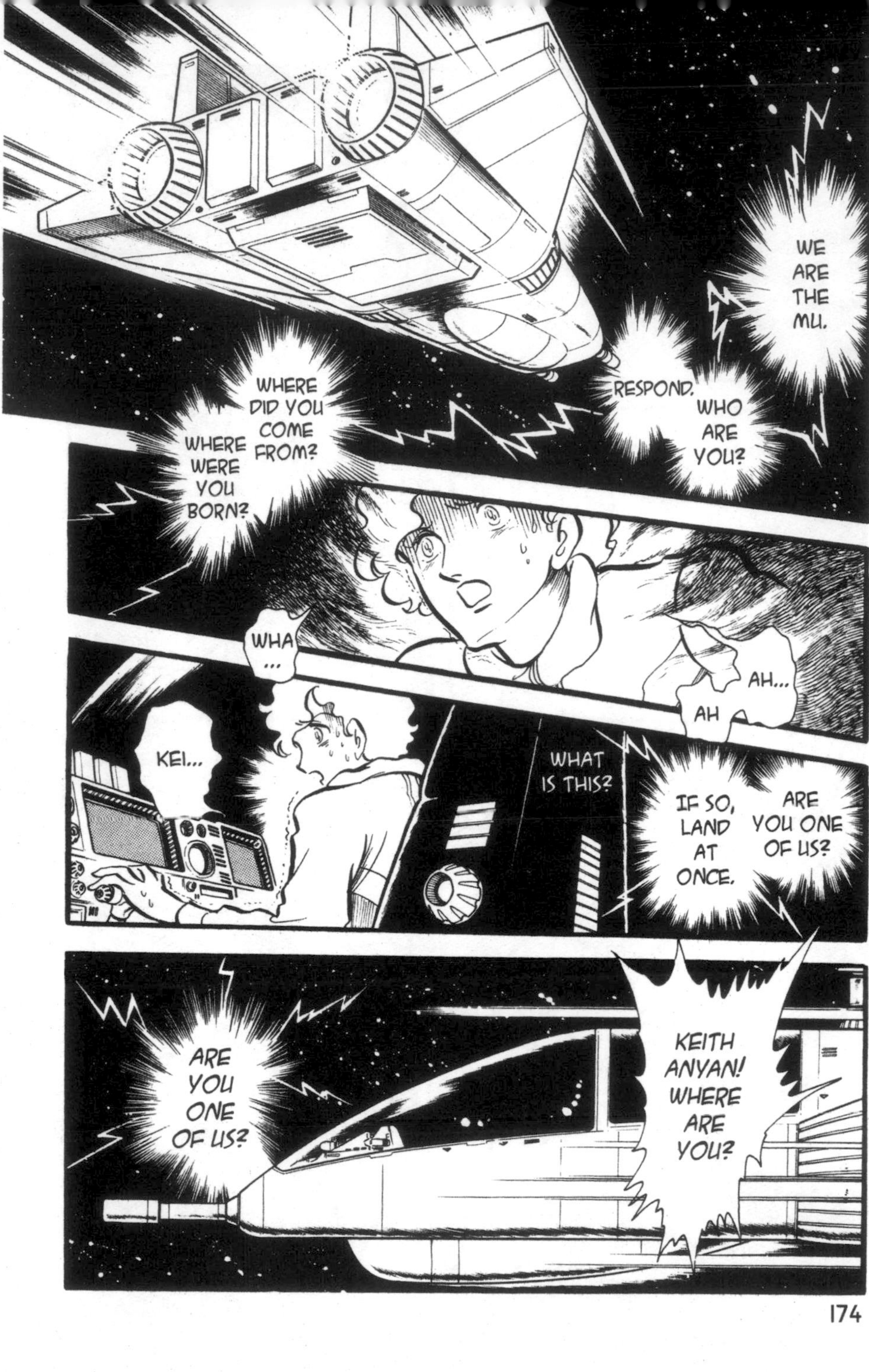
WE ARE THE MU.
RESPOND. WHO ARE YOU?
WHERE DID YOU COME FROM?
WHERE WERE YOU BORN?
AH...
AH
WHA...
ARE YOU ONE OF US?
IF SO, LAND AT ONCE.
WHAT IS THIS?
KEI...
KEITH ANYAN! WHERE ARE YOU?
ARE YOU ONE OF US?

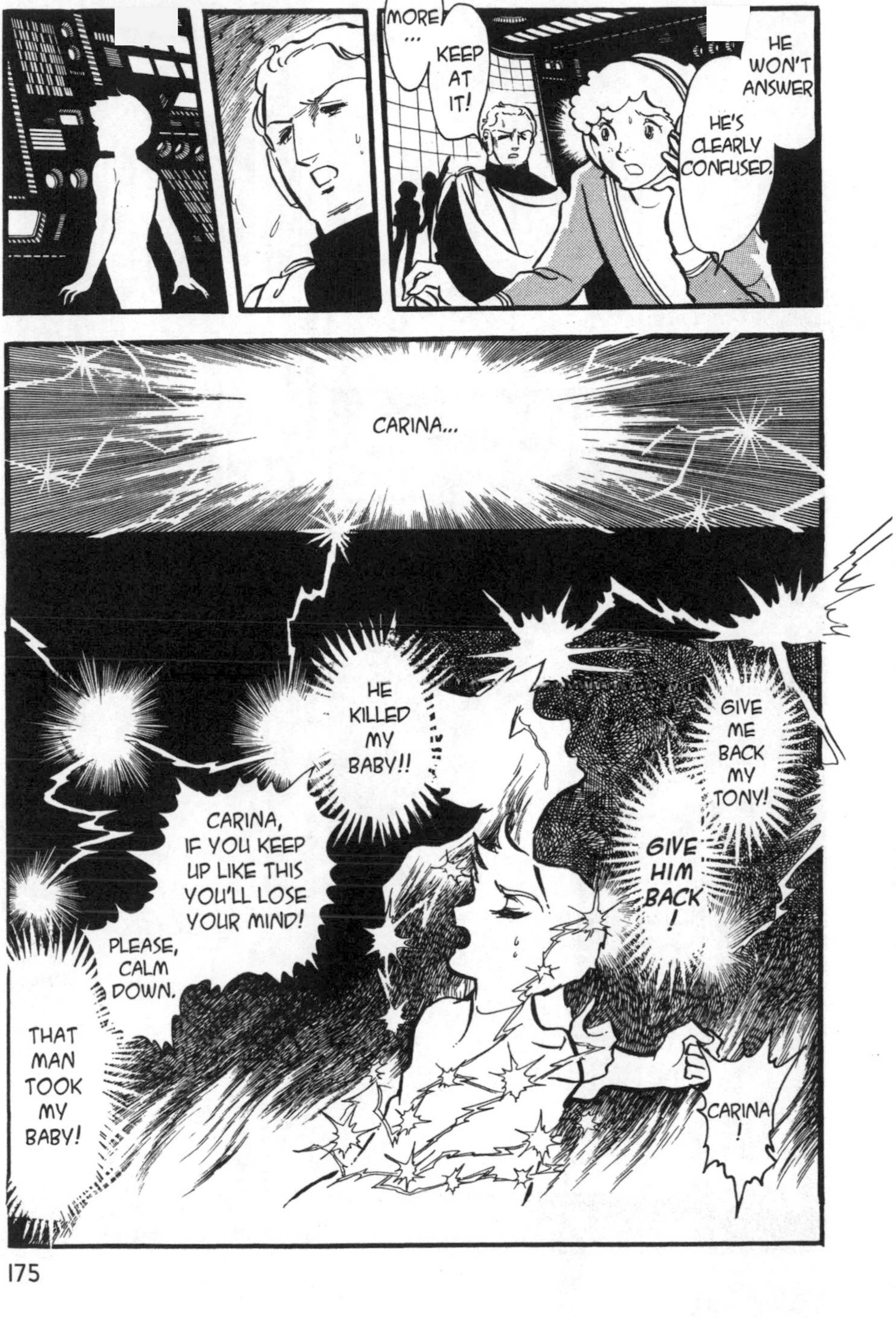
HE WON'T ANSWER
HE'S CLEARLY CONFUSED.
KEEP AT IT!
MORE ...
CARINA...
GIVE ME BACK MY TONY!
GIVE HIM BACK!
HE KILLED MY BABY!!
CARINA, IF YOU KEEP UP LIKE THIS YOU'LL LOSE YOUR MIND!
PLEASE, CALM DOWN.
CARINA!
THAT MAN TOOK MY BABY!

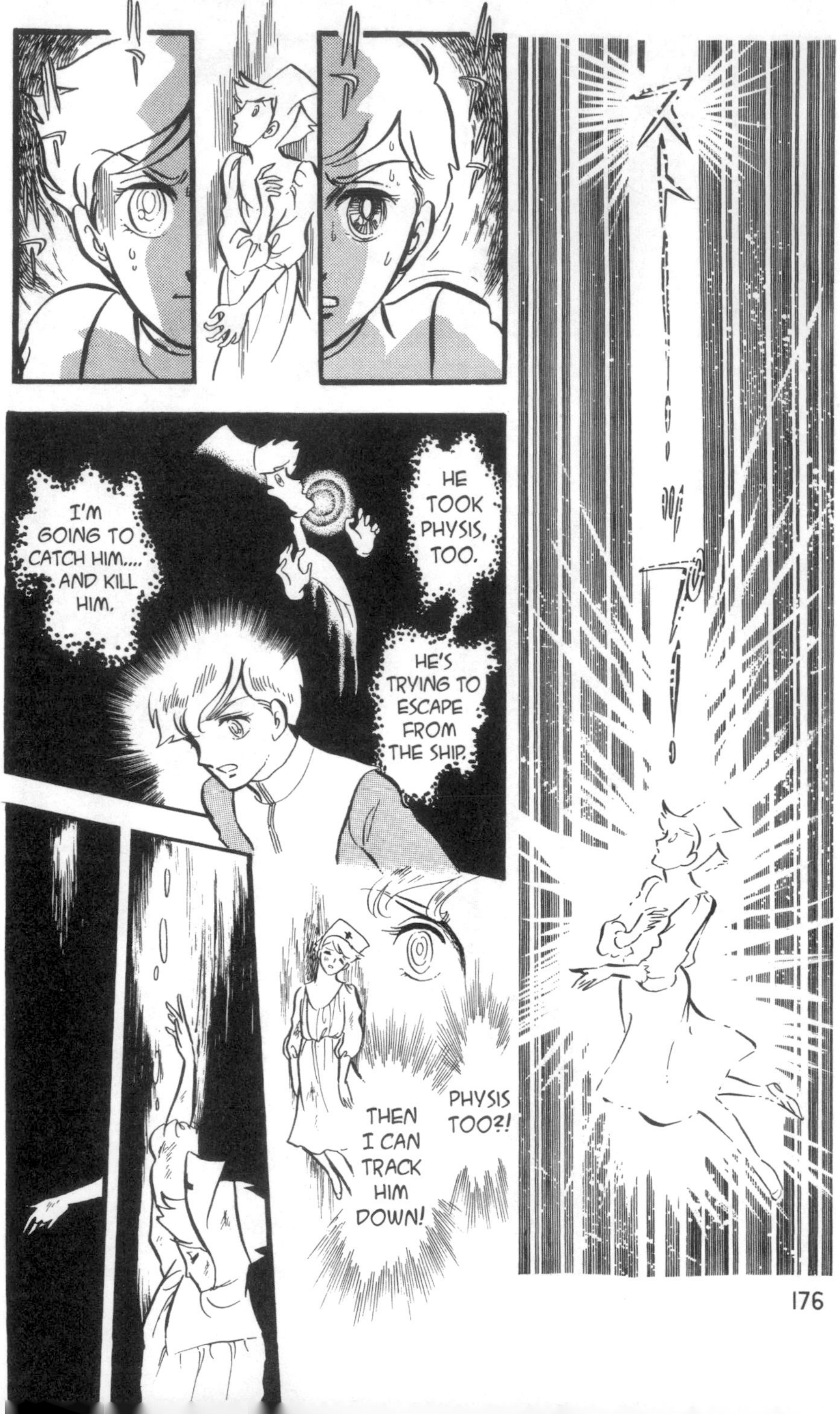
HE TOOK PHYSIS, TOO.
I'M GOING TO CATCH HIM.... AND KILL HIM.
HE'S TRYING TO ESCAPE FROM THE SHIP.
PHYSIS TOO?!
THEN I CAN TRACK HIM DOWN!

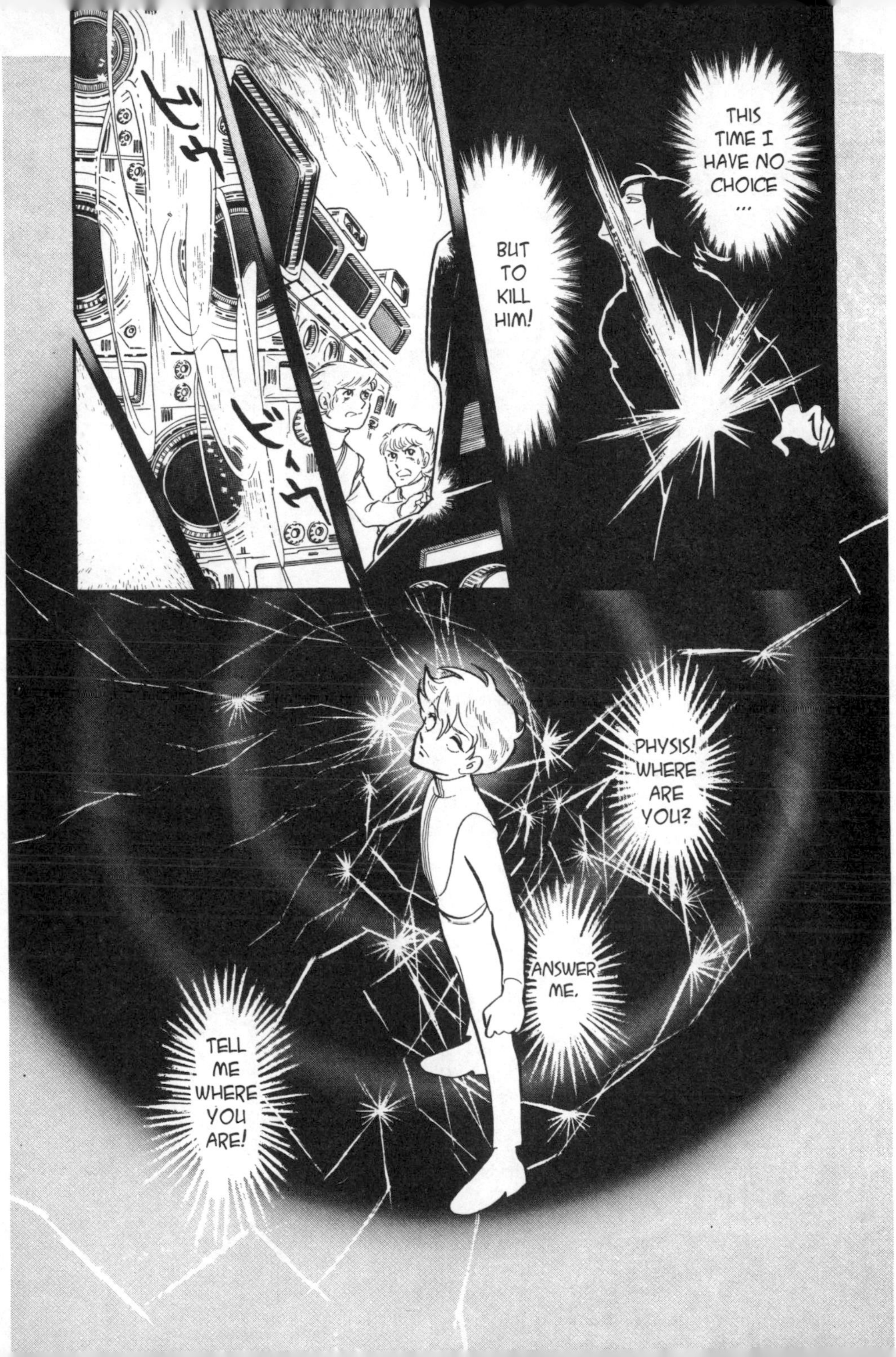
THIS TIME I HAVE NO CHOICE ...
BUT TO KILL HIM!
PHYSIS! WHERE ARE YOU?
ANSWER ME.
TELL ME WHERE YOU ARE!

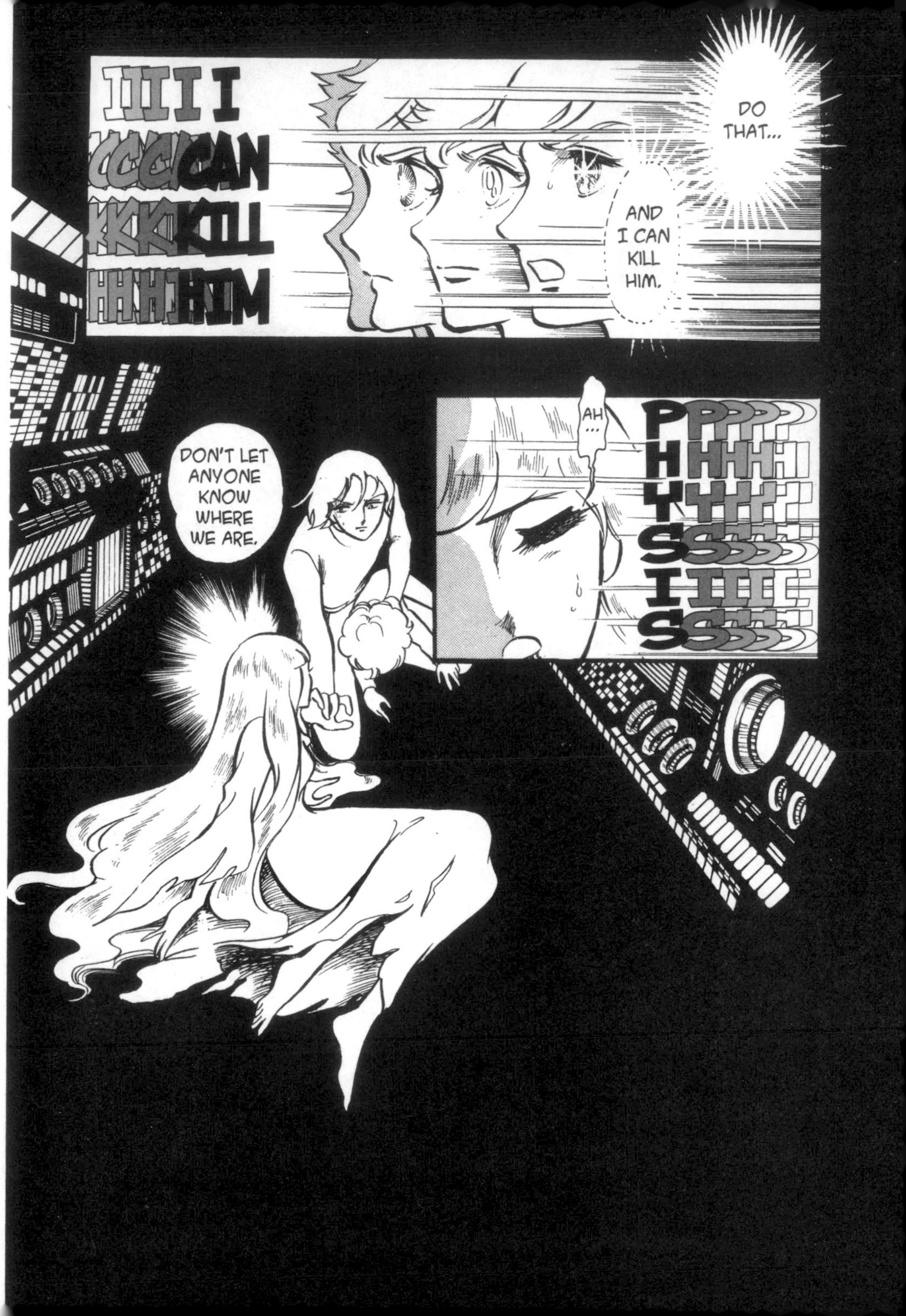
DO THAT...
AND I CAN KILL HIM.
IIII CCCCAN KKKKILL HHHHIM
AH...
PHYSIS
DON'T LET ANYONE KNOW WHERE WE ARE.

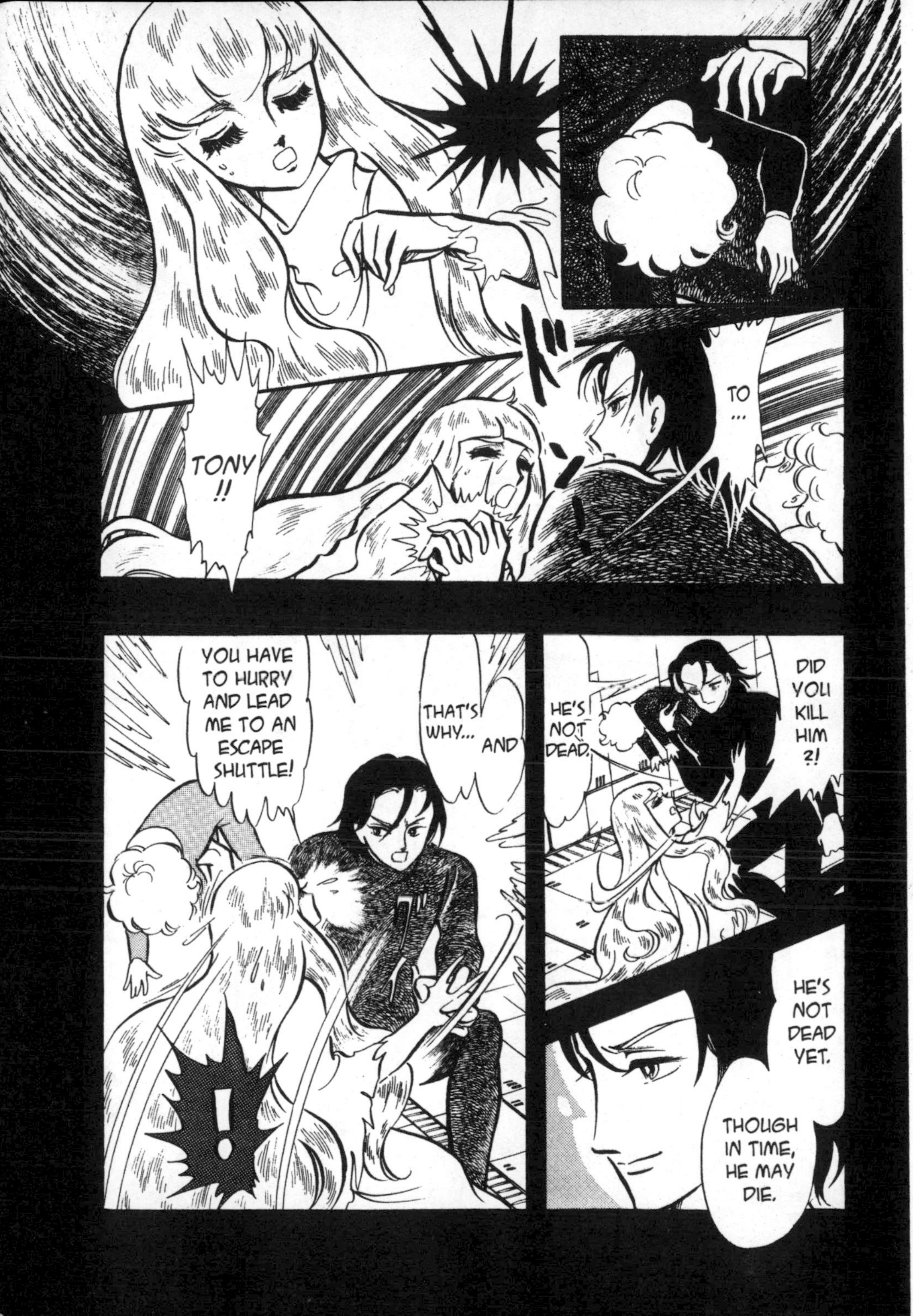
TO ...
TONY !!
DID YOU KILL HIM ?!
HE'S NOT DEAD.
HE'S NOT DEAD YET.
THOUGH IN TIME, HE MAY DIE.
AND
THAT'S WHY...
YOU HAVE TO HURRY AND LEAD ME TO AN ESCAPE SHUTTLE!
!

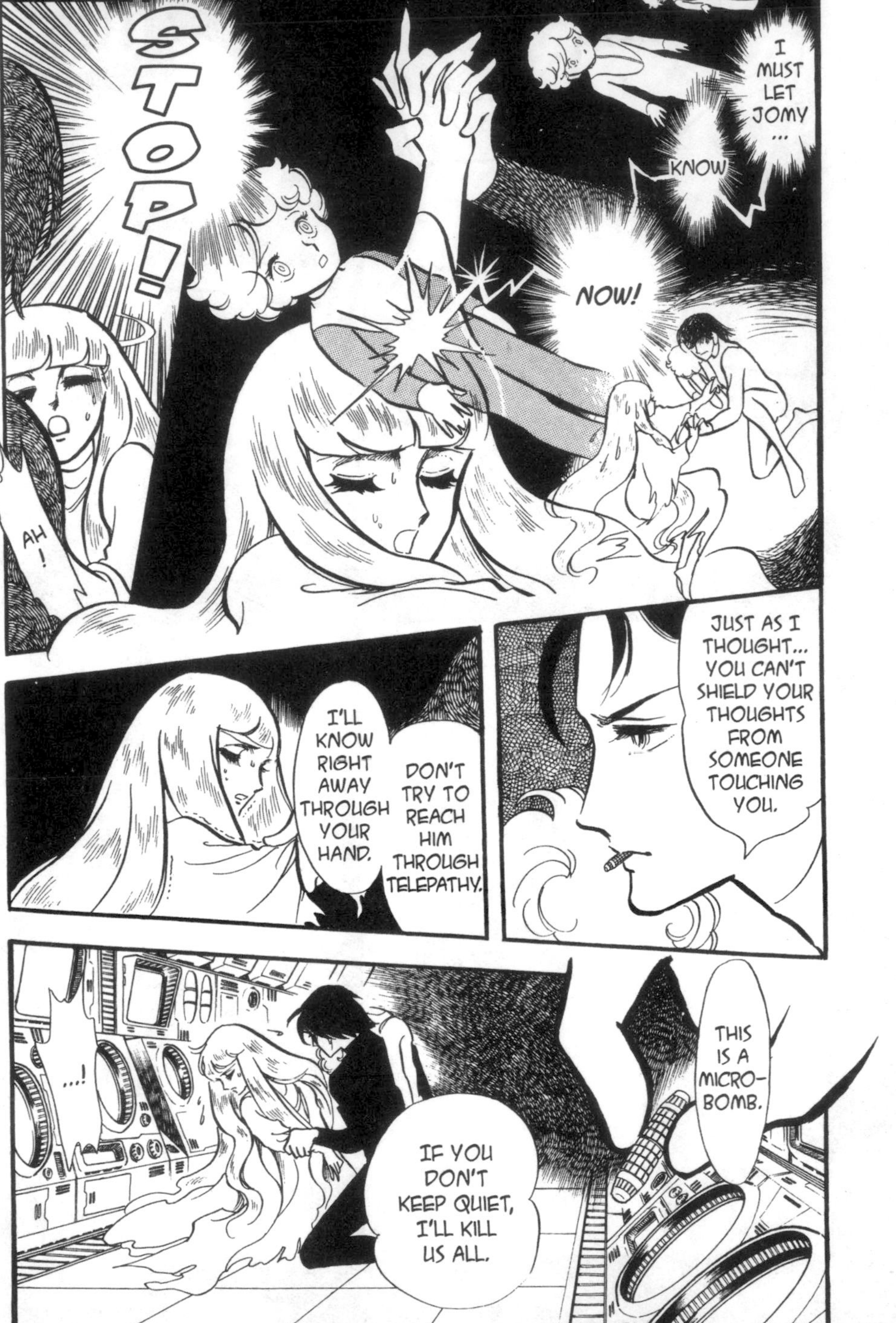
I MUST LET JOMY ...
KNOW
STOP!
NOW!
AH!
JUST AS I THOUGHT... YOU CAN'T SHIELD YOUR THOUGHTS FROM SOMEONE TOUCHING YOU.
DON'T TRY TO REACH HIM THROUGH TELEPATHY.
I'LL KNOW RIGHT AWAY THROUGH YOUR HAND.
THIS IS A MICRO-BOMB.
IF YOU DON'T KEEP QUIET, I'LL KILL US ALL.
...!

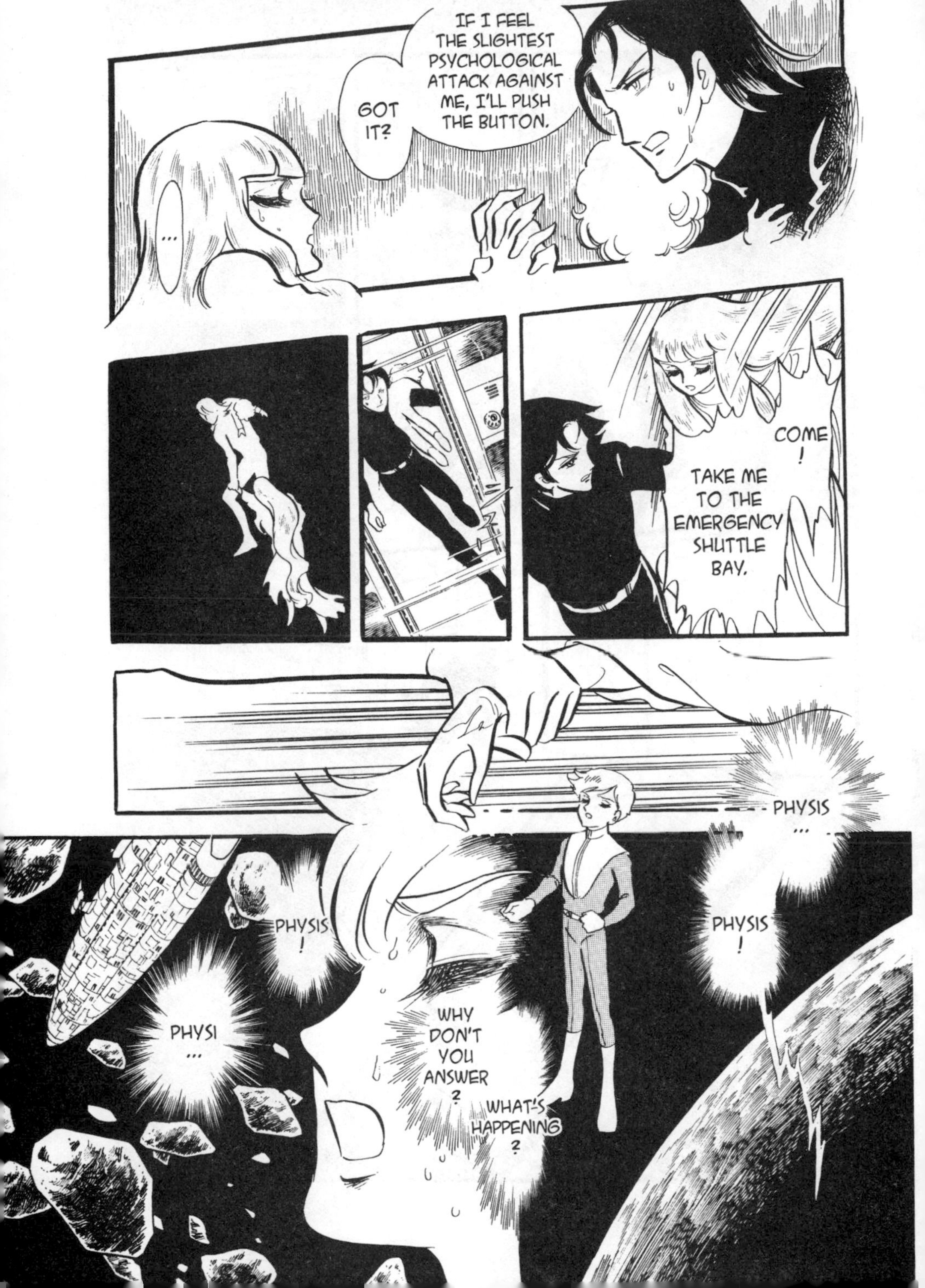
IF I FEEL THE SLIGHTEST PSYCHOLOGICAL ATTACK AGAINST ME, I'LL PUSH THE BUTTON.
GOT IT?
...
COME!
TAKE ME TO THE EMERGENCY SHUTTLE BAY.
PHYSIS...
PHYSIS!
PHYSIS!
PHYSI...
WHY DON'T YOU ANSWER?
WHAT'S HAPPENING?

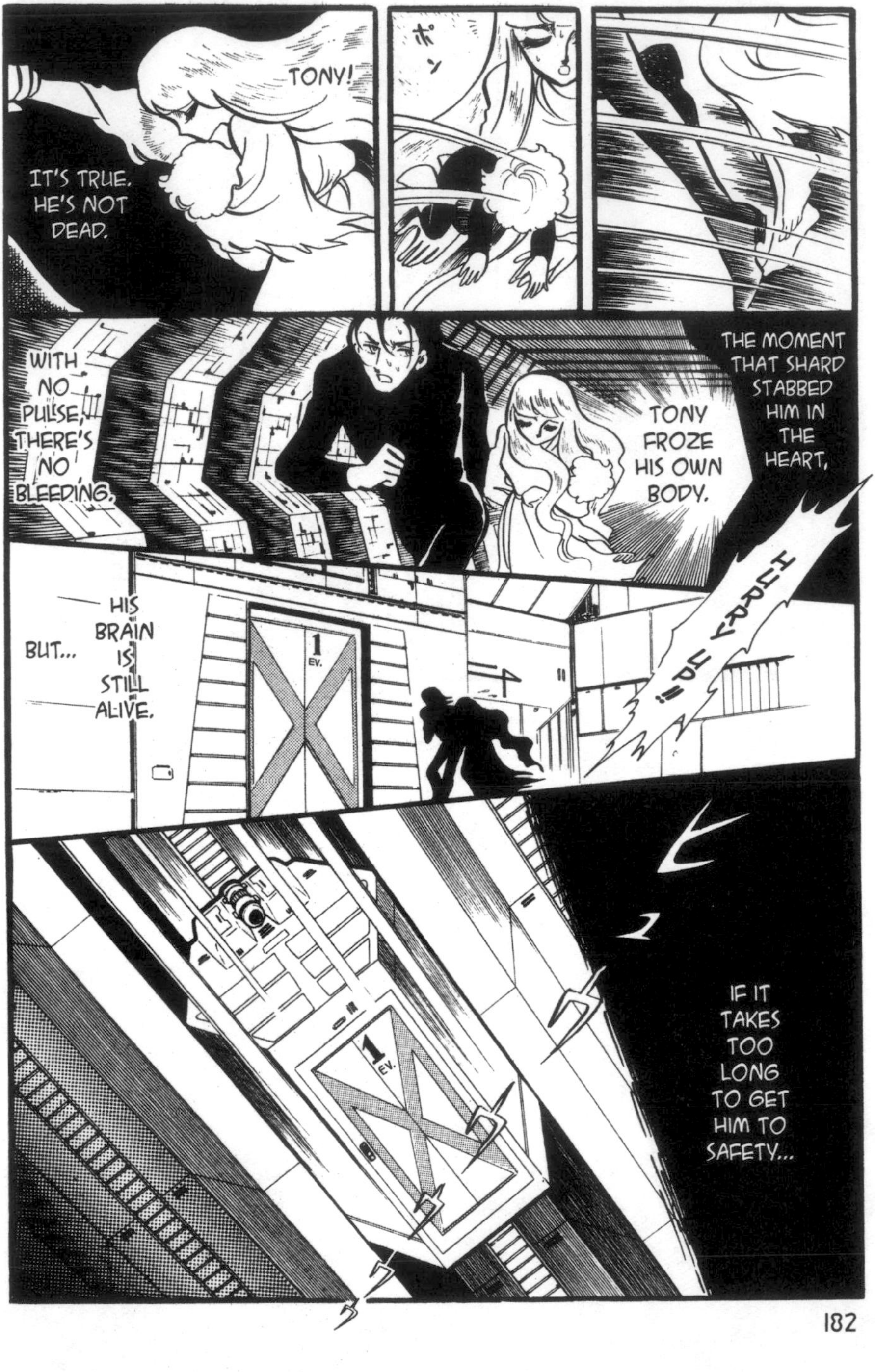

ポン
TONY!
IT'S TRUE. HE'S NOT DEAD.
THE MOMENT THAT SHARD STABBED HIM IN THE HEART,
TONY FROZE HIS OWN BODY.
WITH NO PULSE, THERE'S NO BLEEDING.
HURRY UP!!
BUT...
— HIS BRAIN IS STILL ALIVE.
IF IT TAKES TOO LONG TO GET HIM TO SAFETY...

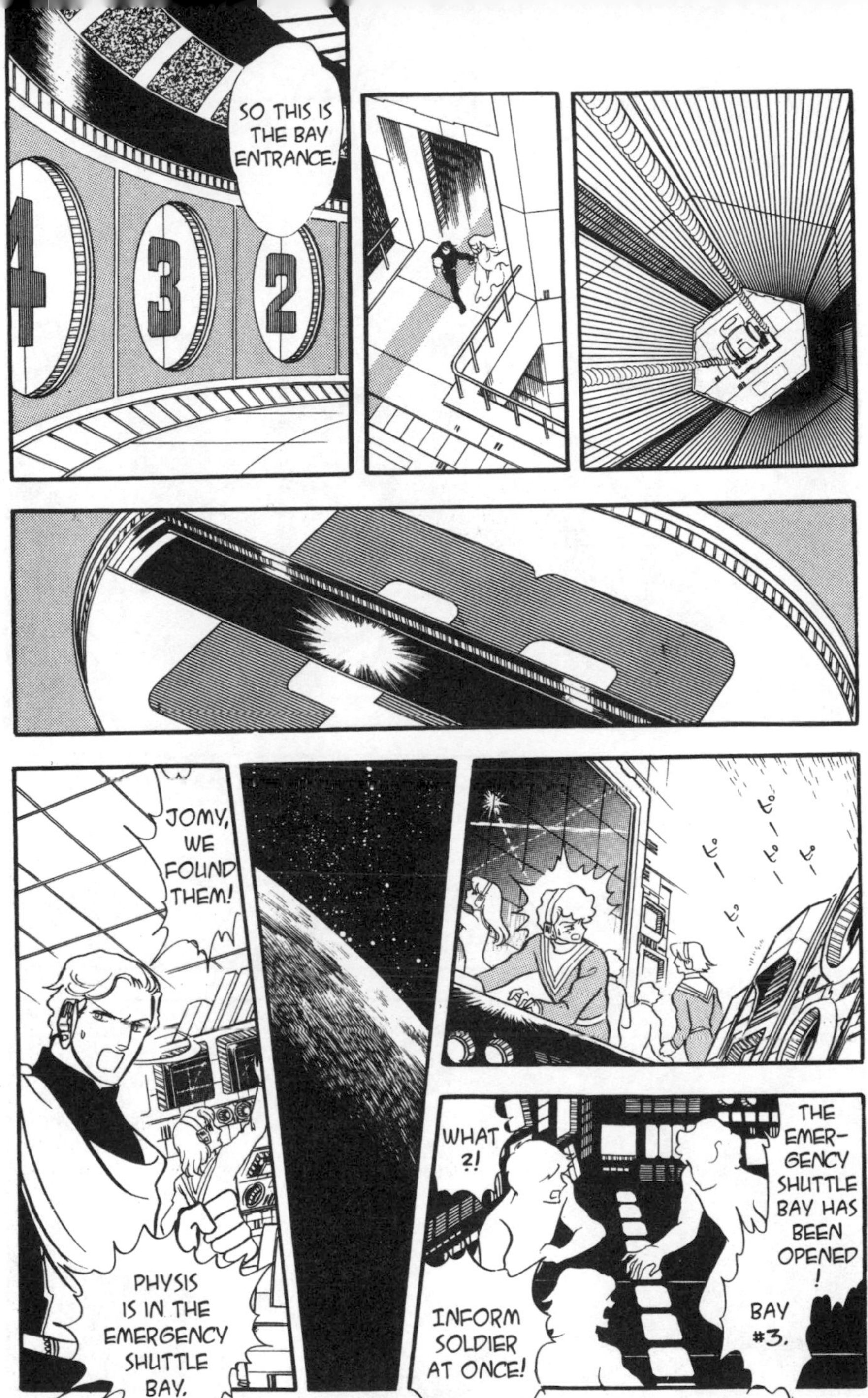
SO THIS IS THE BAY ENTRANCE.
THE EMERGENCY SHUTTLE BAY HAS BEEN OPENED!
BAY #3.
WHAT?!
INFORM SOLDIER AT ONCE!
JOMY, WE FOUND THEM!
PHYSIS IS IN THE EMERGENCY SHUTTLE BAY.

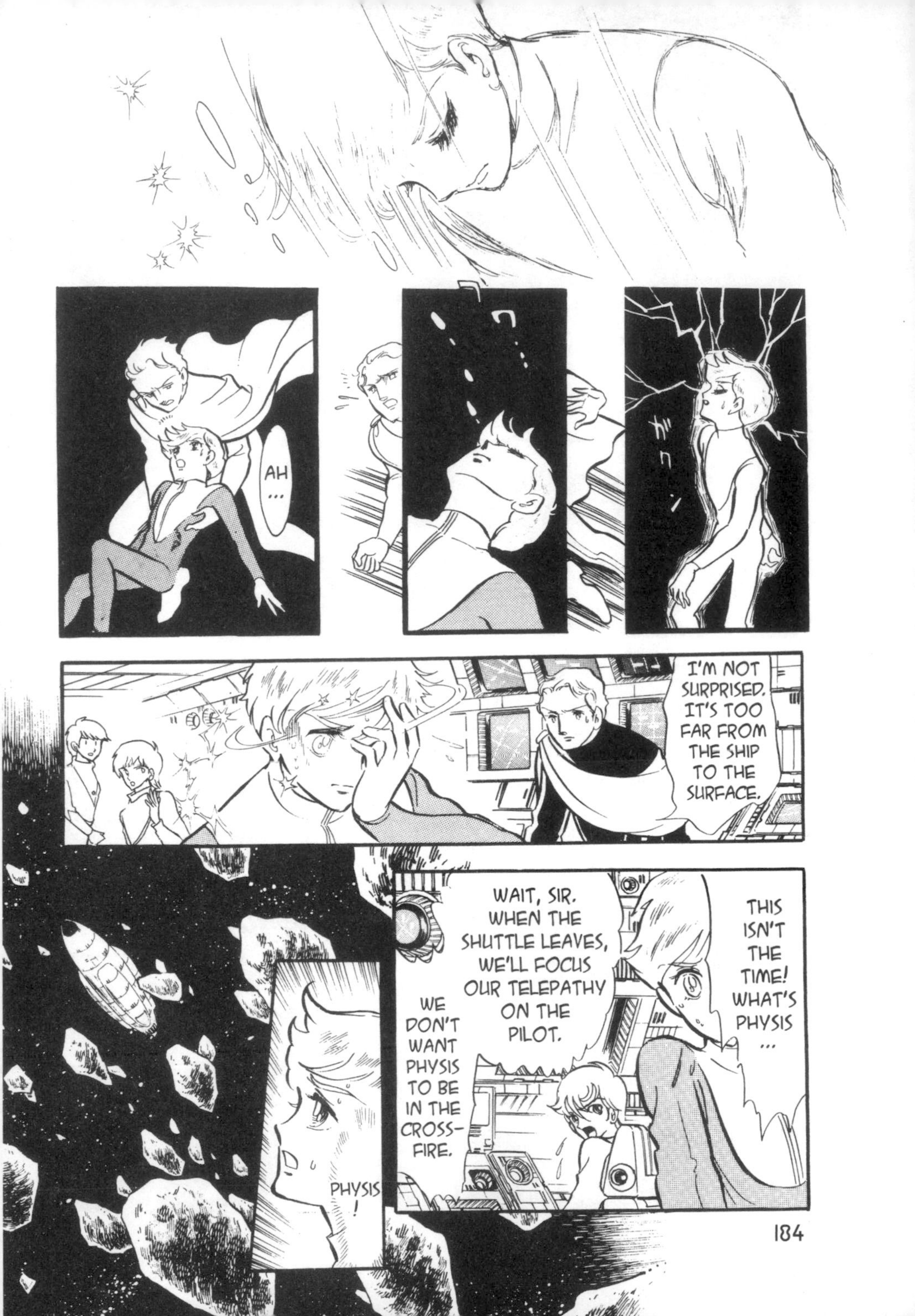
ガクン
AH ...
I'M NOT SURPRISED. IT'S TOO FAR FROM THE SHIP TO THE SURFACE.
THIS ISN'T THE TIME! WHAT'S PHYSIS ...
WAIT, SIR. WHEN THE SHUTTLE LEAVES, WE'LL FOCUS OUR TELEPATHY ON THE PILOT.
WE DON'T WANT PHYSIS TO BE IN THE CROSS-FIRE.
PHYSIS!

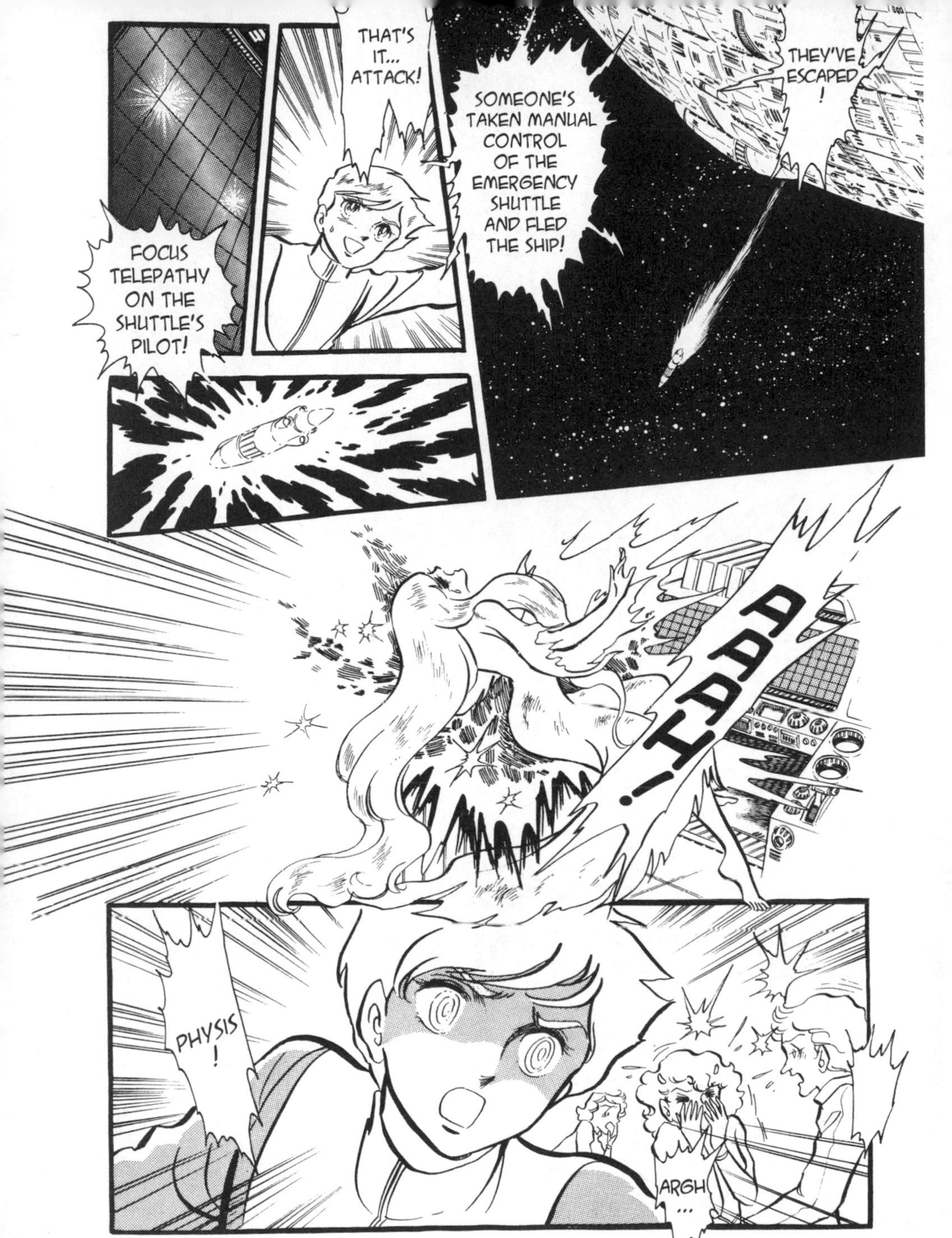
THEY'VE ESCAPED!
SOMEONE'S TAKEN MANUAL CONTROL OF THE EMERGENCY SHUTTLE AND FLED THE SHIP!
THAT'S IT... ATTACK!
FOCUS TELEPATHY ON THE SHUTTLE'S PILOT!
AAAAH!!
ARGH...
PHYSIS!

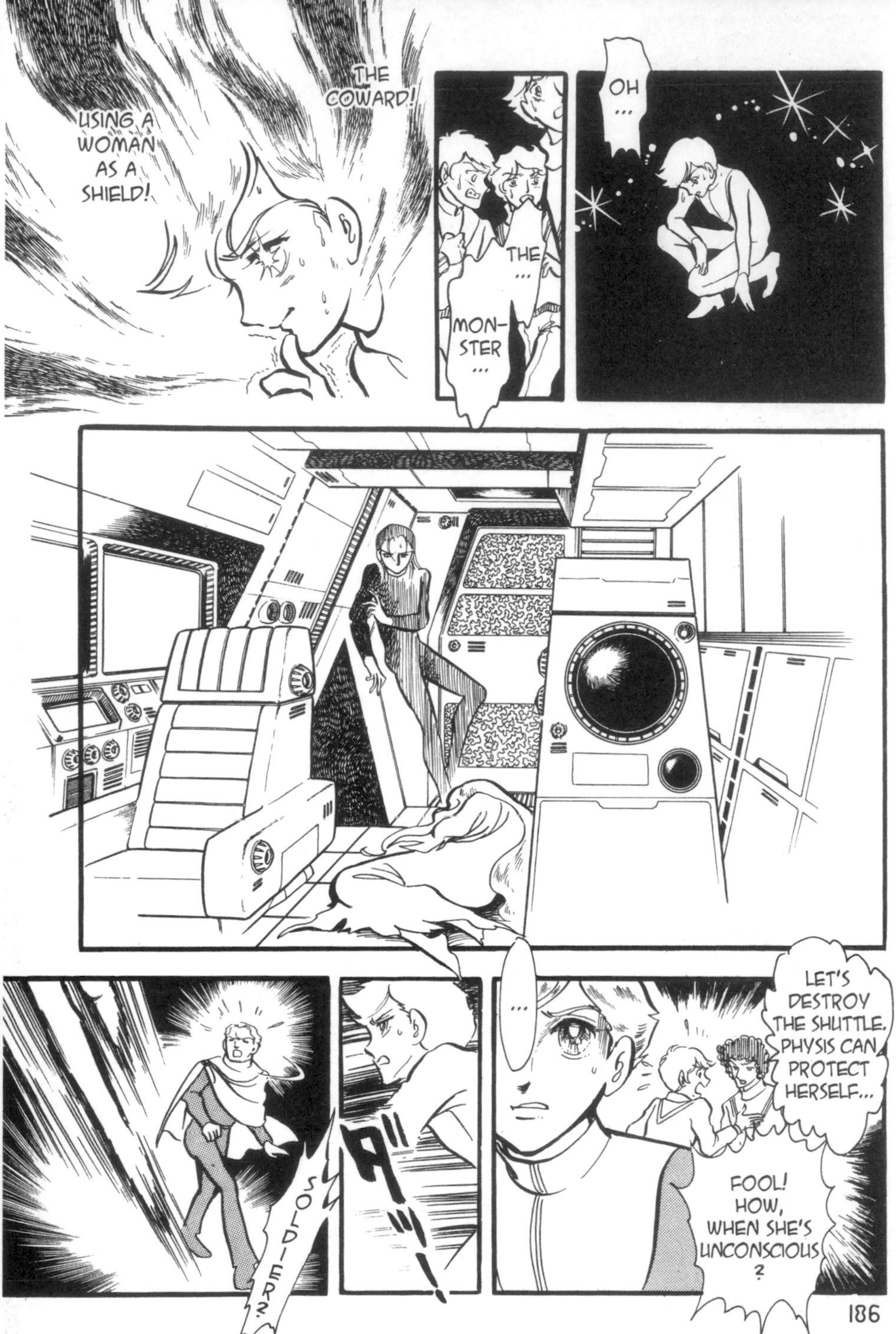
OH ...
THE ... MONSTER ...
THE COWARD!
USING A WOMAN AS A SHIELD!
LET'S DESTROY THE SHUTTLE. PHYSIS CAN PROTECT HERSELF...
...
FOOL! HOW, WHEN SHE'S UNCONSCIOUS?
A!!
SOLDIER?

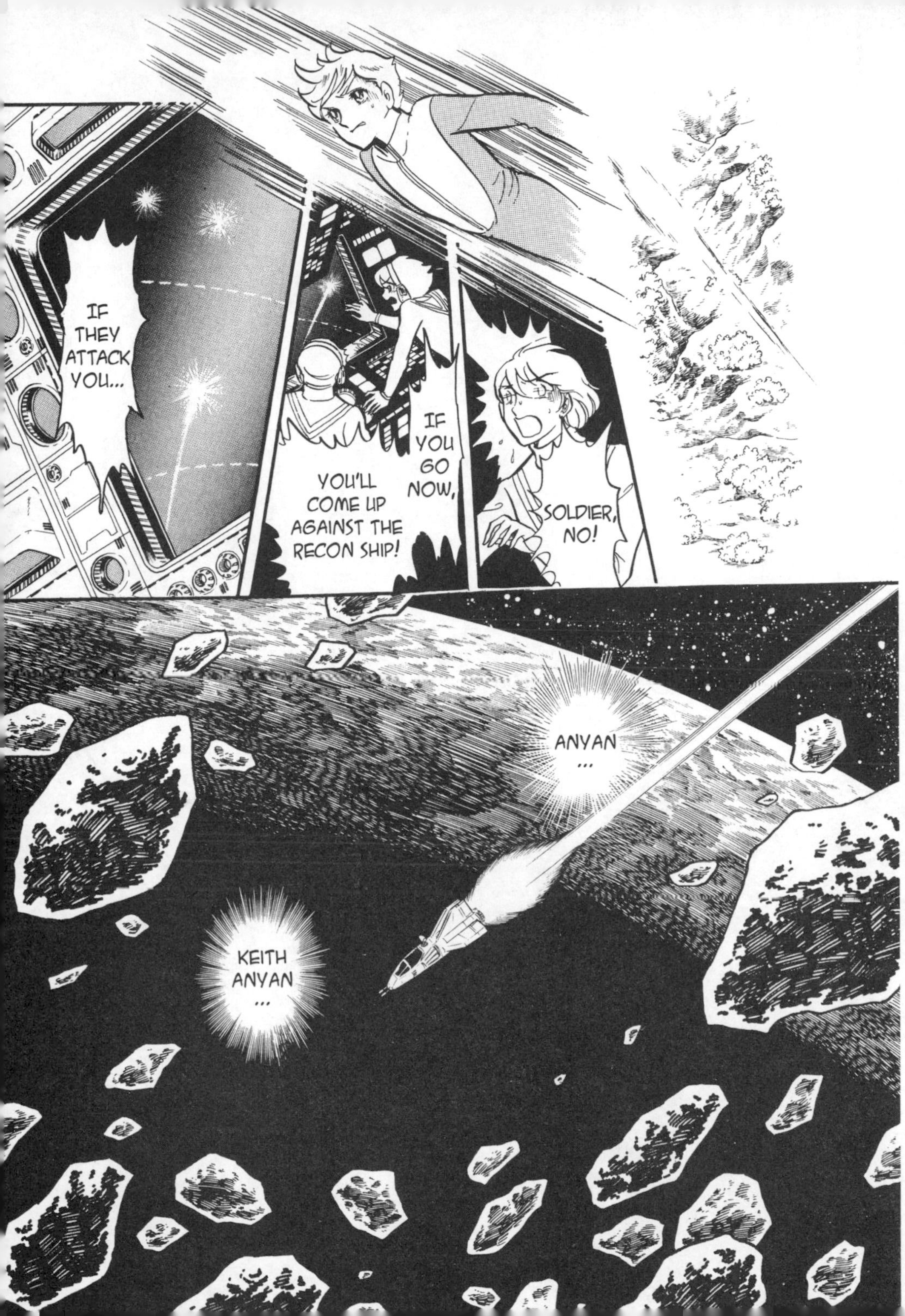
SOLDIER, NO!
IF YOU GO NOW,
YOU'LL COME UP AGAINST THE RECON SHIP!
IF THEY ATTACK YOU...
ANYAN ...
KEITH ANYAN ...

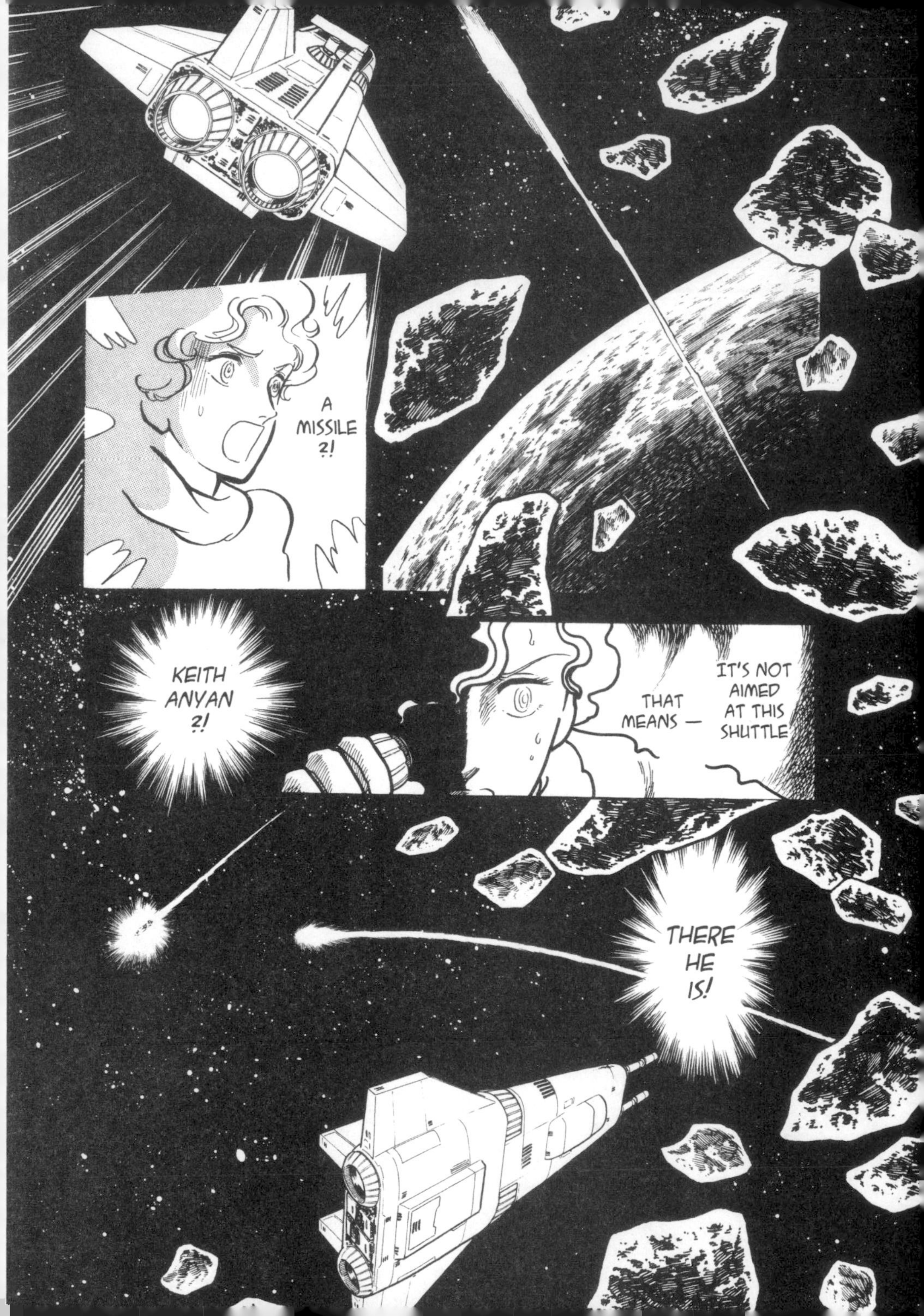
A MISSILE ?!
IT'S NOT AIMED AT THIS SHUTTLE
THAT MEANS —
KEITH ANYAN ?!
THERE HE IS!

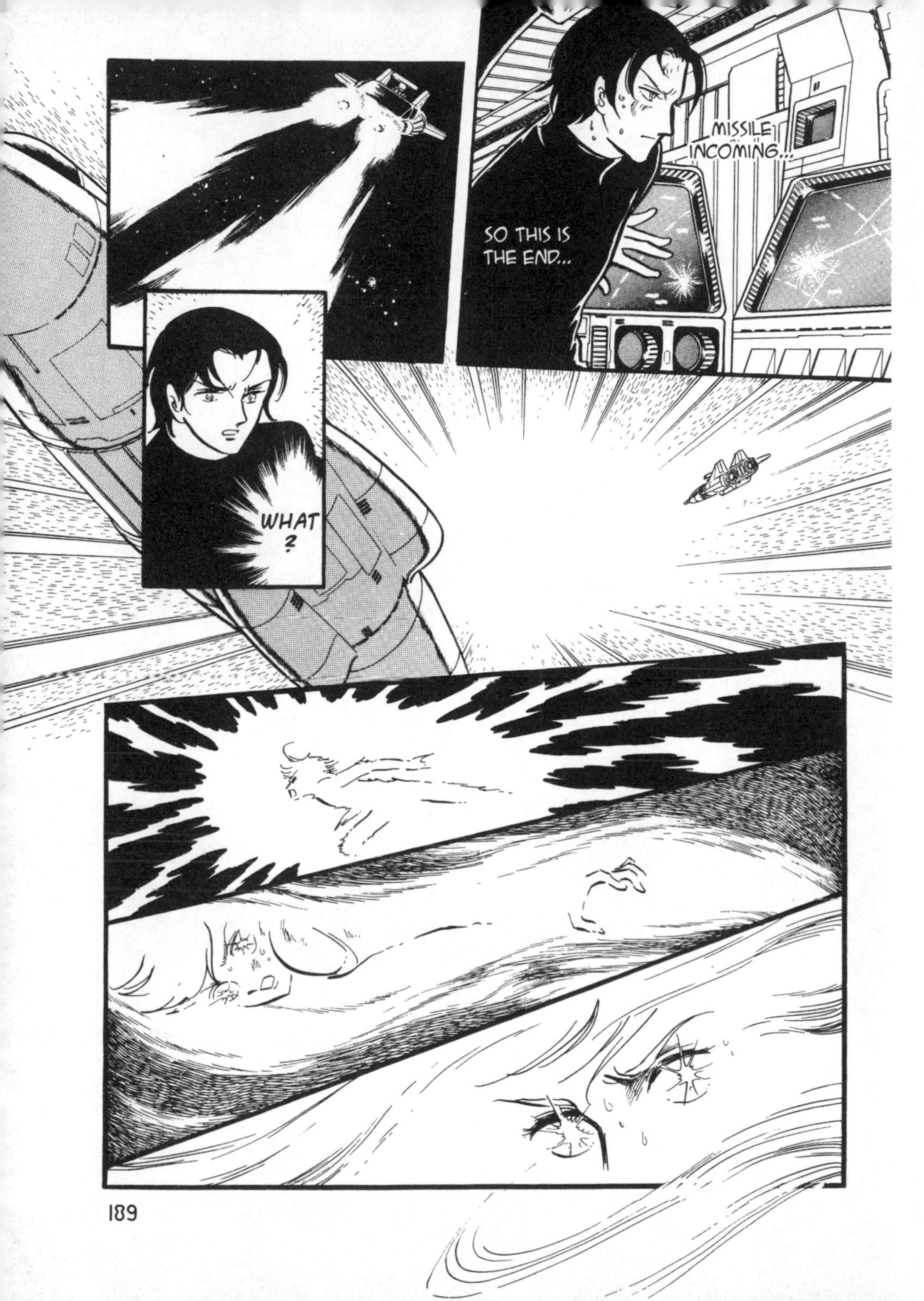
MISSILE INCOMING...
SO THIS IS THE END...
WHAT?

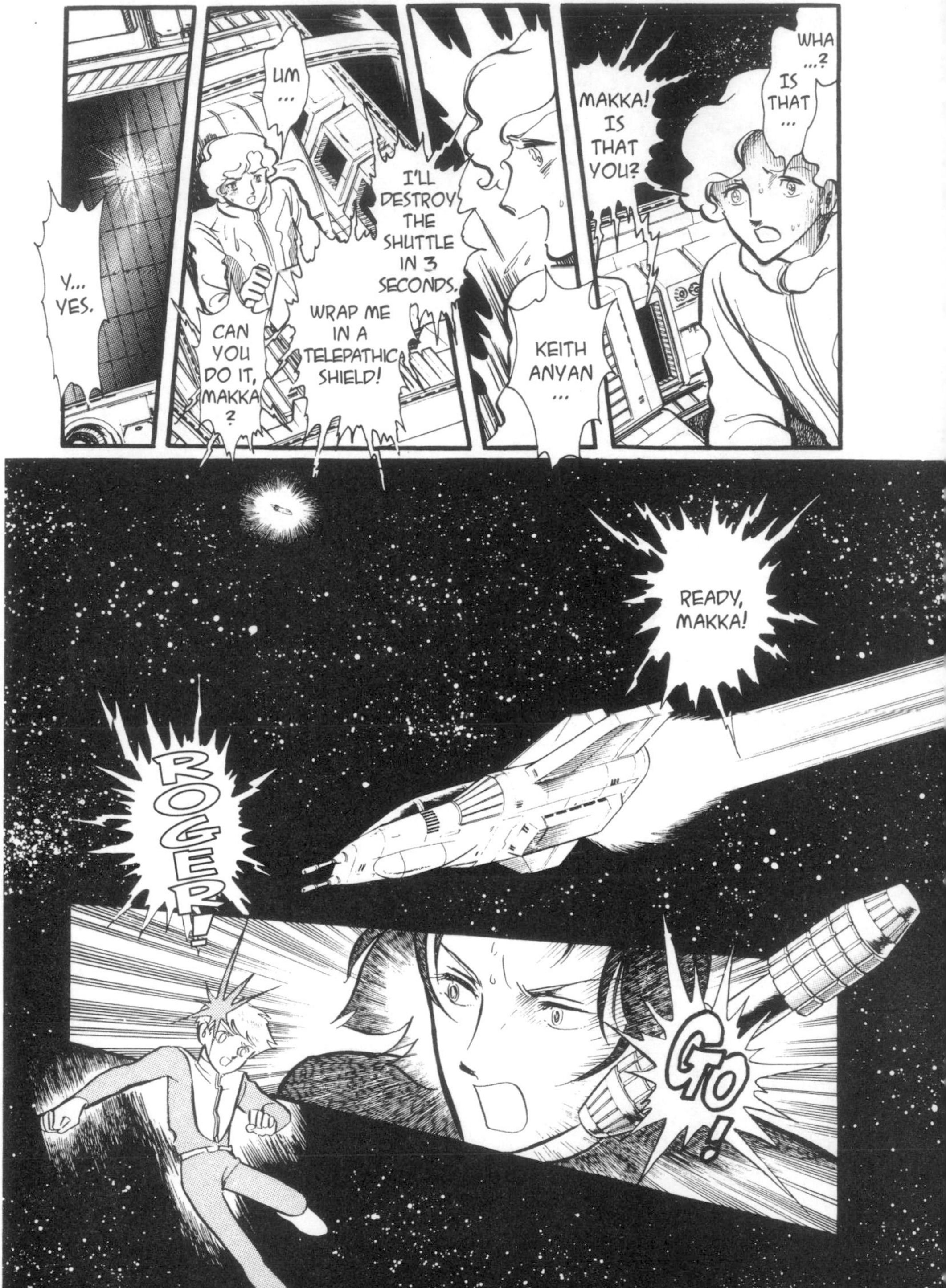
WHA ...?
IS THAT ...
MAKKA! IS THAT YOU?
KEITH ANYAN ...
I'LL DESTROY THE SHUTTLE IN 3 SECONDS.
UM ...
WRAP ME IN A TELEPATHIC SHIELD!
CAN YOU DO IT, MAKKA?
Y... YES.
READY, MAKKA!
ROGER!
GO!

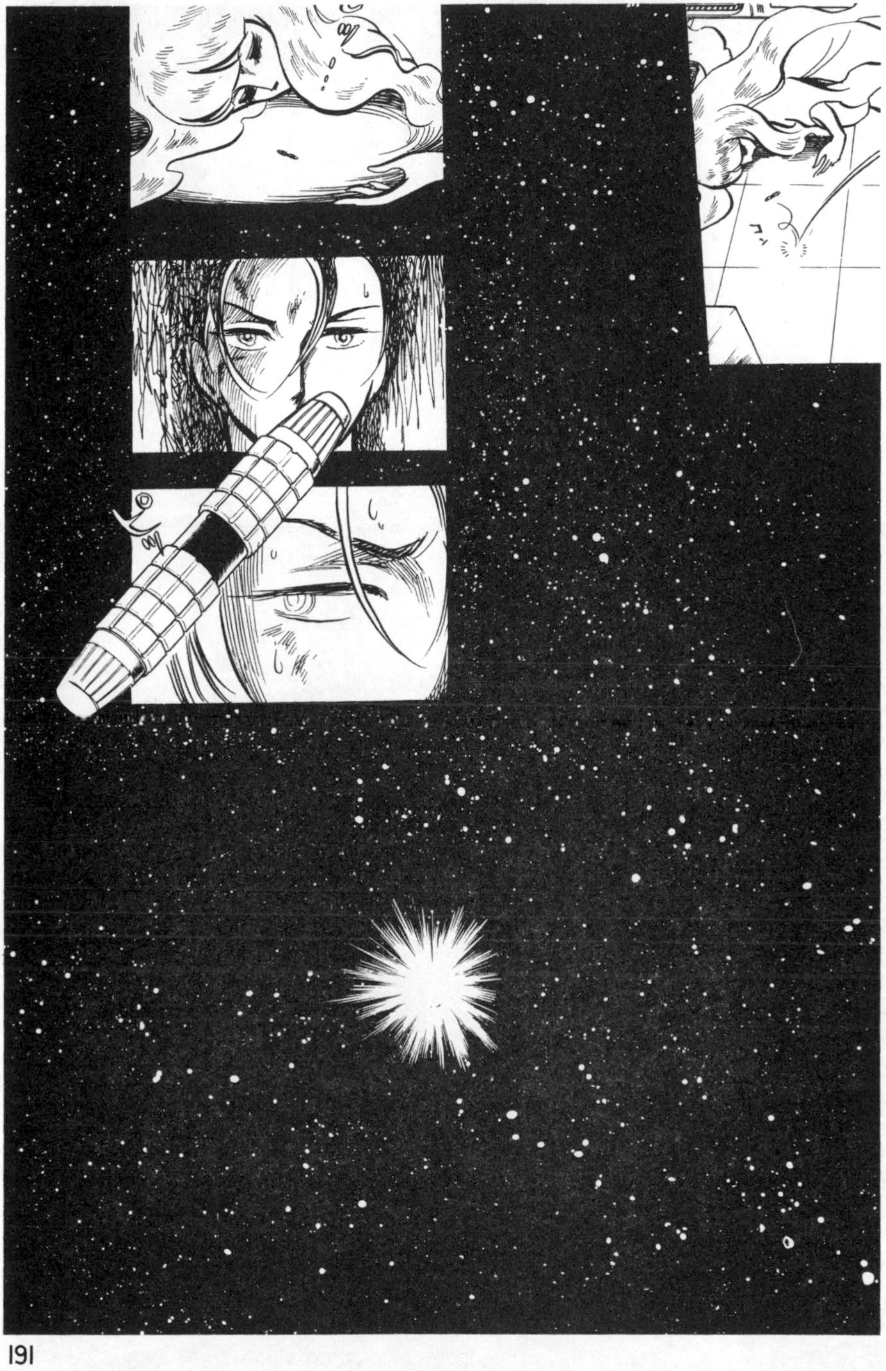
コン

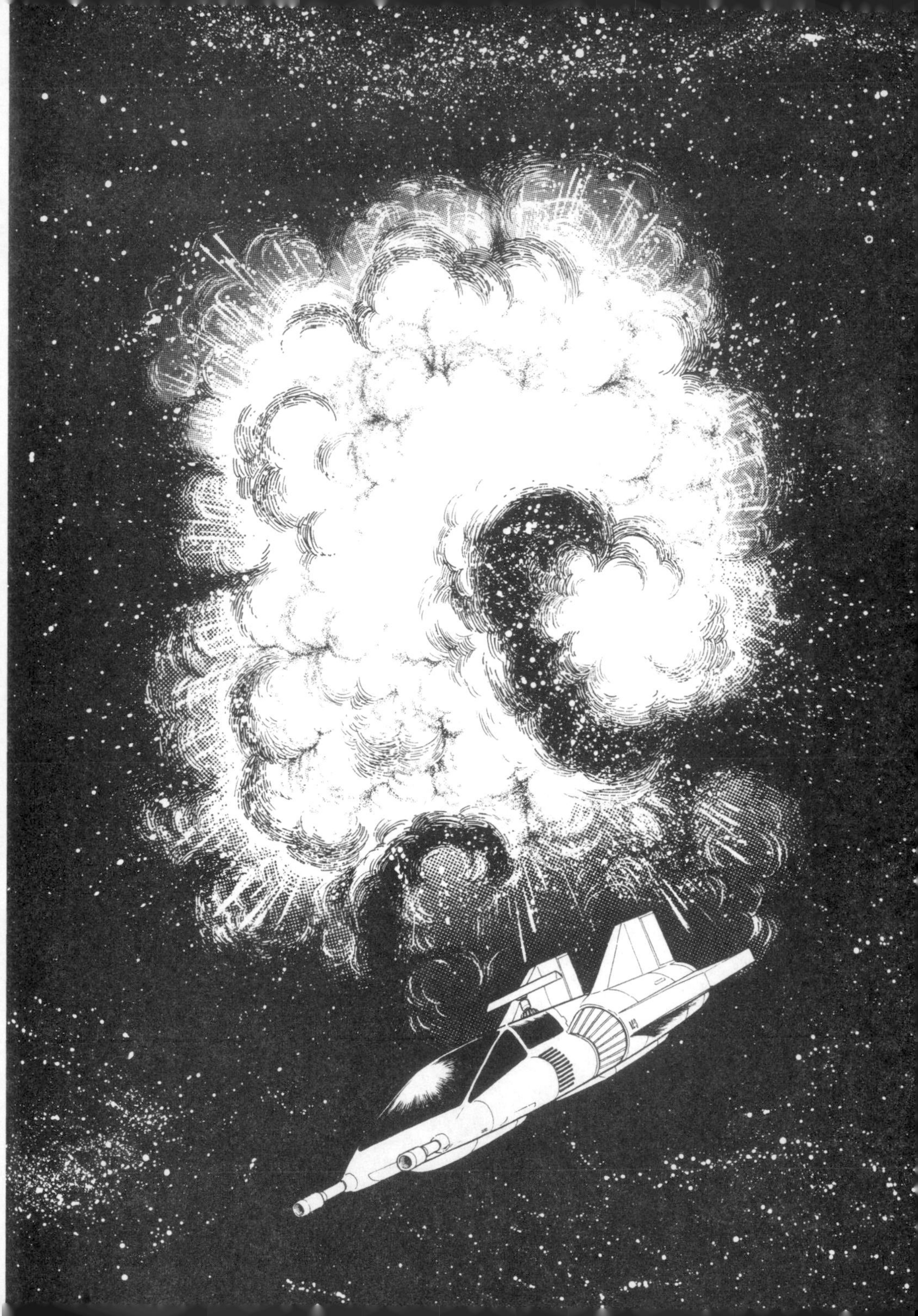

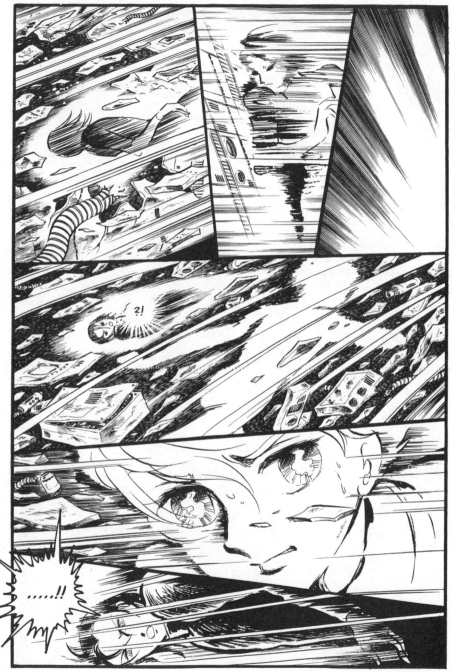

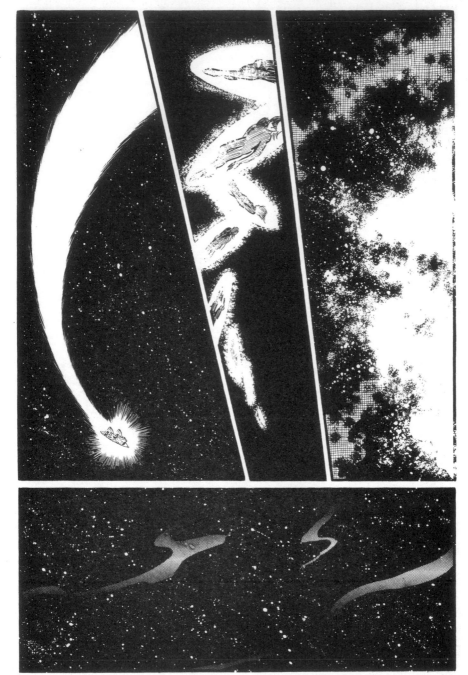

194

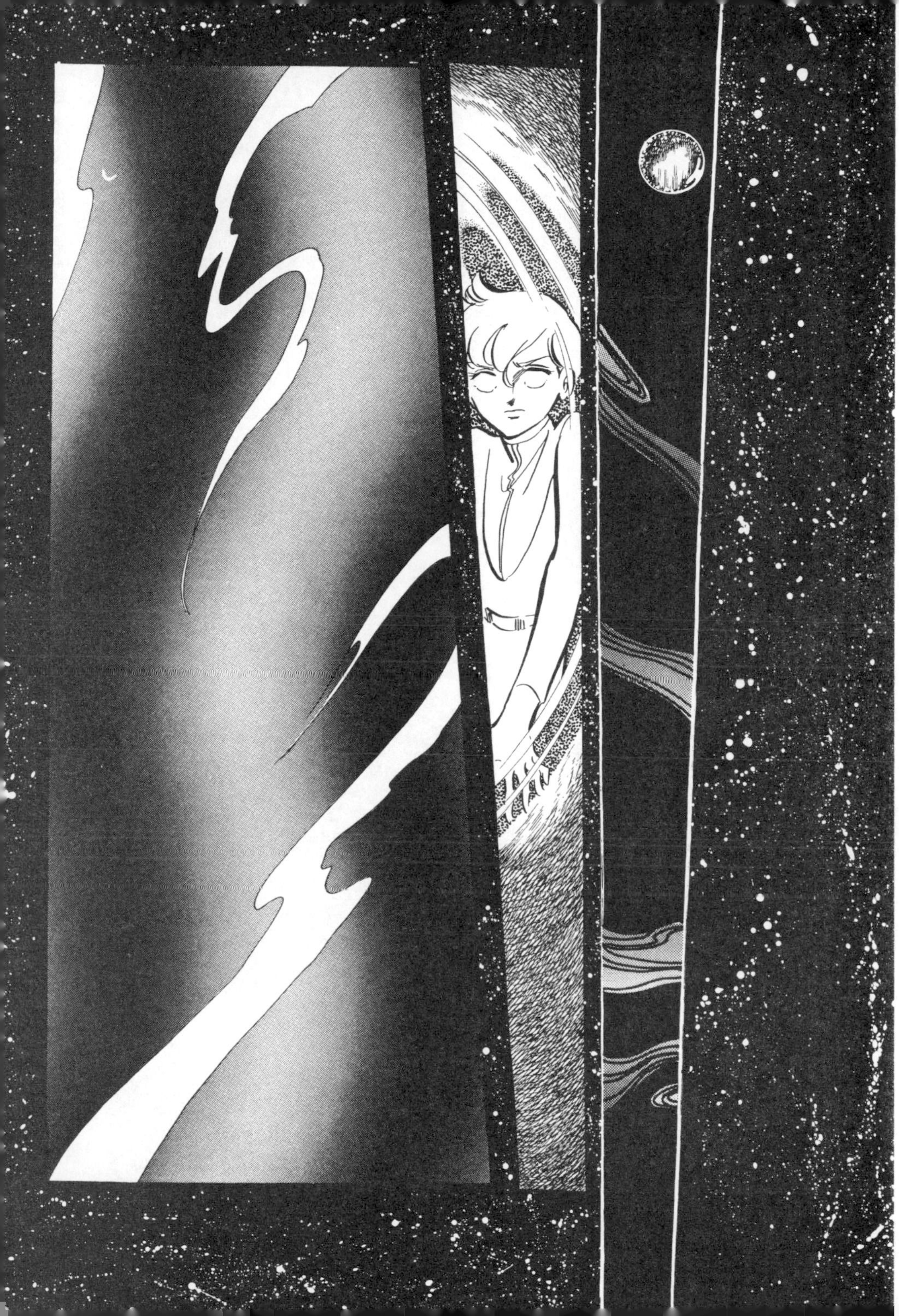

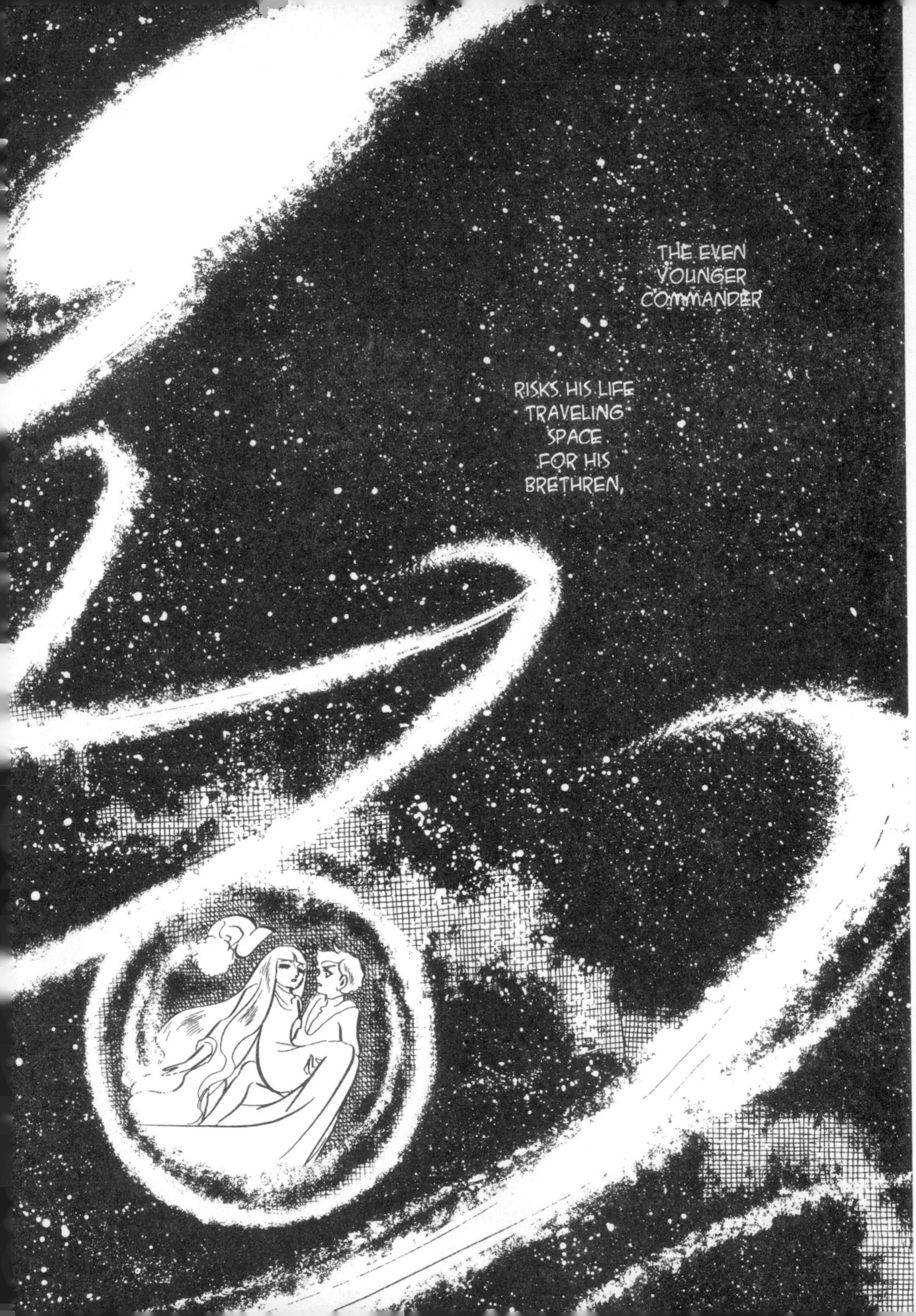
THE EVEN YOUNGER COMMANDER
RISKS HIS LIFE TRAVELING SPACE FOR HIS BRETHREN,

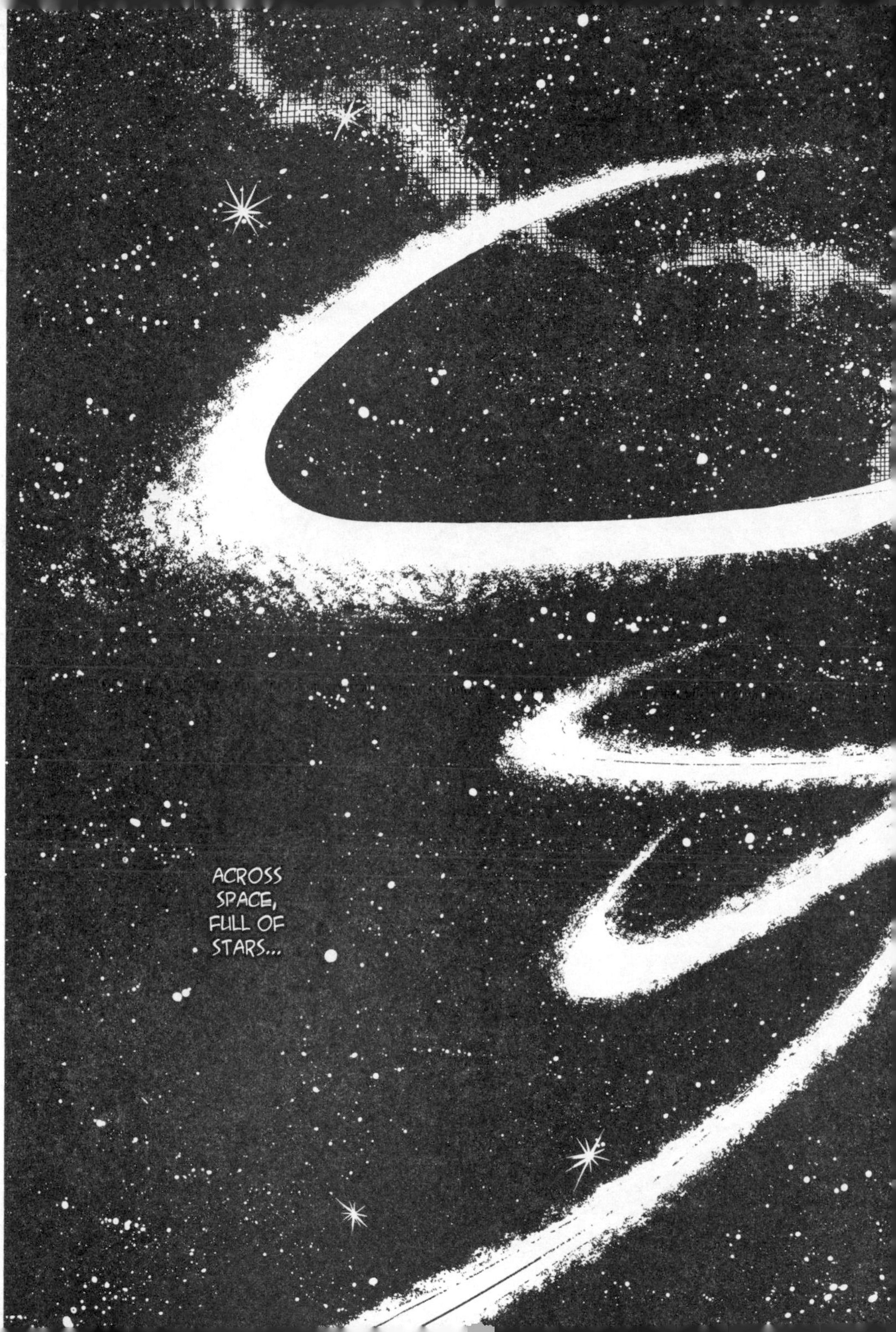
ACROSS SPACE, FULL OF STARS...

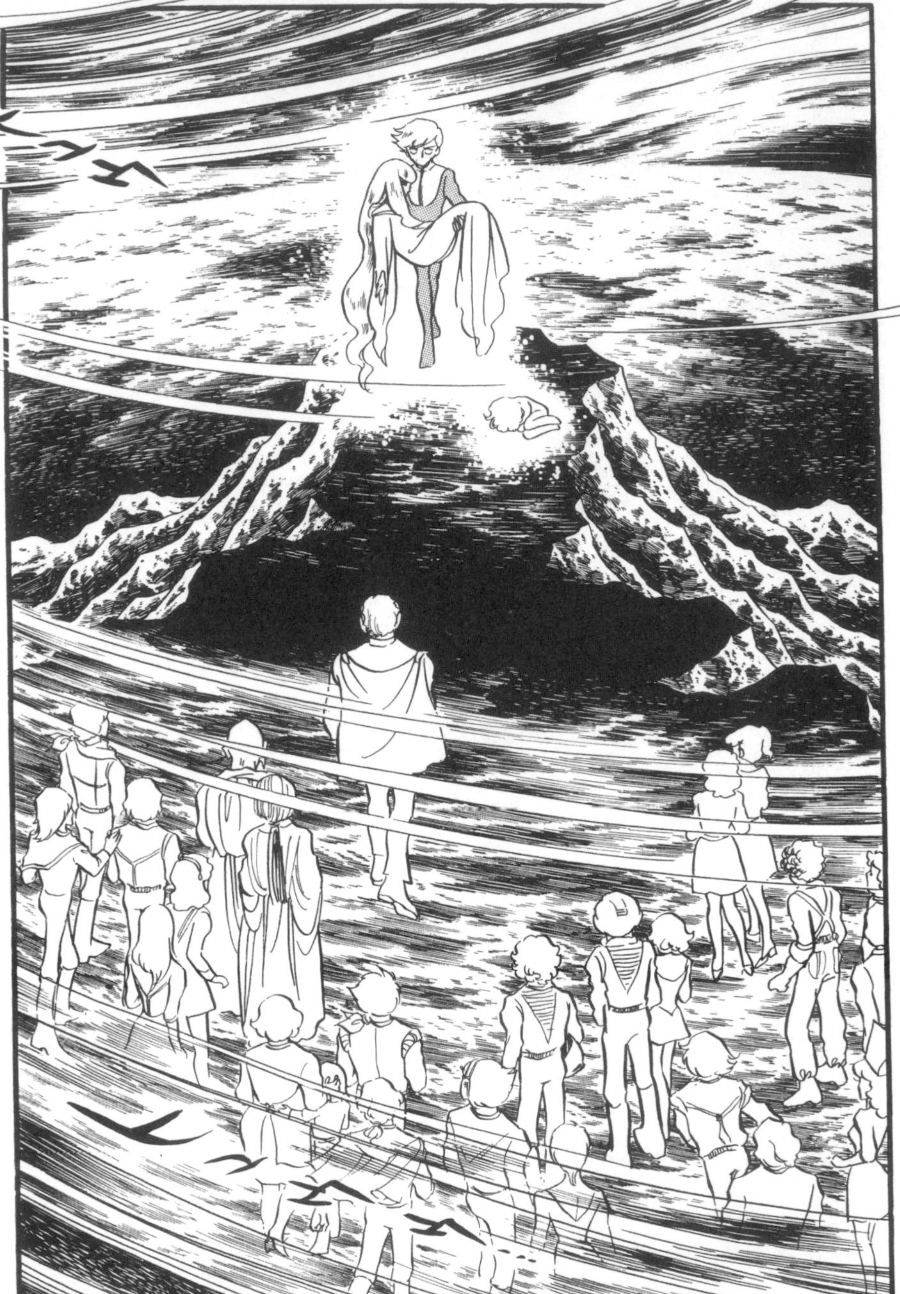
ヒュゥム
ヒュゥムム…

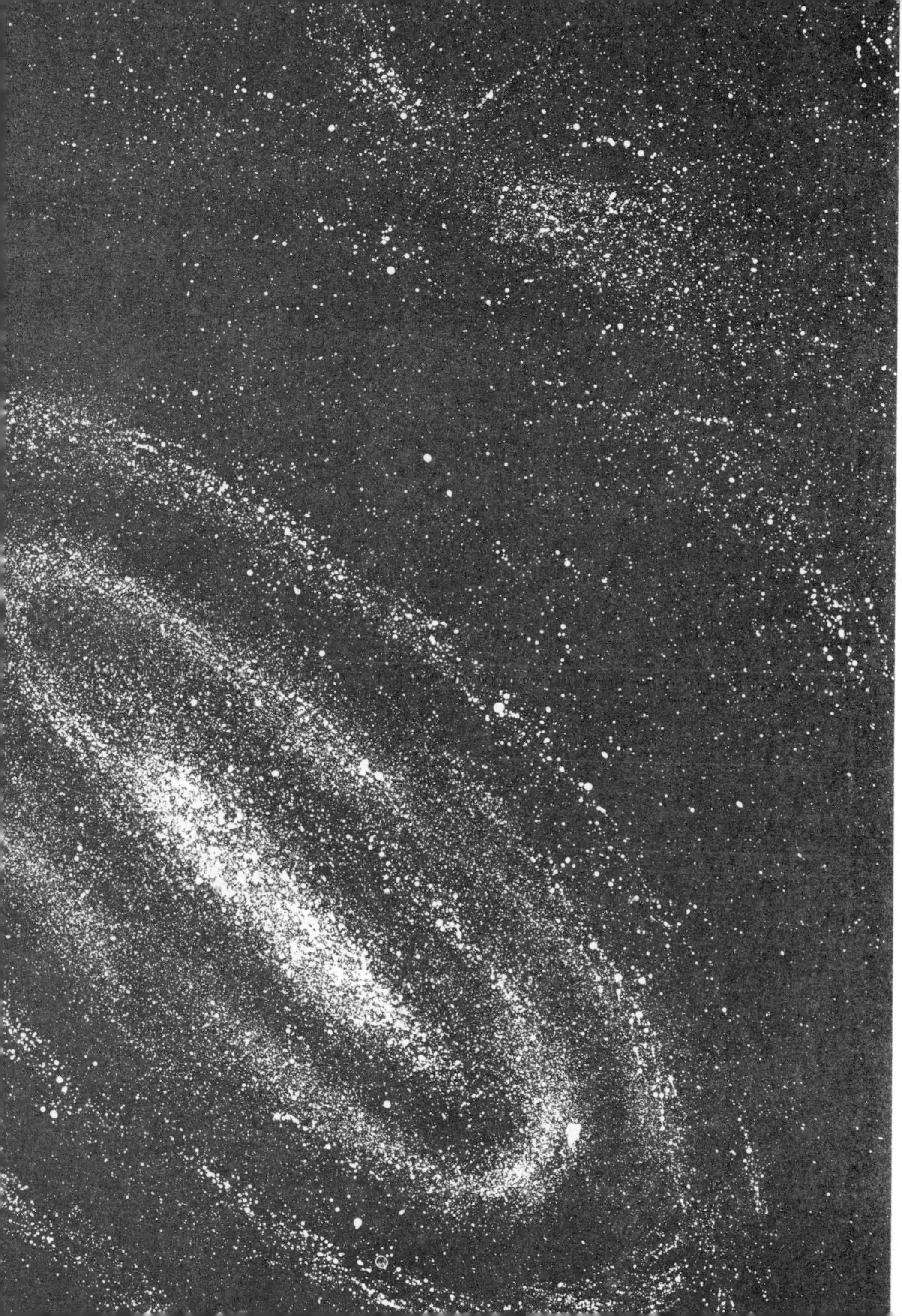

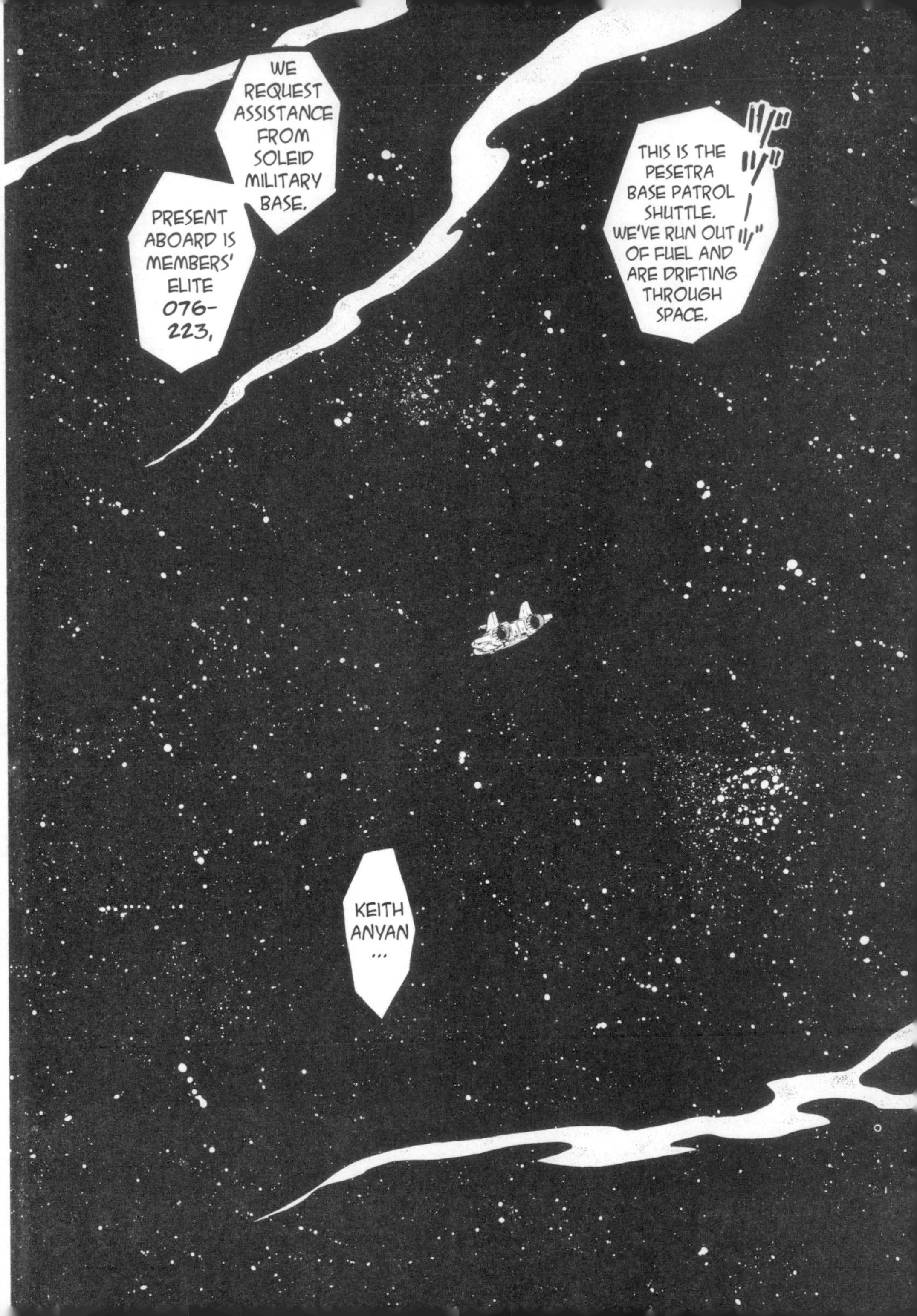
THIS IS THE PESETRA BASE PATROL SHUTTLE. WE'VE RUN OUT OF FUEL AND ARE DRIFTING THROUGH SPACE.
WE REQUEST ASSISTANCE FROM SOLEID MILITARY BASE.
PRESENT ABOARD IS MEMBERS' ELITE 076-223,
KEITH ANYAN ...

PART 4

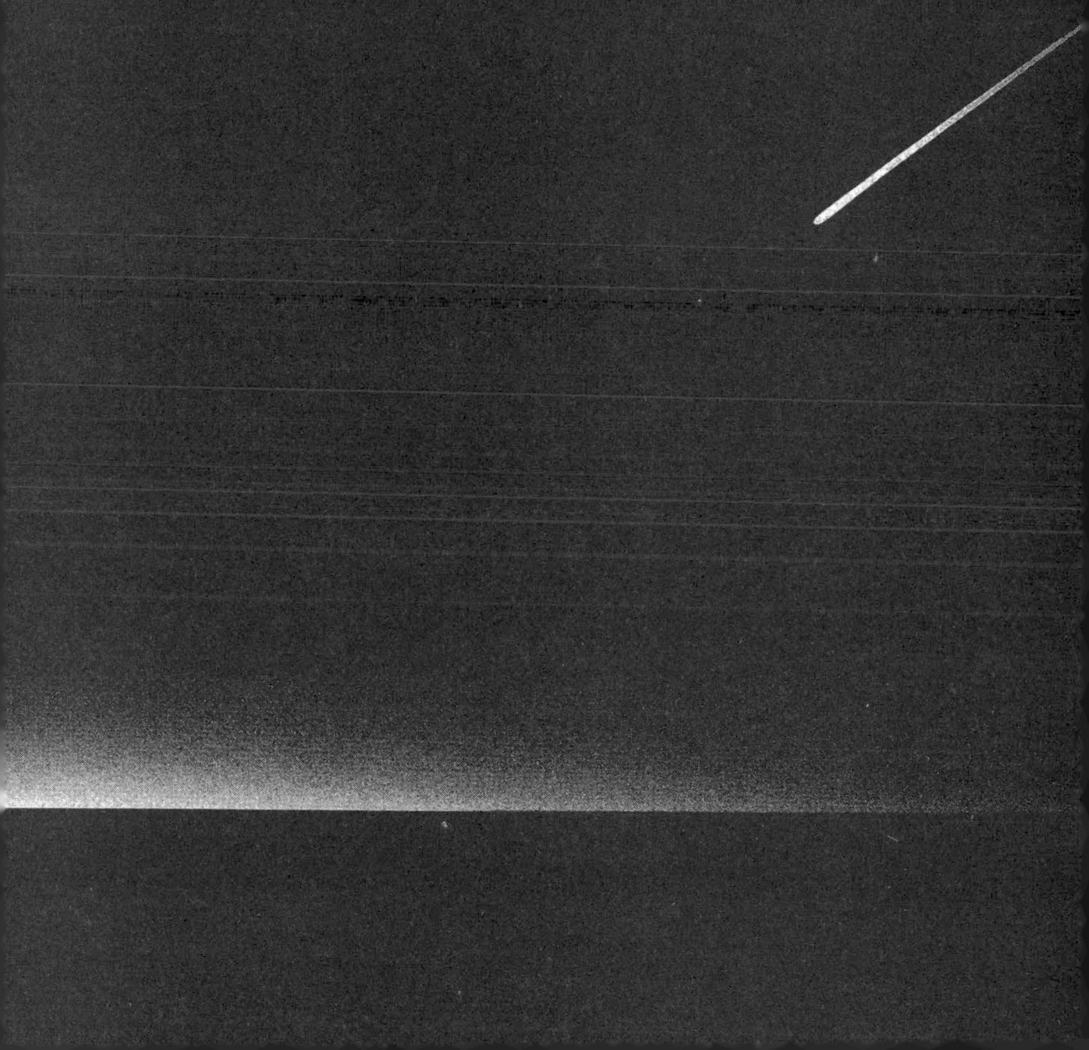

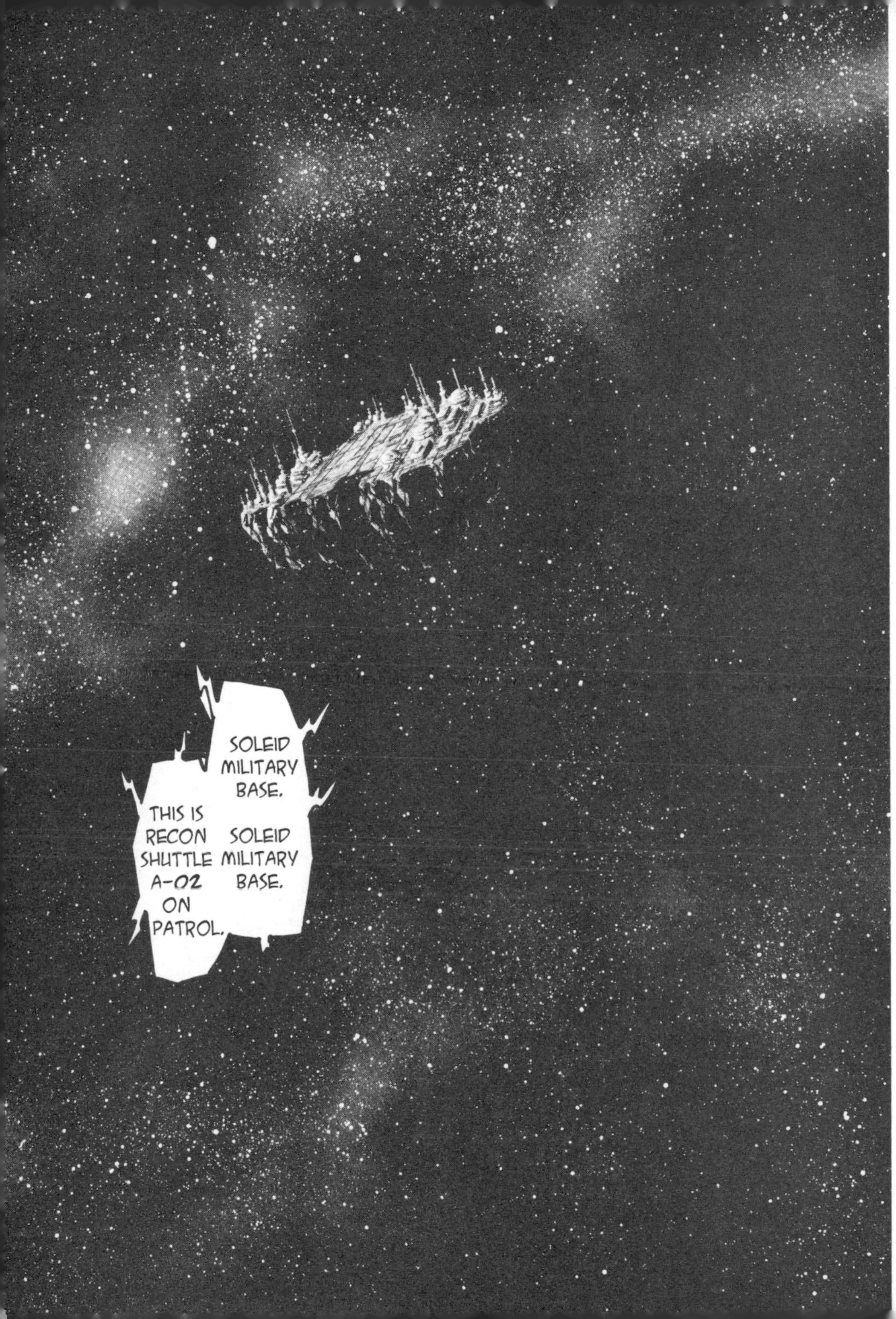
SOLEID MILITARY BASE.
SOLEID MILITARY BASE.
THIS IS RECON SHUTTLE A-02 ON PATROL.

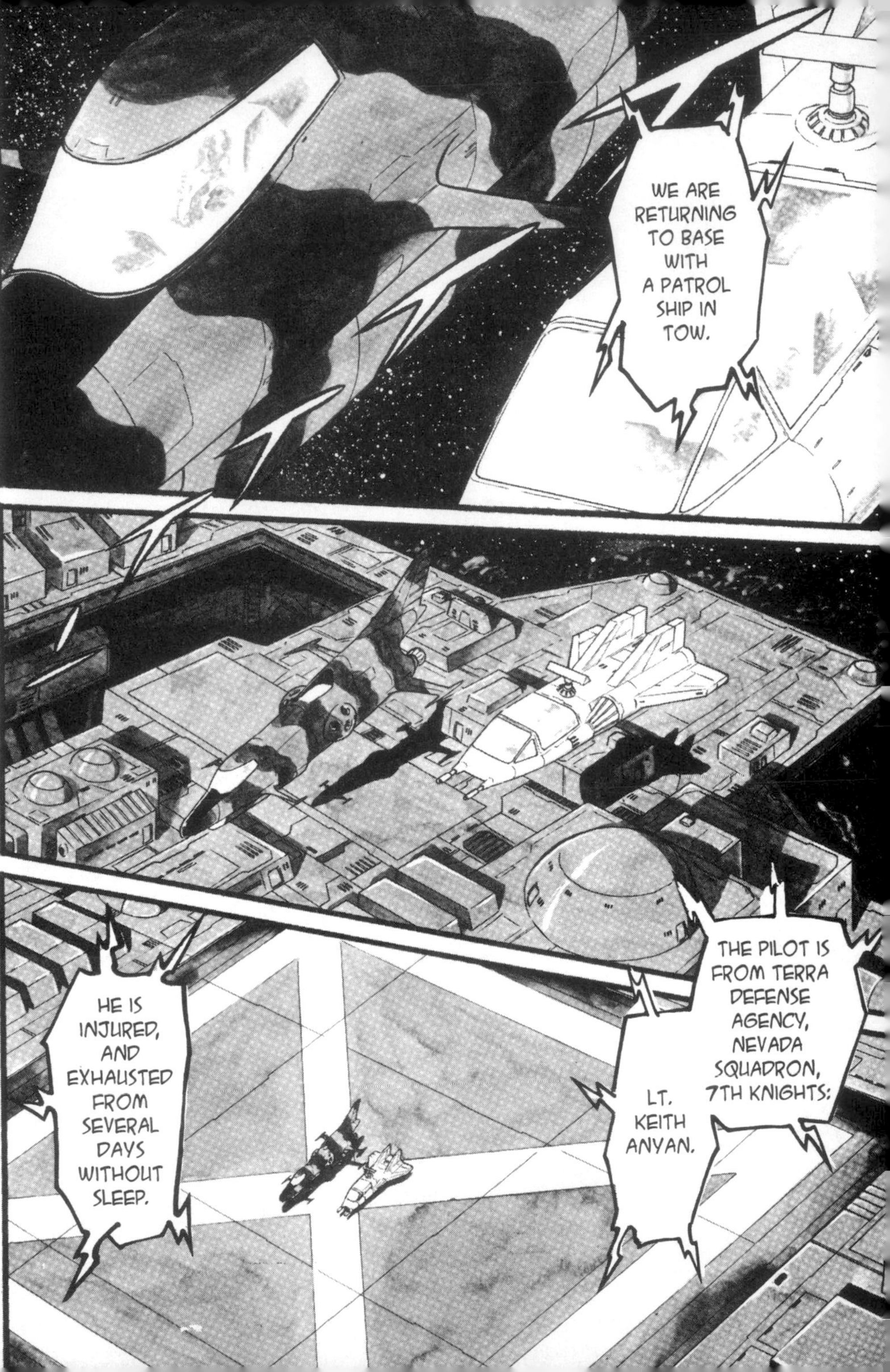
WE ARE RETURNING TO BASE WITH A PATROL SHIP IN TOW.
THE PILOT IS FROM TERRA DEFENSE AGENCY, NEVADA SQUADRON, 7TH KNIGHTS:
LT. KEITH ANYAN.
HE IS INJURED, AND EXHAUSTED FROM SEVERAL DAYS WITHOUT SLEEP.

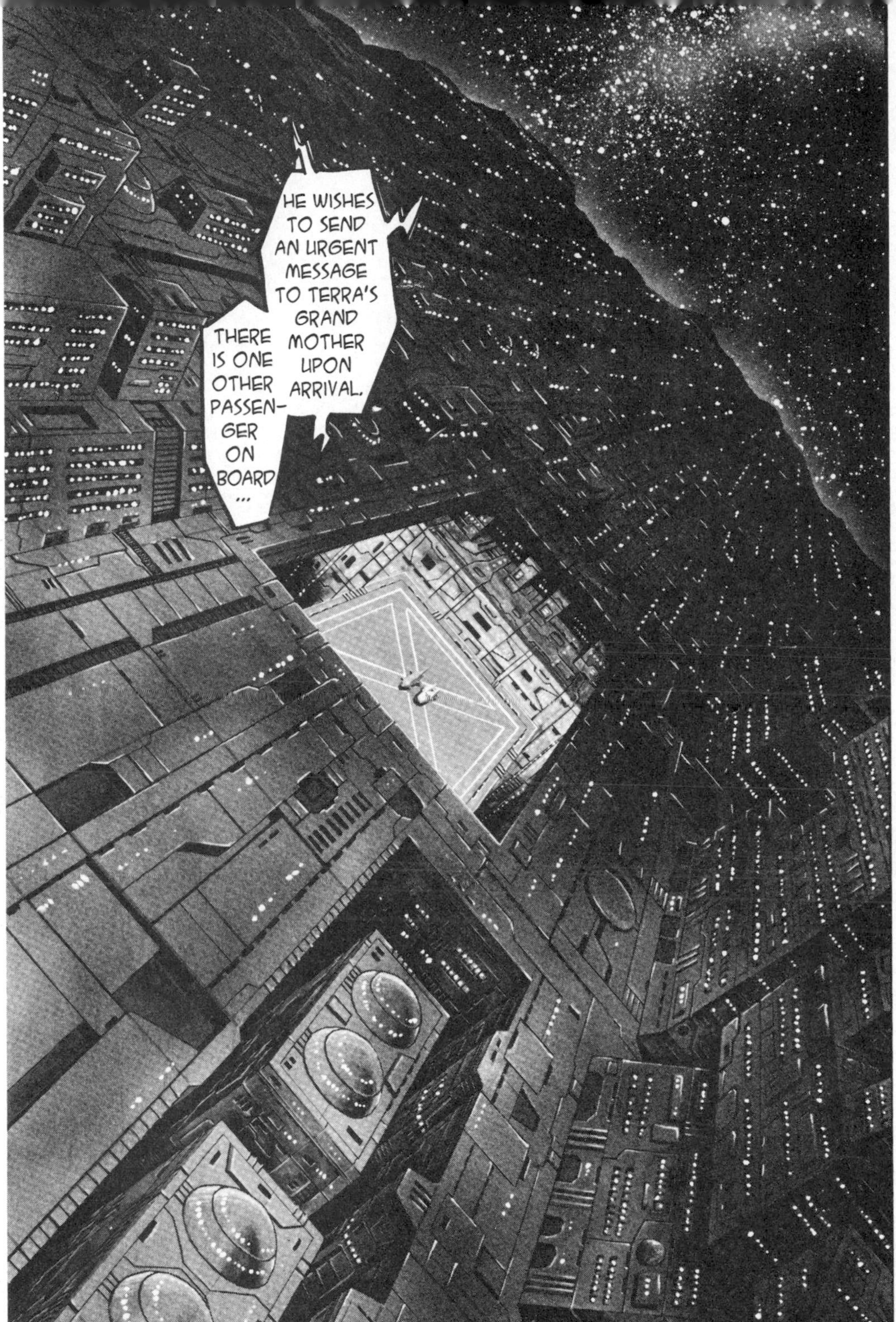
HE WISHES TO SEND AN URGENT MESSAGE TO TERRA'S GRAND MOTHER UPON ARRIVAL.
THERE IS ONE OTHER PASSEN-GER ON BOARD ...

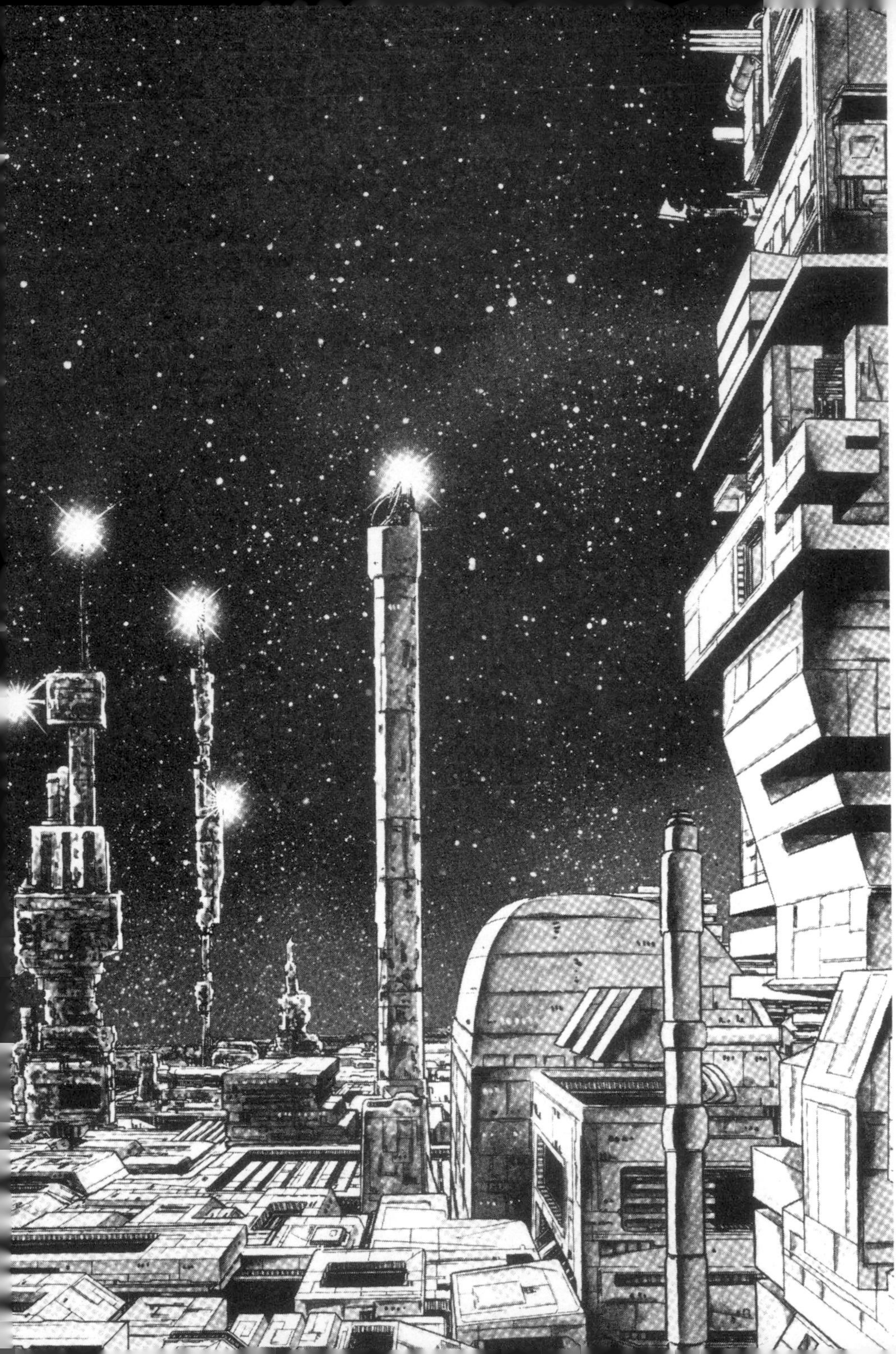

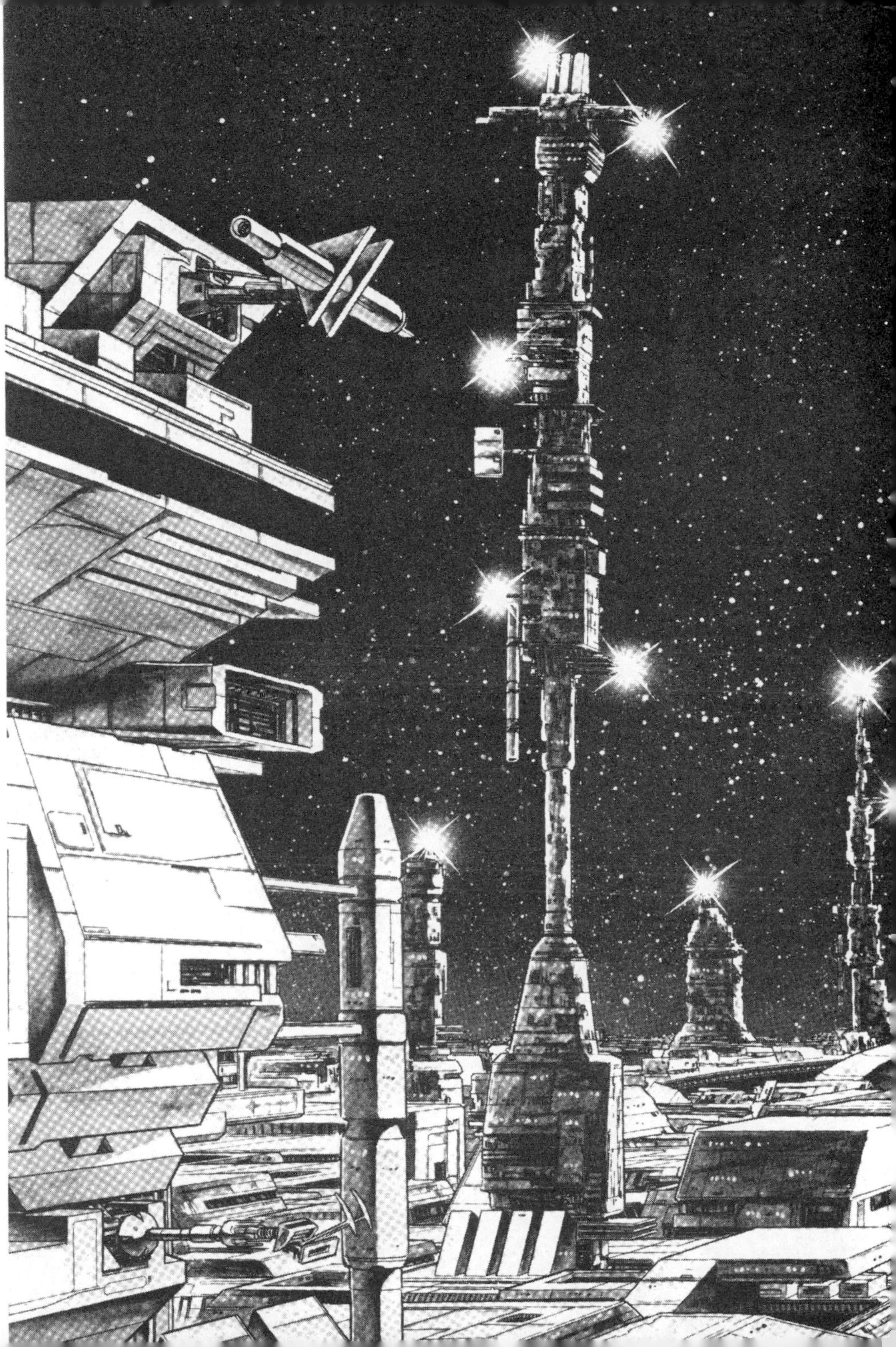

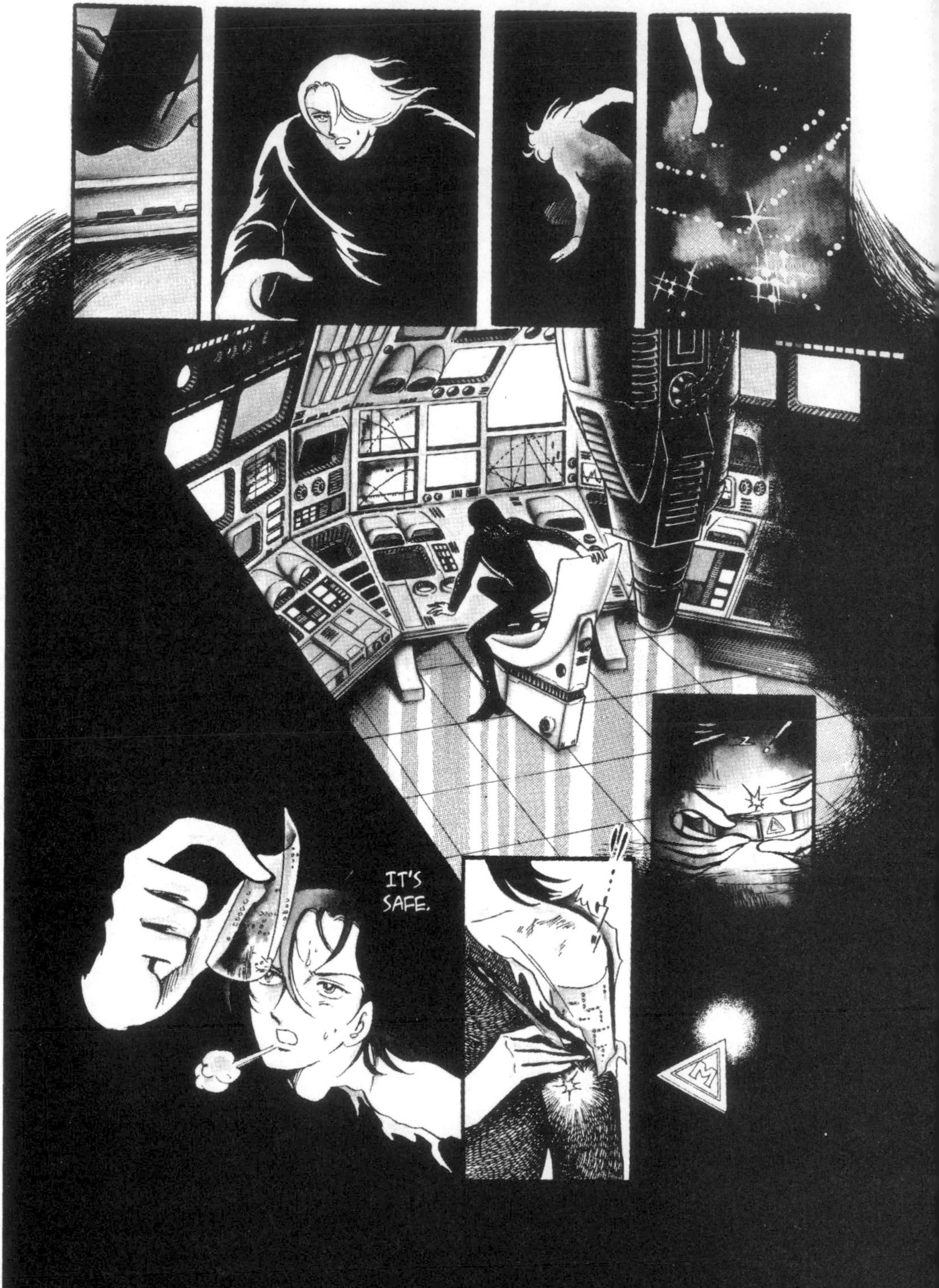
IT'S SAFE.

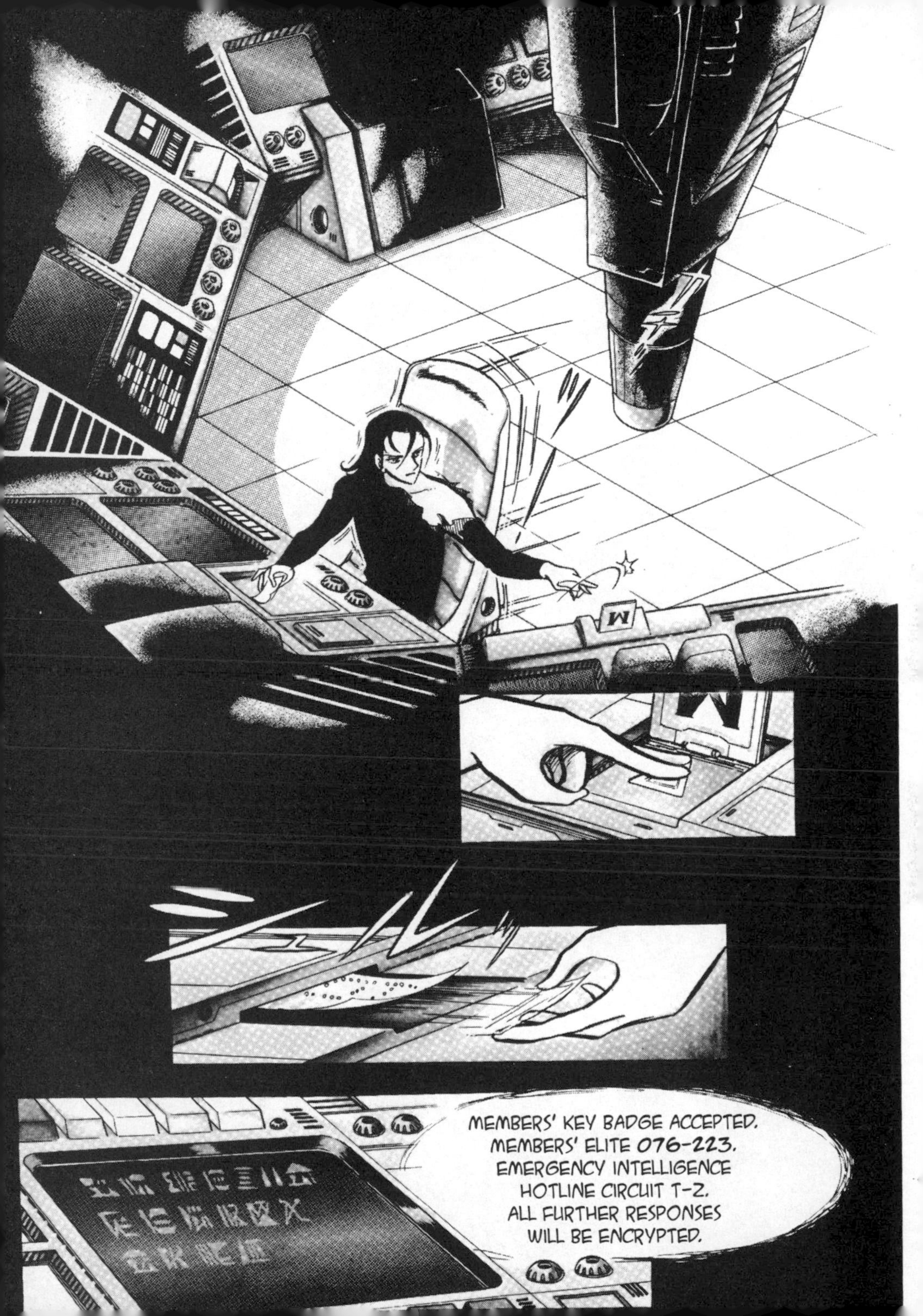
MEMBERS' KEY BADGE ACCEPTED. MEMBERS' ELITE 076-223. EMERGENCY INTELLIGENCE HOTLINE CIRCUIT T-2. ALL FURTHER RESPONSES WILL BE ENCRYPTED.

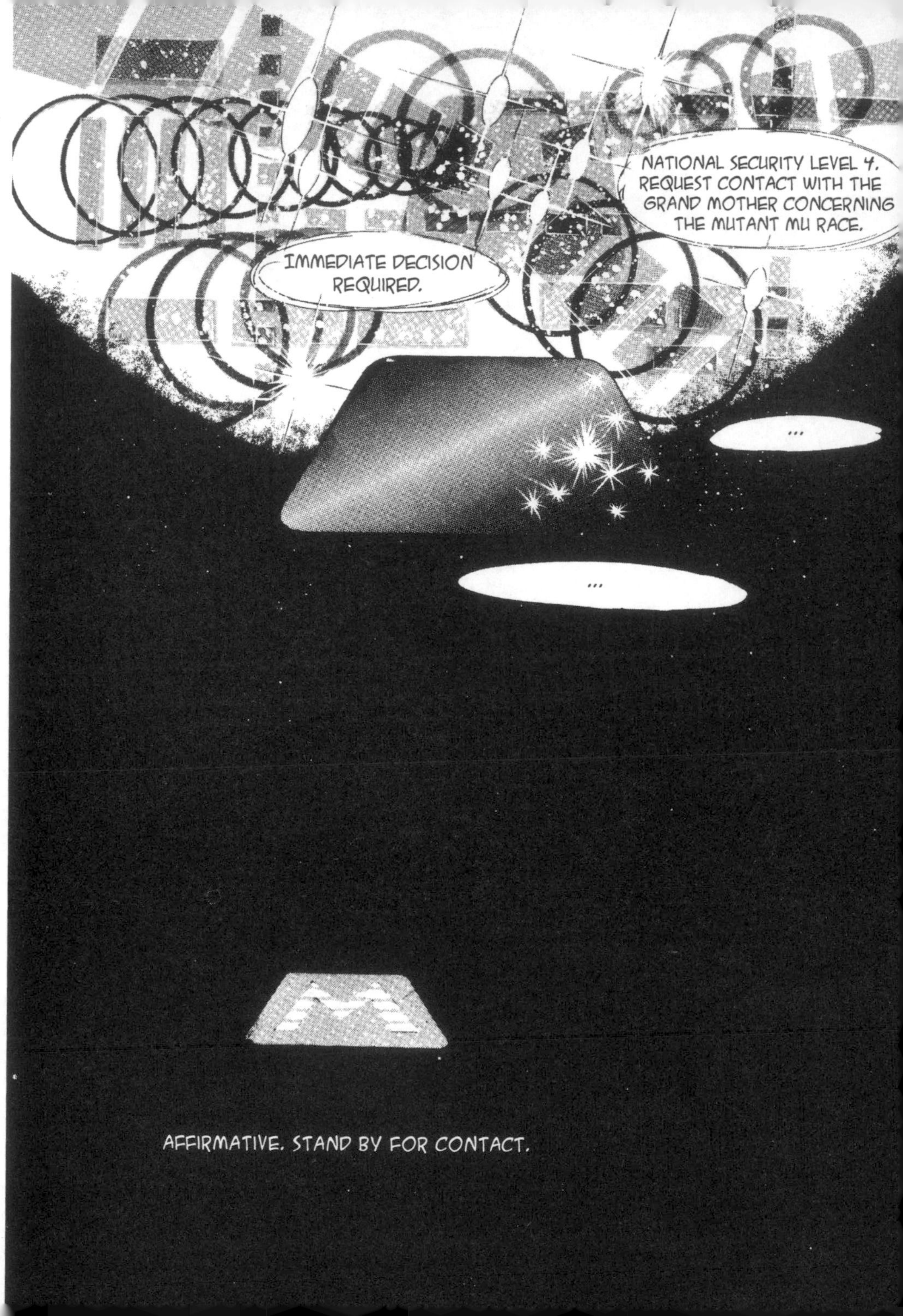
NATIONAL SECURITY LEVEL 4. REQUEST CONTACT WITH THE GRAND MOTHER CONCERNING THE MUTANT MU RACE.
IMMEDIATE DECISION REQUIRED.
...
...
AFFIRMATIVE. STAND BY FOR CONTACT.

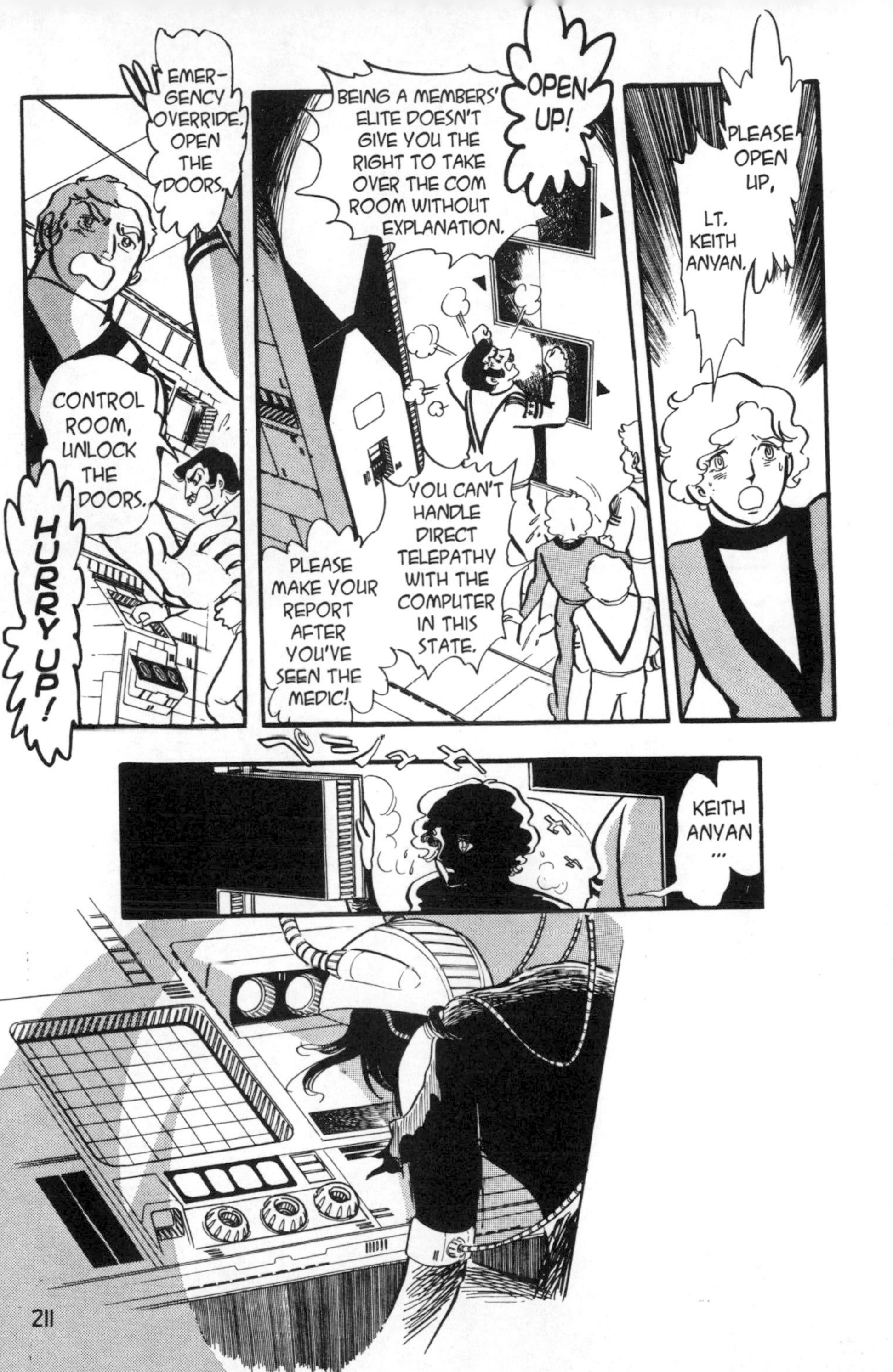
PLEASE OPEN UP,
LT. KEITH ANYAN.
OPEN UP!
BEING A MEMBERS' ELITE DOESN'T GIVE YOU THE RIGHT TO TAKE OVER THE COM ROOM WITHOUT EXPLANATION.
YOU CAN'T HANDLE DIRECT TELEPATHY WITH THE COMPUTER IN THIS STATE.
PLEASE MAKE YOUR REPORT AFTER YOU'VE SEEN THE MEDIC!
EMERGENCY OVERRIDE. OPEN THE DOORS.
CONTROL ROOM, UNLOCK THE DOORS.
HURRY UP!
KEITH ANYAN ...

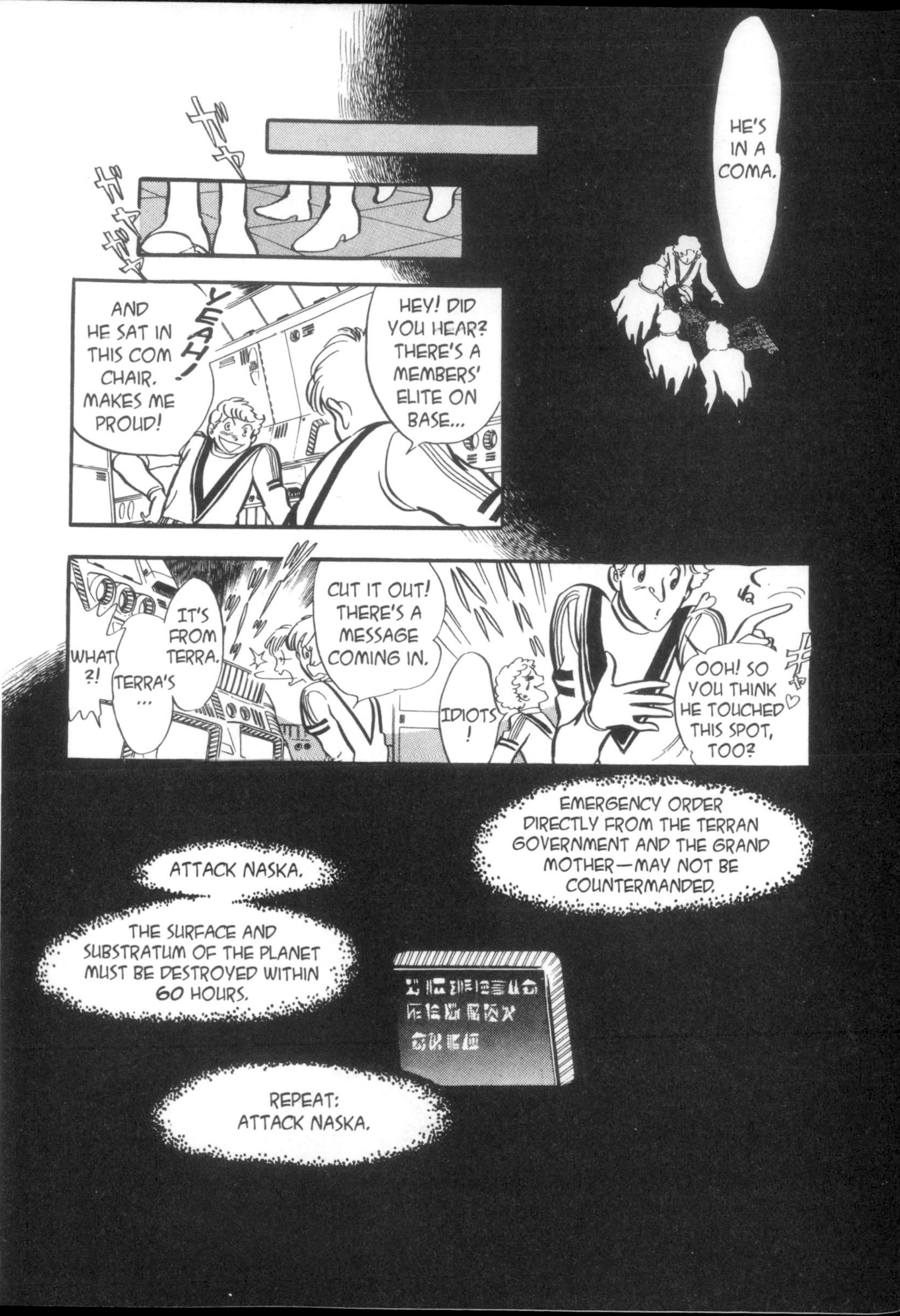
HE'S IN A COMA.
HEY! DID YOU HEAR? THERE'S A MEMBERS' ELITE ON BASE...
YEAH!
AND HE SAT IN THIS COM CHAIR. MAKES ME PROUD!
OOH! SO YOU THINK HE TOUCHED THIS SPOT, TOO?
IDIOTS!
CUT IT OUT! THERE'S A MESSAGE COMING IN.
IT'S FROM TERRA.
TERRA'S ...
WHAT?!
EMERGENCY ORDER DIRECTLY FROM THE TERRAN GOVERNMENT AND THE GRAND MOTHER—MAY NOT BE COUNTERMANDED.
ATTACK NASKA.
THE SURFACE AND SUBSTRATUM OF THE PLANET MUST BE DESTROYED WITHIN 60 HOURS.
REPEAT: ATTACK NASKA.

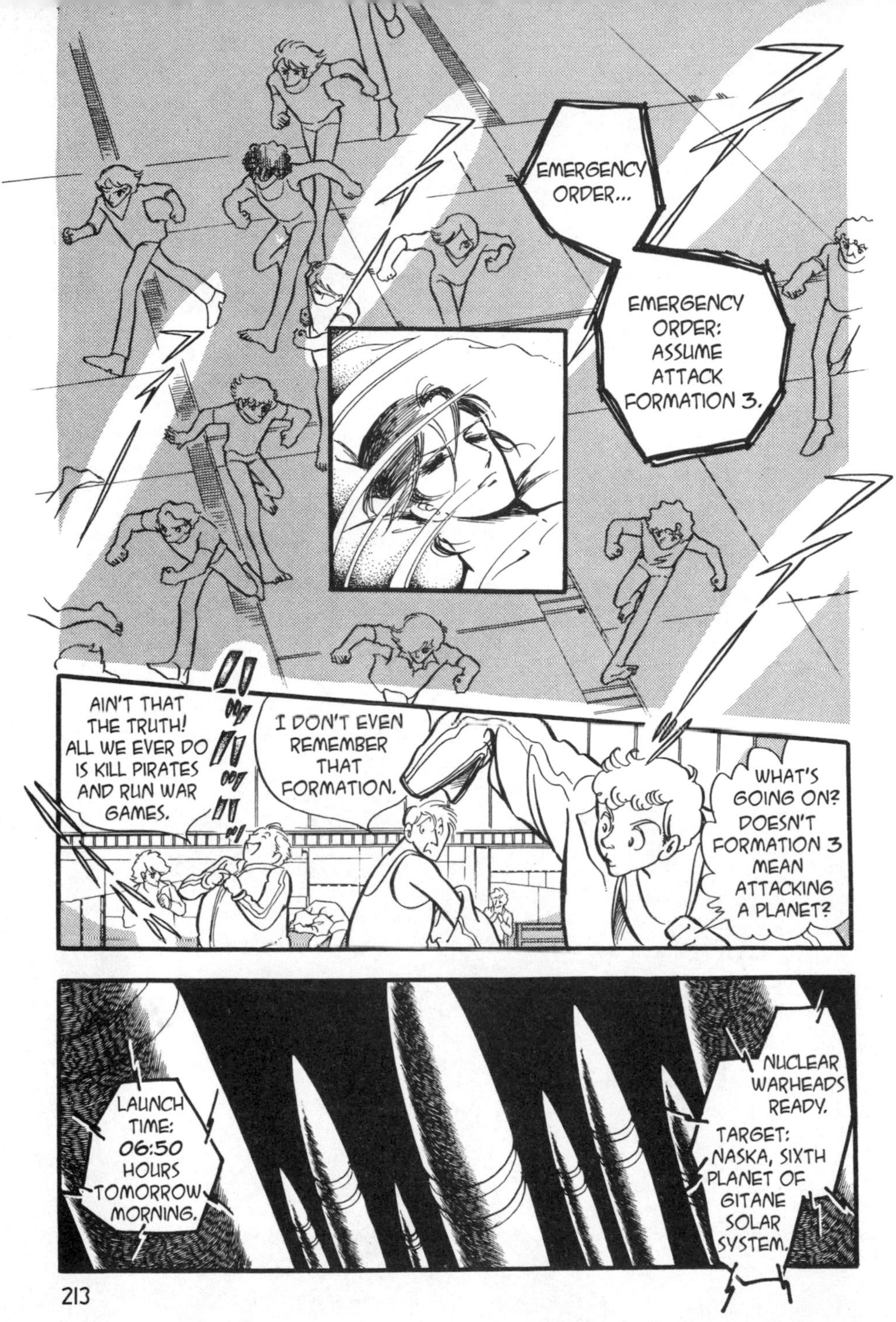
EMERGENCY ORDER...
EMERGENCY ORDER: ASSUME ATTACK FORMATION 3.
WHAT'S GOING ON? DOESN'T FORMATION 3 MEAN ATTACKING A PLANET?
I DON'T EVEN REMEMBER THAT FORMATION.
AIN'T THAT THE TRUTH! ALL WE EVER DO IS KILL PIRATES AND RUN WAR GAMES.
NUCLEAR WARHEADS READY.
TARGET: NASKA, SIXTH PLANET OF GITANE SOLAR SYSTEM.
LAUNCH TIME: 06:50 HOURS TOMORROW MORNING.

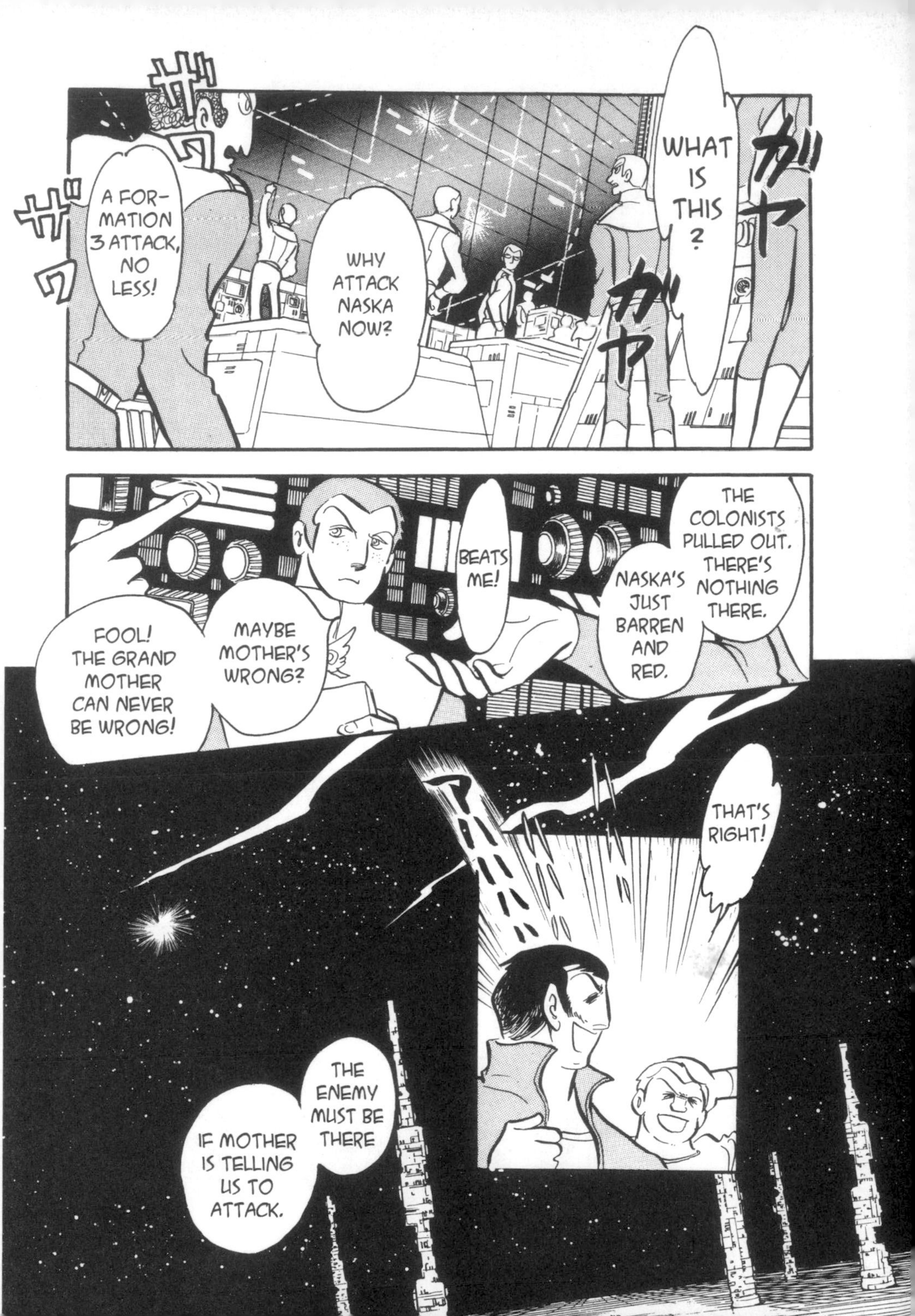
WHAT IS THIS?
ガヤ
ガヤ
WHY ATTACK NASKA NOW?
A FOR-MATION 3 ATTACK, NO LESS!
ザワ
ザワ
THE COLONISTS PULLED OUT. THERE'S NOTHING THERE.
NASKA'S JUST BARREN AND RED.
BEATS ME!
MAYBE MOTHER'S WRONG?
FOOL! THE GRAND MOTHER CAN NEVER BE WRONG!
THAT'S RIGHT!
THE ENEMY MUST BE THERE
IF MOTHER IS TELLING US TO ATTACK.

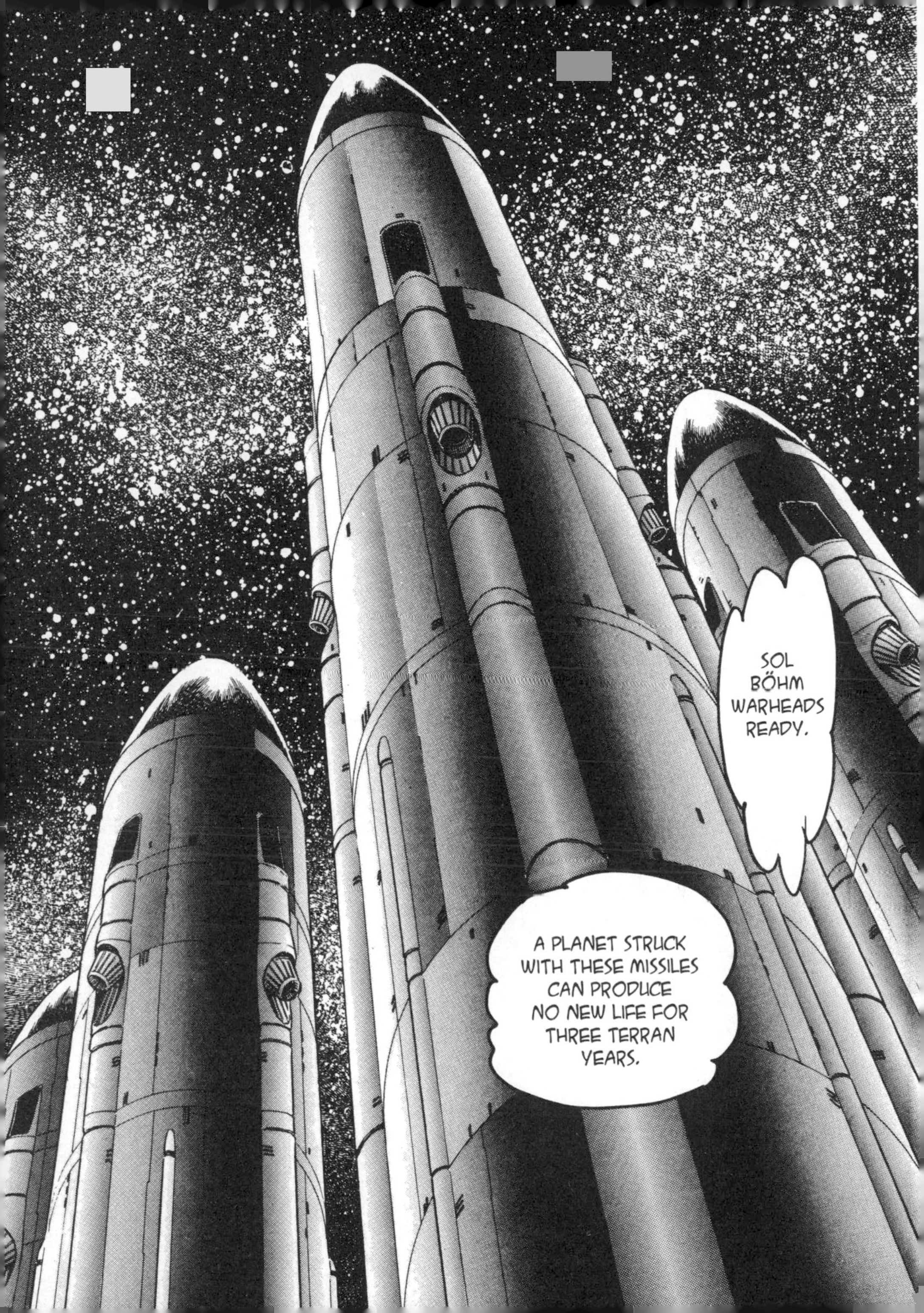
SOL BÖHM WARHEADS READY.
A PLANET STRUCK WITH THESE MISSILES CAN PRODUCE NO NEW LIFE FOR THREE TERRAN YEARS.

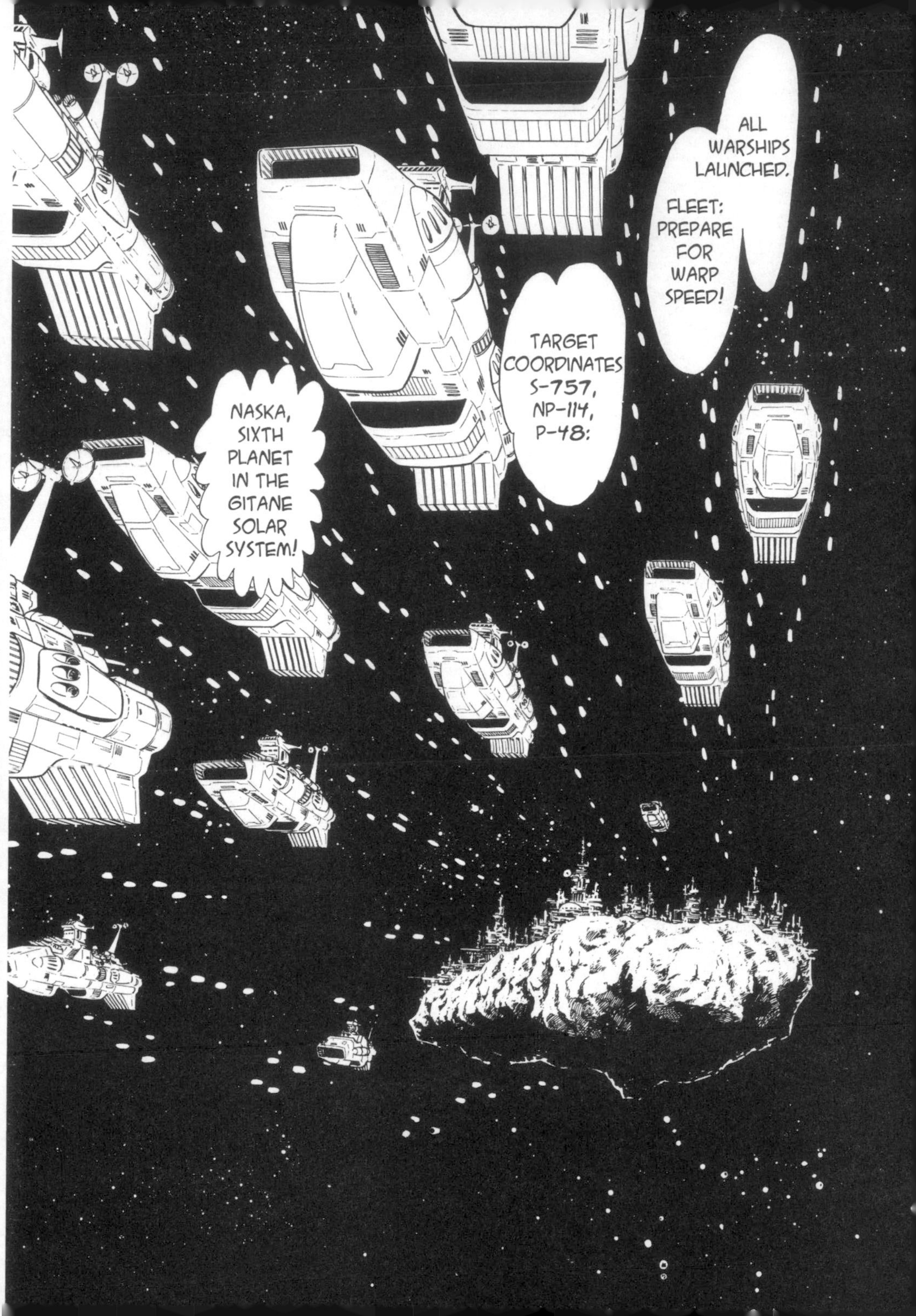
ALL WARSHIPS LAUNCHED. FLEET: PREPARE FOR WARP SPEED!
TARGET COORDINATES S-757, NP-114, P-48:
NASKA, SIXTH PLANET IN THE GITANE SOLAR SYSTEM!

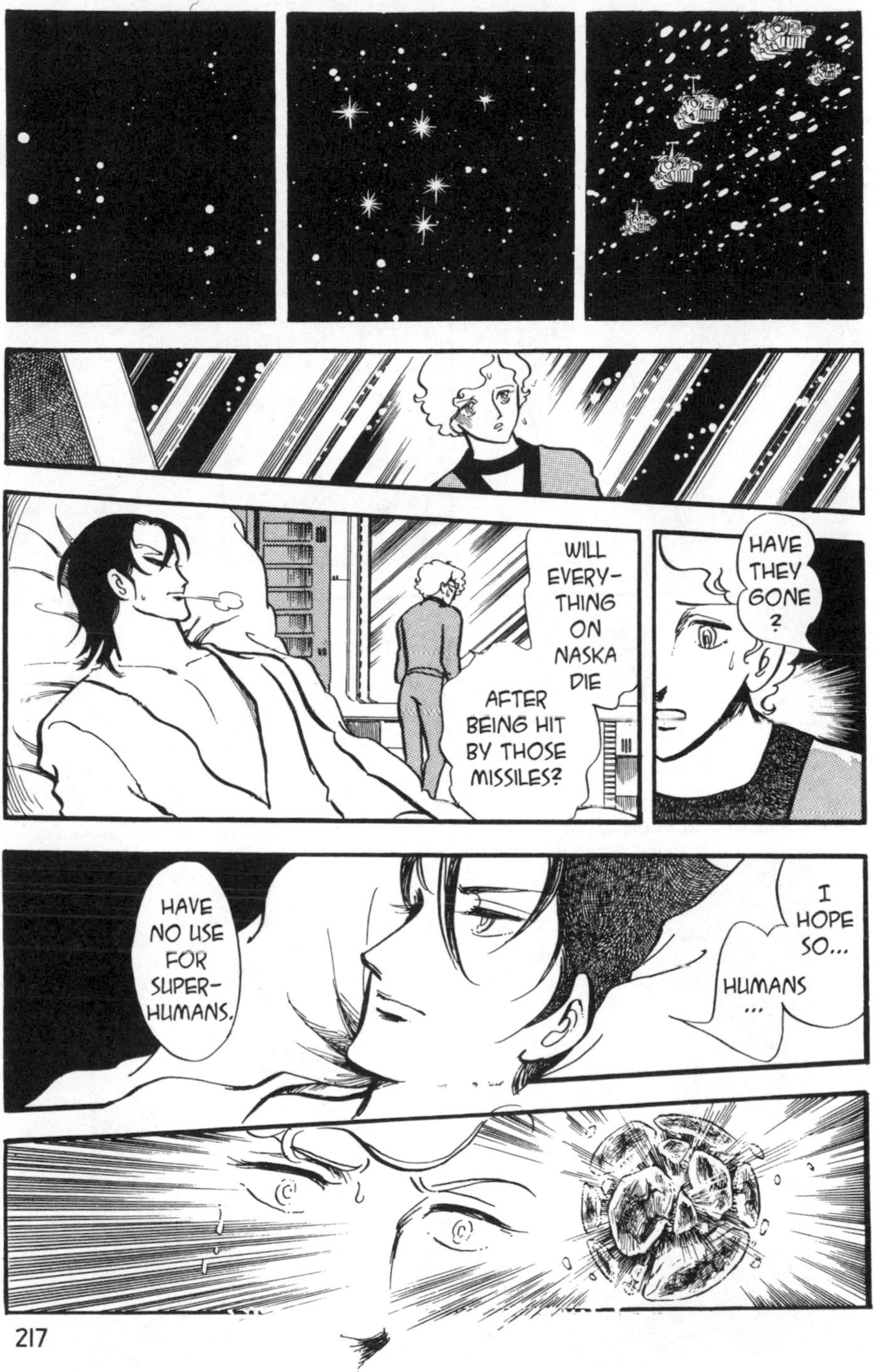
HAVE THEY GONE?
WILL EVERYTHING ON NASKA DIE
AFTER BEING HIT BY THOSE MISSILES?
I HOPE SO...
HUMANS ...
HAVE NO USE FOR SUPER-HUMANS.

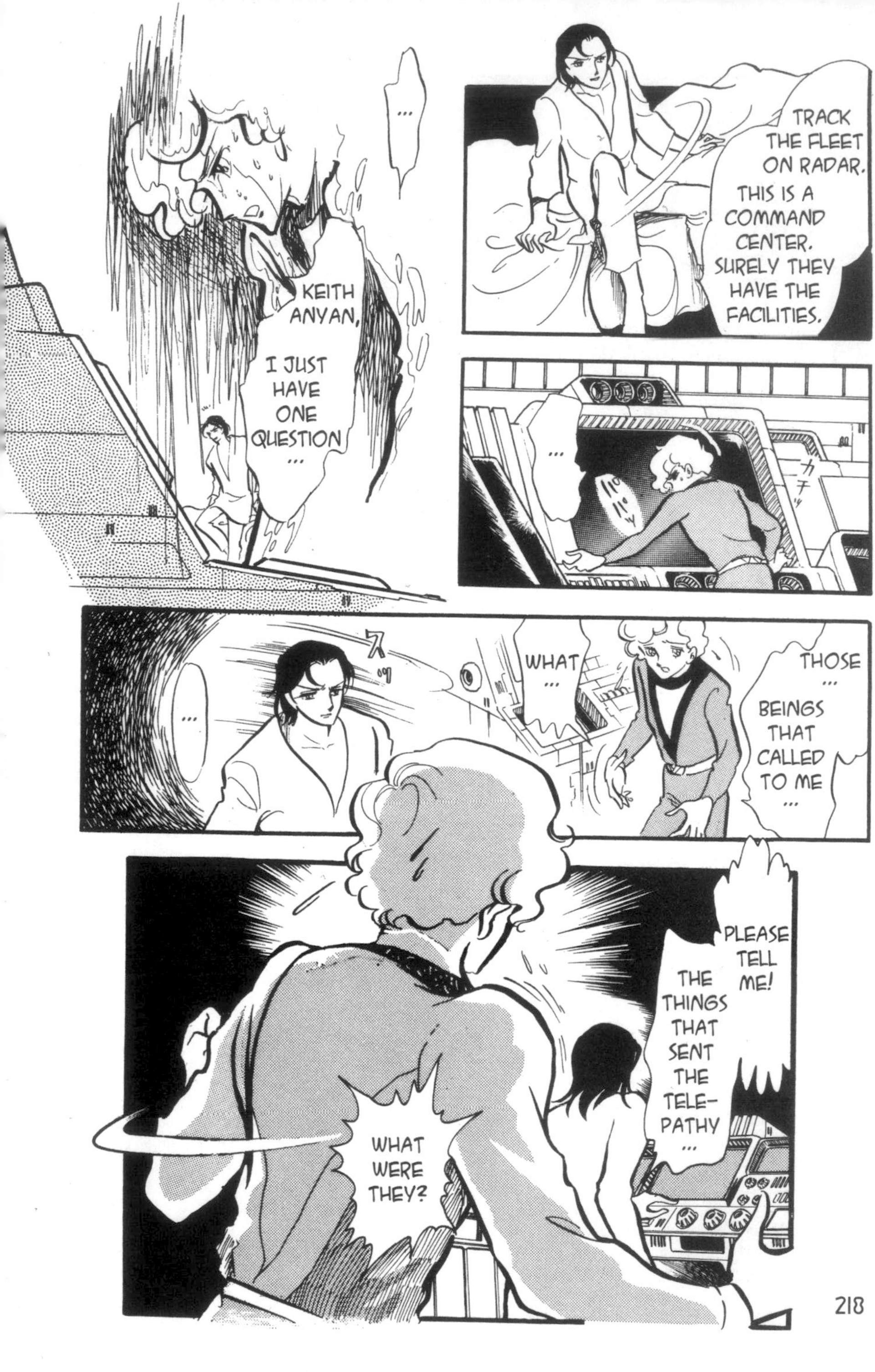

TRACK THE FLEET ON RADAR.
THIS IS A COMMAND CENTER. SURELY THEY HAVE THE FACILITIES.
...
...
KEITH ANYAN,
I JUST HAVE ONE QUESTION ...
THOSE ...
BEINGS THAT CALLED TO ME ...
WHAT ...
...
PLEASE TELL ME!
THE THINGS THAT SENT THE TELEPATHY ...
WHAT WERE THEY?

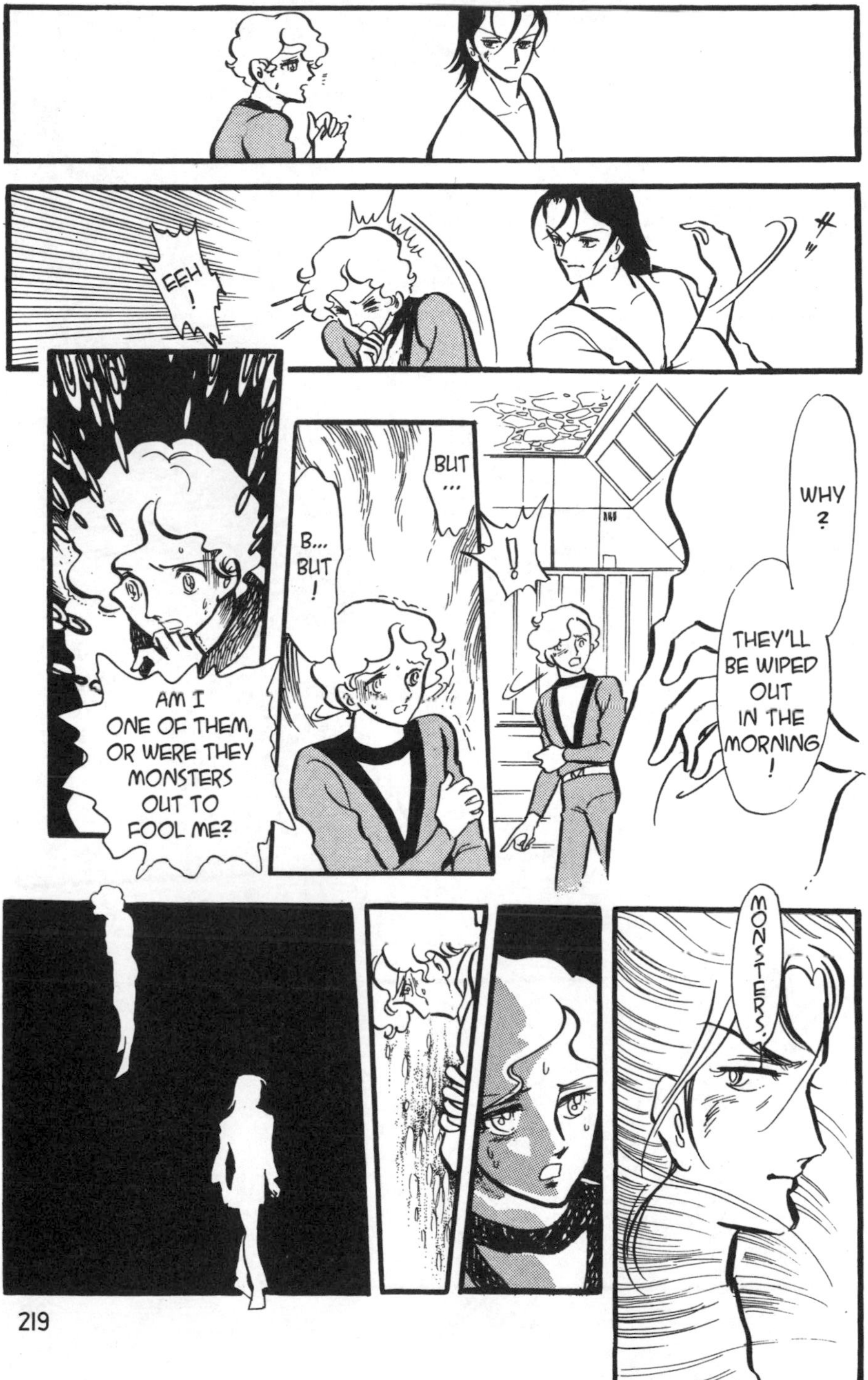
EEH!
WHY?
THEY'LL BE WIPED OUT IN THE MORNING!
!
BUT...
B... BUT!
AM I ONE OF THEM, OR WERE THEY MONSTERS OUT TO FOOL ME?
MONSTERS...

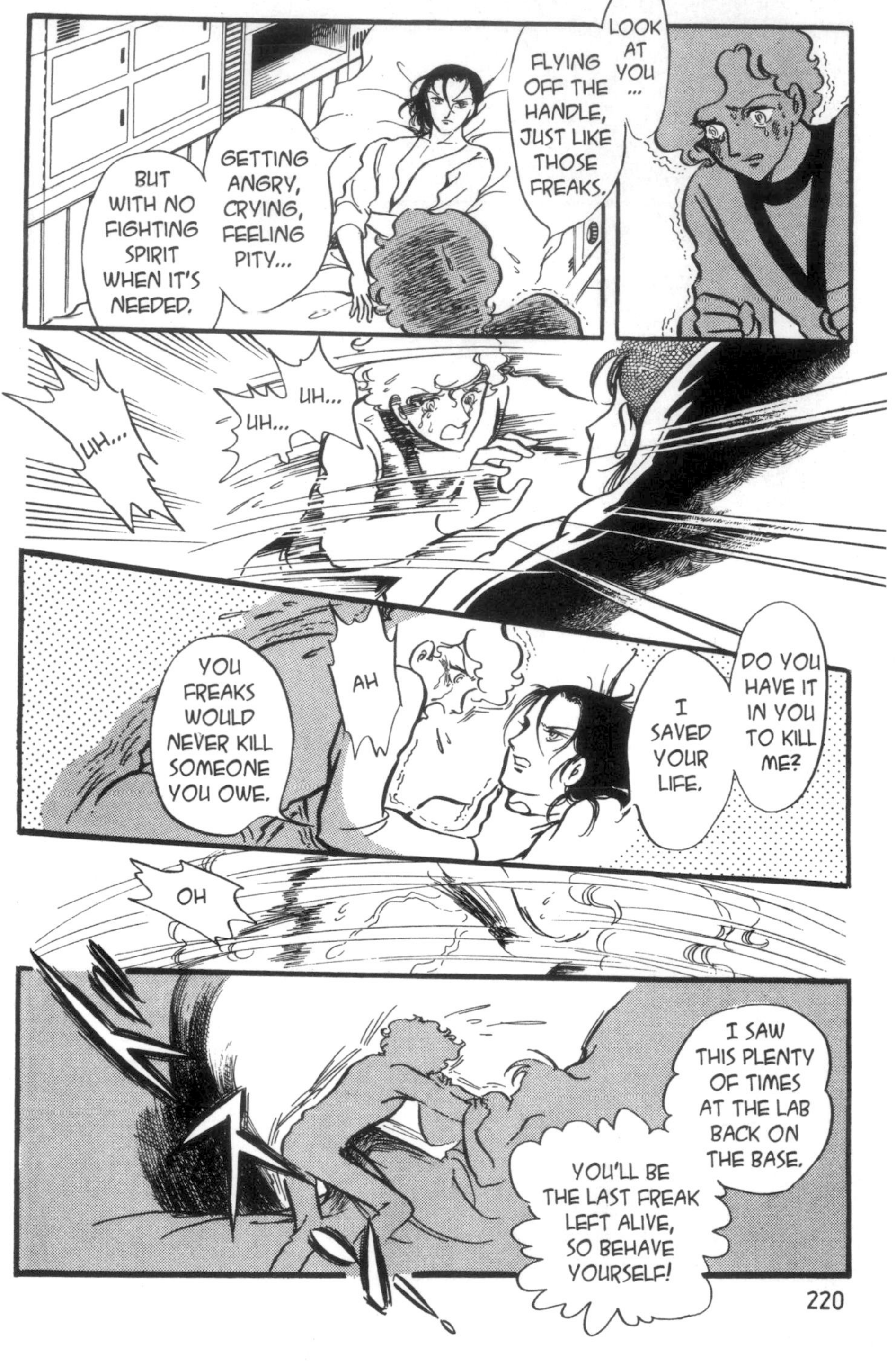
LOOK AT YOU ...
FLYING OFF THE HANDLE, JUST LIKE THOSE FREAKS.
GETTING ANGRY, CRYING, FEELING PITY...
BUT WITH NO FIGHTING SPIRIT WHEN IT'S NEEDED.
UH...
UH...
UH...
DO YOU HAVE IT IN YOU TO KILL ME?
I SAVED YOUR LIFE.
AH
YOU FREAKS WOULD NEVER KILL SOMEONE YOU OWE.
OH
I SAW THIS PLENTY OF TIMES AT THE LAB BACK ON THE BASE.
YOU'LL BE THE LAST FREAK LEFT ALIVE, SO BEHAVE YOURSELF!

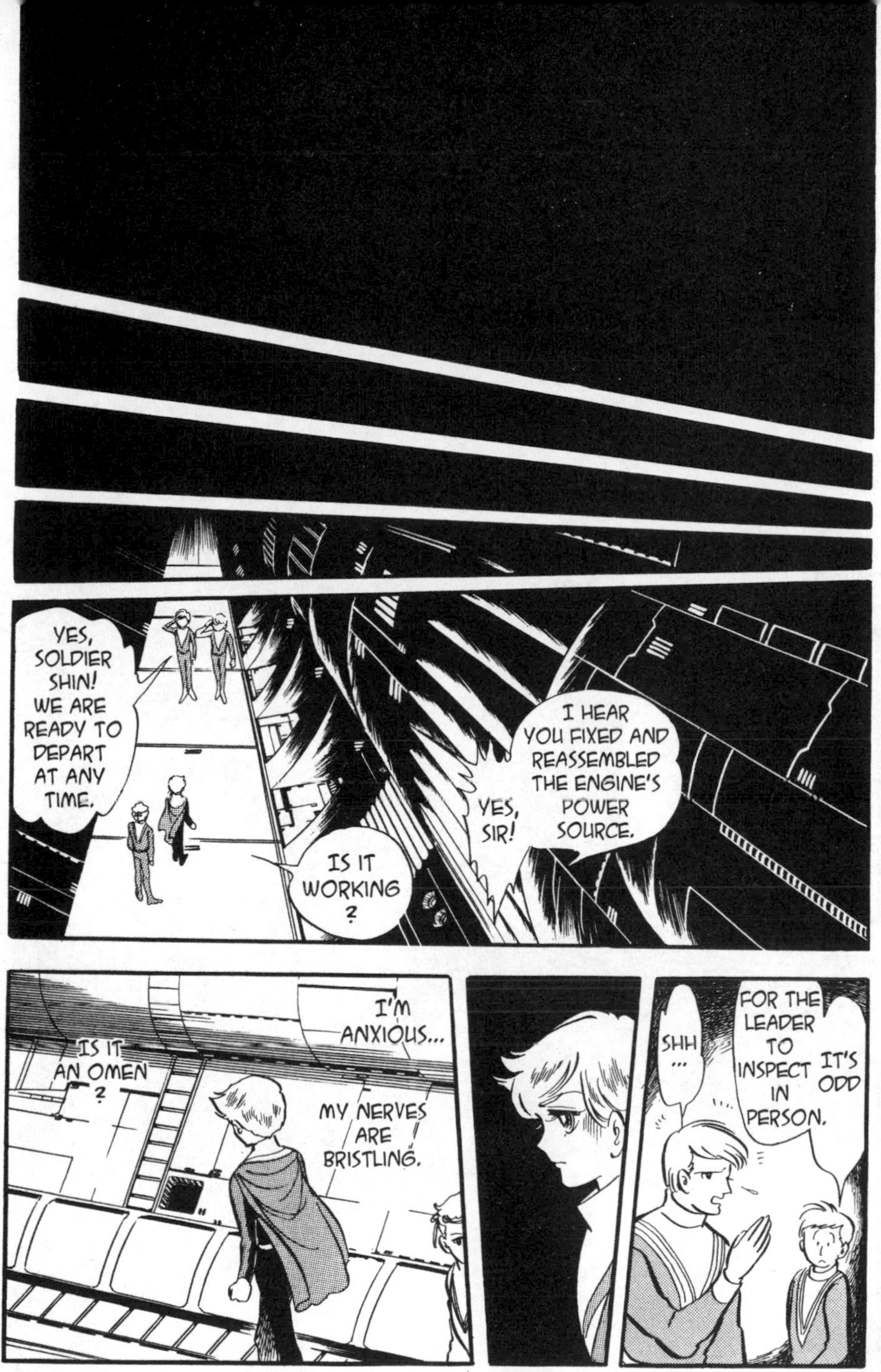
I HEAR YOU FIXED AND REASSEMBLED THE ENGINE'S POWER SOURCE.
YES, SIR!
IS IT WORKING?
YES, SOLDIER SHIN! WE ARE READY TO DEPART AT ANY TIME.
IT'S ODD
FOR THE LEADER TO INSPECT IN PERSON.
SHH...
I'M ANXIOUS...
IS IT AN OMEN?
MY NERVES ARE BRISTLING.

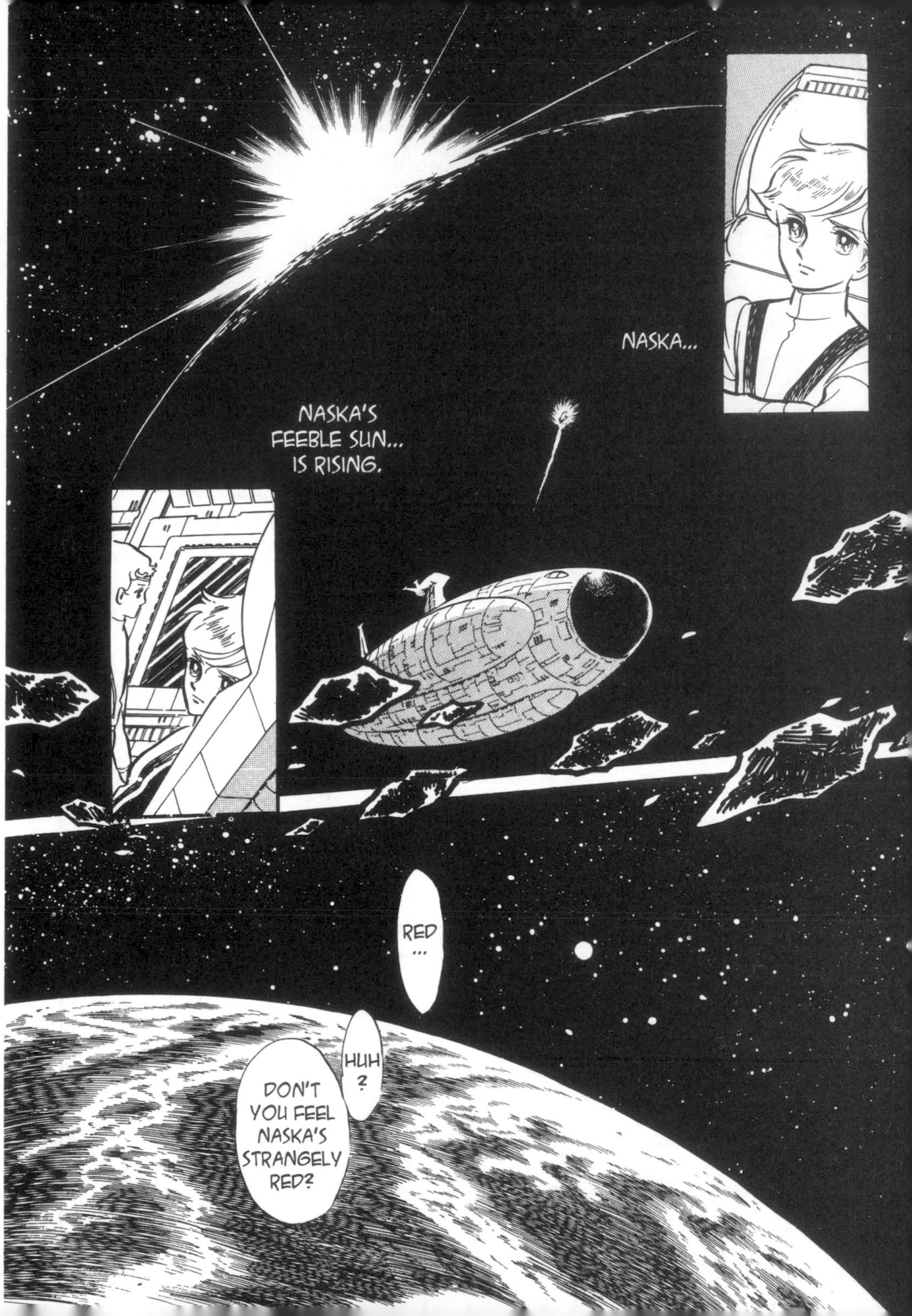
NASKA...
NASKA'S FEEBLE SUN... IS RISING.
RED ...
HUH?
DON'T YOU FEEL NASKA'S STRANGELY RED?

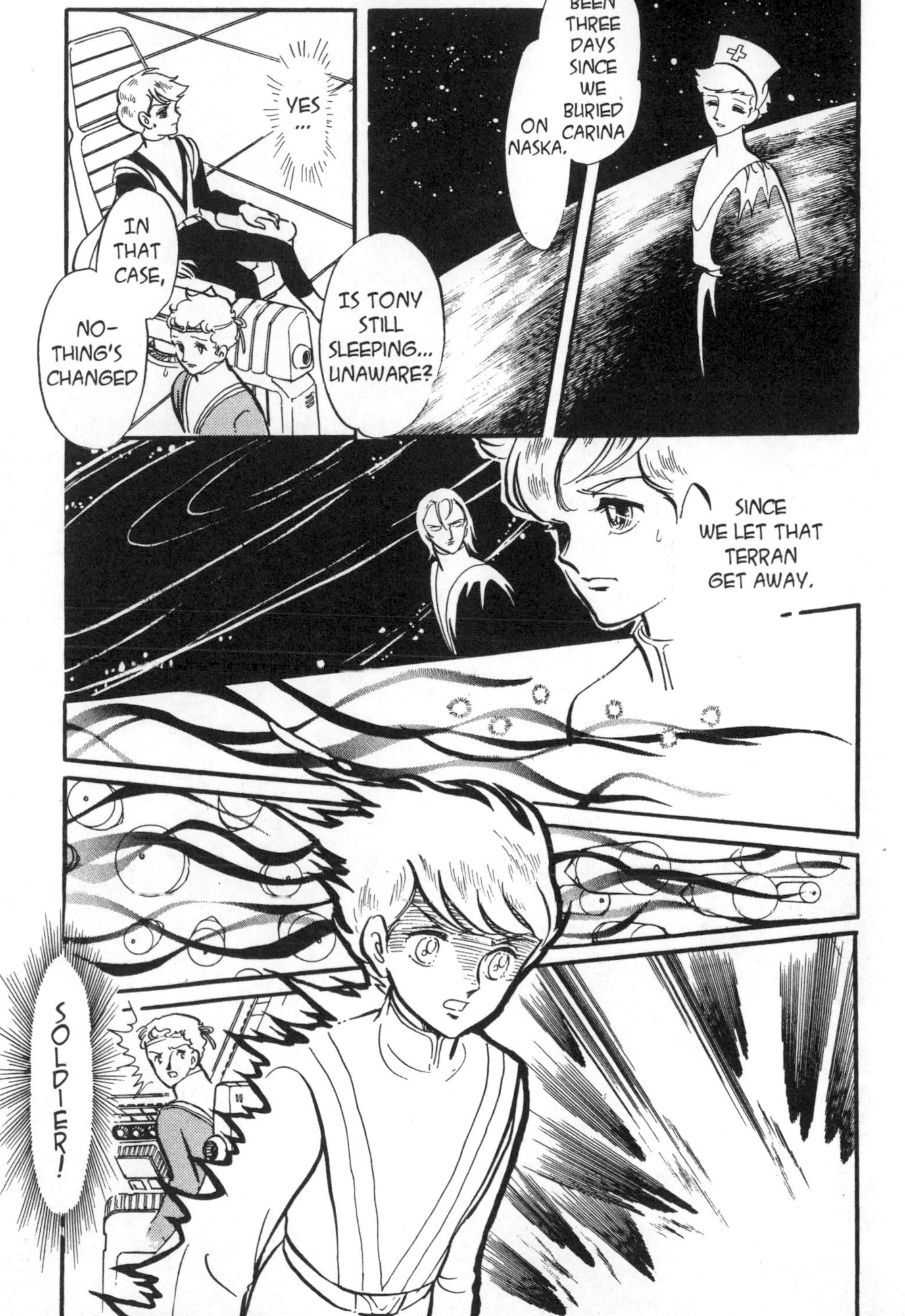
IT'S BEEN THREE DAYS SINCE WE BURIED CARINA
ON NASKA.
IS TONY STILL SLEEPING... UNAWARE?
YES ...
IN THAT CASE,
NO-THING'S CHANGED
SINCE WE LET THAT TERRAN GET AWAY.
SOLDIER!

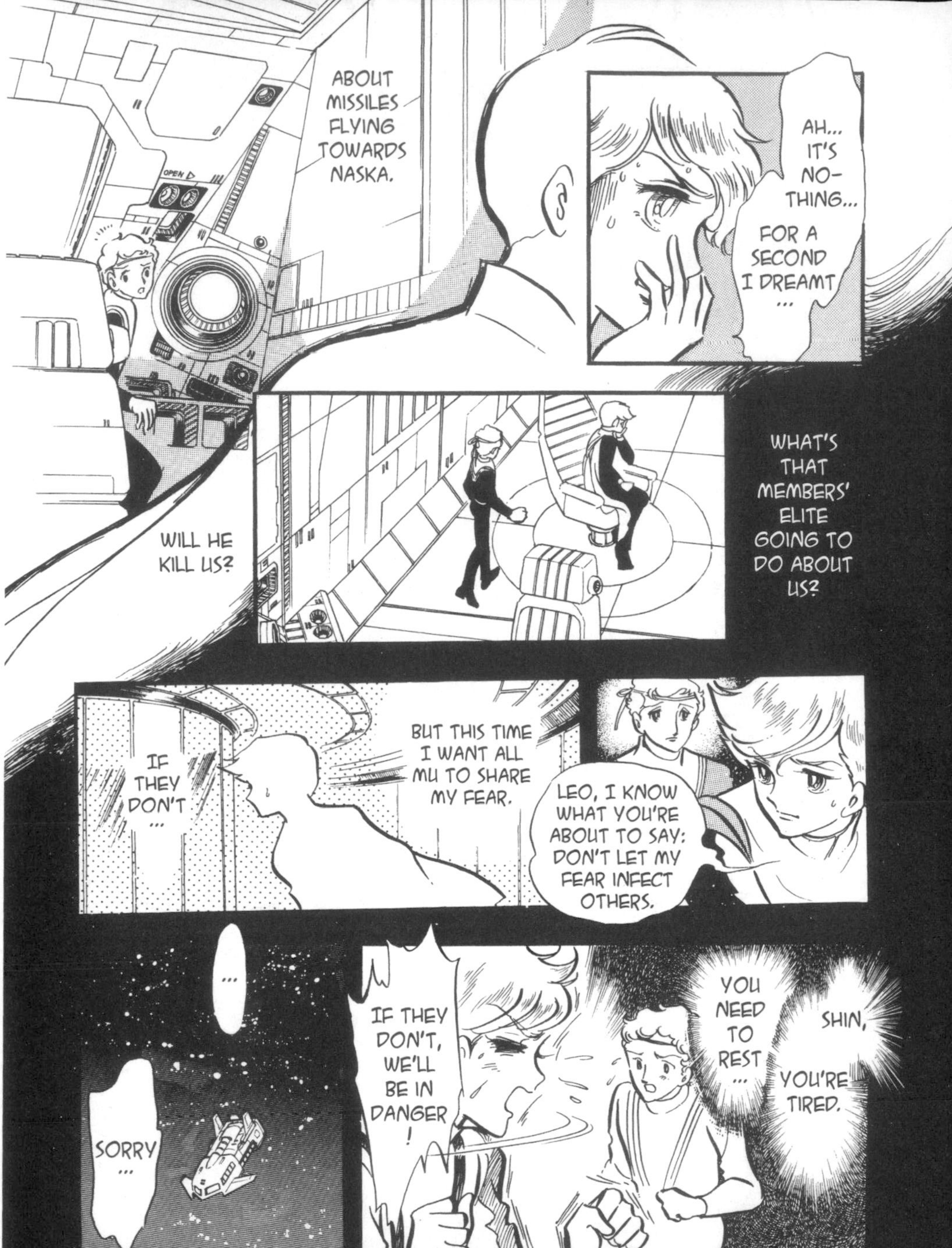
AH... IT'S NO-THING...
FOR A SECOND I DREAMT ...
ABOUT MISSILES FLYING TOWARDS NASKA.
WHAT'S THAT MEMBERS' ELITE GOING TO DO ABOUT US?
WILL HE KILL US?
LEO, I KNOW WHAT YOU'RE ABOUT TO SAY: DON'T LET MY FEAR INFECT OTHERS.
BUT THIS TIME I WANT ALL MU TO SHARE MY FEAR.
IF THEY DON'T ...
SHIN,
YOU'RE TIRED.
YOU NEED TO REST ...
IF THEY DON'T, WE'LL BE IN DANGER !
...
SORRY ...

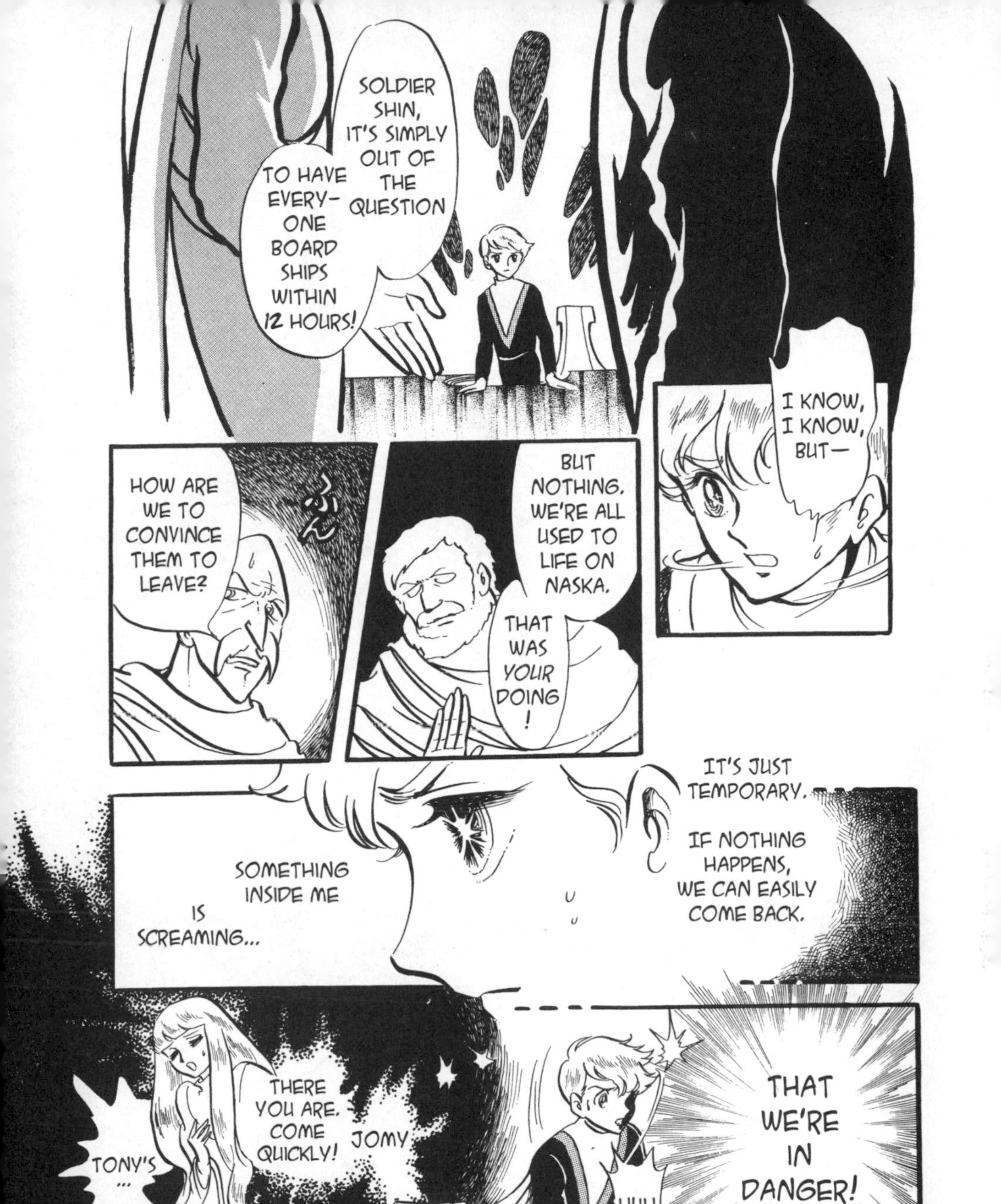
SOLDIER SHIN, IT'S SIMPLY OUT OF THE QUESTION
TO HAVE EVERY-ONE BOARD SHIPS WITHIN 12 HOURS!
I KNOW, I KNOW, BUT—
BUT NOTHING. WE'RE ALL USED TO LIFE ON NASKA.
THAT WAS YOUR DOING!
HOW ARE WE TO CONVINCE THEM TO LEAVE?
IT'S JUST TEMPORARY.
IF NOTHING HAPPENS, WE CAN EASILY COME BACK.
SOMETHING INSIDE ME IS SCREAMING...
THAT WE'RE IN DANGER!
HUH?
JOMY
THERE YOU ARE. COME QUICKLY!
TONY'S...

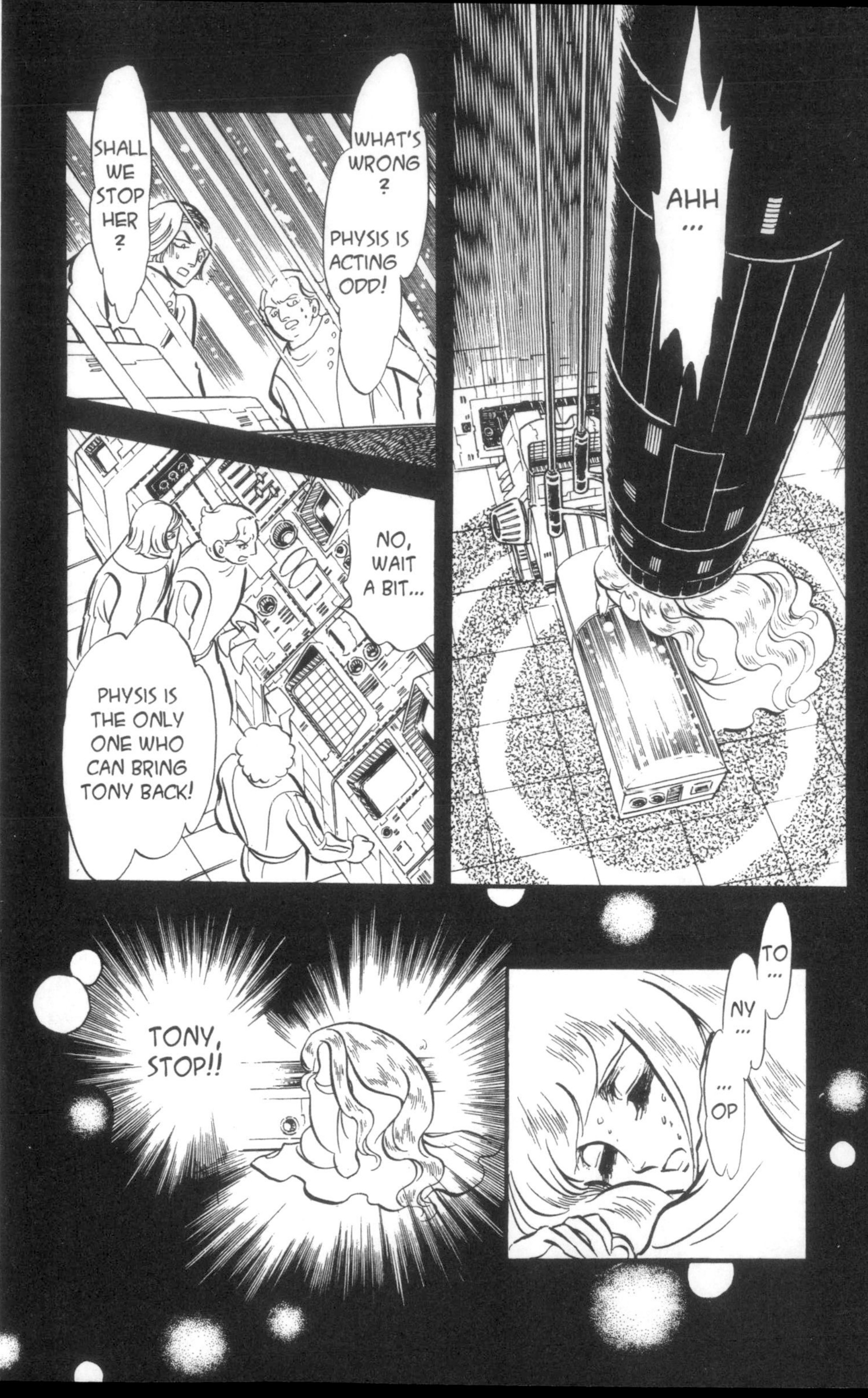
AHH ...
WHAT'S WRONG ?
PHYSIS IS ACTING ODD!
SHALL WE STOP HER ?
NO, WAIT A BIT...
PHYSIS IS THE ONLY ONE WHO CAN BRING TONY BACK!
TO ...
NY ...
... OP
TONY, STOP!!

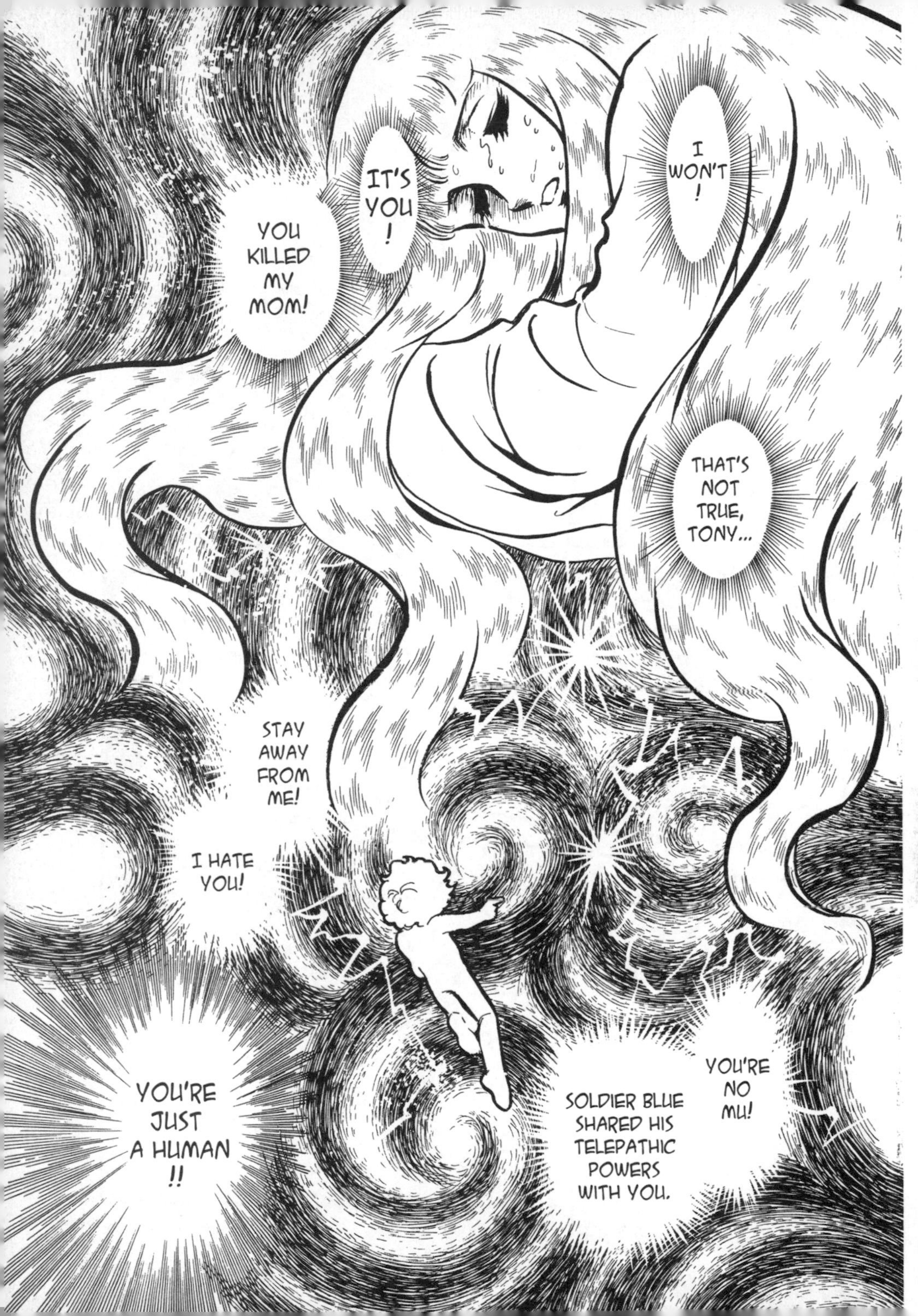
I WON'T!
IT'S YOU!
YOU KILLED MY MOM!
THAT'S NOT TRUE, TONY...
STAY AWAY FROM ME!
I HATE YOU!
YOU'RE NO MU!
SOLDIER BLUE SHARED HIS TELEPATHIC POWERS WITH YOU.
YOU'RE JUST A HUMAN!!

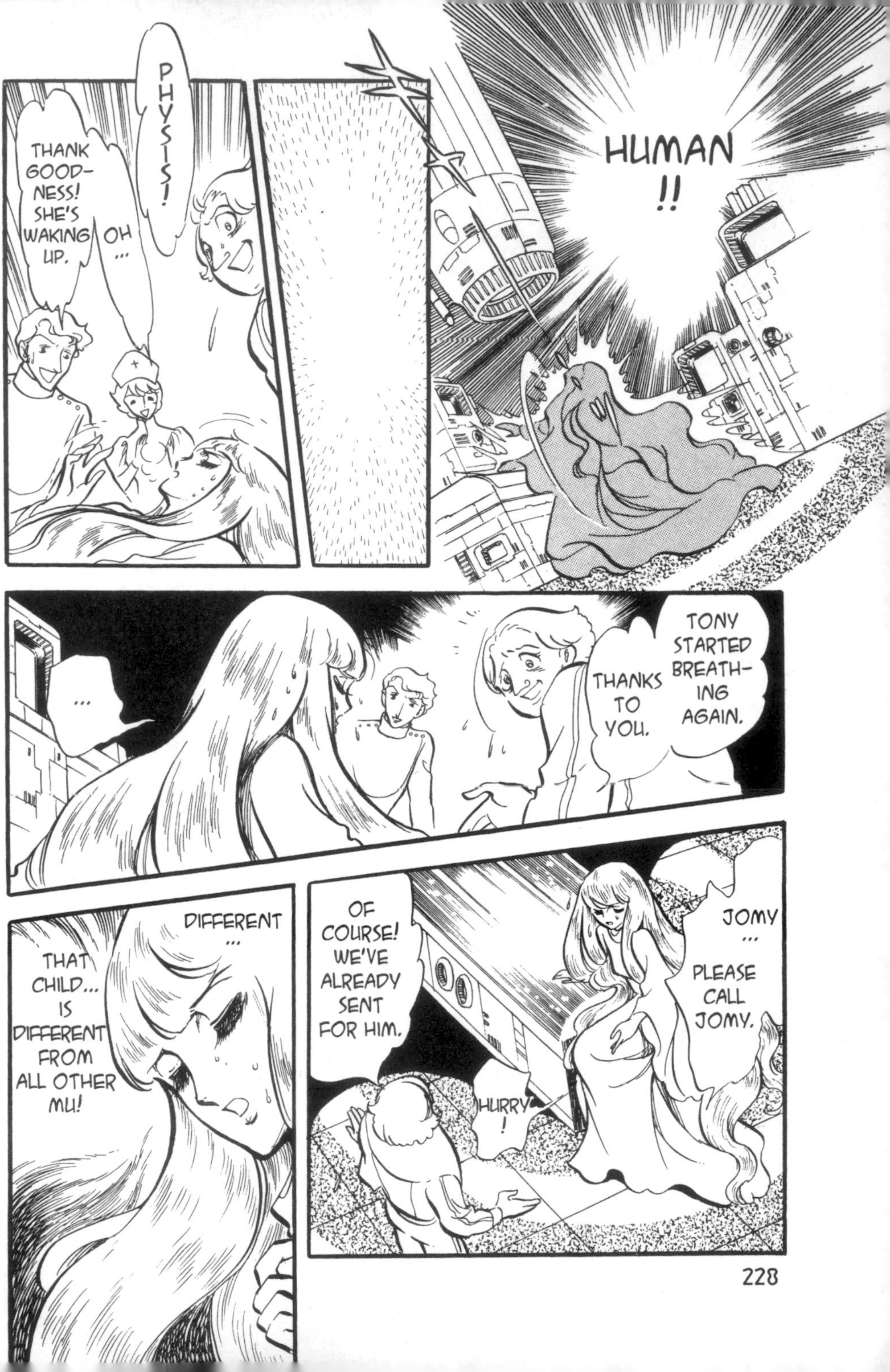
HUMAN !!
PHYSIS!
OH ...
THANK GOODNESS! SHE'S WAKING UP.
TONY STARTED BREATHING AGAIN.
THANKS TO YOU.
...
JOMY ...
PLEASE CALL JOMY.
OF COURSE! WE'VE ALREADY SENT FOR HIM.
HURRY!
DIFFERENT ...
THAT CHILD... IS DIFFERENT FROM ALL OTHER MU!

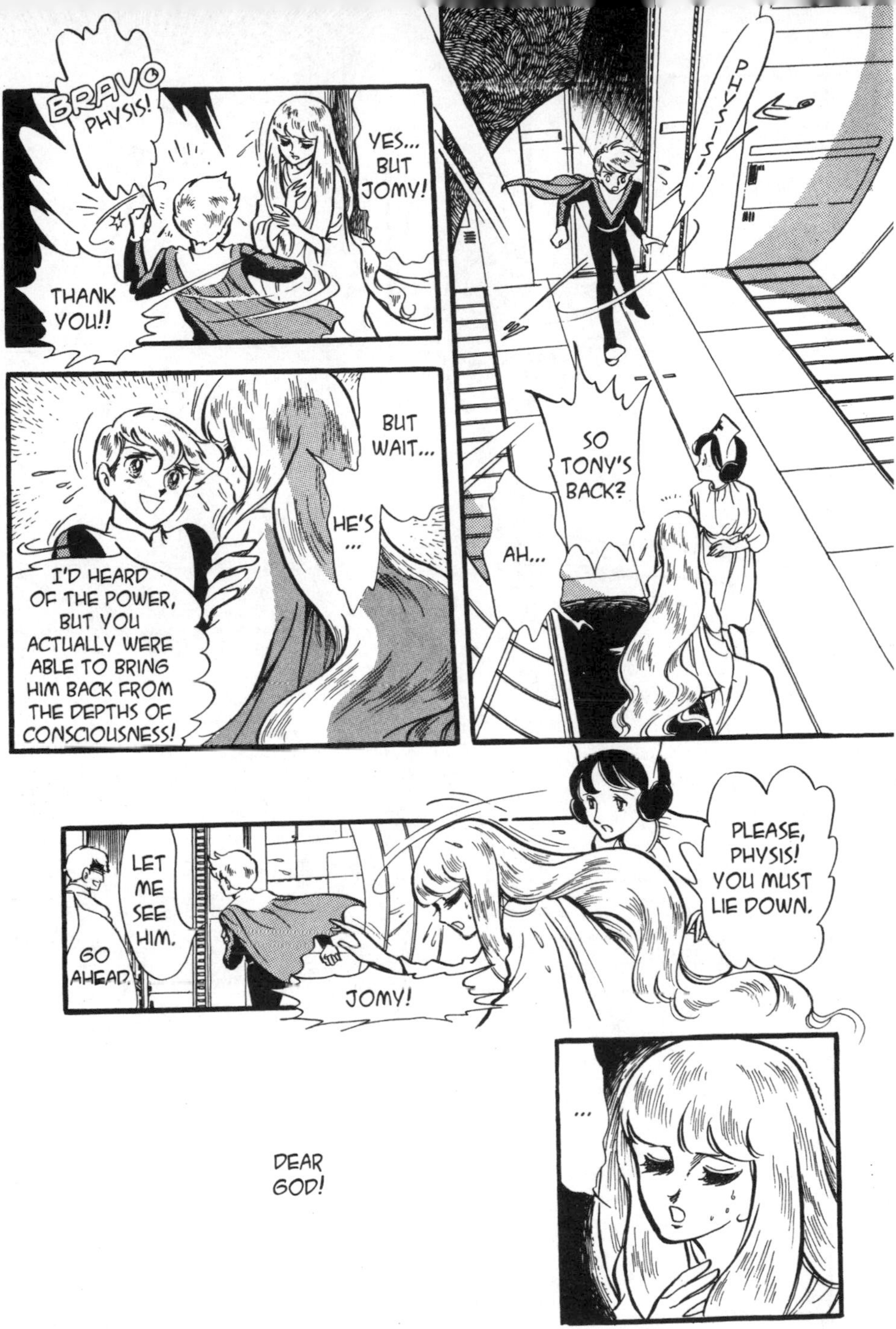
PHYSIS!
SO TONY'S BACK?
AH...
BRAVO PHYSIS!
THANK YOU!!
YES... BUT JOMY!
BUT WAIT...
HE'S ...
I'D HEARD OF THE POWER, BUT YOU ACTUALLY WERE ABLE TO BRING HIM BACK FROM THE DEPTHS OF CONSCIOUSNESS!
PLEASE, PHYSIS! YOU MUST LIE DOWN.
JOMY!
LET ME SEE HIM.
GO AHEAD.
...
DEAR GOD!

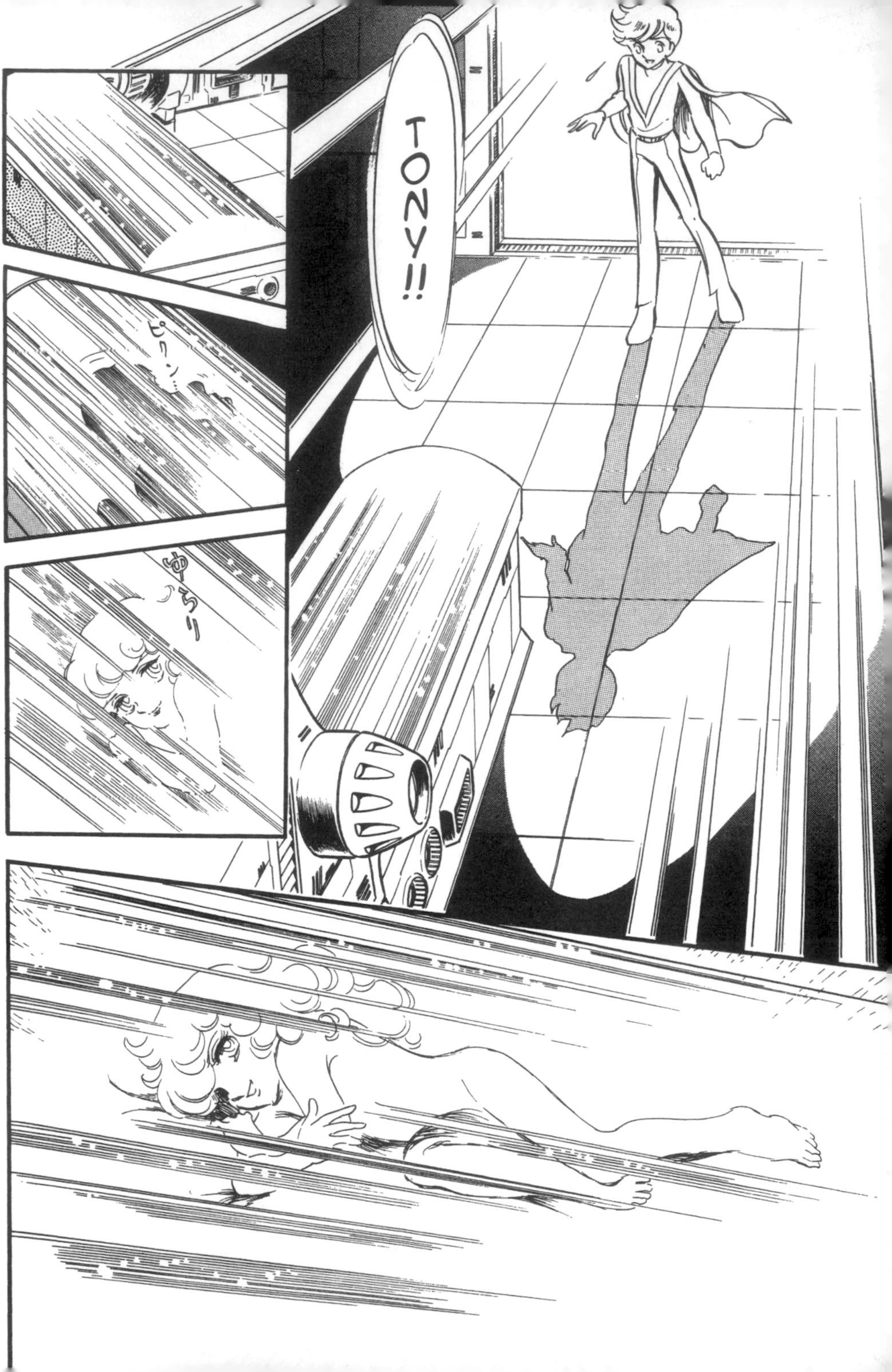
TONY!!
ピク・ン…
ゆらり

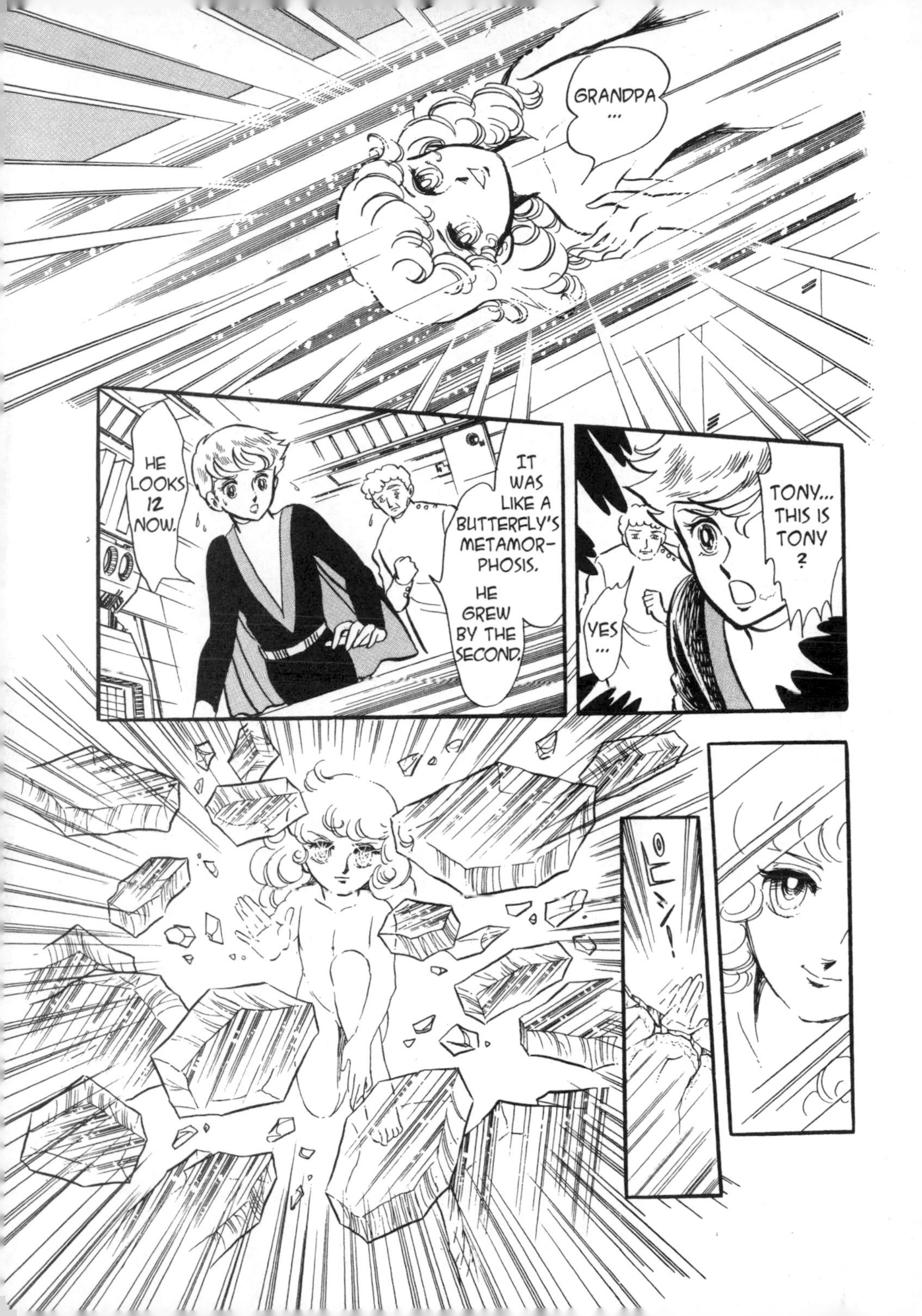
GRANDPA ...
TONY... THIS IS TONY ?
YES ...
IT WAS LIKE A BUTTERFLY'S METAMORPHOSIS.
HE GREW BY THE SECOND.
HE LOOKS 12 NOW.

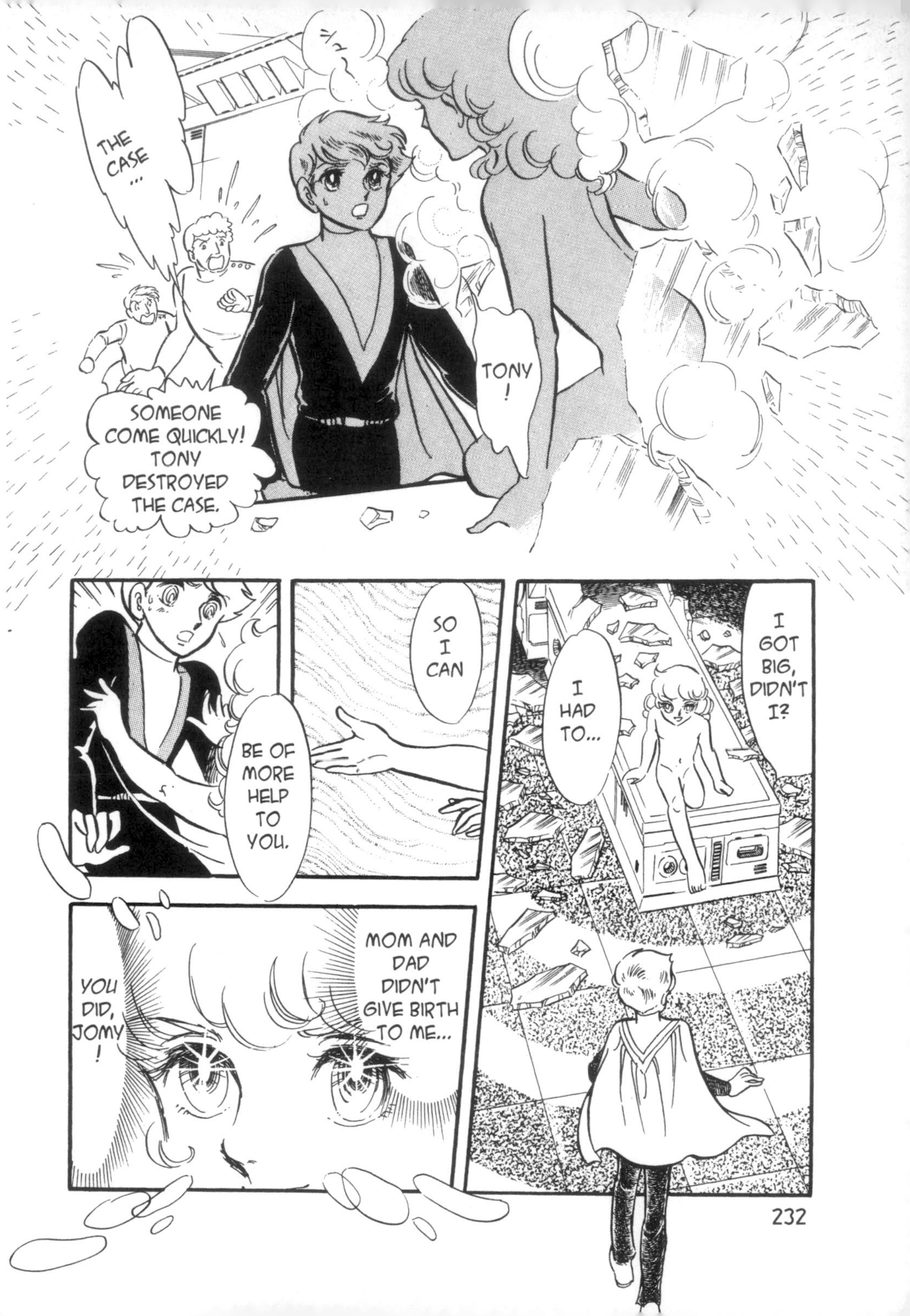
TONY!
THE CASE ...
SOMEONE COME QUICKLY! TONY DESTROYED THE CASE.
I GOT BIG, DIDN'T I?
I HAD TO...
SO I CAN
BE OF MORE HELP TO YOU.
MOM AND DAD DIDN'T GIVE BIRTH TO ME...
YOU DID, JOMY!

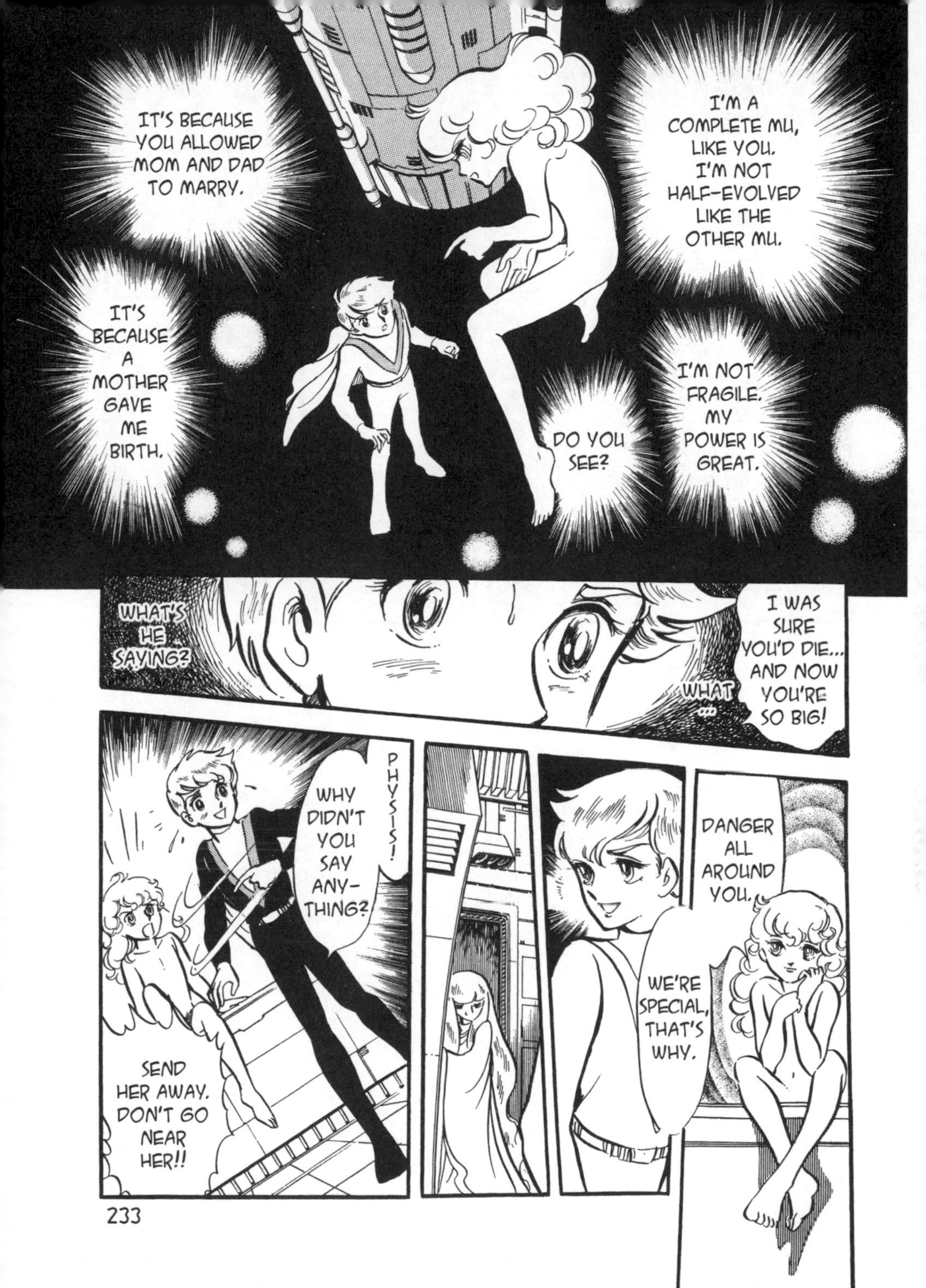
I'M A COMPLETE MU, LIKE YOU. I'M NOT HALF-EVOLVED LIKE THE OTHER MU.
IT'S BECAUSE YOU ALLOWED MOM AND DAD TO MARRY.
I'M NOT FRAGILE. MY POWER IS GREAT.
IT'S BECAUSE A MOTHER GAVE ME BIRTH.
DO YOU SEE?
I WAS SURE YOU'D DIE... AND NOW YOU'RE SO BIG!
WHAT...
WHAT'S HE SAYING?
DANGER ALL AROUND YOU.
WE'RE SPECIAL, THAT'S WHY.
PHYSIS!
WHY DIDN'T YOU SAY ANYTHING?
SEND HER AWAY. DON'T GO NEAR HER!!

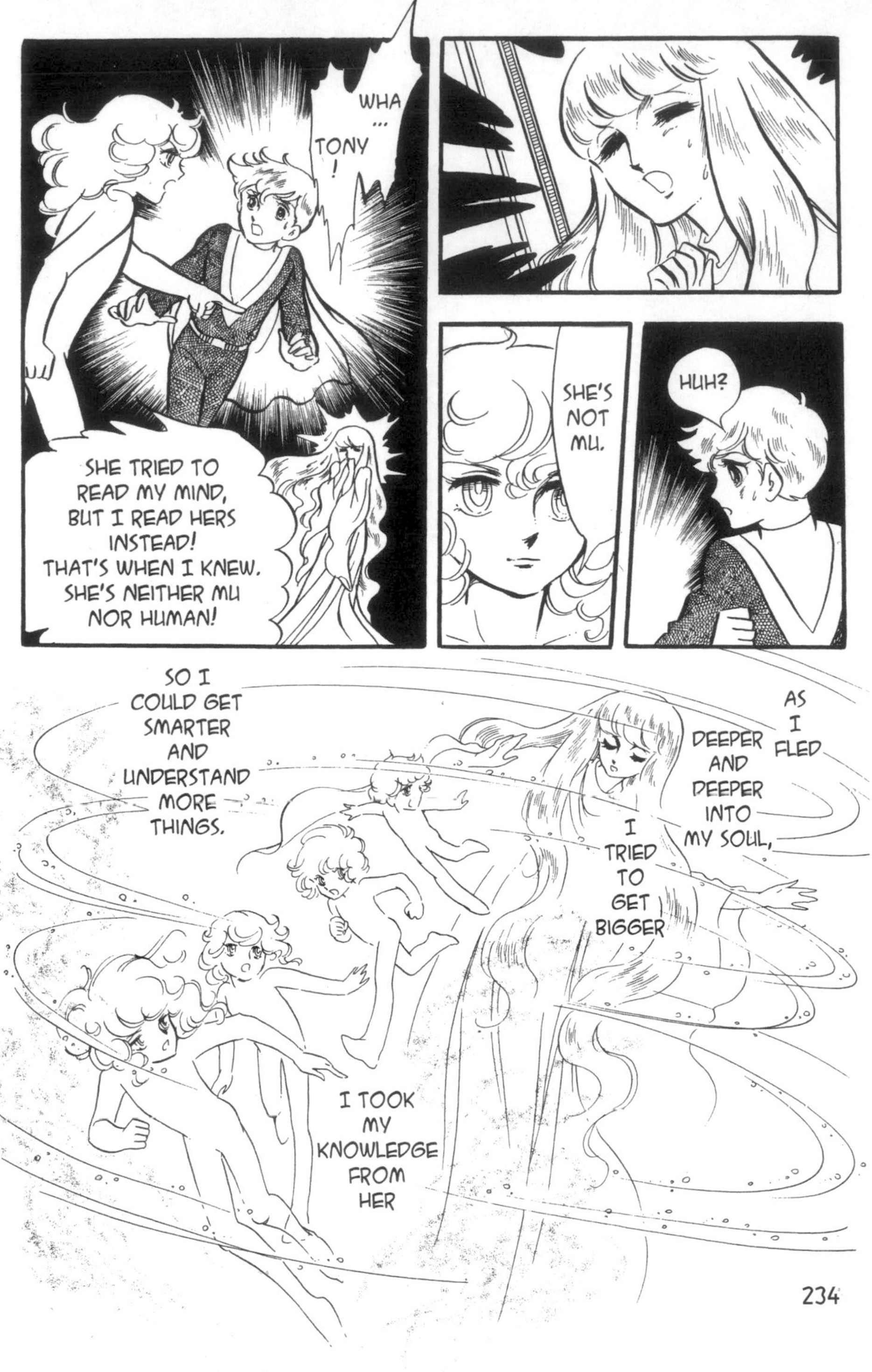
HUH?
SHE'S NOT MU.
WHA... TONY!
SHE TRIED TO READ MY MIND, BUT I READ HERS INSTEAD! THAT'S WHEN I KNEW. SHE'S NEITHER MU NOR HUMAN!
AS I FLED
DEEPER AND DEEPER INTO MY SOUL,
I TRIED TO GET BIGGER
SO I COULD GET SMARTER AND UNDERSTAND MORE THINGS.
I TOOK MY KNOWLEDGE FROM HER

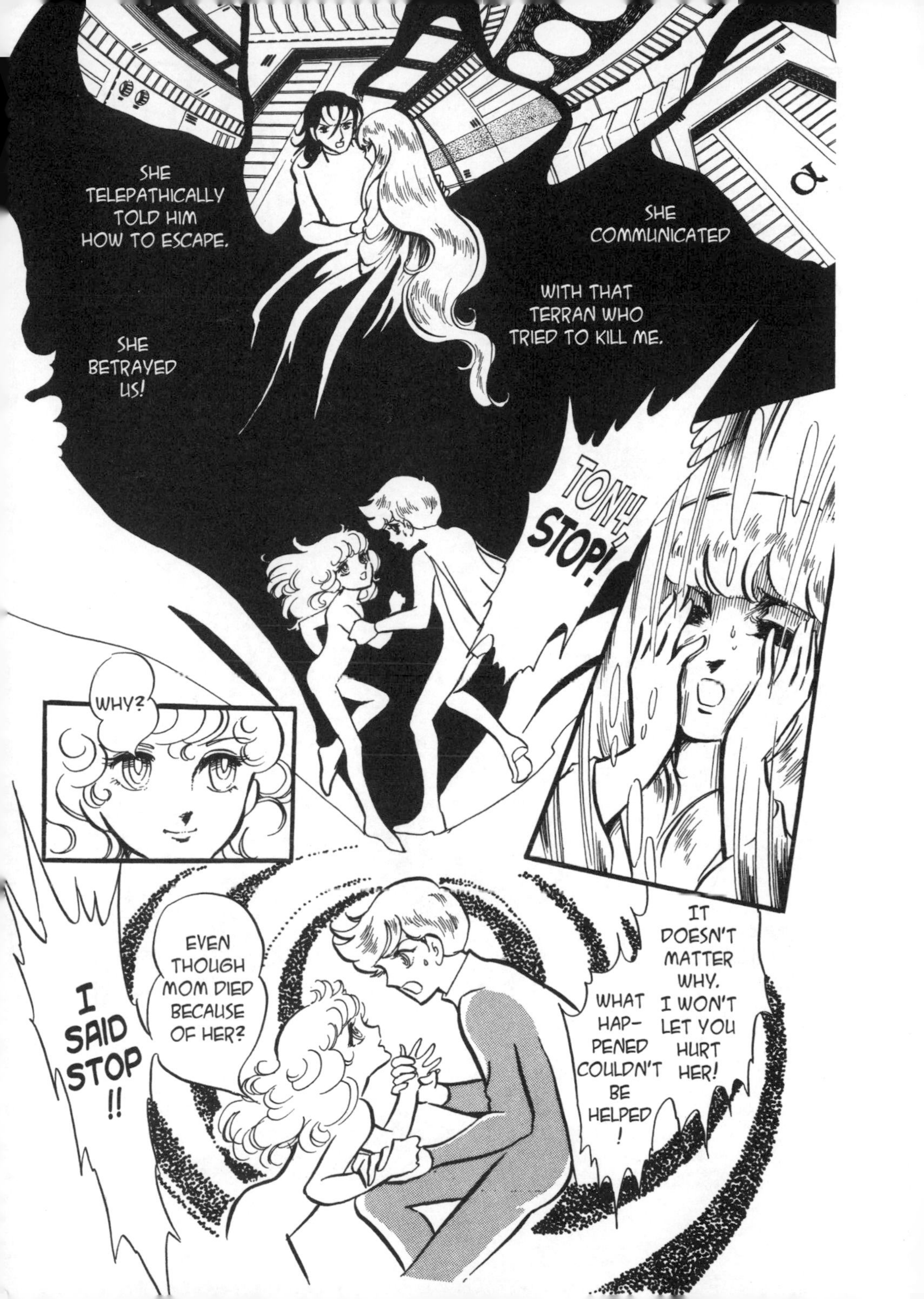
SHE COMMUNICATED
WITH THAT TERRAN WHO TRIED TO KILL ME.
SHE TELEPATHICALLY TOLD HIM HOW TO ESCAPE.
SHE BETRAYED US!
TONY, STOP!
WHY?
IT DOESN'T MATTER WHY. I WON'T LET YOU HURT HER!
WHAT HAP-PENED COULDN'T BE HELPED!
EVEN THOUGH MOM DIED BECAUSE OF HER?
I SAID STOP!!

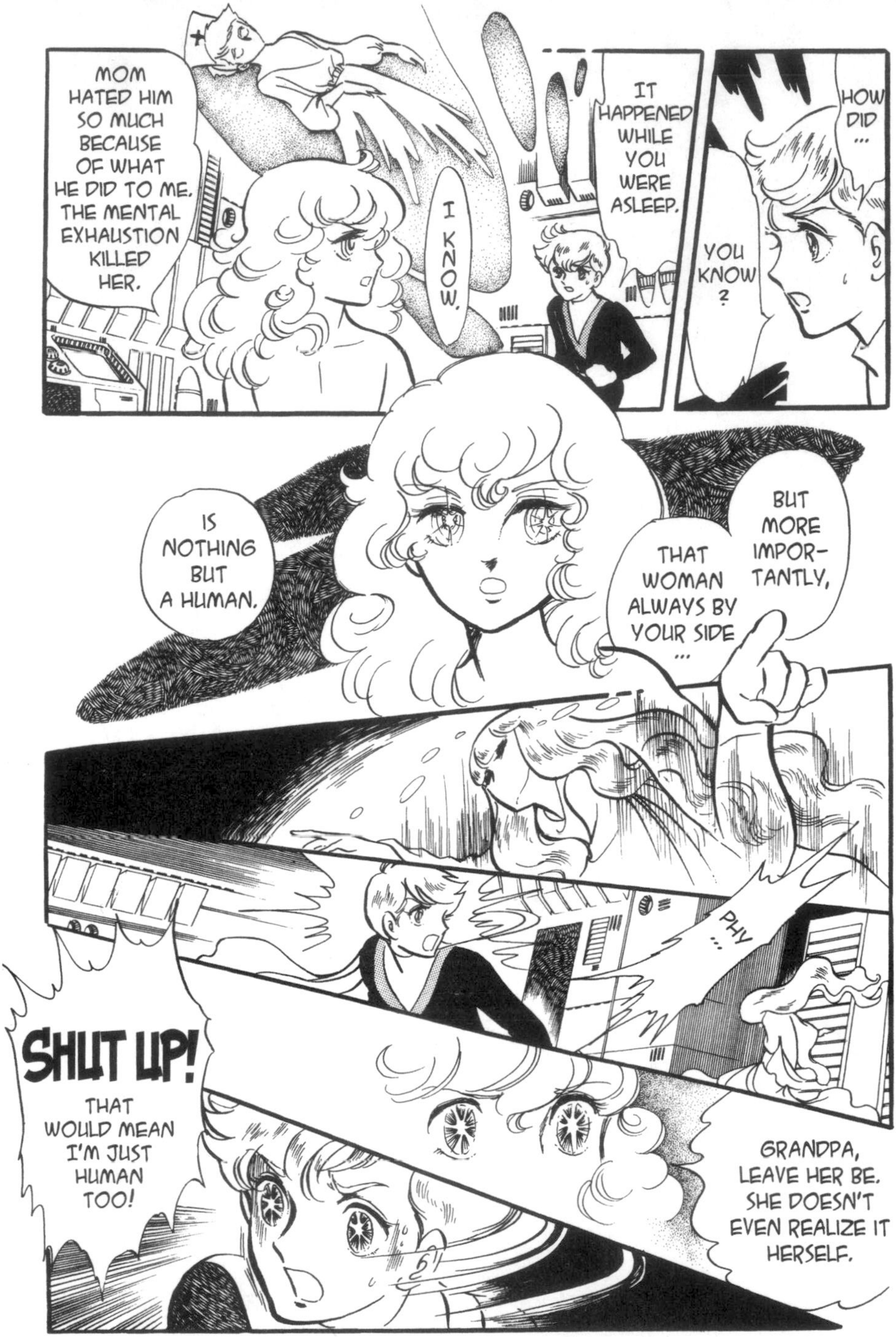
HOW DID ...
YOU KNOW ?
IT HAPPENED WHILE YOU WERE ASLEEP.
I KNOW.
MOM HATED HIM SO MUCH BECAUSE OF WHAT HE DID TO ME. THE MENTAL EXHAUSTION KILLED HER.
BUT MORE IMPOR-TANTLY,
THAT WOMAN ALWAYS BY YOUR SIDE ...
IS NOTHING BUT A HUMAN.
PHY ...
SHUT UP!
THAT WOULD MEAN I'M JUST HUMAN TOO!
GRANDPA, LEAVE HER BE. SHE DOESN'T EVEN REALIZE IT HERSELF.

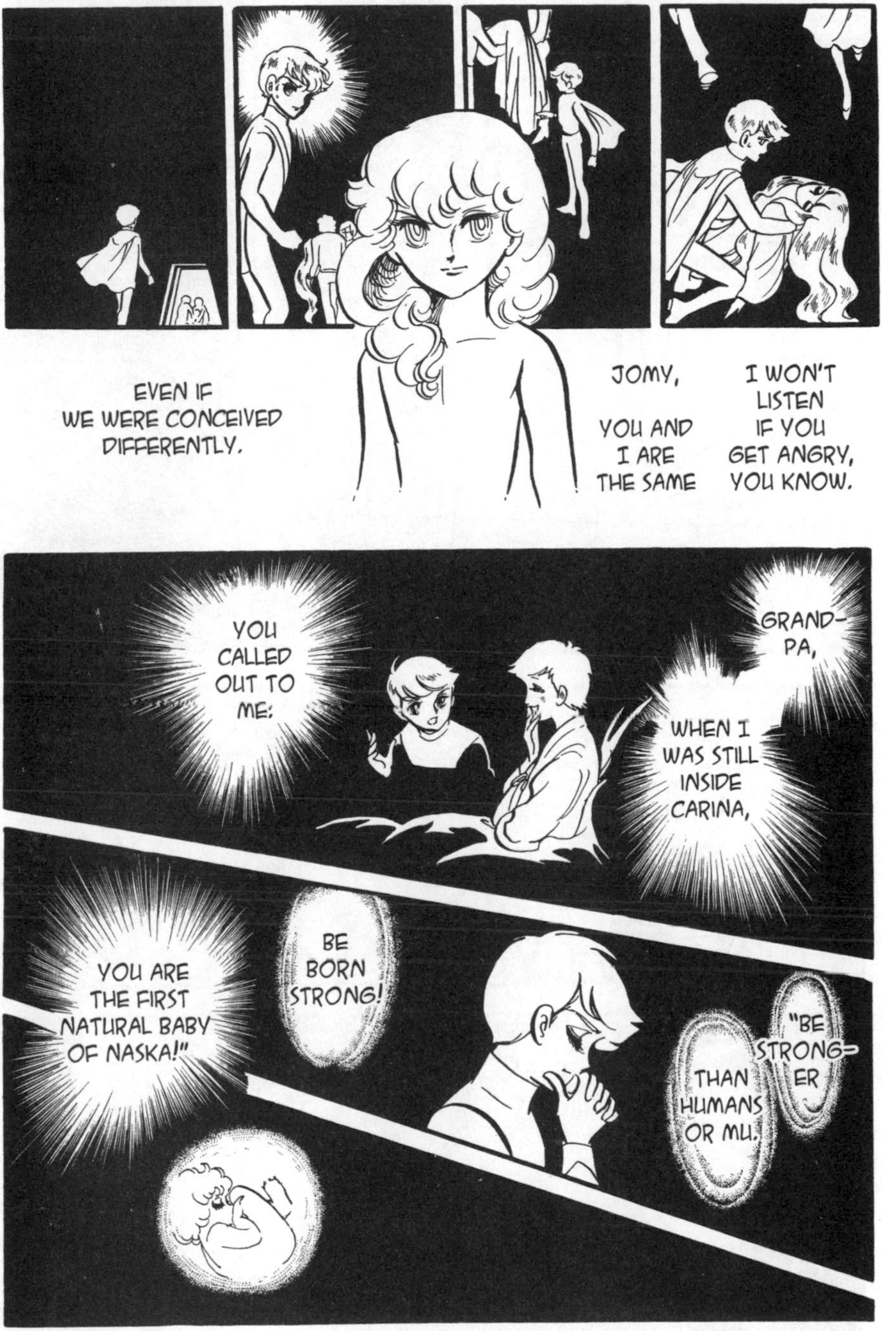
I WON'T LISTEN IF YOU GET ANGRY, YOU KNOW.
JOMY,
YOU AND I ARE THE SAME
EVEN IF WE WERE CONCEIVED DIFFERENTLY.
GRAND-PA,
WHEN I WAS STILL INSIDE CARINA,
YOU CALLED OUT TO ME:
"BE STRONG-ER
THAN HUMANS OR MU.
BE BORN STRONG!
YOU ARE THE FIRST NATURAL BABY OF NASKA!"

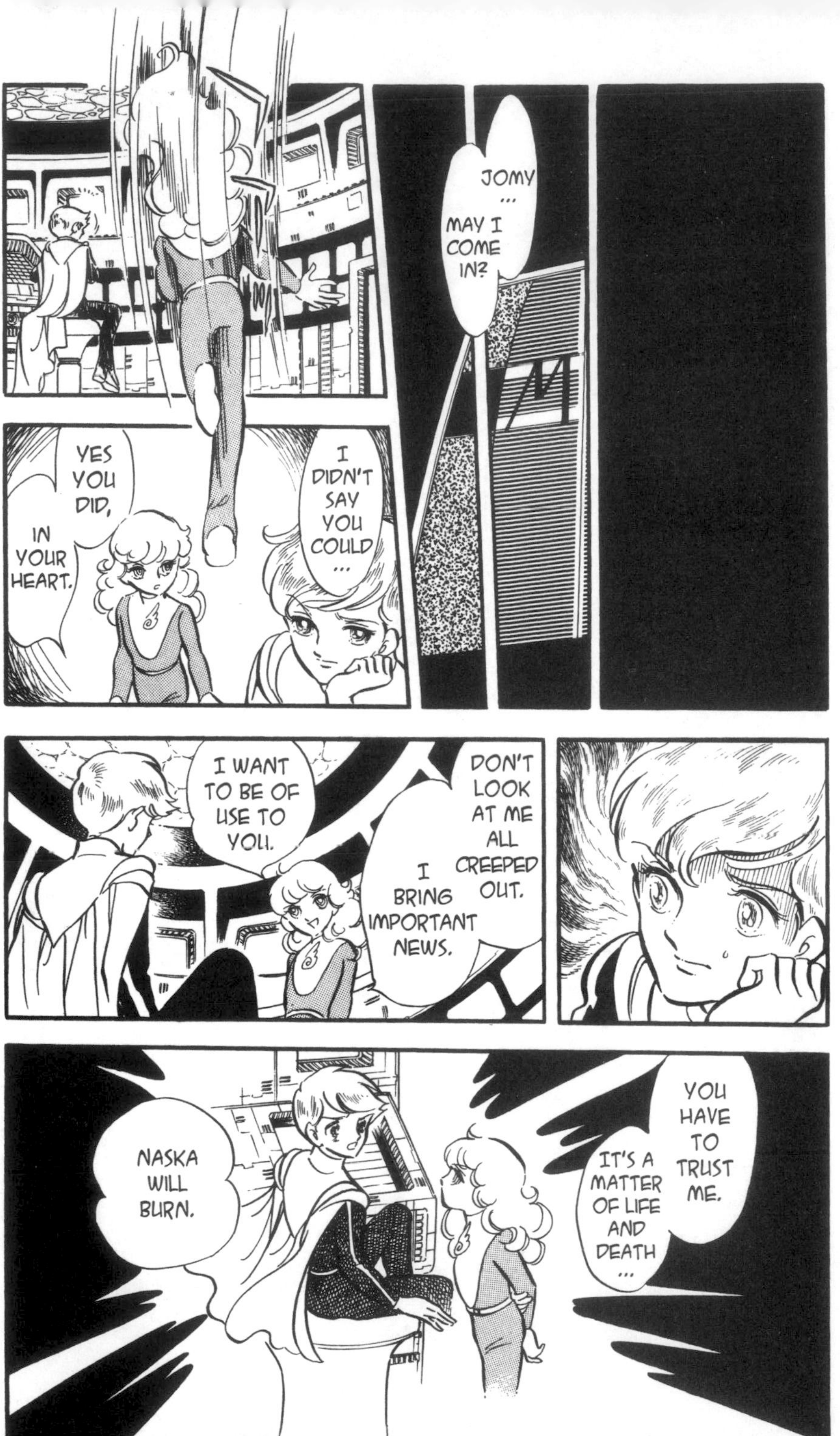
JOMY ... MAY I COME IN?
I DIDN'T SAY YOU COULD ...
YES YOU DID, IN YOUR HEART.
DON'T LOOK AT ME ALL CREEPED OUT.
I BRING IMPORTANT NEWS.
I WANT TO BE OF USE TO YOU.
YOU HAVE TO TRUST ME.
IT'S A MATTER OF LIFE AND DEATH ...
NASKA WILL BURN.

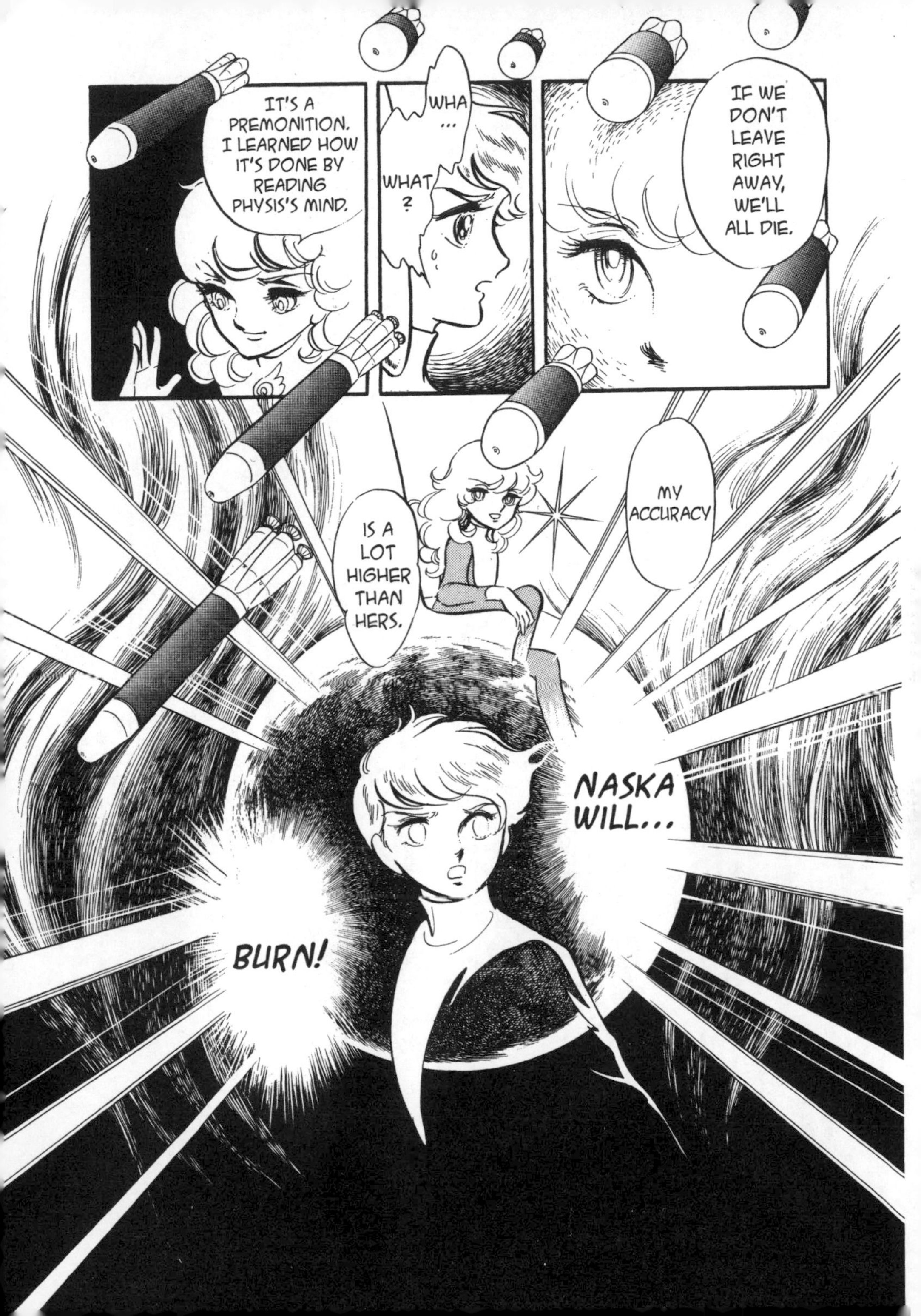
IF WE DON'T LEAVE RIGHT AWAY, WE'LL ALL DIE.
WHA...
WHAT?
IT'S A PREMONITION. I LEARNED HOW IT'S DONE BY READING PHYSIS'S MIND.
MY ACCURACY
IS A LOT HIGHER THAN HERS.
NASKA WILL...
BURN!

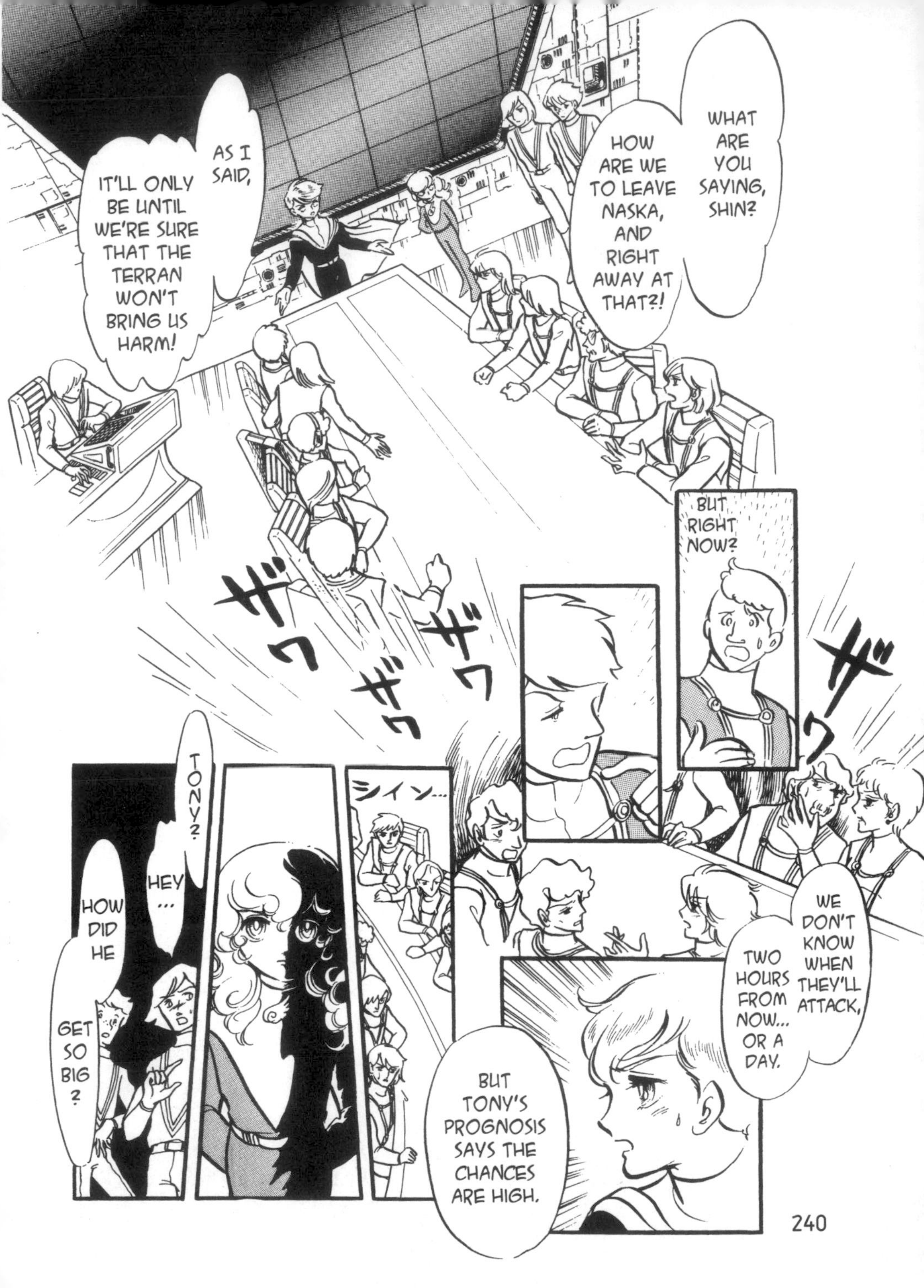
WHAT ARE YOU SAYING, SHIN?
HOW ARE WE TO LEAVE NASKA, AND RIGHT AWAY AT THAT?!
AS I SAID,
IT'LL ONLY BE UNTIL WE'RE SURE THAT THE TERRAN WON'T BRING US HARM!
ザワ
ザワ
ザワ
BUT RIGHT NOW?
ザワ
WE DON'T KNOW WHEN THEY'LL ATTACK,
TWO HOURS FROM NOW... OR A DAY.
BUT TONY'S PROGNOSIS SAYS THE CHANCES ARE HIGH.
シイン...
TONY?
HEY...
HOW DID HE GET SO BIG?

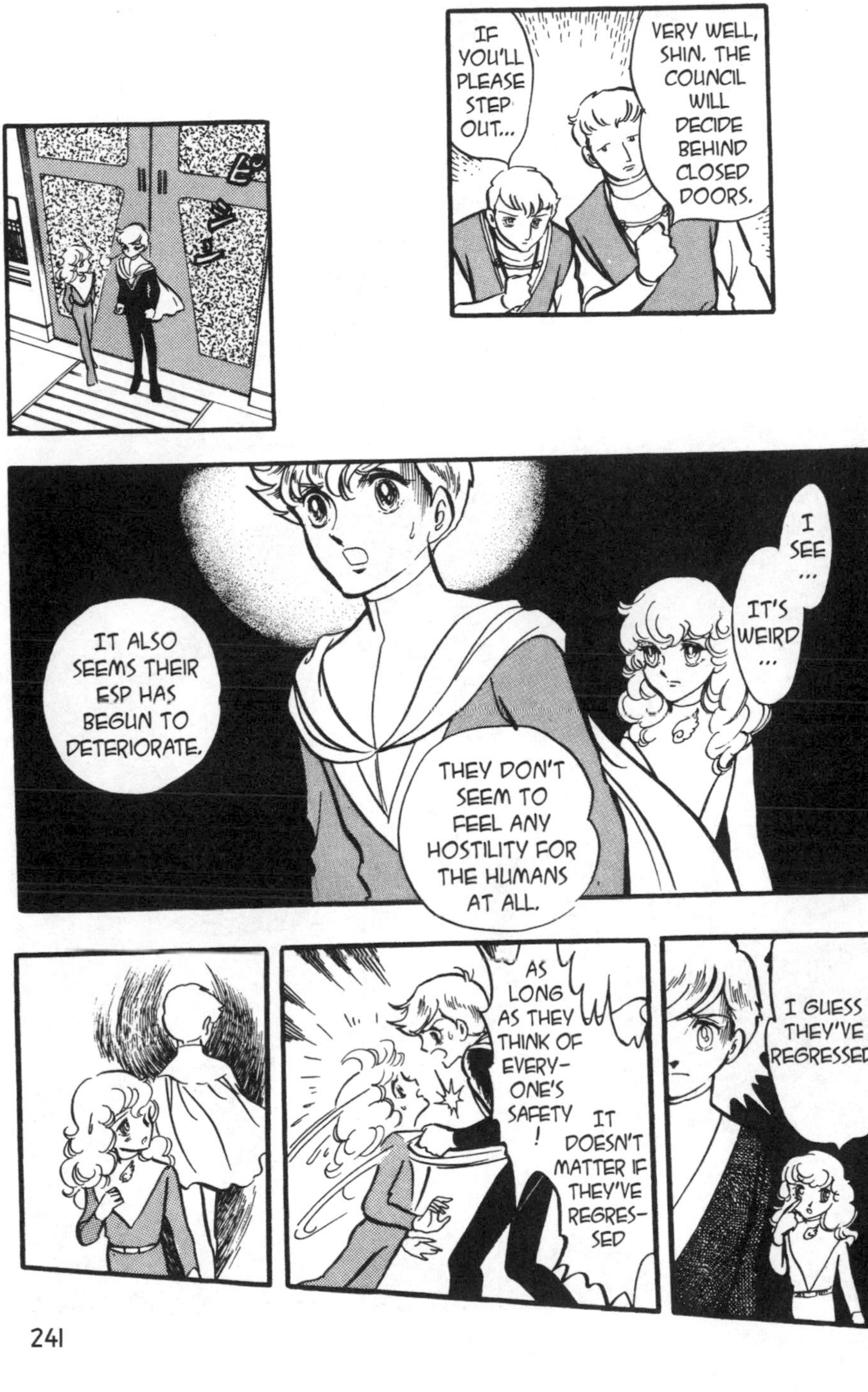
VERY WELL, SHIN. THE COUNCIL WILL DECIDE BEHIND CLOSED DOORS.
IF YOU'LL PLEASE STEP OUT...
I SEE ...
IT'S WEIRD ...
THEY DON'T SEEM TO FEEL ANY HOSTILITY FOR THE HUMANS AT ALL.
IT ALSO SEEMS THEIR ESP HAS BEGUN TO DETERIORATE.
I GUESS THEY'VE REGRESSED.
AS LONG AS THEY THINK OF EVERY-ONE'S SAFETY !
IT DOESN'T MATTER IF THEY'VE REGRES-SED

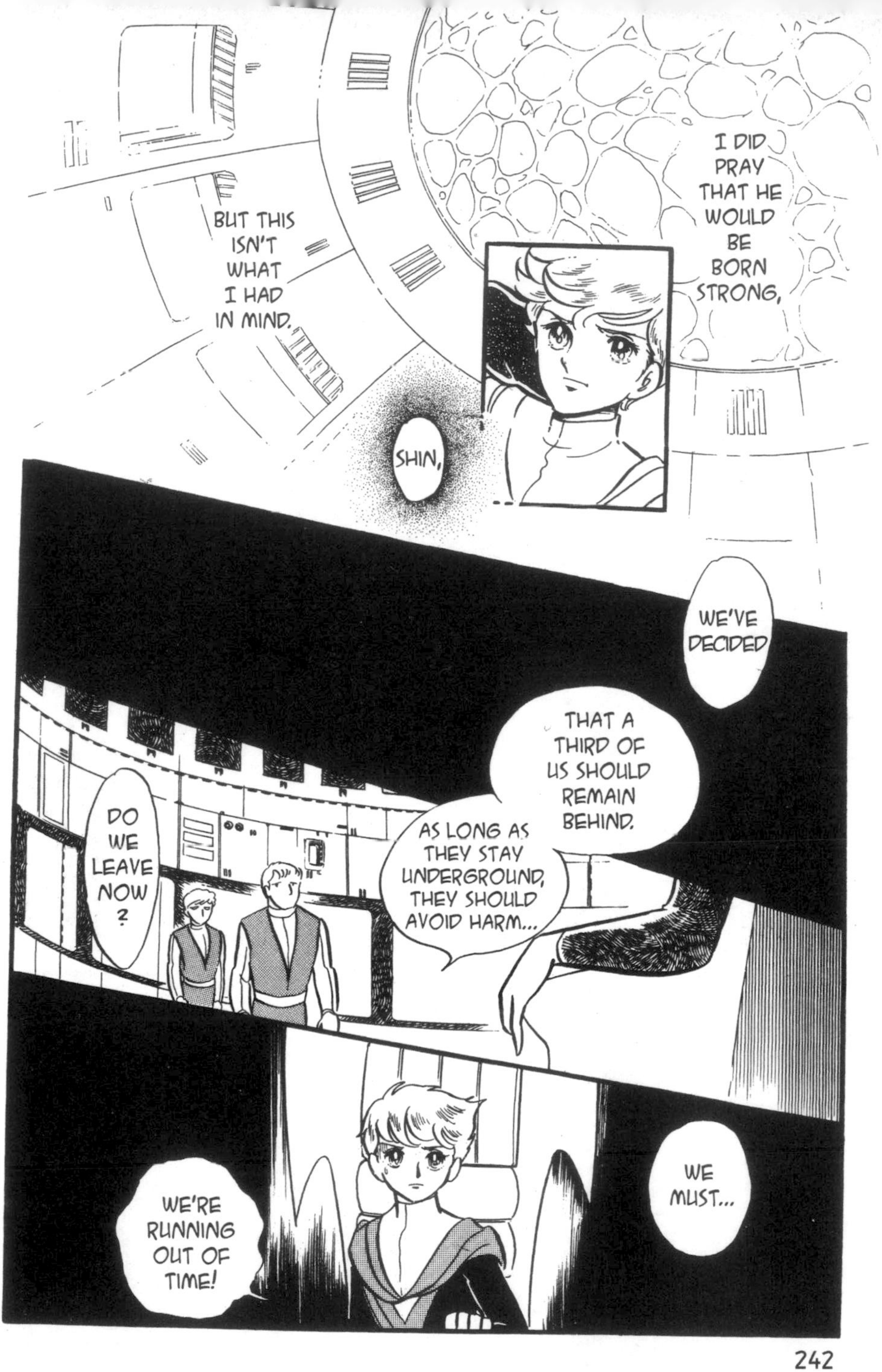
I DID PRAY THAT HE WOULD BE BORN STRONG,
BUT THIS ISN'T WHAT I HAD IN MIND.
SHIN,
WE'VE DECIDED
THAT A THIRD OF US SHOULD REMAIN BEHIND.
AS LONG AS THEY STAY UNDERGROUND, THEY SHOULD AVOID HARM...
DO WE LEAVE NOW?
WE MUST...
WE'RE RUNNING OUT OF TIME!

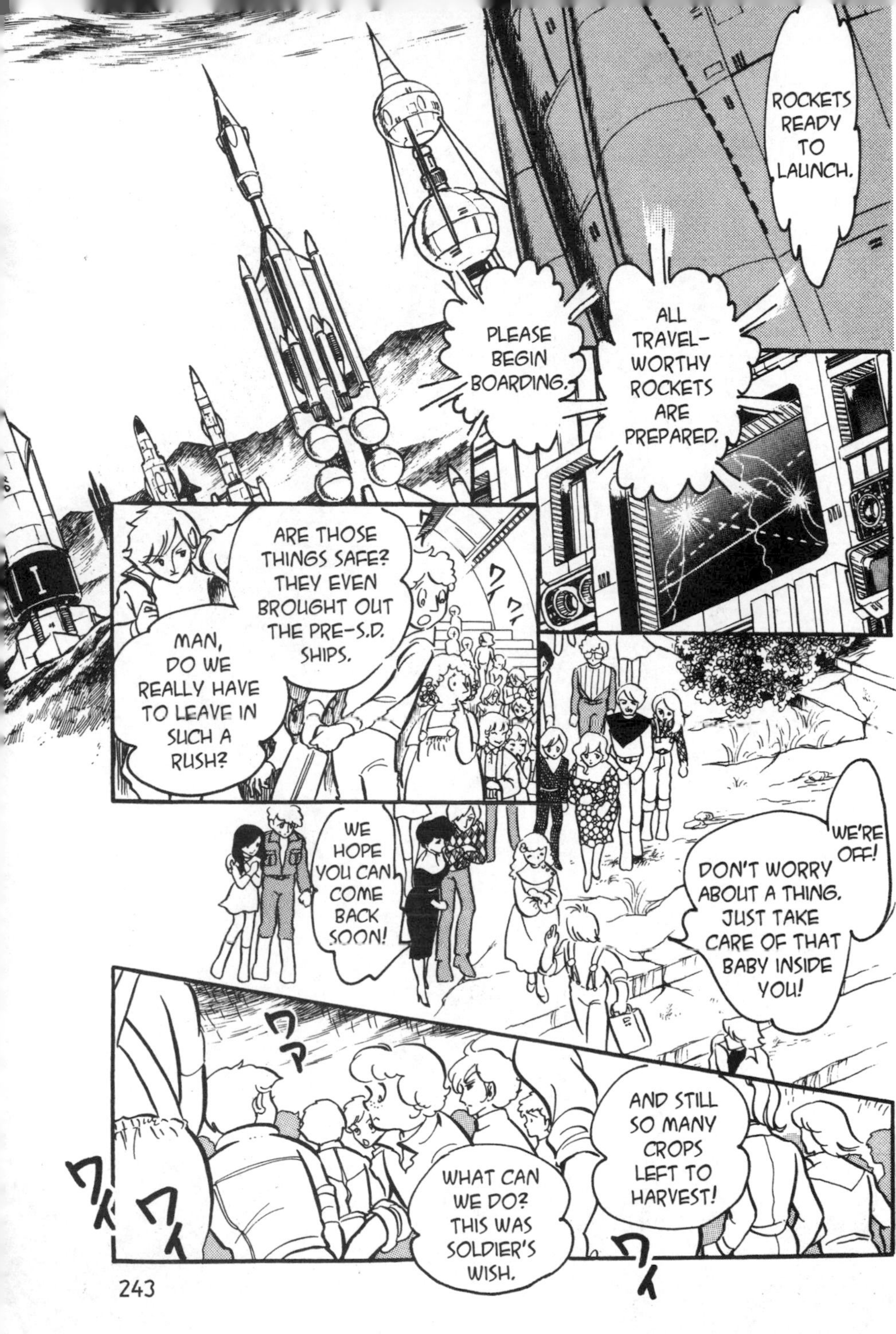
ROCKETS READY TO LAUNCH.
ALL TRAVEL-WORTHY ROCKETS ARE PREPARED.
PLEASE BEGIN BOARDING.
ARE THOSE THINGS SAFE? THEY EVEN BROUGHT OUT THE PRE-S.D. SHIPS.
MAN, DO WE REALLY HAVE TO LEAVE IN SUCH A RUSH?
WE'RE OFF!
DON'T WORRY ABOUT A THING. JUST TAKE CARE OF THAT BABY INSIDE YOU!
WE HOPE YOU CAN COME BACK SOON!
AND STILL SO MANY CROPS LEFT TO HARVEST!
WHAT CAN WE DO? THIS WAS SOLDIER'S WISH.
ワイ
ワァ
ワイ ワイ

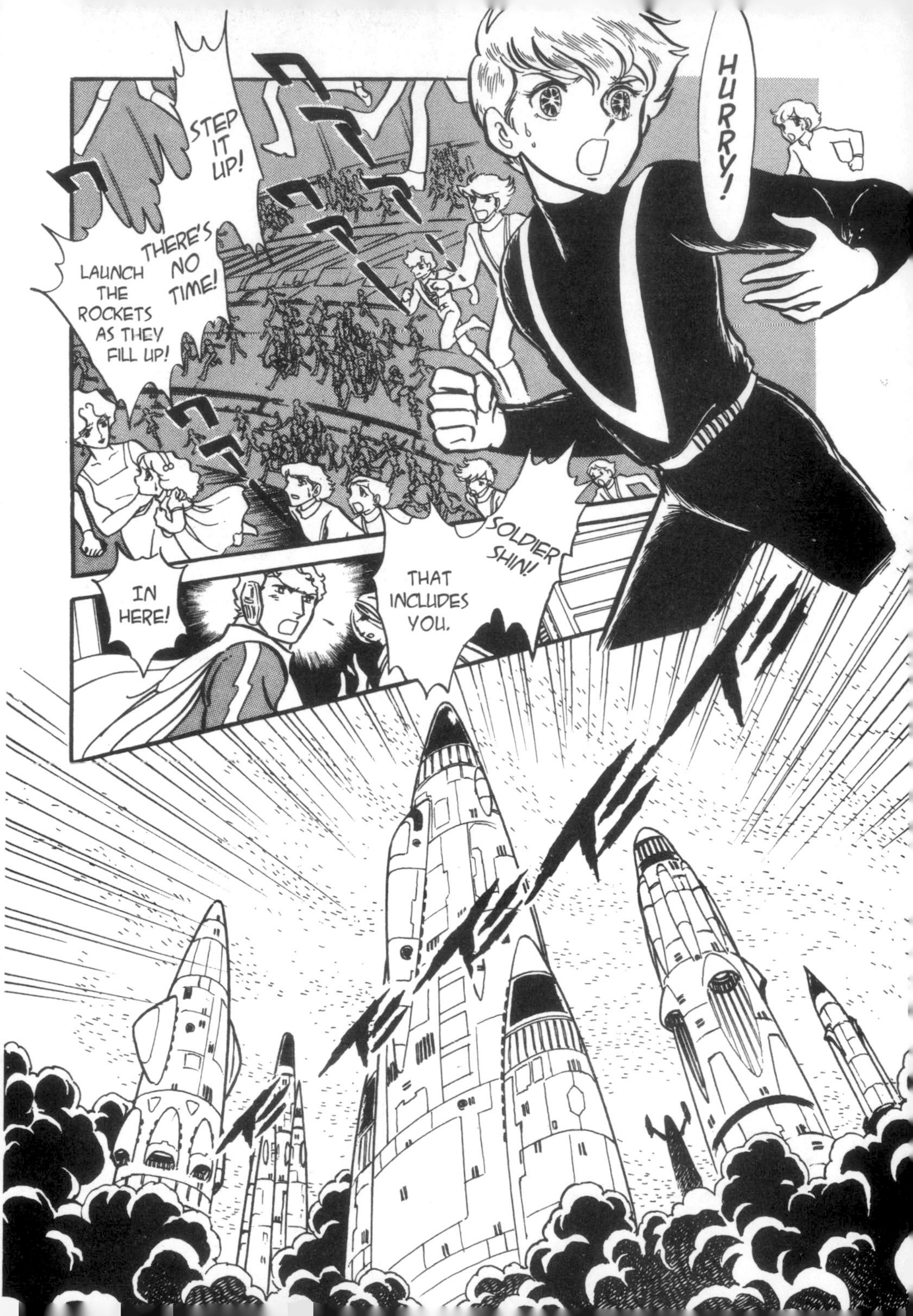
HURRY!
STEP IT UP!
THERE'S NO TIME!
LAUNCH THE ROCKETS AS THEY FILL UP!
SOLDIER SHIN!
THAT INCLUDES YOU.
IN HERE!

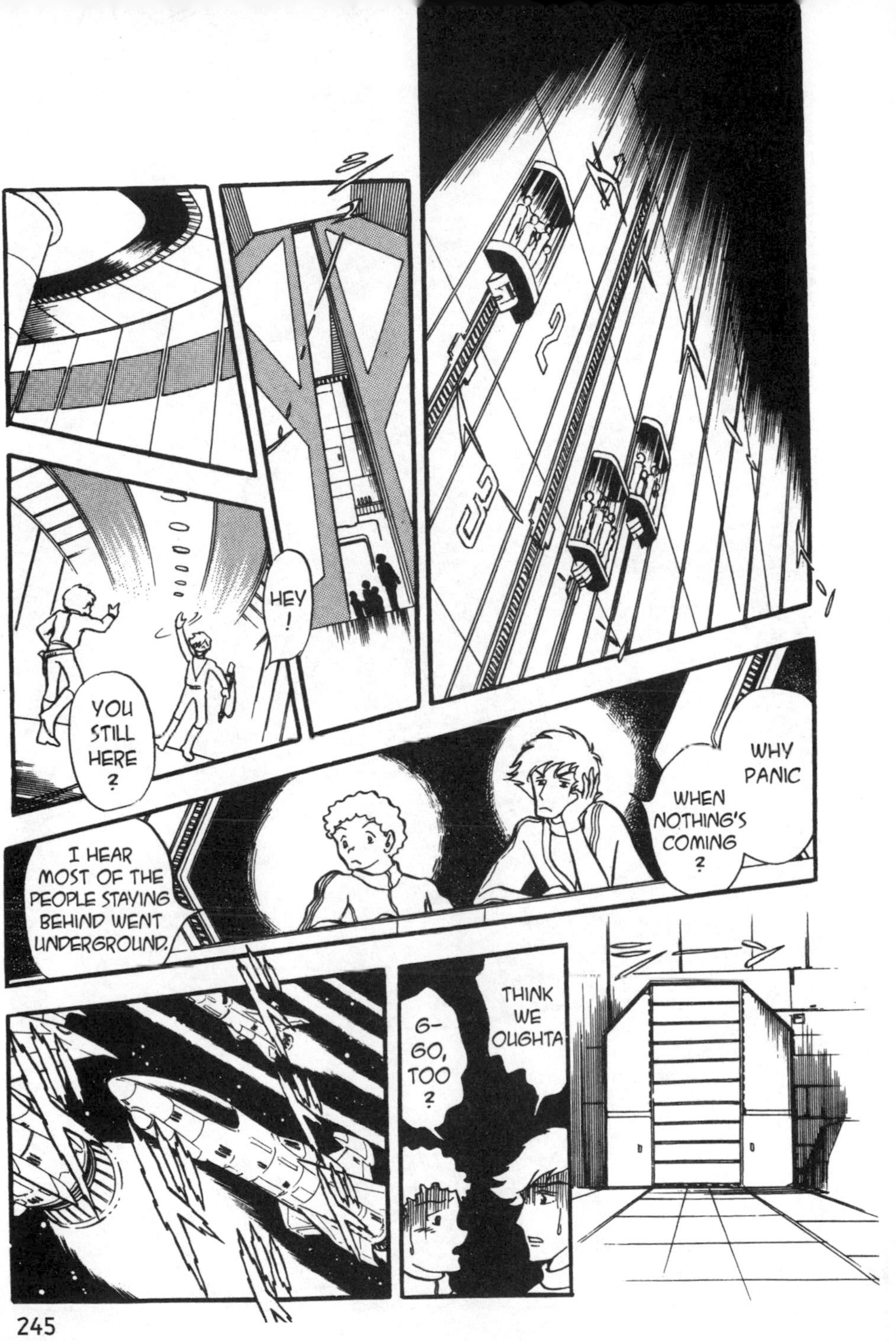
HEY!
YOU STILL HERE?
WHY PANIC WHEN NOTHING'S COMING?
I HEAR MOST OF THE PEOPLE STAYING BEHIND WENT UNDERGROUND.
THINK WE OUGHTA
G-GO, TOO?

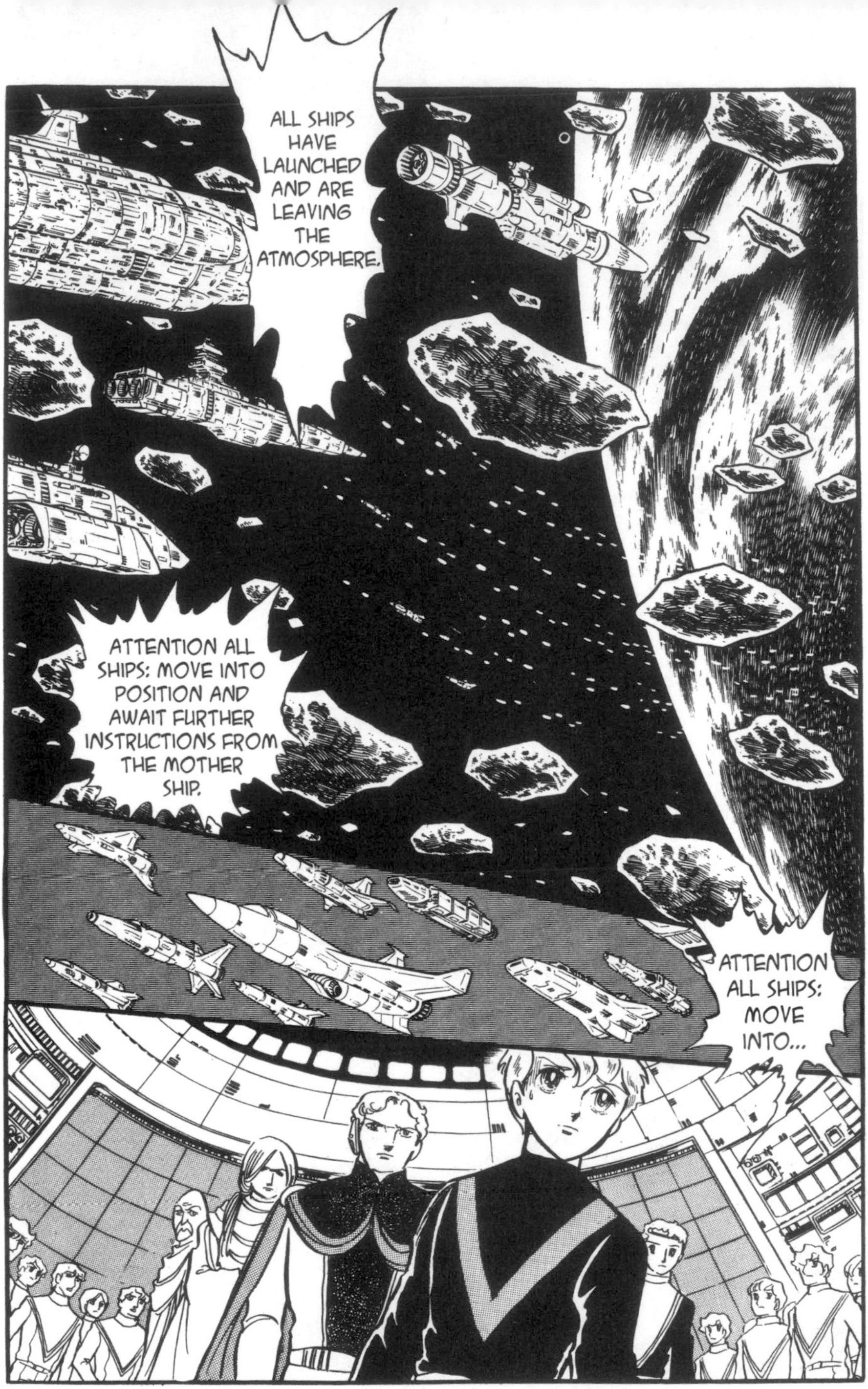
ALL SHIPS HAVE LAUNCHED AND ARE LEAVING THE ATMOSPHERE.
ATTENTION ALL SHIPS: MOVE INTO POSITION AND AWAIT FURTHER INSTRUCTIONS FROM THE MOTHER SHIP.
ATTENTION ALL SHIPS: MOVE INTO...

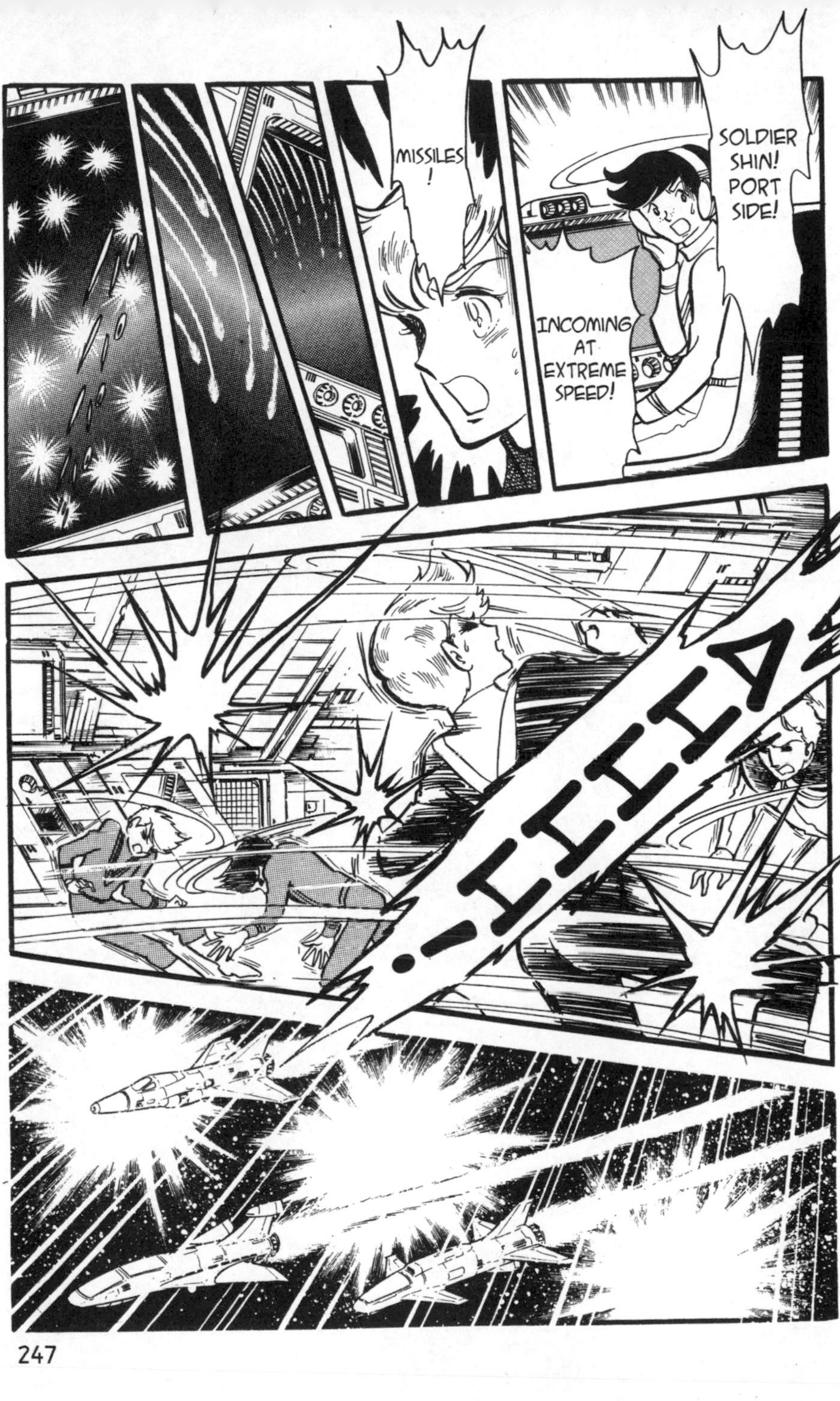
SOLDIER SHIN! PORT SIDE!
INCOMING AT EXTREME SPEED!
MISSILES!
AIIII!

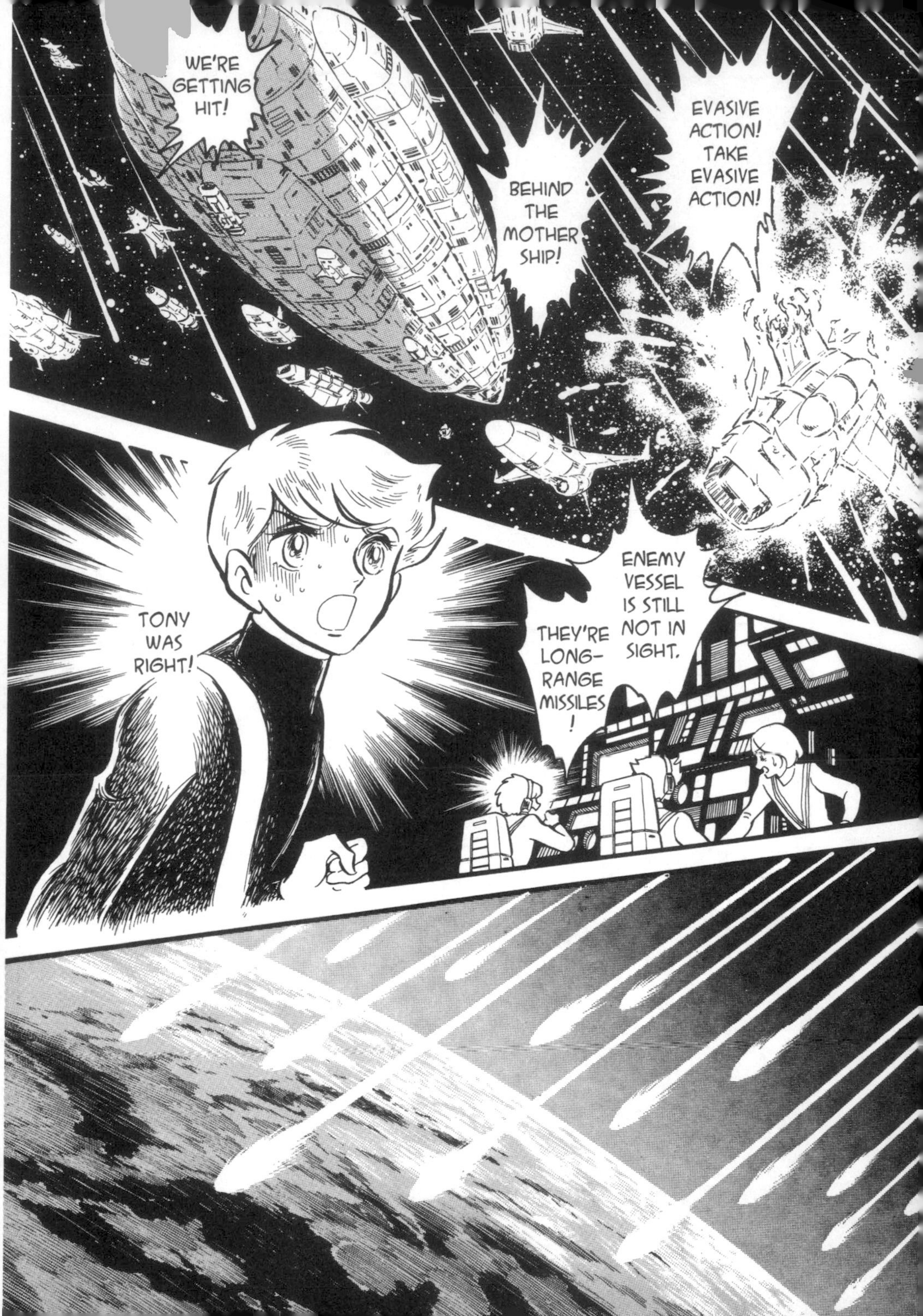
EVASIVE ACTION! TAKE EVASIVE ACTION!
BEHIND THE MOTHER SHIP!
WE'RE GETTING HIT!
ENEMY VESSEL IS STILL NOT IN SIGHT.
THEY'RE LONG-RANGE MISSILES!
TONY WAS RIGHT!

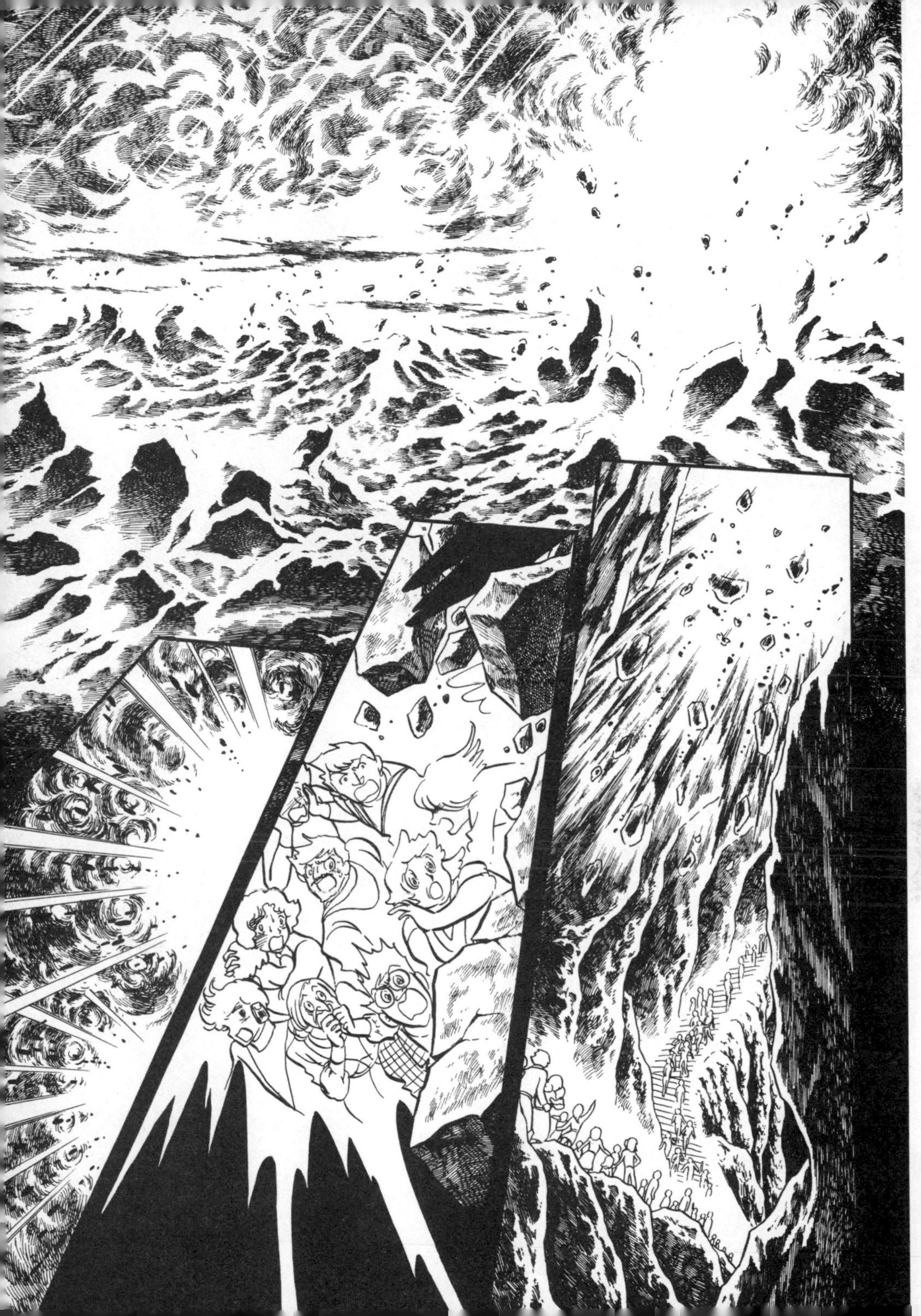

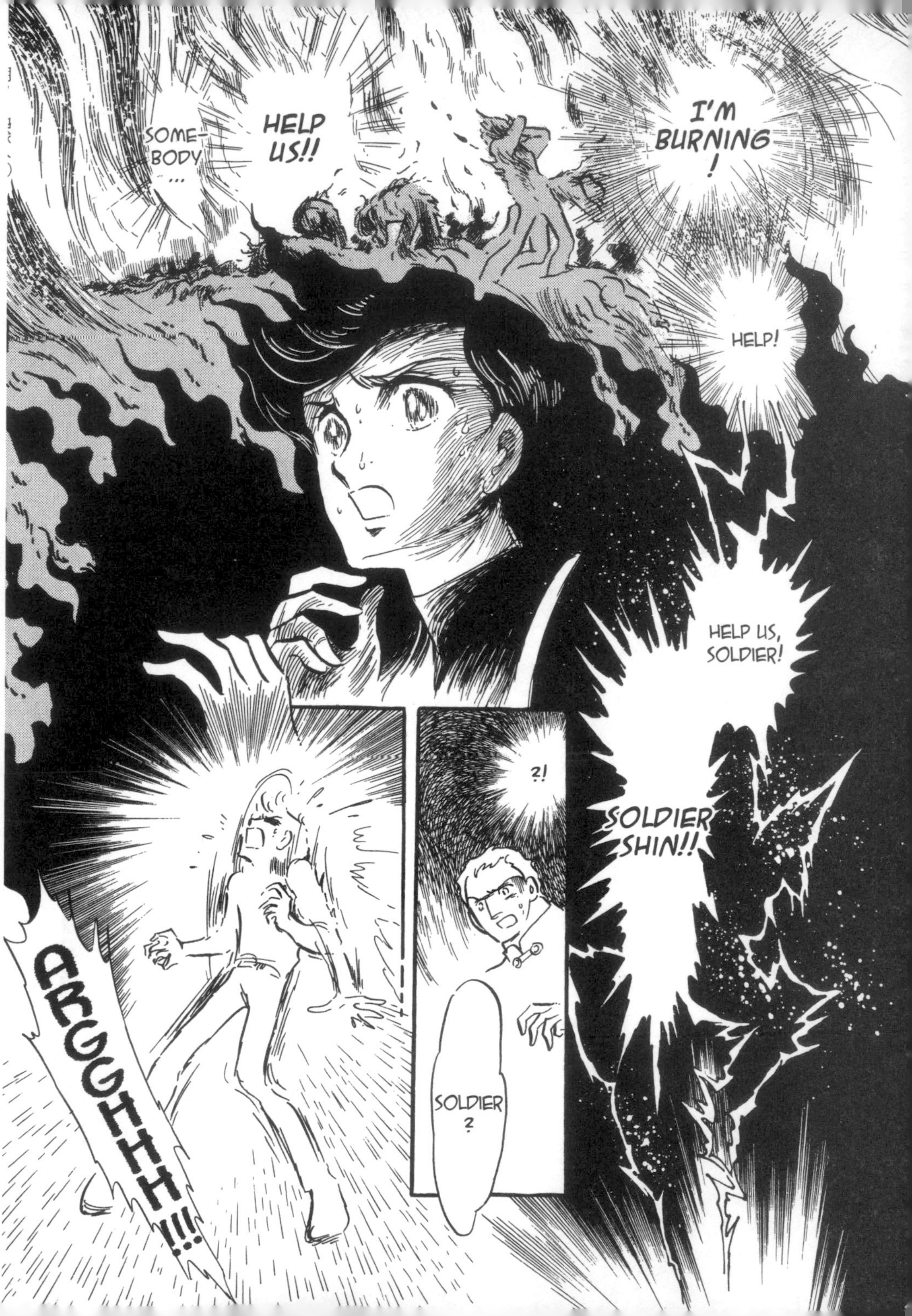

I'M BURNING!
HELP US!!
SOME-BODY...
HELP!
HELP US, SOLDIER!
SOLDIER SHIN!!
?!
SOLDIER?
ARGGHHH!!!

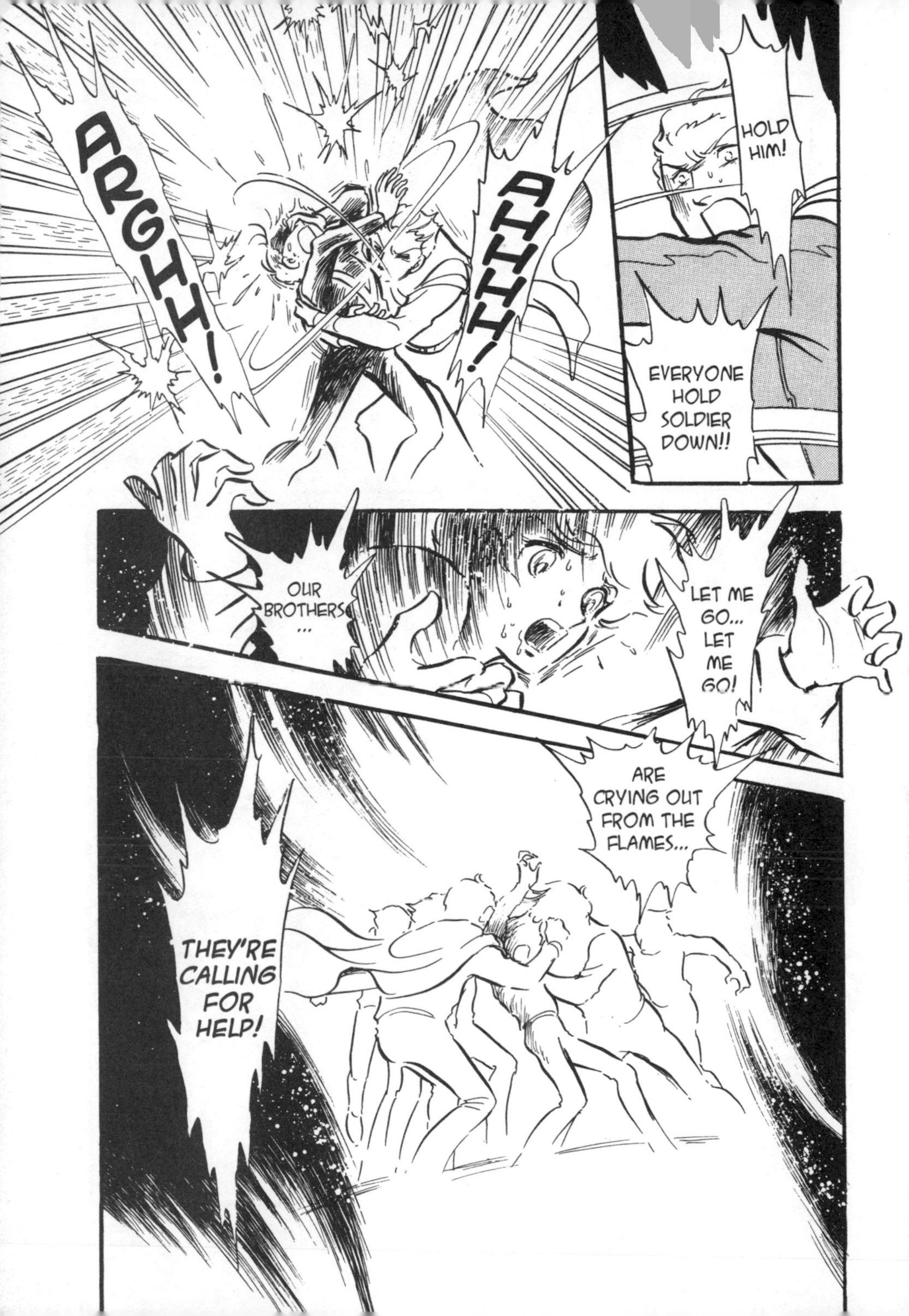
HOLD HIM!
EVERYONE HOLD SOLDIER DOWN!!
AHHHH!
ARGHH!
LET ME GO... LET ME GO!
OUR BROTHERS...
ARE CRYING OUT FROM THE FLAMES...
THEY'RE CALLING FOR HELP!

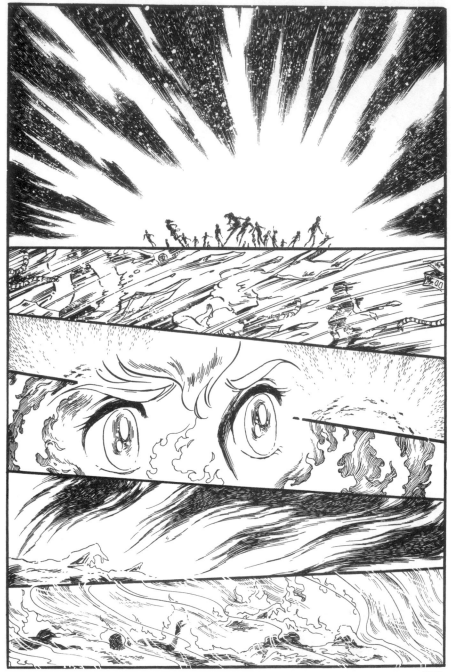

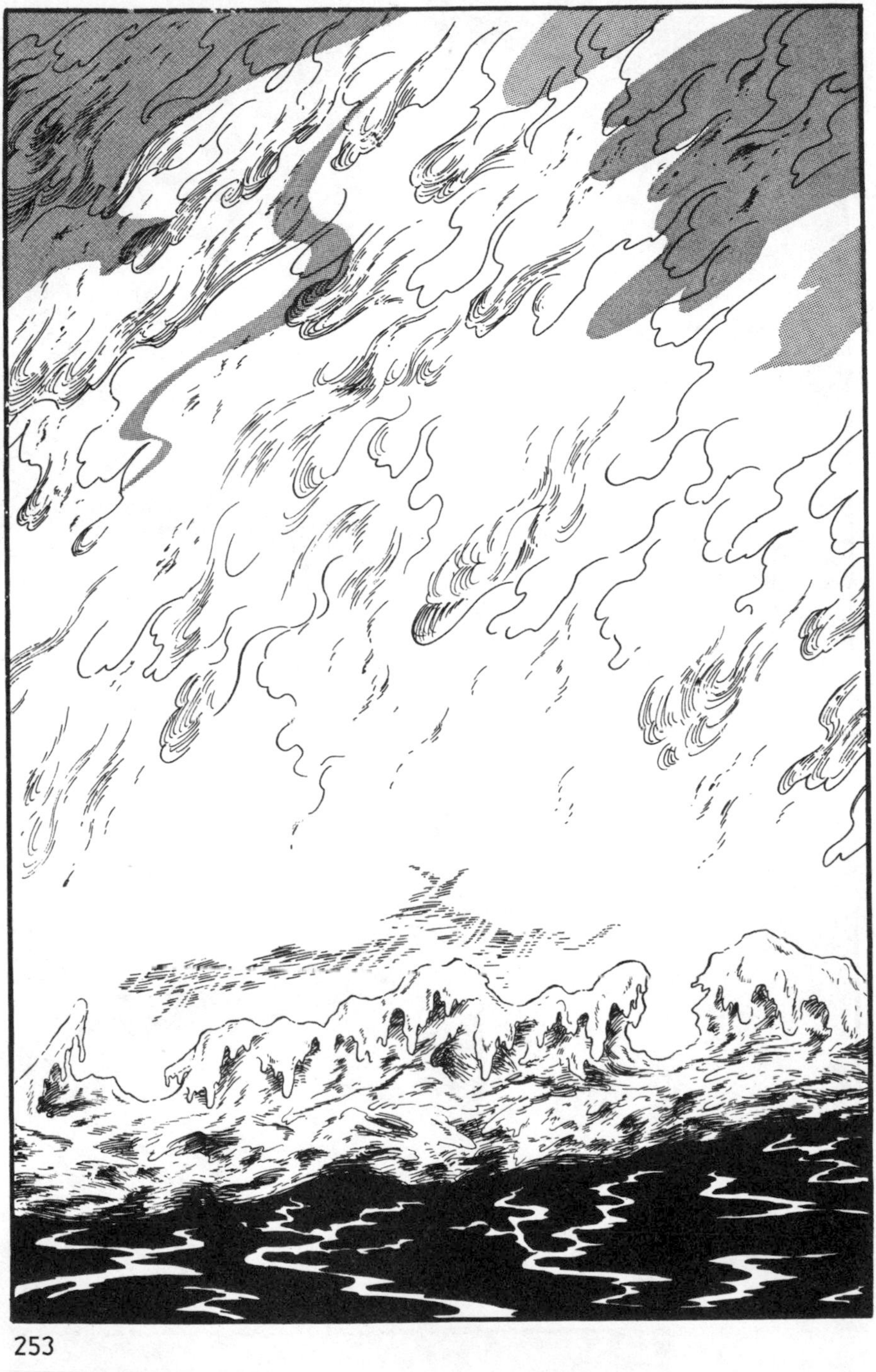

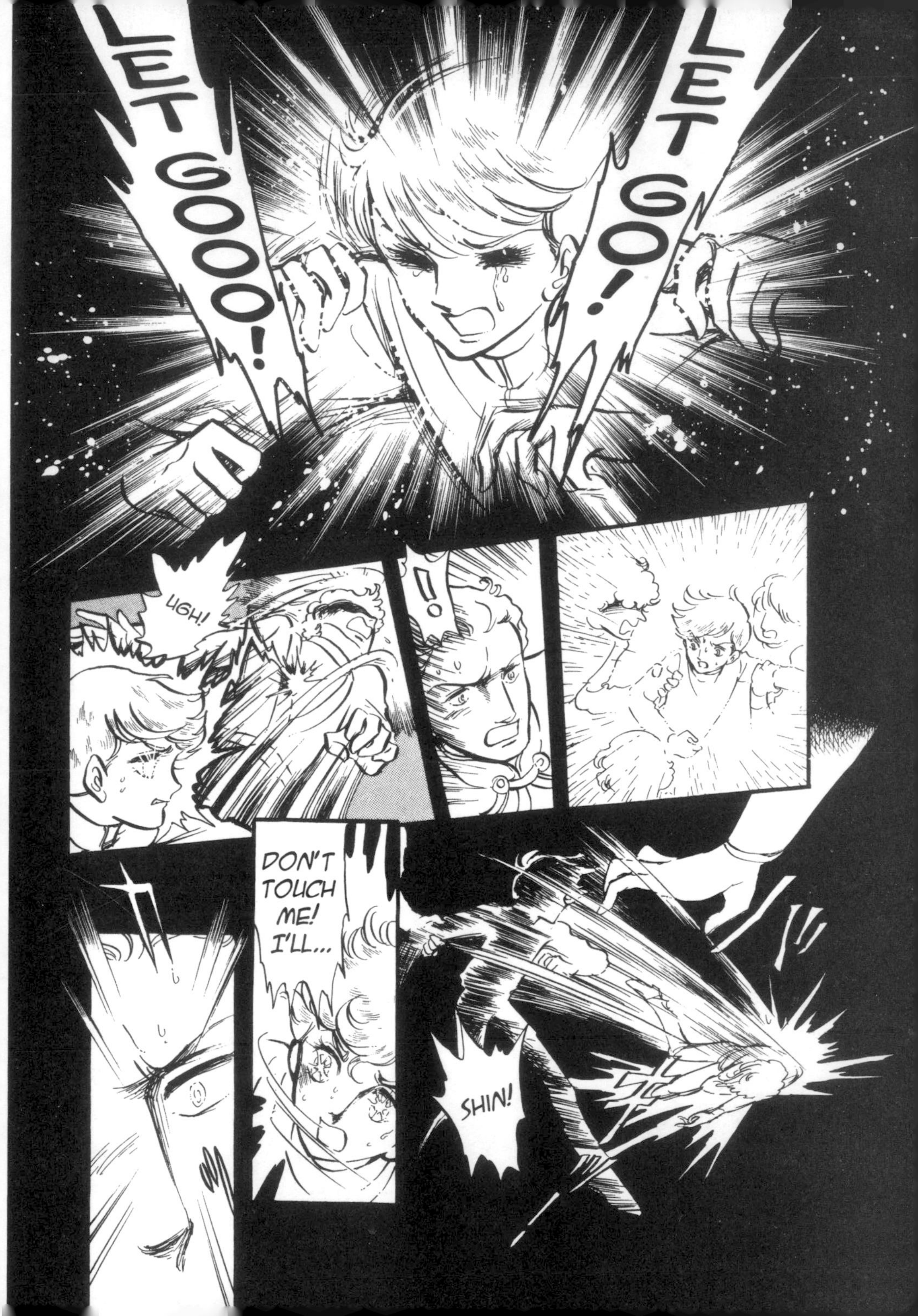
LET GO!
LET GOOOO!
!
UGH!
SHIN!
DON'T TOUCH ME! I'LL...

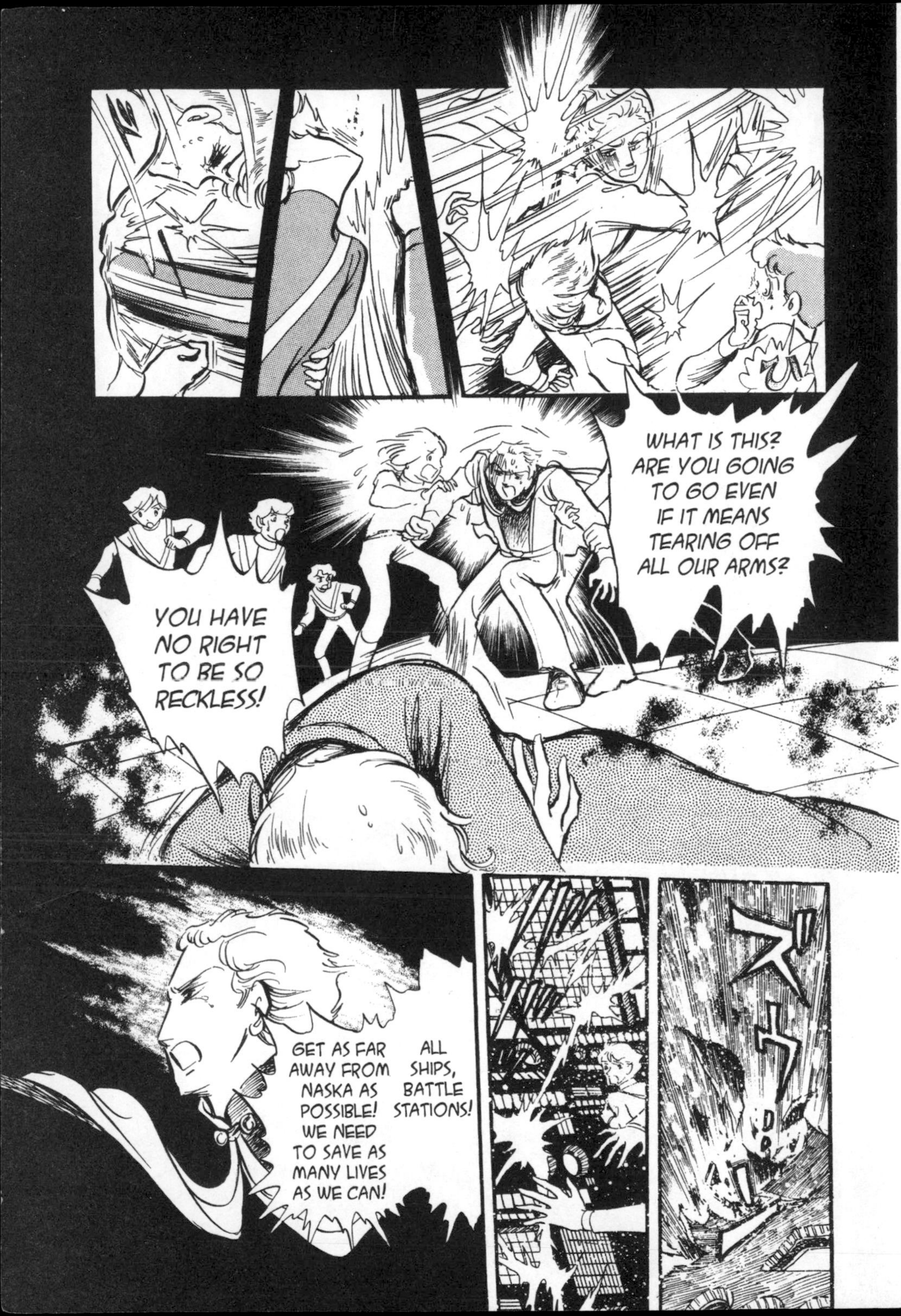
WHAT IS THIS? ARE YOU GOING TO GO EVEN IF IT MEANS TEARING OFF ALL OUR ARMS?
YOU HAVE NO RIGHT TO BE SO RECKLESS!
ALL SHIPS, BATTLE STATIONS!
GET AS FAR AWAY FROM NASKA AS POSSIBLE! WE NEED TO SAVE AS MANY LIVES AS WE CAN!

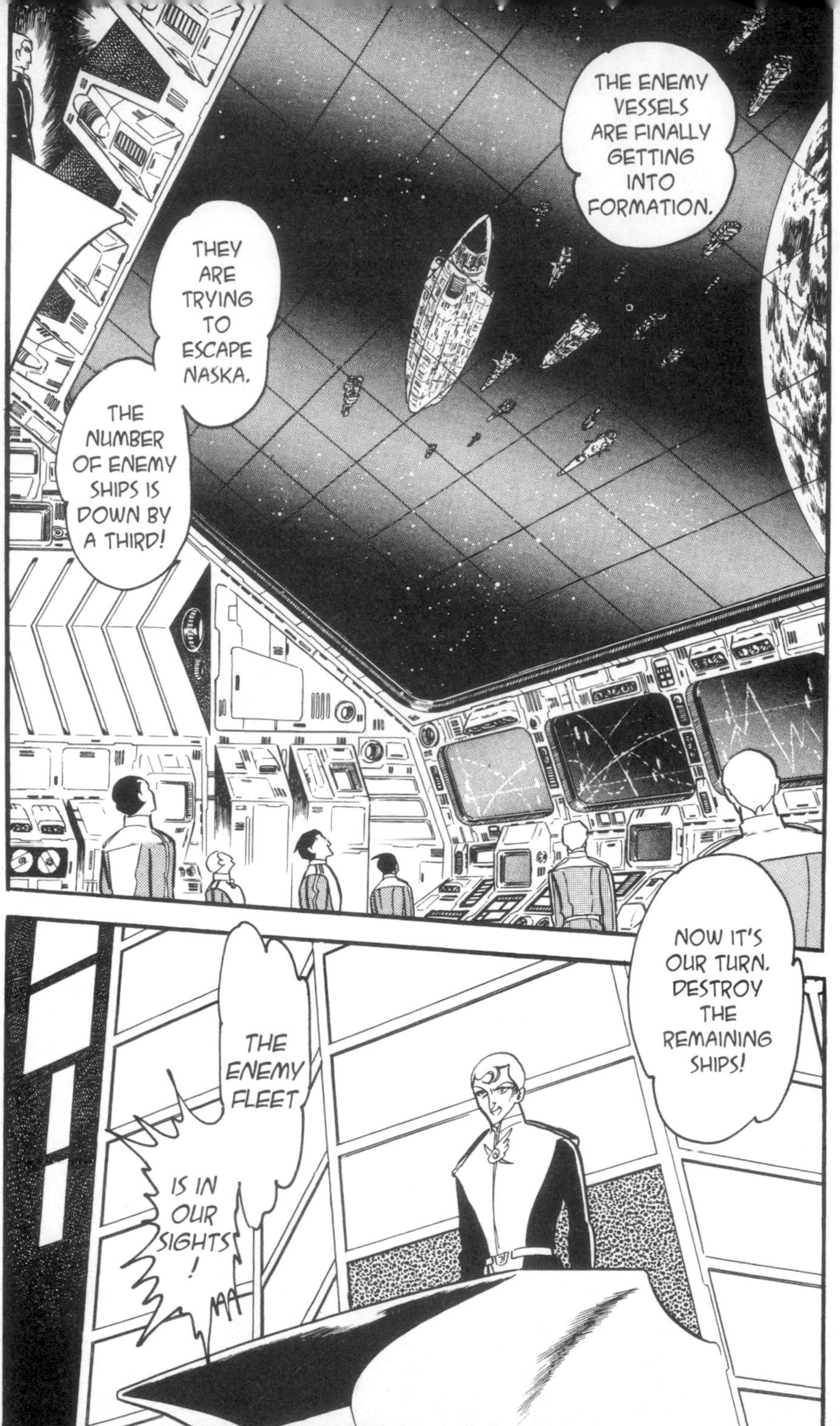
THE ENEMY VESSELS ARE FINALLY GETTING INTO FORMATION.
THEY ARE TRYING TO ESCAPE NASKA.
THE NUMBER OF ENEMY SHIPS IS DOWN BY A THIRD!
NOW IT'S OUR TURN. DESTROY THE REMAINING SHIPS!
THE ENEMY FLEET
IS IN OUR SIGHTS!

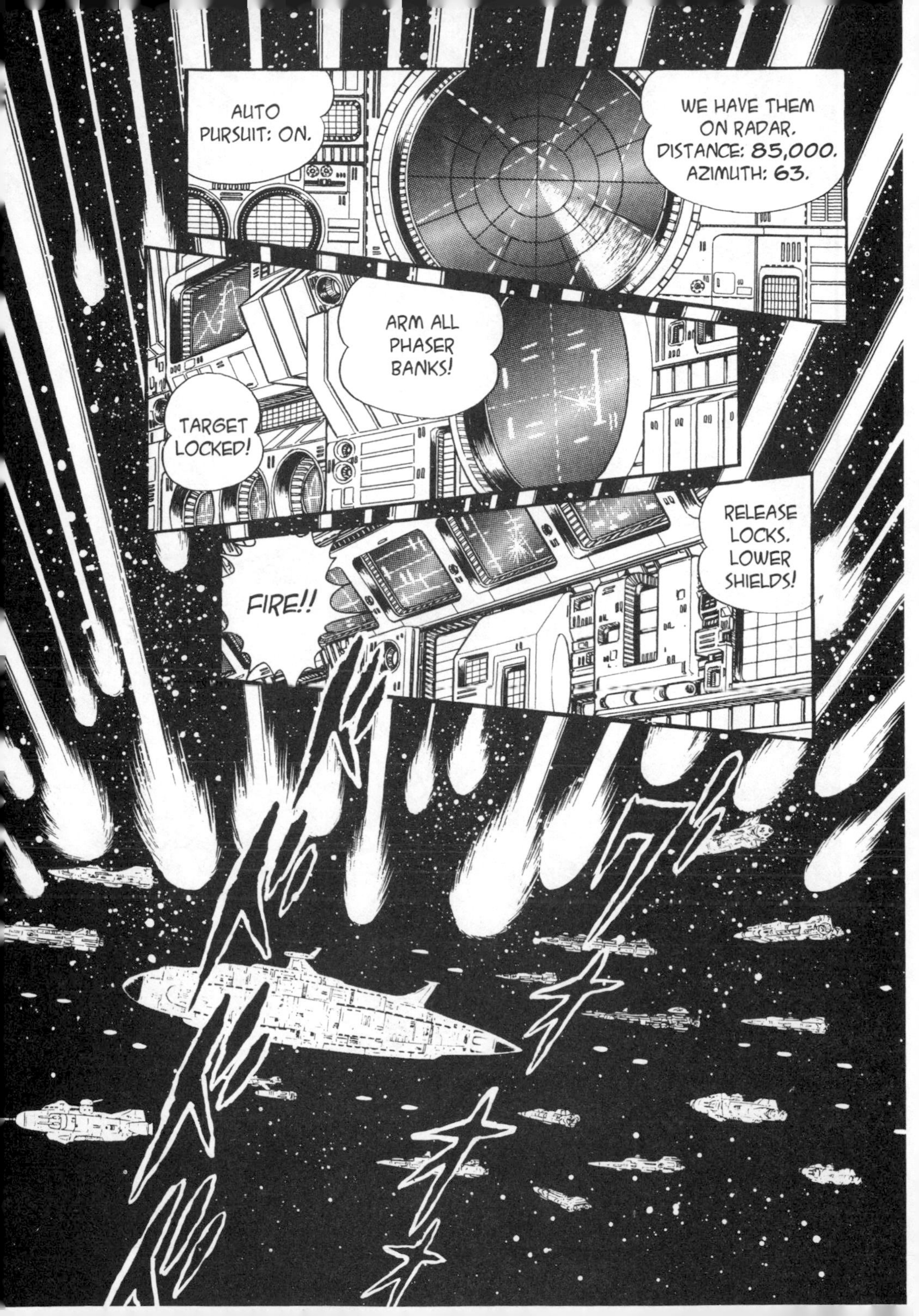
WE HAVE THEM ON RADAR. DISTANCE: 85,000. AZIMUTH: 63.
AUTO PURSUIT: ON.
ARM ALL PHASER BANKS!
TARGET LOCKED!
RELEASE LOCKS. LOWER SHIELDS!
FIRE!!

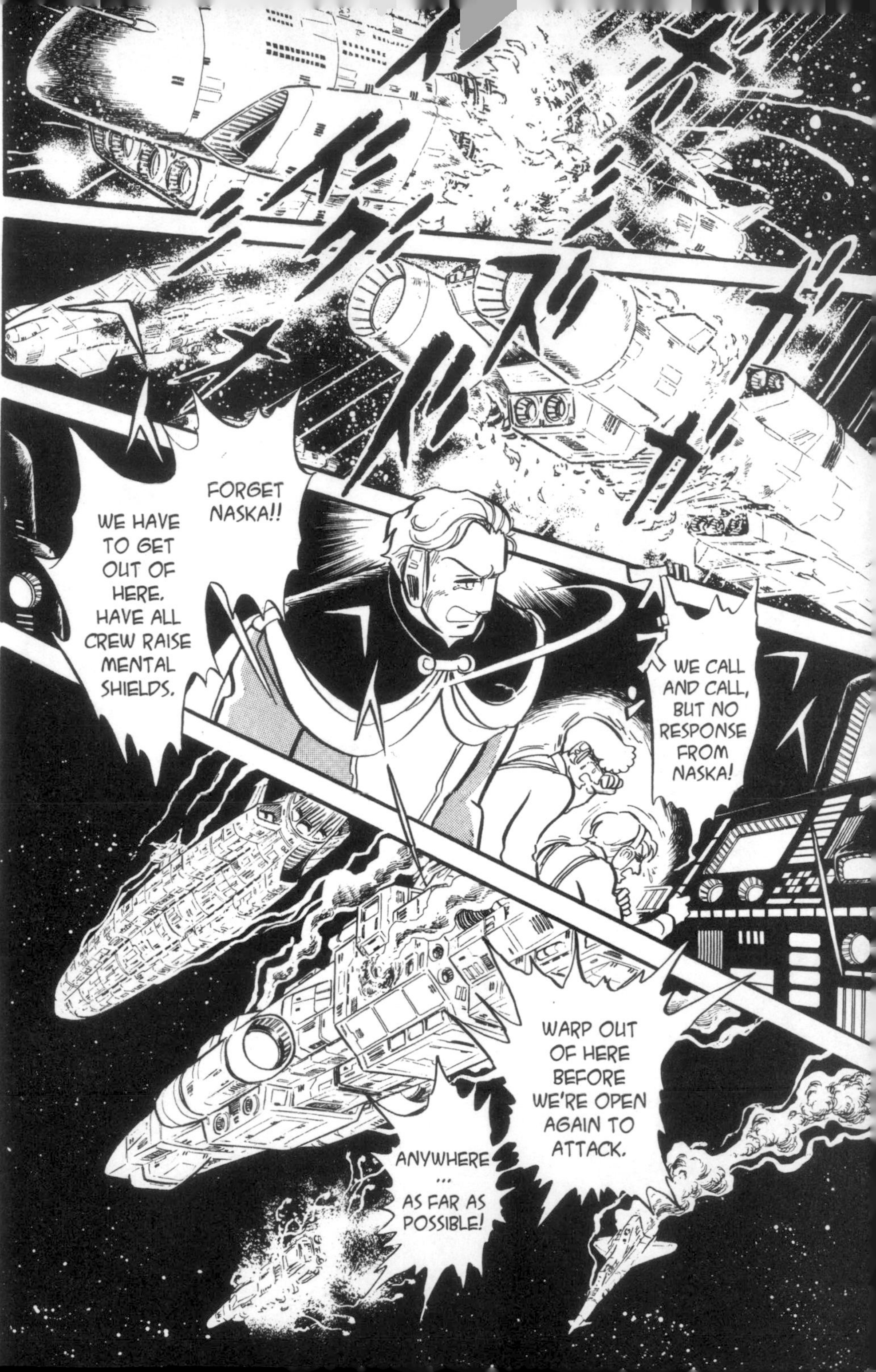
WE CALL AND CALL, BUT NO RESPONSE FROM NASKA!
FORGET NASKA!!
WE HAVE TO GET OUT OF HERE. HAVE ALL CREW RAISE MENTAL SHIELDS.
WARP OUT OF HERE BEFORE WE'RE OPEN AGAIN TO ATTACK.
ANYWHERE ... AS FAR AS POSSIBLE!

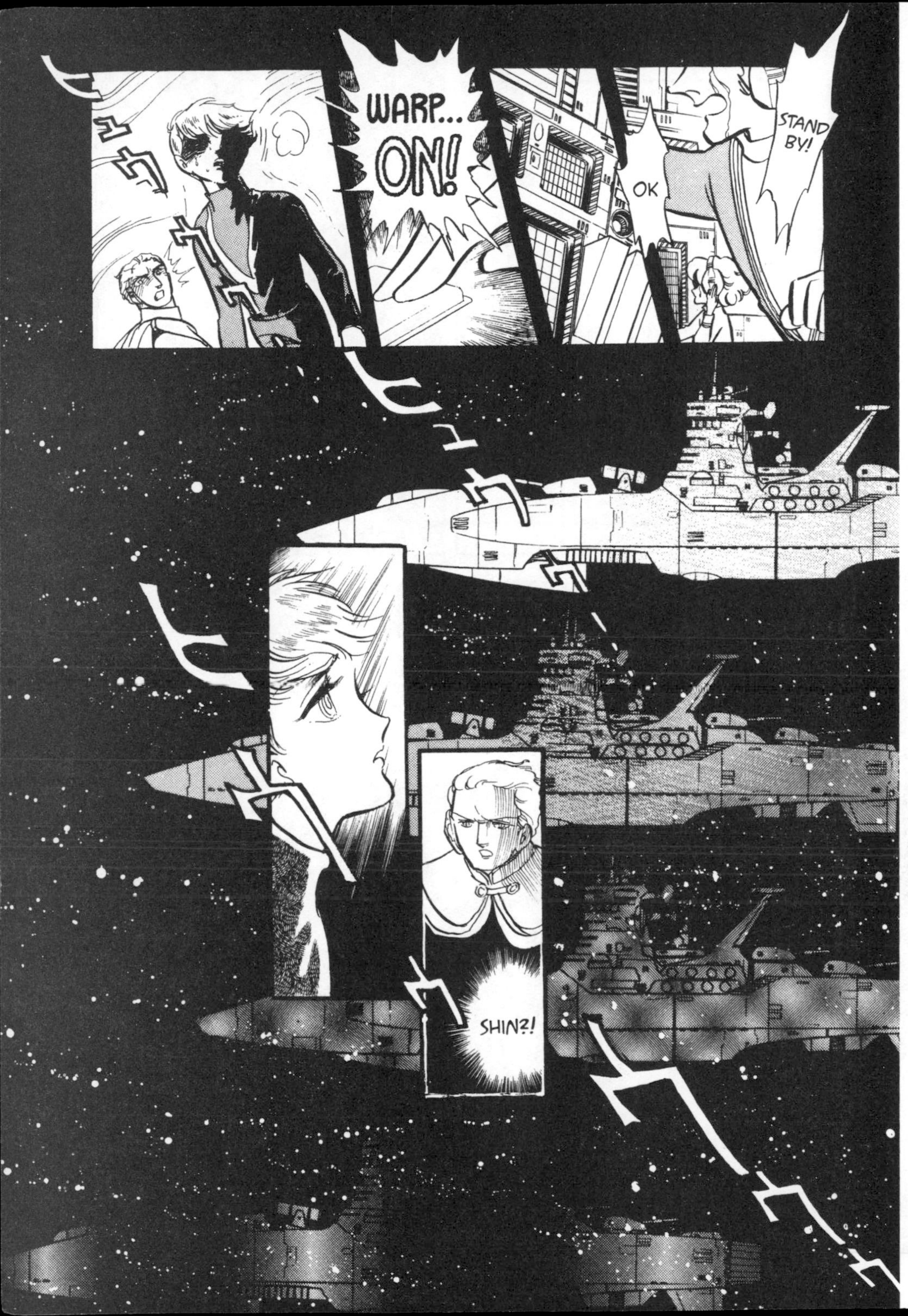
STAND BY!
OK
WARP... ON!
SHIN?!

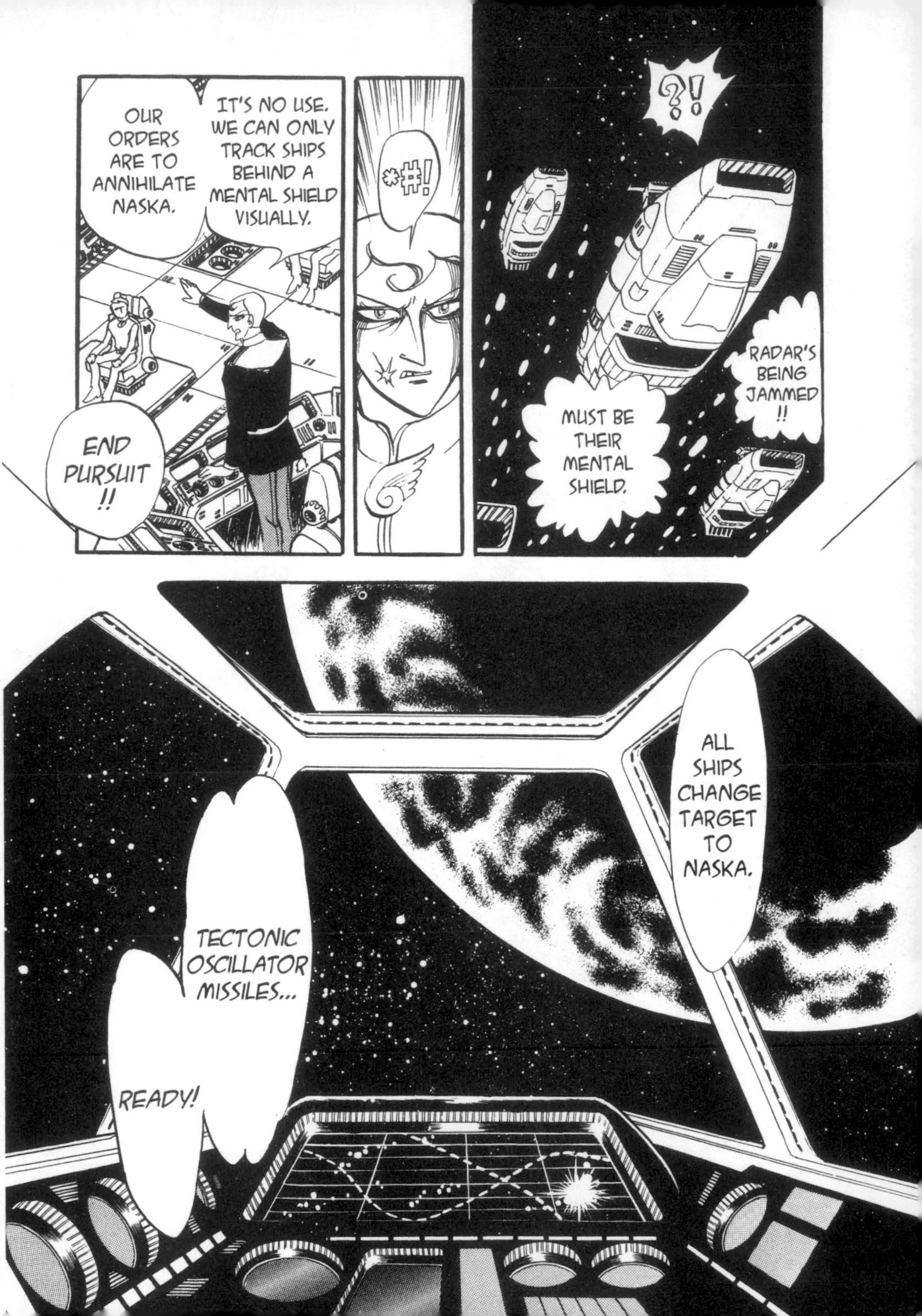
?!
RADAR'S BEING JAMMED !!
MUST BE THEIR MENTAL SHIELD.
*#!
IT'S NO USE. WE CAN ONLY TRACK SHIPS BEHIND A MENTAL SHIELD VISUALLY.
OUR ORDERS ARE TO ANNIHILATE NASKA.
END PURSUIT !!
ALL SHIPS CHANGE TARGET TO NASKA.
TECTONIC OSCILLATOR MISSILES...
READY!

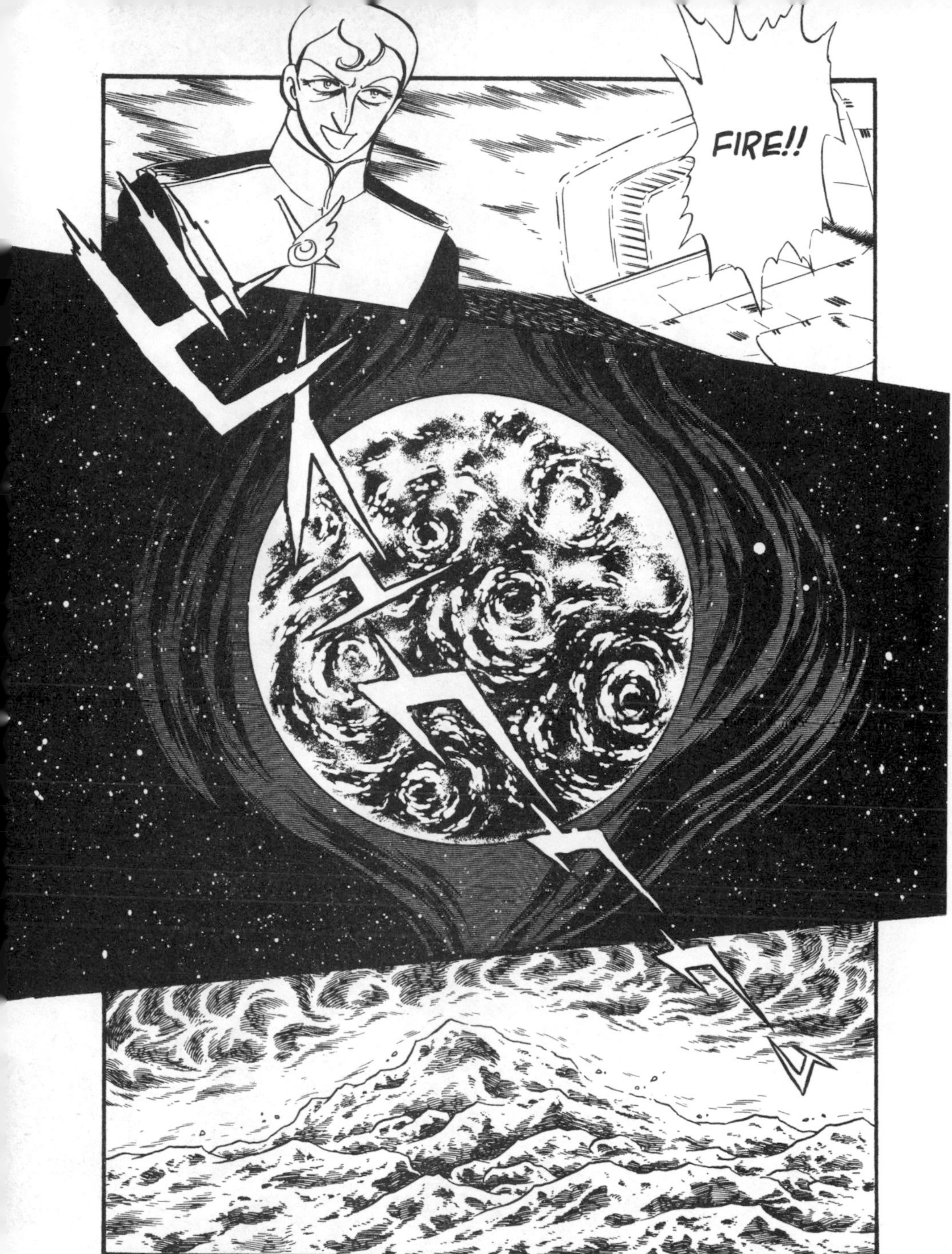
FIRE!!

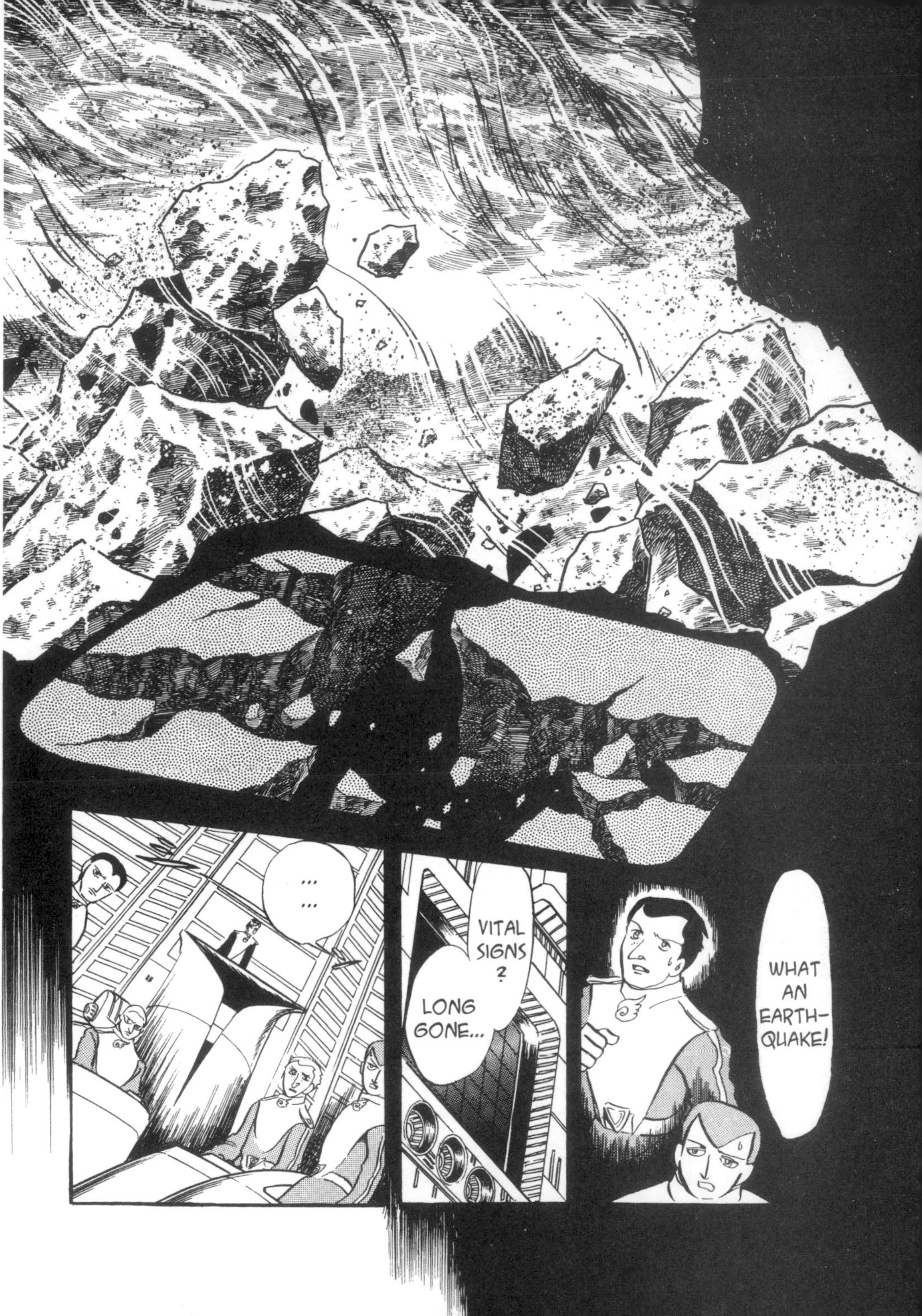
WHAT AN EARTH-QUAKE!
VITAL SIGNS?
LONG GONE...
... ...

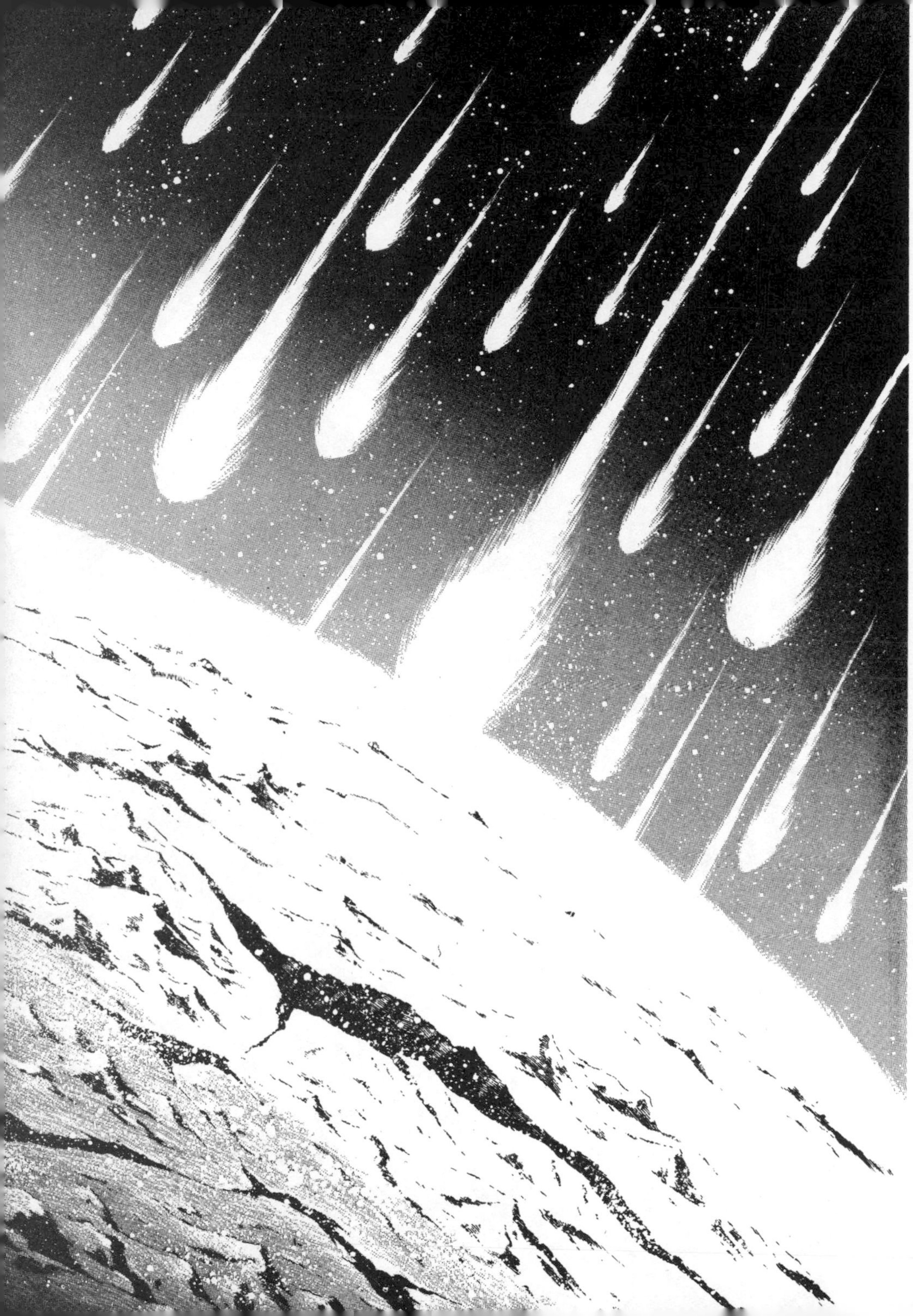

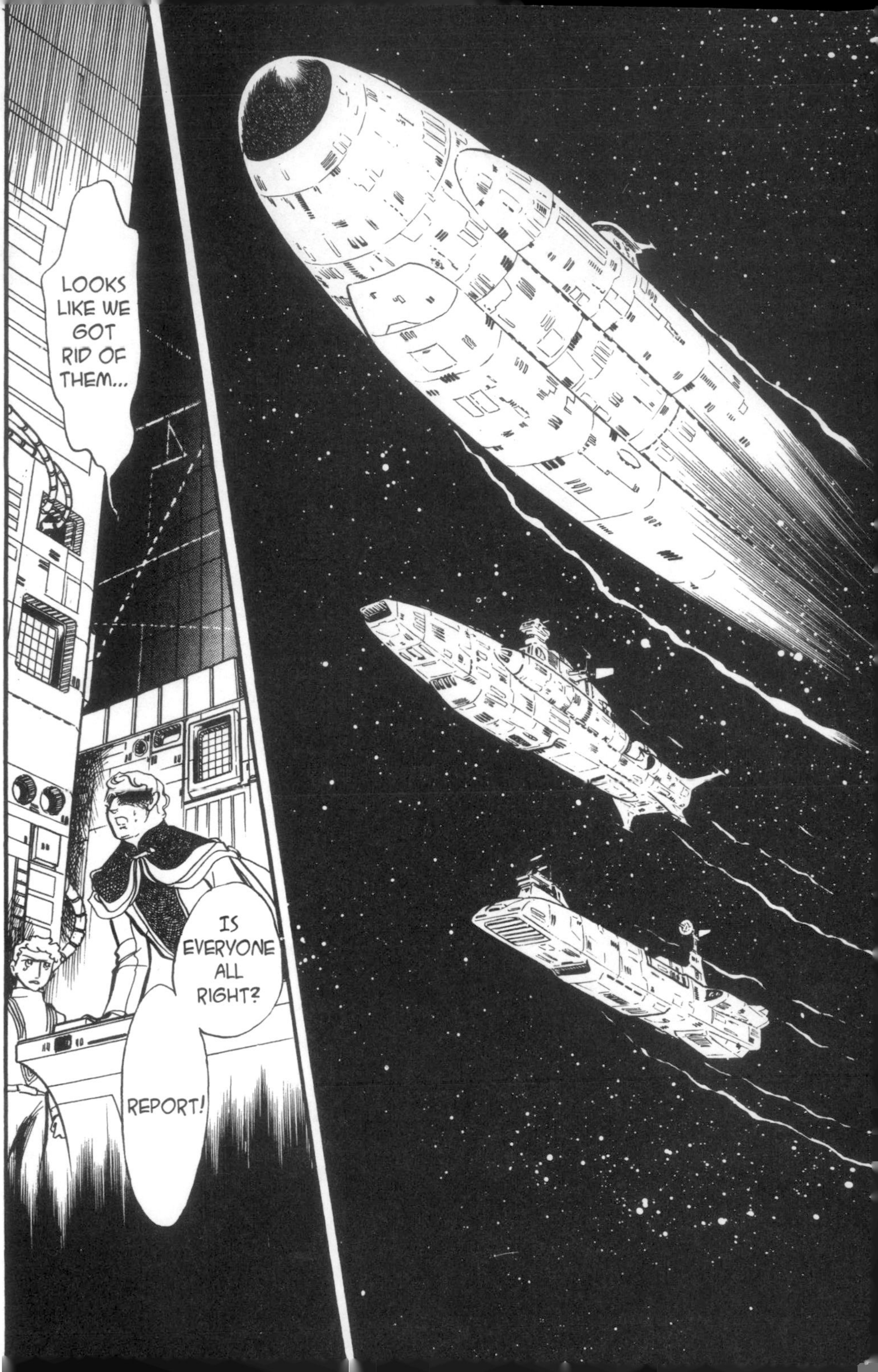
LOOKS LIKE WE GOT RID OF THEM...
IS EVERYONE ALL RIGHT?
REPORT!

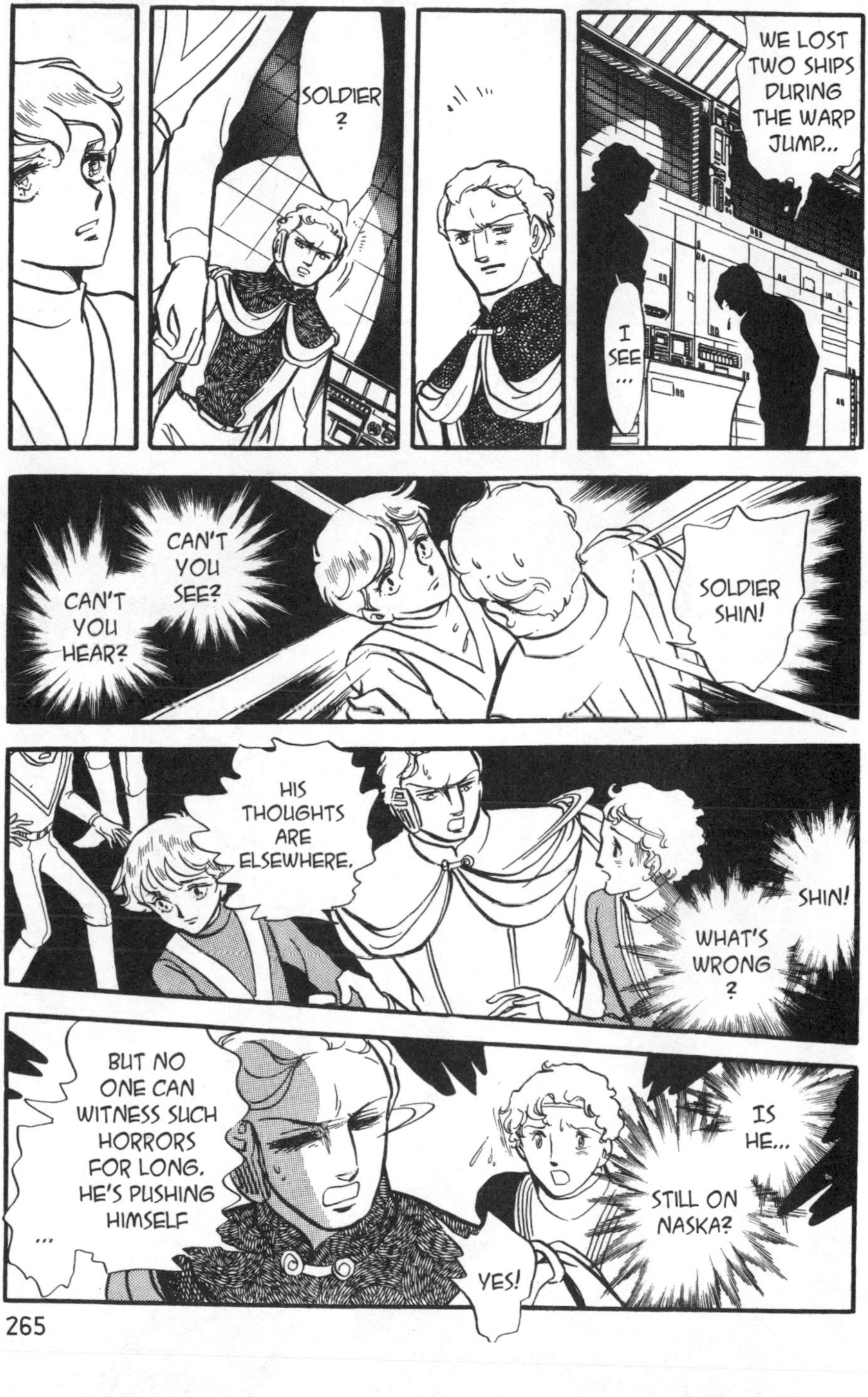
WE LOST TWO SHIPS DURING THE WARP JUMP...
I SEE ...
SOLDIER ?
SOLDIER SHIN!
CAN'T YOU SEE?
CAN'T YOU HEAR?
SHIN!
WHAT'S WRONG ?
HIS THOUGHTS ARE ELSEWHERE.
IS HE...
STILL ON NASKA?
YES!
BUT NO ONE CAN WITNESS SUCH HORRORS FOR LONG. HE'S PUSHING HIMSELF
...

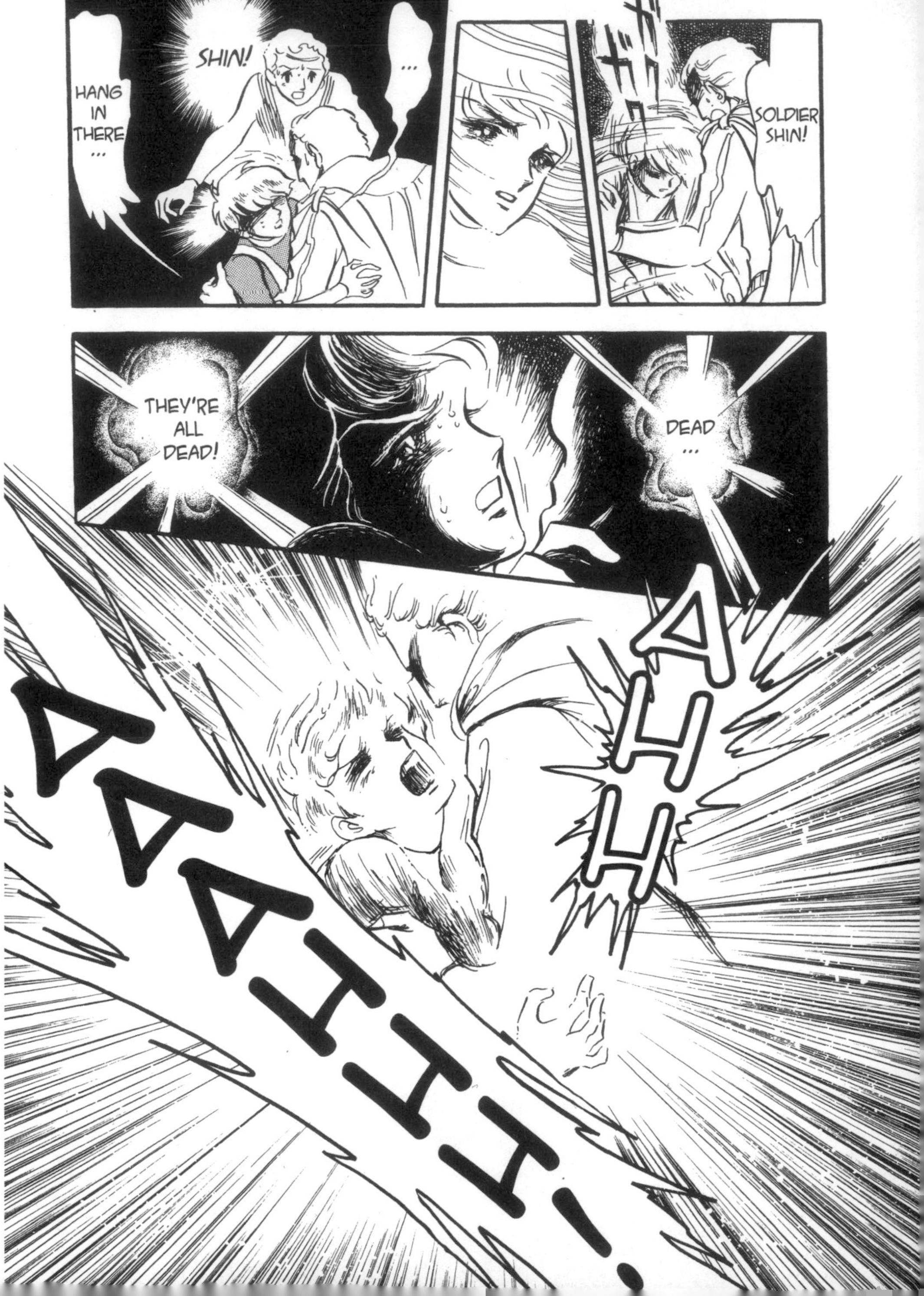
SOLDIER SHIN!
...
SHIN!
HANG IN THERE ...
DEAD ...
THEY'RE ALL DEAD!
AHHH
AAAHHH!!

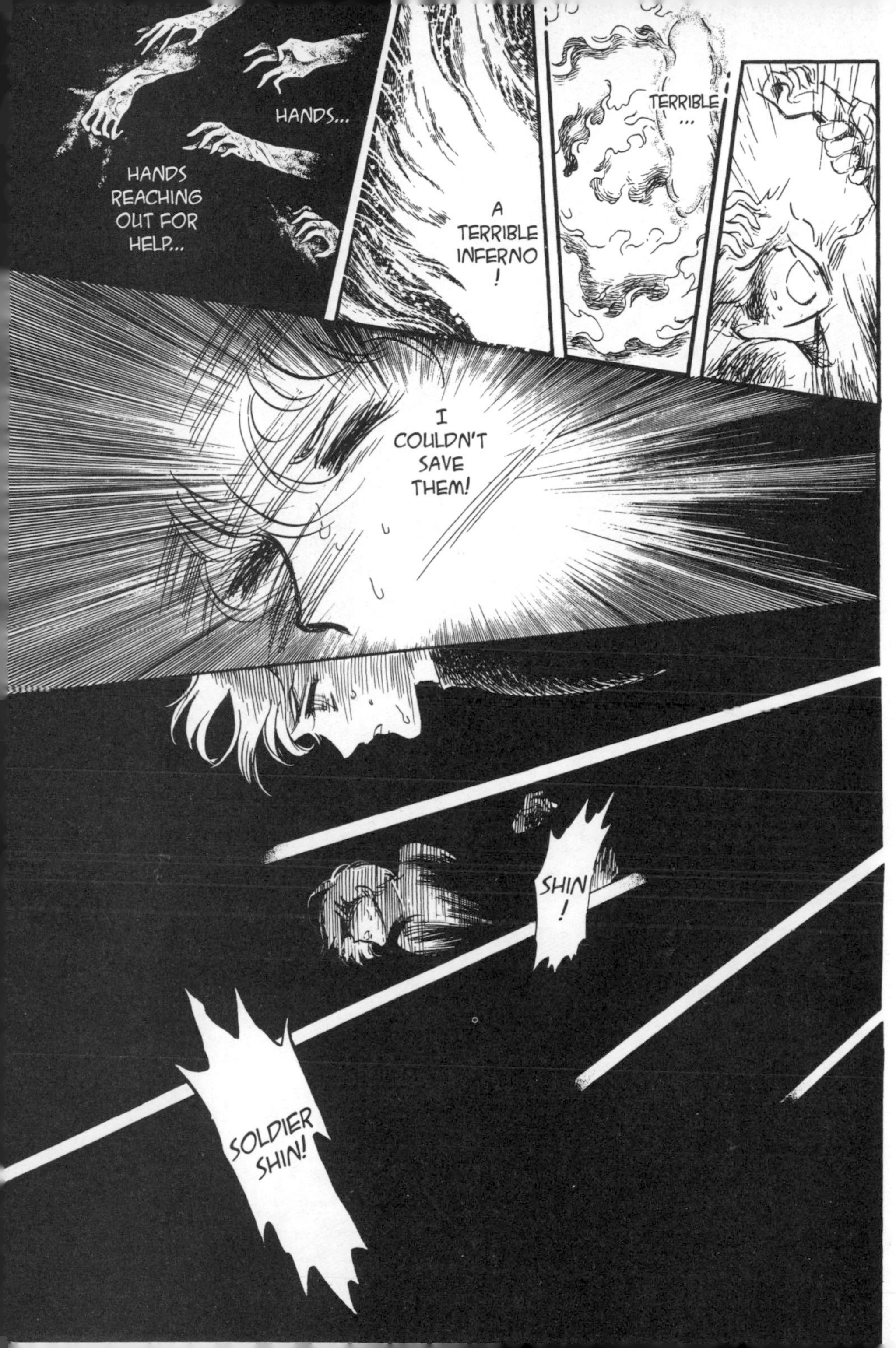
TERRIBLE ...
A TERRIBLE INFERNO !
HANDS...
HANDS REACHING OUT FOR HELP...
I COULDN'T SAVE THEM!
SHIN !
SOLDIER SHIN!

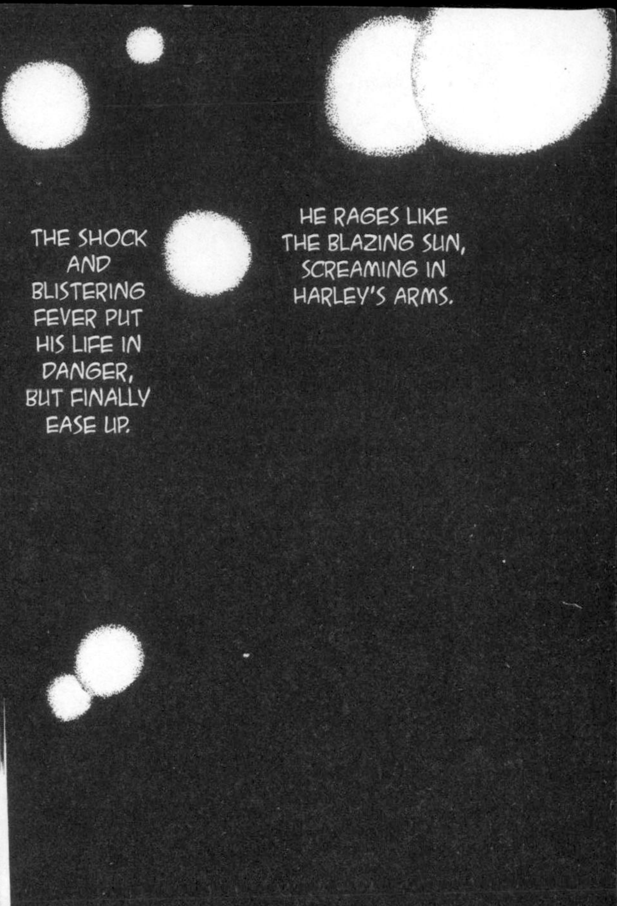
HE RAGES LIKE THE BLAZING SUN, SCREAMING IN HARLEY'S ARMS.
THE SHOCK AND BLISTERING FEVER PUT HIS LIFE IN DANGER, BUT FINALLY EASE UP.
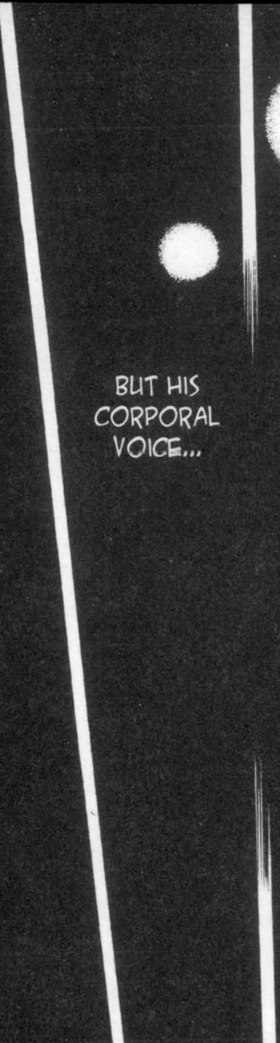
BUT HIS CORPORAL VOICE...
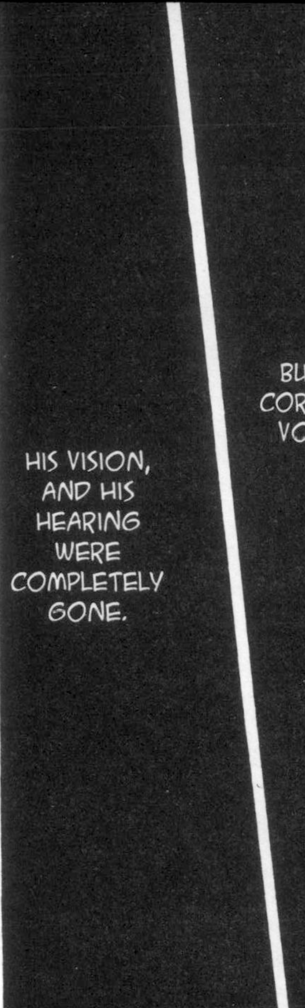
HIS VISION, AND HIS HEARING WERE COMPLETELY GONE.
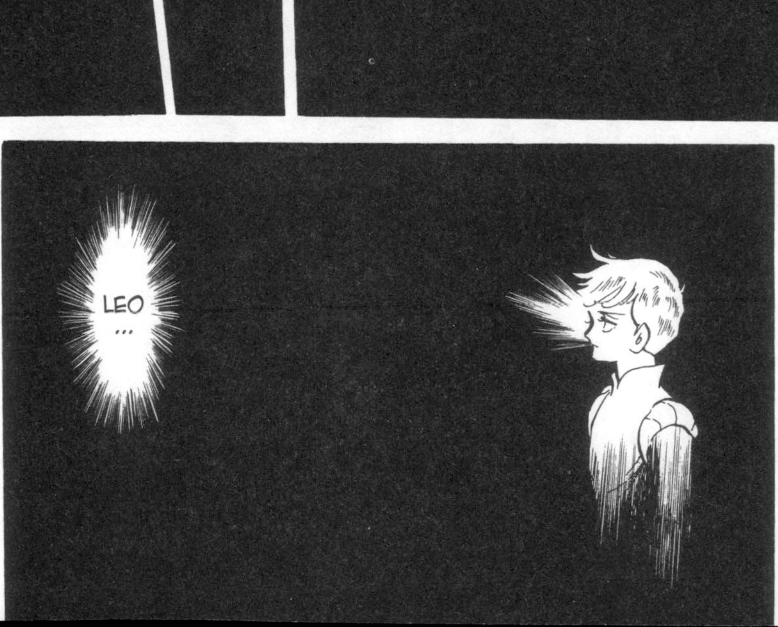
LEO ...

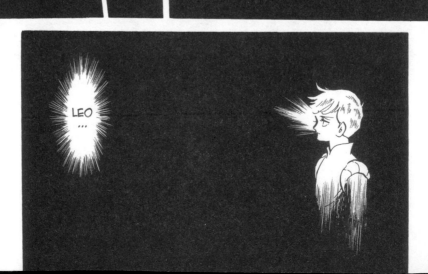

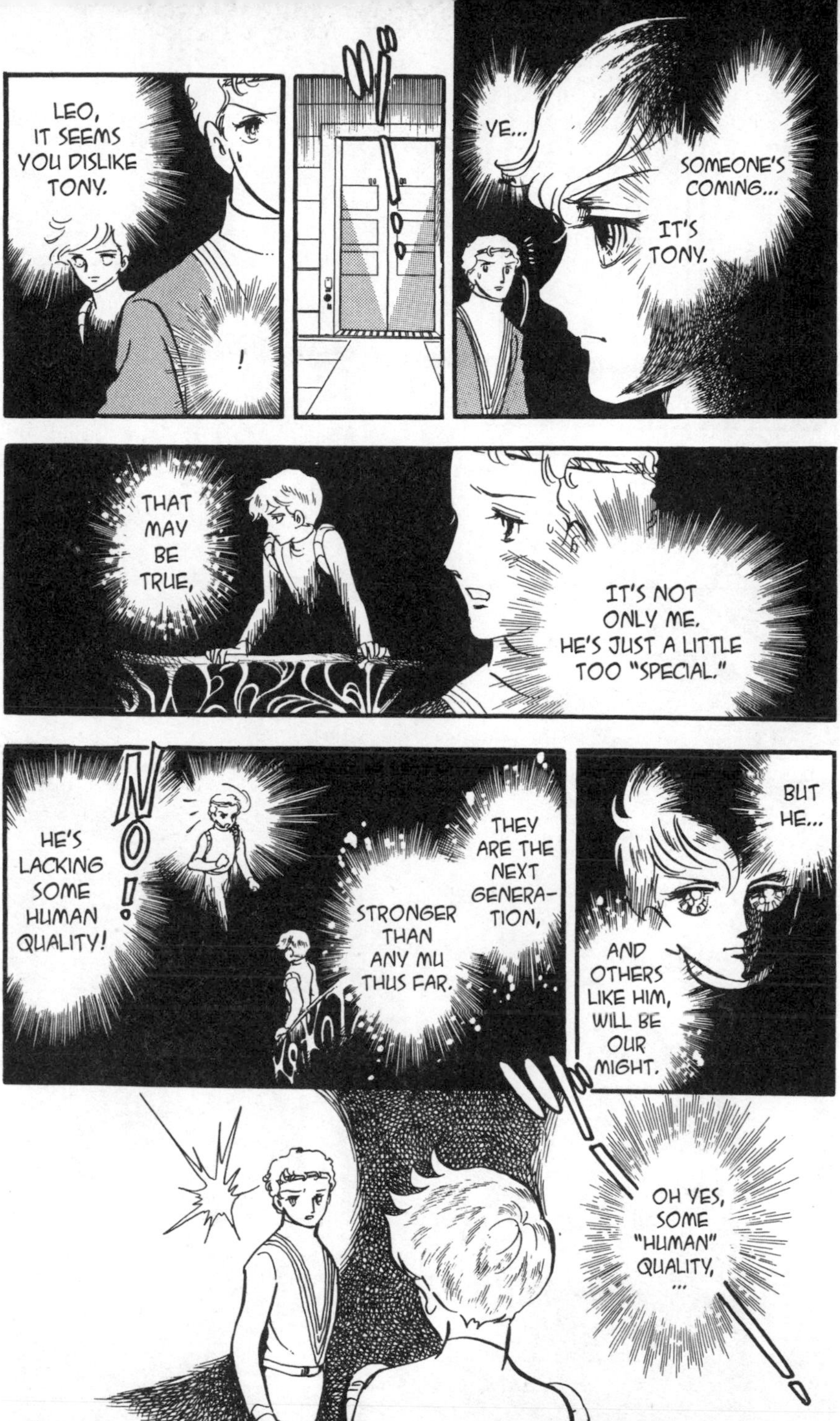
YE...
SOMEONE'S COMING...
IT'S TONY.
LEO, IT SEEMS YOU DISLIKE TONY.
!
IT'S NOT ONLY ME. HE'S JUST A LITTLE TOO "SPECIAL."
THAT MAY BE TRUE,
BUT HE...
AND OTHERS LIKE HIM, WILL BE OUR MIGHT.
THEY ARE THE NEXT GENERATION,
STRONGER THAN ANY MU THUS FAR.
NO!
HE'S LACKING SOME HUMAN QUALITY!
OH YES, SOME "HUMAN" QUALITY, ...

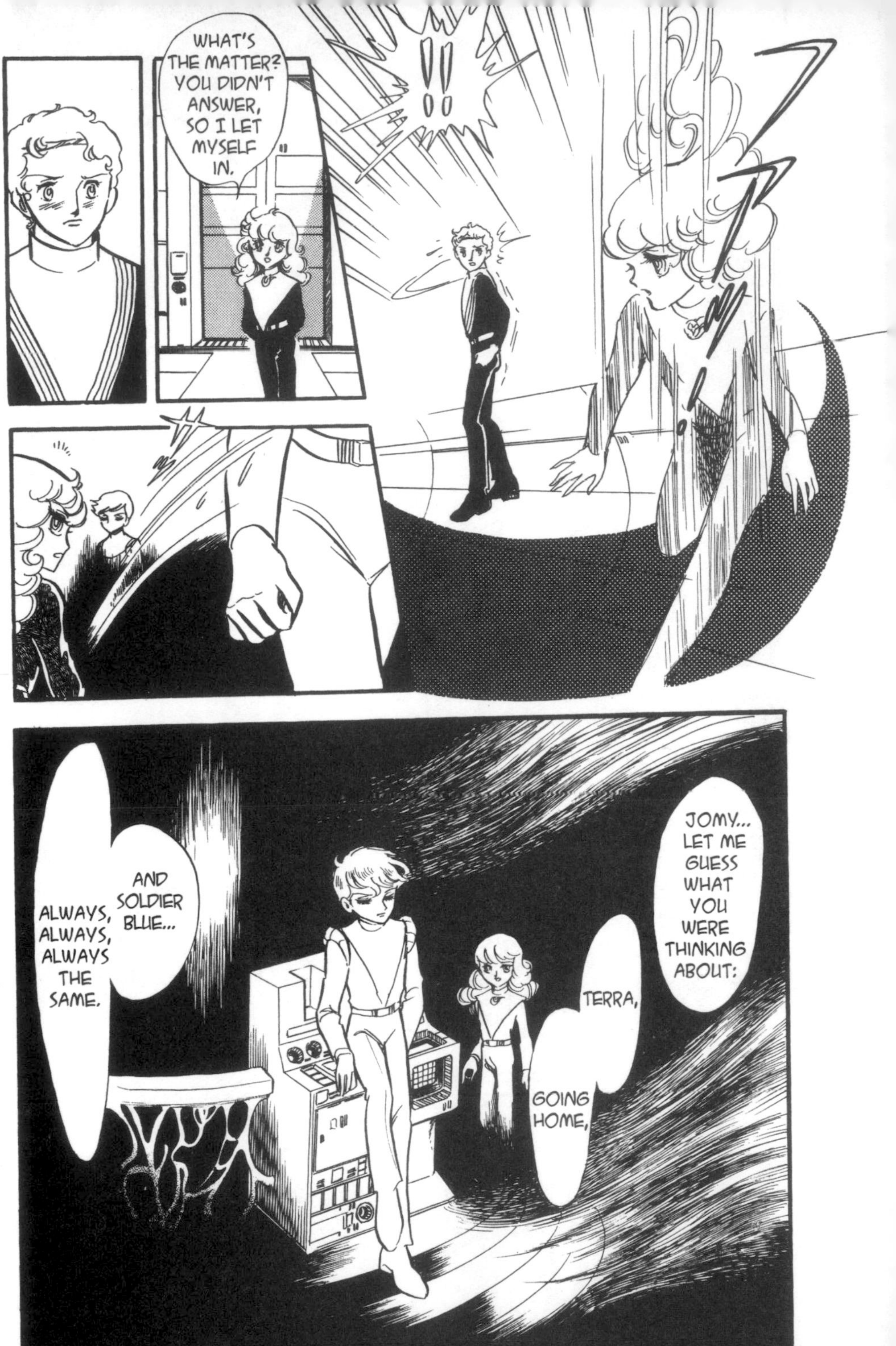
!!
WHAT'S THE MATTER? YOU DIDN'T ANSWER, SO I LET MYSELF IN.
JOMY... LET ME GUESS WHAT YOU WERE THINKING ABOUT:
TERRA,
GOING HOME,
AND SOLDIER BLUE...
ALWAYS, ALWAYS, ALWAYS THE SAME.

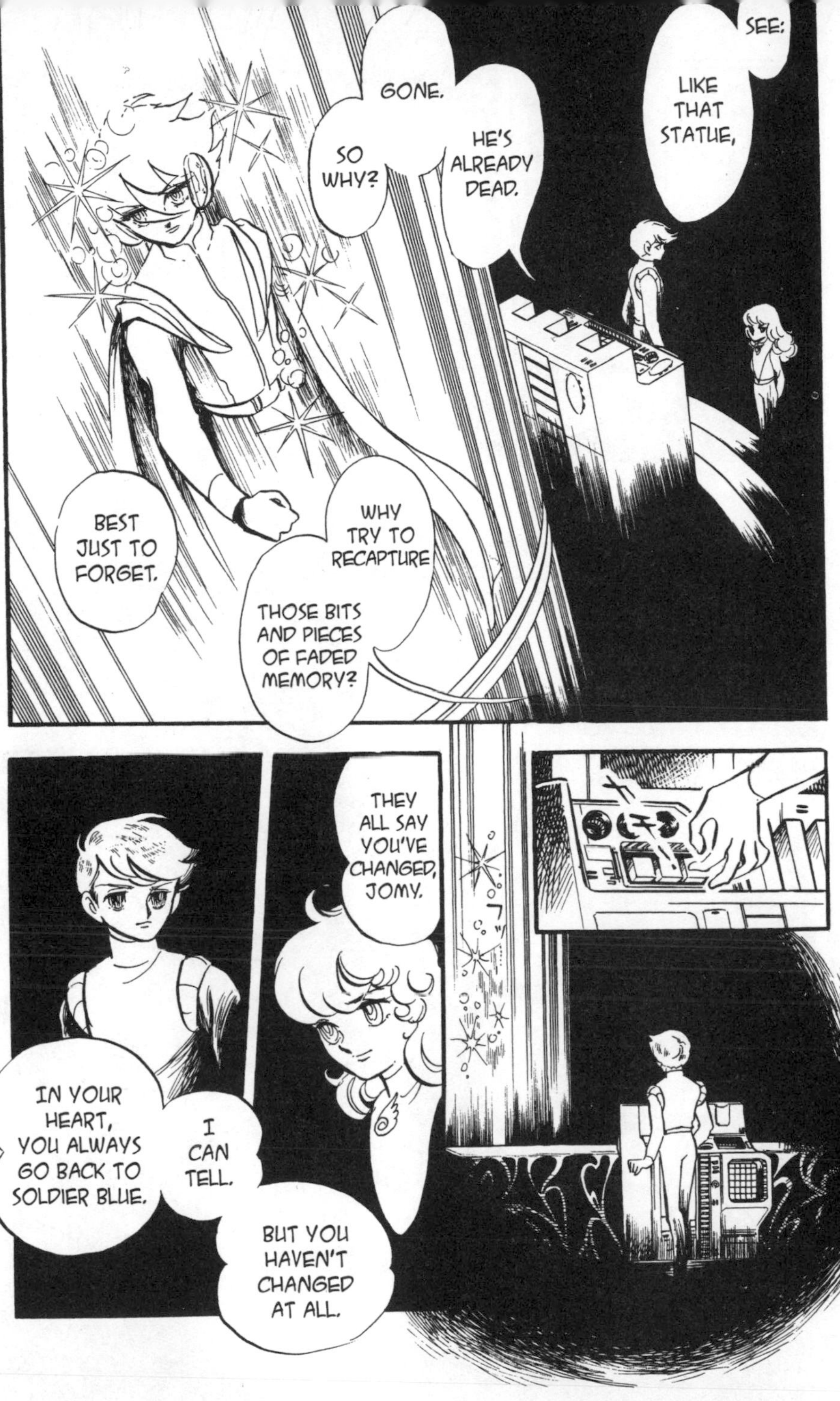
SEE:
LIKE THAT STATUE,
HE'S ALREADY DEAD.
GONE.
SO WHY?
WHY TRY TO RECAPTURE
THOSE BITS AND PIECES OF FADED MEMORY?
BEST JUST TO FORGET.
THEY ALL SAY YOU'VE CHANGED, JOMY.
BUT YOU HAVEN'T CHANGED AT ALL.
I CAN TELL.
IN YOUR HEART, YOU ALWAYS GO BACK TO SOLDIER BLUE.

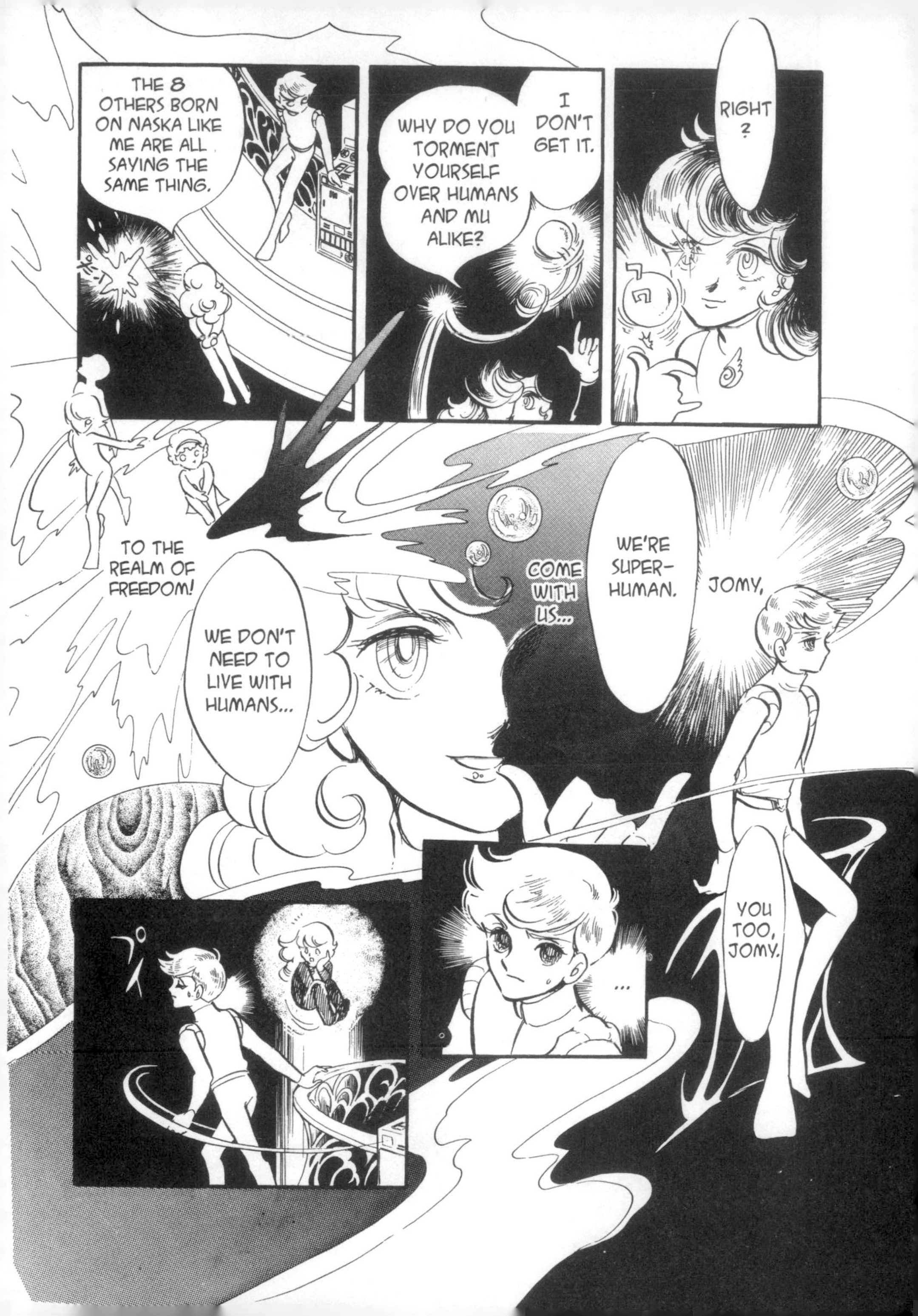
RIGHT ?
I DON'T GET IT.
WHY DO YOU TORMENT YOURSELF OVER HUMANS AND MU ALIKE?
THE 8 OTHERS BORN ON NASKA LIKE ME ARE ALL SAYING THE SAME THING.
JOMY,
WE'RE SUPER-HUMAN.
COME WITH US...
WE DON'T NEED TO LIVE WITH HUMANS...
TO THE REALM OF FREEDOM!
YOU TOO, JOMY.
...

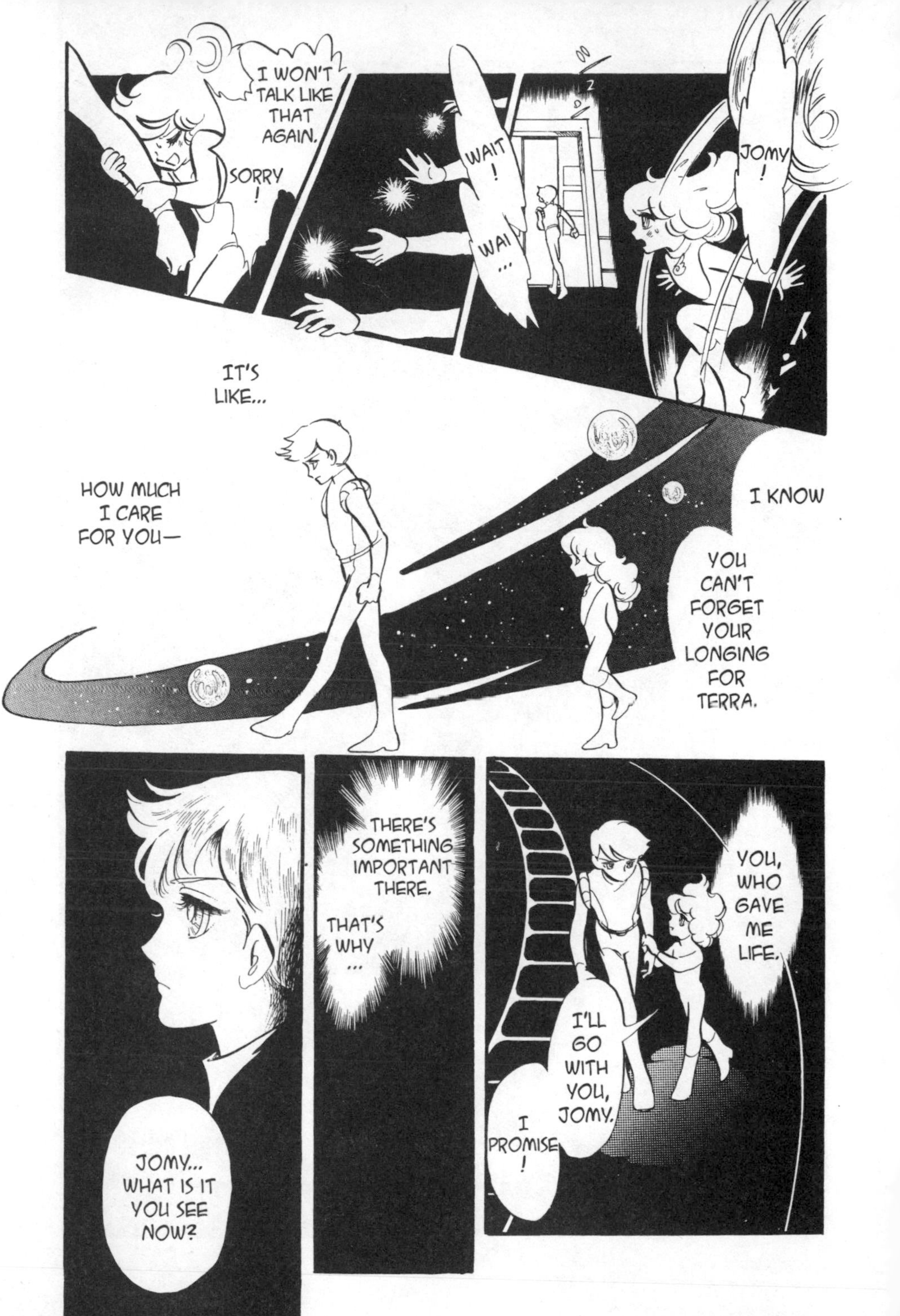
JOMY!
WAIT!
WAI...
I WON'T TALK LIKE THAT AGAIN.
SORRY!
I KNOW
YOU CAN'T FORGET YOUR LONGING FOR TERRA.
IT'S LIKE...
HOW MUCH I CARE FOR YOU—
YOU, WHO GAVE ME LIFE.
I'LL GO WITH YOU, JOMY.
I PROMISE!
THERE'S SOMETHING IMPORTANT THERE.
THAT'S WHY...
JOMY... WHAT IS IT YOU SEE NOW?

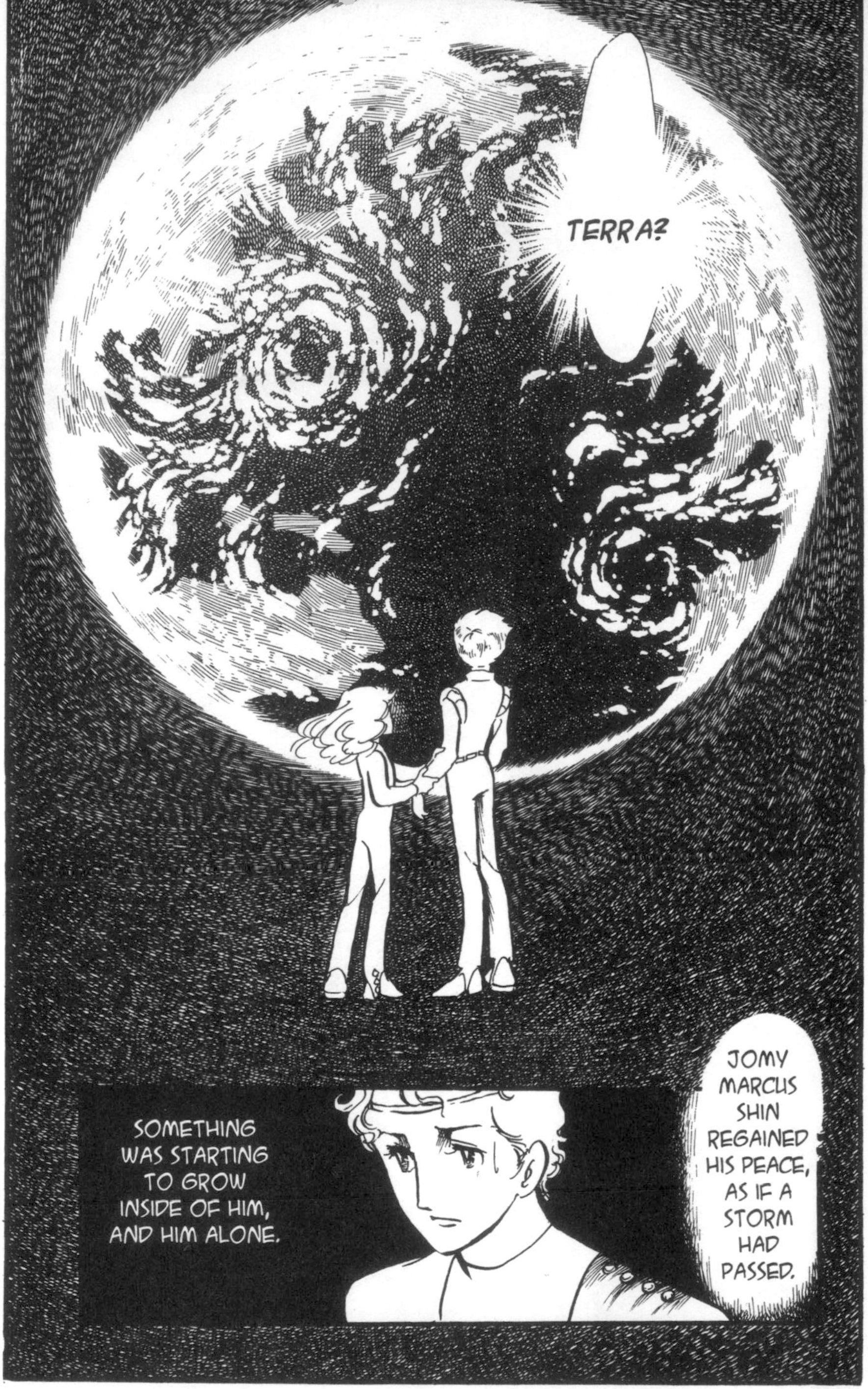
TERRA?
JOMY MARCUS SHIN REGAINED HIS PEACE, AS IF A STORM HAD PASSED.
SOMETHING WAS STARTING TO GROW INSIDE OF HIM, AND HIM ALONE.

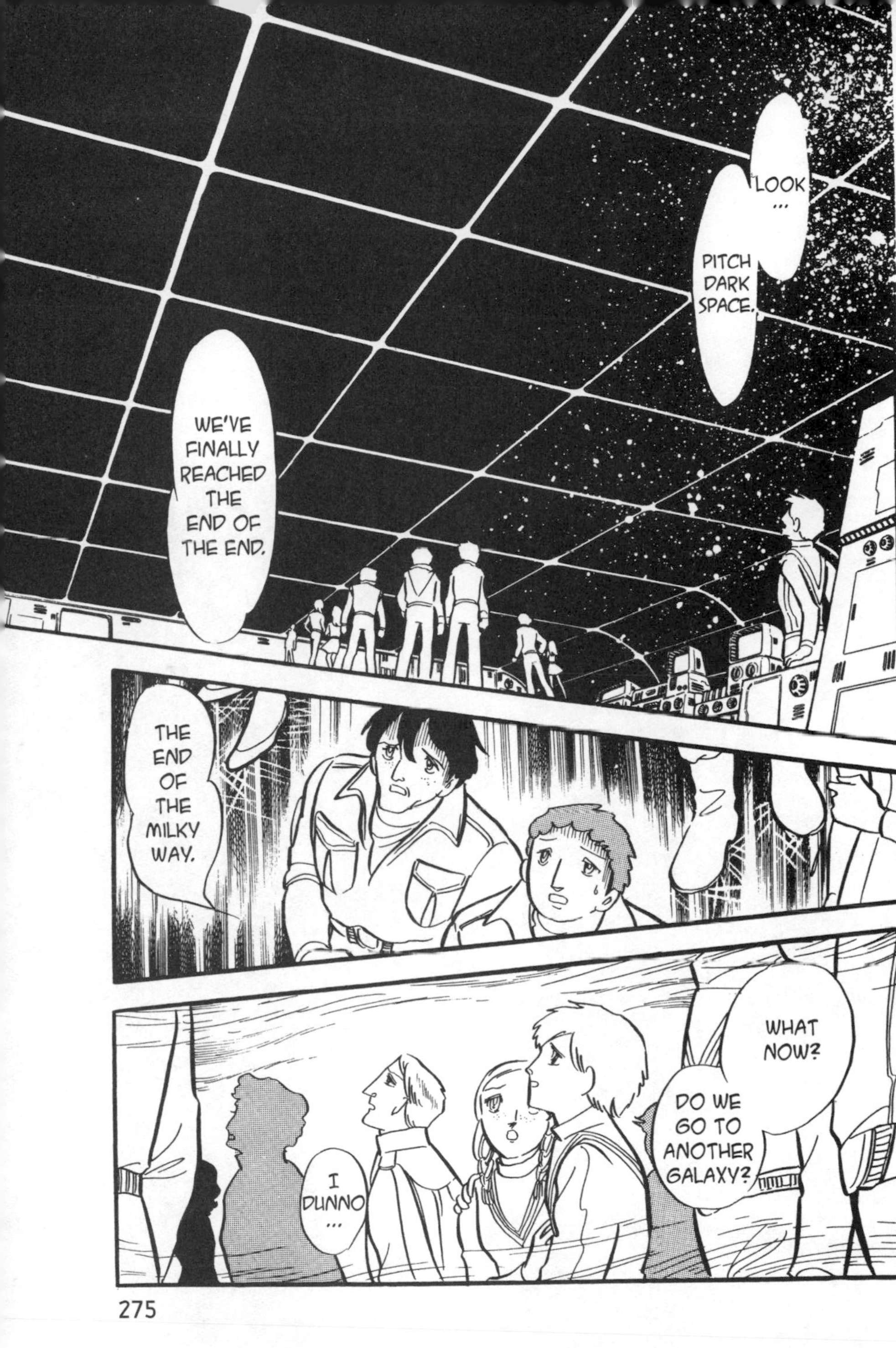
LOOK ...
PITCH DARK SPACE.
WE'VE FINALLY REACHED THE END OF THE END.
THE END OF THE MILKY WAY.
WHAT NOW?
DO WE GO TO ANOTHER GALAXY?
I DUNNO ...

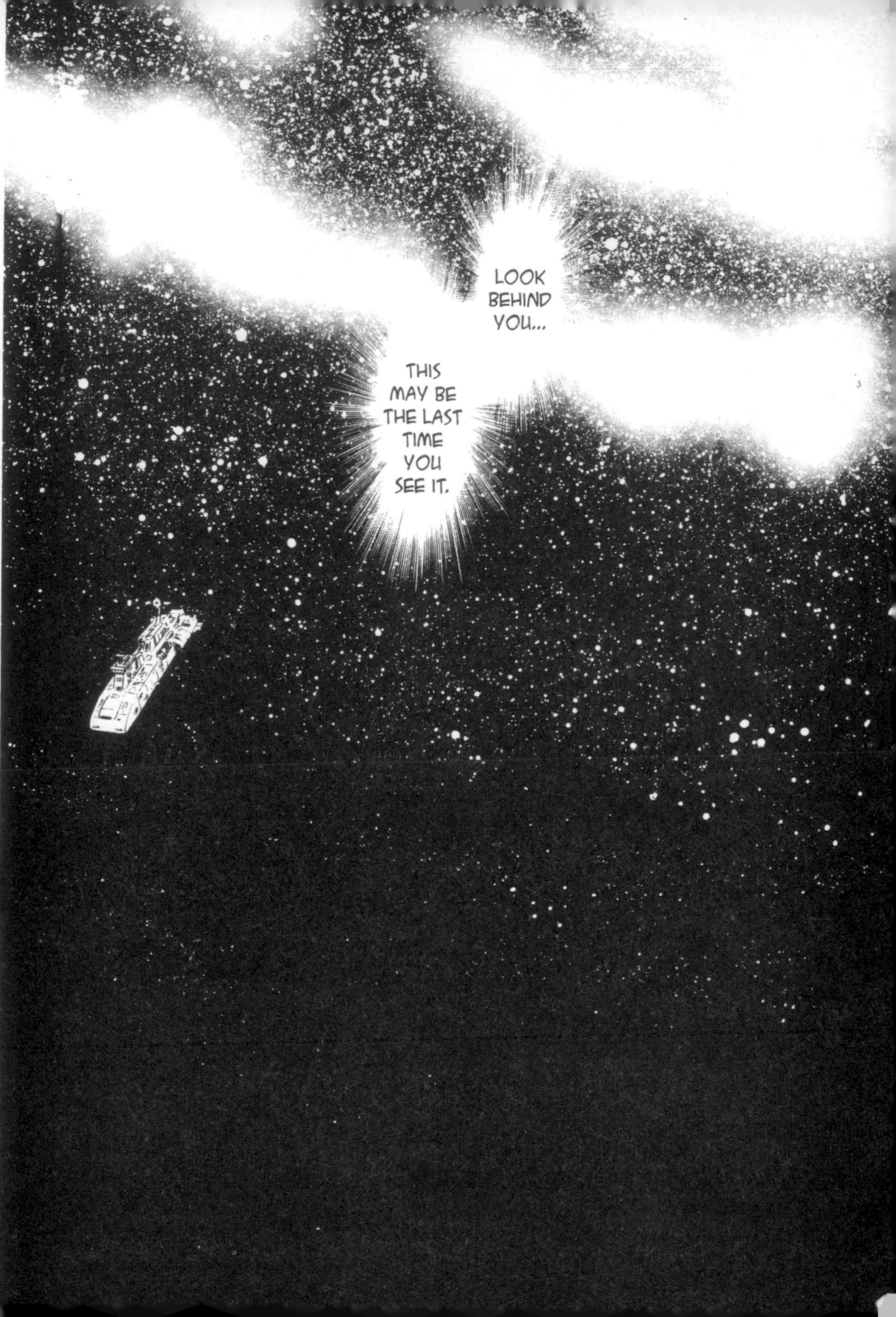
LOOK BEHIND YOU...
THIS MAY BE THE LAST TIME YOU SEE IT.

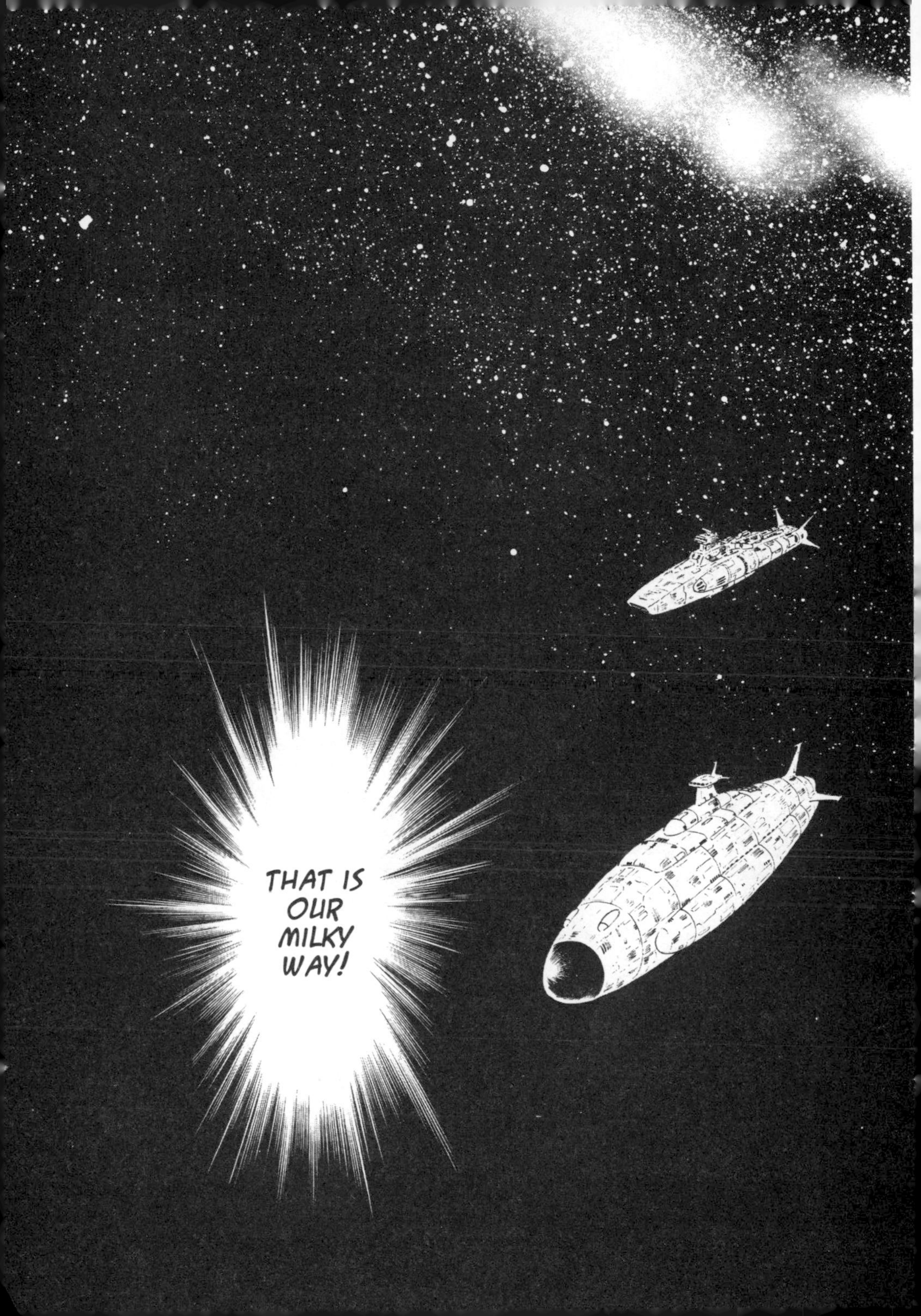
THAT IS OUR MILKY WAY!

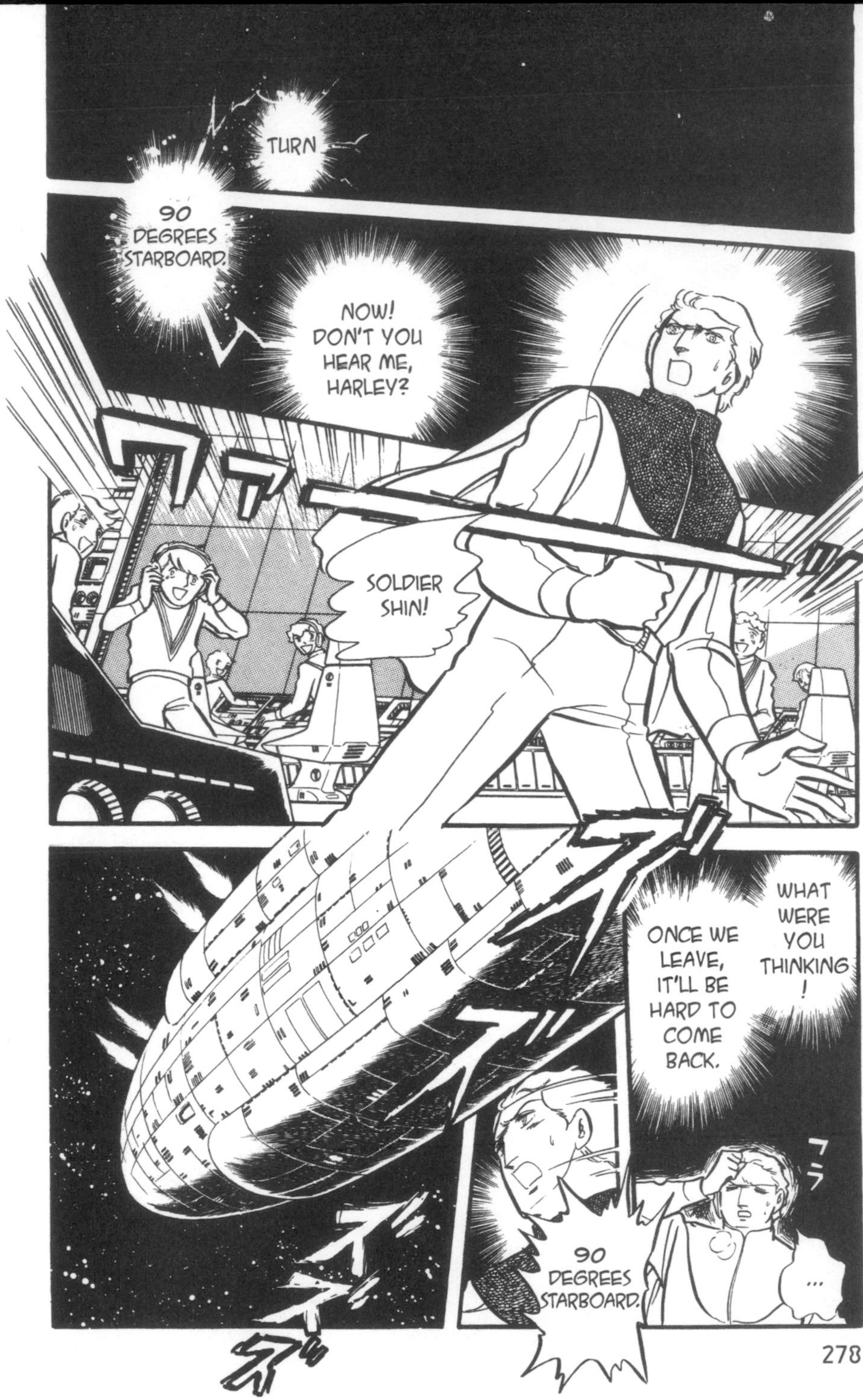
TURN
90 DEGREES STARBOARD.
NOW! DON'T YOU HEAR ME, HARLEY?
SOLDIER SHIN!
WHAT WERE YOU THINKING!
ONCE WE LEAVE, IT'LL BE HARD TO COME BACK.
...
90 DEGREES STARBOARD.

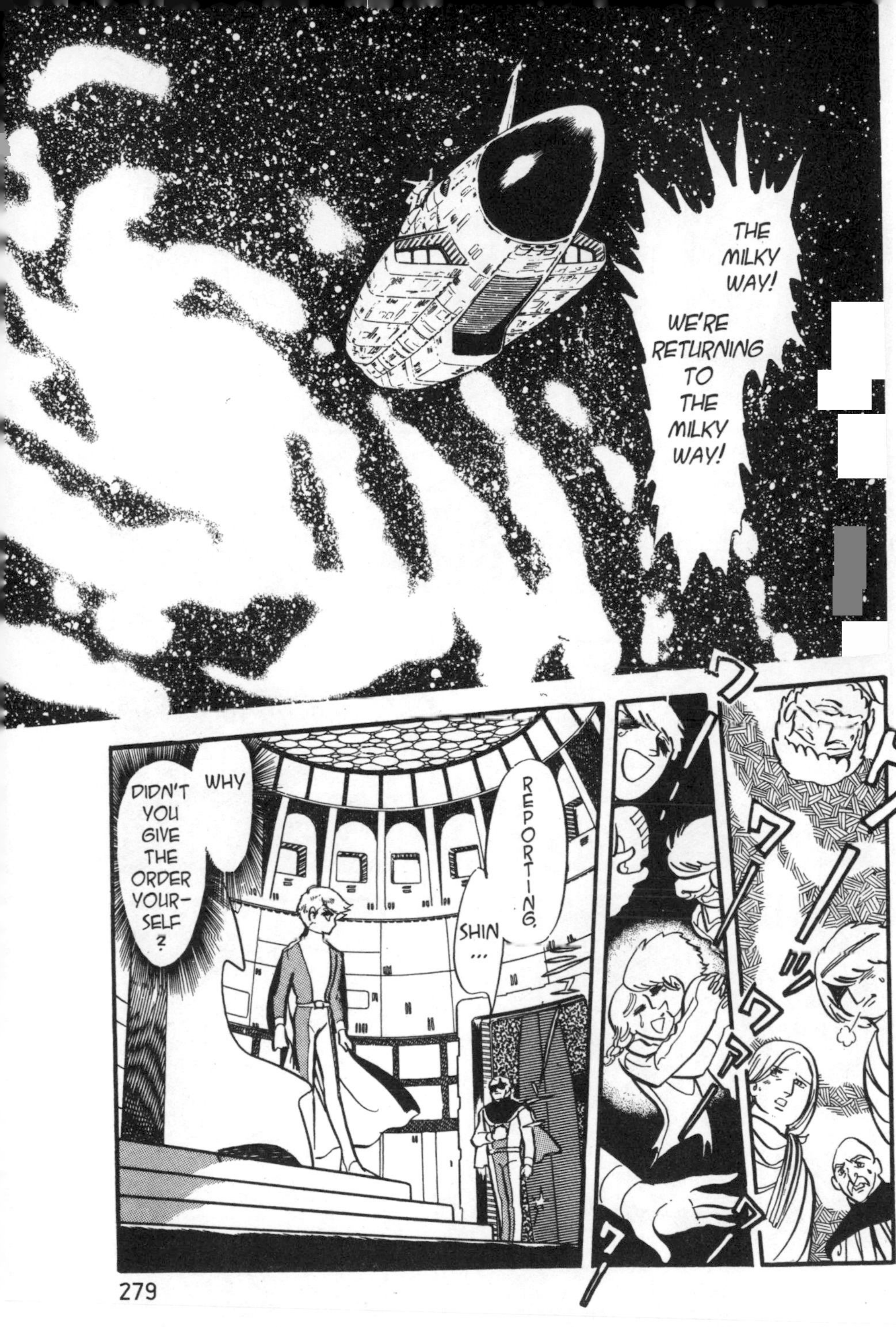
THE MILKY WAY!
WE'RE RETURNING TO THE MILKY WAY!
REPORTING, SHIN...
WHY DIDN'T YOU GIVE THE ORDER YOURSELF?

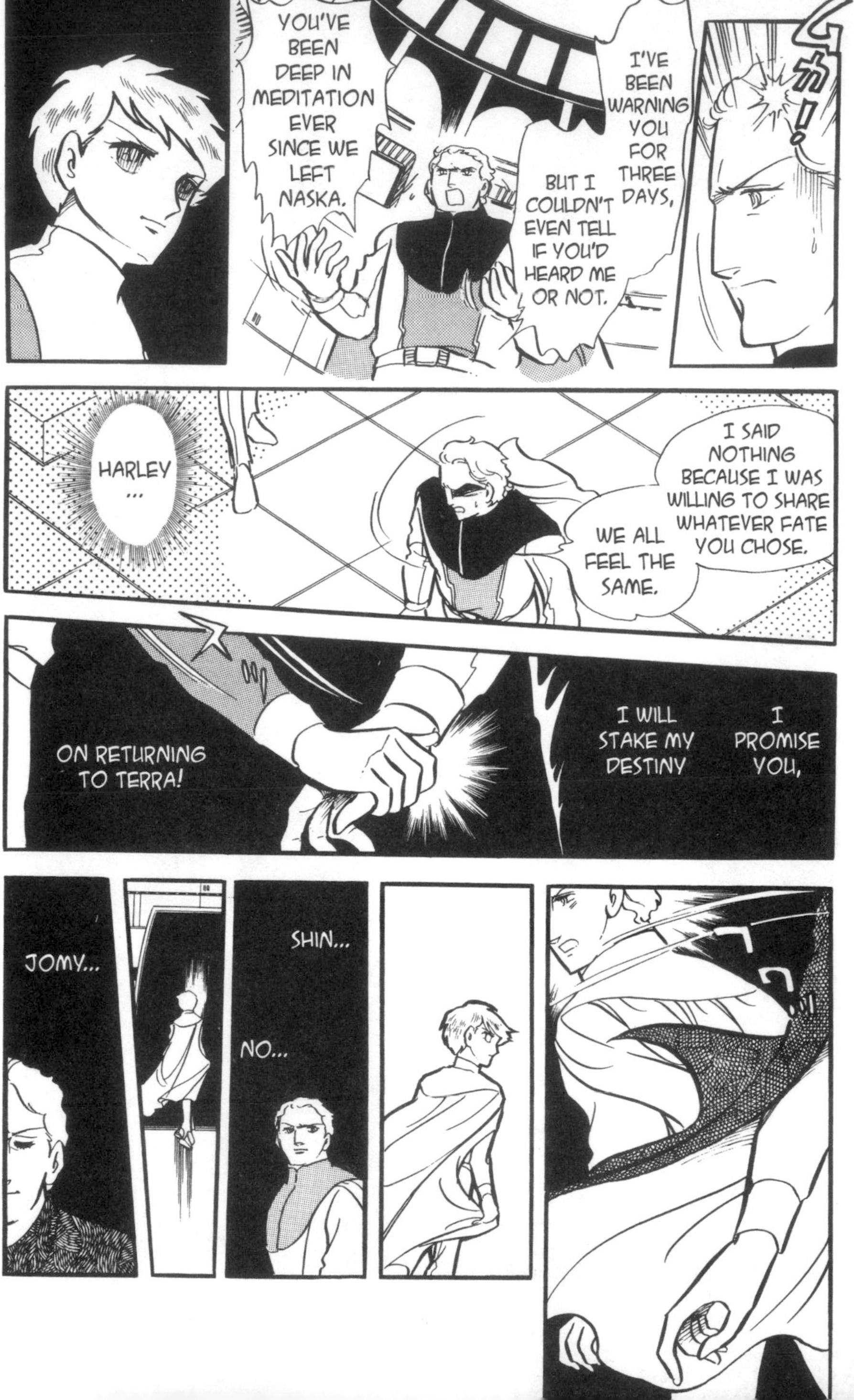

ムカ!
YOU'VE BEEN DEEP IN MEDITATION EVER SINCE WE LEFT NASKA.
I'VE BEEN WARNING YOU FOR THREE DAYS,
BUT I COULDN'T EVEN TELL IF YOU'D HEARD ME OR NOT.
I SAID NOTHING BECAUSE I WAS WILLING TO SHARE WHATEVER FATE YOU CHOSE.
WE ALL FEEL THE SAME.
HARLEY ...
I PROMISE YOU,
I WILL STAKE MY DESTINY
ON RETURNING TO TERRA!
SHIN...
NO...
JOMY...

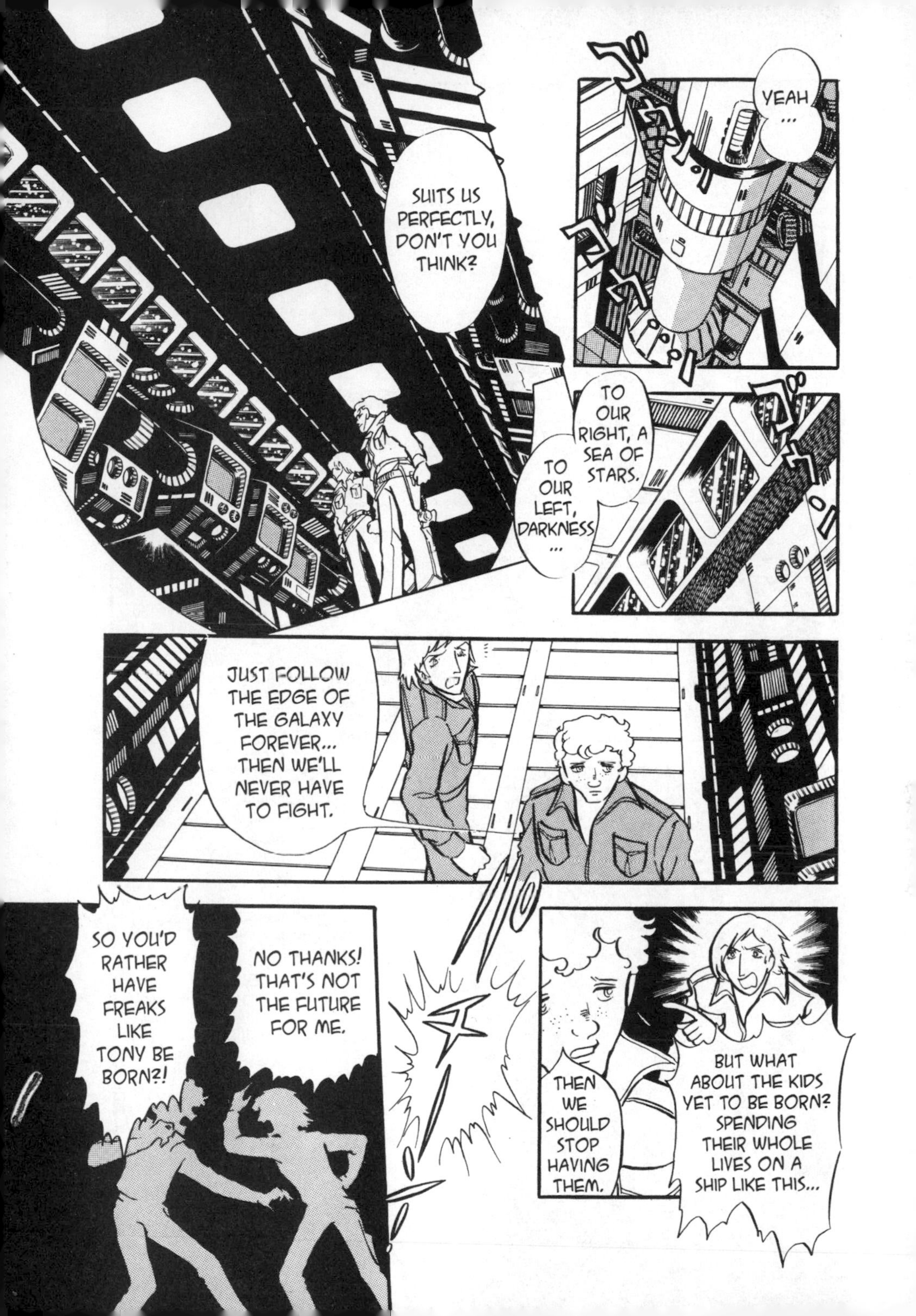
YEAH ...
TO OUR RIGHT, A SEA OF STARS.
TO OUR LEFT, DARKNESS ...
SUITS US PERFECTLY, DON'T YOU THINK?
JUST FOLLOW THE EDGE OF THE GALAXY FOREVER... THEN WE'LL NEVER HAVE TO FIGHT.
BUT WHAT ABOUT THE KIDS YET TO BE BORN? SPENDING THEIR WHOLE LIVES ON A SHIP LIKE THIS...
THEN WE SHOULD STOP HAVING THEM.
NO THANKS! THAT'S NOT THE FUTURE FOR ME.
SO YOU'D RATHER HAVE FREAKS LIKE TONY BE BORN?!

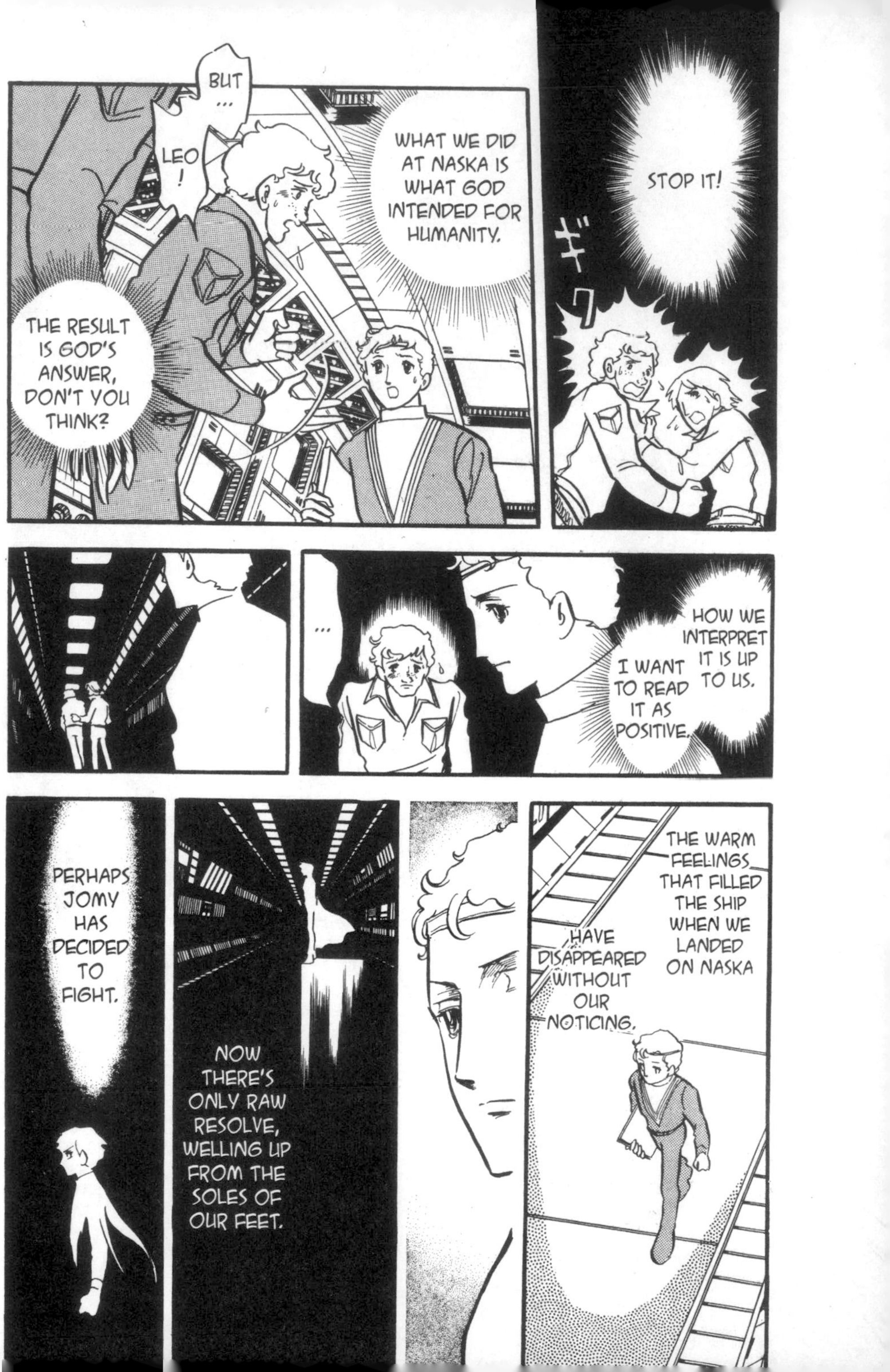
STOP IT!
ギク
WHAT WE DID AT NASKA IS WHAT GOD INTENDED FOR HUMANITY.
BUT ...
LEO !
THE RESULT IS GOD'S ANSWER, DON'T YOU THINK?
HOW WE INTERPRET IT IS UP TO US.
I WANT TO READ IT AS POSITIVE.
...
THE WARM FEELINGS THAT FILLED THE SHIP WHEN WE LANDED ON NASKA
HAVE DISAPPEARED WITHOUT OUR NOTICING.
NOW THERE'S ONLY RAW RESOLVE, WELLING UP FROM THE SOLES OF OUR FEET.
PERHAPS JOMY HAS DECIDED TO FIGHT.

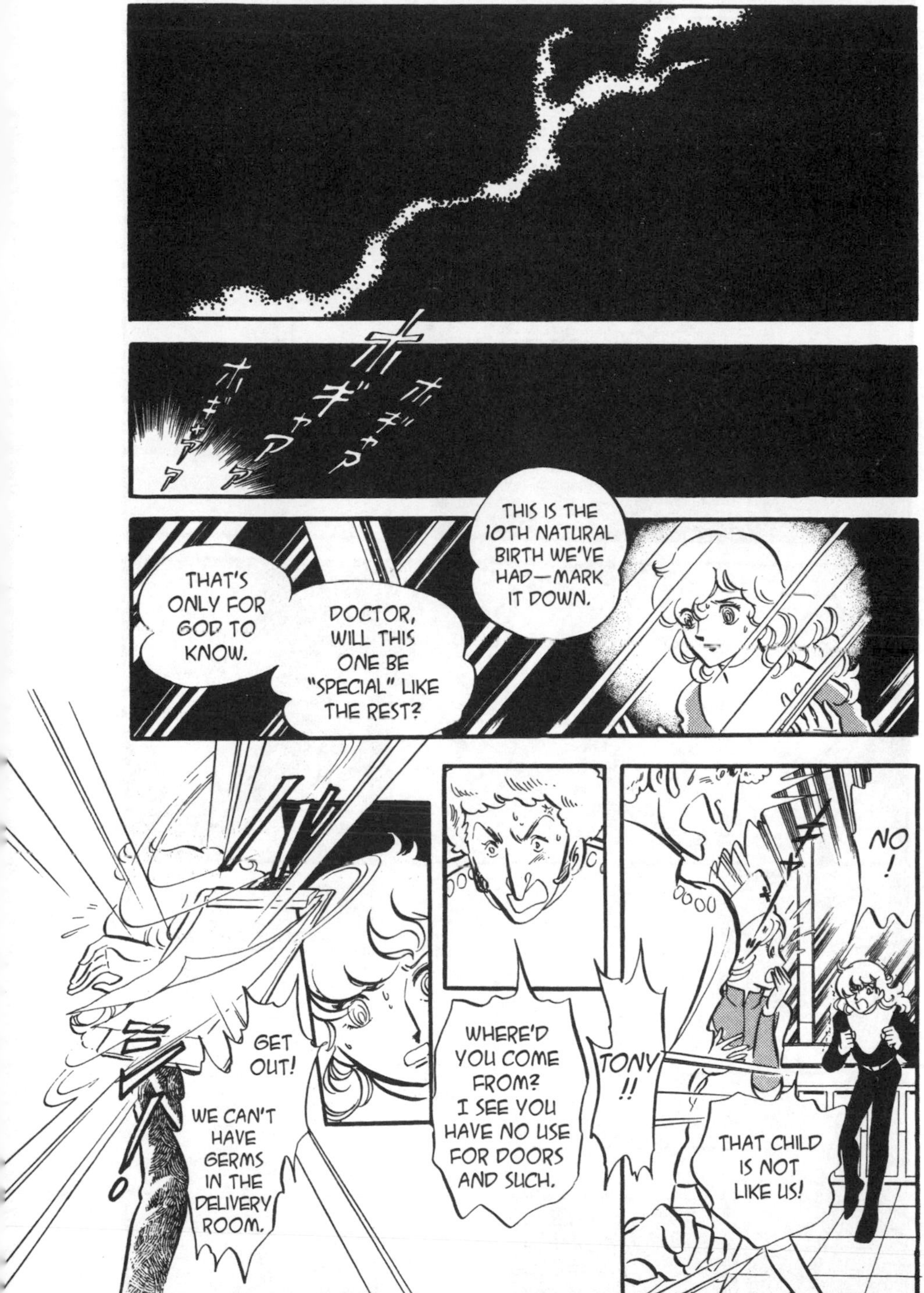
ホギャア
ホギャアア
ホギャアア
THIS IS THE 10TH NATURAL BIRTH WE'VE HAD—MARK IT DOWN.
DOCTOR, WILL THIS ONE BE "SPECIAL" LIKE THE REST?
THAT'S ONLY FOR GOD TO KNOW.
NO!
TONY!!
THAT CHILD IS NOT LIKE US!
WHERE'D YOU COME FROM? I SEE YOU HAVE NO USE FOR DOORS AND SUCH.
GET OUT!
WE CAN'T HAVE GERMS IN THE DELIVERY ROOM.

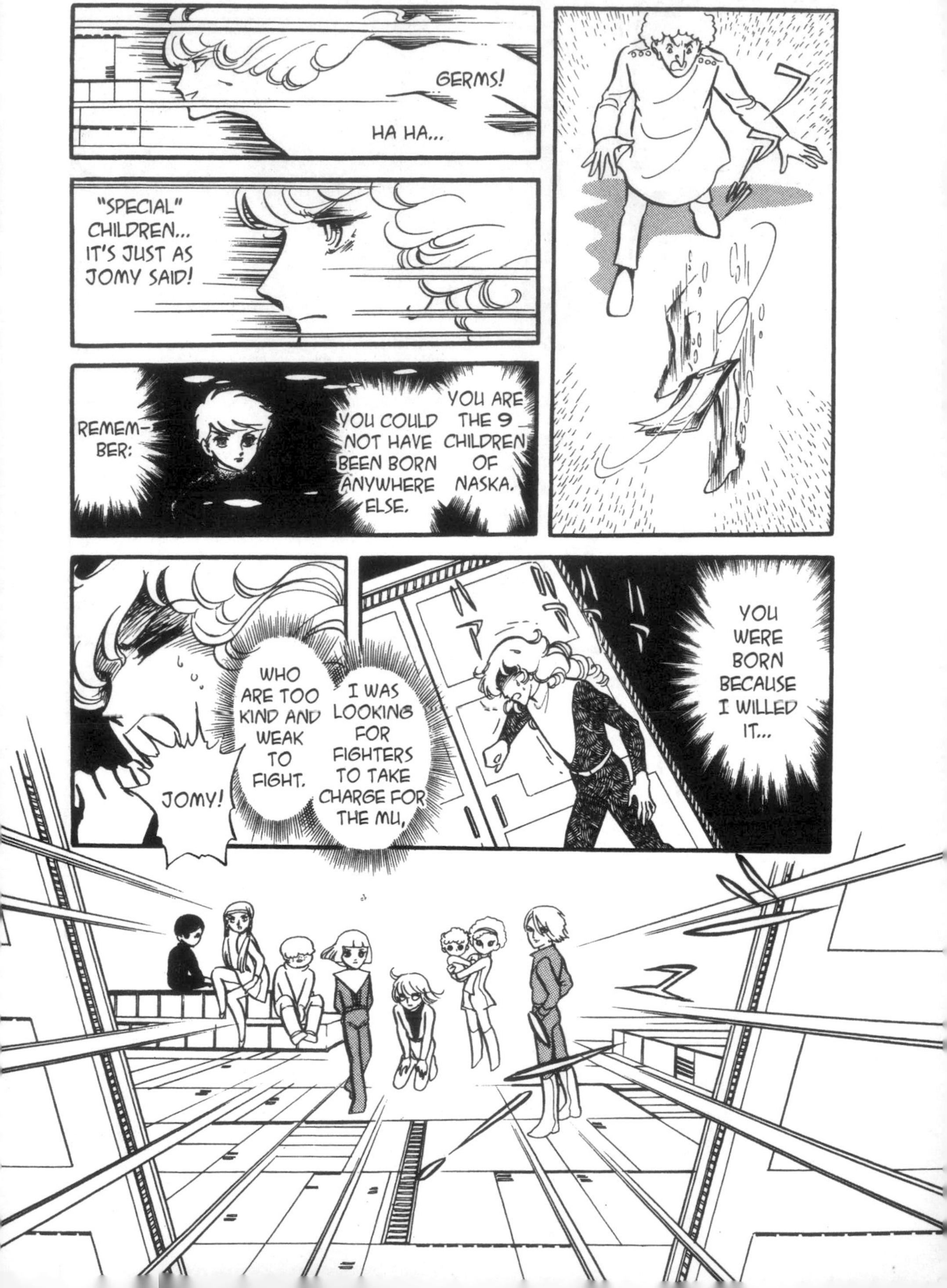
GERMS!
HA HA...
"SPECIAL" CHILDREN... IT'S JUST AS JOMY SAID!
YOU ARE THE 9 CHILDREN OF NASKA.
YOU COULD NOT HAVE BEEN BORN ANYWHERE ELSE.
REMEM-BER:
YOU WERE BORN BECAUSE I WILLED IT...
I WAS LOOKING FOR FIGHTERS TO TAKE CHARGE FOR THE MU,
WHO ARE TOO KIND AND WEAK TO FIGHT.
JOMY!

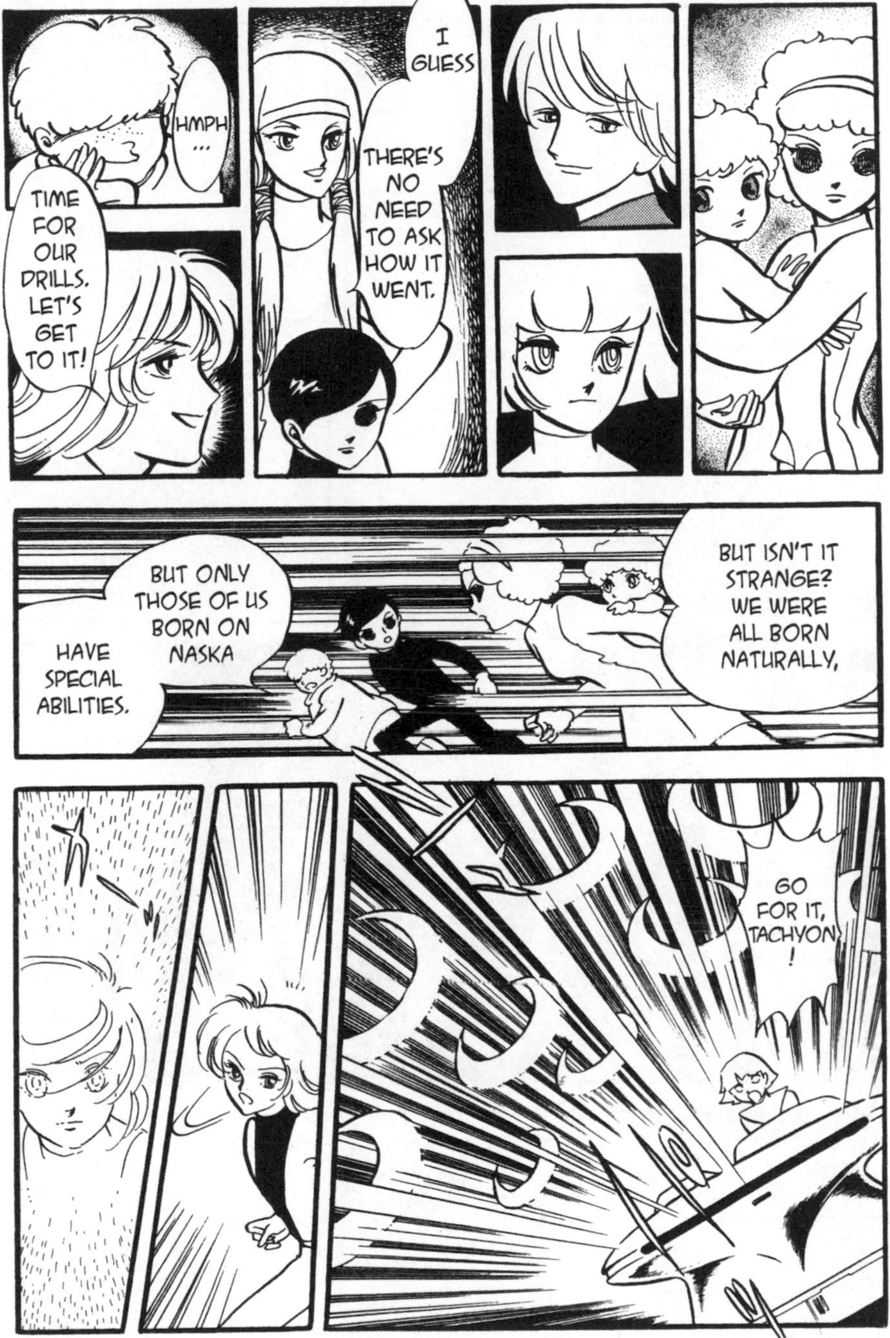
I GUESS
THERE'S NO NEED TO ASK HOW IT WENT.
HMPH ...
TIME FOR OUR DRILLS. LET'S GET TO IT!
BUT ISN'T IT STRANGE? WE WERE ALL BORN NATURALLY,
BUT ONLY THOSE OF US BORN ON NASKA
HAVE SPECIAL ABILITIES.
GO FOR IT, TACHYON!

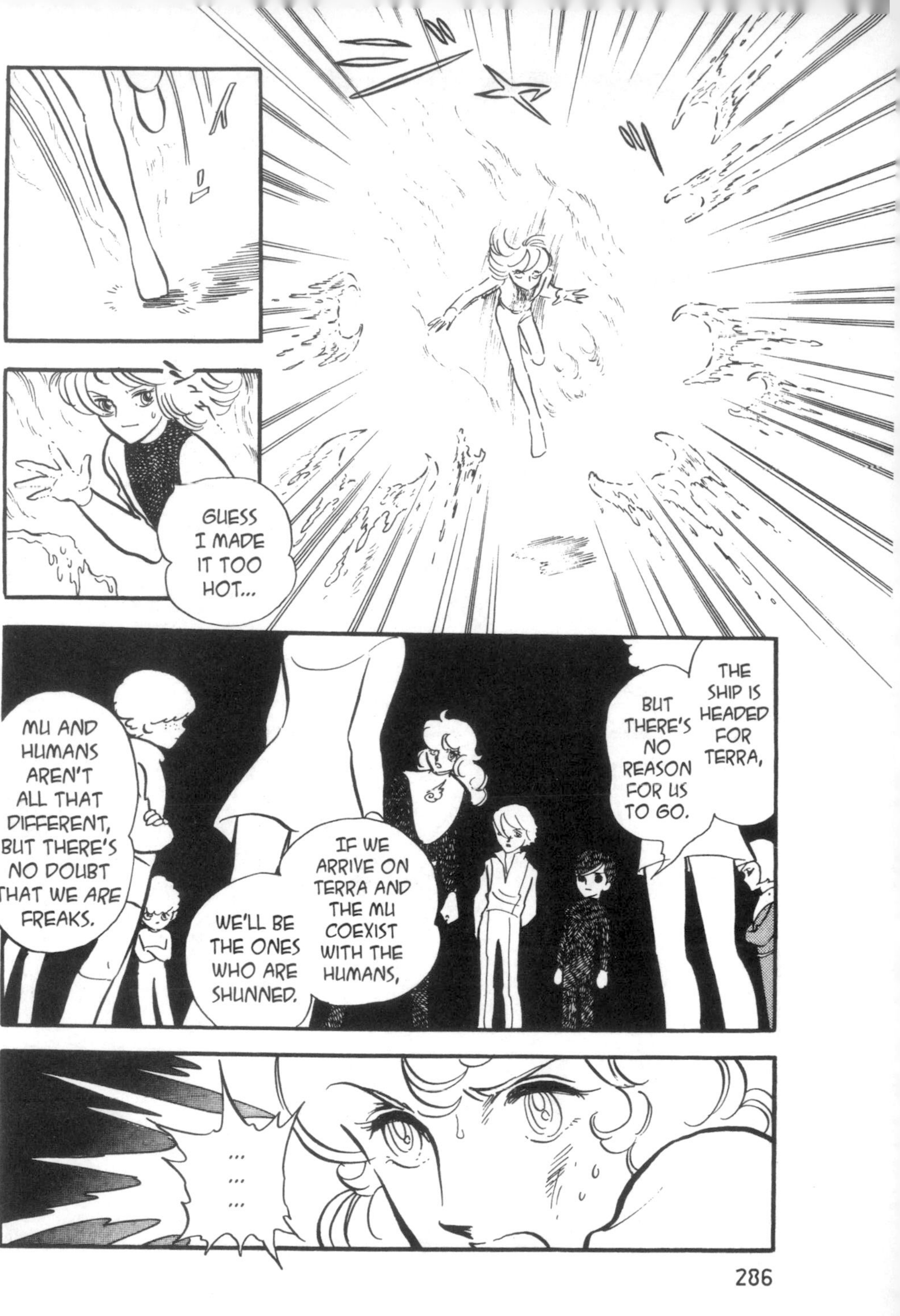
GUESS I MADE IT TOO HOT...
THE SHIP IS HEADED FOR TERRA,
BUT THERE'S NO REASON FOR US TO GO.
IF WE ARRIVE ON TERRA AND THE MU COEXIST WITH THE HUMANS,
WE'LL BE THE ONES WHO ARE SHUNNED.
MU AND HUMANS AREN'T ALL THAT DIFFERENT, BUT THERE'S NO DOUBT THAT WE ARE FREAKS.
...
...
...

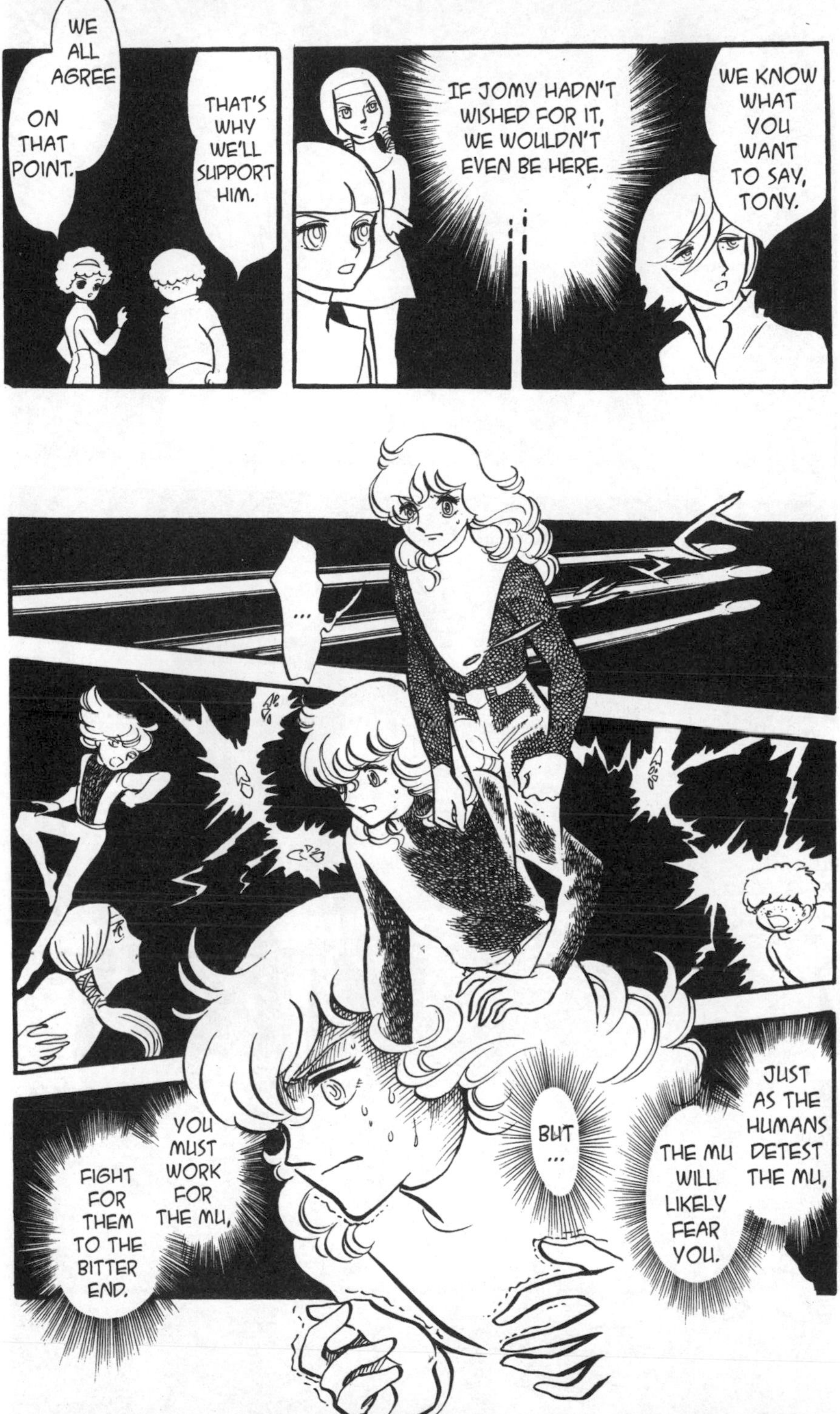
WE KNOW WHAT YOU WANT TO SAY, TONY.
IF JOMY HADN'T WISHED FOR IT, WE WOULDN'T EVEN BE HERE.
THAT'S WHY WE'LL SUPPORT HIM.
WE ALL AGREE ON THAT POINT.
...
JUST AS THE HUMANS DETEST THE MU,
THE MU WILL LIKELY FEAR YOU.
BUT ...
YOU MUST WORK FOR THE MU,
FIGHT FOR THEM TO THE BITTER END.

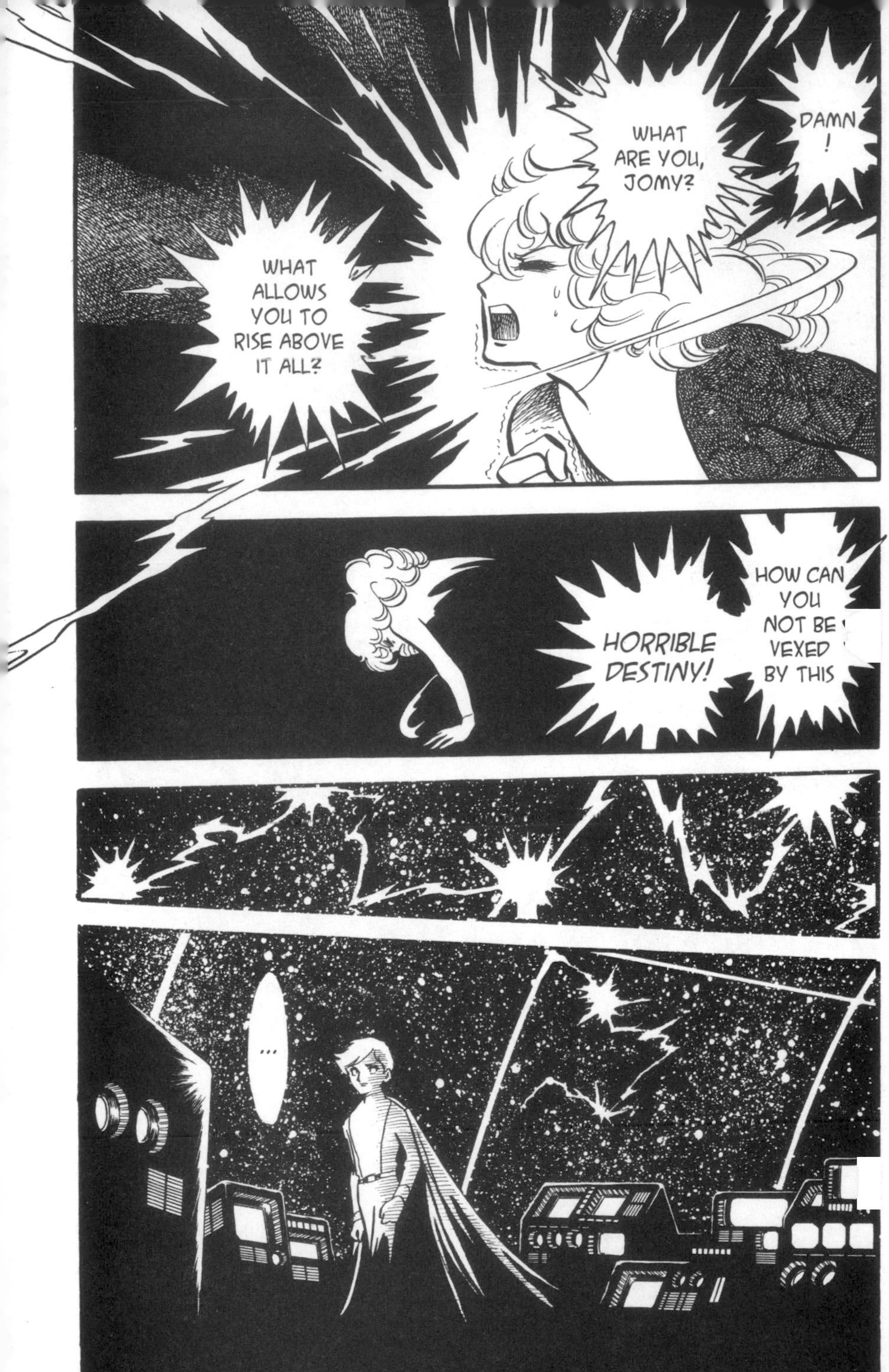
DAMN!
WHAT ARE YOU, JOMY?
WHAT ALLOWS YOU TO RISE ABOVE IT ALL?
HOW CAN YOU NOT BE VEXED BY THIS
HORRIBLE DESTINY!
...

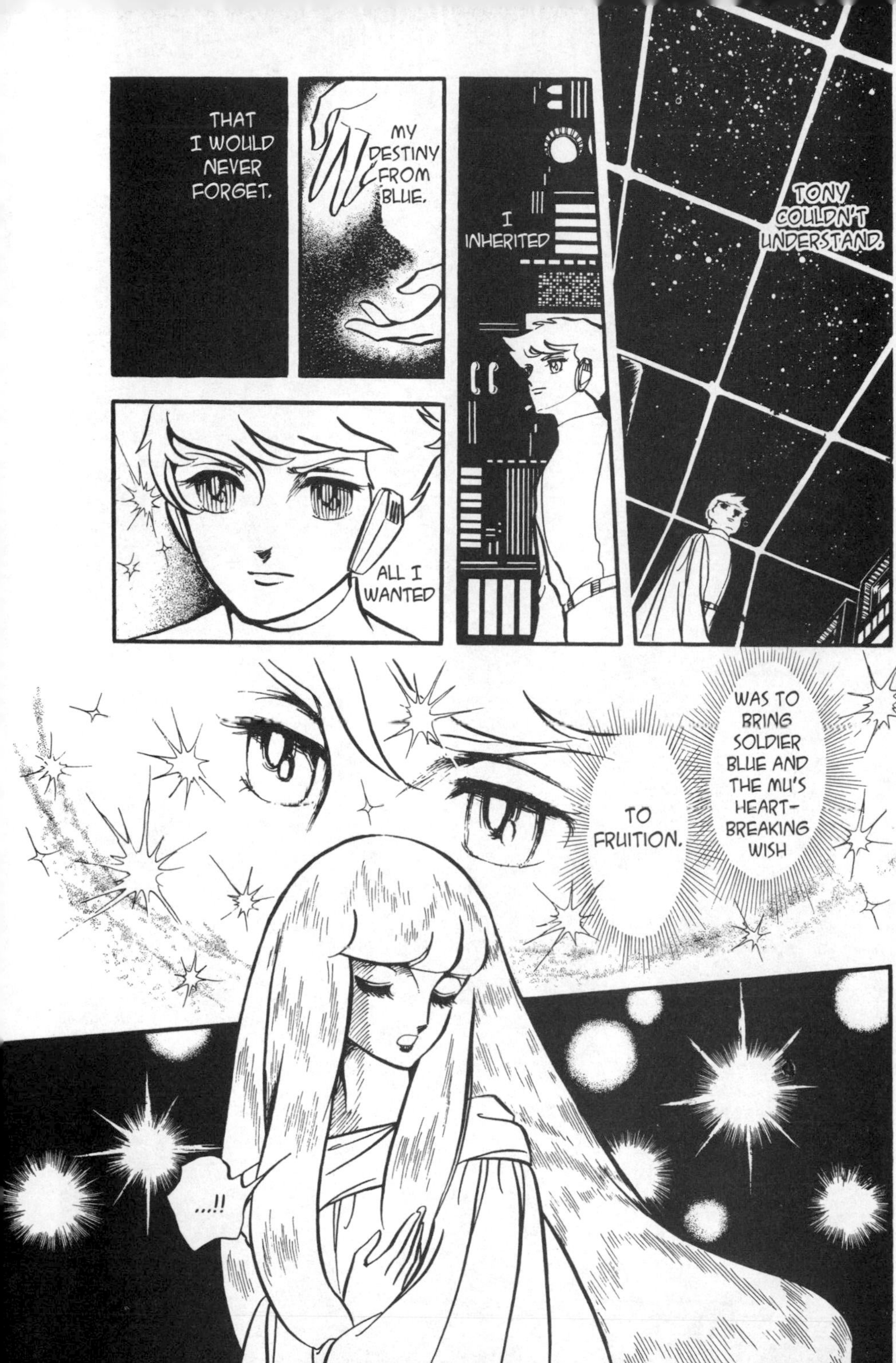

TONY COULDN'T UNDERSTAND.
I INHERITED
MY DESTINY FROM BLUE.
THAT I WOULD NEVER FORGET.
ALL I WANTED
WAS TO BRING SOLDIER BLUE AND THE MU'S HEART-BREAKING WISH
TO FRUITION.
...!!

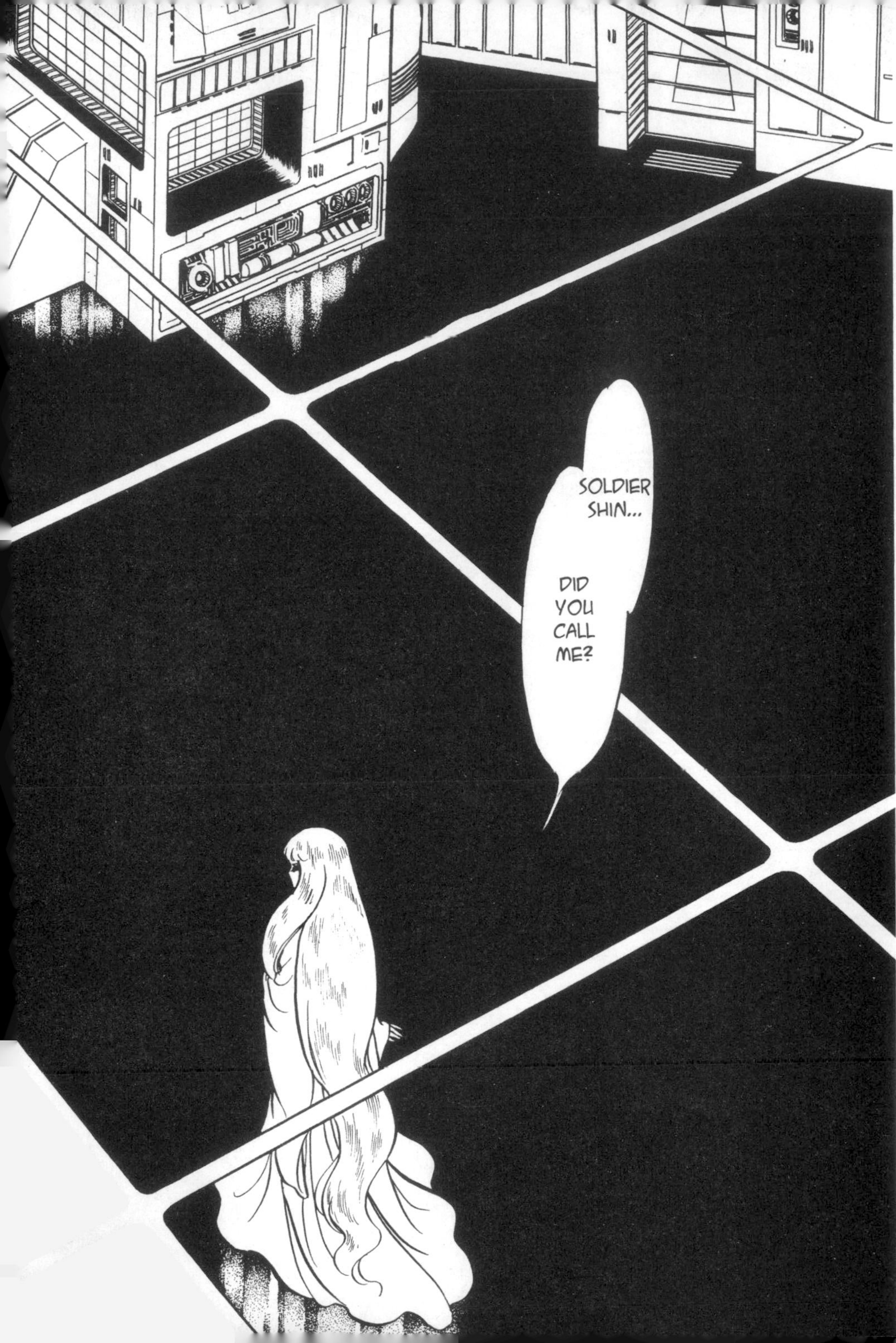
SOLDIER SHIN...
DID YOU CALL ME?

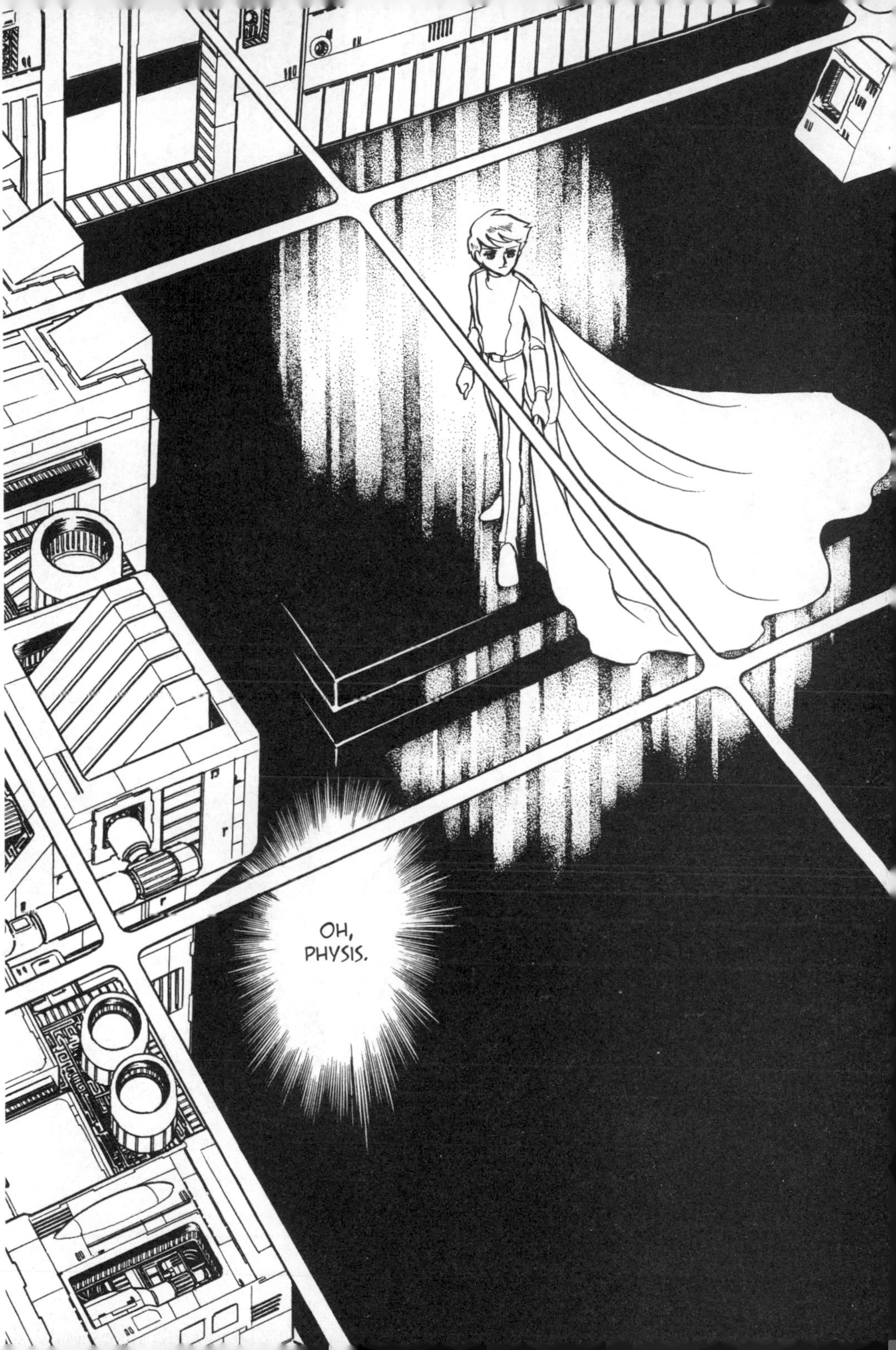
OH, PHYSIS.

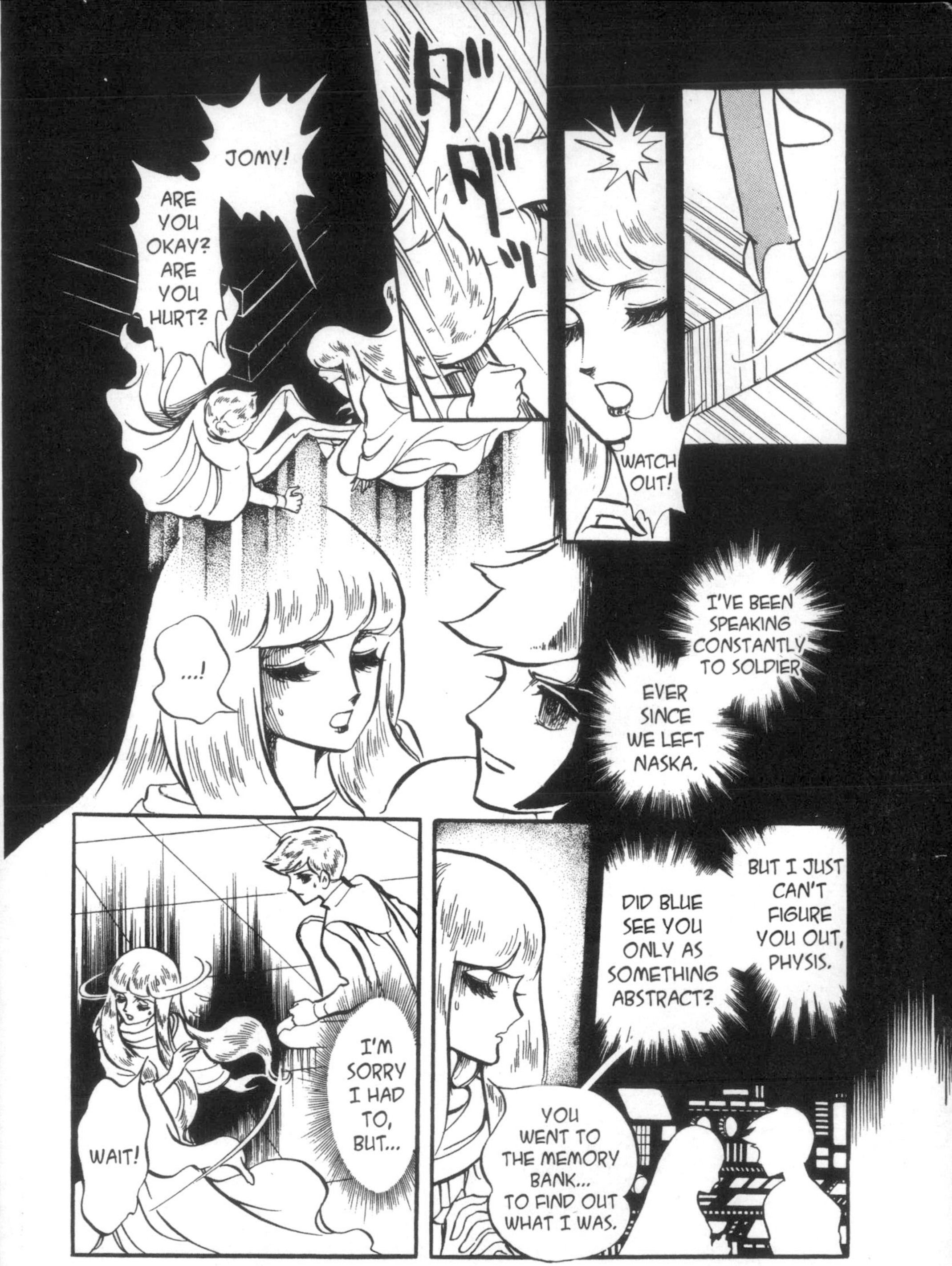
WATCH OUT!
ダダーッ
JOMY!
ARE YOU OKAY? ARE YOU HURT?
I'VE BEEN SPEAKING CONSTANTLY TO SOLDIER
EVER SINCE WE LEFT NASKA.
...!
BUT I JUST CAN'T FIGURE YOU OUT, PHYSIS.
DID BLUE SEE YOU ONLY AS SOMETHING ABSTRACT?
YOU WENT TO THE MEMORY BANK... TO FIND OUT WHAT I WAS.
I'M SORRY I HAD TO, BUT...
WAIT!

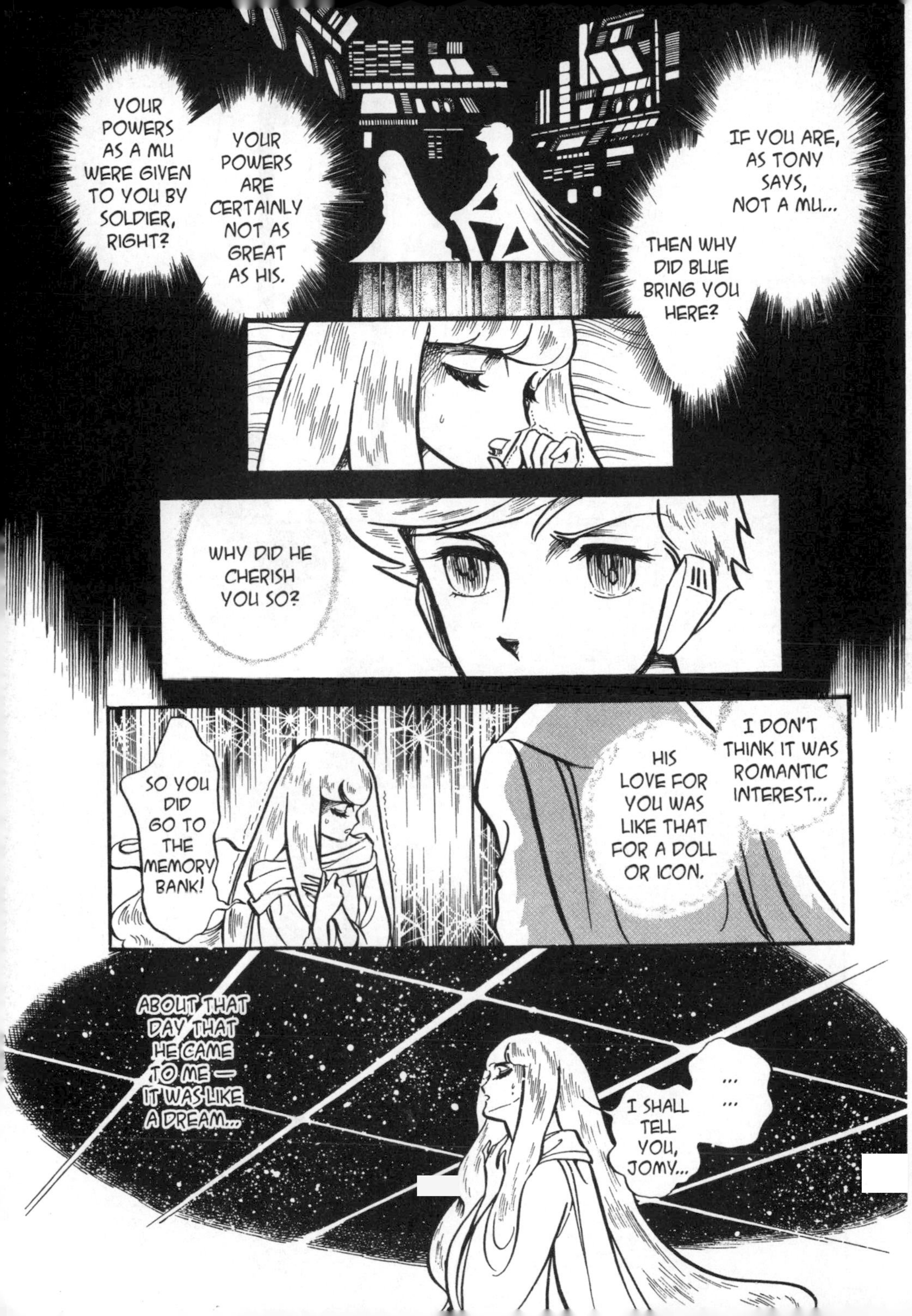
IF YOU ARE, AS TONY SAYS, NOT A MU...
THEN WHY DID BLUE BRING YOU HERE?
YOUR POWERS ARE CERTAINLY NOT AS GREAT AS HIS.
YOUR POWERS AS A MU WERE GIVEN TO YOU BY SOLDIER, RIGHT?
WHY DID HE CHERISH YOU SO?
I DON'T THINK IT WAS ROMANTIC INTEREST...
HIS LOVE FOR YOU WAS LIKE THAT FOR A DOLL OR ICON.
SO YOU DID GO TO THE MEMORY BANK!
... ...
I SHALL TELL YOU, JOMY...
ABOUT THAT DAY THAT HE CAME TO ME — IT WAS LIKE A DREAM...

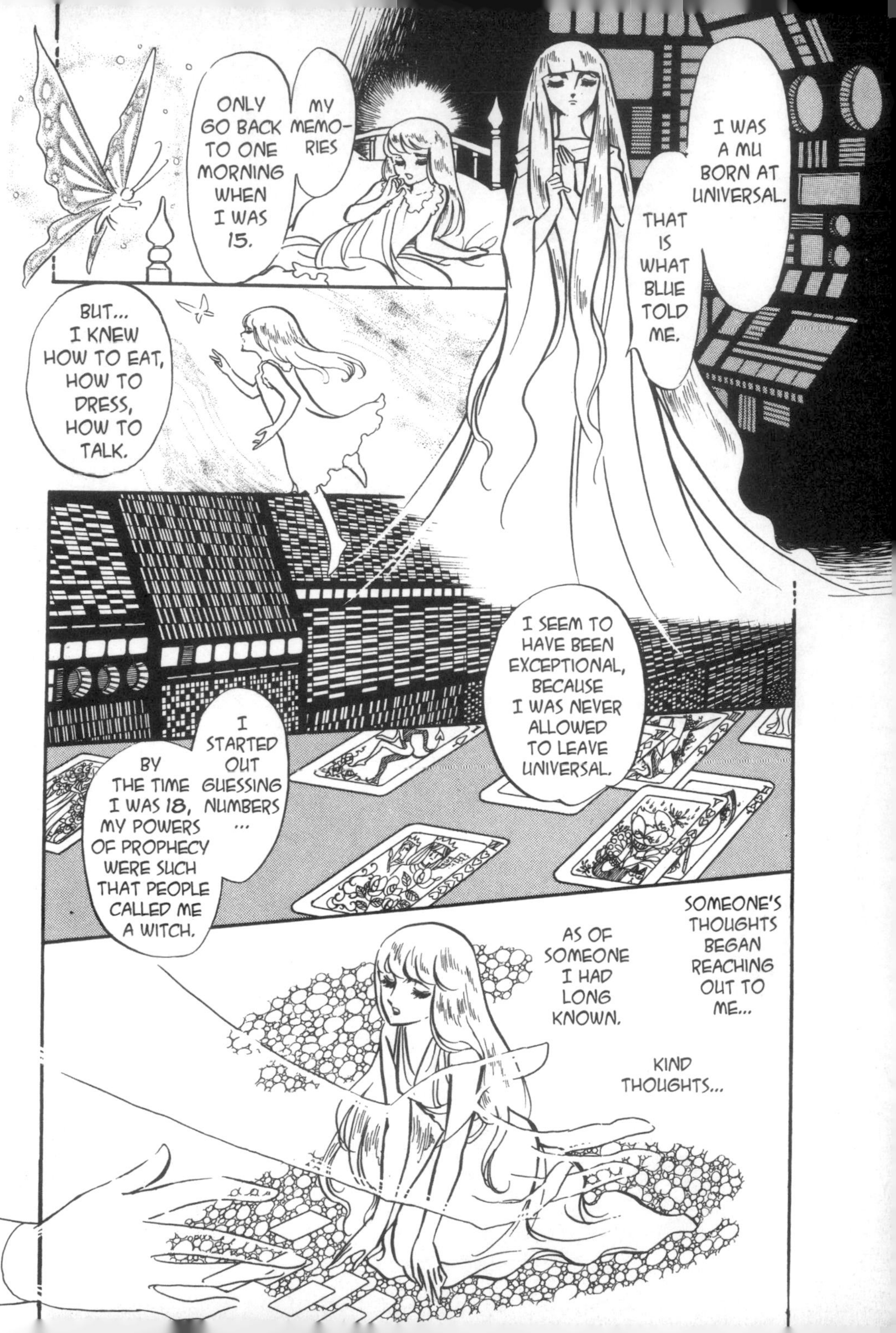
I WAS A MU BORN AT UNIVERSAL.
THAT IS WHAT BLUE TOLD ME.
MY MEMORIES
ONLY GO BACK TO ONE MORNING WHEN I WAS 15.
BUT... I KNEW HOW TO EAT, HOW TO DRESS, HOW TO TALK.
I SEEM TO HAVE BEEN EXCEPTIONAL, BECAUSE I WAS NEVER ALLOWED TO LEAVE UNIVERSAL.
I STARTED OUT GUESSING NUMBERS...
BY THE TIME I WAS 18, MY POWERS OF PROPHECY WERE SUCH THAT PEOPLE CALLED ME A WITCH.
SOMEONE'S THOUGHTS BEGAN REACHING OUT TO ME...
AS OF SOMEONE I HAD LONG KNOWN.
KIND THOUGHTS...

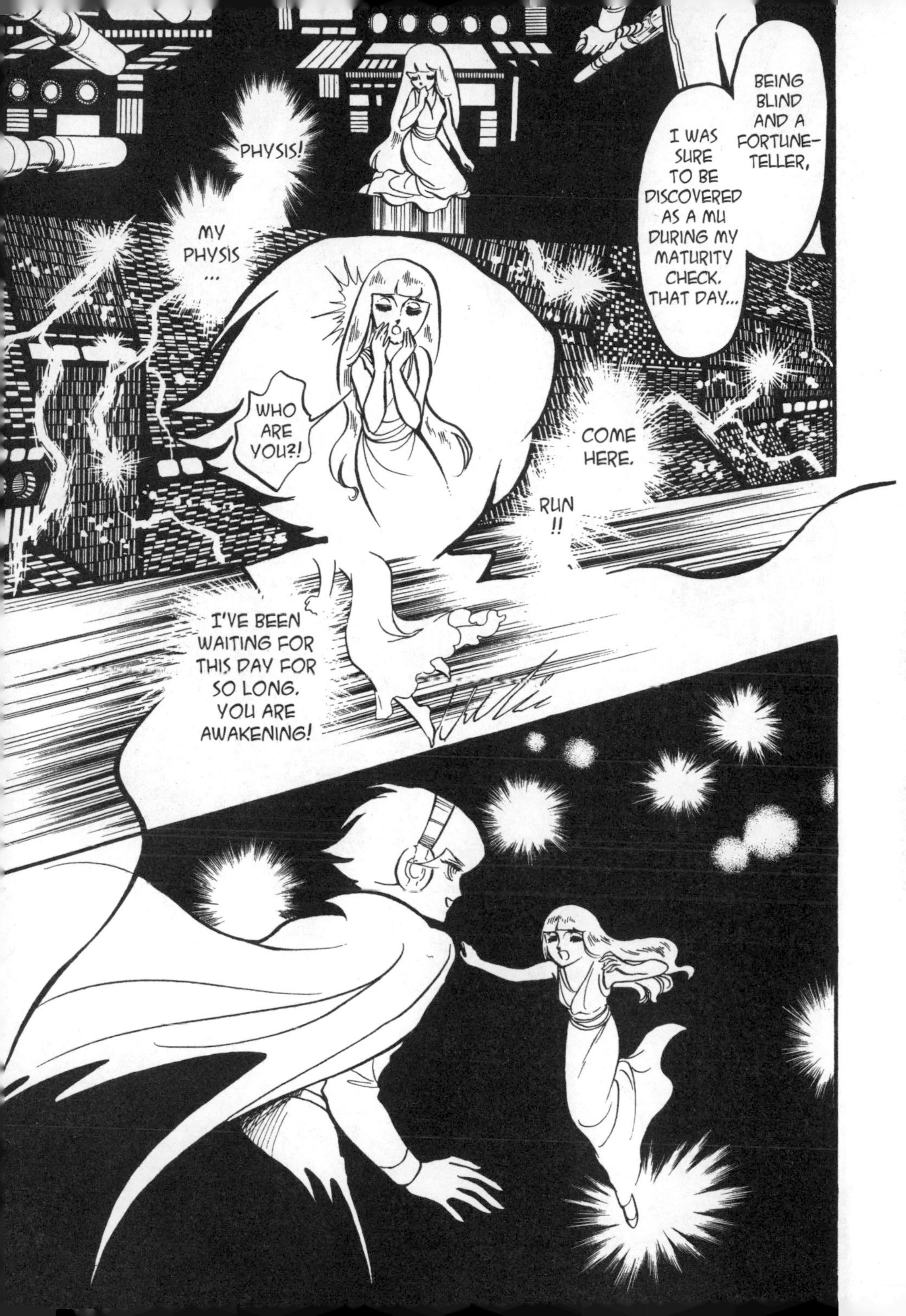
BEING BLIND AND A FORTUNE-TELLER, I WAS SURE TO BE DISCOVERED AS A MU DURING MY MATURITY CHECK. THAT DAY...
PHYSIS!
MY PHYSIS ...
COME HERE.
WHO ARE YOU?!
RUN !!
I'VE BEEN WAITING FOR THIS DAY FOR SO LONG. YOU ARE AWAKENING!

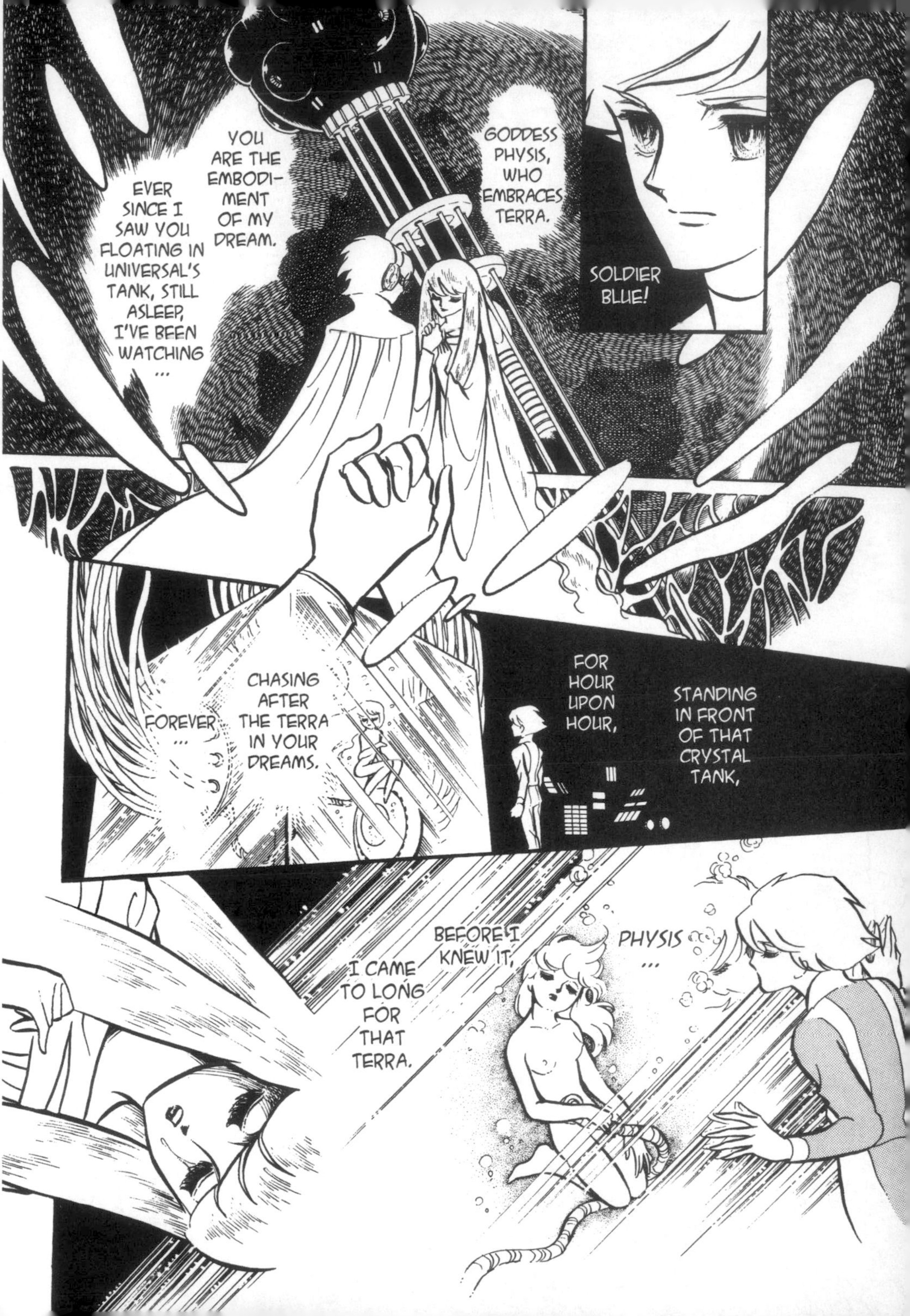
SOLDIER BLUE!
GODDESS PHYSIS, WHO EMBRACES TERRA.
YOU ARE THE EMBODI- MENT OF MY DREAM.
EVER SINCE I SAW YOU FLOATING IN UNIVERSAL'S TANK, STILL ASLEEP, I'VE BEEN WATCHING ...
STANDING IN FRONT OF THAT CRYSTAL TANK,
FOR HOUR UPON HOUR,
CHASING AFTER THE TERRA IN YOUR DREAMS.
FOREVER ...
PHYSIS ...
BEFORE I KNEW IT,
I CAME TO LONG FOR THAT TERRA.

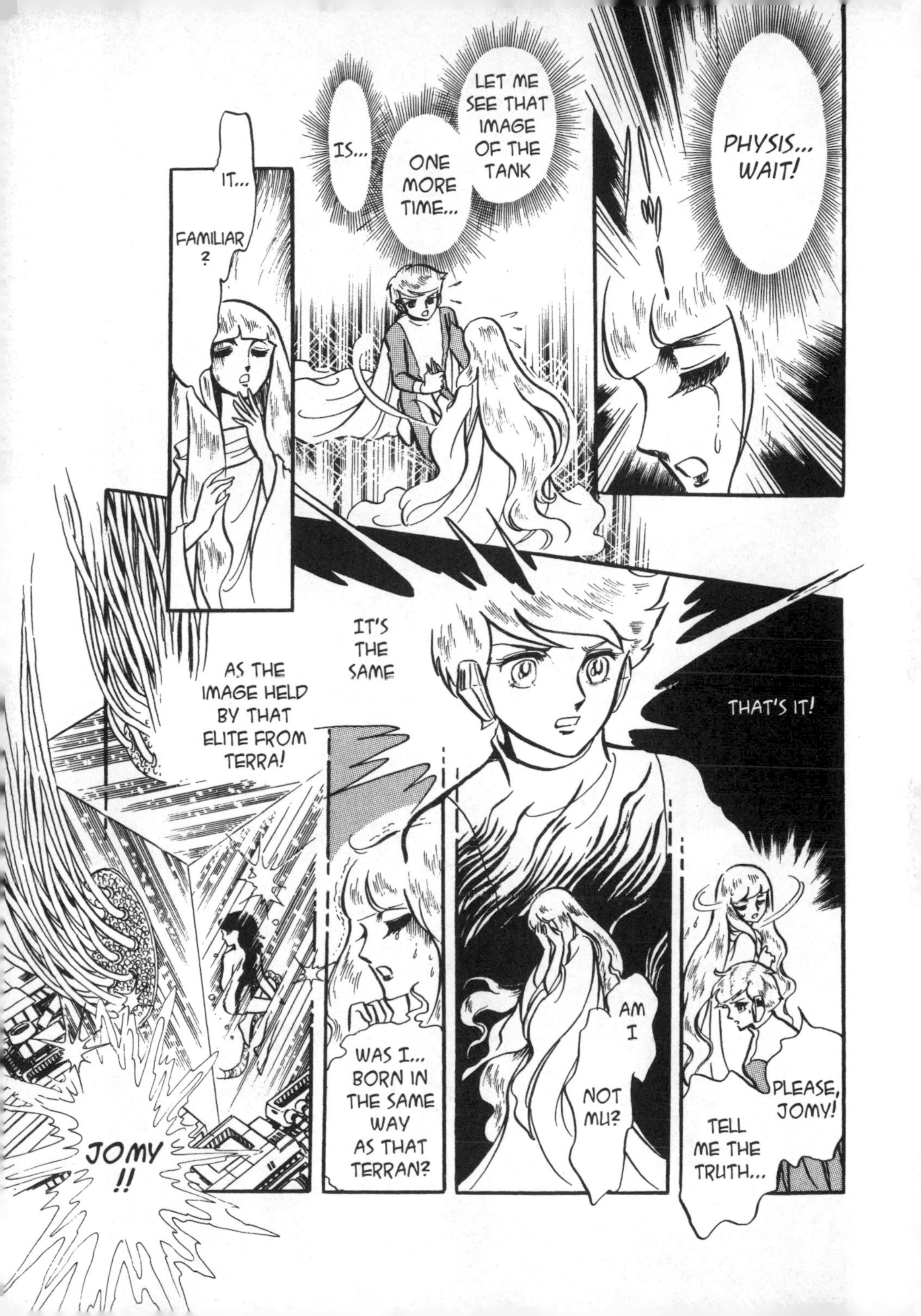
PHYSIS... WAIT!
LET ME SEE THAT IMAGE OF THE TANK
ONE MORE TIME...
IS...
IT...
FAMILIAR?
THAT'S IT!
IT'S THE SAME
AS THE IMAGE HELD BY THAT ELITE FROM TERRA!
PLEASE, JOMY!
TELL ME THE TRUTH...
AM I
NOT MU?
WAS I... BORN IN THE SAME WAY AS THAT TERRAN?
JOMY!!

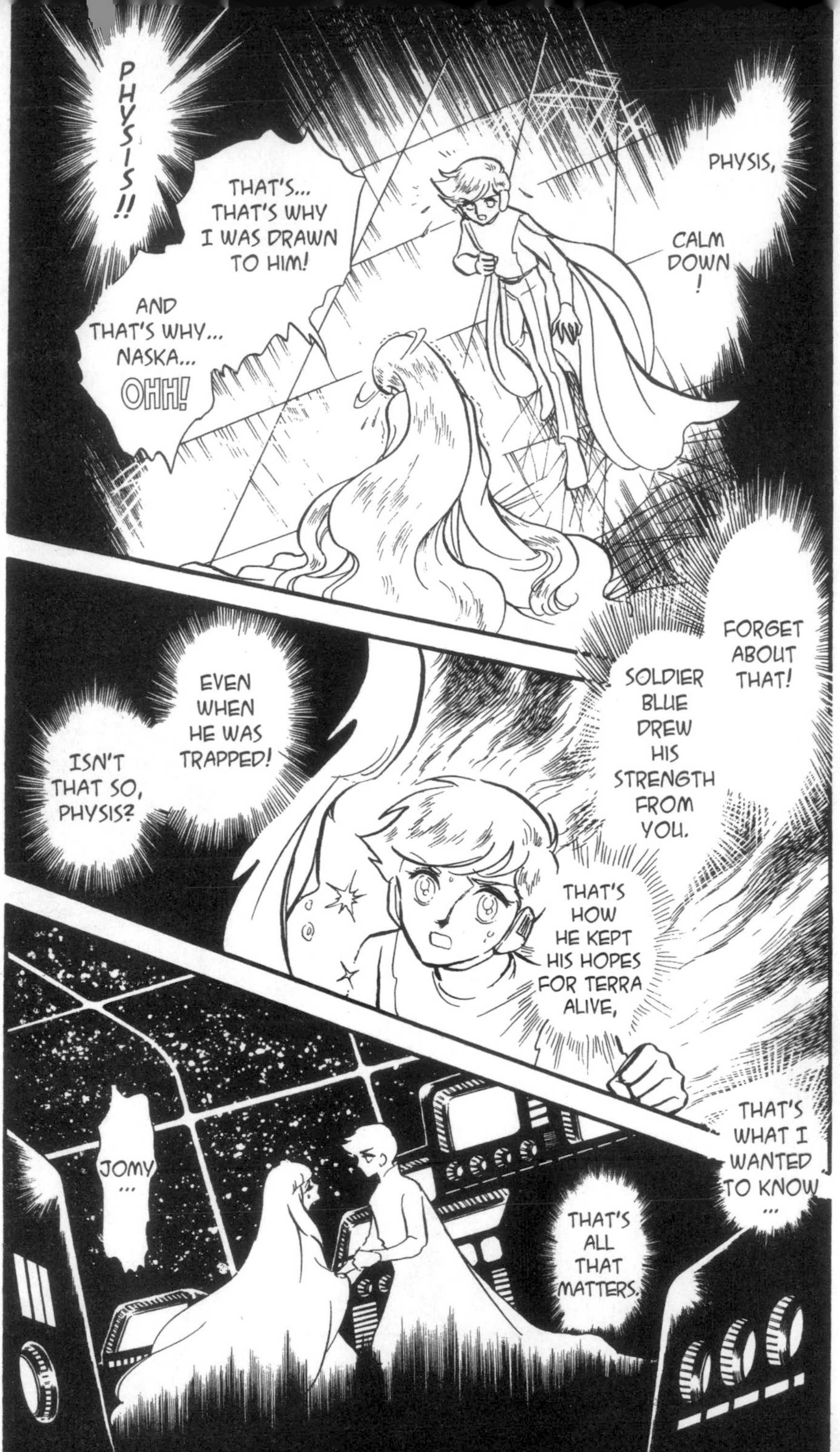
PHYSIS,
CALM DOWN!
PHYSIS!!
THAT'S... THAT'S WHY I WAS DRAWN TO HIM!
AND THAT'S WHY... NASKA...
OHH!
FORGET ABOUT THAT!
SOLDIER BLUE DREW HIS STRENGTH FROM YOU.
THAT'S HOW HE KEPT HIS HOPES FOR TERRA ALIVE,
EVEN WHEN HE WAS TRAPPED!
ISN'T THAT SO, PHYSIS?
THAT'S WHAT I WANTED TO KNOW...
THAT'S ALL THAT MATTERS.
JOMY...

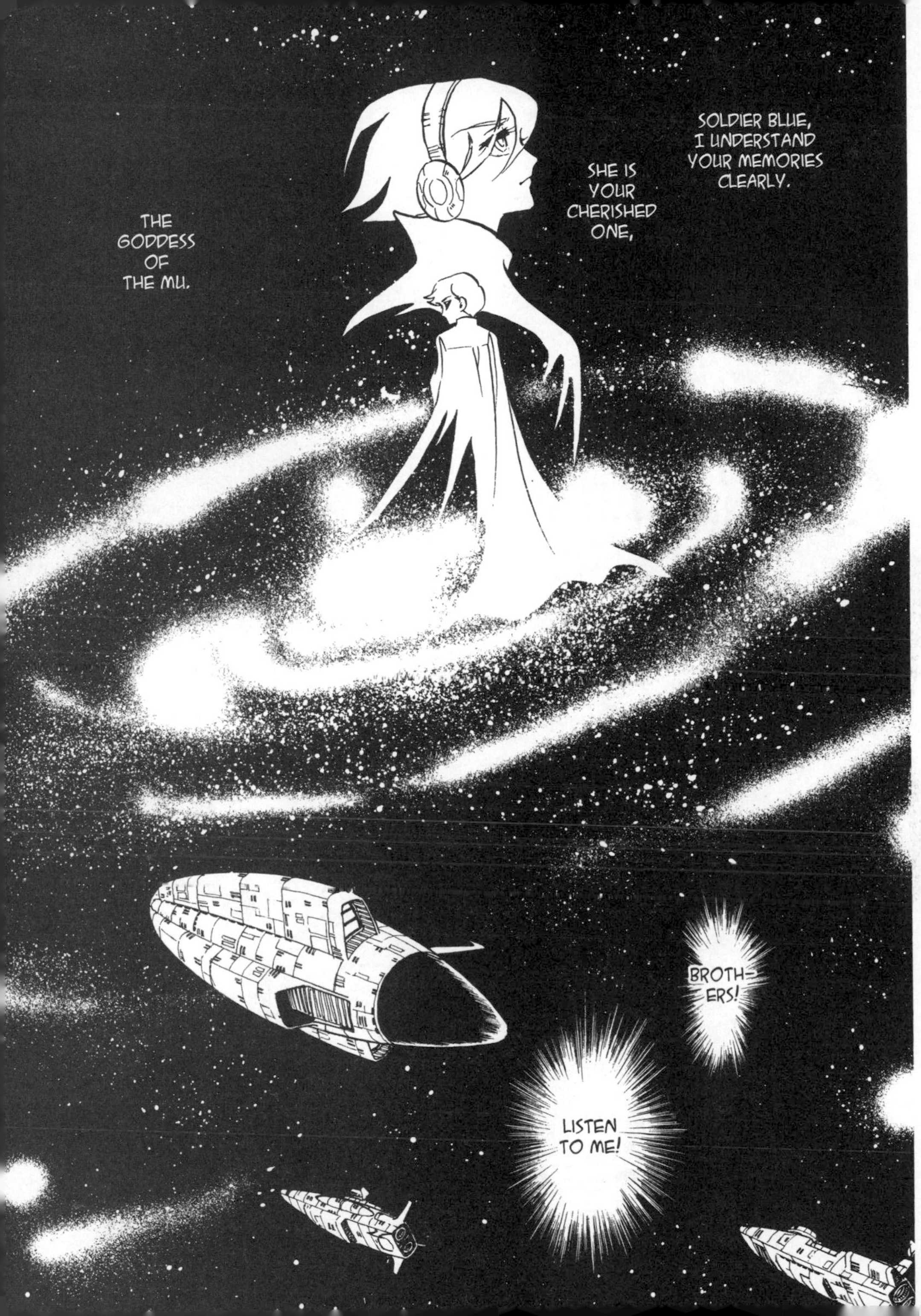
SOLDIER BLUE, I UNDERSTAND YOUR MEMORIES CLEARLY.
SHE IS YOUR CHERISHED ONE,
THE GODDESS OF THE MU.
BROTH-ERS!
LISTEN TO ME!

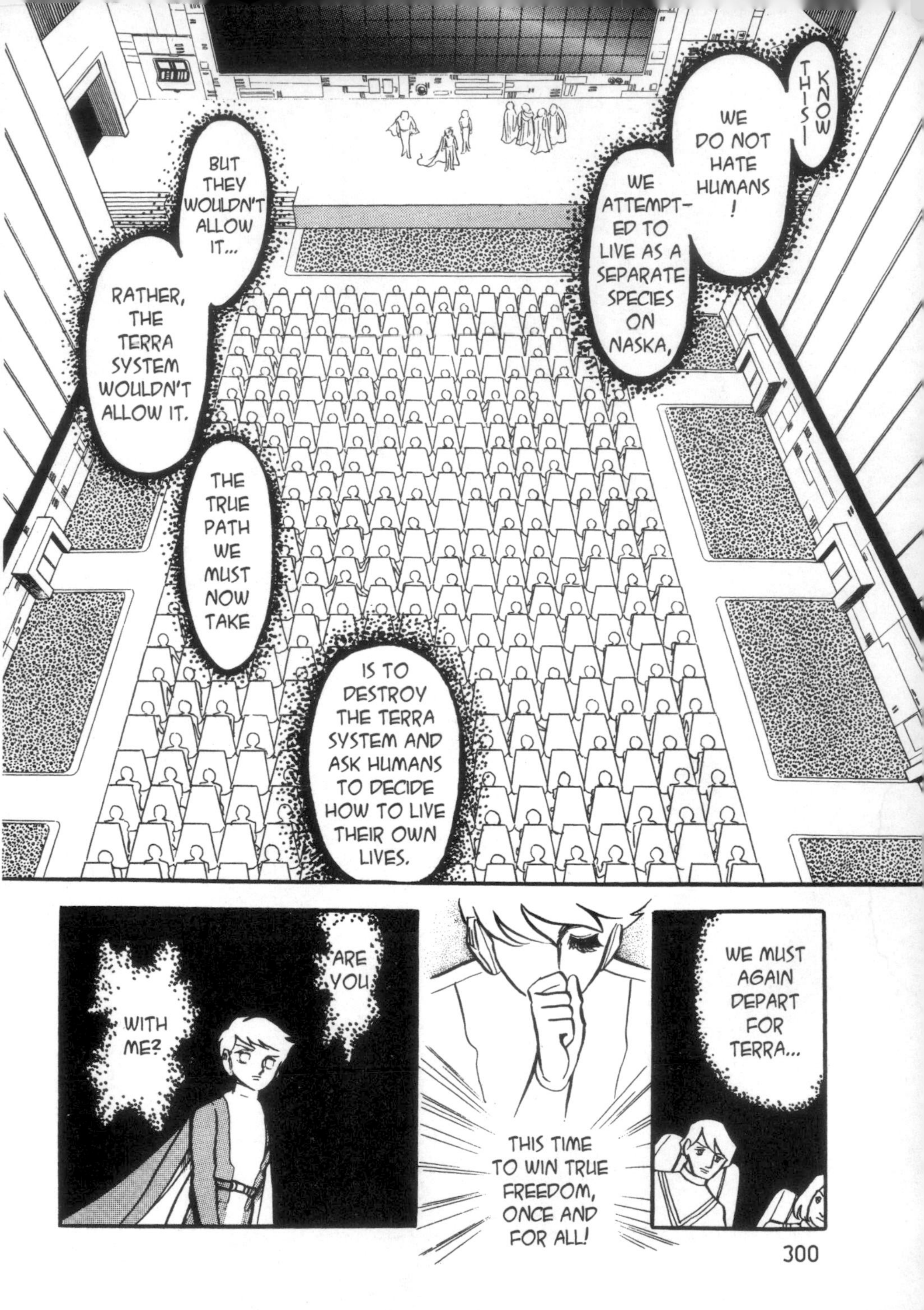
THIS I KNOW
WE DO NOT HATE HUMANS!
WE ATTEMPTED TO LIVE AS A SEPARATE SPECIES ON NASKA,
BUT THEY WOULDN'T ALLOW IT...
RATHER, THE TERRA SYSTEM WOULDN'T ALLOW IT.
THE TRUE PATH WE MUST NOW TAKE
IS TO DESTROY THE TERRA SYSTEM AND ASK HUMANS TO DECIDE HOW TO LIVE THEIR OWN LIVES.
WE MUST AGAIN DEPART FOR TERRA...
THIS TIME TO WIN TRUE FREEDOM, ONCE AND FOR ALL!
ARE YOU
WITH ME?

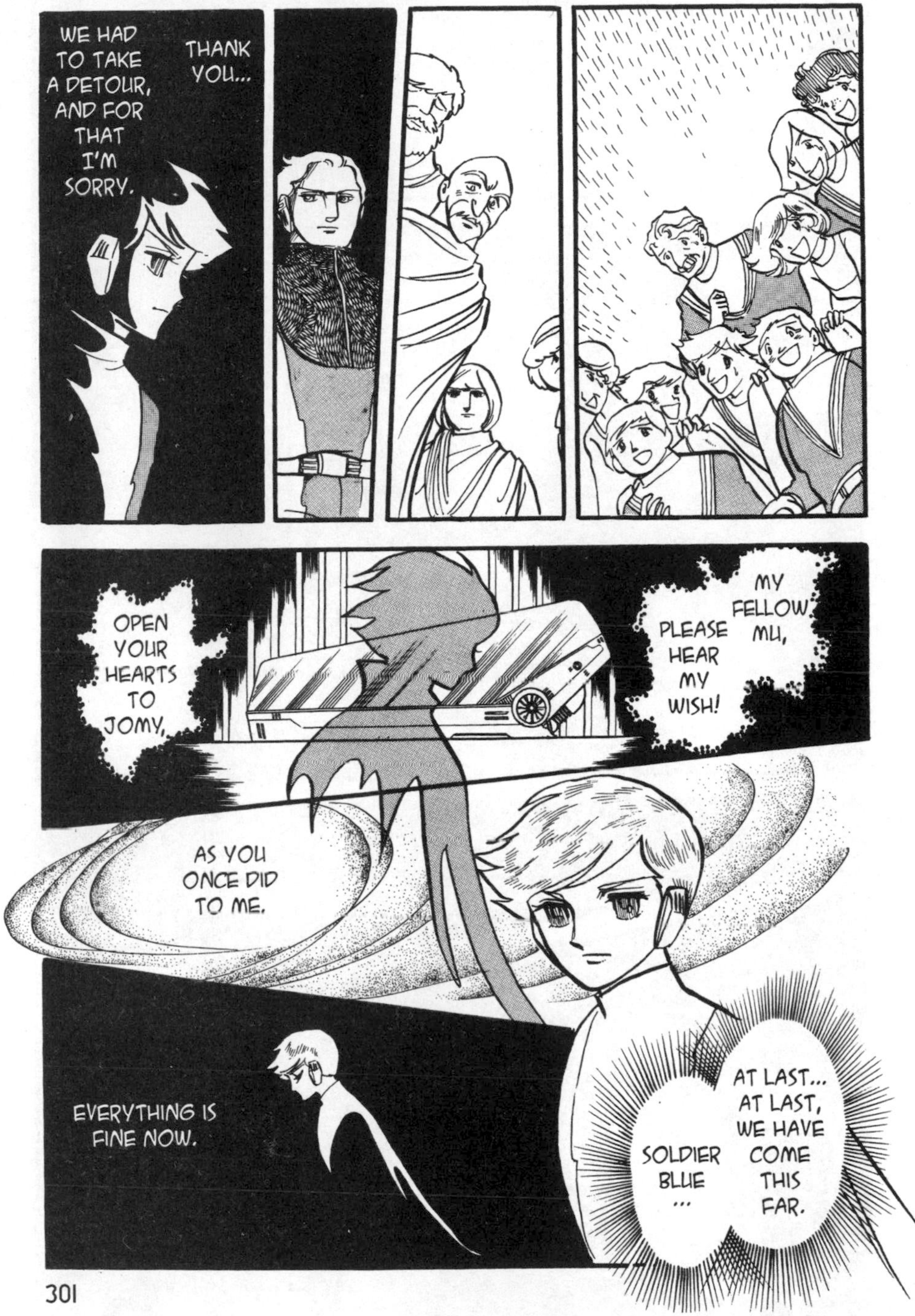
THANK YOU...
WE HAD TO TAKE A DETOUR, AND FOR THAT I'M SORRY.
MY FELLOW MU, PLEASE HEAR MY WISH!
OPEN YOUR HEARTS TO JOMY,
AS YOU ONCE DID TO ME.
AT LAST... AT LAST, WE HAVE COME THIS FAR.
SOLDIER BLUE ...
EVERYTHING IS FINE NOW.

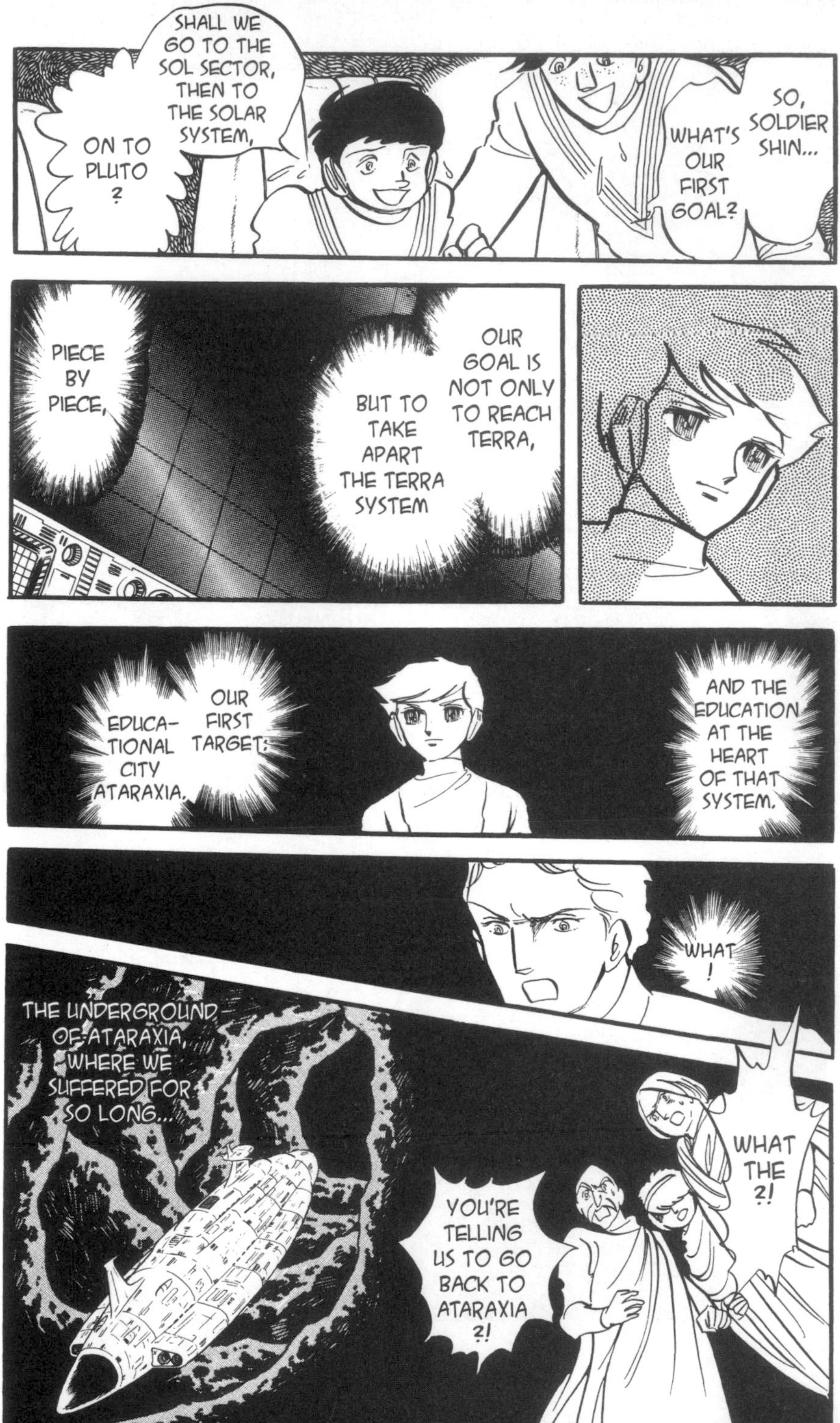
SO, SOLDIER SHIN...
WHAT'S OUR FIRST GOAL?
SHALL WE GO TO THE SOL SECTOR, THEN TO THE SOLAR SYSTEM,
ON TO PLUTO?
OUR GOAL IS NOT ONLY TO REACH TERRA,
BUT TO TAKE APART THE TERRA SYSTEM
PIECE BY PIECE,
AND THE EDUCATION AT THE HEART OF THAT SYSTEM.
OUR FIRST TARGET:
EDUCATIONAL CITY ATARAXIA.
WHAT!
WHAT THE?!
YOU'RE TELLING US TO GO BACK TO ATARAXIA?!
THE UNDERGROUND OF ATARAXIA, WHERE WE SUFFERED FOR SO LONG...

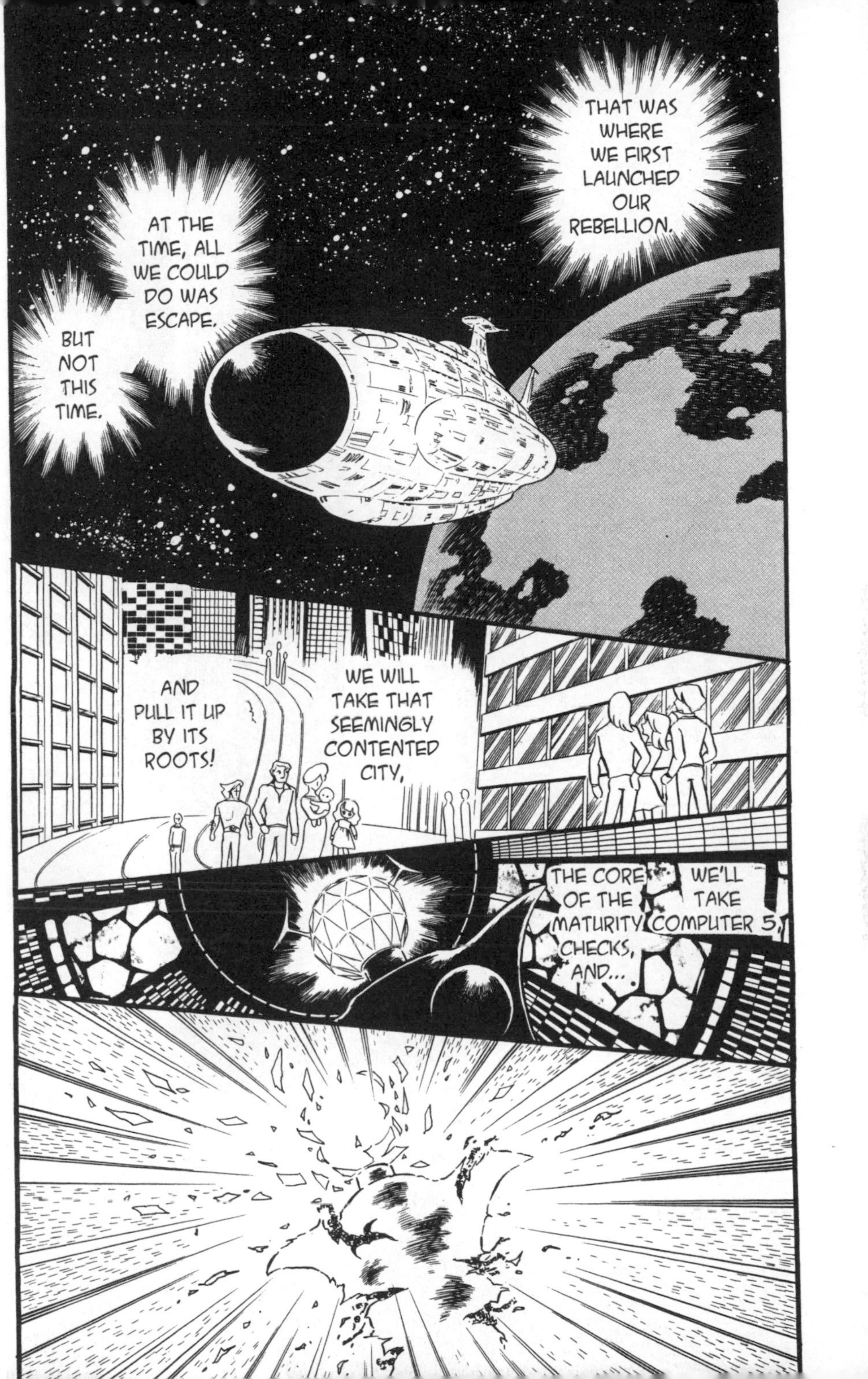
THAT WAS WHERE WE FIRST LAUNCHED OUR REBELLION.
AT THE TIME, ALL WE COULD DO WAS ESCAPE.
BUT NOT THIS TIME.
WE WILL TAKE THAT SEEMINGLY CONTENTED CITY,
AND PULL IT UP BY ITS ROOTS!
WE'LL TAKE COMPUTER 5,
THE CORE OF THE MATURITY CHECKS, AND...

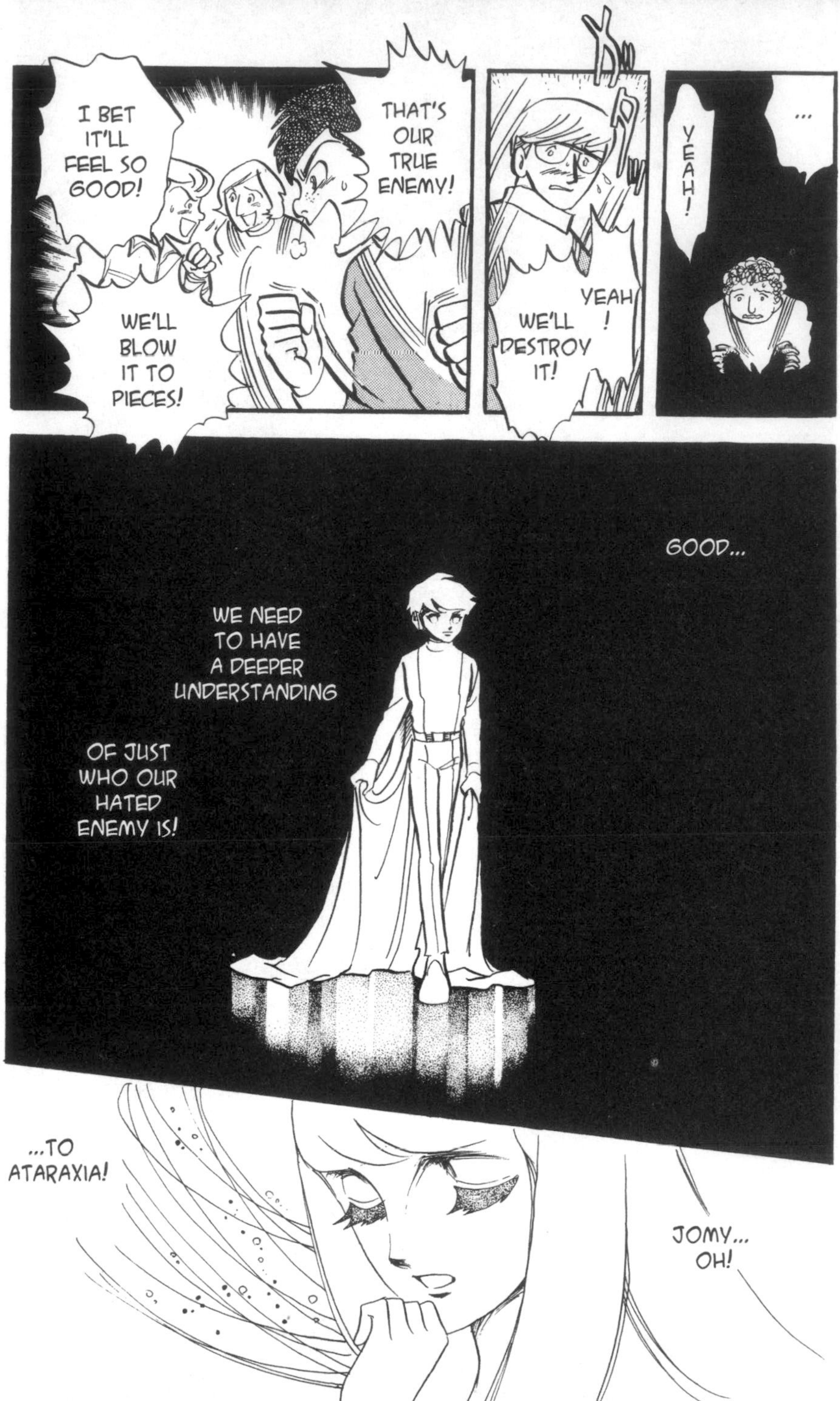
...
YEAH!
YEAH!
WE'LL DESTROY IT!
THAT'S OUR TRUE ENEMY!
I BET IT'LL FEEL SO GOOD!
WE'LL BLOW IT TO PIECES!
GOOD...
WE NEED TO HAVE A DEEPER UNDERSTANDING
OF JUST WHO OUR HATED ENEMY IS!
...TO ATARAXIA!
JOMY... OH!

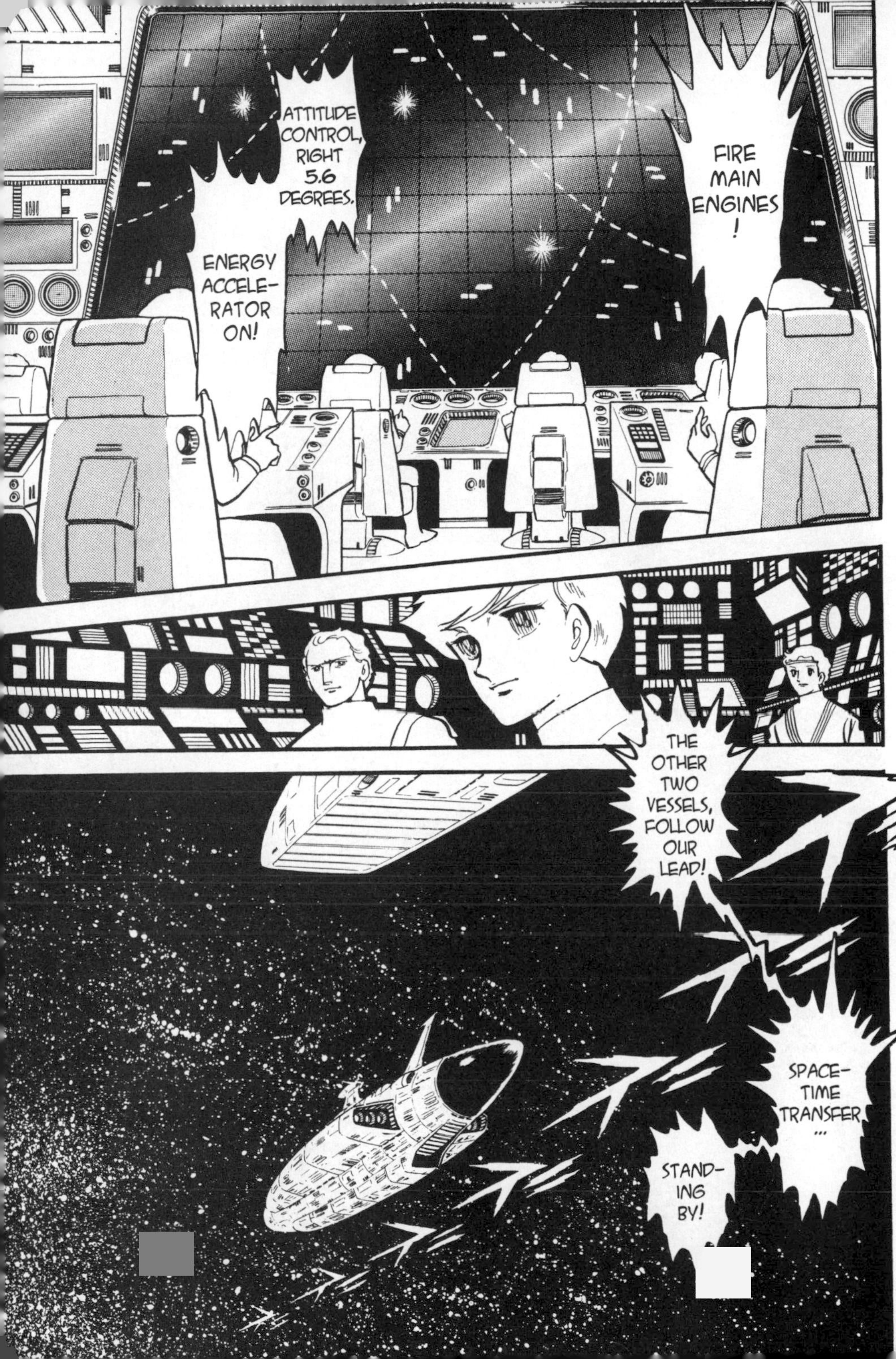
FIRE MAIN ENGINES!
ATTITUDE CONTROL, RIGHT 5.6 DEGREES.
ENERGY ACCELE-RATOR ON!
THE OTHER TWO VESSELS, FOLLOW OUR LEAD!
SPACE-TIME TRANSFER...
STAND-ING BY!

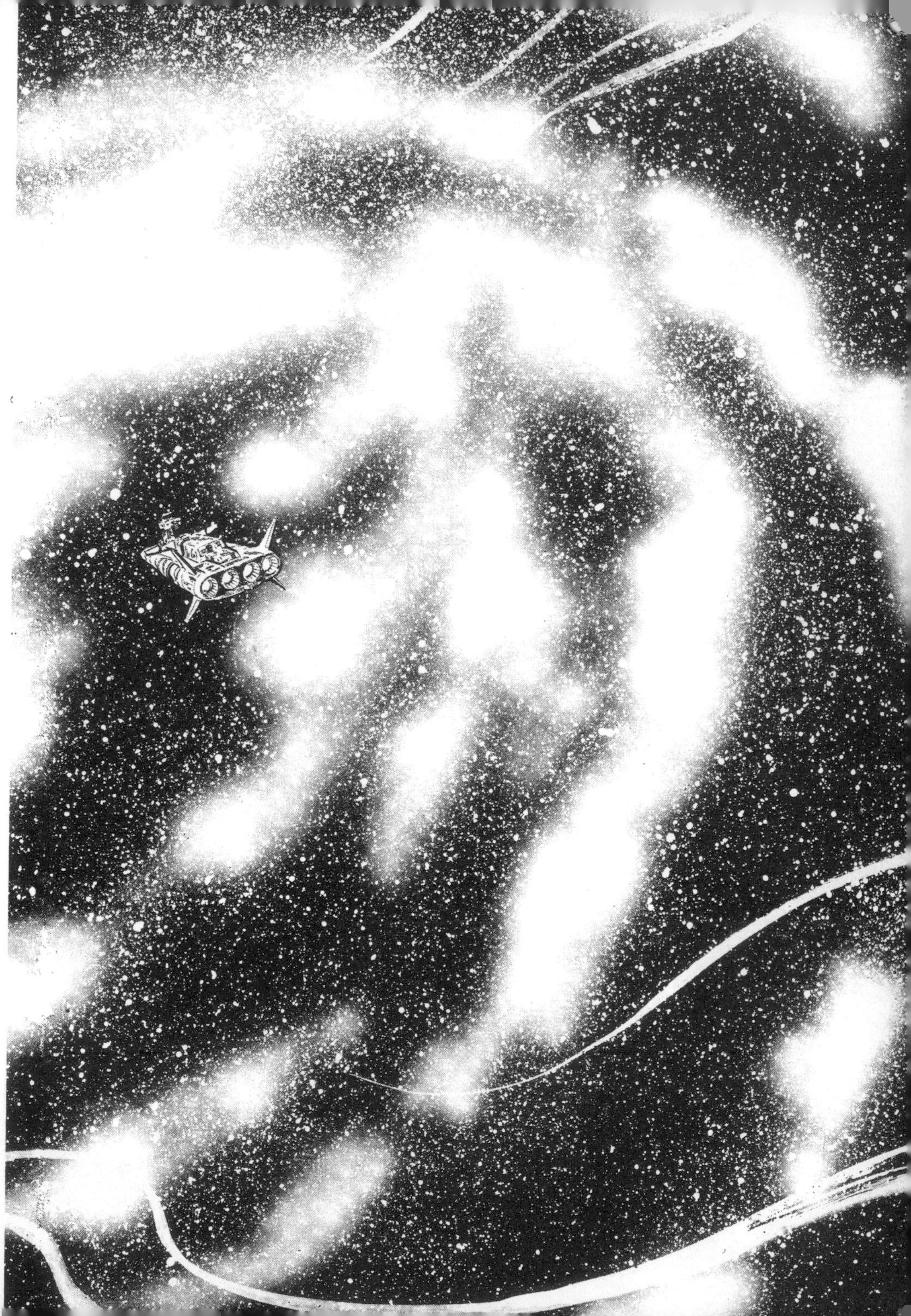

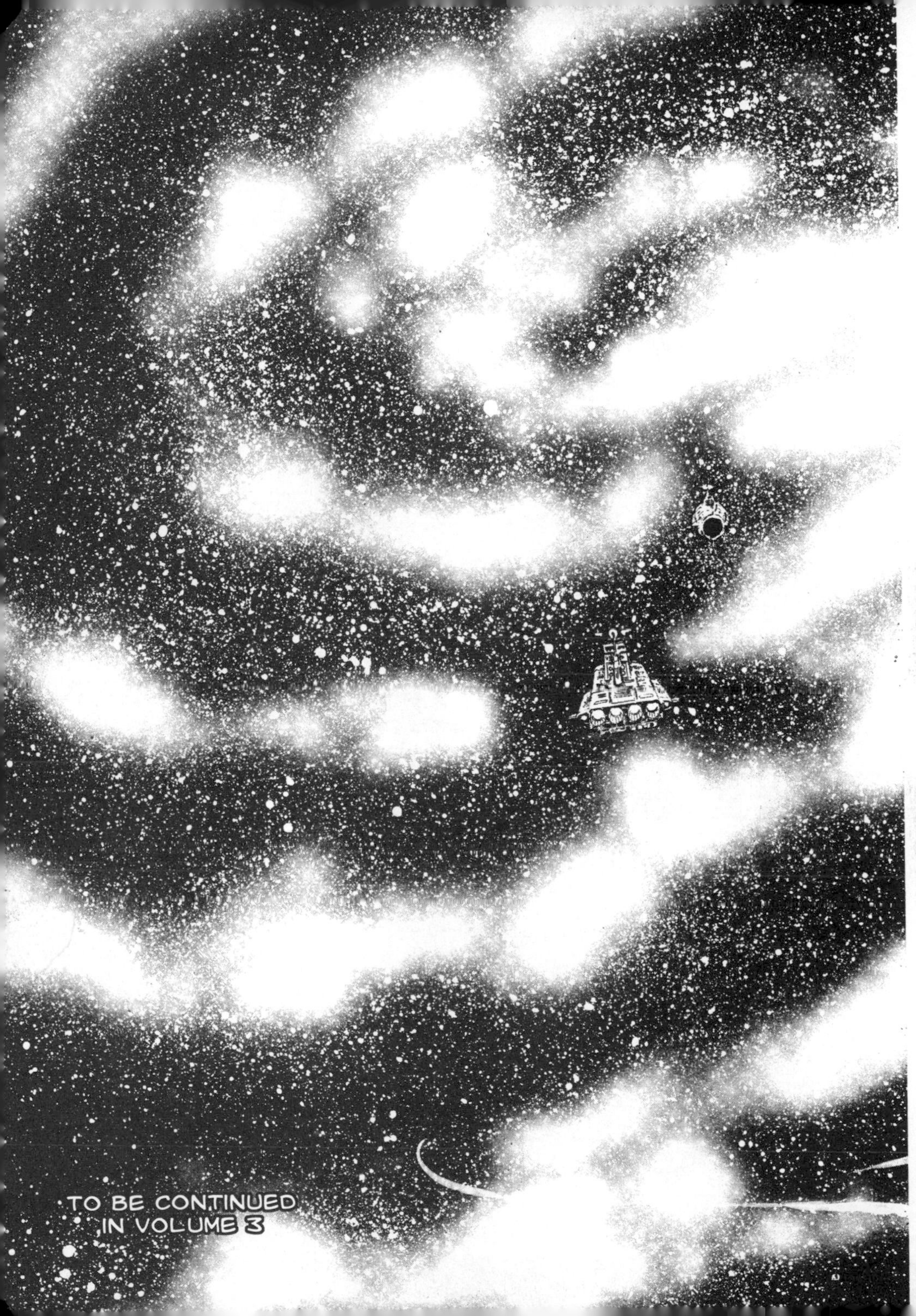
TO BE CONTINUED
IN VOLUME 3

NOW IN PAPERBACK TOO

All Volumes: 6 x 8, $14.95/$21.00

Volume 1
On Sale

Volume 2
On Sale

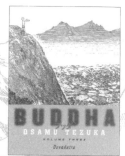

Volume 3
On Sale

Volume 4
November 2006

Volume 5
January 2007

Volume 6
March 2007

Volume 7
May 2007

Volume 8
July 2007

Buddha, the winner of two Eisners and a Harvey Award, is manga pioneer Osamu Tezuka's epic 8-volume biography of one of the world's most important religious figures.

"A rousing tale of intrepid heroes, horrid villains and wicked supernatural creatures. A fast read."
—*Publishers Weekly*

"Enormously entertaining" —*Orlando Sentinel*

"A swashbuckling fantasy...action is always center stage...intense...dreamlike."
—*Seattle Times*

"Japan's answer to *The Lord of the Rings*"
—*The Globe and Mail*

THE GUIN SAGA

KAORU KURIMOTO

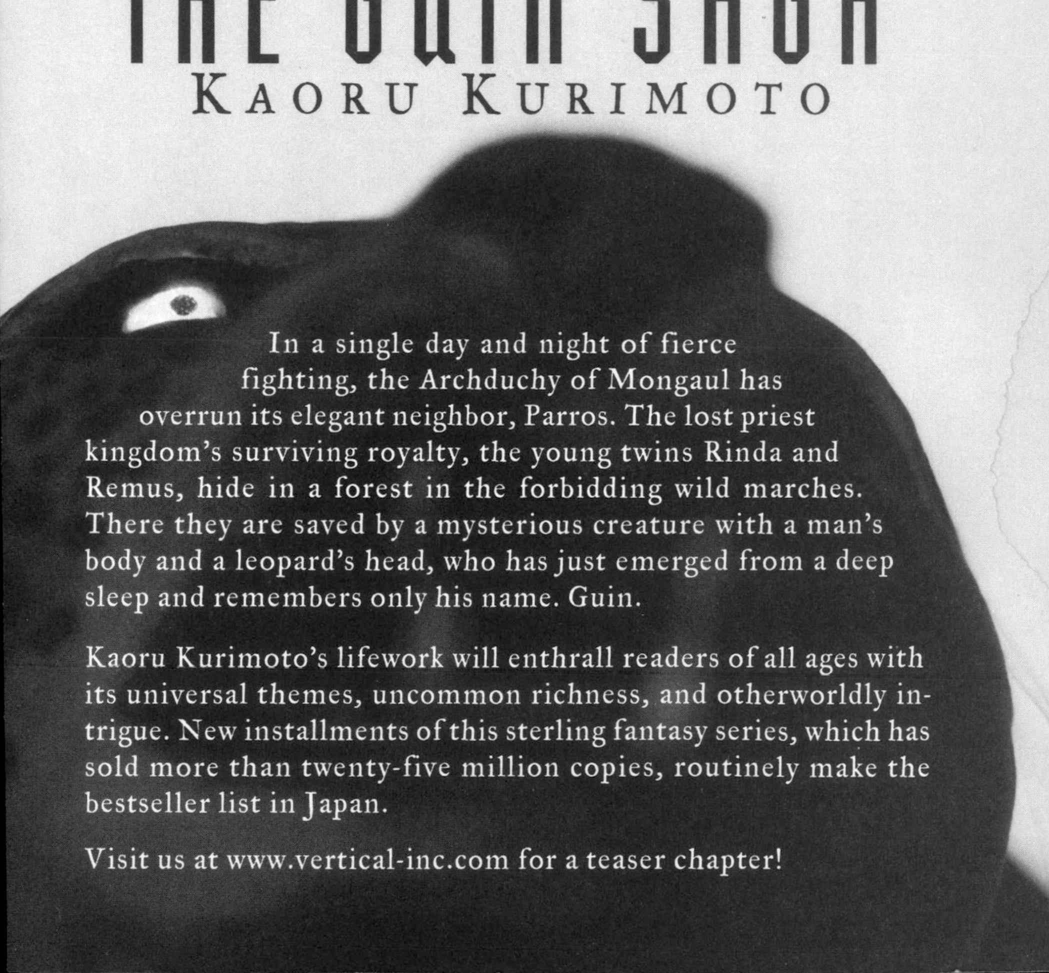

In a single day and night of fierce fighting, the Archduchy of Mongaul has overrun its elegant neighbor, Parros. The lost priest kingdom's surviving royalty, the young twins Rinda and Remus, hide in a forest in the forbidding wild marches. There they are saved by a mysterious creature with a man's body and a leopard's head, who has just emerged from a deep sleep and remembers only his name. Guin.

Kaoru Kurimoto's lifework will enthrall readers of all ages with its universal themes, uncommon richness, and otherworldly intrigue. New installments of this sterling fantasy series, which has sold more than twenty-five million copies, routinely make the bestseller list in Japan.

Visit us at www.vertical-inc.com for a teaser chapter!

If you want to be a cutie...

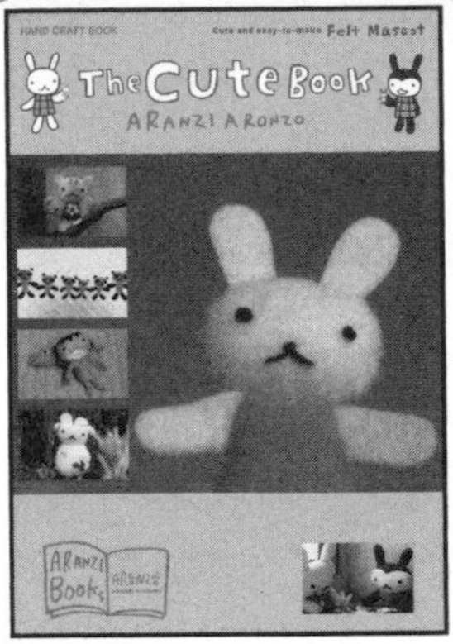

The Cute Book
ARANZI ARONZO

The Cute Book

Category: Crafts & Hobbies
Format: Hardcover
On Sale Date: February 2007
Price: $12.95
ISBN: 978-1-932234-68-8
Meet the cute, the bad, and the spritely!

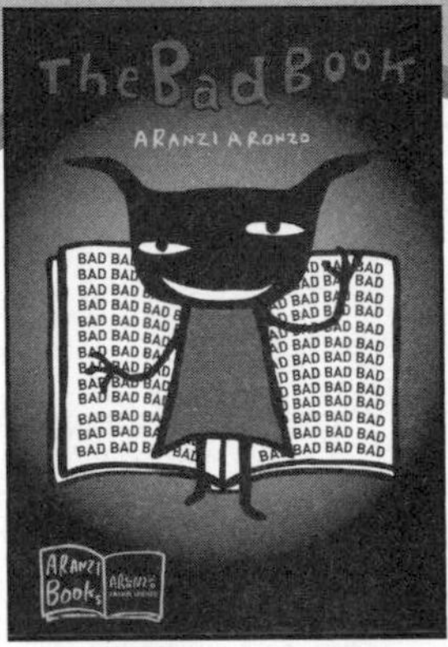

The Bad Book
ARANZI ARONZO

The Bad Book

Category: Crafts & Hobbies
Format: Hardcover
On Sale Date: February 2007
Price: $12.95
ISBN: 978-1-932234-69-5
Who wants to hang out with Bad Guy and Liar? Aranzi Aranzo does!

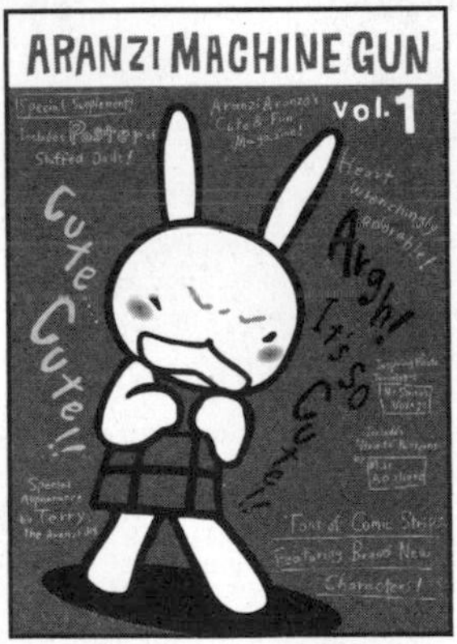

ARANZI MACHINE GUN
vol.1
Cute Cute!!
Argh! It's so Cute!!

ARANZI MACHINE GUN vol.1

Category: Crafts & Hobbies
Format: Trade Paperback
On Sale Date: June 2007
Price: $9.95
ISBN: 978-1-932234-72-5

...you've gotta be crafty

Japanese books, including manga like this one,
are meant to be read from right to left.

So the front cover is actually the back cover, and vice-versa.

To read this book, please flip it over and start in the top right-hand corner.
Read the panels, and the bubbles in the panels, from right to left,
then drop down to the next row and repeat.

It may make you dizzy at first,
but forcing your brain to do things backwards makes you smarter in the long run.
We swear.